# Lecture Notes in Computer Science 14584

The series Lecture Notes in Computer Science (LNCS), including its subseries Lecture Notes in Artificial Intelligence (LNAI) and Lecture Notes in Bioinformatics (LNBI), has established itself as a medium for the publication of new developments in computer science and information technology research, teaching, and education.

LNCS enjoys close cooperation with the computer science R & D community, the series counts many renowned academics among its volume editors and paper authors, and collaborates with prestigious societies. Its mission is to serve this international community by providing an invaluable service, mainly focused on the publication of conference and workshop proceedings and postproceedings. LNCS commenced publication in 1973.

Christina Pöpper · Lejla Batina
Editors

# Applied Cryptography and Network Security

22nd International Conference, ACNS 2024
Abu Dhabi, United Arab Emirates, March 5–8, 2024
Proceedings, Part II

*Editors*
Christina Pöpper
New York University Abu Dhabi
Abu Dhabi, United Arab Emirates

Lejla Batina
Radboud University Nijmegen
Nijmegen, The Netherlands

ISSN 0302-9743 ISSN 1611-3349 (electronic)
Lecture Notes in Computer Science
ISBN 978-3-031-54772-0 ISBN 978-3-031-54773-7 (eBook)
https://doi.org/10.1007/978-3-031-54773-7



This Springer imprint is published by the registered company Springer Nature Switzerland AG
The registered company address is: Gewerbestrasse 11, 6330 Cham, Switzerland

Paper in this product is recyclable.

# Preface

ACNS 2024, the 22nd International Conference on Applied Cryptography and Network Security, was held in Abu Dhabi, United Arab Emirates, on March 5–8, 2024. The conference covered all technical aspects of applied cryptography, network and computer security and privacy, representing both academic research work as well as developments in industrial and technical frontiers.

The conference had two submission deadlines, in July and October 2023. We received a total of 238 submissions over the two cycles (230 unique submissions incl. eight major revisions from the first submission cycle that were resubmitted as revisions in the second submission cycle). From all submissions, the Program Committee (PC) selected 54 papers for publication in the proceedings of the conference, some after minor or major revisions. This led to an acceptance rate of 23.5%.

The two program chairs were supported by a PC consisting of 76 leading experts in all aspects of applied cryptography and security whose expertise and work were crucial for the paper selection process. Each submission received around 4 reviews from the committee. Strong conflict of interest rules ensured that papers were not handled by PC members with a close personal or professional relationship with the authors. The program chairs were not allowed to submit papers and did not handle any submissions they were in conflict with. There were an additional 55 external reviewers, whose expertise the PC relied upon in the selection of papers. The review process was conducted as a double-blind peer review. The authors of 10 submissions rejected from the July deadline, but considered promising, were encouraged to resubmit to the October deadline after major revisions of their paper. From these 10 papers invited for a major revision, 8 papers got resubmitted to the second cycle, 5 of which were finally accepted.

Alongside the presentations of the accepted papers, the program of ACNS 2024 featured three invited talks given by Elisa Bertino, Nadia Heninger, and Gene Tsudik. The three volumes of the conference proceedings contain the revised versions of the 54 papers that were selected, together with the abstracts of the invited talks.

Following a long tradition, ACNS gives a best student paper award to encourage promising students to publish their best results at the conference. The award recipients share a monetary prize of 2,000 EUR generously sponsored by Springer.

Many people contributed to the success of ACNS 2024. We would like to thank the authors for submitting their research results to the conference. We are very grateful to the PC members and external reviewers for contributing their knowledge and expertise and for the tremendous amount of work and time involved in reviewing papers, contributing to the discussions, and shepherding the revisions. We are greatly indebted to Mihalis Maniatakos and Ozgur Sinanoglu, the ACNS'24 General Chairs, for their efforts and overall guidance as well as all the members of the organization committee. We thank the steering committee, Moti Yung and Jianying Zhou, for their direction and valuable advice throughout the preparation of the conference. We also thank the team at Springer for handling the publication of these conference proceedings, as well as Shujaat Mirza for working on the preparation of the proceedings volumes.

March 2024

Lejla Batina
Christina Pöpper

# Organization

## General Co-chairs

| | |
|---|---|
| Michail Maniatakos | New York University Abu Dhabi, UAE |
| Ozgur Sinanoglu | New York University Abu Dhabi, UAE |

## Program Committee Co-chairs

| | |
|---|---|
| Christina Pöpper | New York University Abu Dhabi, UAE |
| Lejla Batina | Radboud University, The Netherlands |

## Steering Committee

| | |
|---|---|
| Jianying Zhou | SUTD, Singapore |
| Moti Yung | Google, USA |

## Local Arrangements Chair

| | |
|---|---|
| Borja García de Soto | New York University Abu Dhabi, UAE |

## Publicity Chair

| | |
|---|---|
| Elias Athanasopoulos | University of Cyprus, Cyprus |

## Web Chair

| | |
|---|---|
| Christoforos Vasilatos | New York University Abu Dhabi, UAE |

## Poster Chair

| | |
|---|---|
| Charalambos Konstantinou | KAUST, KSA |

## Registration Chair

Rafael Song — New York University Abu Dhabi, UAE

## Workshop Chair

Martin Andreoni — Technology Innovation Institute, UAE

## Publication Chair

Shujaat Mirza — New York University, USA

## Student Travel Grants Chair

Lilas Alrahis — New York University Abu Dhabi, UAE

## Program Committee

| | |
|---|---|
| Adwait Nadkarni | William & Mary, USA |
| Alexander Koch | CNRS and IRIF, Université Paris Cité, France |
| Alexandra Dmitrienko | University of Wuerzburg, Germany |
| Amr Youssef | Concordia University, Canada |
| An Braeken | Vrije Universiteit Brussel, Belgium |
| Anna Lisa Ferrara | University of Molise, Italy |
| Archita Agarwal | MongoDB, USA |
| Atefeh Mohseni Ejiyeh | UCSB, USA |
| Benjamin Dowling | University of Sheffield, UK |
| Chao Sun | Osaka University, Japan |
| Chiara Marcolla | Technology Innovation Institute, UAE |
| Chitchanok Chuengsatiansup | The University of Melbourne, Australia |
| Christine Utz | CISPA Helmholtz Center for Information Security, Germany |
| Christoph Egger | Université Paris Cité and CNRS and IRIF, France |
| Claudio Soriente | NEC Laboratories Europe, Spain |
| Colin Boyd | NTNU-Norwegian University of Science and Technology, Norway |
| Daniel Dinu | Intel |
| Daniel Gardham | University of Surrey, UK |

| | |
|---|---|
| Daniel Slamanig | Universität der Bundeswehr München, Germany |
| Dave Singelee | KU Leuven, Belgium |
| Devashish Gosain | MPI-INF, Germany |
| Diego F. Aranha | Aarhus University, Denmark |
| Dimitrios Vasilopoulos | IMDEA Software Institute, Spain |
| Dominique Schröder | Friedrich-Alexander Universität Erlangen-Nürnberg, Germany |
| Eleftheria Makri | Leiden University, The Netherlands |
| Elena Dubrova | Royal Institute of Technology, Sweden |
| Elena Kirshanova | Technology Innovation Institute, UAE |
| Elif Bilge Kavun | University of Passau, Germany |
| Fatemeh Ganji | Worcester Polytechnic Institute, USA |
| Florian Hahn | University of Twente, The Netherlands |
| Francisco Rodríguez-Henríquez | Technology Innovation Institute, UAE |
| Ghassan Karame | Ruhr University Bochum, Germany |
| Gustavo Banegas | Qualcomm, France |
| Hyungsub Kim | Purdue University, USA |
| Jean Paul Degabriele | Technology Innovation Institute, UAE |
| Jianying Zhou | Singapore University of Technology and Design, Singapore |
| João S. Resende | University of Porto, Portugal |
| Karim Eldefrawy | SRI International, USA |
| Katerina Mitrokotsa | University of St. Gallen, Switzerland |
| Katharina Krombholz | CISPA Helmholtz Center for Information Security, Germany |
| Kazuo Sakiyama | UEC, Tokyo, Japan |
| Kehuan Zhang | The Chinese University of Hong Kong, China |
| Khurram Bhatti | Information Technology University (ITU), Pakistan |
| Lukasz Chmielewski | Masaryk University, Czech Republic |
| Mainack Mondal | Indian Institute of Technology, Kharagpur, India |
| Marc Manzano | SandboxAQ, USA |
| Matthias J. Kannwischer | QSMC, Taiwan |
| Melissa Azouaoui | NXP Semiconductors, Germany |
| Monika Trimoska | Eindhoven University of Technology, The Netherlands |
| Monowar Hasan | Washington State University, USA |
| Mridula Singh | CISPA Helmholtz Center for Information Security, Germany |
| Murtuza Jadliwala | University of Texas at San Antonio, USA |
| Nabil Alkeilani Alkadri | CISPA Helmholtz Center for Information Security, Germany |

| | |
|---|---|
| Nils Ole Tippenhauer | CISPA Helmholtz Center for Information Security, Germany |
| Olga Gadyatskaya | Leiden University, The Netherlands |
| Paulo Barreto | University of Washington – Tacoma, USA |
| Pino Caballero-Gil | University of La Laguna, Spain |
| Pooya Farshim | IOG & Durham University, UK |
| Sathvik Prasad | North Carolina State University, USA |
| Sebastian Köhler | University of Oxford, UK |
| Shahram Rasoolzadeh | Radboud University, The Netherlands |
| Sherman S. M. Chow | The Chinese University of Hong Kong, China |
| Silvia Mella | Radboud University, The Netherlands |
| Sinem Sav | Bilkent University, Turkey |
| Sofía Celi | Brave Software, Portugal |
| Sudipta Chattopadhyay | Singapore University of Technology and Design, Singapore |
| Sushmita Ruj | University of New South Wales, Australia |
| Tako Boris Fouotsa | EPFL, Switzerland |
| Tibor Jager | University of Wuppertal, Germany |
| Tien Tuan Anh Dinh | Deakin University, Australia |
| Tran Quang Duc | Hanoi University of Science and Technology, Vietnam |
| Valeria Nikolaenko | A16Z Crypto Research, USA |
| Vera Rimmer | KU Leuven, Belgium |
| Willy Susilo | University of Wollongong, Australia |
| Xiapu Luo | The Hong Kong Polytechnic University, China |
| Zheng Yang | Southwest University, China |

## Additional Reviewers

Afonso Vilalonga
Alexander Karenin
Anshu Yadav
Astrid Ottenhues
Beatrice Biasioli
Behzad Abdolmaleki
Benjamin Terner
Callum London
Enrique Argones Rúa
Erkan Tairi
Fabio Campos
Gareth T. Davies
Gora Adj
Gregor Seiler
Jean-Philippe Bossuat
Jelle Vos
Jenit Tomy
Jérôme Govinden
Jiafan Wang
Jodie Knapp
Joel Frisk Gärtner
Jorge Chávez-Saab
Karl Southern
Laltu Sardar
Laurane Marco
Li Duan

Lorenz Panny
Marcus Brinkmann
Nada El Kassem
Nan Cheng
Nusa Zidaric
Octavio Pérez Kempner
Okan Seker
Patrick Harasser
Paul Huynh
Paul Gerhart
Pradeep Mishra
Quan Yuan
Raghav Bhaskar
Ritam Bhaumik
Robert Merget
Sacha Servan-Schreiber
Sebastian Faller
Sebastian Ramacher
Semyon Novoselov
Shahram Rasoolzadeh
Sylvain Chatel
Tianyu Li
Valerio Cini
Victor Miller
Viktoria Ronge
Vir Pathak
Vojtech Suchanek
Vukašin Karadžić
Yangguang Tian

# Abstracts of Keynote Talks

# Applying Machine Learning to Securing Cellular Networks

Elisa Bertino

Purdue University, Indiana, USA

**Abstract.** Cellular network security is more critical than ever, given the increased complexity of these networks and the numbers of applications that depend on them, including telehealth, remote education, ubiquitous robotics and autonomous vehicles, smart cities, and Industry 4.0. In order to devise more effective defenses, a recent trend is to leverage machine learning (ML) techniques, which have become applicable because of today's advanced capabilities for collecting data as well as high-performance computing systems for training ML models. Recent large language models (LLMs) are also opening new interesting directions for security applications. In this talk, I will first present a comprehensive threat analysis in the context of 5G cellular networks to give a concrete example of the magnitude of the problem of cellular network security. Then, I will present two specific applications of ML techniques for the security of cellular networks. The first application focuses on the use of natural language processing techniques to the problem of detecting inconsistencies in the "natural specifications" of cellular network protocols. The second application addresses the design of an anomaly detection system able to detect the presence of malicious base stations and determine the type of attack. Then I'll conclude with a discussion on research directions.

# Real-World Cryptanalysis

Nadia Heninger

University of California, San Diego, USA

**Abstract**. Cryptography has traditionally been considered to be one of the strong points of computer security. However, a number of the public-key cryptographic algorithms that we use are fragile in the face of implementation mistakes or misunderstandings. In this talk, I will survey "weapons of math destruction" that have been surprisingly effective in finding broken cryptographic implementations in the wild, and some adventures in active and passive network measurement of cryptographic protocols.

# CAPTCHAs: What Are They Good For?

Gene Tsudik

University of California, Irvine, USA

**Abstract.** Since about 2003, CAPTCHAs have been widely used as a barrier against bots, while simultaneously annoying great multitudes of users worldwide. As their use grew, techniques to defeat or bypass CAPTCHAs kept improving, while CAPTCHAs themselves evolved in terms of sophistication and diversity, becoming increasingly difficult to solve for both bots and humans. Given this long-standing and still-ongoing arms race, it is important to investigate usability, solving performance, and user perceptions of modern CAPTCHAs. This talk will discuss two such efforts:

In the first part, we explore CAPTCHAs in the wild by evaluating users' solving performance and perceptions of unmodified currently-deployed CAPTCHAs. We obtain this data through manual inspection of popular websites and user studies in which 1,400 participants collectively solved 14,000 CAPTCHAs. Results show significant differences between the most popular types of CAPTCHAs: surprisingly, solving time and user perception are not always correlated. We performed a comparative study to investigate the effect of experimental context – specifically the difference between solving CAPTCHAs directly versus solving them as part of a more natural task, such as account creation. Whilst there were several potential confounding factors, our results show that experimental context could have an impact on this task, and must be taken into account in future CAPTCHA studies. Finally, we investigate CAPTCHA-induced user task abandonment by analyzing participants who start and do not complete the task.

In the second part of this work, we conduct a large-scale (over 3,600 distinct users) 13-month real-world user study and post-study survey. The study, performed at a large public university, was based on a live account creation and password recovery service with currently prevalent captcha type: reCAPTCHAv2. Results show that, with more attempts, users improve in solving checkbox challenges. For website developers and user study designers, results indicate that the website context directly influences (with statistically significant differences) solving time between password recovery and account creation. We consider the impact of participants' major and education level, showing that certain majors exhibit better performance, while, in general, education level has a direct impact on solving time. Unsurprisingly, we discover that participants find image challenges to be annoying, while checkbox challenges are perceived as easy. We also show that, rated via System Usability Scale (SUS), image tasks are viewed as "OK", while checkbox tasks are viewed as "good". We explore the cost and security of reCAPTCHAv2 and conclude that it has an immense cost and no security. Overall, we believe that this study's results prompt a natural conclusion: reCAPTCHAv2 and similar reCAPTCHA technology should be deprecated.

# Contents – Part II

## Post-quantum



## Cryptographic Protocols II



## Wireless and Networks

# Post-quantum

# Automated Issuance of Post-Quantum Certificates: A New Challenge

Alexandre Augusto Giron[1(✉)], Frederico Schardong[2,3], Lucas Pandolfo Perin[4], Ricardo Custódio[2], Victor Valle[2], and Victor Mateu[4]

[1] Federal University of Technology - Parana (UTFPR), Toledo-PR, Brazil
alexandregiron@utfpr.edu.br
[2] Federal University of Santa Catarina (UFSC), Florianópolis-SC, Brazil
[3] Instituto Federal do Rio Grande do Sul (IFRS), Rolante-RS, Brazil
[4] Technology Innovation Institute (TII), Abu Dhabi, UAE

**Abstract.** The Automatic Certificate Management Environment protocol (ACME) has significantly contributed to the widespread use of digital certificates in safeguarding the authenticity and privacy of Internet data. These certificates are required for implementing the Transport Layer Security (TLS) protocol. However, it is well known that the cryptographic algorithms employed in these certificates will become insecure with the emergence of quantum computers. This study assesses the challenges in transitioning ACME to the post-quantum landscape using Post-Quantum Cryptography (PQC). To evaluate the cost of ACME's PQC migration, we create a simulation environment for issuing PQC-only and hybrid digital certificates. Our experiments reveal performance drawbacks associated with the switch to PQC or hybrid solutions. However, considering the high volume of certificates issued daily by organizations like Let's Encrypt, the performance of ACME is of utmost importance. To address this concern, we propose a novel challenge method for ACME. Compared to the widely used HTTP-01 method, our findings indicate an average PQC certificate issuance time that is 4.22 times faster, along with a potential reduction of up to 35% in communication size.

**Keywords:** Post-Quantum Cryptography · ACME Protocol · Certificate Management

## 1 Introduction

Encrypted data channels play a crucial role in ensuring data privacy on the Internet. One of the most widely used protocols for implementing these channels is the Transport Layer Security (TLS) [21]. However, the rapid and reliable issuance of digital certificates at minimal cost and the management of associated cryptographic keys throughout their lifecycle presents a bottleneck in the large-scale adoption of TLS. The widespread deployment of the protocol became


C. Pöpper and L. Batina (Eds.): ACNS 2024, LNCS 14584, pp. 3–23, 2024.
https://doi.org/10.1007/978-3-031-54773-7_1

possible only with the emergence of the Let's Encrypt project. Let's Encrypt's Certificate Authority (CA) has issued over 1 billion digital certificates and continues to experience substantial growth [6]. The success of Let's Encrypt can be attributed to the automation of all necessary steps for issuing and renewing digital certificates. The automation of certificate issuance is facilitated by the Automatic Certificate Management Environment (ACME) protocol [1].

TLS and ACME protocols rely on classical cryptography to guarantee their security properties. However, the existence of Shor's quantum algorithm [27] gives an expiry date to the current protocols dated at the time a Cryptographically Relevant Quantum Computer (CRQC) [13] exists. This computer could compromise digital certificates and Key Exchange (KEX) mechanisms based on classical Public Key Cryptography (PKC). Consequently, attackers could collect transmitted data today with the anticipation of decrypting it using a CRQC in the future, a scenario known as "store-now-decrypt-later" attacks [3]. Such attacks would impact the security of existing protocols and applications dependent on TLS before a CRQC exists.

It is necessary to replace vulnerable algorithms to mitigate the quantum threats to classical cryptography. The cryptographic algorithms that can execute on a classical computer and offer security against attackers with access to a CRQC are called Post-Quantum Cryptography (PQC) [2]. The security of these cryptographic schemes relies on mathematical problems with no known efficient solutions for both quantum and classical computation. There is currently a significant global effort to evaluate and standardize post-quantum schemes. Regarding the adoption of these schemes, two primary strategies have emerged. The first strategy involves directly replacing classical algorithms with post-quantum ones. The second strategy, "hybrid mode" [3], utilizes both classical and post-quantum algorithms. Proponents of hybrid methods argue that post-quantum algorithms are relatively new and have not undergone the same level of scrutiny as classical algorithms. Their reasoning states that by including a classical algorithm alongside a post-quantum one, the security properties of the cryptographic protocol can still be guaranteed in case of a flaw or cryptanalytic attack on the post-quantum algorithm.

The transition from classical to PQC presents several challenges. One of the most relevant ones is the significantly increased size of cryptographic objects, such as public keys and signatures, and their impact on the protocol performance. For example, certain post-quantum algorithms like Classic McEliece are impractical for regular TLS handshakes due to the size of their public keys. To address this issue, researchers have conducted numerous benchmarks of PQC in network protocols like TLS [18,28], and others have proposed protocol changes to better accommodate PQC [24,25]. Such changes and evaluations are crucial to understand the performance implications imposed by PQC in advance. Therefore, adapting and evaluating protocol changes must be undertaken prior to the arrival of quantum computers to ensure a smooth transition to PQC.

Although several PQC-based TLS proposals and experiments have been proposed, we could not find any proposal for PQC in the context of ACME.

Therefore, the impacts of using post-quantum schemes in such a scenario still need to be explored. In this paper, we address this gap by providing the following contributions:

1. We integrate PQC schemes, namely Dilithium, Falcon, and Sphincs+, along with hybrid modes, into ACME implementations and the required libraries. Our modified implementations are publicly available.
2. We evaluate ACME using geographically-distant peers, where the server is close to the Let's Encrypt CA location. Such a distance allows us to compare and estimate the impact of PQC on certificate issuance in a more realistic scenario.
3. To expedite the certificate issuance process, we propose an alternative ACME challenge which can be used for issuing both classical and PQC certificates.
4. We analyze the time and communication costs associated with our proposed challenge, demonstrating that it reduces issuance time and byte cost for certificates with both classical and post-quantum cryptography.

The remainder of this paper is organized as follows. Section 2 presents the necessary background concepts for understanding this work. Section 3 discusses quantum threats in ACME, the details of PQC integration, and the evaluation methodology. Section 4 presents our proposed ACME challenge design, its evaluation, and a discussion of the obtained results. Finally, Sect. 5 provides concluding remarks and outlines potential future work.

## 2 Background

First, we present the main characteristics of TLS and ACME. After that, we describe PQC concepts and the standardization process conducted by NIST. Finally, we conclude this section by showing related works about PQC adoption in network protocols.

### 2.1 TLS Version 1.3

Formerly known as Secure Sockets Layer (SSL), the TLS protocol, in its current version (1.3), is described in RFC 8446 [21]. TLS provides a communication channel with confidentiality and authentication assurances between two peers: a client (e.g., a browser) and a server (e.g., a web server). TLS requires the server to provide authentication credentials when establishing a connection, while client authentication is optional.

The TLS 1.3 specification divides the protocol into three parts: (1) a Handshake protocol; (2) a Record protocol; and (3) an Alert protocol. The first part covers how the two communicating peers establish a session, aided by an Authenticated Key Exchange (AKE) and cryptographic computations ordered in a Key Schedule [21]. The second part covers how peers use their session data (and keys) to exchange application data securely, typically utilizing Authenticated Encryption with Associated Data (AEAD) algorithms. The last part covers how the peers should handle alert messages and protocol exceptions.

The mechanics of a complete TLS 1.3 handshake are as follows. First, a TLS client initiates the handshake by sending a `ClientHello` message. The message can include several pieces of information, such as supported algorithms, cipher suites, and an extension message called `keyshare`. The `keyshare` is an ephemeral Elliptic Curve Diffie-Hellman (ECDH) public key used to create shared secrets for deriving symmetric keys. Upon receiving the `ClientHello`, the server responds with a set of messages: `ServerHello`, `Certificate`, `CertificateVerify`, `EncryptedExtensions`, and `Finished`. The server hello includes information about algorithm selection, the corresponding ECDH `keyshare`, and additional extensions (if available). The server provides a set of certificates, a digital signature, and an HMAC [15] to authenticate over the handshake transcript data (`Certificate`, `CertificateVerify`, and `Finished` messages, respectively). Except for the `ServerHello`, all messages are encrypted using keys derived from the `keyshare` pair. The `EncryptedExtensions` message, sent immediately after the `ServerHello`, is also encrypted.

The client receives the server's response and processes it. It verifies the handshake signature, validates the certificates, and the `Finished` message. Additionally, the client checks if the server's reply includes the optional `CertificateRequest` message. If it does, the client will authenticate using a certificate and a handshake signature with its private key. Otherwise, it sends the mandatory `Finished` message and any desired application data to the server, concluding the handshake and initiating secure communication. TLS is commonly used in upper-layer network protocols like HTTPS and network applications like OpenVPN. In this work, we focus on using TLS by the ACME protocol.

## 2.2 ACMEv2 Characteristics

The Automated Certificate Management Environment (ACME) protocol is defined in RFC 8555 [1]. ACME offers services for verifying identity over the Internet and managing certificates. The primary objective of the protocol is to minimize the need for human intervention in configuring web servers and handling certificates. ACME enables an ACME server (controlled by an Issuer CA) to issue a Domain-Validated (DV) digital certificate to the ACME client. The issuance and domain validation processes are fully automated. Currently in its version 2, ACME plays a crucial role in Let's Encrypt, one of the largest CAs on the Internet. Moreover, many certification authorities and PKI vendors, such as ZeroSSL [30], are adopting the ACME protocol in their products because it simplifies and enhances the quality of service provided to their customers.

ACME relies on two communication channels: (1) the ACME Channel, protected by TLS; and (2) the Validation channel, which depends on the validation method. An ACME client uses TLS to request the issuance of one or more DV certificates from an ACME server. ACME servers store ACME client accounts associated with a public-key pair that clients use to authenticate themselves to the server. However, the server only issues a certificate after the client proves control over the desired identifier to be certified, i.e., the domain name. To accomplish this, the client must solve an ACME challenge. RFC 8555 [1] specifies the HTTP and DNS challenge types, and RFC 8737 [26] describes the TLS-ALPN challenge. Generally, a challenge is considered fulfilled if (a) the client proves control of the private key associated with the ACME account and (b) the client proves control of the domain name in question.

ACME protocol messages are based on the JSON Web Signature (JWS) standard [9] and transmitted through HTTPS/TLS requests. Typically, ACME HTTPS requests are signed using the account's private key, while the public key is usually not included in the JWS body. However, when creating a new account or revoking a certificate, the "jwk" field (i.e., the public key) is included in the request. Other requests identify keys using a "Key ID" ("kid") field in the request [9]. This way, the server can determine which key to verify subsequent requests.

Figure 1 illustrates the necessary ACME messages for issuing an X.509 certificate. The issuance process is divided into three steps: (1) account creation; (2) challenge; and (3) issuance. Communication between the ACME client and server occurs through HTTPS requests, requiring the ACME client to trust the ACME server. This trust is established by the ACME client's confidence in the server's certificate chain, which includes intermediate and root CAs. Typically, root CAs are pre-installed in the client's certificate repository.

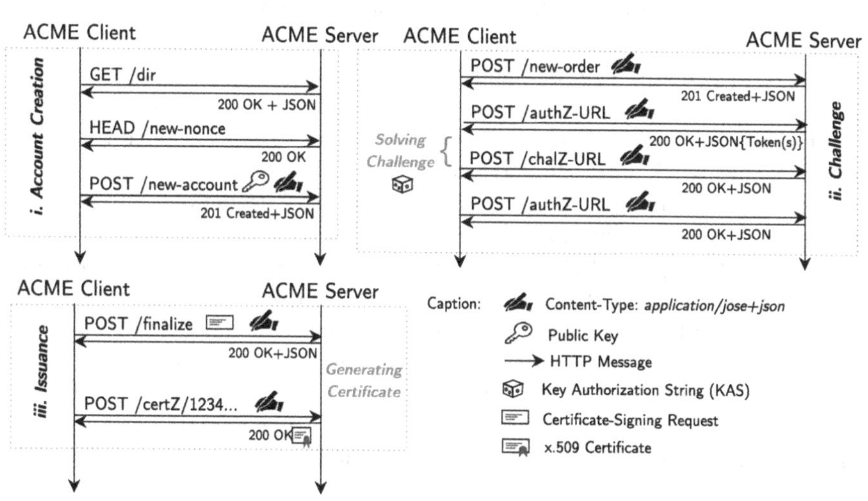


**Fig. 1.** ACME Issuance Overview

The client initiates an account creation request with the ACME server in the first step. The client's account can optionally include contact information and is associated with a key pair generated by the client. To initiate the creation process, the client requests server resources by sending a `GET /dir` message. The server responds with an HTTP code (typically 200 for success) and a JSON payload. The JSON payload contains the URLs for the desired resources and the Terms of Service. If it is the client's first connection, a new nonce is required. The client obtains the nonce by sending a `HEAD /new-nonce` message. This nonce is used to protect against possible replay attacks. The registration is concluded with a `POST /new-account` request. At this point, it is important to note that the ACME server does not have any means to confirm the claimed identity other than the newly registered authentication key, referred to as the "account key". Subsequent HTTP requests from the client must be signed with the account key.

The second step aims to prove the client's identity through an Identifier Validation Challenge [1]. The ACME protocol specification focuses on domain name identifiers. There are different types of challenges available, such as HTTP-01, DNS-01, and TLS-ALPN-01, with HTTP-01 being the most commonly used [5]. In general, to complete the challenge, the client must demonstrate possession of the account key and control over the identifier. In the case of HTTP-01, the client must serve a file over HTTP containing the Key Authorization String (KAS). A KAS is formed by concatenating a 128-bit random token (previously generated by the server), a dot separator ('.'), and the base64-encoded key fingerprint. The ACME server retrieves and checks the file over HTTP to validate the challenge. Refer to Appendix A for additional details on HTTP-01.

Figure 1 provides an abstract representation of the challenge-solving step. First, the client requests a new certificate by sending a `POST /new-order` message. The server's response includes information about the available challenges, their respective URLs, and the KAS for each challenge. Each challenge requires a unique KAS generated on demand, meaning authorization requests can fail, and the client may need to retry them. Additionally, each challenge has a state (e.g., pending, valid, deactivated), allowing the server to expect multiple requests using the same KAS until the certificate is issued. Therefore, the client must check the status of the desired KAS by sending a `POST /authZ/...` request and then proceed with the relevant challenge.

After completing the challenge, the client sends a `POST /chal/...` message to inform the server that the challenge has been completed, and it waits for the server to validate the challenge. The client can check the challenge's status by sending `POST /authZ/...` requests. Once the challenge is deemed valid by the server, it is considered completed. The server stores the authorization and marks it as valid for a specific period (not controlled by RFC 8555 [1]).

The issuance step, as depicted in Fig. 1, is the final part of the process. The client sends a `POST /finalize` message, which includes a PKCS#10 Certificate-Signing Request (CSR) [17], to the server. It is important to note that the account key pair used for the CSR generation differs from the one used for the account registration. Specifically, the CSR must not contain a public key for any known account. The server validates the CSR and generates the certificate. Finally, the client can download the issued certificate using a `POST /certZ/...`

message, often referred to as "POST-AS-GET" [1]. Once the client has obtained the certificate, the ACME client's request flow is complete. ACME client implementations like Certbot [8] typically store and automatically configure the certificate(s) in the web server repository. It enables the seamless activation of an HTTPS-secured web server with just a few command-line instructions. Additionally, Certbot configures automatic certificate renewal, thereby simplifying certificate management operations. It is worth mentioning that RFC 8555 does not distinguish between certificate issuance and renewal, meaning the renewal process starts with a new request to `/new-order`.

### 2.3 Post-Quantum Cryptography

Post-Quantum Cryptography (PQC) or Quantum-Safe Cryptography is an area of research that focuses on developing cryptographic algorithms that are resistant to attacks from quantum computers. Traditional public-key schemes based on problems such as the Discrete Logarithm Problem (DLP), Elliptic Curve Discrete Logarithm Problem (ECDLP), and Integer Factorization Problem (IFP), are considered to be vulnerable to attacks by quantum computers, specifically Shor's algorithm [27].

The threat of quantum computers to current cryptographic systems raises concerns about the confidentiality and authentication of data transmitted over the internet. While the impact on confidentiality is more immediate, as an adversary can gather encrypted data today and decrypt it in the future with the help of a quantum computer, the impact on authentication is less urgent since quantum adversaries cannot retroactively impersonate past communications [3].

In this context, efforts are underway to standardize post-quantum algorithms. One notable initiative is led by the National Institute of Standards and Technology (NIST) [14]. NIST has been running a standardization process for PQC algorithms, including key exchange, public-key encryption, and digital signatures. The initial choice of standards includes Kyber for key exchange and public-key encryption, as well as Dilithium, Falcon, and Sphincs+ for digital signatures. These algorithms have gone through multiple rounds of evaluation, and the process is currently in the fourth round, with additional schemes under scrutiny [16].

Regarding the impact on the ACME protocol and TLS, the transition to post-quantum cryptography will involve replacing current signature algorithms with post-quantum digital signature schemes. However, the transition process is expected to take significant time, as it requires coordination among various entities such as certificate authorities (CAs), client and server implementations, and browsers. Therefore, it is crucial to experiment, evaluate, and plan for a smooth transition to post-quantum cryptography in ACME and TLS [10]. Table 1 provides an overview of the post-quantum signature schemes expected to be standardized by NIST, along with their sizes and corresponding security levels.

There is limited work specifically focusing on the issuance of post-quantum certificates. Two main methods have been proposed for implementing hybrid post-quantum certificates within the X.509 standard format. One method involves concatenating cryptographic objects, such as public keys and signatures, while the other adds PQC algorithm information as X.509 extensions. The second method uses non-critical extensions and minimizes the risk of compatibility issues with legacy implementations that do not support post-quantum algorithms. Security analyses have been conducted to evaluate the effectiveness of these combining methods [4]. The impact of post-quantum certificates on PKI operations and TLS connections has been discussed in the literature, highlighting concerns about performance, particularly when dealing with the certificate chain. However, there are often no objections to using the hybrid mode, which combines both classical and post-quantum algorithms, regarding performance penalties [11,20].

**Table 1.** Currently digital signature schemes to be standardized by the NIST PQC process.

| Algorithm Parameter Set Name | NIST SecurityLevel | Public key size + Signature size (bytes) |
|---|---|---|
| `Dilithium2` | 1 | 3732 |
| `Dilithium3` | 3 | 5245 |
| `Dilithium5` | 5 | 7187 |
| `Falcon-512` | 1 | 1587 |
| `Falcon-1024` | 5 | 3123 |
| `SPHINCS+-SHAKE256-128s-simple` | 1 | 7888 |
| `SPHINCS+-SHAKE256-128f-simple` | 1 | 17120 |
| `SPHINCS+-SHAKE256-192f-simple` | 3 | 35712 |
| `SPHINCS+-SHAKE256-192s-simple` | 3 | 16272 |
| `SPHINCS+-SHAKE256-256f-simple` | 5 | 49920 |
| `SPHINCS+-SHAKE256-256s-simple` | 5 | 29856 |

## 3 Quantum Threat and PQC Adoption

We begin by examining the threats to ACME security in the presence of a quantum computer in Sect. 3.1. Subsequently, we delve into implementation and design specifics in Sect. 3.2. Finally, we explore the implications of evaluating ACME with PQC in Sect. 3.3.

### 3.1 Quantum Threats in ACME

The ACME protocol relies on PKC to ensure its cryptographic properties. Consequently, once a CRQC exists, the protocol would become insecure. While the threat exists, the transition to PQC may not be as urgent for ACME compared to other cases, given that most interactions are certificate-related. However, RFC 8555 [1] specifies that a secure channel, often implemented using

TLS, must be used for client requests to the server. Therefore, a quantum-safe ACME implementation depends on a quantum-safe TLS. To prevent "store-now-decrypt-later" attacks, a quantum-safe Key Exchange (KEX) algorithm must be used before a CRQC arrives. It is worth noting that the challenge validation channel in ACME does not necessarily require TLS.

One of the benefits that ACME provides to clients is the ability to reuse valid authorizations. After completing a challenge, a client can reuse the authorization to issue a new certificate more efficiently. This feature allows clients to issue certificates at their convenience, not necessarily immediately after challenge validation. However, it introduces a potential vulnerability in the form of a store-now-decrypt-later attack. An attacker could collect TLS-encrypted ACME messages and, in the future, exploit a hypothetical quantum attack on the TLS layer to gain access to the ACME information containing challenge authorization details. Since RFC 8555 [1] leaves the deactivation of authorizations up to implementations, many challenge authorizations could remain valid for an extended period. As a result, an attacker could exploit old valid authorizations to issue unauthorized certificates. Figure 2 illustrates the attack. Therefore, the authorization reuse feature needs careful redesign considering the existence of future CRQCs. More details about authorizations and their validity times are discussed in Sect. 4.3.

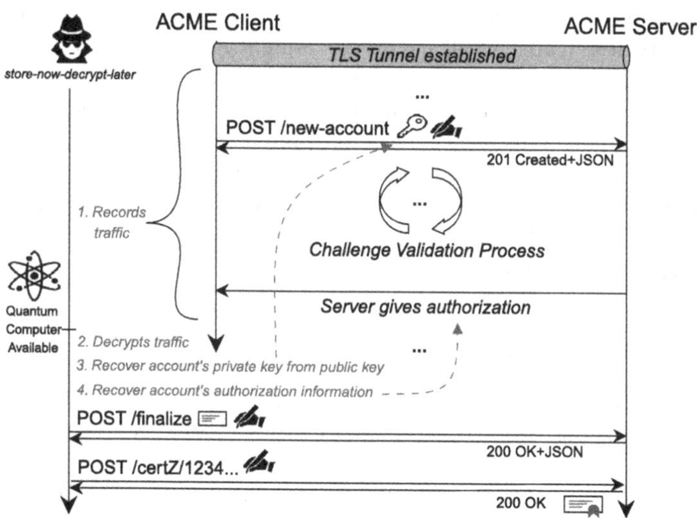


**Fig. 2.** Unauthorized issuance of a certificate with the help of a quantum computer.

Both attack scenarios, targeting classical certificates and the classical communication channel, can be mitigated by using PQC.

### 3.2 Integrating PQC Algorithms

We selected PQC implementations from the Open Quantum-Safe project `liboqs` [29]. Since our project is developed using the Go language, we used the liboqs-go binding [19]. We integrated them into Pebble's ACME server and LEGO ("Let's Encrypt Client and ACME Library in Go"). Pebble is suitable for testing ACME client implementations. For reproducibility, our ACME implementations and test scripts are publicly available[1]. We used the selected standard candidates from the NIST PQC standardization process for integration:

- **Kyber**: for Key Exchange in TLS, using security levels 1, 3 and 5.
- **Dilithium** and **Falcon**: we use the same algorithm and security level parameters in all required cryptographic objects. Namely: ACME client account keys and CSR; ACME server digital certificate (TLS level); issued certificates; and the certificate chains of issued certificates (Root CA certificate and Intermediate CA certificate). For simplicity, we did not change Pebble's certificate chain size for TLS. We only alter Pebble's TLS chain to use PQC algorithms without adding a new Intermediate CA certificate.
- **Sphincs+**: due to its increased signature sizes, we restrict Sphincs+ only for the Root CA certificate. We omit Root CA certificates in TLS handshakes, so Sphincs+ increased sizes are not transmitted in the handshake. Sphincs+ selected parameters are: `SHAKE` for the hash function, "s" for compact signatures and improved verification timings, and "simple" for performance.
- **Hybrid modes**: using NIST P-curves, namely `P256`, combined by concatenating with Kyber, Dilithium, and Falcon cryptographic objects. For simplicity, we opted to concatenate cryptographic objects into certificates (public keys and signatures). Hybrids are recommended because the confidence in PQC security is not well established yet [3], but also because RFC 8555 states "MUST/SHOULD implement" for some classical algorithms [1], thus keeping our integration close to the specification. We refer to the hybrid mode using the'H' letter (e.g., "Dilithium H.").

### 3.3 Impacts of PQC in ACME

To better understand the consequences of using PQC in ACME, we run several experiments using two geographically distant Google N2 Virtual Machines (VMs) with identical configurations (8 GB memory, two vCPUs). The ACME client VM was hosted in Osasco, São Paulo, Brazil, while the ACME server location was based on one of Let's Encrypt's data centers in Salt Lake City, Utah, USA. The average round-trip time (RTT) for this geographically distant network was measured to be 157 ms. The number of successful requests was computed by employing 1024 threads to POST requests to the `/finalize` endpoint for six minutes. Each thread simulated a different client sending CSRs, thereby increasing the server's load during certificate issuance. We set `ulimit -n 1048576` to enhance the server's load test configuration.

[1] https://github.com/AAGiron/acme-newchallenge.

Figure 3 illustrates the impacts of PQC observed during a load test experiment. For automation purposes, the default option is to generate a CSR during protocol execution, which we refer to as the "CSR-on-the-fly" test. This approach includes key generation and signing computational times, resulting in delayed clients and fewer successful requests handled by the server. Alternatively, using a pre-computed CSR can reduce the PQC impact at the cost of some of ACME's automation properties.

From the CA's perspective, the results demonstrated a noticeable impact when deploying PQC in the standard ACME configuration. The reduced number of successfully handled requests implies fewer certificates generated and issued by the ACME server. Furthermore, larger PQC objects can congest the network earlier than the baseline configuration (see Sect. 4.3).

It is worth noting that our experiments did not provide an exact measurement of the number of certificates issued per second due to the protocol's design (e.g., "REST-based" implementation, polling times, etc.). However, our load test is representative as it involves handling multiple signed requests, CSR generation by client threads, and verification by the server.

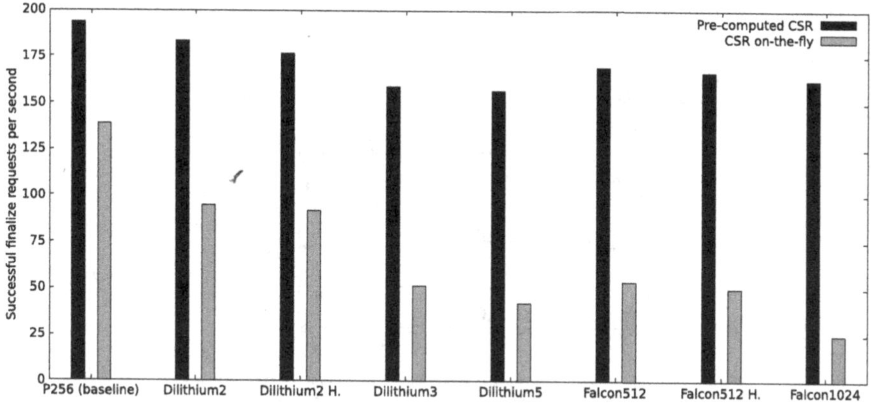


**Fig. 3.** Load test experiment with and without CSR cryptographic operations.

## 4 Proposed ACME Challenge

In order to speed up the issuance of digital certificates, we propose an alternate ACME challenge. In this section, we present our proposed ACME challenge (Sect. 4.1). After that, we evaluate and compare our proposed challenge against standard ACME certificate issuance and renewal. Lastly, we discuss the experimental findings in Sect. 4.3.

### 4.1 Design Details

We can consider two general scenarios when an ACME client $C$ will ask an ACME server $S$ for a new certificate. In the first scenario, $C$ already has a classical certificate, so $C$ can ask: (a) for a renewal, using the same ACME account; (b) for a new classical certificate (new account); or (c) a new PQC (or hybrid) certificate. In the second scenario, $C$ does not have a classical certificate: in this case, $C$ can only ask for a new PQC (or hybrid) certificate.

In the first scenario, we assume that $C$ already has a previously issued certificate. Having a certificate means that these ACME peers have a relationship that could be used to optimize the certificate issuance process. In the second scenario, there is no previous relationship available. Therefore, for the second scenario, $C$ must comply with all ACME requirements, i.e., fulfill the account creation, challenge validation, and issuance steps.

As described in Sect. 2.2, the issuance flow has several digitally-signed requests between peers. Using PQC signatures in such requests would increase protocol communication costs and impact the overall interaction between those peers. Also, one could take advantage of the scenario in which the server already has a certificate. To speed up the issuance process, we propose a new ACME challenge, depicted in Fig. 4.

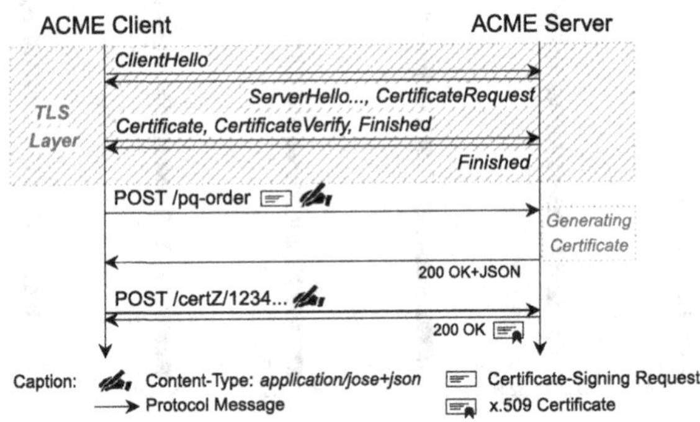


**Fig. 4.** Proposed ACME Challenge

Note that our proposal is valid for the scenario in which ACME clients already have a certificate. We provide an alternative to the original `/new-order` ACME server endpoint, called `/pq-order`. This new endpoint (at the server) expects a CSR in an HTTP POST message, as the usual `/finalize` endpoint. The main difference is that it requires a mutually authenticated TLS handshake. Mutual authentication means that the ACME client authenticates directly in the TLS layer, proving that it possesses the private key of that certificate. If the client successfully authenticates to the server, the server can issue the new (PQC or hybrid) certificate, replying with the URL where the certificate can be downloaded.

The fact that the ACME client already possesses a certificate plays a crucial role in this approach. For example, let $C_{classic-cert}$ be the certificate the client is willing to use in the TLS authentication layer, and $C_{pqc-cert}$ the certificate the client requests. If $C_{classic-cert}$ was issued by the same ACME server where $C_{pqc-cert}$ will be requested, then the peer trust relationship is already established. The ACME server will trust $C_{classic-cert}$ (in the pre-quantum scenario), so additional configuration or protocol messages are unnecessary. In this example, the ACME client can ask for a PQC certificate with this new challenge in a single request. Comparatively, we remove (at least) 4 signed requests from the ACME flow and replace the challenge with TLS client authentication using the $C_{classic-cert}$.

Since the `/pq-order` is an endpoint of the ACME server, clients perform POST requests with their account information accompanied by a CSR. In this case, the CSR can be created using a PQC algorithm (hybrid or not), allowing the issuance of a post-quantum certificate. Note, however, that the signature present in the request also uses a post-quantum algorithm. Appendix B gives an example of a POST message. Additionally, our proposed challenge applies to clients willing to issue a classical certificate, if desired.

Regarding the request validation, the server uses the algorithm name, nonce, and key ID (`kid`) information to search for the required account information. Note that the `kid` field can be replaced by the public key in a field called `jwk` for verifying the message. The optional `certhash` value is a way of binding the request to the particular certificate used in the TLS mutual authentication. In this way, the server can check if the hash is on his list of issued certificates and if it belongs to the corresponding account in the request. Alternatively, the ACME server can obtain the client certificate from the TLS layer and compare domain names and hashes. Golang provides access directly through the standard library [12]. The ACME server processes the CSR as usual. If the validation is successful, the server can issue the certificate.

**Security Considerations.** RFC 8555 describes a threat model against active and passive attackers considering two communication channels: the ACME channel, using TLS for security, and the Validation channel, which is dependent on the ACME challenge (e.g., HTTP). Since the validation channel is bound to the signatures transferred in the ACME channel, abusing only the validation channel should not be enough to impersonate a client (i.e., obtain a valid authorization).

Regarding the ACME channel, the only thing we changed is that it uses PQC algorithms. On the other hand, our proposed challenge replaces the available validation channels from the original ACME challenges with a mutually authenticated TLS connection channel. Note that our proposed challenge requires a valid mutual authentication TLS session and a valid signature in the request. Therefore, our challenge keeps the binding between the validation and ACME channels, thus not deviating from the RFC's threat model. The main requirement is a mandatory client authentication policy since client authentication is optional in TLS. An additional consideration is to avoid TLS Post-Handshake

Authentication [21] because the ACME server can issue the certificate only after the mutually authenticated connection is established.

Our proposed challenge assumes that who owns a certified (and valid) key pair for a particular domain owns the identifier in question, i.e., the domain. This might not be directly applicable in some cases, such as hosting providers. For example, when the domain ownership is transferred, the original owner could use the certificate to obtain a new one through our proposed challenge. Although this is a problem, it could be mitigated by simply revoking the certificate before transferring a domain. If revoked, the certificate can not be used to authenticate in our proposed challenge. Therefore, the server will not issue a new certificate in this case. This requirement implies keeping the certificate's validity period within the granted domain ownership validity period.

### 4.2 Issuance and Renewal Timings

We use the same experiment methodology as described in Sect. 3.3. In this case, the issuance time was measured at the client and encompassed all ACME steps (depicted in Fig. 1) until the client obtained its certificate. The renewal time was considered as a new issuance process by requesting the `/new-order` endpoint without creating a new account. Consequently, this metric measured the time from the `/new-order` POST request until the client received the certificate. Both renewal and issuance times were computed from 500 protocol executions (resulting in 500 certificates per algorithm instance) to obtain the average and standard deviation statistics.

Figure 5 shows the issuance and renewal times for ACME with baseline (classical) and PQC compared to our proposed challenge. The bars correspond to average timings, and the graph includes standard deviation information (above the bars). All standard deviations obtained from our proposed challenge executions are below 10 ms, whereas in standard ACME, it reaches 1.4 s. All bars are below the baseline standard deviation (using NIST's P256), which suggests no PQC transition impact in the timings perceived by the ACME client.

From the ACME client's perspective, Fig. 5 shows that the average impact in PQC is not significant. Here the network time dominates, and ACME's query-response nature increases the variations (as shown by the standard deviations). Sphincs+, `Dilithium3`, `Dilithium5`, and `Falcon-1024` also do not greatly influence the timings, so these configurations are also viable. On average, it took near to 7.5 s to issue a classical, PQC, or hybrid certificate.

On the other hand, our results suggest that the issuance and renewal time can be significantly reduced using our proposed challenge. The issuance times are, on average, 4.22x faster compared to the commonly-used HTTP challenge. Renewals are also much faster: without the account creation time, our renewals are near or below 1 s (on average), regardless of the algorithm selected for the new certificate (P256 or PQC). We highlight that our proposed challenge can be used generically, both for renewing classical certificates or issuing PQC certificates.

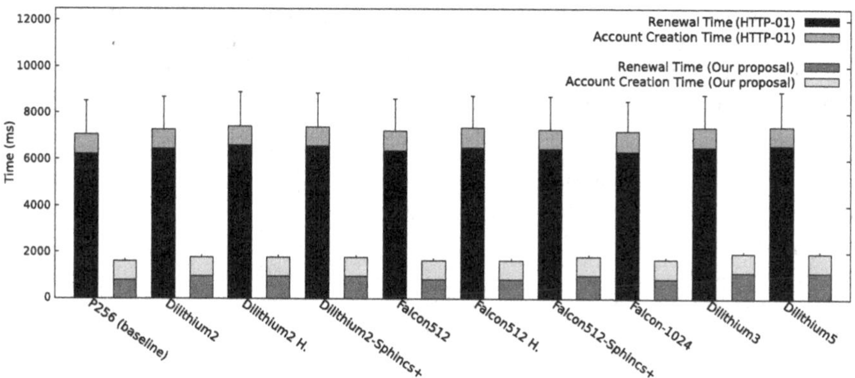


**Fig. 5.** Issuance and renewal average timings for different PQC algorithm instantiations. Note: Issuance time is the sum of Account Creation and Renewal time.

### 4.3 Discussion

In the context of PQC, we expected a significant slowdown in issuance and renewal times due to the increased sizes of PQC instances. For example, using `Dilithium2` imposes a payload size of 64.21 KiB on the network. However, this payload size is divided among several request messages in ACME (as depicted in Fig. 1). Assuming at least seven signed requests in ACME, each carrying less than 10 KB (except for certificate download), the data can be transported within a single round trip without requiring additional RTTs, assuming a standard TCP/IP network stack. Furthermore, we are not transmitting the Sphincs+ certificate, which saves bytes and keeps the size below network limits, such as the TCP window size. While literature shows scenarios where PQC imposes additional RTTs in other designs [28], issuance times depend not only on RTTs but also on the variable number of requests and waiting times. Our results indicate that the average issuance time for PQC was close to the baseline.

We were able to modify ACME and achieved better performance under reasonable assumptions, such as the client already having a classical certificate. By transitivity, having control of the certificate that certifies a domain demonstrates control over that domain, even if the certificate's private key is not stored on the server. In this scenario, our proposed modification reduced the byte costs of ACME. Table 2 illustrates the impacts of PQC on ACME and the sizes of our proposed challenge. Since not all ACME requests are used in our challenge, it reduces network RTTs. Compared to the original ACME flow, our challenge saves 35.39% and 32.14% for `Dilithium2` and `Falcon-512` instantiations, respectively.

It is important to note that our challenge differs from the TLS-ALPN-01 challenge. Defined in RFC 8737 [26], the ACME client generates a self-signed X.509 certificate with the challenge information, such as the KAS, and starts the TLS server under its control. The ACME server performs a handshake with this new TLS server to check the required information. However, the TLS-ALPN-01 challenge focuses on cases where the web service providing content is separate

**Table 2.** Comparison of sizes of ACME client requests, sampled from a pcapng capture file. Note: "Total (ACME)" excludes repeated requests (like POST /authZ); however, in practice, more bytes are transmitted (see Sect. 2.2). Certificate sizes include server and intermediate CA certificate.

| Request | Request is in our challenge? | P256 (baseline) size (bytes) | Dilithium2 size (bytes) | Falcon-512 size (bytes) |
|---|---|---|---|---|
| GET /dir | ✓ | 223 | 223 | 223 |
| HEAD /new-nonce | ✓ | 207 | 207 | 207 |
| POST /new-account | ✓ | 718 | 6097 | 3010 |
| POST /new-order | ✗ | 594 | 3747 | 1399 |
| POST /pq-order | ✓ | 1194 | 10558 | 4336 |
| POST /authZ | ✗ | 624 | 3776 | 1423 |
| POST /challZ | ✗ | 627 | 3779 | 1425 |
| POST /finalize | ✗ | 1088 | 10648 | 4417 |
| POST-AS-GET /certZ | ✓ | 649 | 3713 | 1361 |
| **Total (ACME*)** | – | **4730** | **32190** | **13465** |
| **Total (Our Challenge)** | – | **2991** | **20798** | **9137** |
| **Certificate size** | – | 1913 | 17838 | 7157 |

from the TLS server, such as reverse proxies. Additionally, the DNS-1 challenge can take up to one hour or up to five minutes under specific conditions [22], making it unsuitable for direct comparison against our challenge. Since the HTTP challenge is the most commonly used, our experiments focused on this scenario.

While our proposed challenge provides faster issuance times, it is not meant to replace other existing ACME challenges. There may be scenarios where our challenge is not suitable. One example is when the client does not have a classical certificate. Another example relates to the validity period of certificates and the reuse of valid authorizations, as allowed in RFC 8555 [1].

RFC 8555 [1] does not impose a limit on the expiration time of authorizations, leaving the validity period of a valid authorization to the implementation. For instance, Let's Encrypt's current policy allows reuse for up to 30 days. Therefore, if an HTTP challenge has been fulfilled, the ACME client has 30 days to issue or renew certificates, improving performance by skipping the challenge step. However, this 30-day policy is subject to change [7] and may vary or be denied in other implementations. On the other hand, our challenge's validity is limited to the certificate's validity period (currently 90 days in Let's Encrypt's policy). In the context of PQC transition, we highly recommend deactivating authorizations of accounts created with classical cryptography. Deactivation is necessary because ACME servers cannot guarantee that the TLS connection established by ACME clients is quantum-safe. Non-PQC TLS usage by clients and valid authorizations facilitate quantum attacks, as discussed in Sect. 3.1.

Nevertheless, our proposal improves performance for issuing certificates (including account creation time) and renewals (assuming the client has an account with the server). In scenarios where our challenge's assumptions hold, ACME clients can utilize our approach for renewing classical certificates faster, or during the PQC transition phase and subsequently renew their PQC certificates. For security reasons, Issuer CA policies can impose usage limits on clients renewing with our challenge. These limits can reduce the impact of a certificate's key compromise, forcing the client to prove ownership using a different challenge.

Our proposed challenge can be further optimized if additional modifications are made at the TLS layer. Specifically, mutual authentication in TLS involves transferring certificates over the network, increasing the size of TLS messages. RFC 7924 [23] specifies certificate caching mechanisms (client or server), which could be employed in ACME's TLS channel to reduce the TLS payload size.

## 5 Final Remarks and Future Work

This work provided a comprehensive evaluation of ACME's performance when secured with PQC algorithms, considering the perspectives of ACME clients (e.g., web servers) and servers (e.g., Issuer CAs). The comparison against classical cryptography highlighted different impacts on these entities.

Regarding challenges required for the certificate issuance process, our proposed design showed favorable results. We achieved smaller communication sizes and decreased network bandwidth by replacing the HTTP challenge and eliminating associated signed requests. To encourage practical adoption, we have made our design and prototype implementation available to the community. We have also provided an RFC-like description of our challenge as a guide for future implementations.

There are interesting opportunities for further research and evaluation of ACME. For instance, investigating ACME's performance in different computing environments, such as the Internet of Things (IoT), would be valuable. Additionally, exploring how ACME performs when issuing certificates for KEMTLS, a key encapsulation mechanism-based TLS, could provide valuable insights. It is worth noting that issuing KEM-based certificates in ACME poses challenges due to the typical usage of CSRs with signature methods. Nonetheless, ACME remains a significant security-enabling protocol that has already benefited various applications and is likely to continue doing so in the future.

**Acknowledgements.** This work was supported by the Federal University of Technology - Parana (UTFPR) and the Technology Innovation Institute (TII).

## Appendix

## A ACME's HTTP-01 Challenge

Figure 6 focus on the HTTP challenge message flow, which is more commonly used, probably due to its simplicity. We omit account creation messages, order and download requests. First, the client obtains the necessary information for the challenge (e.g., KAS) with the steps presented in Fig. 1. Basically, the client places the KAS file in (one or more) HTTP servers that it controls. Therefore, the KAS binds the HTTP server to the ACME client's account. Then, the client notifies the server with a POST to `/challZ` endpoint. The validation steps include checking the response (e.g., if the domain name matches the previous order information) and, most importantly: (i) if the KAS inside the downloaded file matches; and (ii) if the digital signatures (in the requests) can be verified using the corresponding account's public key. Otherwise, the challenge fails.

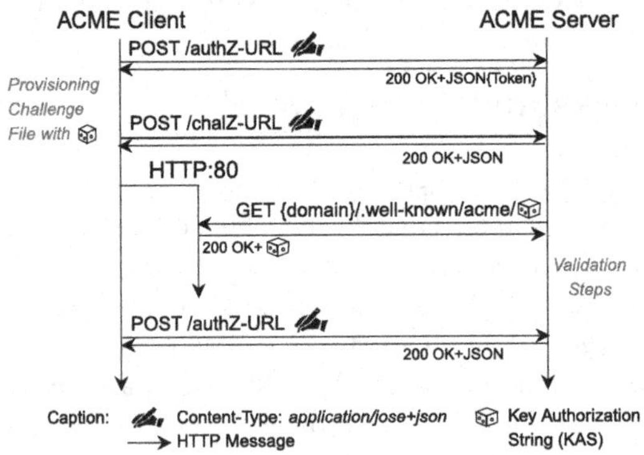


**Fig. 6.** HTTP challenge flow

In practice, the HTTP challenge (and the other types) can consume more POST requests to `/authZ` endpoint than shown in Fig. 6. The ACME client will repeat such a POST request until the status of the order is "valid" (or "invalid" in the case of an error). This can increase network traffic when considering multiple clients at the same time. Moreover, Although the most common option, the HTTP-01 challenge is not the best option for issuing multiple certificates for multiple servers and if firewalls are blocking HTTP port (80).

## B POST Request Example

Figure 7 shows an example of a POST request to `/pq-order` (in our proposed ACME challenge). We followed the notation of the `/new-order` endpoint [1]. The main differences are: we removed the order's validity period, when focusing on the PQC transition, due to the uncertainty of when quantum computers will arrive; and we included an (optional) `certhash` field in the protected header. Both protected and payload fields have integrity guarantees (e.g., by signing). In this example, `Dilithium2` is the PQC algorithm used for signing. The CSR included in the payload in this case use a post-quantum signature algorithm. However, we note that one could also use classical algorithms in the POST and CSR, aiming at renewing classical certificates.

```
POST /acme/pq-order HTTP/1.1
 Host: example.com
 Content-Type: application/jose+json
 {
  "protected": base64url({
   "alg": "Dilithium2",
   "kid": "https://example.com/acme/acct/evOfKhNU60wg",
   "nonce": "5XJ1L3lEkMG7tR6pA00clA",
   "url": "https://example.com/acme/pq-order",
   "certhash": "89f308210c7c7820b...947c3188dedba6e3"
  }),
  "payload": base64url({
   "csr": "MIIBPTCBxAIBADBFMQ...KdZeGsysoCo4H9P",
    "identifiers": [
     { "type": "dns", "value": "www.teste.org" },
     { "type": "dns", "value": "teste.org" }
    ],
  }),
  "signature": "H6ZXtGjTZyUnPeKn...wEA4TklBdh3e454g"
 }
```

**Fig. 7.** POST request example

The POST message uses the account's private key to sign the protected and payload JSON fields. This complies to JSON Web Signature (JWS) [9] requirements. After validating the POST message, the server issues the certificate and returns to the client the URL for the certificate's location (similarly as in standard ACME). In this way, the ACME client can ask for a classical or PQC certificate with our proposed challenge in a single request.

## References


1. Barnes, R., Hoffman-Andrews, J., McCarney, D., Kasten, J.: Automatic Certificate Management Environment (ACME). RFC 8555, RFC Editor (2019)
2. Bernstein, D.J., Lange, T.: Post-quantum cryptography. Nature **549**(7671), 188–194 (2017)
3. Bindel, N., Braun, J., Gladiator, L., Stöckert, T., Wirth, J.: X. 509-compliant hybrid certificates for the post-quantum transition. J. Open Sour. Software **4**(40), 1606 (2019)
4. Bindel, N., Herath, U., McKague, M., Stebila, D.: Transitioning to a quantum-resistant public key infrastructure. In: Lange, T., Takagi, T. (eds.) PQCrypto 2017. LNCS, vol. 10346, pp. 384–405. Springer, Cham (2017). https://doi.org/10.1007/978-3-319-59879-6_22
5. Encrypt, L.: Challenge types (2020). https://letsencrypt.org/docs/challenge-types/
6. Encrypt, L.: Let's Encrypt Stats (2022). https://letsencrypt.org/pt-br/stats/
7. Forum, L.E.C.: The lifecycle of a valid authorization (2019). https://community.letsencrypt.org/t/the-lifecycle-of-a-valid-authorization/101387/2
8. Foundation, E.F.: Certbot - get your site on https (2022). https://certbot.eff.org/
9. Jones, M., Bradley, J., Sakimura, N.: JSON Web Signature (JWS). RFC 7515, RFC Editor (2015). http://www.rfc-editor.org/rfc/rfc7515.txt, http://www.rfc-editor.org/rfc/rfc7515.txt

10. Joseph, D., et al.: Transitioning organizations to post-quantum cryptography. Nature **605**(7909), 237–243 (2022). https://doi.org/10.1038/s41586-022-04623-2
11. Kampanakis, P., Panburana, P., Daw, E., Geest, D.V.: The Viability of Post-quantum X.509 Certificates. Cryptology ePrint Archive, Paper 2018/063 (2018). https://eprint.iacr.org/2018/063, https://eprint.iacr.org/2018/063
12. LLC, G.: Go Standard Library (2023). https://pkg.go.dev/std
13. Mosca, M., Piani, M.: Quantum Threat Timeline Report 2020 (2020). https://globalriskinstitute.org/publications/quantum-threat-timeline-report-2020/. Accessed 20 Jul 2021
14. NIST: Post-quantum Cryptography (2016). https://csrc.nist.gov/Projects/Post-Quantum-Cryptography. Accessed 26 Jun 2021
15. NIST: HMAC - Glossary (2022). https://csrc.nist.gov/glossary/term/hmac. Accessed 01 Nov 2022
16. NIST: PQC Standardization Process: Announcing four candidates to be standardized, plus fourth round candidates (2022). https://csrc.nist.gov/News/2022/pqc-candidates-to-be-standardized-and-round-4. Accessed 02 Nov 2022
17. Nystrom, M., Kaliski, B.: PKCS #10: Certification Request Syntax Specification Version 1.7. RFC 2986, RFC Editor (2000)
18. Paquin, C., Stebila, D., Tamvada, G.: Benchmarking post-quantum cryptography in TLS. In: Ding, J., Tillich, J.-P. (eds.) PQCrypto 2020. LNCS, vol. 12100, pp. 72–91. Springer, Cham (2020). https://doi.org/10.1007/978-3-030-44223-1_5
19. Project, O.Q.S.: liboqs-go: Go bindings for liboqs (2022). https://github.com/open-quantum-safe/liboqs-go. Accessed 25 Jan 2022
20. Raavi, M., Chandramouli, P., Wuthier, S., Zhou, X., Chang, S.Y.: Performance characterization of post-quantum digital certificates. In: 2021 International Conference on Computer Communications and Networks (ICCCN), Athens, Greece, pp. 1–9. IEEE (2021). https://doi.org/10.1109/ICCCN52240.2021.9522179
21. Rescorla, E.: The Transport Layer Security (TLS) Protocol Version 1.3. RFC 8446, RFC Editor (2018)
22. Rudra, A.: How long does it take for DNS to update? DNS Propagation (2022). https://powerdmarc.com/how-long-does-it-take-for-dns-to-update/
23. Santesson, S., Tschofenig, H.: Transport Layer Security (TLS) Cached Information Extension. RFC 7924, RFC Editor (2016)
24. Schwabe, P., Stebila, D., Wiggers, T.: Post-Quantum TLS Without Handshake Signatures, New York, NY, USA, pp. 1461–1480. Association for Computing Machinery (2020). https://doi.org/10.1145/3372297.3423350
25. Schwabe, P., Stebila, D., Wiggers, T.: More efficient post-quantum KEMTLS with pre-distributed public keys. In: Bertino, E., Shulman, H., Waidner, M. (eds.) ESORICS 2021. LNCS, vol. 12972, pp. 3–22. Springer, Cham (2021). https://doi.org/10.1007/978-3-030-88418-5_1
26. Shoemaker, R.: Automated Certificate Management Environment (ACME) TLS Application-Layer Protocol Negotiation (ALPN) Challenge Extension. RFC 8737, RFC Editor (2020)
27. Shor, P.W.: Algorithms for quantum computation: discrete logarithms and factoring. In: Proceedings 35th Annual Symposium on Foundations of Computer Science, Santa Fe, NM, USA, pp. 124–134. IEEE, IEEE (1994)
28. Sikeridis, D., Kampanakis, P., Devetsikiotis, M.: Assessing the overhead of post-quantum cryptography in TLS 1.3 and SSH. In: Proceedings of the 16th International Conference on emerging Networking Experiments and Technologies, New York, NY, USA, pp. 149–156. Association for Computing Machinery (2020)

29. Stebila, D., Mosca, M.: Post-quantum key exchange for the internet and the open quantum safe project. In: Avanzi, R., Heys, H. (eds.) SAC 2016. LNCS, vol. 10532, pp. 14–37. Springer, Cham (2017). https://doi.org/10.1007/978-3-319-69453-5_2
30. ZeroSSL: Free SSL Certificates and SSL tools (2022). https://zerossl.com/

# Algorithmic Views of Vectorized Polynomial Multipliers – NTRU Prime

Vincent Hwang[1,3(✉)], Chi-Ting Liu[2(✉)], and Bo-Yin Yang[3(✉)]

[1] Max Planck Institute for Security and Privacy, Bochum, Germany
vincentvbh7@gmail.com
[2] National Taiwan University, Taipei, Taiwan
gting906@gmail.com
[3] Academia Sinica, Taipei, Taiwan
by@crypto.tw

**Abstract.** In this paper, we explore the cost of vectorization for multiplying polynomials with coefficients in $\mathbb{Z}_q$ for an odd prime $q$, as exemplified by NTRU Prime, a postquantum cryptosystem that found early adoption due to its inclusion in OpenSSH.

If there is a large power of two dividing $q-1$, we can apply radix-2 Cooley–Tukey fast Fourier transforms to multiply polynomials in $\mathbb{Z}_q[x]$. The radix-2 nature admits efficient vectorization. Conversely, if 2 is the only power of two dividing $q-1$, we can apply Schönhage's and Nussbaumer's FFTs to craft radix-2 roots of unity, but these double the number of coefficients.

We show how to avoid the doubling while maintaining the vectorization friendliness with Good–Thomas, Rader's, and Bruun's FFTs. In particular, in `sntrup761`, the most common instance of NTRU Prime we have $q = 4591$, and we exploit the existing Fermat-prime factor of $q-1$ for Rader's FFT and power-of-two factor of $q+1$ for Bruun's FFT.

Polynomial multiplications in $\mathbb{Z}_{4591}[x]/\left\langle x^{761} - x - 1\right\rangle$ is still a worthwhile target because while out of the NIST PQC competition, `sntrup761` is still going to be used with OpenSSH by default in the near future.

Our polynomial multiplication outperforms the state-of-the-art vector-optimized implementation by $6.1\times$. For `ntrulpr761`, our keygen, encap, and decap are $2.98\times$, $2.79\times$, and $3.07\times$ faster than the state-of-the-art vector-optimized implementation. For `sntrup761`, we outperform the reference implementation significantly.

**Keywords:** Good–Thomas FFT · Rader's FFT · Bruun's FFT · NTRU Prime · Vectorization

## 1 Introduction

At PQCrypto 2016, the National Institute of Standards and Technology (NIST) announced the Post-Quantum Cryptography Standardization Process for replacing existing standards for public-key cryptography with quantum-resistant cryptosystems. For lattice-based cryptosystems, polynomial multiplications have


C. Pöpper and L. Batina (Eds.): ACNS 2024, LNCS 14584, pp. 24–46, 2024.
https://doi.org/10.1007/978-3-031-54773-7_2

been the most time-consuming operations. Recently standardized [AAC+22] Dilithium, Kyber, and Falcon wrote number–theoretic transforms (NTTs) into their specifications in response.

OpenSSH 9.0 defaults to NTRU Prime[1]. However, in NTRU Prime the polynomial ring doesn't allow NTT-based multiplications naturally. State-of-the-art vectorized implementations introduced various techniques extending coefficient rings, or computed the results over $\mathbb{Z}$. In each of these approaches, empirically small-degree polynomial multiplications is always an important bottleneck. We study the compatibility of vectorization and various algorithmic techniques in the literature and choose the ARM Cortex-A72 implementing the Armv8-A architecture[2] for this work. We are interested in vectorized polynomial multiplications for NTRU Prime. [BBCT22] showed that a vectorized generic polynomial multiplication takes $\sim 1.5\times$ time of a "generic by small (ternary coefficients)" one with AVX2. [BBCT22] applied Schönhage and Nussbaumer to ease vectorization. Schönhage and Nussbaumer double the sizes of the coefficient rings and lead to a larger number of small-degree polynomial multiplications. We explain how to avoid the doubling with Good–Thomas, Rader's, and Bruun's FFTs.

We implement our ideas on Cortex-A72 implementing Armv8.0-A with the vector instruction set Neon. However, we emphasize that our approaches are built around the notion of vectorization and not a specific architecture.

### 1.1 Contributions

We summarize our contributions as follows.

- We formalize the needs of vectorization commonly involved in vectorized implementations.
- We propose vectorized polynomial multipliers essentially quartering and halving the number of small-dimensional polynomial multiplications after FFTs.
- We propose novel accumulative (subtractive) variants of Barrett multiplication absorbing the follow up addition (subtraction).
- We implement the ideas with the SIMD technology Neon in Armv8.0-A on a Cortex-A72. Our fastest polynomial multiplier outperforms the state-of-the-art optimized implementation by a factor of $6.1\times$.
- In addition to the polynomial multiplication, we vectorize the sorting network, polynomial inversions, encoding, and decoding subroutines used in `ntrulpr761` and `sntrup761`. For `ntrulpr761`, our key generation, encapsulation, and decapsulation are $2.98\times$, $2.79\times$, and $3.07\times$ faster than the state-of-the-art optimized implementation. For `sntrup761`, we outperform the reference implementation significantly.

[1] https://marc.info/?l=openssh-unix-dev&m=164939371201404&w=2.

[2] ARMv8-A, which naturally comes with the SIMD technology Neon, is currently the most prevalent architecture for mobile devices and is used for all Apple hardware.

### 1.2 Code

Our source code can be found at https://github.com/vector-polymul-ntru-ntrup/NTRU_Prime under the CC0 license.

### 1.3 Structure of This Paper

Section 2 goes through the preliminaries. Section 3 surveys FFTs. Section 4 describes our implementations. We show the performance numbers in Sect. 5.

## 2 Preliminaries

Section 2.1 describes the polynomials rings in NTRU Prime, Sect. 2.2 describes our target platform Cortex-A72, and Sect. 2.3 describes the modular arithmetic.

### 2.1 Polynomials in NTRU Prime

The NTRU Prime submission comprises two families: Streamlined NTRU Prime and NTRU LPRime. Both operate on the polynomial ring $\mathbb{Z}_q[x]/\langle x^p - x - 1\rangle$ where $q$ and $p$ are primes such that the ring is a finite field. We target the polynomial multiplications for parameter sets `sntrup761` and `ntrulpr761` where $q = 4591$ and $p = 761$. One should note that `sntrup761`, which is used by OpenSSH, uses a (Quotient) NTRU structure, and requires inversions in $\mathbb{Z}_3[x]/\langle x^{761} - x - 1\rangle$ and $\mathbb{Z}_{4591}[x]/\langle x^{761} - x - 1\rangle$. We refer the readers to the specification [BBC+20] for more details. With no other assumptions on the inputs, we call a polynomial multiplication "big by big". If one of the inputs is guaranteed to be ternary, we call it "big by small". We optimize both although the former is required only if we apply the fast constant-time GCD [BY19] to the inversions in the key generation of `sntrup761`. The fast constant-time GCD is left as a future work.

### 2.2 Cortex-A72

Our target platform is the ARM Cortex-A72, implementing the 64-bit Armv8.0-A instruction set architecture. It is a superscalar Central Processing Unit (CPU) with an in-order frontend and an out-of-order backend. Instructions are first decoded into $\mu$ops in the frontend and dispatched to the backend, which contains these eight pipelines: `L` for loads, `S` for stores, `B` for branches, `I0/I1` for integer instructions, `M` for multi-cycle integer instructions, and `F0/F1` for Single-Instruction-Multiple-Data (SIMD) instructions. The frontend can only dispatch at most three $\mu$ops per cycle. Furthermore, in a single cycle, the frontend dispatches at most one $\mu$op using `B`, at most two $\mu$ops using `I0/I1`, at most two $\mu$ops using `M`, at most one $\mu$op using `F0`, at most one $\mu$op using `F1`, and at most two $\mu$ops using `L/S` [ARM15, Sect. 4.1].

We mainly focus on the pipelines `F0`, `F1`, `L`, and `S` for performance. `F0/F1` are both capable of various additions, subtractions, permutations, comparisons, minimums/maximums, and table lookups[3]. However, multiplications can only be dispatched to `F0`, and shifts to `F1`. The most heavily-loaded pipeline is clearly the critical path. If there are more multiplications than shifts, we much prefer instructions that can use either pipeline to go to `F1` since the time spent in `F0` will dominate our runtime. Conversely, with more shifts than multiplications, we want to dispatch most non-shifts to `F0`. In practice, we interleave instructions dispatched to the pipeline with the most workload with other pipelines (or even `L/S`)—and pray. Our experiment shows that this approach generally works well. In the case of `chacha20` implementing `randombytes` for benchmarking [BHK+22], we even consider a compiler-aided mixing of `I0/I1`, `F0/F1`, *and* `L/S`[4]. The idea also proved valuable for `Keccak` on some other Cortex-A cores [BK22, Table 1].

**SIMD Registers.** The 64-bit Armv8-A has 32 architectural 128-bit SIMD registers with each viewable as packed 8-, 16-, 32-, or 64-bit elements ([ARM21, Fig. A1-1]), denoted by suffixes `.16B` `.8H`, `.4S`, and `.2D` on the register name, respectively.

### Armv8-A Vector Instructions

*Multiplications.* A plain `mul` multiplies corresponding vector elements and returns same-sized results. There are many variants of multiplications: `mla/mls` computes the same product vector and accumulates to or subtracts from the destination. There are high-half products `sqdmulh` and `sqrdmulh`. The former computes the double-size products, doubles the results, and returns the upper halves. The latter first rounds to the upper halves before returning them. There are long multiplications `s{mul,mla,mls}l{,2}`. `smull` multiplies the corresponding signed elements from the lower 64-bit of the source registers and places the resulting double-width vector elements in the destination register. It is usually paired with an `smull2` using the upper 64-bit instead. Their accumulating and subtracting variants are `s{mla,mls}l{,2}`. We will not use the unsigned counterparts `u{mul,mla,mls}l{,2}`.

*Shifts.* `shl` shifts left; `sshr` arithmetically shifts right; `srshr` rounds the results after shifting. We won't use the unsigned `ushr` and `urshr`.

*Additions/Subtractions.* For basic arithmetic, the usual `add/sub` adds/subtracts the corresponding elements. Long variants `s{add,sub}l{,2}` add or subtract the corresponding elements from the lower or upper 64-bit halves and signed-extend into double-width results[5].

[3] There are some exceptions, including `addv`, `smaxv`, `sadalp`. We are not using them in this paper and refer to [ARM15] for more details.

[4] We write some assembly and only obtain comparable performance. So we keep the implementations with intrinsics instead for readability.

[5] There are several options for signed-extending vector elements—`saddl{,2}` and `ssubl{,2}` which go to either `F0/F1`, `sxtl{,2}` to `F1`, and `smull{,2}` going to `F0`.

*Permutations.* Then we have permutations—`uzp{1,2}` extracts the even and odd positions respectively from a pair of vectors and concatenates the results into a vector. `ext` extracts the lowest elements (there is an immediate operand specifying the number of bytes) of the second source vector (as the high part) and concatenates to the highest elements of the first source vector. `zip{1,2}` takes the bottom and top halves of a pair of vectors and riffle-shuffles them into the destination.

### 2.3 Modular Arithmetic

**Algorithm 1.** Barrett reduction.

This is [BHK+22, Algorithm 11].

**Input:** $\mathtt{a} = a$.

**Output:** $\mathtt{a} = a - \left\lfloor \frac{a \left\lfloor \frac{2^e \mathtt{R}}{q} \right\rceil}{2^e \mathtt{R}} \right\rceil q \equiv a \bmod {}^{\pm}q$.

sqdmulh t, a, $\left\lfloor \frac{2^e \mathtt{R}}{q} \right\rceil$
srshr t, t, #$(e+1)$
mls a, t, $q$

**Algorithm 2.** Barrett multiplication.

This is [BHK+22, Algorithm 10].

**Input:** $\mathtt{a} = a$.

**Output:** $\mathtt{a} = ab - \left\lfloor \frac{a \left\lfloor \frac{b\mathtt{R}}{q} \right\rceil_2}{\mathtt{R}} \right\rceil q \equiv ab \bmod {}^{\pm}q$.

sqrdmulh t, a, $\frac{\left\lfloor \frac{b\mathtt{R}}{q} \right\rceil_2}{2}$
mul a, a, $b$
mls a, t, $q$

Let $q$ be an odd modulus, and $\mathtt{R}$ be the size of the arithmetic. We describe the modular reductions and multiplications for computing in $\mathbb{Z}_q$. Barrett reduction [Bar86] reduces a value $a$ by approximating $a \bmod {}^{\pm}q$ with $a - \left\lfloor \frac{a \cdot \left\lfloor \frac{2^e \mathtt{R}}{q} \right\rceil}{2^e \mathtt{R}} \right\rceil$ (cf. Algorithm 1). For multiplying an unknown $a$ with a fixed value $b$, we compute $ab - \left\lfloor \frac{a \left\lfloor \frac{b\mathtt{R}}{q} \right\rceil_2}{\mathtt{R}} \right\rceil q \equiv ab \bmod {}^{\pm}q$ (Barrett multiplication [BHK+22]) where $\lfloor \rceil_2$ is the function mapping a real number $r$ to $2 \left\lfloor \frac{r}{2} \right\rceil$ (cf. Algorithm 2). We give novel multiply-add/sub variants of Barrett multiplication in Algorithms 3 and 4. Algorithm 3 (resp. Algorithm 4) computes a representation of $a + bc$ (resp. $a - bc$) by merging a `mul` with an `add` (resp. a `sub`) into an `mla` (resp. `mls`), saving 1 instruction.

**Algorithm 3.** `Barrett_mla`.

**Input:** $\mathtt{a} = a$.

**Output:** $\mathtt{a} = a + bc - \left\lfloor \frac{b \left\lfloor \frac{c\mathtt{R}}{q} \right\rceil_2}{\mathtt{R}} \right\rceil q$.

sqrdmulh t, $b$, $\frac{\left\lfloor \frac{c\mathtt{R}}{q} \right\rceil_2}{2}$
mla a, $b$, $c$
mls a, t, $q$

**Algorithm 4.** `Barrett_mls`.

**Input:** $\mathtt{a} = a$.

**Output:** $\mathtt{a} = a - bc + \left\lfloor \frac{b \left\lfloor \frac{c\mathtt{R}}{q} \right\rceil_2}{\mathtt{R}} \right\rceil q$.

sqrdmulh t, $b$, $\frac{\left\lfloor \frac{c\mathtt{R}}{q} \right\rceil_2}{2}$
mls a, $b$, $c$
mla a, t, $q$

# 3 Fast Fourier Transforms

We go through the mathematics behind various fast Fourier transforms (FFTs) and emphasize their defining conditions. This section is structured as follows. Section 3.1 reviews the Chinese remainder theorem for polynomial rings and discrete Fourier transform (DFT). We then survey various FFTs, including Cooley–Tukey in Sect. 3.2, Bruun and its finite field counterpart in Sect. 3.3, Good–Thomas in Sect. 3.4, Rader in Sect. 3.5, and Schönhage and Nussbaumer in Sect. 3.6. We use number–theoretic transform (NTT) as a synonym of FFT.

## 3.1 The Chinese Remainder Theorem (CRT) for Polynomial Rings

Let $n = \prod_l n_l$, and $\boldsymbol{g}_{i_0,\dots,i_{h-1}} \in R[x]$ be coprime polynomials for all indices $(i_l)_{l=0\cdots h-1}$ where $0 \le i_l < n_l$. The CRT gives us a chain of isomorphisms

$$\frac{R[x]}{\left\langle \prod_{i_0,\dots,i_{h-1}} \boldsymbol{g}_{i_0,\dots,i_{h-1}} \right\rangle} \cong \prod_{i_0} \frac{R[x]}{\left\langle \prod_{i_1,\dots,i_{h-1}} \boldsymbol{g}_{i_0,\dots,i_{h-1}} \right\rangle} \cong \cdots \cong \prod_{i_0,\dots,i_{h-1}} \frac{R[x]}{\left\langle \boldsymbol{g}_{i_0,\dots,i_{h-1}} \right\rangle}.$$

Multiplying in $\prod_{i_0,\dots,i_{h-1}} R[x] \Big/ \left\langle \boldsymbol{g}_{i_0,\dots,i_{h-1}} \right\rangle$ is cheap if the polynomial modulus is small. If the isomorphism chain is also cheap, we improve the polynomial multiplications in $R[x] \Big/ \left\langle \prod_{i_0,\dots,i_{h-1}} \boldsymbol{g}_{i_0,\dots,i_{h-1}} \right\rangle$. For small $n_l$'s, it is usually cheap to decompose a polynomial ring into a product of $n_l$ polynomial rings.

Transformations will be described with the words “radix”, “split”, and “layer”. We demonstrated below for $h = 2$. Suppose we have isomorphisms

$$R[x] \Big/ \left\langle \prod_{i_0,i_1} \boldsymbol{g}_{i_0,i_1} \right\rangle \overset{\eta_0}{\cong} \prod_{i_0} R[x] \Big/ \left\langle \prod_{i_1} \boldsymbol{g}_{i_0,i_1} \right\rangle \overset{\eta_1}{\cong} \prod_{i_0,i_1} R[x] / \langle \boldsymbol{g}_{i_0,i_1} \rangle$$

where $i_0 \in \{0, \dots, n_0 - 1\}$ and $i_1 \in \{0, \dots, n_1 - 1\}$. We call $\eta_0$ a *radix-$n_0$ split* and an implementation of $\eta_0$ a radix-$n_0$ computation, and similarly for $\eta_1$. Usually, we implement several isomorphisms together to minimize memory operations. The resulting computation is called a *multi-layer* computation. Suppose we implement $\eta_0$ and $\eta_1$ with a single pair of loads and stores, and $\eta_0$ and $\eta_1$ both rely on X, a shape of computations, then the resulting multi-layer computation is called a *2-layer* X. If additionally $n_0 = n_1$, the computation is a *2-layer radix-$n_0$* X, and similarly for more layers.

## 3.2 Cooley–Tukey FFT

In a Cooley–Tukey FFT [CT65], we have $\zeta \in R$, $\omega_n \in R$ a principal $n$th root of unity, $n$ coprime to char$(R)$, and $\boldsymbol{g}_{i_0,\dots,i_{h-1}} = x - \zeta \omega_n^{\sum_l i_l \prod_{j<l} n_j} \in R[x]$.

Since $\prod_{i_0,\dots,i_{h-1}} \boldsymbol{g}_{i_0,\dots,i_{h-1}} = x^n - \zeta^n$, the efficiency of multiplying polynomials in $R[x]/\langle x^n - \zeta^n \rangle$ boils down to the efficiency of the isomorphisms indexed by $i_l$'s. Furthermore, it is a *cyclic* NTT if $\zeta^n = 1$.

### 3.3 Bruun-Like FFTs

[Bru78] first introduced the idea of factoring into trinomials $\boldsymbol{g}_{i_0,\dots,i_{h-1}}$ when $n$ is a power of two—to reduce the number of multiplications in $R$ while operating over $\mathbb{C}$. [Mur96] generalized this to arbitrary even $n$. For our implementations, we need the results on factoring $x^{2^k} + 1 \in \mathbb{F}_q[x]$ when $q \equiv 3 \pmod 4$ [BGM93] and composed multiplications of polynomials in $\mathbb{F}_q[x]$ [BC87]. Factoring $x^n - 1$ over $\mathbb{F}_q$ is actively researched [BGM93, Mey96, TW13, MVdO14, WYF18, WY21].

**Review: The Original Bruun's FFT ($\boldsymbol{R} = \mathbb{C}$).** We choose $\boldsymbol{g}_{i_0,\dots,i_{h-1}} = x^2 - \left(\zeta\omega_n^{\sum_l i_l \prod_{j<l} n_j} + \zeta^{-1}\omega_n^{-\sum_l i_l \prod_{j<l} n_j}\right) x + 1$ so $x^{2n} - (\zeta^n + \zeta^{-n})\, x^n + 1 = \prod_{i_0,\dots,i_{h-1}} \boldsymbol{g}_{i_0,\dots,i_{h-1}}$. This provides us an alternative factorization for $x^{4n} - 1 = (x^{2n} - 1)(x^{2n} + 1)$ by choosing $\zeta^n = \omega_4$. For a complex number with norm 1, since the sum of its inverse and itself is real, we only need arithmetic in $\mathbb{R}$ to reach $\prod_{i_0,\dots,i_{h-1}} \mathbb{C}[x] \Big/ \left\langle \boldsymbol{g}_{i_0,\dots,i_{h-1}(x)} \right\rangle$.

**$\boldsymbol{R} = \mathbb{F}_q$ where $\boldsymbol{q} \equiv 3 \pmod 4$.** We need Theorem 1 for our implementations.

**Theorem 1 ([BGM93, Theorem 1]).** Let $q \equiv 3 \pmod 4$ and $2^w$ be the highest power of two in $q+1$. If $k < w$, then $x^{2^k} + 1$ factors into irreducible trinomials $x^2 + \gamma x + 1$ in $\mathbb{F}_q[x]$. Else (i.e., $k \geq w$) $x^{2^k} + 1$ factors into irreducible trinomials $x^{2^{k-w+1}} + \gamma x^{2^{k-w}} - 1$ in $\mathbb{F}_q[x]$.

Given $\boldsymbol{f}_0, \boldsymbol{f}_1 \in \mathbb{F}_q[x]$, we define their "composed multiplication" as $(\boldsymbol{f}_0 \odot \boldsymbol{f}_1) := \prod_{\boldsymbol{f}_0(\alpha)=0} \prod_{\boldsymbol{f}_1(\beta)=0} (x - \alpha\beta)$ where $\alpha, \beta$ run over all the roots of $\boldsymbol{f}_0, \boldsymbol{f}_1$ in an extension field of $\mathbb{F}_q$.We need the following from [BC87]:

**Lemma 1 ([BC87, Eq. 8]).** $\prod_{i_0} \boldsymbol{f}_{0,i_0} \odot \prod_{i_1} \boldsymbol{f}_{1,i_1} = \prod_{i_0,i_1} (\boldsymbol{f}_{0,i_0} \odot \boldsymbol{f}_{1,i_1})$ holds for any sequences of polynomials $\boldsymbol{f}_{0,i_0}, \boldsymbol{f}_{1,i_1} \in \mathbb{F}_q[x]$.

**Lemma 2 ([BC87, Eq. 5]).** If $\boldsymbol{f}_0 = \prod_\alpha (x - \alpha) \in \mathbb{F}_q[x]$, then for any $\boldsymbol{f}_1 \in \mathbb{F}_q[x]$, we have $\boldsymbol{f}_0 \odot \boldsymbol{f}_1 = \prod_\alpha \alpha^{\deg(\boldsymbol{f}_1)} \boldsymbol{f}_1(\alpha^{-1}x) \in \mathbb{F}_q[x]$.

**Lemma 3.** Let $r$ be odd, $x^r - 1 = \prod_{i_0} (x - \omega_r^{i_0}) \in \mathbb{F}_q[x]$, and $x^{2^k} - 1 = \prod_{i_1} \boldsymbol{f}_{i_1} \in \mathbb{F}_q[x]$. We have $x^{2^k r} - 1 = \prod_{i_0} \left(x^{2^k} - \omega_r^{2^k i_0}\right) = \prod_{i_0,i_1} \omega_r^{i_0 \deg(\boldsymbol{f}_{i_1})} \boldsymbol{f}_{i_1}(\omega_r^{-i_0} x)$.

*Proof.* First observe $x^{2^k r} - 1 = (x^r - 1) \odot \left(x^{2^k} - 1\right)$[6]. By Lemma 1, this equals $\prod_{i_0} \left((x - \omega_r^{i_0}) \odot \left(x^{2^k} - 1\right)\right) = \prod_{i_0,i_1} \left((x - \omega_r^{i_0}) \odot \boldsymbol{f}_{i_1}\right)$. According to

[6] $\forall$ coprime $q_0, q_1$, $\left\{\omega_{q_0}^{i_0} \omega_{q_1}^{i_1} | 0 \leq i_0 < q_0, 0 \leq i_1 < q_1\right\} = \left\{\omega_{q_0 q_1}^{i} | 0 \leq i < q_0 q_1\right\}$ in the splitting field of $x^{q_0 q_1} - 1$.

Lemma 2, $(x - \omega_r^{i_0}) \odot \left(x^{2^k} - 1\right) = x^{2^k} - \omega_r^{2^k i_0}$ and $(x - \omega_r^{i_0}) \odot \boldsymbol{f}_{i_1} = \omega_r^{i_0 \deg(\boldsymbol{f}_{i_1})} \boldsymbol{f}_{i_1}(\omega_r^{-i_0} x)$ as desired.

In summary, by Lemma 3 we have the following isomorphisms:

$$\frac{\mathbb{F}_q[x]}{\langle x^{2^k r} - 1\rangle} \cong \frac{\mathbb{F}_q[x]}{\left\langle \prod_{i_0} \left(x^{2^k} - \omega_r^{2^k i_0}\right)\right\rangle} \cong \frac{\mathbb{F}_q[x]}{\left\langle \prod_{i_0, i_1} \omega_r^{i_0 \deg(\boldsymbol{f}_{i_1})} \boldsymbol{f}_{i_1}(\omega_r^{-i_0} x)\right\rangle}.$$

**Radix-2 Bruun's Butterflies and Inverses.** Define $\mathbf{Bruun}_{\alpha,\beta}$ as follows:

$$\mathbf{Bruun}_{\alpha,\beta} : \begin{cases} \frac{R[x]}{\langle x^4 + (2\beta - \alpha^2)x^2 + \beta^2\rangle} & \to \frac{R[x]}{\langle x^2 + \alpha x + \beta\rangle} \times \frac{R[x]}{\langle x^2 - \alpha x + \beta\rangle} \\ a_0 + a_1 x + a_2 x^2 + a_3 x^3 & \mapsto ((\hat{a}_0 + \hat{a}_1 x), (\hat{a}_2 + \hat{a}_3 x)) \end{cases}$$

where

$$\begin{cases} (\hat{a}_0, \hat{a}_1) = & (a_0 - \beta a_2 + \alpha\beta a_3, a_1 + (\alpha^2 - \beta) a_3 - \alpha a_2), \\ (\hat{a}_2, \hat{a}_3) = & (a_0 - \beta a_2 - \alpha\beta a_3, a_1 + (\alpha^2 - \beta) a_3 + \alpha a_2). \end{cases}$$

We compute $(a_0 - \beta a_2, a_1 + (\alpha^2 - \beta) a_3, \alpha a_2, \alpha\beta a_3)$, swap the last two values implicitly, and do an addition-subtraction (cf. Fig. 1). Notice that we can use `Barrett_mla` and `Barrett_mls` whenever a product is followed by only one accumulation $(a_1 + (\alpha^2 - \beta) a_3)$ or subtraction $(a_0 - \beta a_2)$.

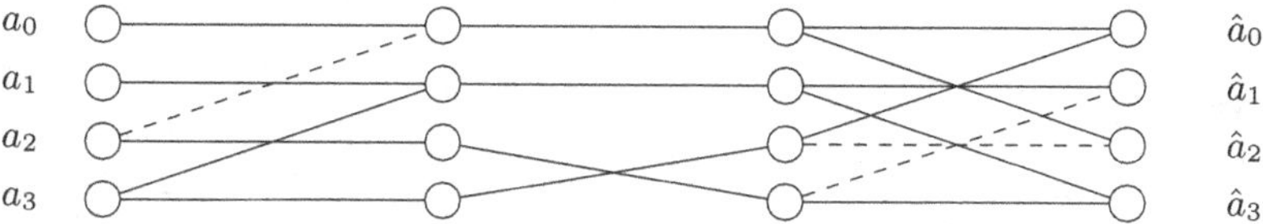


**Fig. 1.** Bruun's butterfly. $(\hat{a}_0, \hat{a}_1, \hat{a}_2, \hat{a}_3) = \mathbf{Bruun}_{\alpha,\beta}(a_0, a_1, a_2, a_3)$.

$$\mathbf{2Bruun}_{\alpha,\beta}^{-1} : \begin{cases} \frac{R[x]}{\langle x^2 + \alpha x + \beta\rangle} \times \frac{R[x]}{\langle x^2 - \alpha x + \beta\rangle} & \to \frac{R[x]}{\langle x^4 + (2\beta - \alpha^2)x^2 + \beta^2\rangle} \\ ((\hat{a}_0 + \hat{a}_1 x), (\hat{a}_2 + \hat{a}_3 x)) & \mapsto 2a_0 + 2a_1 x + 2a_2 x^2 + 2a_3 x^3 \end{cases}$$

correspondingly defines the inverse, where

$$\begin{cases} 2(a_0, a_1) = & (\hat{a}_0 + \hat{a}_2 + (\hat{a}_3 - \hat{a}_1)\,\alpha^{-1}\beta, \hat{a}_1 + \hat{a}_3 - (\hat{a}_0 - \hat{a}_2)\,\alpha^{-1}\beta^{-1}\,(\alpha^2 - \beta)), \\ 2(a_2, a_3) = & ((\hat{a}_3 - \hat{a}_1)\,\alpha^{-1}, (\hat{a}_0 - \hat{a}_2)\,\alpha^{-1}\beta^{-1}). \end{cases}$$

We compute $(\hat{a}_0 + \hat{a}_2, \hat{a}_1 + \hat{a}_3, \hat{a}_0 - \hat{a}_2, \hat{a}_3 - \hat{a}_1)$, swap the last two values implicitly, multiply the constants $\alpha^{-1}, \beta, \alpha^{-1}\beta^{-1}$, and $(\alpha^2 - \beta)$, and add-sub (cf. Fig. 2). Both $\mathbf{Bruun}_{\alpha,\beta}$ and $\mathbf{2Bruun}_{\alpha,\beta}^{-1}$ take 4 multiplications.

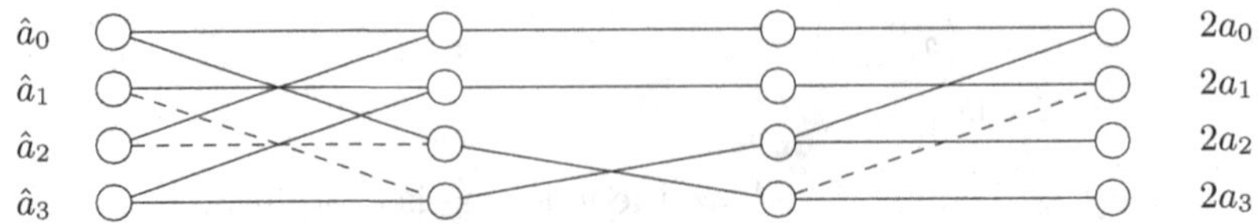


**Fig. 2.** Bruun's Inverse butterfly. $(2a_0, 2a_1, 2a_2, 2a_3) = 2\mathbf{Bruun}^{-1}_{\alpha,\beta}(\hat{a}_0, \hat{a}_1, \hat{a}_2, \hat{a}_3)$.

We will use three special cases of Bruun's butterflies.

**$\mathbf{Bruun}_{\sqrt{2},1}$:** The initial split of $x^{2^k}+1$ is $\mathbf{Bruun}_{\sqrt{2},1}$. Since $\beta = \alpha^2 - \beta = 1$, we only need two multiplications by $\times\sqrt{2}$.

**$\mathbf{Bruun}_{\alpha,\pm 1}$:** We avoid multiplying with $\beta = \pm 1$ in $\mathbf{Bruun}_{\alpha,\pm 1}$ and $2\mathbf{Bruun}^{-1}_{\alpha,\pm 1}$.

**$\mathbf{Bruun}_{\alpha,\frac{\alpha^2}{2}}$:** We save no multiplications, but only use 2 constants $\alpha$ and $\frac{\alpha^2}{2}$ instead of 4. It is used in the split of $x^{2^k} + \omega_r^{2^k i}$ for an odd $r$.

### 3.4 Good–Thomas FFTs

A Good–Thomas FFT [Goo58] converts cyclic FFTs and convolutions into multi-dimensional ones for coprime $n_l$'s. For the polynomial ring $R[x]/\langle x^n - 1\rangle$, we implement $R[x]/\langle x^n - 1\rangle \cong \prod_{i_0,\ldots,i_{h-1}} R[x]/\langle x - \prod_l \omega_{n_l}^{i_l}\rangle$ with a multi-dimensional FFT induced by the equivalences $x \sim \prod_l u_l$ and $\forall l, u_l^{n_l} \sim 1$. Formally, we have

$$\frac{R[x]]}{\langle x^n - 1\rangle} \cong \frac{R[x, u_0, \ldots, u_{h-1}]}{\langle x - \prod_l u_l, u_0^{n_0} - 1, \ldots, u_{h-1}^{n_{h-1}} - 1\rangle}$$

$$\cong \prod_{i_0,\ldots,i_{h-1}} \frac{R[x, u_0, \ldots, u_{h-1}]}{\left\langle x - \prod_l u_l, u_0 - \omega_{n_0}^{i_0}, \ldots, u_{h-1} - \omega_{n_{h-1}}^{i_{h-1}}\right\rangle} \cong \prod_{i_0,\ldots,i_{h-1}} \frac{R[x]}{\left\langle x - \prod_l \omega_{n_l}^{i_l}\right\rangle}.$$

We illustrate the idea for $h = 2, n_0 = 2$, and $n_1 = 3$. Let $P_{(14)}$ be the permutation matrix exchanging the 1st and the 4th rows. We write the size-6 FFT matrix as follows:

$$P_{(14)}\begin{pmatrix} 1 & 1 & 1 & 1 & 1 & 1 \\ 1 & \omega_6 & \omega_6^2 & \omega_6^3 & \omega_6^4 & \omega_6^5 \\ 1 & \omega_6^2 & \omega_6^4 & 1 & \omega_6^2 & \omega_6^4 \\ 1 & \omega_6^3 & 1 & \omega_6^3 & 1 & \omega_6^3 \\ 1 & \omega_6^4 & \omega_6^2 & 1 & \omega_6^4 & \omega_6^2 \\ 1 & \omega_6^5 & \omega_6^4 & \omega_6^3 & \omega_6^2 & \omega_6 \end{pmatrix} P_{(14)} = \begin{pmatrix} 1 & 1 & 1 & 1 & 1 & 1 \\ 1 & \omega_6^4 & \omega_6^2 & 1 & \omega_6^4 & \omega_6^2 \\ 1 & \omega_6^2 & \omega_6^4 & 1 & \omega_6^2 & \omega_6^4 \\ 1 & 1 & 1 & \omega_6^3 & \omega_6^3 & \omega_6^3 \\ 1 & \omega_6^4 & \omega_6^2 & \omega_6^3 & \omega_6 & \omega_6^5 \\ 1 & \omega_6^2 & \omega_6^4 & \omega_6^3 & \omega_6^5 & \omega_6 \end{pmatrix} = \begin{pmatrix} 1 & 1 \\ 1 & -1 \end{pmatrix} \otimes \begin{pmatrix} 1 & 1 & 1 \\ 1 & \omega_6^4 & \omega_6^2 \\ 1 & \omega_6^2 & \omega_6^4 \end{pmatrix}.$$

### 3.5 Rader's FFT for Odd Prime $p$

Suppose $\omega_p \in R$ for an odd prime $p$. [Rad68] introduced how to map a polynomial $\sum_i a_i x^i \in R[x]/\langle x^p - 1\rangle$ to the tuple $(\hat{a}_j) := \left(\sum_i a_i \omega_p^{ij}\right) \in \prod_i R[x]/\langle x - \omega_p^i\rangle$

with a size-$(p-1)$ cyclic convolution. Let $g$ be a generator of $\mathbb{Z}_p^*$ and write $j = g^k$ and $i = g^{-\ell}$. Then $\hat{a}_{g^k} - a_0 = \hat{a}_j - a_0 = \sum_{i=1}^{p-1} a_i \omega_p^{ij} = \sum_{\ell=0}^{p-2} a_{g^{-\ell}} \omega_p^{g^{k-\ell}}$ for $k = 0, \ldots, p-2$.

The sequence $\left(\sum_{\ell=0}^{p-2} a_{g^{-\ell}} \omega_p^{g^{k-\ell}}\right)_{j=0,\ldots,p-2}$ is the size-$(p-1)$ cyclic convolution of sequences $\left(a_{g^{-i}}\right)_{i=0,\ldots,p-2}$ and $\left(\omega_p^{g^i}\right)_{i=0,\ldots,p-2}$. For example, let $p=5$. We have $(1,2,3,4) = (2^4, 2, 2^3, 2^2)$ and

$$\begin{pmatrix} \hat{a}_2 - a_0 \\ \hat{a}_4 - a_0 \\ \hat{a}_3 - a_0 \\ \hat{a}_1 - a_0 \end{pmatrix} = \begin{pmatrix} \omega_5 & \omega_5^2 & \omega_5^4 & \omega_5^3 \\ \omega_5^3 & \omega_5 & \omega_5^2 & \omega_5^4 \\ \omega_5^4 & \omega_5^3 & \omega_5 & \omega_5^2 \\ \omega_5^2 & \omega_5^4 & \omega_5^3 & \omega_5 \end{pmatrix} \begin{pmatrix} a_3 \\ a_4 \\ a_2 \\ a_1 \end{pmatrix}.$$

### 3.6 Schönhage's and Nussbaumer's FFTs

Instead of isomorphisms based on CRT, we sometimes compute chains of monomorphisms and determine the unique inverse image from the product of two images. Given polynomials $\boldsymbol{a}, \boldsymbol{b} \in R[x]/\langle \boldsymbol{g} \rangle$ where $\boldsymbol{g}$ is a degree-$n_0 n_1$ polynomial, we introduce $y = x^{n_1}$, and write $\boldsymbol{a}$ and $\boldsymbol{b}$ as polynomials in $R[x,y]/\langle x^{n_1} - y, \boldsymbol{g}_0 \rangle$ where $\boldsymbol{g}_0|_{y=x^{n_1}} = \boldsymbol{g}(x)$. In other words, $\boldsymbol{a}(y) := \sum_{i_0=0}^{n_0-1} \left(\sum_{i=0}^{n_1-1} a_{i+i_0 n_1} x^i\right) y^{i_0} \in R[x,y]/\langle x^{n_1} - y, \boldsymbol{g}_0 \rangle$. We recap transforms when $R[x,y]/\langle x^{n_1} - y, \boldsymbol{g}_0 \rangle$ does not naturally split.

We want an injection $R[x]/\langle x^{n_1} - y \rangle \hookrightarrow \bar{R}$ such that $R[x,y]/\langle x^{n_1} - y, \boldsymbol{g}_0 \rangle \hookrightarrow \bar{R}[y]/\langle \boldsymbol{g}_0 \rangle$ is a monomorphism with $\bar{R}[y]/\langle \boldsymbol{g}_0 \rangle \cong \prod_j \bar{R}[y]/\langle \boldsymbol{g}_{0,j} \rangle$. A Schönhage FFT [Sch77] is when $\boldsymbol{g}_0 | (y^{n_0} - 1)$, and $\bar{R} = R[x]/\langle \boldsymbol{h} \rangle$ with $\boldsymbol{h} | \Phi_{n_0}(x)$ (the $n_0$-th cyclotomic polynomial). E.g., "cyclic Schönhage" for powers of two $n_0$, $n_1 = \frac{n_0}{4}$, $\boldsymbol{g}_0 = y^{n_0} - 1$, and $\boldsymbol{h} = x^{2n_1} + 1$ is:

$$\frac{R[x]}{\langle x^{n_0 n_1} - 1 \rangle} \cong \frac{\frac{R[x]}{\langle x^{n_1} - y \rangle}[y]}{\langle y^{n_0} - 1 \rangle} \hookrightarrow \frac{\frac{R[x]}{\langle x^{2n_1} + 1 \rangle}[y]}{\langle y^{n_0} - 1 \rangle} \triangleq \frac{\bar{R}[y]}{\langle y^{n_0} - 1 \rangle} \cong \prod_i \frac{\bar{R}[y]}{\langle y - x^i \rangle}.$$

We can also exchange the roles of $x$ and $y$ and get Nussbaumer's FFT [Nus80]. We map $R[x,y]/\langle x^{n_1} - y, \boldsymbol{g}_0 \rangle \hookrightarrow R[x,y]/\langle \boldsymbol{h}, \boldsymbol{g}_0 \rangle$ for $\boldsymbol{g}_0 | \Phi_{2n_1}(y)$ and $\boldsymbol{h} | (x^{2n_1} - 1)$. This can be illustrated for powers of two $n_0 = n_1$, $\boldsymbol{h} = x^{2n_1} - 1$, and $\boldsymbol{g}_0 = y^{n_0} + 1$:

$$\frac{R[x]}{\langle x^{n_0 n_1} + 1 \rangle} \cong \frac{R[x,y]}{\langle x^{n_1} - y, y^{n_0} + 1 \rangle} \hookrightarrow \frac{\frac{R[y]}{\langle y^{n_0} + 1 \rangle}[x]}{\langle x^{2n_1} - 1 \rangle} \triangleq \frac{\tilde{R}[x]}{\langle x^{2n_1} - 1 \rangle} \cong \prod_i \frac{\tilde{R}[x]}{\langle x - y^i \rangle}.$$

Our presentation is motivated by [Ber01, Sect. 9, Paragraph "High-radix variants"] and [vdH04, Sect. 3].

## 4 Implementations

In this section, we discuss our ideas for multiplying polynomials over $\mathbb{Z}_{4591}$. For brevity, we assume $R = \mathbb{Z}_{4591}$ in this section. The state-of-the-art vectorized "big by big" polynomial multiplication in NTRU Prime [BBCT22] computed the product in $R[x]/\langle(x^{1024}+1)(x^{512}-1)\rangle$ with Schönhage and Nussbaumer. This leads to 768 size-8 base multiplications where all of them are negacyclic convolutions. [BBCT22] justified the choice as follows:

> ... since $4591-1 = 2\cdot 3^3\cdot 5\cdot 17$, no simple root of unity is available for recursive radix-2 FFT tricks. ... They ([ACC+21]) performed radix-3, radix-5, and radix-17 NTT stages in their NTT (defined in $R[x]/\langle x^{1530}-1\rangle$). We instead use a radix-2 algorithm that efficiently utilizes the full ymm registers (for vectorization) in the Haswell architecture.

We propose transformations (essentially) *quartering* and *halving* the number of coefficients involved in base multiplications for vectorization. Our first transformation computes the result in $R[x]/\langle x^{1536}-1\rangle$. We apply Good–Thomas with $\omega_3 \in R$ for a more rapid decrease of the sizes of polynomial rings, Schönhage for radix-2 butterflies, and Bruun over $R[x]/\langle x^{32}+1\rangle$. This leads to 384 size-8 base multiplications defined over trinomial moduli. Our second transformation computes the result in $R[x]/\langle x^{1632}-1\rangle$. We show how to incorporate Rader for radix-17 butterflies and Good–Thomas for the coprime factorization $17\cdot 3\cdot 2$. For computing the size-16 weighted convolutions, we split with Cooley–Tukey and Bruun for $R[x]/\langle x^{16} \pm \omega_{102}^{i}\rangle$. Since no coefficient ring extensions are involved, this leads to 96 size-8 base multiplication with binomial moduli, 96 size-8 base multiplications with trinomial moduli, and six size-16 base multiplications with binomial moduli.

Section 4.1 formalizes the needs of vectorization, and Sect. 4.2 goes through our implementation `Good--Thomas` for big-by-small polynomial multiplications. We then go through big-by-big polynomial multiplications. Section 4.3 goes through our implementation `Good--Schönhage--Bruun`, and Sect. 4.4 goes through our implementation `Good--Rader--Bruun`.

### 4.1 The Needs of Vectorization

We formalize "the needs of vectorization" to justify how we choose among transformations. In the literature, power-of-two-sized FFTs are oftenly described as easily vectorizable. In this paper, we explicitly state and relate them to the designs of vectorization-friendly polynomial multiplications. Our definition is based on our programming experience.

We assume that a reasonable vector instruction set should provide the following features accessible to programmers:

- Several vector registers each holding a large number of bits of data. Commonly, each register holds $2^k$ bits.
- Several vector arithmetic instructions computing $2^k$-bit data from $2^k$-bit data while regarding each $2^k$-bit data as packed elements.
  - If input and output are regarded as packed $2^{k'}$-bit data, we call the instruction a single-width instruction.

- If input is regarded as packed $2^{k'-1}$-bit data and output is regarded as packed $2^{k'}$-bit data, we call the instruction a widening instruction.
- If input is regarded as packed $2^{k'}$-bit data and output is regarded as packed $2^{k'-1}$-bit data, we call the instruction a narrowing instruction.

The terminologies "widening" and "narrowing" come from [ARM21]. For a $k' \leq k$, we are interested in the number of elements $v = 2^{k-k'}$ contained in a vector register. Intuivitely, we want to compute with minimal number of data shuffling while maintaining the vectorization feature: if we want to add up several pairs $(a_i, b_i)$ of elements, we assign $(a_i)$ to one vector register and $(b_i)$ to another one and issue a vector addtion, similarly for subtractions, multiplications, and bitwise operations. We formalize this intuition for algebra homomorphisms.

Let $\pi$ be a platform-dependent set of module homomorphisms. We'll specify $\pi = \pi(\texttt{neon})$ in the case of Neon shortly. Let $f$ be an algebra homomorphism. We call $f$ "vectorization friendly" if $f$ is a composition of homomorphisms of the form $g \otimes \text{id}_v \otimes d$ for $g$ an algebra homomorphism, $d$ a composition of elements from $\pi$. Since $g \otimes \text{id}_v$ operates over several chunks of $v$-sets, we need no permutations for this part. For the set $\pi$, we define it with the matrix view for simplicity. $\pi$ is defined as the set of module homomorphisms representable as a $v' \times v'$ diagonal matrix or a size-$v'$ cyclic/negacyclic shift for $v'$ a multiple of $v$.

In this paper, we start with $R[x] \Big/ \Big\langle \boldsymbol{g}\left(x^{v'}\right) \Big\rangle \cong R[y] \Big/ \Big\langle x^{v'} - y, \boldsymbol{g}(y) \Big\rangle$ for $v'$ a multiple of $v$ and transform accordingly.

### 4.2 Good–Thomas FFT in "Big×Small" Polynomial Multiplications

We recall below the design principle of vectorization–friendly Good–Thomas from [AHY22], and describe our implementation `Good--Thomas` for the "big by small" polynomial multiplications. For a cyclic convolution $R[x]/\langle x^{v n_0 n_1} - 1\rangle$ where $n_0$ and $n_1$ coprime, and $v$ a multiple of the number of coefficients in a vector, one introduces the equivalences $x^v \sim uw$, $u^{n_0} \sim w^{n_1} \sim 1$. Usually, one picks $n_0$ and $n_1$ carefully for fast computations. In the simplest form, one picks $n_0$ as a power of 2 and $n_1 = 3$. Our `Good--Thomas` computes the polynomial multiplication in $\mathbb{Z}[x]/\langle x^{1536} - 1\rangle$ with $(v, n_0, n_1) = (4, 128, 3)$ where $v = 4$ comes from the fact that each Neon SIMD register holds four 32-bit values. After reaching $\mathbb{Z}[x, u, w]/\langle x^4 - uw, u^3 - 1, w^{128} - 1\rangle$, we want to compute size-3 NTT over $u^3 - 1$ and size-128 NTT over $w^{128} - 1$. It suffices to choose a large modulus $q'$ with a principal 384-th root of unity. We choose $q'$ as a 32-bit modulus bounding the maximum value of the product in $\mathbb{Z}[x]/\langle x^{1536} - 1\rangle$. Obviously, our `Good--Thomas` supports any "big-by-small" polynomial multiplications with size less than or equal to 1536.

### 4.3 Good–Thomas, Schönhage's, and Bruun's FFT

This section describes our `Good--Schönhage--Bruun`. We briefly recall the AVX2-optimized "big by big" polynomial multiplication by [BBCT22]. They computed the product in $R[x]/\langle(x^{512}-1)(x^{1024}+1)\rangle$. They first applied Schönhage as follows.

$$\frac{R[x]}{\langle(x^{512}-1)(x^{1024}+1)\rangle} \cong \frac{\frac{R[x]}{\langle x^{32}-y\rangle}[y]}{\langle(y^{16}-1)(y^{32}+1)\rangle}$$
$$\hookrightarrow \frac{\frac{R[x]}{\langle x^{64}+1\rangle}[y]}{\langle(y^{16}-1)(y^{32}+1)\rangle} \cong \prod_{i=0,1,3,j=0,\ldots,15} \frac{\frac{R[x]}{\langle x^{64}+1\rangle}[y]}{\langle y-x^{2i+8j}\rangle}.$$

They then applied Nussbaumer for multiplying in $\frac{R[x]}{\langle x^{64}+1\rangle}$ as follows.

$$\frac{R[x]}{\langle x^{64}+1\rangle} \cong \frac{\frac{R[x]}{\langle x^{8}-z\rangle}[z]}{\langle z^{8}+1\rangle} \hookrightarrow \frac{\frac{R[x]}{\langle x^{16}-1\rangle}[z]}{\langle z^{8}+1\rangle} \cong \frac{\frac{R[z]}{\langle z^{8}+1\rangle}[x]}{\langle x^{16}-1\rangle} \cong \prod_{k=0,\ldots,15} \frac{\frac{R[z]}{\langle z^{8}+1\rangle}[x]}{\langle x-z^{k}\rangle}.$$

The vectorization-friendliness of Schönhage is obvious. In principle, Nussbaumer is vectorization-friendly since it shares the same computation as Schönhage after transposing.

**Truncated Schönhage vs Good–Thomas and Schönhage.** We first discuss an optimization of Schönhage if there is a principal root of unity with order coprime to the one defining Schönhage.

*How it Works, Mathematically.* In $R=\mathbb{Z}_{4591}$, we know that there is a principal 3rd root of unity $\omega_3 \in R$. Instead of computing in $R[x]/\langle(x^{512}-1)(x^{1024}+1)\rangle$, we apply Schönhage and Good–Thomas FFTs to $R[x]/\langle x^{1536}-1\rangle$. By definition, if $\boldsymbol{\omega}$ is a principal $2^k$-th root of unity, then $\omega_3\boldsymbol{\omega}$ is a principal $3\cdot 2^k$-th root of unity. Let's define $\bar{R}=R[x]/\langle x^{32}+1\rangle$. We introduce a principal 32-th root of unity $\boldsymbol{\omega}_{32}=x^2$ as follows:

$$\frac{R[x]}{\langle x^{1536}-1\rangle} \cong \frac{\frac{R[x]}{\langle x^{16}-y\rangle}[y]}{\langle y^{96}-1\rangle} \hookrightarrow \frac{\bar{R}[y]}{\langle y^{96}-1\rangle}.$$

Then $\omega_3\boldsymbol{\omega}_{32}$ is a principal 96-th root of unity implementing $\bar{R}[y]/\langle y^{96}-1\rangle \cong \prod_{i=0,1,2,j=0,\ldots,31} \bar{R}[y]\Big/\Big\langle y-\omega_3^i\boldsymbol{\omega}_{32}^j\Big\rangle$. However, one should not implement this isomorphism with Cooley–Tukey FFT. Observe that multiplication by $\boldsymbol{\omega}_{32}=x^2$ requires negating and permuting whereas multiplication by $\omega_3$ requires actual modular multiplication. Cooley–Tukey FFT requires one to multiply $\omega_3^i\boldsymbol{\omega}_{32}^j$ which is unreasonably complicated while optimizing for $i,j\neq 0$. We apply Good–Thomas FFT implementing $\bar{R}[y]/\langle y^{96}-1\rangle \cong \bar{R}[y]/\langle y-uw, u^3-1, w^{32}-1\rangle$. Obviously, we only need multiplications by powers of $\omega_3$ and $\boldsymbol{\omega}_{32}$ and not $\omega_3\boldsymbol{\omega}_{32}$. See Table 1 for an overview of available approaches.

**Table 1.** Approaches for computing the size-1536 product of two polynomials drawn from $R[x]/\langle x^{761} - x - 1\rangle$.

| Approach | Domain | Image | Twiddle factors |
|---|---|---|---|
| Truncated Schönhage [BBCT22] | $\frac{R[x]}{\langle (x^{1024}+1)(x^{512}-1)\rangle}$ | $\left(\frac{R[x]}{\langle x^{64}+1\rangle}\right)^{48}$ | $x^{2i}$ |
| Cooley–Tukey and Schönhage | $\frac{R[x]}{\langle x^{1536}-1\rangle}$ | $\left(\frac{R[x]}{\langle x^{32}+1\rangle}\right)^{96}$ | $\omega_3^i x^{2j}$ |
| **Good–Thomas and Schönhage** | $\frac{R[x]}{\langle x^{1536}-1\rangle}$ | $\left(\frac{R[x]}{\langle x^{32}+1\rangle}\right)^{96}$ | $\omega_3^i, x^{2j}$ |

*How it Works, Concretely.* We detail the implementation as follows.

- We transform the input array `in[761]` into a temporary array `out[3][32][32]`, where `out[`$i$`][`$j$`][0-31]` is the size-32 polynomial in $\frac{R[x]}{\langle x^{32}+1, u-\omega_3^i, w-x^{2j}\rangle}$. Concretely, we combine the permutations of Good–Thomas and Schönhage as `out[`$i$`][`$j$`][`$k$`] = in[`$(16(64i + 33j) \bmod 96) + k$`]` if $(16(64i + 33j) \bmod 96) + k < 761$ and zero otherwise. This step is the foundation of the implicit permutations [ACC+21].
- For input `small`, we start with the 8-bit form of the polynomial. Since coefficients are in $\{\pm 1, 0\}$, we first perform five layers of radix-2 butterflies without any modular reductions. The initial three layers of radix-2 butterflies are combined with the implicit permutations. For the last two layers of radix-2 butterflies, we use `ext` if the root is not a power of $x^{16}$. For the last layer of radix-2 butterflies, we merge the sign-extension and add-sub pairs into the sequence `saddl`, `saddl2`, `ssubl`, `ssubl2`. We then apply one layer of radix-3 butterflies based on the improvement of [DV78, Equation 8]. We compute the radix-3 NTT $(\hat{v}_0, \hat{v}_1, \hat{v}_2)$ of size-32 polynomials $(v_1, v_2, v_3)$ as:

$$\begin{cases} \hat{v}_0 = v_0 + v_1 + v_2, \\ \hat{v}_1 = (v_0 - v_2) + \omega_3(v_1 - v_2), \\ \hat{v}_2 = (v_0 - v_1) - \omega_3(v_1 - v_2). \end{cases}$$

- For the input `big`, we use the 16-bit form and perform one layer of radix-3 butterflies followed by five layers of radix-2 butterflies. This implies only 1536 coefficients are involved in radix-3 butterflies instead of 3072 as for the input `small`. We first apply one layer of radix-3 butterflies and two layers of radix-2 butterflies followed by one layer of Barrett reductions while permuting implicitly for Good–Thomas and Schönhage. Then, we perform three layers of radix-2 butterflies and another layer of Barrett reductions.

**Nussbaumer vs Bruun.** Next, we discuss efficient polynomial multiplications in $R[x]/\langle x^{32} + 1\rangle$. [BBCT22] applied Nussbaumer to $R[x]/\langle x^{64} + 1\rangle$. We state without proof that applying Nussbaumer to $R[x]/\langle x^{32} + 1\rangle$ results in 8 polynomial multiplications in $R[z]/\langle z^8 + 1\rangle$. We instead apply Bruun's FFT resulting

**Algorithm 5.** Radix-2 butterfly with symbolic root $x^2$.

**Input:** Size-32 8-bit polynomials $a = \mathtt{a0} + \mathtt{a1}x^{16}, b = \mathtt{b0} + \mathtt{b1}x^{16}$, where $\mathtt{a0}, \mathtt{a1}, \mathtt{b0}, \mathtt{b1}$ are SIMD registers containing:

$$\begin{cases} \mathtt{a0} = a_7 || \cdots || a_0, \\ \mathtt{a1} = a_{15} || \cdots || a_8, \\ \mathtt{b0} = b_7 || \cdots || b_0, \\ \mathtt{b1} = b_{15} || \cdots || b_8. \end{cases}$$

**Output:** $\mathtt{a0} + \mathtt{a1}x^{16} = (a + bx^2) \bmod (x^{32} + 1), \mathtt{b0} + \mathtt{b1}x^{16} = (a - bx^2) \bmod (x^{32} + 1)$

```
ext   v0.16b, b0.16b, b1.16b, #14      ▷ v0 = b29||···||b14
neg   b1.16b, b1.16b
ext   v1.16b, b1.16b, b0.16b, #14      ▷ v1 = b13||···||b0||(−b31)||(−b30)
sub   b0.16b, a0.16b, v0.16b
sub   b1.16b, a1.16b, v1.16b           ▷ b0 + b1x^16 = (a − x^2 b) mod (x^32 + 1)
add   a0.16b, a0.16b, v0.16b
add   a1.16b, a1.16b, v1.16b           ▷ a0 + a1x^16 = (a + x^2 b) mod (x^32 + 1)
```

in multiplications in rings $R[x]/\langle x^8 + \alpha x^4 + 1\rangle$ for 4 different $\alpha$. Since

$$\begin{aligned} x^{32} + 1 &= (x^{16} + 1229x^2 + 1)(x^{16} - 1229x^2 + 1) \\ &= (x^8 + 58x^4 + 1)(x^8 - 58x^4 + 1)(x^8 + 2116x^4 + 1)(x^8 - 2116x^4 + 1), \end{aligned}$$

we apply $\mathbf{Bruun}_{1229,1}$ followed by $\mathbf{Bruun}_{58,1}$ and $\mathbf{Bruun}_{2116,1}$. We have slower FFT and base multiplications, but we do only half as many as in [BBCT22]. See Table 2 for comparisons.

**Table 2.** Approaches for multiplying in $R[x]/\langle x^{64} + 1\rangle$ and $R[x]/\langle x^{32} + 1\rangle$.

| Approach | Domain | Image | Twiddle factors |
|---|---|---|---|
| Nussbaumer [BBCT22] | $\frac{R[x]}{\langle x^{64}+1\rangle}$ | $\left(\frac{R[z]}{\langle z^8+1\rangle}\right)^{16}$ | $z^i$ |
| Nussbaumer | $\frac{R[x]}{\langle x^{32}+1\rangle}$ | $\left(\frac{R[z]}{\langle z^8+1\rangle}\right)^{8}$ | $z^{2i}$ |
| **Bruun** | $\frac{R[x]}{\langle x^{32}+1\rangle}$ | $\prod_{i=0,1} \prod \frac{R[x]}{\langle x^8 \pm \alpha_i x^4+1\rangle}$ | Elements in $R$. |

Then, we perform $96 \cdot 4 = 384$ size-8 base multiplications and compute the inverses of Bruun's, Schönhage's, and Good–Thomas FFT.

### 4.4 Good–Thomas, Rader's, and Bruun's FFT

In the previous section, we replace Nussbaumer with Bruun. This section shows how to replace Schönhage with Rader while computing in $R[x]/\langle x^{1632} - 1\rangle$. We name the resulting computation `Good--Rader--Bruun`.

**Schönhage vs Rader-17.** We first observe that the Schönhage in [BBCT22] reduced a size-1536 problem to several size-64 problems. We are looking for a multiple of 17 close to $\frac{1536}{64} = 48$. We choose 51 since one can define a size-51 cyclic NTT nicely over $\mathbb{Z}_q$ and optimize further by extending the size-51 cyclic NTT to size-102. For the size-102 cyclic NTT, we apply the 3-dimensional Good–Thomas FFT by identifying $(\omega_{17}, \omega_3, \omega_2) = (\omega_{102}^{e_0}, \omega_{102}^{e_1}, \omega_{102}^{e_2})$ as the principal roots of unity where $(e_0, e_1, e_2)$ is the unique tuple satisfying $\forall a \in \mathbb{Z}_{102}, a \equiv e_0(a \bmod 17) + e_1(a \bmod 3) + e_2(a \bmod 2) \pmod{102}$. Algorithm 6 is an illustration. Radix-2 and radix-3 computations are straightforward. For the radix-17 cyclic FFT, we apply Rader's FFT. Algorithm 7 illustrates the multi-dimensional cyclic FFT. Obviously, the above computation is vectorization–friendly.

**Algorithm 6.** Good–Thomas, in practice merged with Algorithm 7.

**Inputs:** `src[1632]`.
**Outputs:** `poly_NTT[17][3][2][16]`.

**for** $i = 0, \ldots, 1631$ **do**
  Let $t = i/16$.
  `poly_NTT`[$t$ mod 17][$t$ mod 3][$t$ mod 2][$i$ mod 16] = `src`[$i$].
**end for**

**Algorithm 7.** FFTs over chunks of 16 coefficients.

**Inputs:** `poly_NTT[17][3][2][16]`.
**Outputs:** `poly_NTT[17][3][2][16]`.

**for** $i_3 \in \{0, \ldots, 15\}$ **do**
  **for** $i_1 \in \{0, 1, 2\}, i_2 \in \{0, 1\}$ **do**
    `rader-17(poly_NTT[0-16]`[$i_1$][$i_2$][$i_3$]).
  **end for**
  **for** $i_0 \in \{0, \ldots, 16\}$ **do**
    `radix-(3, 2)(poly_NTT`[$i_0$]`[0-2][0-1]`[$i_3$]).
  **end for**
**end for**

**Generalize Bruun Over $x^{2^k} + c$ for $c \neq \pm 1$.** The composed multiplication over a finite field shows that the remaining factorization follows the same pattern of factorizing $R[x]/\langle x^{16} \pm 1 \rangle$. The isomorphism $R[x]/\langle x^{16} - \omega_{102}^{2i} \rangle \cong \prod R[x]/\langle x^8 \pm \omega_{102}^{i} \rangle$ is obvious. Since we also have $\prod_i R[x]/\langle x^{16} - \omega_{102}^{2i+1} \rangle \cong \prod_i R[x]/\langle x^{16} + \omega_{102}^{2i} \rangle$ by permuting, it suffices to understand the isomorphisms defined on $R[x]/\langle x^{16} + \omega_{102}^{2i} \rangle$. Applying Lemma 3, we have $R[x]/\langle x^{16} + \omega_{102}^{2i} \rangle \cong \prod R[x]/\langle x^8 \pm \sqrt{2}\omega_{102}^{128i} x^4 + \omega_{102}^{256i} \rangle$.

Finally, the remaining computing task is multiplication in $R[x]/\langle x^8 + \alpha x^4 + \beta\rangle$ for some $\alpha, \beta \in R$. We extend the idea of [CHK+21, Algorithm 17] by altering between multiplying in $R[x]$ and reducing modulo $x^8 + \alpha x^4 + \beta$.

# 5 Results

We present the performance numbers in this section. We focus on polynomial multiplications, leaving the fast constant-time GCD [BY19] as future work.

## 5.1 Benchmark Environment

We use the Raspberry Pi 4 Model B featuring the quad-core Broadcom BCM2711 chipset. It comes with a 32 kB L1 data cache, a 48 kB L1 instruction cache, and a 1 MB L2 cache and runs at 1.5 GHz. For hashing, we use the `aes`, `sha2`, and `fips202` from PQClean [KSSW] without any optimizations due to the lack of corresponding cryptographic units. For the randombytes, [BHK+22] used the `randombytes` from SUPERCOP which in turn used `chacha20`. We extract the conversion from `chacha20` into `randombytes` from SUPERCOP and replace `chacha20` with our optimized implementations using the pipelines `I0/I1`, `F0/F1`. We use the cycle counter of the PMU for benchmarking. Our programs are compilable with GCC 10.3.0, GCC 11.2.0, Clang 13.1.6, and Clang 14.0.0. We report numbers for the binaries compiled with GCC 11.2.0.

**Table 3.** Overview of polynomial multiplications in `ntrulpr761/sntrup761`.

| Armv8-A Neon | | x86 AVX2 | |
|---|---|---|---|
| Implementation | Cycles | Implementation | Cycles |
| Big-by-small polynomial multiplications | | | |
| `Good--Thomas` | 47 696 | [BBCT22] | 16 992 |
| [Haa21] | 242 585 | | |
| Big-by-big polynomial multiplications | | | |
| `Good--Rader--Bruun` | 39 788 | [BBCT22] | 25 113 |
| `Good--Schönhage--Bruun` | 50 398 | | |

### 5.2 Performance of Vectorized Polynomial Multiplications

Table 3 summarizes the performance of vectorized polynomial multiplications.

**Table 4.** Detailed `Good--Schönhage--Bruun` cycle counts including reducing to $\frac{\mathbb{Z}_{4591}[x]}{\langle x^{761}-x-1\rangle}$.

| Good--Schönhage--Bruun | | | |
|---|---|---|---|
| Operation | Count | Cycles | Total cycles |
| `polymul` | - | - | 50 398 |
| `Good-Schönhage-3-2x2` | 1 | 1 708 | 1 708 |
| `Schönhage-3x2` | 3 | 1 246 | 3738 |
| `Good-Schönhage-5x2` | 1 | 1 527 | 1 527 |
| `Radix-3` | 1 | 2 084 | 2 084 |
| `Bruun` | 24 | 291 | 6 984 |
| `Trinomial-8x8` | 12 | 1 115 | 13 380 |
| `Bruun inverse` | 12 | 409 | 4 908 |
| `Schönhage-2x4 inverse` | 3 | 1 304 | 3 912 |
| `Good-Schönhage-2-3 inverse` | 1 | 7 653 | 7 653 |

For NTRU Prime, our `Good--Rader--Bruun` performs the best. It is followed by `Good--Thomas` and `Good--Schönhage--Bruun`. Notice that `Good--Rader--Bruun` requires no extensions or changes of coefficient rings. The closest instances in the literature regarding vectorization are the `Good--Thomas` and `Schönhage--Nussbaumer` by [BBCT22], and `Good--Thomas` by [Haa21]. [BBCT22]'s, [Haa21], and our `Good--Thomas` compute "big by small" polynomial multiplications. We outperform [Haa21] `Good--Thomas` by a factor of 6.1× since they implemented the base multiplications with scalar code using the C % operator. On the other hand, [BBCT22]'s `Schönhage--Nussbaumer` and our `Good--Schönhage--Bruun` compute "big by big" polynomial multiplications. Regarding the impact of switching "big by small" to "big by big", [BBCT22]'s `Schönhage--Nussbaumer` takes $\frac{25113}{16992} \approx 147.79\%$ cycles of their own `Good--Thomas` [BBCT22, Sect. 3.4.2] while our `Good--Schönhage--Bruun` takes only $\frac{50398}{47696} \approx 105.67\%$ cycles of our own `Good--Thomas`. Essentially, this demonstrates the benefit of vectorization-friendly Good–Thomas and Bruun over truncated [vdH04] Schönhage and Nussbaumer.

**Table 5.** Detailed cycle counts of `Good--Rader--Bruun`, excluding reductions to $\mathbb{Z}_{4591}[x]/\langle x^{761} - x - 1\rangle$.

| Good--Rader--Bruun | | | |
|---|---|---|---|
| Operation | Count | Cycles | Total |
| polymul | - | - | 37 475 |
| Good-Rader-17 | 24 | 407 | 9 768 |
| Radix-(3, 2) | 2 | 2 339 | 4 678 |
| CT | 2 | 570 | 1 140 |
| Bruun | 2 | 838 | 1 676 |
| Weighted-8x8 | 12 | 244 | 2 928 |
| Trinomial-8x8 | 12 | 328 | 3 936 |
| $\texttt{CT}^{-1}$ | 1 | 592 | 592 |
| $\texttt{Bruun}^{-1}$ | 1 | 989 | 989 |
| Weighted-16x16 | 1 | 1 019 | 1 019 |
| $\texttt{Radix-(3, 2)}^{-1}$ | 1 | 2 341 | 2 341 |
| $\texttt{Good-Rader-17}^{-1}$ | 12 | 543 | 6 516 |

We also provide the detailed cycle counts of the polynomial multiplications. For the "big by big" polynomial multiplications in `sntrup761/ntrulpr761`, Table 5 details the numbers of `Good--Rader--Bruun` and Table 4 details the numbers of `Good--Schönhage--Bruun`.

### 5.3 Performance of Schemes

Before comparing the overall performance, we first illustrate the performance numbers of some other critical subroutines. Most of our optimized implementations of these subroutines are not seriously optimized except for parts involving polynomial multiplications. We simply translate existing techniques and AVX2-optimized implementations into Neon. Table 6 summarizes the performance of inversions, encoding, and decoding.

**Table 6.** Performance of inversions, encoding, and decoding in NTRU Prime.

| Operation | Ref | Ours |
|---|---|---|
| sntrup761/ntrulpr761 | | |
| Rq_recip3 | 116 353 545 | 5 811 777 |
| R3_recip | 127 578 811 | 587 407 |
| Rq_encode | 17 753 | 2 084 |
| Rq_decode | 31 715 | 3 914 |
| Rounded_encode | 14 707 | 3 145 |
| Rounded_decode | 31 832 | 3 445 |
| crypto_sort_uint32 | 186 867 | 21 659 |

**Inversions, Sorting Network, Encoding, and Decoding.** For `sntrup761`, we need one inversion over $\mathbb{Z}_{4591}$ and one inversion over $\mathbb{Z}_3$. We bitslice the inversion over $\mathbb{Z}_3$, and identify and vectorize the hottest loop in the inversion over $\mathbb{Z}_{4591}$. Additionally, we translate AVX2-optimized sorting network, encoding, and decoding into Neon. Notice that inversions over $\mathbb{Z}_2$, $\mathbb{Z}_3$, and $\mathbb{Z}_{4591}$, sorting networks, encoding, and decoding are implemented in a generic sense. With fairly little effort, they can be used for other parameter sets.

**Performance of `sntrup761/ntrulpr761`.** Table 7 summarizes the overall performance. For `ntrulpr761`, our key generation, encapsulation, and decapsulation are 2.98×, 2.79×, and 3.07× faster than [Haa21]. For `sntrup761`, we outperform the reference implementation significantly. Finally, Table 8 details the performance.

**Constant-Time Concerns.** There are no input-dependent branches in our code. Our program is constant-time only if one believes the documentation [ARM15]. The source code from [Haa21] and Armv8-A works [NG21, BHK+22], indicate the requirement of the same assumption. In the most relevant documented Neon implementations, our code is constant-time, but this is never strictly guaranteed[7] even with Data-Independent Timing (DIT). If ARM decides to extend the domain of DIT to relevant multiplication instructions used in this paper, our code is guaranteed to be constant-time once the DIT flag is set. Furthermore, literally all the lattice-based post-quantum cryptosystems will be benefit from this since the constant-time concerns arise from the basic building blocks implementing modular multiplications.

**Table 7.** Overall cycles of `sntrup761/ntrulpr761`.

| `sntrup761` | | | |
|---|---|---|---|
| Operation | Key generation | Encapsulation | Decapsulation |
| Ref | 273 598 470 | 29 750 035 | 89 968 342 |
| `Good--Rader--Bruun` | 6 333 403 | 147 977 | 158 233 |
| `Good--Thomas` | 6 340 758 | 153 465 | 182 271 |
| `Good--Schönhage--Bruun` | 6 345 787 | 163 305 | 193 626 |
| **`ntrulpr761`** | | | |
| Operation | Key generation | Encapsulation | Decapsulation |
| Ref | 29 853 635 | 59 572 637 | 89 185 030 |
| [Haa21] | 775 472 | 1 150 294 | 1 417 394 |
| `Good--Rader--Bruun` | 260 606 | 412 629 | 461 250 |
| `Good--Thomas` | 269 590 | 422 102 | 471 014 |
| `Good--Schönhage--Bruun` | 272 738 | 436 965 | 499 559 |

[7] ARM's DIT flag, according to https://developer.arm.com/documentation/ddi0595/2021-06/AArch64-Registers/DIT--Data-Independent-Timing, does not guarantee the high half multiplications `sqrdmulh` and `sqdmulh` to be constant-time.

**Acknowledgments.** This work was supported in part by the Academia Sinica Investigator Award AS-IA-109-M01, and Taiwan's National Science and Technology Council grants 112-2634-F-001-001-MBK and 112-2119-M-001-006.

# A Detailed Performance Numbers

**Table 8.** Detailed performance numbers of **sntrup761** and **ntrulpr761** with **Good--Rader--Bruun**. Only performance-critical subroutines are shown.

| sntrup761 | | ntrulpr761 | |
|---|---|---|---|
| Operation | Cycles | Operation | Cycles |
| crypto_kem_keypair | 6 333 403 | crypto_kem_keypair | 260 606 |
| ZKeyGen | 6 248 089 | ZKeyGen | 247 919 |
| | | XKeyGen | 243 332 |
| KeyGen | 6 194 194 | KeyGen | 112 496 |
| Rq_recip3 | 5 811 777 | | |
| R3_recip | 587 407 | | |
| Rq_mult_small | 39 829 | Rq_mult_small | 39 829 |
| sort | 22 369 | sort | 21 243 |
| randombytes | 86 932 | randombytes | 44 713 |
| | | aes | 127 203 |
| Rq_encode | 2 084 | Rounded_encode | 3 145 |
| sha2 | 13 207 | sha2 | 16 386 |
| crypto_kem_enc | 147 977 | crypto_kem_enc | 412 629 |
| ZEncrypt | 48 639 | ZEncrypt | 383 991 |
| | | XEncrypt | 374 695 |
| Encrypt | 40 650 | Encrypt | 83 487 |
| Rq_mult_small | 39 829 | Rq_mult_small (2×) | 2× 39 829 |
| | | aes | 253 597 |
| | | sort | 21 773 |
| | | sha2 | 2 914 |
| Rq_decode | 3 914 | Rounded_decode | 3 445 |
| Rounded_encode | 3 145 | Rounded_encode | 3 145 |
| randombytes | 45 109 | | |
| sha2 | 29 713 | sha2* | 26 548 |
| sort | 21 659 | | |
| crypto_kem_dec | 158 233 | crypto_kem_dec | 461 250 |
| ZDecrypt | 88 054 | ZDecrypt | 47 573 |
| Decrypt | 83 892 | XDecrypt (defined as Decrypt) | 43 799 |
| Rq_mult_small | 39 829 | Rq_mult_small | 39 829 |
| R3_mult | 42 059 | | |
| Rounded_decode | 3 445 | Rounded_decode | 3 445 |
| ZEncrypt | 48 639 | ZEncrypt | 383 991 |
| sha2 | 18 111 | sha2* | 16 982 |

* The numbers of sha2 cycles of XEncrypt are included.

## References


[AAC+22] Alagic, G., et al.: NISTIR8413 – status report on the second round of the nist post-quantum cryptography standardization process (2022). https://doi.org/10.6028/NIST.IR.8413-upd1

[ACC+21] Alkim, E., et al.: Polynomial multiplication in NTRU Prime comparison of optimization strategies on cortex-M4. IACR Trans. Cryptogr. Hardware Embed. Syst. **2021**(1), 217–238 (2021). https://tches.iacr.org/index.php/TCHES/article/view/8733

[AHY22] Alkim, E., Hwang, V., Yang, B.Y.: Multi-parameter support with NTTs for NTRU and NTRU Prime on cortex-M4. IACR Trans. Cryptogr. Hardware Embed. Syst. 349–371 (2022)

[ARM15] ARM. Cortex-A72 Software Optimization Guide (2015). https://developer.arm.com/documentation/uan0016/a/

[ARM21] ARM. Arm Architecture Reference Manual, Armv8, for Armv8-A architecture profile (2021). https://developer.arm.com/documentation/ddi0487/gb/?lang=en

[Bar86] Barrett, P.: Implementing the Rivest Shamir and Adleman public key encryption algorithm on a standard digital signal processor. In: Odlyzko, A.M. (ed.) CRYPTO 1986. LNCS, vol. 263, pp. 311–323. Springer, Heidelberg (1986). https://doi.org/10.1007/3-540-47721-7_24

[BBC+20] Bernstein, D.J., et al.: NTRU Prime. In: Submission to the NIST Post-Quantum Cryptography Standardization Project [?] (2020). https://ntruprime.cr.yp.to/

[BBCT22] Bernstein, D.J., Brumley, B.B., Chen, M.S., Tuveri, N.: OpenSSLNTRU: faster post-quantum TLS key exchange. In: 31st USENIX Security Symposium (USENIX Security 2022), pp. 845–862 (2022)

[BC87] Brawley, J.V., Carlitz, L.: Irreducibles and the composed product for polynomials over a finite field. Disc. Math. **65**(2), 115–139 (1987)

[Ber01] Bernstein, D.J.: Multidigit multiplication for mathematicians (2001)

[BGM93] Blake, I.F., Gao, S., Mullin, R.C.: Explicit factorization of $x^{2^k} + 1$ over $\mathbb{F}_p$ with prime $p \equiv 3 \ mod \ 4$. Appl. Algebra Eng. Commun. Comput. **4**(2), 89–94 (1993)

[BHK+22] Becker, H., Hwang, V., Kannwischer, M.J., Yang, B.Y., Yang, S.Y.: Neon NTT: faster Dilithium, Kyber, and Saber on cortex-A72 and apple M1. IACR Trans. Cryptogr. Hardware Embed. Systems **2022**(1), 221–244 (2022). https://tches.iacr.org/index.php/TCHES/article/view/9295

[BK22] Becker, H., Kannwischer, M.J.: Hybrid scalar/vector implementations of Keccak and SPHINCS+ on AArch64. Cryptology ePrint Archive (2022)

[Bru78] Bruun, G.: z-transform DFT filters and FFT's. IEEE Trans. Acoust. Speech Signal Process. **26**(1), 56–63 (1978)

[BY19] Bernstein, D.J., Yang, B.Y.: Fast constant-time GCD computation and modular inversion. IACR Trans. Cryptogr. Hardware Embed. Syst. **2019**(3), 340–398 (2019). https://tches.iacr.org/index.php/TCHES/article/view/8298

[CHK+21] Chung, C.M.M., Hwang, V., Kannwischer, M.J., Seiler, G., Shih, C.J., Yang, B.Y.: NTT multiplication for NTT-unfriendly rings new speed records for Saber and NTRU on Cortex-M4 and AVX2. IACR Trans. Cryptogr. Hardware Embed. Syst. **2021**(2), 159–188 (2021). https://tches.iacr.org/index.php/TCHES/article/view/8791

[CT65] Cooley, J.W., Tukey, J.W.: An algorithm for the machine calculation of complex fourier series. Math. Comput. **19**(90), 297–301 (1965)

[DV78] Dubois, E., Venetsanopoulos, A.: A new algorithm for the radix-3 FFT. IEEE Trans. Acoust. Speech Signal Process. **26**(3), 222–225 (1978)

[Goo58] Good, I.J.: The interaction algorithm and practical Fourier analysis. J. Roy. Stat. Soc.: Ser. B (Methodol.) **20**(2), 361–372 (1958)

[Haa21] Haasdijk, J.: Optimizing NTRU LPRime on the ARM Cortex - A72 (2021). https://github.com/jhaasdijk/KEMobi

[KSSW] Kannwischer, M.J., Schwabe, P., Stebila, D., Wiggers, T.: PQClean. https://github.com/PQClean

[Mey96] Meyn, H.: Factorization of the cyclotomic polynomial $x^{2^n}+1$ over finite fields. Finite Fields Appl. **2**(4), 439–442 (1996)

[Mur96] Murakami, H.: Real-valued fast discrete Fourier transform and cyclic convolution algorithms of highly composite even length. In: 1996 IEEE International Conference on Acoustics, Speech, and Signal Processing Conference Proceedings, vol. 3, pp. 1311–1314 (1996)

[MVdO14] Martínez, F.E., Vergara, C.R., de Oliveira, L.B.: Explicit factorization of $x^n - 1 \in \mathbb{F}_q[x]$. arXiv preprint arXiv:1404.6281 (2014)

[NG21] Nguyen, D.T., Gaj, K.: Optimized software implementations of CRYSTALS-Kyber, NTRU, and Saber using NEON-based special instructions of ARMv8,. In: Third PQC Standardization Conference (2021)

[Nus80] Nussbaumer, H.: Fast polynomial transform algorithms for digital convolution. IEEE Trans. Acoust. Speech Signal Process. **28**(2), 205–215 (1980)

[Rad68] Rader, C.M.: Discrete Fourier transforms when the number of data samples is prime. Proc. IEEE **56**(6), 1107–1108 (1968)

[Sch77] Schönhage, A.: Schnelle multiplikation von polynomen über körpern der charakteristik 2. Acta Informatica **7**(4), 395–398 (1977)

[TW13] Tuxanidy, A., Wang, Q.: Composed products and factors of cyclotomic polynomials over finite fields. Des. Codes Crypt. **69**(2), 203–231 (2013)

[vdH04] van der Hoeven, J.: The truncated Fourier transform and applications. In: Proceedings of the 2004 International Symposium on Symbolic and Algebraic Computation, pp. 290–296 (2004)

[WY21] Yansheng, W., Yue, Q.: Further factorization of $x^n - 1$ over a finite field (II). Disc. Math. Algor. Appl. **13**(06), 2150070 (2021)

[WYF18] Yansheng, W., Yue, Q., Fan, S.: Further factorization of $x^n - 1$ over a finite field. Finite Fields Appl. **54**, 197–215 (2018)

# Efficient Quantum-Safe Distributed PRF and Applications: Playing DiSE in a Quantum World

Sayani Sinha[1(✉)], Sikhar Patranabis[2], and Debdeep Mukhopadhyay[1,3]

[1] Indian Institute of Technology Kharagpur, Kharagpur, India
sayanisinhamid@kgpian.iitkgp.ac.in, debdeep@cse.iitkgp.ac.in
[2] IBM Research, Bangalore, India
sikhar.patranabis@ibm.com
[3] New York University, Abu Dhabi, UAE

**Abstract.** We propose the first *distributed* version of a simple, efficient, and provably quantum-safe pseudorandom function (PRF). The distributed PRF (DPRF) supports arbitrary threshold access structures based on the hardness of the well-studied Learning with Rounding (LWR) problem. Our construction (abbreviated as PQDPRF) practically outperforms not only existing constructions of DPRF based on lattice-based assumptions, but also outperforms (in terms of evaluation time) existing constructions of: (i) classically secure DPRFs based on discrete-log hard groups, and (ii) quantum-safe DPRFs based on any generic quantum-safe PRF (e.g. AES). The efficiency of PQDPRF stems from the extreme simplicity of its construction, consisting of a simple inner product computation over $\mathbb{Z}_q$, followed by a rounding to a smaller modulus $p < q$. The key technical novelty of our proposal lies in our proof technique, where we prove the correctness and post-quantum security of PQDPRF (against semi-honest corruptions of any less than threshold number of parties) for a polynomial $q/p$ (equivalently, "modulus to modulus")-ratio.

Our proposed DPRF construction immediately enables efficient yet quantum-safe instantiations of several practical applications, including key distribution centers, distributed coin tossing, long-term encryption of information, etc. We showcase a particular application of PQDPRF in realizing an efficient yet quantum-safe version of distributed symmetric-key encryption (DiSE – originally proposed by Agrawal et al. in CCS 2018), which we call PQ – DiSE. For semi-honest adversarial corruptions across a wide variety of corruption thresholds, PQ – DiSE substantially outperforms existing instantiations of DiSE based on discrete-log hard groups and generic PRFs (e.g. AES). We illustrate the practical efficiency of our PQDPRF via prototype implementation of PQ – DiSE.


C. Pöpper and L. Batina (Eds.): ACNS 2024, LNCS 14584, pp. 47–78, 2024.
https://doi.org/10.1007/978-3-031-54773-7_3

# 1 Introduction

**Threshold Cryptography.** The privacy guarantees of any (computationally secure) cryptosystem fundamentally rely on the secure storage of a secret key. If the secret key is stored on a single server, this server becomes the single point of vulnerability, i.e., if an adversary successfully manages to corrupt the server, the secret key is retrieved and the security of the whole system is compromised. Threshold cryptography provides a solution to this problem by allowing the secret key to remain distributed among multiple (say, $T$) servers in the form of several key shares. Among them, if $t$ servers (for $1 < t \leq T$) can collaborate with their respective key shares to successfully perform the cryptographic computation without any knowledge of the actual secret key, we call it $(t, T)$-threshold cryptography. An underlying threshold secret sharing algorithm makes sure that collaboration of at least $t$ servers is necessary to reconstruct the secret, or in other words, less than $t$ servers together can not reconstruct the secret. Hence, if an adversary manages to corrupt $(t-1)$ number of servers (at most) in a $(t, T)$-threshold cryptosystem, the system still continues to remain secure, as the adversary can not retrieve the actual secret from secret shares of $(t-1)$ servers.

In this paper, we focus on threshold cryptographic systems [8,14] where the secret key is shared once during the initial setup phase (either by a trusted dealer or in a decentralized manner) and is *never* explicitly reconstructed in the clear. Subsequently, any cryptographic computation is performed in two phases: (a) first, each of the participating $t$ servers does the some *partial computation* with its own key share, and then (b) these partial computations are combined together either by one of the participating servers or a separate evaluating entity to get the final result. Crucially, the combination process should leak no additional information about the secret key beyond what is revealed by the final output.

**Threshold PRF and Applications.** In a threshold or distributed PRF, the PRF key is distributed across multiple (say, $T$) parties, and evaluations can be performed on any given input in a distributed manner by a threshold $t \in [2, T]$ number of parties. Informally, the primitive retains its pseudorandomness guarantees against any adversary that corrupts $t' < t$ parties. Some applications of a distributed PRF are as follows.

- **Distributed KDC** [28]**:** Key Distribution Center (KDC) provides keys to the users in a network that shares sensitive data. Usually, there is a dedicated key between the KDC and each user in the network. Whenever two users have to communicate securely, one of them requests a key to the KDC. KDC chooses a random key and sends it to each of the two parties, keeping it encrypted with their respective dedicated keys. The users can then decrypt it and retrieve the key for the secure communication session between them. This approach was introduced by Needham and Schroeder in [30], and KDC has been widely implemented in Kerberos System[1]. However, KDC is a single point of vulnerability as it stores the dedicated keys of all the users. KDC, being a single

[1] https://web.mit.edu/kerberos/.

point of contact, also suffers from the availability problem whenever there is a need for communication between multiple pairs of users or communication is needed among a set of more than two parties. To avoid these scenarios, distributed KDC is considered, which consists of multiple (say, $T$) servers to service the key requests, and a user can contact any available subset of $t$ servers out of them and receive a key irrespective of which particular subset it contacted. Distributed PRF is a building block of distributed KDC [28].
- **DiSE** [1,19]**:** A formal construction of threshold distributed symmetric-key encryption (DiSE) was proposed in [1], where a user has to contact $t$-out-of-$T$ servers for both encryption and decryption. The construction is discussed in detail later in Sect. 4.1 as an application context of threshold PRF.

**Post-quantum Security.** Once physical quantum computer comes to existence [7], various quantum algorithms [22,32,33] can be used to break classical cryptosystems built on the hardness assumption of mathematical problems like integer factorization, discrete logarithm. Lattice-based cryptography offers security against cryptanalytic attack by quantum computers. Although NIST[2] launched standardization process of quantum-safe asymmetric-key cryptography, need for standard post-quantum symmetric-key cryptography [12] still persists. As PRF is a building block of various symmetric-key primitives, we take a step towards this goal by constructing a simple but efficient quantum-safe threshold PRF.

### 1.1 Related Works and Our Contributions

The concept of shared evaluation of a PRF was initially proposed in [26], albeit for restricted threshold access structures. This was generalized to arbitrary threshold access structures in follow-up works [28,29,31], with new applications in [1,19]. Now we highlight our contributions in this paper in the context of related works.

**First Practically Efficient Quantum-Safe Distributed PRF.** We provide the first non-interactive *distributed* version of a simple but efficient quantum-safe PRF (PQDPRF) in random oracle model based on lattice-based Learning with Rounding (LWR) assumption. Such efficient straight-forward construction of quantum-safe distributed PRF with polynomial ratio between input and output modulus is the first of its kind to the best of our knowledge. We claim novelty of our contribution with respect to existing works as follows.

- Efficient DPRFs with their possible application areas have been proposed [28, 31], but they are not quantum-safe.
- LWR assumption was introduced in [10] along with a proposed PRF in standard model, but their construction was inefficient as it required superpolynomial modulus-to-modulus ratio. Also, the aspect of thresholdization was not captured there.

[2] National Institute of Standards and Technology.

- Some other PRF contructions based on variants of LWE assumption [9,15,17] can further be used in constructing threshold PRF. "Universal thresholdizer" tool by [14] can be used to construct threshold PRF from an underlying threshold FHE protocol. However, none of them is a straightforward and efficient approach to designing quantum-safe threshold PRF.
- A robust non-interactive lattice-based DPRF construction with theoretically efficient parameters is proposed in [25] for adaptive corruption settings. Although our construction is in the semi-honest setting against static corruptions, its main advantage lies in its simplicity, superior practical efficiency, and ease of implementation as compared to the scheme in [25]. In particular, our proposed construction provides a practically efficient quantum-safe drop-in replacement for AES/DDH-based DPRFs for applications (e.g., DiSE [1], distributed KDC [28]) where robustness can be achieved more efficiently and directly at the application level instead of trying to achieve the same at the DPRF level, requiring costlier and more mathematically involved techniques.

We prove the correctness, consistency, and security of our proposed PQDPRF, described in Sect. 3.2 and Sect. 3.3.

**A Practical Use-Case of Proposed Distributed PRF.** We validate the efficacy of proposed PQDPRF by plugging it into existing DiSE (distributed symmetric-key encryption) protocol [1], to get an improved quantum-safe version of DiSE, which we call PQ – DiSE. We also show that our proposed LWR-based DPRF, apart from being quantum-safe, is more efficient than other DPRFs (i.e., DDH-based DPRF and AES-based DPRF) previously used in DiSE, and consequently, PQ – DiSE outperforms DiSE in terms of throughput (number of encryptions per second). We emphasize that, to the best of our knowledge, no prior work has actually explored practical implementations and prototype realizations of applications such as in [1,19] based on quantum-safe distributed PRFs from lattice-based assumptions.

## 2 Preliminaries and Background

This section presents notations and background material.

### 2.1 Notation

The notation $x \leftarrow \mathcal{X}$ signifies that $x$ is sampled according to distribution $\mathcal{X}$, whereas $x \xleftarrow{R} X$ means that, $x$ is uniform random choice over set $X$. Upper case (e.g., $\mathbf{A}$) and lower case (e.g., $\mathbf{a}$) variables in bold denote a matrix and a vector, respectively. With two vectors $\mathbf{a}, \mathbf{b} \in \mathbb{Z}_q^n$, $\langle \mathbf{a}, \mathbf{b} \rangle = \sum_{i=1}^{n} a_i b_i \pmod q$ represents their vector dot product modulo $q$. The cardinality of a set $S$ is denoted by $|S|$. The notation $[n]$ for some $n \in \mathbb{N}$ denotes the set $\{1, \ldots, n\}$. For any $y \in \mathbb{Z}_q$, the round-off operation, denoted by $\lfloor y \rceil_p$ gives the nearest integral value of $(y \cdot \frac{p}{q})$ in $\mathbb{Z}_p$; in particular, if $(y \cdot \frac{p}{q})$ has a fractional part exactly equal to 0.5, we choose to always round it down to $\lfloor y \cdot \frac{p}{q} \rfloor$ to avoid ambiguity. We can apply the round-off operator to vectors and matrices as well to denote element-wise round-off operation. A negligible function of $\lambda$ is denoted by $\text{negl}(\lambda)$; $\text{poly}(\lambda)$ denotes a polynomial function of $\lambda$. Terms "threshold PRF" and "distributed PRF" are used alternatively throughout the paper.

## 2.2 Some Terminologies and Definitions

Here, we provide definitions of some terminologies that have been used frequently in the paper.

**Threshold Access Structure.** Let $\mathcal{P} = \{P_1, \ldots, P_T\}$ be a set of $T$ parties, and suppose that some secret $k$ is distributed among them in form of secret shares. Access structure is a set consisting of all "valid" subsets $\overline{\mathcal{P}} \subseteq \mathcal{P}$ of parties that can recover the secret $k$ by combining their key shares together. For any $t, T \in \mathbb{N}$ $(t \leq T)$, a minimal $(t, T)$-threshold access structure over $\mathcal{P}$ is defined as a collection of valid subsets of the form $\mathbb{A}_{t,T} = \{\overline{\mathcal{P}} \subseteq \mathcal{P} : |\overline{\mathcal{P}}| = t\}$, such that we have $|\mathbb{A}_{t,T}| = \binom{T}{t}$ as the number of valid subsets.

**Monotone Boolean Formula (MBF).** A Boolean formula is monotone if it has a single output and it consists of only AND and OR combination of Boolean variables. Note that any $(t, T)$-threshold access structure $\mathbb{A}_{t,T}$ can be represented by a MBF. The fact that a particular collaboration of $t$ parties is able to reconstruct the secret, is captured by Boolean formula of the form $(x_1 \wedge \ldots \wedge x_t)$ and that any such $t$-collaboration is a way of reconstruction, is captured by ORing $\binom{T}{t}$ such terms. For e.g., $\mathbb{A}_{3,4}$ is represented by $(x_1 \wedge x_2 \wedge x_3) \vee (x_1 \wedge x_2 \wedge x_4) \vee (x_1 \wedge x_3 \wedge x_4) \vee (x_2 \wedge x_3 \wedge x_4)$.

**Pseudo Random Function (PRF).** We recall the formal definition of a pseudorandom function (PRF). Let $\mathcal{F} : \mathcal{K} \times \mathcal{X} \to \mathcal{Y}$ be a family of pseudo random functions and $\mathcal{F}' = \{f' | f' : \mathcal{X} \to \mathcal{Y}\}$ be the set of all possible functions with the same domain and range. Let us assume that, $f_k \in \mathcal{F}$ uses a uniform random secret $k \xleftarrow{R} \mathcal{K}$ and, on input $x \in \mathcal{X}$, outputs $f_k(x)$, using both $k$ and $x$. Then, the advantage of any PPT distinguisher $\mathcal{D}$ is negligible, i.e.,

$$\left| \mathsf{Pr}[\mathcal{D}^{f_k(\cdot)}(1^\lambda) = 1] - \mathsf{Pr}[\mathcal{D}^{f'(\cdot)}(1^\lambda) = 1] \right| \leq \text{negl}(\lambda),$$

where $\lambda$ is a security parameter. The first probability is taken over uniform choice of $k$ and randomness of $\mathcal{D}$, and the second probability is taken over uniform choice of $f'$ and randomness of $\mathcal{D}$.

**Weak Pseudo Random Function.** A PRF is weak if its output is pseudorandom, only when the inputs are uniformly random over the input space. This is in contrast to the case of (strong) PRF, where indistinguishability holds for any input from the input space. However a weak PRF can be converted to a PRF by relying on existence of a random oracle. If $f_k(\cdot) : \mathcal{K} \times \mathcal{X} \to \mathcal{Y}$ is a weak PRF and $\mathcal{H} : \{0,1\}^\star \to \mathcal{X}$ is a hash function modeled as a random oracle, then $g_k(\cdot) = f_k(\mathcal{H}(\cdot))$ is a PRF [28].

**Learning with Rounding (LWR) Problem.** LWR problem is a "derandomized" version of Learning with Errors (LWE) problem, first introduced in [10]. Given a parameter $n \in \mathbb{N}$, two moduli $q, p \in \mathbb{N}$ such that $q > p \geq 2$, the LWR distribution $L_s$ for a secret $\mathbf{s} \in \mathbb{Z}_q^n$ is defined over $\mathbb{Z}_q^n \times \mathbb{Z}_p$ of the form $(\mathbf{a}, b)$, where we choose $\mathbf{a} \xleftarrow{R} \mathbb{Z}_q^n$ and then calculate $b = \lfloor \langle \mathbf{a}, \mathbf{s} \rangle \rceil_p$. The decision LWR problem is to distinguish samples of $L_\mathbf{s}$ from uniformly random samples of $\mathbb{Z}_q^n \times \mathbb{Z}_p$.

### 2.3 Distributed PRF (DPRF)

If the evaluation of a PRF is performed in a distributed way, we call it a distributed PRF. In this case, the secret $k$ of the PRF always remains distributed as shares among multiple parties. Here, we define distributed PRF formally.

**Definition 1 (Distributed Pseudo Random Function** (DPRF)**).** *Let $\mathcal{P} = \{P_1, \ldots, P_T\}$ be a set of $T$ parties, and let $\mathbb{S}$ be a class of threshold access structures on $\mathcal{P}$. A threshold PRF scheme for $\mathbb{S}$ over an input space $\mathcal{X}$ and key space $\mathcal{K}$ is a tuple of probabilistic polynomial-time algorithms as follows,*

$$\mathsf{DPRF} = (\mathsf{DPRF.Setup}, \mathsf{DPRF.PartialEval}, \mathsf{DPRF.FinalEval}).$$

$\underline{\mathsf{DPRF.Setup}(1^\lambda, \mathbb{A})}$: *On input the security parameter $\lambda$ and an access structure $\mathbb{A} \in \mathbb{S}$, this algorithm generates a key $k \xleftarrow{R} \mathcal{K}$, and then generates multiple key shares of $k$ corresponding to $\mathbb{A}$. At the end of key sharing among $T$ parties, the actual key $k$ is not stored anywhere. Each party has to store one or more than one key share depending on the particular threshold secret sharing scheme used.*

$\underline{\mathsf{DPRF.PartialEval}(x, P_i, A)}$: *On input a valid subset $A \in \mathbb{A}$, an input $x \in \mathcal{X}$ and a party $P_i \in A$, the appropriate key share (say, $k_i$) of $P_i$ corresponding to $A$ is chosen and a partial evaluation $f_{k_i}(x)$ is returned.*

$\underline{\mathsf{DPRF.FinalEval}(A, \{f_{k_i}(x)\}_{P_i \in A})}$: *On input a valid subset $A \in \mathbb{A}$ and all the partial evaluations by parties $P_i \in A$, this algorithm combines them to get the final PRF evaluation. The actual combination procedure depends upon the reconstruction property of the underlying threshold secret sharing scheme.*

**Correctness and Consistency.** A $(t, T)$-distributed PRF with $f_k(\cdot)$ as its underlying PRF is *correct* if given an input, its distributed evaluation by any valid subset $A \in \mathbb{A}$ outputs the same value as would be obtained by directly evaluating $f_k(\cdot)$ on the same input except with negligible probability, i.e.,

$$\mathsf{Pr}[\mathsf{DPRF.FinalEval}(A, \{\mathsf{DPRF.PartialEval}(x, P_i, A)\}_{P_i \in A}) = f_k(x)] \geq 1 - \text{negl}(\lambda).$$

A $(t, T)$-distributed PRF is *consistent* if distributed evaluation on a given input by any two distinct valid subsets $S_1, S_2 \in \mathbb{A}$ outputs the same value except with negligible probability, i.e.,

$$\begin{aligned} \big|\mathsf{Pr}[&\mathsf{DPRF.FinalEval}(S_1, \{\mathsf{DPRF.PartialEval}(x, P_i, S_1)\}_{P_i \in S_1}) \\ &\neq \mathsf{DPRF.FinalEval}(S_2, \{\mathsf{DPRF.PartialEval}(x, P_j, S_2)\}_{P_j \in S_2})]\big| \leq \text{negl}(\lambda). \end{aligned}$$

Note that the correctness of $(t, T)$-distributed PRF implies its consistency, but not the other way around.

**Security.** We borrow the notion of DPRF security from [28].

*The Adversarial Model.* We assume a probabilistic polynomial time (PPT) adversary that can statically corrupt (i.e., announces the set of corrupt parties before the partial evaluation query phase starts) at most $(t-1)$ number of parties and each party if corrupted, is honest but curious.

*The Security Notion.* Let $\mathcal{P} = \{P_1, \ldots, P_T\}$ be the set of $T$ parties and $\mathcal{A}$ be a PPT adversary as described above. Let $\mathcal{P}'$ be a statically corrupted set such that, $|\mathcal{P}'| = (t-1)$. Hence, after $\mathsf{DPRF.Setup}(1^\lambda, \mathbb{A}_{t,T})$ is run, $\mathcal{A}$ has access to key shares of each $P_i \in \mathcal{P}'$. We say that DPRF is secure if the winning probability of $\mathcal{A}$ against a challenger $\mathcal{C}$ in the following game is negligible.

Game:

1. $\mathcal{A}$ sends a query input $x \in \mathcal{X}$ to $\mathcal{C}$. $\mathcal{C}$ sends $(f_k(x), \{f_{k_i}(x)\}_{P_i \in \mathcal{P} \setminus \mathcal{P}'})$ to $\mathcal{A}$, where $f_{k_i}(x) = \mathsf{DPRF.PartialEval}(x, P_i, \mathcal{P}' \bigcup P_i)$.
2. The above step is repeated at most a priori bounded number of times for adaptive choice of query input $x \in \mathcal{X}$.
3. $\mathcal{A}$ sends a new challenge query $x^\star$ (different from query phase inputs) to $\mathcal{C}$.
4. $\mathcal{C}$ chooses a random bit $b \xleftarrow{R} \{0, 1\}$. If $b = 0$, it sends $f_k(x^\star)$ to $\mathcal{A}$, otherwise, it sends some $y \xleftarrow{R} \mathcal{Y}$ to $\mathcal{A}$, where $\mathcal{Y}$ is the range of underlying PRF.
5. $\mathcal{A}$ has to output a distinguishing bit $b'$.

$\mathcal{A}$ wins the game, if $b = b'$.

### 2.4 $(t, T)$-Threshold Secret Sharing

A threshold secret sharing scheme is an essential underlying primitive to build a distributed PRF protocol. A $(t, T)$-threshold secret sharing scheme shares a key $k$ among these $T$ parties in such a way that any $t$ or more parties are able to reconstruct it from their respective shares, though collaboration of less than $t$ parties does not suffice. We choose to use Benaloh-Leichter Linear Integer Secret Sharing Scheme (LISSS) as described in [20]. The secret sharing scheme is "linear integer" because key shares can be linearly combined to get the actual secret back in a way that the coefficients of the linear combination are integers. These coefficients used during the reconstruction of the secret are called *recovery coefficients*. Though the original Benaloh-Leichter LISSS shares a scalar secret, it can naturally be extended to share a secret in vector form. As we deal with secrets belonging to $\mathbb{Z}_q^n$ in later sections, we describe the LISSS scheme in the context of sharing a secret vector $\mathbf{k} \in \mathbb{Z}_q^n$ here.

**Preprocessing.** Here, we discuss some necessary preprocessing steps for threshold secret sharing.

**Formation of Distribution Matrix M**: Formation of distribution matrix **M** depends upon the MBF, representing a $(t, T)$-threshold access structure. As any MBF is a combination of AND and OR of Boolean variables, we need to focus on the three following cases.

*Each Boolean variable* $x_i$ corresponds to a singleton matrix with 1 as its only element.

*AND-ing of* $\mathbf{M_{f_a}}$ *and* $\mathbf{M_{f_b}}$*:* Let $\mathbf{M_{f_a}}$ with dimension $d_a \times e_a$ and $\mathbf{M_{f_b}}$ with dimension $d_b \times e_b$ be the distribution matrices for Boolean formulae $f_a$ and $f_b$ respectively. Then we form $\mathbf{M_{f_a \wedge f_b}}$ as follows:

| | | | |
|---|---|---|---|
| $c_a$ | $c_a$ | $C_a$ | 0 |
| 0 | $c_b$ | 0 | $C_b$ |

Here, $c_a$ and $c_b$ denote the first column of $\mathbf{M_{f_a}}$ and $\mathbf{M_{f_b}}$ respectively. $C_a$ and $C_b$ denote the rest of the columns of $\mathbf{M_{f_a}}$ and $\mathbf{M_{f_b}}$ respectively. $\mathbf{M_{f_a \wedge f_b}}$ has dimension $(d_a + d_b) \times (e_a + e_b)$.

*OR-ing of* $\mathbf{M_{f_a}}$ *and* $\mathbf{M_{f_b}}$*:* Let $\mathbf{M_{f_a}}$ with dimension $d_a \times e_a$ and $\mathbf{M_{f_b}}$ with dimension $d_b \times e_b$ be the distribution matrices for Boolean formulae $f_a$ and $f_b$ respectively. Then we form $\mathbf{M_{f_a \vee f_b}}$ as follows:

| | | |
|---|---|---|
| $c_a$ | $C_a$ | 0 |
| $c_b$ | 0 | $C_b$ |

Here, $c_a$ and $c_b$ denote the first column of $\mathbf{M_{f_a}}$ and $\mathbf{M_{f_b}}$ respectively. $C_a$ and $C_b$ denote the rest of the columns of $\mathbf{M_{f_a}}$ and $\mathbf{M_{f_b}}$ respectively. $\mathbf{M_{f_a \vee f_b}}$ has dimension $(d_a + d_b) \times (e_a + e_b - 1)$.

It can be easily verified that, the distribution matrix **M** for $(t, T)$-threshold secret sharing has dimension $d \times e$, where $d = \binom{T}{t} t$ and $e = (1 + \binom{T}{t}(t-1))$.

**Formation of Share Matrix $\boldsymbol{\rho}$:** $\boldsymbol{\rho}$ is a matrix with dimension $e \times n$. Its first row is populated from the $n$ elements of the actual secret vector $\mathbf{k} \in \mathbb{Z}_q^n$. The rest of the elements of the matrix are filled uniformly randomly from $\mathbb{Z}_q$.

**Sharing.** First we compute the matrix $\mathbf{M}\boldsymbol{\rho}$ that has $d = \binom{T}{t} t$ rows. Each of the rows is a unique key share. Note that the number of $t$-sized subset of $\mathcal{P}$ is $\binom{T}{t}$ and each of the $t$ parties in a $t$-sized subset will hold a keyshare corresponding to that specific group, which justifies $d = \binom{T}{t} t$ to be the total number of unique keyshares. For ease of explanation, we identify each keyshare with the following two attributes: (1) party_id ( which party the key share belongs to), (2) group_id (which $t$-sized group the key share is used for). By enumerating over all $t$-sized subsets and tagging them with corresponding enumerating serial numbers, we get group_id's of all $t$-sized subsets.

Now sharing of $d$ rows among $T$ parties happens in the following manner: we consider $d = \binom{T}{t}t$ rows as $\binom{T}{t}$ chunks of rows of size $t$. Now for $i \in [\binom{T}{t}]$, we pick $i^{th}$ such chunk at a time and assign each of the $t$ rows to parties belonging to the subset with group_id $i$. For example, in a (3, 5)-threshold secret sharing, subset $\{P_1, P_2, P_3\}$ has group_id 1, so first three rows of $\mathbf{M}_{\boldsymbol{\rho}}$ are assigned to $P_1, P_2, P_3$ respectively. $\{P_1, P_2, P_4\}$ has group_id 2, so next three rows of $\mathbf{M}_{\boldsymbol{\rho}}$ are assigned to $P_1, P_2, P_4$ respectively and so on.

**Reconstruction.** Any $t$-sized group of parties, with their key shares, should be able to reconstruct $\mathbf{k}$. Given $\mathcal{P}' = \{P_{i_1}, P_{i_2}, \ldots, P_{i_t}\} \subset \mathcal{P}$ with $i_1 < \cdots < i_t$, each of the $t$ parties will have one key share with group_id corresponding to $\mathcal{P}'$. Let us denote these $t$ key shares as $\{\mathbf{k}_{i_1}, \ldots, \mathbf{k}_{i_t}\}$. In any $t$-sized group, the party with minimum value of party_id is called the group_leader. Hence, $P_{i_1}$ is the group_leader here. In this LISSS the recovery coefficient is 1 for the group_leader and -1 for the rest of the $(t-1)$ parties. The key $\mathbf{k}$ can be reconstructed as $\mathbf{k} = \mathbf{k}_{i_1} - \sum_{j=2}^{t} \mathbf{k}_{i_j}$. We exploit this reconstruction property in final evaluation of $(t, T)$-threshold PRF.

**Size of Secret Shares.** After applying $(t, T)$-threshold secret sharing on $\mathbf{k} \in \mathbb{Z}_q^n$, each party gets $\binom{T-1}{t-1}$ key shares to store. So each party has to store $\binom{T-1}{t-1} \cdot n \cdot \lceil \log_2 q \rceil$ bits in total.

## 3 Our Contribution: Proposed Distributed PRF

In this section, we first describe a post-quantum secure PRF in the random oracle model. Next, in Sect. 3.2, we construct a distributed version of the same PRF such that, if the key is distributed among $T$ parties, participation of all $T$ parties is necessary to evaluate the PRF on a given input. We call it $(T, T)$-distributed PRF, denoted with $\mathsf{PQDPRF}_{\mathsf{T,T}}$. In Sect. 3.3, we provide a generalized construction of quantum-safe $(t, T)$-distributed PRF, denoted with $\mathsf{PQDPRF}_{\mathsf{t,T}}$, where participation of all $T$ parties is no longer a necessity, but the collaboration of at least $t$ ($t \leq T$) parties is required to evaluate the PRF on any given input. In general, PQDPRF refers to both of these schemes in subsequent sections. We elaborate on the choice of parameters for PQDPRF in Sect. 3.4. Section 3.5 compares our work with existing lattice-based DPRF [25].

### 3.1 Underlying Quantum-Safe PRF

We discuss the straightforward construction of underlying quantum-safe PRF from the Learning with Rounding (LWR) assumption in the following.

**The PRF Construction**
**Fixed parameters:**
- Key: $\mathbf{k} \xleftarrow{R} \mathcal{K}$, where $\mathcal{K} = \mathbb{Z}_q^n$. [Secret]
- $q \in \mathbb{N}$, modulus of input space. [Public]
- $p \in \mathbb{N}$, modulus of output space. [Public]

**Input:** $\mathbf{x} \in \mathcal{X} = \mathbb{Z}_q^n$
**Evaluation:** $f_{\mathbf{k}}(\mathbf{x}) = \lfloor\langle\mathcal{H}(\mathbf{x}), \mathbf{k}\rangle\rceil_p$, where $\mathcal{H} : \{0,1\}^\star \rightarrow \mathbb{Z}_q^n$ is a hash function, modeled as a random oracle.

**Choice of LWR over LWE.** To realize a distributed PRF, we typically need an algebraically structured PRF with some kind of "deterministic homomorphism" between key space and output space. Unfortunately, it is hard to achieve such an algebraically structured PRF from standard LWE. For example, the natural LWE-based (weak) PRF would be: $f_{\mathbf{k}}(\mathbf{x}) = \langle\mathbf{x}, \mathbf{k}\rangle + e$, where the error $e$ needs to be deterministic, and thus needs to be generated using some (weak) PRF as $e = g_{\mathbf{k}}(\mathbf{x})$. Now, unless $g$ is thresholdizable, $f$ can not be thresholdized. Hence, in order to avoid this circular requirement, we resort to LWR, where the rounding operation enables deterministic homomorphism. Several advantages of choosing LWR over LWE in the construction of PRF have been discussed in [27].

**Post-quantum Security of the PRF.** We discuss the security of underlying PRF here.

**Theorem 1.** *The above construction of PRF is secure in the random oracle model if the LWR assumption holds.*

*Proof.* We assume a distinguisher $\mathcal{D}$ which distinguishes PRF outputs on a polynomial number of inputs of its choice from outputs of a truly random function on the same set of inputs. Assuming that an LWR challenger $\mathcal{C}$ chooses to always generate samples either from an LWR distribution with fixed secret $\mathbf{k} \in \mathcal{K}$ or from uniform random distribution over $\mathbb{Z}_q^n \times \mathbb{Z}_p$, we build another distinguisher $\mathcal{D}'$ to distinguish LWR samples from uniformly random samples generated by $\mathcal{C}$ in the following manner:

- $\mathcal{D}$ sends an input $\mathbf{x}_i$ of its choice to $\mathcal{D}'$.
- $\mathcal{D}'$ requests for a sample of the form $(\mathbf{a}_i, b_i) \in \mathbb{Z}_q^n \times \mathbb{Z}_p$ from $\mathcal{C}$.
- Upon receiving $(\mathbf{a}_i, b_i)$, $\mathcal{D}'$ now programs the random oracle such that $\mathcal{H}(\mathbf{x}_i) = \mathbf{a}_i$. It returns $b_i$ to $\mathcal{D}$ as the output for input $\mathbf{x}_i$.
- After polynomial repetitions of above three steps, $\mathcal{D}$ returns a distinguishing bit $\mathsf{b}$.
- $\mathcal{D}'$ forwards the same bit $\mathsf{b}$ as distinguishing bit to $\mathcal{C}$.

If $\mathcal{C}$ chooses to generate all $(\mathbf{a}_i, b_i)$ samples from LWR distribution, $b_i$ is indeed PRF output for an input $\mathbf{x}_i$, since $b_i = \lfloor\langle\mathbf{a}_i, \mathbf{k}\rangle\rceil_p = \lfloor\langle\mathcal{H}(\mathbf{x}_i), \mathbf{k}\rangle\rceil_p = f_{\mathbf{k}}(\mathbf{x}_i)$. On the other hand if $\mathcal{C}$ chooses to generate samples from uniform distribution, $b_i$ is a TRF (truly random function) output for input $\mathbf{x}_i$. Hence, if $\mathcal{D}$ guesses $\mathsf{b}$ correctly with non-negligible probability, $\mathcal{D}'$ wins the game against $\mathcal{C}$ with non-negligible probability, thus breaking the LWR assumption. Therefore, by contradiction, we conclude that the above PRF construction is secure due to LWR assumption with the same moduli $p, q$.

Furthermore, the proposed PRF is a post-quantum secure construction in random oracle model[3], since it relies upon quantum-safe LWR assumption. □

**Polynomial Modulus-to-Modulus Ratio of LWR Parameters.** During the introduction of the LWR assumption [10], the hardness of decision-LWR problem, when derived from the hardness of the well-established decision-LWE problem, required a superpolynomial (in security parameter) "$\frac{q}{p}$" ratio while keeping the dimension ($n$) and modulus ($q$) same and allowing unbounded number ($m$) of adversarial queries. Later, several works [6,11] focused on new reduction techniques from LWE problem to LWR problem, which would require only polynomial "$\frac{q}{p}$" ratio, but allow a priori bounded number of adversarial queries and a multiplicative decrease in dimension. Another work [27] proposed a (non-practical) variant of LWR problem where reduction from LWE allows an unbounded number of adversarial queries while achieving a polynomial "$\frac{q}{p}$" ratio. However [5] proposes a dimension-preserving reduction from LWE to LWR problem requiring only polynomial "$\frac{q}{p}$" ratio allowing a priori bounded number of queries. Formally, we summarize the following theorem from Theorem 1.1 of [5].

**Theorem 2 (Theorem 1.1 of [5]).** *Let $\lambda$ be the security parameter. Let $\Psi$ be a $B$-bounded LWE noise distribution over $\mathbb{Z}$ and $p, q = \text{poly}(\lambda)$, $m = \text{poly}(\lambda)$, $n \in \mathbb{N}$ with $\frac{q}{p} \geq mB\lambda$. Suppose a PPT adversary $\mathcal{A}$ can distinguish LWR samples with parameter $(n, q, p, m)$ from uniform random samples with advantage $\epsilon \geq \lambda^{-c}$ for some constant $c \geq 1$. In that case, there must exist another adversary $\mathcal{A}'$ which can distinguish LWE samples with parameters $(n, q, m, \Psi)$ from uniform random samples with advantage $\epsilon' = \epsilon(mB)^{-c}$.*

We conclude from the above theorem that it is possible to obtain a hard instance of decision-LWR problem from a hard instance of LWE problem with the same set of parameters $(n, q)$ and polynomially large "$\frac{q}{p}$" ratio.

**Concrete Choice of LWR Parameters.** Although the theoretical analysis above implies a technical gap between the hardness of LWE problem and LWR problem, no practical attack on LWR exploits this gap to perform better than an attack on LWE with the same set of parameters. Hence, several LWR-based constructions [18,21], including NIST candidates (e.g., SABER) make a more aggressive choice of LWR parameters than what is suggested by the theoretical analysis, to build practically efficient cryptosystems. We follow the same approach while providing a concrete choice of LWR parameters for our construction in Sect. 3.4. Since the existing attacks on LWR do not capture the loss in security while traversing from an LWE-based construction to an LWR-based construction, we first find a set of LWE parameters for which LWE problem is hard to

[3] We assume quantum adversary with classical access to random oracle here [13].

solve. Then we use them as LWR parameters while maintaining polynomial "$\frac{q}{p}$" ratio.

### 3.2 Proposed (T, T)-Distributed PRF

Here, we propose the formal construction of $(T, T)$-distributed PRF, based on the PRF described in 3.1, and discuss its proof of correctness, consistency, and security.

**Construction 1** (Post-quantum Secure $(T, T)$-Distributed Pseudo Random Function ($\mathsf{PQDPRF_{T,T}}$)). $\mathsf{PQDPRF_{T,T}}$ *is a post-quantum secure $(T, T)$-distributed PRF over an input space (or, domain) $\mathcal{X} = \mathbb{Z}_q^n$ and key space $\mathcal{K} = \mathbb{Z}_q^n$. The range of PRF is $\mathcal{Y} = \mathbb{Z}_p$. Here $q, p \in \mathbb{N}$ are publicly known moduli of input and output space respectively; $q_1 \in \mathbb{N}$ $(p < q_1 < q)$ is another public modulus to be used during partial evaluation. Assume, $\mathcal{H} : \{0,1\}^\star \to \mathbb{Z}_q^n$ is a hash function modeled as a random oracle. Also, let us assume $\mathcal{P} = \{P_1, \ldots, P_T\}$ to be the set of $T$ parties. The access structure $\mathbb{A}_{T,T}$ here is a singleton set, such that, $\mathbb{A}_{T,T} = \{\mathcal{P}\}$. The protocol consists of the following three PPT algorithms,*

$$\mathsf{PQDPRF_{T,T}} = (\mathsf{PQDPRF_{T,T}.Setup}, \mathsf{PQDPRF_{T,T}.PartialEval}, \mathsf{PQDPRF_{T,T}.FinalEval}).$$

$\underline{\mathsf{PQDPRF_{T,T}.Setup}(1^\lambda, \mathbb{A}_{T,T})}$: *First, on input security parameter $\lambda$, a key $\mathbf{k} \xleftarrow{R} \mathcal{K}$ is generated. Next, it is distributed among $T$ parties using additive secret sharing such that each party $P_i \in \mathcal{P}$ gets a key share $\mathbf{k_i}$ and $\sum_{i=1}^{T} \mathbf{k_i} = \mathbf{k}$.*

$\underline{\mathsf{PQDPRF_{T,T}.PartialEval}(\mathbf{x}, P_i)}$: *For a given input $\mathbf{x}$, each party $P_i$ partially evaluates the PRF with its own share $\mathbf{k_i}$ as follows: $f_{\mathbf{k_i}}(\mathbf{x}) = \lfloor \langle \mathcal{H}(\mathbf{x}), \mathbf{k_i} \rangle \rceil_{q_1}$, and broadcasts it to other $(T-1)$ parties.*

$\underline{\mathsf{PQDPRF_{T,T}.FinalEval}(\{f_{\mathbf{k_i}}(\mathbf{x})\}_{i \in [T]})}$: *Each party having its own partial evaluation and partial evaluations of rest $(T-1)$ parties, computes the final evaluation of the PRF on the given input $\mathbf{x}$ as follows: $f_{\mathbf{k}}(\mathbf{x}) = \lfloor \sum_{i=1}^{T} f_{\mathbf{k_i}}(\mathbf{x}) \rceil_p$.*

**Remark.** The construction $\mathsf{PQDPRF_{T,T}}$ requires a *two-layered rounding*; first from modulo $q$ to $q_1$ during partial evaluation, and then from modulo $q_1$ to $p$ during final evaluation.

**Proof of Correctness and Consistency.** Here, we formally prove the correctness of our proposed $\mathsf{PQDPRF_{T,T}}$. Let us express direct and distributed PRF evaluation as

$$f_{\mathbf{k}}^{\mathsf{dir}}(\mathbf{x}) = \lfloor \langle \mathcal{H}(\mathbf{x}), \mathbf{k} \rangle \rceil_p, \quad f_{\{\mathbf{k_i}\}_{i \in [T]}}^{\mathsf{dist}}(\mathbf{x}) = \lfloor \sum_{i=1}^{T} \lfloor \langle \mathcal{H}(\mathbf{x}), \mathbf{k_i} \rangle \rceil_{q_1} \rceil_p.$$

*Claim.* The difference between direct PRF evaluation and distributed PRF evaluation on some input $x$ is strictly upper bounded by 1 with high probability, i.e.,

$$\left| f_{\{\mathbf{k_i}\}_{i \in [T]}}^{\mathsf{dist}}(\mathbf{x}) - f_{\mathbf{k}}^{\mathsf{dir}}(\mathbf{x}) \right| < 1.$$

*Proof.* Note that by definition of round-off operation (Sect. 2.1), for any $y \in \mathbb{Z}_q$, we can express $\lfloor y \rceil_p$ as $\frac{p}{q}y + e$, where $-0.5 \leq e < 0.5$.

Now, assuming $\mathbf{r} = \mathcal{H}(\mathbf{x})$, the direct evaluation can be written as,

$$f_{\mathbf{k}}^{\mathsf{dir}}(\mathbf{x}) = \lfloor \langle \mathbf{r}, \mathbf{k} \rangle \rceil_p = \frac{p}{q} \langle \mathbf{r}, \mathbf{k} \rangle + e',$$

where $-0.5 \leq e' < 0.5$. The distributed evaluation can be expressed as,

$$\begin{aligned} f_{\{\mathbf{k_i}\}_{i \in [T]}}^{\mathsf{dist}}(\mathbf{x}) &= \lfloor \sum_{i=1}^{T} \lfloor \langle \mathbf{r}, \mathbf{k_i} \rangle \rceil_{q_1} \rceil_p = \lfloor \sum_{i=1}^{T} (\langle \mathbf{r}, \mathbf{k_i} \rangle \cdot \frac{q_1}{q} + e_i) \rceil_p \\ &= \lfloor \frac{q_1}{q} \sum_{i=1}^{T} \langle \mathbf{r}, \mathbf{k_i} \rangle + \sum_{i=1}^{T} e_i \rceil_p \leq \lfloor \frac{q_1}{q} \langle \mathbf{r}, \mathbf{k} \rangle + \frac{T}{2} \rceil_p \\ &= \frac{p}{q_1} (\frac{q_1}{q} \langle \mathbf{r}, \mathbf{k} \rangle + \frac{T}{2}) + e = \frac{p}{q} \langle \mathbf{r}, \mathbf{k} \rangle + \frac{p}{q_1} \cdot \frac{T}{2} + e, \end{aligned}$$

where, each $-0.5 \leq e_i < 0.5$ and $-0.5 \leq e < 0.5$. Thus,

$$\begin{aligned} & f_{\{\mathbf{k_i}\}_{i \in [T]}}^{\mathsf{dist}}(\mathbf{x}) - f_{\mathbf{k}}^{\mathsf{dir}}(\mathbf{x}) \leq \frac{p}{q_1} \cdot \frac{T}{2} + e - e' \\ \implies & \left| f_{\{\mathbf{k_i}\}_{i \in [T]}}^{\mathsf{dist}}(\mathbf{x}) - f_{\mathbf{k}}^{\mathsf{dir}}(\mathbf{x}) \right| \leq \left| \frac{p}{q_1} \cdot \frac{T}{2} \right| + |e - e'| \end{aligned}$$

As $e, e' \in [-0.5, 0.5)$, $|e - e'| < 1$ holds true. Subsequently in Sect. 3.4 we discuss choice of values $p$, $q_1$ such that $\epsilon = \frac{p}{q_1} \cdot \frac{T}{2}$ is small enough and $|e - e'| + \epsilon$ does not exceed 1. □

Now, as both $f_{\{\mathbf{k_i}\}_{i \in [T]}}^{\mathsf{dist}}(\mathbf{x})$ and $f_{\mathbf{k}}^{\mathsf{dir}}(\mathbf{x})$ are integers, we can conclude that their values are same except with a negligible probability. Thus, the correctness of our proposed distributed PRF is satisfied.

Please note that in the case of $(T, T)$-distributed PRF, $\mathbb{A}_{T,T}$ is a singleton set, and hence, the consistency of $\mathsf{PQDPRF}_{\mathsf{T,T}}$ is trivially satisfied.

**Proof of Security.** We recall the definition of security for a DPRF in the random oracle model in Sect. 2.3. We provide the formal statement on the security of the proposed DPRF in the following.

**Theorem 3.** *Our proposed* $\mathsf{PQDPRF}_{\mathsf{T,T}}$ *is secure if the underlying PRF is secure.*

*Proof Overview.* The underlying PRF, described in Sect. 3.1, is secure based on the LWR assumption (see Theorem 1). The hardness of the LWR problem is argued in Theorem 2 from the hardness of LWE problem. In the proposed DPRF, as described in Construction 1, we rely on the hardness of the same LWR instance, on which the underlying PRF relies. As the construction is in a $(T, T)$-threshold scenario, we follow the security notion of Sect. 2.3 and assume maximal corruption by the adversary. In other words, we assume a PPT adversary that has corrupted $(T-1)$ parties and gained access to their key shares. Apart from the actual PRF evaluation for each query input, it is also allowed to see the partial evaluations of the honest parties for each queried input. The crux of the proof of security for the proposed DPRF (over and above the security of the underlying PRF) is to prove that the partial evaluation of an honest party does not leak any meaningful information about the honest party's key share. To prove this, we propose a strategy to simulate the partial evaluation of the honest party without using its actual key share, and then show that the distributions of the real and simulated partial evaluations are statistically indistinguishable.

*Proof of Theorem* 3. We define four hybrids $\mathsf{Hybrid}_0$, $\mathsf{Hybrid}_1$, $\mathsf{Hybrid}_2$ and $\mathsf{Hybrid}_3$ (see the hybrid diagrams in the following page), such that in each hybrid, the game is between a PPT adversary $\mathcal{A}$ and a challenger $\mathcal{C}$. We assume $\mathcal{P} = \{P_1, \ldots, P_T\}$ to be a set of $T$ parties. The adversary $\mathcal{A}$ has corrupted $(T-1)$ parties among them (say, $P_2, \ldots, P_T$ without loss of generality). So, $P_1$ is the only honest party, and its key share $\mathbf{k_1}$ is unknown to the adversary. Each hybrid consists of a query phase and a challenge phase. Only a priori bounded number of queries are allowed in the query phase, whereas the challenge phase consists of a single challenge. In the first hybrid ($\mathsf{Hybrid}_0$), the adversary sees the actual partial evaluations in the query phase, and in the challenge phase, it sees the actual DPRF evaluation on challenge input. In the last hybrid ($\mathsf{Hybrid}_3$), the adversary still sees the actual partial evaluations in the query phase, but in the challenge phase, it sees a truly random value. We aim to prove indistinguishability of $\mathsf{Hybrid}_3$ from $\mathsf{Hybrid}_0$, such that the adversary can not distinguish the output of the proposed DPRF and the output of a truly random function for the challenge input $\mathbf{x}^\star$ even in the presence of direct PRF evaluation and partial evaluation by the honest party ($P_1$) on a bounded number of uniform random query inputs. For the sake of argument, we introduce two intermediate hybrids. In $\mathsf{Hybrid}_1$, the adversary sees simulated partial evaluations in the query phase, but in the challenge phase, it still sees the actual DPRF evaluation on the challenge input. In the next hybrid ($\mathsf{Hybrid}_2$), the adversary keeps on seeing simulated partial evaluations in the query phase, whereas, in the challenge phase, it sees a truly random value.

We prove the indistinguishability between the chain of hybrids in the form of some lemmas, which, in turn, proves the theorem. □

**Indistinguishability Between Chain of Hybrids**

**Lemma 1.** $\mathsf{Hybrid}_1$ *is statistically indistinguishable from* $\mathsf{Hybrid}_0$.

*Proof.* These two hybrids differ in the query phase, as in the first case the adversary $\mathcal{A}$ sees the actual partial evaluation by the honest party, while in the second case, $\mathcal{A}$ sees the simulated partial evaluation.

Actual partial evaluation in $\mathsf{Hybrid}_0$: $f_{\mathbf{k_1}}(\mathbf{x}) = \lfloor \langle \mathbf{r}, \mathbf{k_1} \rangle \rceil_{q_1}$.

| Query Phase | Challenge Phase |
|---|---|
| The adversary $\mathcal{A}$ sends a query input $\mathbf{x}$ to the challenger $\mathcal{C}$. In response, $\mathcal{C}$ sends $f_{\mathbf{k}}(\mathbf{x})$ and $f_{\mathbf{k_1}}(\mathbf{x})$ to $\mathcal{A}$, where $\mathbf{r} = \mathcal{H}(\mathbf{x})$, $f_{\mathbf{k}}(\mathbf{x}) = \lfloor \langle \mathbf{r}, \mathbf{k} \rangle \rceil_p$, $\boxed{f_{\mathbf{k_1}}(\mathbf{x}) = \lfloor \langle \mathbf{r}, \mathbf{k_1} \rangle \rceil_{q_1}.}$ | $\mathcal{A}$ sends a challenge input $\mathbf{x}^\star$. In response, it receives $\boxed{f_{\mathbf{k}}(\mathbf{x}^\star)}$ from $\mathcal{C}$. |

Hybrid$_0$

| Query Phase | Challenge Phase |
|---|---|
| $\mathcal{A}$ sends a query input $\mathbf{x}$ to $\mathcal{C}$. In response, $\mathcal{C}$ sends $f_{\mathbf{k}}(\mathbf{x})$ and $f^{\mathsf{sim}}_{\mathbf{k_1}}(\mathbf{x})$ to $\mathcal{A}$, where $\mathbf{r} = \mathcal{H}(\mathbf{x})$, $f_{\mathbf{k}}(\mathbf{x}) = \lfloor \langle \mathbf{r}, \mathbf{k} \rangle \rceil_p$, $\boxed{f^{\mathsf{sim}}_{\mathbf{k_1}}(\mathbf{x}) = \lfloor f_{\mathbf{k}}(\mathbf{x}) \cdot \frac{q}{p} - \sum_{i=2}^{T} \langle \mathbf{r}, \mathbf{k_i} \rangle \rceil_{q_1}.}$ | The adversary sends a challenge input $\mathbf{x}^\star$. In response, it receives $\boxed{f_{\mathbf{k}}(\mathbf{x}^\star)}$ from the challenger. |

Hybrid$_1$

| Query Phase | Challenge Phase |
|---|---|
| $\mathcal{A}$ sends a query input $\mathbf{x}$ to $\mathcal{C}$. In response, $\mathcal{C}$ sends $f_{\mathbf{k}}(\mathbf{x})$ and $f_{\mathbf{k_1}}(\mathbf{x})$ to $\mathcal{A}$, where $\mathbf{r} = \mathcal{H}(\mathbf{x})$, $f_{\mathbf{k}}(\mathbf{x}) = \lfloor \langle \mathbf{r}, \mathbf{k} \rangle \rceil_p$, $\boxed{f_{\mathbf{k_1}}(\mathbf{x}) = \lfloor \langle \mathbf{r}, \mathbf{k_1} \rangle \rceil_{q_1}.}$ | $\mathcal{A}$ sends a challenge input $\mathbf{x}^\star$. In response, it receives from $\mathcal{C}$ $\boxed{y^\star \xleftarrow{R} \mathbb{Z}_p.}$ |

Hybrid$_3$

| Query Phase | Challenge Phase |
|---|---|
| The adversary sends a query input $\mathbf{x}$ to the challenger. In response, the challenger sends $f_{\mathbf{k}}(\mathbf{x})$ and $f^{\mathsf{sim}}_{\mathbf{k_1}}(\mathbf{x})$ to the adversary, where $\mathbf{r} = \mathcal{H}(\mathbf{x})$, $f_{\mathbf{k}}(\mathbf{x}) = \lfloor \langle \mathbf{r}, \mathbf{k} \rangle \rceil_p$, $\boxed{f^{\mathsf{sim}}_{\mathbf{k_1}}(\mathbf{x}) = \lfloor f_{\mathbf{k}}(\mathbf{x}) \cdot \frac{q}{p} - \sum_{i=2}^{T} \langle \mathbf{r}, \mathbf{k_i} \rangle \rceil_{q_1}.}$ | $\mathcal{A}$ sends a challenge input $\mathbf{x}^\star$. In response, it receives from $\mathcal{C}$ $\boxed{y^\star \xleftarrow{R} \mathbb{Z}_p.}$ |

Hybrid$_2$

Simulated partial evaluation in Hybrid$_1$:

$$f^{\mathsf{sim}}_{\mathbf{k_1}}(\mathbf{x}) = \lfloor f_{\mathbf{k}}(\mathbf{x}) \cdot \frac{q}{p} - \sum_{i=2}^{T} \langle \mathbf{r}, \mathbf{k_i} \rangle \rceil_{q_1} = \lfloor \lfloor \langle \mathbf{r}, \mathbf{k} \rangle \rceil_p \cdot \frac{q}{p} - \sum_{i=2}^{T} \langle \mathbf{r}, \mathbf{k_i} \rangle \rceil_{q_1}$$
$$= \lfloor \langle \mathbf{r}, \mathbf{k} \rangle - e - \sum_{i=2}^{T} \langle \mathbf{r}, \mathbf{k_i} \rangle \rceil_{q_1} = \lfloor \langle \mathbf{r}, \mathbf{k_1} \rangle - e \rceil_{q_1}.$$

Now we will prove that, the error term $e$ in the expression of $f^{\mathsf{sim}}_{\mathbf{k_1}}(\mathbf{x})$ can be rewritten as $\langle \mathbf{r}, \mathbf{k}' \rangle$ for some $\mathbf{k}' \in \{0,1\}^n$, such that,

$$f^{\mathsf{sim}}_{\mathbf{k_1}}(\mathbf{x}) = \lfloor \langle \mathbf{r}, \mathbf{k_1} \rangle - e \rceil_{q_1} = \lfloor \langle \mathbf{r}, \mathbf{k_1} \rangle - \langle \mathbf{r}, \mathbf{k}' \rangle \rceil_{q_1} = \lfloor \langle \mathbf{r}, \mathbf{k_1} - \mathbf{k}' \rangle \rceil_{q_1} = \lfloor \langle \mathbf{r}, \mathbf{k}'_1 \rangle \rceil_{q_1},$$

which essentially has the same distribution as of $f_{\mathbf{k_1}}(\mathbf{x})$. Note that $e = \langle \mathbf{r}, \mathbf{k} \rangle - \lfloor \langle \mathbf{r}, \mathbf{k} \rangle \rceil_p \cdot \frac{q}{p}$ is non-zero with high probability and it is independent of $\mathbf{k_1}$. So,

$\mathbf{k}'$ satisfying $e = \langle \mathbf{r}, \mathbf{k}' \rangle$ is independent of $\mathbf{k_1}$. Hence although, $\mathbf{k}_1' = \mathbf{k_1} - \mathbf{k}'$, $\mathbf{k}_1'$ and $\mathbf{k_1}$ are independent of each other.

Since actual partial evaluation $f_{\mathbf{k_1}}(\mathbf{x}) = \lfloor \langle \mathbf{r}, \mathbf{k_1} \rangle \rceil_{q_1}$ in $\mathsf{Hybrid}_0$ and simulated partial evaluation $f_{\mathbf{k_1}}^{\mathsf{sim}}(\mathbf{x}) = \lfloor \langle \mathbf{r}, \mathbf{k}_1' \rangle \rceil_{q_1}$ in $\mathsf{Hybrid}_1$ come from the same distribution, $\mathsf{Hybrid}_1$ is statistically indistinguishable from $\mathsf{Hybrid}_0$. □

What remains to be proved is the following claim.

*Claim.* Given $\mathbf{r} \in \mathbb{Z}_q^n$, and an error term $e \in \mathbb{Z}_q$, $e$ can be represented as $\langle \mathbf{r}, \mathbf{k}' \rangle$ for some $\mathbf{k}' \in \{0,1\}^n$.

*Proof.* We recall a simple application of leftover hash lemma [2,23,24], which states that given an additive group $G$, and $n$ elements of that group $g_1, \ldots, g_n$, an arbitrary subset sum of those group elements is statistically indistinguishable from a random group element $g \xleftarrow{R} G$. In other words, for a random $\mathbf{k} \xleftarrow{R} \{0,1\}^n$ with high entropy, $\sum_{i=1}^{n} k_i g_i$ is uniformly random over $G$, provided $n \geq 3 \log |G|$.

Analogously, $\mathbb{Z}_q$ is an additive group with $q$ elements. For any $\mathbf{r} \in \mathbb{Z}_q^n$ and $\mathbf{k}' \in \{0,1\}^n$, $\langle \mathbf{r}, \mathbf{k}' \rangle$ represents a subset sum of group elements, which is uniformly random over $\mathbb{Z}_q$ by leftover hash lemma, for unknown $\mathbf{k}'$ and $n \geq 3 \log q$.

Now let us assume that $e$ can not be represented as $\langle \mathbf{r}, \mathbf{k}' \rangle$, which implies that there exists at least one $e \in \mathbb{Z}_q$, that can not be produced from the subset sum $\sum_{i=1}^{n} k_i' r_i$, thus leading to the violation of leftover hash lemma.

Hence by contradiction we can say that for any $e \in \mathbb{Z}_q$, there exists a $\mathbf{k}'$, such that $\langle \mathbf{r}, \mathbf{k}' \rangle = e$. □

**Lemma 2.** $\mathsf{Hybrid}_2$ *is computationally indistinguishable from* $\mathsf{Hybrid}_1$.

*Proof.* The challenger $\mathcal{C}$ in both these hybrids, responds to a query input $\mathbf{x}$ with $f_{\mathbf{k}}(\mathbf{x})$ and $f_{\mathbf{k_1}}^{\mathsf{sim}}(\mathbf{x})$. As $f_{\mathbf{k_1}}^{\mathsf{sim}}(\mathbf{x})$ is not a function of $\mathbf{k_1}$, it is never able to leak any meaningful information about $\mathbf{k_1}$ to the adversary $\mathcal{A}$. Hence the problem of distinguishing $\mathsf{Hybrid}_2$ from $\mathsf{Hybrid}_1$ reduces to the problem of distinguishing the PRF output of the form $\lfloor \langle \mathcal{H}(\mathbf{x}), \mathbf{k} \rangle \rceil_p$ from the output of a truly random function in the challenge phase, which is hard since the underlying PRF has already been discussed to be secure due to hardness of LWR problem (Theorem 1). Thus, we conclude that $\mathsf{Hybrid}_2$ is indistinguishable from $\mathsf{Hybrid}_1$. Also, since our DPRF relies on the hardness of the same LWR instance, on which the underlying PRF relies, no loss in security is incurred owing to the choice of LWR parameters for PQDPRF. □

**Lemma 3.** $\mathsf{Hybrid}_3$ *is statistically indistinguishable from* $\mathsf{Hybrid}_2$.

*Proof.* Lemma 2 implies the proof of this lemma. □

Finally, Lemma 1, Lemma 2, and Lemma 3 together establish the fact that $\mathsf{Hybrid}_0$ is indistinguishable from $\mathsf{Hybrid}_3$, which implies that, $\mathcal{A}$ can not distinguish PRF output from the output of a truly random function even after seeing actual partial evaluations of the honest party for bounded number of query inputs, thus completing the proof of Theorem 3. Hence, the proposed $(T, T)$-distributed PRF is secure.

### 3.3 Generalised (t, T)-Threshold PRF

Now we extend the protocol described in the previous section for a more general setting of $(t, T)$-threshold PRF, where $2 \leq t \leq T$.

**Construction 2** (Post-quantum Secure $(t, T)$-distributed Pseudo Random Function ($\mathsf{PQDPRF_{t,T}}$)). $\mathsf{PQDPRF_{t,T}}$ *is a post-quantum secure $(t, T)$-threshold PRF, whose input space $\mathcal{X}$, key space $\mathcal{K}$ and range $\mathcal{Y}$ are same as of* $\mathsf{PQDPRF_{T,T}}$. *Here $q, p \in \mathbb{N}$ are publicly known moduli of input and output space respectively, while $q_1 \in \mathbb{N}$ $(p < q_1 < q)$ is the publicly known modulus of partial evaluation. Let $\mathcal{H} : \{0,1\}^\star \rightarrow \mathbb{Z}_q^n$ be a hash function modeled as a random oracle. With the key $\mathbf{k} \in \mathcal{K}$, distributed beforehand among $T$ parties of the set $\mathcal{P} = \{P_1, \ldots, P_T\}$ by some threshold secret sharing procedure, we expect any subset of $\mathcal{P}$ having size at least $t$ to be able to collaboratively evaluate the PRF on a given input $\mathbf{x} \in \mathcal{X}$. $\mathbb{A}_{t,T} = \{A \subset \mathcal{P} : |A| = t\}$ is the threshold access structure with $|\mathbb{A}_{t,T}| = \binom{T}{t}$. Any set with cardinality more than $t$ is not explicitly considered as a member of $\mathbb{A}_{t,T}$, because one can pick any $t$ number of parties from that set and perform the threshold evaluation on a given input. Hence, it is redundant to keep $A \subset \mathcal{P}$ with $|A| > t$ as a member of $\mathbb{A}_{t,T}$.* $\mathsf{PQDPRF_{t,T}}$ *consists of three PPT algorithms,*

$$\mathsf{PQDPRF_{t,T}} = (\mathsf{PQDPRF_{t,T}.Setup}, \mathsf{PQDPRF_{t,T}.PartialEval}, \mathsf{PQDPRF_{t,T}.FinalEval}).$$

$\underline{\mathsf{PQDPRF_{t,T}.Setup}(1^\lambda, \mathbb{A}_{t,T})}$: *On input security parameter $\lambda$ and the threshold access structure $\mathbb{A}_{t,T}$, a key $\mathbf{k} \xleftarrow{R} \mathcal{K}$ is generated first. Next, it is distributed among $T$ parties with a threshold secret sharing scheme, as described in Sect. 2.4, after which, each $P_i \in \mathcal{P}$ has to store $\binom{T-1}{t-1}$ number of shares, each corresponding to one of the $\binom{T-1}{t-1}$ number of $t$-sized subset of $\mathcal{P}$, that $P_i$ belongs to. Notice that the original key $\mathbf{k}$ is destroyed and stored nowhere once the threshold secret sharing is done.*

$\underline{\mathsf{PQDPRF_{t,T}.PartialEval}(\mathbf{x}, P_i, \mathcal{P}')}$: *For a given input $\mathbf{x}$ and a valid $t$-sized subset $\mathcal{P}' \in \mathbb{A}_{t,T}$, party $P_i \in \mathcal{P}'$ partially evaluates the PRF with its own share $\mathbf{k_i}$ corresponding to the subset $\mathcal{P}'$ as $f_{\mathbf{k_i}}(\mathbf{x}) = \lfloor \langle \mathcal{H}(\mathbf{x}), \mathbf{k_i} \rangle \rceil_{q_1}$, and broadcasts it to other collaborating parties in $\mathcal{P}' \setminus P_i$.*

$\underline{\mathsf{PQDPRF_{t,T}.FinalEval}(\mathcal{P}', \{f_{\mathbf{k_i}}(\mathbf{x})\}_{i \in [T]})}$: *Each party $P_i \in \mathcal{P}'$ having its own partial evaluation and partial evaluations of rest of the $(t-1)$ parties, computes the final evaluation of the PRF on the given input $\mathbf{x}$ as $f_{\mathbf{k}}(\mathbf{x}) = \lfloor \sum_{P_i \in \mathcal{P}'} c_i f_{\mathbf{k_i}}(\mathbf{x}) \rceil_p$. Here, $c_i$'s are the recovery coefficients and according to the threshold secret sharing scheme, described in Sect. 2.4, recovery coefficient of the* group_leader *(the party in $\mathcal{P}'$ with minimum* party_id*) is 1 and recovery coefficient of each of the other parties in $\mathcal{P}' \setminus P_i$ is -1.*

**Proof of Correctness and Consistency.** Correctness of $\mathsf{PQDPRF_{t,T}}$ can be proved essentially in the same way as of $\mathsf{PQDPRF_{T,T}}$, which in turn implies its consistency (see Appendix A.1 for details).

**Proof of Security.** The idea of the proof remains essentially the same as the proof of security of $(T, T)$-distributed PRF (Sect. 3.2). We provide the detailed proof of security of $\mathsf{PQDPRF}_{t,T}$ in Appendix A.2.

### 3.4 Choice of Parameters

The security of our proposed DPRF directly relies on the security of underlying PRF (Theorem 3), which in turn relies on the hardness of decision-LWR problem (Theorem 1). Hence, we need to find a suitable set of parameters $n$, $p$, $q$ for which LWR problem is hard.

While an approach for determining LWR parameters $(n, p, q)$ from LWE parameters $(n, q, \alpha)$ (where $\alpha$ is the rate of Gaussian LWE noise) could be to follow the theoretical analysis of LWE-to-LWR reduction maintaining polynomial "$\frac{q}{p}$" ratio with a priori bounded number of samples (Theorem 2), we find the line of works in [18,21] more suitable to choose LWR parameters for practical instantiations. While analyzing the concrete hardness of LWR problem, they convert the LWR samples to LWE samples by multiplying the sample with $\frac{q}{p}$ and then analyze the cost of known attacks to solve LWE. The works [4,16,18,21] based on LWE or LWR assumption considers only primal and dual attacks as number of samples($m$) in their case is at most $2n$. However, there are several known attacks against LWE [3] and none of the attacks on LWR exploits the theoretical gap between the hardness of LWE and LWR problem to perform better than an attack on LWE. So, we focus on finding parameters $(n, q, \alpha)$, for which the LWE problem is hard with $m$ number of samples. Here, we consider a larger a priori bounded value of $m$, which can be interpreted as the allowed number of samples during LWE-to-LWR reduction or the allowed number of queries in the query phase of security game of DPRF. Note that *lattice estimator*[4] [3] evaluates the hardness of LWE problem for a given set of parameters based on its resistance against all practical attack methods. We use *lattice estimator* to find a suitable LWE parameter choice $n = 512, q = 2^{32}, \alpha = 2^{-17}, m = 2^{25}$ with secret distribution being uniform over $\mathbb{Z}_n^q$, and LWE noise distribution being Gaussian with standard deviation $\alpha q$, such that all the known attack methods have run time more than $2^{160}$, which indicates that these parameter choices provide 160 bit of classical security. We accordingly choose our LWR parameters $n = 512, q = 2^{32}$.

**Table 1.** Parameters used in PQDPRF implementation

| Parameter | Value |
|---|---|
| Modulus of input space ($\mathcal{X}$) of PQDPRF ($q$) | $2^{32}$ |
| Modulus of partial evaluation space ($q_1$) | $2^{28}$ |
| Modulus of output space ($\mathcal{Y}$) of PQDPRF ($p$) | $2^{10}$ |
| Dimension of key in PQDPRF ($n$) | 512 |

[4] https://github.com/malb/lattice-estimator.

Now what remains is to choose a suitable value of modulus $p$ and $q_1$ ($p < q_1 < q$) such that (1) $\frac{q}{p}$ is polynomial in security parameter and (2) $\frac{p}{q_1}$ is sufficiently small to ensure the correctness of our proposed DPRF. We observe that choosing $p = 2^{10}$, $q_1 = 2^{28}$ makes the value of $\frac{p}{q_1}$ sufficiently small. Also note that the ratio $\frac{q}{p} = 2^{22}$ is still polynomial in security parameter $\lambda = 160$.

Finally, we provide our concrete choice of parameters for the proposed DPRF in Table 1. We continue using this set of parameters while using it in PQ – DiSE.

### 3.5 Proposed PQDPRF vs. the Lattice-Based DPRF in [25]

A robust construction of lattice-based distributed PRF in adaptive corruption settings with theoretically efficient parameters in the standard model was proposed in [25], which builds upon LWE-to-LWR reductions preserving polynomial large modulus-to-noise ratios [6,11]. On the contrary, our construction is in the random oracle model and is targeted for semi-honest settings against static corruption. Hence, a direct experimental comparison is not feasible. However, the fact that our construction is in the random oracle model makes it more efficient, and hence, more suitable for real-world applications.

We compare the overheads of a single DPRF evaluation in [25] vs a single DPRF evaluation in our case for the same LWR parameters $(n, q, p)$. In [25] the PRF evaluation assumes a $L$-bit input and the evaluation (see Eq 2 of Sect. 3.2) requires (i) $L$ matrix multiplications with each matrix in $\mathbb{Z}_q^{m\times m}$, which needs a $O(\log L)$-depth circuit with $\omega(m^2)$ field operations per matrix multiplication (leading to a total cost of $L \cdot \omega(m^2)$ field operations), (ii) A matrix multiplication between two matrices of dimension $n \times m$ and $m \times m$ respectively (leading to a cost of $\omega(mn)$ field operations), (iii) A matrix-vector multiplication where the matrix has dimension $n \times m$ and the vector has dimension $n$ (leading to a cost of $O(mn)$ field operations). So, the overall cost of single PRF evaluation in [25] is $L \cdot \omega(m^2)$. On the other hand a single PRF evaluation in our case (see Sect. 3.1) requires multiplying two vectors of $\mathbb{Z}_q^n$ which only costs $O(n)$ field operations. In the case of the DPRFs obtained by distributing the evaluation of the above PRFs, the above cost analysis still applies for a single partial evaluation done by each of the parties.

We now present a back-of-the-envelope calculation to compare these overheads for typical parameters used in practical applications (e.g., $n = 512$, $q = 2^{32}$ for LWR hardness, an input length of $L = n \log q$ and dimension $m = 2n \log q$). In this case, the number of field operations required for a single PRF evaluation (equivalently, a single DPRF partial evaluation) in [25] is at least $10^{10}\times$ larger than that for our construction. This clearly establishes that our construction is practically more efficient.

We defer the performance comparison of the proposed DPRF with other (more practically efficient) existing DPRFs (namely the AES-based DPRF and the quantum-broken DDH-based DPRF) till Sect. 5, where the experimental results are provided in the context of an application (DiSE).

## 4 Application

The LWR-based distributed PRF, that we propose and discuss in detail in the previous section, can be plugged into various real-world applications of distributed PRF. In this work, we particularly focus on the DiSE (Distributed Symmetric Encryption) protocol, originally proposed in [1] and view it as an application of DPRF. We validate our proposed LWR-based DPRF by using it in DiSE to make it quantum-safe and call it PQ – DiSE. For the sake of exposition, we dedicate one subsection below to recall the original DiSE protocol of [1] and then discuss the proposed PQ – DiSE in the following subsection.

### 4.1 An Overview of the DiSE Protocol

Like any other encryption scheme, the distributed symmetric-key encryption (DiSE) scheme also consists of three PPT algorithms: (i) Setup, (ii) Encrypt and (iii) Decrypt, but with a difference that, both Encrypt and Decrypt are distributed, i.e., encryption and decryption are performed by, instead of a single server, a number of servers in distributed manner. In a $(t, T)$-DiSE, any $t(< T)$ parties among the $T$ parties are contacted with a request of encryption or decryption and each of them contributes some partially computed values, which are then combined in order to get the end result of encryption or decryption.

**Definition 2 (Distributed Symmetric-key Encryption (DiSE)).** *Let $\mathcal{P} = \{P_i\}_{i\in[T]}$ be the set of parties/servers to perform DPRF evaluation.* DiSE *protocol internally uses the following cryptographic primitives as its building blocks:*
*(i) A DPRF* $\mathsf{DP} = (\mathsf{DP.Setup}, \mathsf{DP.PartialEval}, \mathsf{DP.FinalEval})$,
*(ii) A PRG (pseudo random generator) of polynomial stretch,*
*(iii) A commitment scheme* $\mathsf{C} = (\mathsf{C.Setup}, \mathsf{C.Com})$.
DiSE *consists of the following three protocols built over these primitives,*

$\mathsf{DiSE.Setup}(1^\lambda, t, T)$: $\mathsf{DP.Setup}(1^\lambda, t, T)$ *is executed to provide evaluation key shares $ek_i$ to $P_i$ $\forall i \in [T]$. Also* $\mathsf{C.Setup}(1^\lambda)$ *outputs public parameters* $pp_{\mathsf{com}}$.

$\mathsf{DiSE.DistEncrypt}(m, S, \{ek_i\}_{P_i\in S})$: *An entity* E *requiring encryption of plaintext $m$ follows the method below.*

- E *contacts a set $S \subset \mathcal{P}$ of servers, such that $|S| = t$ and provides them with* $\alpha = \mathsf{C.Com}(m, pp_{\mathsf{com}}; \rho)$, *where $\rho$ is randomness used in commitment.*
- *Now* $z_i = \mathsf{DP.PartialEval}(\alpha, P_i, S)$ *is generated parallelly by each $P_i \in S$ with its evaluation key share $ek_i$ and sent back to* E.
- E *now computes* $w = \mathsf{DP.FinalEval}(S, \{z_i\}_{P_i\in S})$ *and then* $e = \mathsf{PRG}(w) \bigoplus (m||\rho)$. *Finally $c = (\alpha, e)$ is the ciphertext of $m$. Here, $w$ can be viewed as the message-specific encryption key.*

$\mathsf{DiSE.DistDecrypt}(c, S, \{ek_i\}_{P_i\in S})$: *Distributed decryption of a ciphertext c is performed by an entity* D *as follows.*

- D *parses c into $(\alpha, e)$ and contacts a set $S \subset \mathcal{P}$ of $t$ servers and provides them with $\alpha$.*

- *Each* $P_i \in S$ *computes* $z_i = \mathsf{DP.PartialEval}(\alpha, P_i, S)$ *with its evaluation key share and sends it to* D.
- D *combines the* $z_i$*'s to retrieve* $w = \mathsf{DP.FinalEval}(S, \{z_i\}_{P_i \in S})$. *Next* $e \bigoplus \mathsf{PRG}(w)$ *gives back* $m||\rho$. *It then checks if* $\alpha$ *is indeed a commitment to* $m$ *with randomness* $\rho$. *If it is, then* $m$ *is returned as the result of distributed decryption.*

**Relation Between DiSE and the Underlying DPRF DP.** We recall a theorem from [1] in order to better understand how the security of DiSE depends upon the underlying distributed PRF (assume that other two primitives PRG and C are already secure).

**Theorem 4.** DiSE *is secure if the underlying DPRF* DP *is secure.*

Informally, the security of a DPRF DP implies that its output retains pseudorandomness even when evaluated in a distributed manner (See Sect. 2.3 for formal security notion). The interesting part of the theorem is that the security of the underlying DPRF DP directly implies the security of the distributed encryption scheme.

**Instantiations of DP.** DiSE [1] use the following two instantiations of DP for semi-honest settings:

- **DDH-based DPRF**: Proposed in [28], DDH-based DPRF is secure due to the hardness of the classical DDH problem. It uses Shamir's secret sharing scheme for sharing the PRF evaluation key among the servers. However, it is vulnerable to quantum attack.
- **AES-based DPRF**: A general construction of DPRF from any existing PRF was proposed in [28]. DiSE uses AES-based DPRF accordingly and proves it to be secure. It uses replicated secret sharing to share the evaluation key among the $T$ servers. Although AES(128)-based DPRF is believed to provide 64-bit quantum security, it is also not built upon any quantum-safe assumption.

The paper [1] compares performances of both these instantiations and concludes that DiSE performs well with AES-based DPRF for lesser values of $T$. Note that none of the underlying DPRF is inherently quantum-safe.

### 4.2 Our Improved PQ – DiSE Protocol

As security of DiSE directly depends upon the security of the underlying DP (Theorem 4), we obtain post-quantum secure version of DiSE (i.e., PQ – DiSE) by instantiating the underlying DP with our proposed post-quantum secure PQDPRF. Our implementation of PQ – DiSE is publicly available here[5].

**Technical Challenges of PQ – DiSE Implementation.** DPRF implementation in original DiSE generates 128-bit DPRF output from 128-bit input, whereas our proposed DPRF generates $\log p = 10$ bit output from $n \cdot \log q = 512 \times 32$ bit

[5] https://github.com/SayaniSinha97/PQDiSE-from-PQDPRF.

input. We face two-fold challenge here: (i) converting 128-bit input to 512×32-bit input in order to apply PQDPRF, and (ii) generating a total of 128 pseudorandom bits in the output. The first challenge is overcome by applying hash function on the input concatenated with a counter value repeatedly until the length of these concatenated hash outputs equals $512 \times 32$ bits. The next challenge is handled by running 13 instances of PQDPRF together in order to obtain $(13 \times 10) = 130$ bits and extract 128 bits as the message-specific encryption key to be used later. We use Blake2[6] to instantiate the hash function, modeled as a random oracle.

**Table 2.** Comparison of key sizes for DPRFs

| DPRFs | Size of secret key (as well as each key share) | Total number of unique key shares | Number of key shares that each party stores | Secret sharing method |
|---|---|---|---|---|
| AES-based | 128-bits | $\binom{T}{t-1}$ | $\binom{T-1}{t-1}$ | Replicated secret sharing |
| DDH-based | 256-bits | $T$ | 1 | Shamir's secret sharing |
| **LWR-based (proposed)** | **512×32-bits** | $\binom{T}{t} \cdot t$ | $\binom{T-1}{t-1}$ | **Benaloh-Leichter LISSS** |

**An Analysis on the Key and Key Shares.** Table 2 provides a comparative analysis on the size of secret key and key shares with respect to the three DPRF instantiations. Even with a larger key-size requirement, our proposed LWR-based DPRF outperforms the other two due to its highly parallelizable nature, as evident from the results in the next section.

## 5 Experimental Result

We now provide a detailed performance analysis of our proposed PQDPRF in PQ − DiSE based on various metrics with respect to DDH-based DPRF and AES-based DPRF, used in DiSE, all in semi-honest adversarial settings. All experiments have been executed on a high-end server with an Intel(R) Xeon(R) Gold 6226 CPU (2.70GHz clock frequency), 96 cores, 256GB RAM. All graphs have their $y$-axis in *logarithmic scale*. During performance evaluation, we disable the use of AES-NI instructions by AES-based DPRF to ensure fair comparison among software implementations of the three DPRFs. We optimize our LWR-based DPRF implementation that involves arithmetic in $\mathbb{Z}_q$ using NTL[7].

**Partial Evaluation Time vs.** $(t, T)$ **Values** [Fig. 1]**.** In any $(t, T)$-distributed PRF scheme, the partial evaluation of the DPRF on a given input is computed parallelly by all $t$ collaborating parties with their respective secret share. Here, we analyze the maximum partial evaluation time required by any of the $t$ participating parties for all three DPRFs under consideration.

[6] https://www.blake2.net/.
[7] https://libntl.org/.

- **AES-based DPRF**: A linear increase in partial evaluation time in a logarithmic $y$-axis actually reflects an exponential increase in time. In AES-based DPRF, computation of partial evaluations by $t$ parties involves all $\binom{T}{t-1}$ key shares; however, the load of computation is not evenly distributed among all $t$ parties. In particular, the maximum computation time increases linearly with $\binom{T-1}{t-1}$.
- **DDH-based and LWR-based DPRF**: Partial evaluation time remains almost constant with increasing $T$ for both these DPRFs. Because, in both cases, given an input, each of the $t$ parties parallelly performs a similar computation with its own secret share. Hence, each of the $t$ parties requires a similar time in computing partial evaluation. Thus, the maximum time taken by any party to complete the partial evaluation phase does not depend upon the value of $t$ or $T$. The graph line of LWR-based DPRF lies slightly below the line of DDH-based DPRF due to the fact that the modular dot product of two vectors in $\mathbb{Z}_q^n$ takes less time than modular exponentiation.

**Final Evaluation Time vs. $(t, T)$ values [Fig. 2].** This graph compares the three DPRFs in terms of final evaluation time required by them with varying $T$.

- The final evaluation time of combining $t$ partial evaluations increases linearly with increasing value of $t$ for all the three DPRFs due to the fact that, in final evaluation phase, LWR-based DPRF involves modular vector addition of $t$ partial evaluations, whereas AES-based DPRF involves XORing of $t$ partial evaluations. XORing, being a lighter operation than vector addition, places AES-based DPRF at a lower position in $y$-axis than LWR-based DPRF. DDH-based DPRF involves exponentiation and then multiplication of $t$ partial evaluations, leading to its higher value along $y$-axis. Note that although the final evaluation time of the proposed LWR-based DPRF is more than that of AES-based DPRF, we argue the efficiency of LWR-based DPRF considering the total (partial + final) evaluation time of both the DPRFs, as we discuss next.

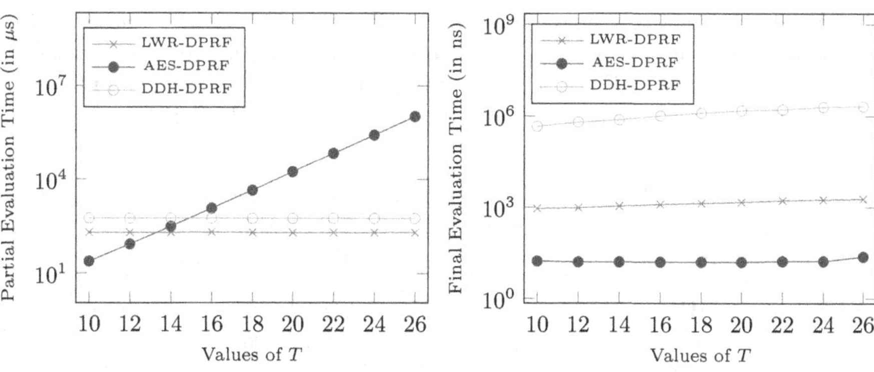


**Fig. 1.** Partial evaluation time of $(\frac{T}{2}, T)$-DPRFs

**Fig. 2.** Final evaluation time of $(\frac{T}{2}, T)$-DPRFs

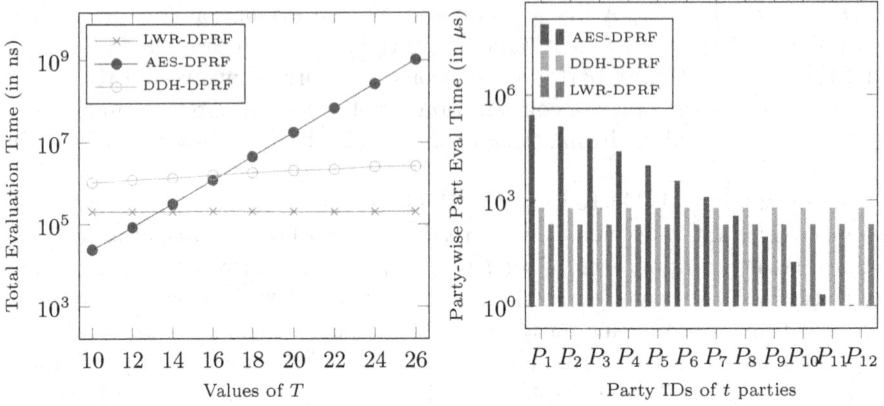


**Fig. 3.** Total evaluation time of $(\frac{T}{2}, T)$-DPRFs

**Fig. 4.** Individual part-eval time for $(12, 24)$-DPRF

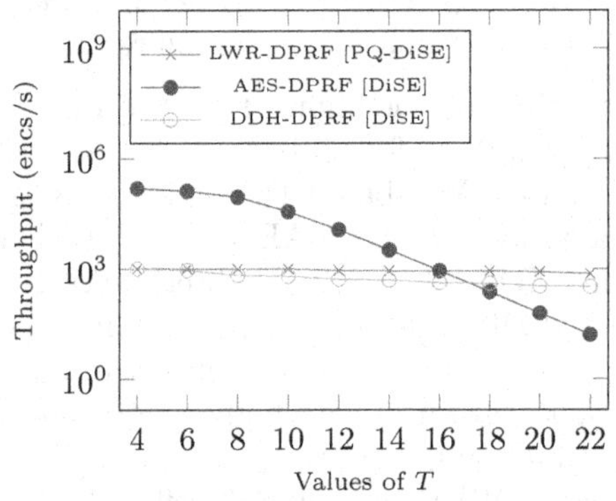


**Fig. 5.** Throughput in PQ-DiSE and DiSE

**Total Evaluation Time vs. $(t, T)$ Values [Fig. 3].** This graph compares the three DPRFs in terms of total (partial + final) evaluation time required by them with varying $T$. Keeping Fig. 1 and Fig. 2 in mind, the plots here are quite self-explanatory and clearly depict the efficiency of the proposed LWR-based DPRF for larger values of $T$.

**Partial Evaluation Time vs. Party-id [Fig. 4].** We plot in this graph the partial evaluation time taken by each of the $t$ collaborating parties in a $t$-sized subset for a specific pair of values, $(t, T) = (12, 24)$.

- **AES-based DPRF**: As mentioned earlier, all the $t$ parties here do not have the same amount of computation load during partial evaluation phase. Without loss of generality, if we denote the collaborating parties with $\{P_1, \ldots, P_t\}$, $P_1$ requires computation using $\binom{T-1}{t-1}$ key shares, $P_2$ requires $\binom{T-2}{t-2}$ key shares and so on. Finally $P_t$ requires $\binom{T-t}{0} = 1$ key share in its partial evaluation,

thus involving all $\binom{T}{t-1}$ key shares. Thus, each participating party has a different computation cost, as depicted in the graph.
- **DDH-based and LWR-based DPRF**: In both cases, each participating party needs only one key share for partial evaluation computation and involves the same modular dot product operation between vectors (LWR-based DPRF) or exponentiation operation (DDH-based DPRF) irrespective of its party-id. This feature can be useful while enabling parallel computation by all participating parties.

**Throughput vs.** $(t, T)$ **Values [Fig. 5].** We plot the throughput (number of encryptions per second) of DiSE using DDH-based and AES-based DPRF and PQ – DiSE using LWR-based DPRF.

- DiSE: When instantiated with AES-based DPRF, its throughput decreases with increasing value of $t, T$, but remains stable with increasing value of $t, T$ if DDH-based DPRF is used.
- PQ – DiSE: Its throughput is stable for all values of $t, T$. It performs slightly better than DiSE using DDH-based DPRF and significantly better than DiSE using AES-based DPRF for larger values of $t, T$.
  ***Explanation:*** Our PQ – DiSE outperforms DiSE in terms of throughput owing to the fact that LWR-based DPRF outperforms AES-based and DDH-based DPRF in terms of evaluation cost as discussed in analysis of Fig. 1.

***Note:*** Although we provide the analysis with respect to $(\frac{T}{2}, T)$-distributed PRF, the graph patterns of Fig. 1, 2, 4, 5 retain for any $1 < t \leq T$. However we prefer $(\frac{T}{2}, T)$-distributed PRF for the sake of analysis, as the value of $\binom{T}{t}$ is the largest for $t = \frac{T}{2}$.

**Concluding Remark.** AES-128 provides 128-bit classical security and 64-bit quantum security (against Grover's algorithm [22]), which is also the security level for the AES-based DPRF implemented in DiSE. One could upgrade to AES-256 to provide stronger quantum security, but this would only degrade the performance of the AES-based DPRF further. The DDH-based DPRF provides 128 bits of classical security, and is quantum-broken. In contrast, our proposed DPRF uses an LWR parameter set that provides the quantum-equivalent of 160-bit classical security (as per the latest lattice estimator) but still outperforms AES-based DPRF for higher values of $T$ and DDH-based DPRF slightly for all values of $T$.

## 6 Conclusion and Future Work

We proposed a $(T, T)$-distributed quantum-safe PRF based on Learning with Rounding (LWR) problem and its generalized $(t, T)$-distributed version in this work. We proved its correctness, consistency as well as security. We also showed how to use our proposed DPRF to obtain an efficient quantum-safe version of DiSE [1], namely PQ – DiSE. We outline some future research directions below.

- **Scalability with an even larger number of parties.** Our $(t, T)$-DPRF requires each party to store $\binom{T-1}{t-1}$ number of key shares after threshold secret sharing, thus suffering from high space complexity. Future works may consider modifying the linear integer secret sharing protocol in order to reduce space complexity and make the DPRF scalable for an even larger number of parties.
- **Adaptive security.** We assumed that the corrupted set of parties is statically fixed before the game begins between the challenger and the adversary. We leave it as an open problem to allow our DPRF to handle the scenario, where parties are corrupted dynamically during the game.
- **Security in Quantum Random Oracle Model.** We leave it as an open problem to prove the security of the proposed LWR-based distributed PRF in the quantum random oracle model, where the quantum adversary has quantum access to the random oracle and, thus is able to query the random oracle with a state in superposition.

**Acknowledgement.** We would like to thank the Prime Minister Research Fellowship (PMRF) funded by the Ministry of Human Resource Development, Government of India, for supporting our research.

# A Generalised $(t, T)$-Threshold PRF

## A.1 Proof of Correctness and Consistency

Correctness of $\mathsf{PQDPRF}_{\mathsf{t,T}}$ can be proved essentially in the same way as of $\mathsf{PQDPRF}_{\mathsf{T,T}}$, which in turn implies its consistency. Let $\mathcal{P} = \{P_i\}_{i\in[T]}$ be a set of $T$ parties, and $\mathbb{A}_{t,T}$ be a threshold access structure defined on it. Without loss of generality let us consider $\mathcal{P}' = \{P_1, \ldots, P_t\} \in \mathbb{A}_{t,T}$ to be a valid $t$-sized subset. Clearly $P_1$ is the $\mathsf{group\_leader}$ of $\mathcal{P}'$. Let $\mathcal{H} : \{0,1\}^\star \to \mathbb{Z}_q^n$ be a hash function modeled as a random oracle. Given an input $\mathbf{x}$, let us denote the direct PRF evaluation with $f_{\mathbf{k}}^{\mathsf{dir}}(\mathbf{x})$ and distributed PRF evaluation by $t$ number of parties in $\mathcal{P}'$ using $\mathsf{PQDPRF}_{\mathsf{t,T}}$ as $f_{\mathbf{k}}^{\mathsf{dist}}(\mathbf{x})$. They are computed as follows.

$$f_{\mathbf{k}}^{\mathsf{dir}}(\mathbf{x}) = \lfloor\langle\mathcal{H}(\mathbf{x}), \mathbf{k}\rangle\rceil_p, \quad f_{\mathbf{k}}^{\mathsf{dist}}(\mathbf{x}) = \lfloor\lfloor\langle\mathcal{H}(\mathbf{x}), \mathbf{k_1}\rangle\rceil_{q_1} - \sum_{i=2}^{t}\lfloor\langle\mathcal{H}(\mathbf{x}), \mathbf{k_i}\rangle\rceil_{q_1}\rceil_p.$$

*Claim.* Difference between direct PRF evaluation ($f_{\mathbf{k}}^{\mathsf{dir}}(\mathbf{x})$) and distributed PRF evaluation ($f_{\mathbf{k}}^{\mathsf{dist}}(\mathbf{x})$) on some input $\mathbf{x}$ is strictly upper bounded by 1, i.e.,

$$\left|f_{\mathbf{k}}^{\mathsf{dist}}(\mathbf{x}) - f_{\mathbf{k}}^{\mathsf{dir}}(\mathbf{x})\right| < 1.$$

*Proof.* Note that by definition of round-off operation (Sect. 2.1), for any $y \in \mathbb{Z}_q$, we can express $\lfloor y\rceil_p$ as $\frac{p}{q}y + e$, where $-0.5 \le e < 0.5$.

We assume $\mathbf{r} = \mathcal{H}(\mathbf{x})$. Now the direct evaluation can be written as,

$$f_{\mathbf{k}}^{\mathsf{dir}}(\mathbf{x}) = \lfloor \langle \mathbf{r}, \mathbf{k} \rangle \rceil_p = \frac{p}{q}\langle \mathbf{r}, \mathbf{k} \rangle + e',$$

where $|e'| \leq 0.5$. The distributed evaluation can be expressed as,

$$\begin{aligned} f_{\mathbf{k}}^{\mathsf{dist}}(\mathbf{x}) &= \lfloor \lfloor \langle \mathbf{r}, \mathbf{k_1} \rangle \rceil_{q_1} - \sum_{i=2}^{t} \lfloor \langle \mathbf{r}, \mathbf{k_i} \rangle \rceil_{q_1} \rceil_p \\ &= \lfloor \langle \mathbf{r}, \mathbf{k_1} \rangle \cdot \frac{q_1}{q} + e_1 - \sum_{i=2}^{t} ((\langle \mathbf{r}, \mathbf{k_i} \rangle \cdot \frac{q_1}{q} + e_i) \rceil_p \\ &= \lfloor \frac{q_1}{q}((\langle \mathbf{r}, \mathbf{k_1} \rangle - \sum_{i=2}^{t} \langle \mathbf{r}, \mathbf{k_i} \rangle) + (e_1 - \sum_{i=2}^{t} e_i) \rceil_p \\ &\leq \lfloor \frac{q_1}{q} \langle \mathbf{r}, \mathbf{k} \rangle + \frac{t}{2} \rceil_p \\ &= \frac{p}{q_1}(\frac{q_1}{q} \langle \mathbf{r}, \mathbf{k} \rangle + \frac{t}{2}) + e \\ &= \frac{p}{q} \langle \mathbf{r}, \mathbf{k} \rangle + \frac{p}{q_1} \cdot \frac{t}{2} + e, \end{aligned}$$

where, each $-0.5 \leq e_i < 0.5$ and $-0.5 \leq e < 0.5$ due to the definition of the round-off operation. Thus,

$$f_{\mathbf{k}}^{\mathsf{dist}}(\mathbf{x}) - f_{\mathbf{k}}^{\mathsf{dir}}(\mathbf{x}) \leq \frac{p}{q_1} \cdot \frac{t}{2} + e - e' \implies \left| f_{\mathbf{k}}^{\mathsf{dist}}(\mathbf{x}) - f_{\mathbf{k}}^{\mathsf{dir}}(\mathbf{x}) \right| \leq \left| \frac{p}{q_1} \cdot \frac{t}{2} \right| + |e - e'|.$$

We choose values of $p$, $t$ and $q_1$ such that, the quantity $\epsilon = \frac{p}{q_1} \cdot \frac{t}{2}$ becomes sufficiently small. As $-0.5 \leq e < 0.5$ and $-0.5 \leq e' < 0.5$, $|e - e'| < 1$ always holds true. Thus, the quantity $\epsilon + |e - e'|$ is highly unlikely to exceed 1. Hence, the difference between direct PRF evaluation and distributed PRF evaluation is strictly upper bounded by 1, i.e.,

$$\left| f_{\mathbf{k}}^{\mathsf{dist}}(\mathbf{x}) - f_{\mathbf{k}}^{\mathsf{dir}}(\mathbf{x}) \right| < 1.$$

□

As both $f_{\mathbf{k}}^{\mathsf{dist}}(\mathbf{x})$ and $f_{\mathbf{k}}^{\mathsf{dir}}(\mathbf{x})$ are integers, we conclude that their values are same except with a negligible probability. Thus correctness of our proposed distributed PRF $\mathsf{PQDPRF}_{\mathsf{t,T}}$ is satisfied.

As correctness of distributed PRF implies its consistency, the proposed $\mathsf{PQDPRF}_{\mathsf{t,T}}$ is consistent. We can see the consistency of the proposed DPRF by a different argument as well. Let us assume two distinct valid subsets $S_1, S_2 \in \mathbb{A}_{t,T}$, such that $f_{\mathbf{k}}^{\mathsf{dist}}(\mathbf{x})\big|_{S_1}$ and $f_{\mathbf{k}}^{\mathsf{dist}}(\mathbf{x})\big|_{S_2}$ are result of DPRF evaluations computed by $S_1$ and $S_2$ respectively. We can write,

$$f_{\mathbf{k}}^{\mathsf{dist}}(\mathbf{x})\big|_{S_1} = \frac{p}{q}\langle \mathbf{r}, \mathbf{k}\rangle + \frac{p}{q_1}\cdot\frac{t}{2} + e_1, \qquad f_{\mathbf{k}}^{\mathsf{dist}}(\mathbf{x})\big|_{S_2} = \frac{p}{q}\langle \mathbf{r}, \mathbf{k}\rangle + \frac{p}{q_1}\cdot\frac{t}{2} + e_2,$$

so that they together imply,

$$\left| f_{\mathbf{k}}^{\mathsf{dist}}(\mathbf{x})\big|_{S_1} - f_{\mathbf{k}}^{\mathsf{dist}}(\mathbf{x})\big|_{S_2} \right| = |e_1 - e_2|\,.$$

Now as $-0.5 \leq e_1 < 0.5$ and $-0.5 \leq e_2 < 0.5$, $|e_1 - e_2| < 1$ always holds true. And both $f_{\mathbf{k}}^{\mathsf{dist}}(\mathbf{x})\big|_{S_1}$ and $f_{\mathbf{k}}^{\mathsf{dist}}(\mathbf{x})\big|_{S_2}$ being integral values, they always evaluate to the same value.

### A.2 Proof of Security

The idea of the proof remains essentially the same as of proof of security of $(T, T)$-distributed PRF (Sect. 3.2). However among $T$ parties of the set $\mathcal{P} = \{P_1, \ldots, P_T\}$, only $t$ parties are required to collaborate to evaluate the PRF on a given input. We assume a PPT adversary $\mathcal{A}$ which has corrupted a subset $\mathcal{P}_C \subset \mathcal{P}$ of size $(t-1)$ and thus acquired all their key shares. We show that, even if $\mathcal{A}$ is able to see the PRF evaluation and all the partial evaluations of the honest parties in $\mathcal{P} \setminus \mathcal{P}_C$ for a priori bounded number of query inputs, it will not be able to distinguish output of the PRF from the output of a truly random function on a challenge input, which is essentially different from the query inputs.

Recall that, after $\mathsf{PQDPRF_{t,T}.Setup}$, each $P_i \in \mathcal{P}$ gets to store $\binom{T-1}{t-1}$ number of secret shares, each corresponding to one of the $t$-sized subsets, that $P_i$ may belong to. In each of the hybrids, if $P_i \in \mathcal{P} \setminus \mathcal{P}_C$ is a honest party, we denote by $\mathbf{k_i}$ its key share corresponding to the $t$-sized group $\{P_i\} \bigcup \mathcal{P}_C$, and by $\mathsf{gl}$, the $\mathsf{group\_leader}$ of $\{P_i\} \bigcup \mathcal{P}_C$.

Now we define four hybrids consisting of game between the PPT adversary $\mathcal{A}$ and a challenger $\mathcal{C}$ as described in the tabular forms for the ease of exposition.

**Indistinguishibility Between the Hybrids**

The indistinguishibility of $\mathsf{Hybrid}_3$ from $\mathsf{Hybrid}_0$ for $(t, T)$-distributed PRF can be proved analogously as done in Sect. 3.2 for $(T, T)$-distributed PRF. Please see the detailed hybrids on the next page.

| Query Phase | Challenge Phase |
|---|---|
| $\mathcal{A}$ sends a query input $\mathbf{x}$ to $\mathcal{C}$. Then, $\mathcal{C}$ responds with $f_{\mathbf{k}}(\mathbf{x})$ and $\{f_{\mathbf{k_i}}(\mathbf{x})\}_{P_i \in \mathcal{P} \setminus \mathcal{P}_C}$, where $\mathbf{r} = \mathcal{H}(\mathbf{x})$, $f_{\mathbf{k}}(\mathbf{x}) = \lfloor \langle \mathbf{r}, \mathbf{k} \rangle \rceil_p$, $\boxed{f_{\mathbf{k_i}}(\mathbf{x}) = \lfloor \langle \mathbf{r}, \mathbf{k_i} \rangle \rceil_{q_1}.}$ | $\mathcal{C}$, on receiving a challenge input $\mathbf{x}^\star$ from $\mathcal{A}$, responds with $\boxed{f_{\mathbf{k}}(\mathbf{x}^\star).}$ |

Hybrid$_0$

| Query Phase | Challenge Phase |
|---|---|
| $\mathcal{A}$ sends a query input $\mathbf{x}$ to $\mathcal{C}$. $\mathcal{C}$ responds with $f_{\mathbf{k}}(\mathbf{x})$ and $\{f_{\mathbf{k_i}}(\mathbf{x})\}_{P_i \in \mathcal{P} \setminus \mathcal{P}_C}$, where $\mathbf{r} = \mathcal{H}(\mathbf{x})$, $f_{\mathbf{k}}(\mathbf{x}) = \lfloor \langle \mathbf{r}, \mathbf{k} \rangle \rceil_p$, $\boxed{f_{\mathbf{k_i}}(\mathbf{x}) = \lfloor \langle \mathbf{r}, \mathbf{k_i} \rangle \rceil_{q_1}.}$ | $\mathcal{C}$, on receiving a challenge input $\mathbf{x}^\star$ from $\mathcal{A}$, responds with a random $\boxed{y^\star \xleftarrow{R} \mathbb{Z}_p.}$ |

Hybrid$_3$

| Query Phase | Challenge Phase |
|---|---|
| On receiving query input $\mathbf{x}$ from $\mathcal{A}$, $\mathcal{C}$ responds with PRF evaluation $f_{\mathbf{k}}(\mathbf{x})$ and simulated partial evaluations for the honest parties $\{f^{\mathsf{sim}}_{\mathbf{k_i}}(\mathbf{x})\}_{P_i \in \mathcal{P} \setminus \mathcal{P}_C}$, where $\mathbf{r} = \mathcal{H}(\mathbf{x})$, $f_{\mathbf{k}}(\mathbf{x}) = \lfloor \langle \mathbf{r}, \mathbf{k} \rangle \rceil_p$, if $i == \mathsf{gl}$, $\boxed{f^{\mathsf{sim}}_{\mathbf{k_i}}(\mathbf{x}) = \lfloor f_{\mathbf{k}}(\mathbf{x}) \cdot \frac{q}{p} + \sum_{P_j \in \mathcal{P}_C} \langle \mathbf{r}, \mathbf{k_j} \rangle \rceil_{q_1},}$ otherwise, $\boxed{f^{\mathsf{sim}}_{\mathbf{k_i}}(\mathbf{x}) = \lfloor \langle \mathbf{r}, \mathbf{k}_{\mathsf{gl}} \rangle - f_{\mathbf{k}}(\mathbf{x}) \cdot \frac{q}{p} - \sum_{P_j \in \mathcal{P}_C, j \neq \mathsf{gl}} \langle \mathbf{r}, \mathbf{k_j} \rangle \rceil_{q_1}.}$ In the above expression, $\mathbf{k_j}$ is the key share of $P_j \in \mathcal{P}_C$ corresponding to $t$-sized group $\{P_i\} \bigcup \mathcal{P}_C$. | $\mathcal{C}$, on receiving a challenge input $\mathbf{x}^\star$ from $\mathcal{A}$, responds with $\boxed{f_{\mathbf{k}}(\mathbf{x}^\star).}$ |

Hybrid$_1$

| Query Phase | Challenge Phase |
|---|---|
| On receiving query input $\mathbf{x}$ from $\mathcal{A}$, $\mathcal{C}$ responds with PRF evaluation $f_{\mathbf{k}}(\mathbf{x})$ and simulated partial evaluations for the honest parties $\{f^{\mathsf{sim}}_{\mathbf{k_i}}(\mathbf{x})\}_{P_i \in \mathcal{P} \setminus \mathcal{P}_C}$, where $\mathbf{r} = \mathcal{H}(\mathbf{x})$, $f_{\mathbf{k}}(\mathbf{x}) = \lfloor \langle \mathbf{r}, \mathbf{k} \rangle \rceil_p$, if $i == \mathsf{gl}$, $\boxed{f^{\mathsf{sim}}_{\mathbf{k_i}}(\mathbf{x}) = \lfloor f_{\mathbf{k}}(\mathbf{x}) \cdot \frac{q}{p} + \sum_{P_j \in \mathcal{P}_C} \langle \mathbf{r}, \mathbf{k_j} \rangle \rceil_{q_1},}$ otherwise, $\boxed{f^{\mathsf{sim}}_{\mathbf{k_i}}(\mathbf{x}) = \lfloor \langle \mathbf{r}, \mathbf{k}_{\mathsf{gl}} \rangle - f_{\mathbf{k}}(\mathbf{x}) \cdot \frac{q}{p} - \sum_{P_j \in \mathcal{P}_C, j \neq \mathsf{gl}} \langle \mathbf{r}, \mathbf{k_j} \rangle \rceil_{q_1}.}$ In the above expression, $\mathbf{k_j}$ is the key share of $P_j \in \mathcal{P}_C$ corresponding to $t$-sized group $\{P_i\} \bigcup \mathcal{P}_C$. | $\mathcal{C}$, on receiving a challenge input $\mathbf{x}^\star$ from $\mathcal{A}$, responds with a random $\boxed{y^\star \xleftarrow{R} \mathbb{Z}_p.}$ |

Hybrid$_2$

## References

1. Agrawal, S., Mohassel, P., Mukherjee, P., Rindal, P.: DISE: distributed symmetric-key encryption. In: Proceedings of the 2018 ACM SIGSAC Conference on Computer and Communications Security, pp. 1993–2010 (2018)
2. Alamati, N., Montgomery, H., Patranabis, S.: Symmetric primitives with structured secrets. In: Boldyreva, A., Micciancio, D. (eds.) CRYPTO 2019. LNCS, vol. 11692, pp. 650–679. Springer, Cham (2019). https://doi.org/10.1007/978-3-030-26948-7_23
3. Albrecht, M.R., Player, R., Scott, S.: On the concrete hardness of learning with errors. J. Math. Cryptol. **9**(3), 169–203 (2015)
4. Alkim, E., Ducas, L., Pöppelmann, T., Schwabe, P.: Post-quantum key {Exchange-A} new hope. In: 25th USENIX Security Symposium (USENIX Security 16), pp. 327–343 (2016)
5. Alperin-Sheriff, J., Apon, D.: Dimension-preserving reductions from LWE to LWR. Cryptology ePrint Archive (2016)
6. Alwen, J., Krenn, S., Pietrzak, K., Wichs, D.: Learning with rounding, revisited. In: Canetti, R., Garay, J.A. (eds.) CRYPTO 2013. LNCS, vol. 8042, pp. 57–74. Springer, Heidelberg (2013). https://doi.org/10.1007/978-3-642-40041-4_4
7. Arute, F., et al.: Quantum supremacy using a programmable superconducting processor. Nature **574**(7779), 505–510 (2019)
8. Asharov, G., Jain, A., López-Alt, A., Tromer, E., Vaikuntanathan, V., Wichs, D.: Multiparty computation with low communication, computation and interaction via threshold FHE. In: Pointcheval, D., Johansson, T. (eds.) EUROCRYPT 2012. LNCS, vol. 7237, pp. 483–501. Springer, Heidelberg (2012). https://doi.org/10.1007/978-3-642-29011-4_29
9. Banerjee, A., Peikert, C.: New and improved key-homomorphic pseudorandom functions. In: Garay, J.A., Gennaro, R. (eds.) CRYPTO 2014. LNCS, vol. 8616, pp. 353–370. Springer, Heidelberg (2014). https://doi.org/10.1007/978-3-662-44371-2_20
10. Banerjee, A., Peikert, C., Rosen, A.: Pseudorandom functions and lattices. In: Pointcheval, D., Johansson, T. (eds.) EUROCRYPT 2012. LNCS, vol. 7237, pp. 719–737. Springer, Heidelberg (2012). https://doi.org/10.1007/978-3-642-29011-4_42
11. Bogdanov, A., Guo, S., Masny, D., Richelson, S., Rosen, A.: On the hardness of learning with rounding over small modulus. In: Kushilevitz, E., Malkin, T. (eds.) TCC 2016. LNCS, vol. 9562, pp. 209–224. Springer, Heidelberg (2016). https://doi.org/10.1007/978-3-662-49096-9_9
12. Bogomolec, X., Underhill, J.G., Kovac, S.A.: Towards post-quantum secure symmetric cryptography: a mathematical perspective. Cryptology ePrint Archive (2019)
13. Boneh, D., Dagdelen, Ö., Fischlin, M., Lehmann, A., Schaffner, C., Zhandry, M.: Random oracles in a quantum world. In: Lee, D.H., Wang, X. (eds.) ASIACRYPT 2011. LNCS, vol. 7073, pp. 41–69. Springer, Heidelberg (2011). https://doi.org/10.1007/978-3-642-25385-0_3
14. Boneh, D., et al.: Threshold cryptosystems from threshold fully homomorphic encryption. In: Shacham, H., Boldyreva, A. (eds.) CRYPTO 2018. LNCS, vol. 10991, pp. 565–596. Springer, Cham (2018). https://doi.org/10.1007/978-3-319-96884-1_19

15. Boneh, D., Lewi, K., Montgomery, H., Raghunathan, A.: Key homomorphic PRFs and their applications. In: Canetti, R., Garay, J.A. (eds.) CRYPTO 2013. LNCS, vol. 8042, pp. 410–428. Springer, Heidelberg (2013). https://doi.org/10.1007/978-3-642-40041-4_23
16. Bos, J., et al.: Frodo: take off the ring! practical, quantum-secure key exchange from LWE. In: Proceedings of the 2016 ACM SIGSAC Conference on Computer and Communications Security, pp. 1006–1018 (2016)
17. Brakerski, Z., Vaikuntanathan, V.: Constrained key-homomorphic PRFs from standard lattice assumptions. In: Dodis, Y., Nielsen, J.B. (eds.) TCC 2015. LNCS, vol. 9015, pp. 1–30. Springer, Heidelberg (2015). https://doi.org/10.1007/978-3-662-46497-7_1
18. Cheon, J.H., Kim, D., Lee, J., Song, Y.: Lizard: cut off the tail! a practical post-quantum public-key encryption from LWE and LWR. In: Catalano, D., De Prisco, R. (eds.) SCN 2018. LNCS, vol. 11035, pp. 160–177. Springer, Cham (2018). https://doi.org/10.1007/978-3-319-98113-0_9
19. Christodorescu, M., Gaddam, S., Mukherjee, P., Sinha, R.: Amortized threshold symmetric-key encryption. In: Proceedings of the 2021 ACM SIGSAC Conference on Computer and Communications Security, pp. 2758–2779 (2021)
20. Damgård, I., Thorbek, R.: Linear integer secret sharing and distributed exponentiation. In: Yung, M., Dodis, Y., Kiayias, A., Malkin, T. (eds.) PKC 2006. LNCS, vol. 3958, pp. 75–90. Springer, Heidelberg (2006). https://doi.org/10.1007/11745853_6
21. D'Anvers, J.-P., Karmakar, A., Sinha Roy, S., Vercauteren, F.: Saber: module-LWR based key exchange, CPA-secure encryption and CCA-secure KEM. In: Joux, A., Nitaj, A., Rachidi, T. (eds.) AFRICACRYPT 2018. LNCS, vol. 10831, pp. 282–305. Springer, Cham (2018). https://doi.org/10.1007/978-3-319-89339-6_16
22. Grover, L.K.: A fast quantum mechanical algorithm for database search. In: Proceedings of the Twenty-Eighth Annual ACM Symposium on Theory of Computing, pp. 212–219 (1996)
23. Impagliazzo, R., Naor, M.: Efficient cryptographic schemes provably as secure as subset sum. J. Cryptol. **9**(4), 199–216 (1996)
24. Impagliazzo, R., Zuckerman, D.: How to recycle random bits. In: FOCS, vol. 30, pp. 248–253 (1989)
25. Libert, B., Stehlé, D., Titiu, R.: Adaptively secure distributed PRFs from LWE. J. Cryptol. **34**(3), 1–49 (2021)
26. Micali, S., Sidney, R.: A simple method for generating and sharing pseudo-random functions, with applications to clipper-like key escrow systems. In: Coppersmith, D. (ed.) CRYPTO 1995. LNCS, vol. 963, pp. 185–196. Springer, Heidelberg (1995). https://doi.org/10.1007/3-540-44750-4_15
27. Montgomery, H.: A nonstandard variant of learning with rounding with polynomial modulus and unbounded samples. In: Lange, T., Steinwandt, R. (eds.) PQCrypto 2018. LNCS, vol. 10786, pp. 312–330. Springer, Cham (2018). https://doi.org/10.1007/978-3-319-79063-3_15
28. Naor, M., Pinkas, B., Reingold, O.: Distributed pseudo-random functions and KDCs. In: Stern, J. (ed.) EUROCRYPT 1999. LNCS, vol. 1592, pp. 327–346. Springer, Heidelberg (1999). https://doi.org/10.1007/3-540-48910-X_23
29. Naor, M., Reingold, O.: Number-theoretic constructions of efficient pseudo-random functions. J. ACM (JACM) **51**(2), 231–262 (2004)
30. Needham, R.M., Schroeder, M.D.: Using encryption for authentication in large networks of computers. Commun. ACM **21**(12), 993–999 (1978)

31. Nielsen, J.B.: A threshold pseudorandom function construction and its applications. In: Yung, M. (ed.) CRYPTO 2002. LNCS, vol. 2442, pp. 401–416. Springer, Heidelberg (2002). https://doi.org/10.1007/3-540-45708-9_26
32. Shor, P.W.: Algorithms for quantum computation: discrete logarithms and factoring. In: Proceedings 35th Annual Symposium on Foundations of Computer Science, pp. 124–134. IEEE (1994)
33. Shor, P.W.: Polynomial-time algorithms for prime factorization and discrete logarithms on a quantum computer. SIAM Rev. **41**(2), 303–332 (1999)

# On the Untapped Potential of the Quantum FLT-Based Inversion

Ren Taguchi[1(✉)] and Atsushi Takayasu[1,2]

[1] The University of Tokyo, Tokyo, Japan
{rtaguchi-495,takayasu-a}@g.ecc.u-tokyo.ac.jp
[2] National Institute of Advanced Industrial Science and Technology, Tokyo, Japan

**Abstract.** Thus far, several papers estimated concrete quantum resources of Shor's algorithm for solving a binary elliptic curve discrete logarithm problem. In particular, the complexity of computing quantum inversions over a binary field $\mathbb{F}_{2^n}$ is dominant when running the algorithm, where $n$ is a degree of a binary elliptic curve. There are two major methods for quantum inversion, i.e., the quantum GCD-based inversion and the quantum FLT-based inversion. Among them, the latter method is known to require more qubits; however, the latter one is valuable since it requires much fewer Toffoli gates and less depth. When $n = 571$, Kim-Hong's quantum GCD-based inversion algorithm (Quantum Information Processing 2023) and Taguchi-Takayasu's quantum FLT-based inversion algorithm (CT-RSA 2023) require $3,473$ qubits and $8,566$ qubits, respectively. In contrast, for the same $n = 571$, the latter algorithm requires only 2.3% of Toffoli gates and 84% of depth compared to the former one. In this paper, we modify Taguchi-Takayasu's quantum FLT-based inversion algorithm to reduce the required qubits. While Taguch-Takayasu's FLT-based inversion algorithm takes an addition chain for $n-1$ as input and computes a sequence whose number is the same as the length of the chain, our proposed algorithm employs an uncomputation step and stores a shorter one. As a result, our proposed algorithm requires only $3,998$ qubits for $n = 571$, which is only 15% more than Kim-Hong's GCD-based inversion algorithm. Furthermore, our proposed algorithm preserves the advantage of FLT-based inversion since it requires only 3.7% of Toffoli gates and 77% of depth compared to Kim-Hong's GCD-based inversion algorithm for $n = 571$.

**Keywords:** ECDLP · quantum cryptanalysis · FLT-based inversion · quantum resource estimate · addition chain

## 1 Introduction

### 1.1 Background

RSA [11] and elliptic-curve cryptography (ECC) [8,9] are the most widely used public-key cryptosystems in practice. The security of RSA and ECC relates


C. Pöpper and L. Batina (Eds.): ACNS 2024, LNCS 14584, pp. 79–100, 2024.
https://doi.org/10.1007/978-3-031-54773-7_4

to the computational complexity of the factorization problem and the elliptic curve discrete logarithm problem (ECDLP). Since there are no algorithms that solve the factorization problem/ECDLP in polynomial time, RSA and ECC are believed to be secure. In 1994, Shor [13] proposed a quantum polynomial time algorithm for solving the problems. Thus, quantum resource estimates and optimized quantum circuits of the algorithm has been actively studied.

In this paper, we focus on the ECDLP over a binary elliptic curve called the binary ECDLP. Banegas et al. [1] presented the first concrete quantum circuits for solving the problem. For this purpose, they proposed a quantum elliptic curve point addition algorithm and *two* quantum inversion algorithms over $\mathbb{F}_{2^n}$, where $n$ is called a degree of a binary field and $n = 163, 233, 283, 571$ are recommended by NIST [2]. Banegas et al. estimated the concrete quantum resource, where they regarded required qubits as the main optimization target. The number of Toffoli gates is their secondary one since the gates are much more expensive than CNOT gates. Since the depth of circuits is also known to be cared as mentioned in [12], we collectively call the required qubits, Toffoli gates, and the depth the main quantum resource throughout the paper. Banegas et al.'s analysis indicates that the quantum resource varies greatly depending on which of their two quantum inversion algorithms is used. They concluded that their *GCD-based* inversion algorithm is better than their *FLT-based* one[1]since the former requires fewer qubits, while the latter requires much fewer Toffoli gates and less depth. When $n = 571$, their GCD-based and FLT-based inversion algorithms require $4,015$ and $9,137$ qubits, respectively, while the latter requires only 2.4% of Toffoli gates and 94%[2] of depth to run Shor's algorithm. A point to note is that the depth of a circuit is not an exact value but an upper bound. In general, it is technically hard to analyze fully parallel quantum computation towards minimizing the depth.

Afterward, there have been several subsequent works that updated the quantum resource estimate by presenting improved quantum inversion algorithms. Kim and Hong [6] proposed a GCD-based inversion algorithm that reduces all main quantum resources of Banegas et al.'s GCD-based algorithm. Although Putranto et al. [10] proposed an FLT-based inversion algorithm that reduces the depth of Banegas et al.'s FLT-based algorithm, it requires more qubits. Taguchi and Takayasu [15] proposed FLT-based inversion algorithms that reduce the depth (resp. required qubits) of Banegas et al.'s (resp. Putranto et al.'s) FLT-based algorithms. On the other hand, these works do not change the relationship between GCD-based and FLT-based inversion algorithms. When $n = 571$, Kim-Hong's GCD-based and Taguchi-Takayasu's FLT-based inversion algorithms require $3,473$ and $8,566$ qubits, respectively, while the latter requires only 2.3% of Toffoli gates and 84% of depth to run Shor's algorithm. Therefore, it is desirable to develop GCD-based (resp. FLT-based) inversion algorithms

[1] FLT is the abbreviation of Fermat's little theorem.

[2] Although Banegas et al. [1] used Hoof's quantum multiplication algorithm [5], we replace it with more efficient Kim et al.'s quantum multiplication algorithm [7] and update their analysis. We use the more efficient algorithm throughout the paper.

that drastically reduce required Toffoli gates and depth (resp. required qubits) of Kim-Hong's GCD-based (resp. Taguchi-Takayasu's FLT-based) algorithms.

## 1.2 Our Contribution

In this paper, we break the relationship between GCD-based and FLT-based inversion algorithms by presenting an FLT-based method that requires much fewer qubits. When $n = 571$, our method requires 3,998 qubits to run Shor's algorithm and reduces all main quantum resources of Banegas et al.'s GCD-based algorithm [1]. Although the required qubits are still more than Kim-Hong's GCD-based algorithm, they are competitive since ours are just 15% more than Kim-Hong. Furthermore, our method preserves the advantage of FLT-based inversion since it requires only 3.7% of Toffoli gates and 77% of depth to run Shor's algorithm compared to Kim-Hong's GCD-based inversion algorithm.

We briefly explain three technical ingredients to obtain the result.

**Register-Bounded Addition Chain.** Taguchi-Takayasu's FLT-based inversion algorithm takes an addition chain as input and computes a sequence whose number is the same as the length of the chain. Briefly speaking, the addition chain represents the sequence of computation. Unfortunately, this procedure wastes the number of ancillary registers since there are several terms that are stored until the end of the computation, while they are used only at an early step of the computation. If we delete such terms, we can save the required qubits; however, an addition chain does not indicate which terms should be deleted and when. For this purpose, we introduce a *register-bounded addition chain*. A register-bounded addition chain is a longer sequence than an addition chain and represents the sequence of computation/uncomputation. We find register-bounded addition chains for NIST recommended degrees $n = 163, 233, 283, 571$ and reduce the required qubits for inversions.

**Modified Elliptic Curve Point Addition Algorithm.** Although a register-bounded addition chain enables us to reduce required qubits, the resulting inversion algorithm requires slightly more qubits than Banegas et al.'s GCD-based inversion algorithm. Since our final target is not an inversion itself but Shor's algorithm, we modify Banegas et al.'s point addition algorithm [1] and further reduce the required qubits for running Shor's algorithm. Interestingly, our proposed point addition algorithm itself does not reduce the required qubits; however, it becomes effective when combined with our inversion algorithm. Specifically, we design our point addition algorithm so that the proposed inversion algorithm and the point addition algorithm share the same ancillary registers.

**Depth Reduction of Quantum Multiple Squaring Circuits.** The above two ingredients enable us to run Shor's algorithm with 3,998 qubits for $n = 571$. However, the algorithm lost the advantage of FLT-based inversion since it requires more depth than GCD-based inversion algorithms. To preserve the advantage, we find how to perform parallel quantum computation during FLT-based inversion and reduce the depth. Since FLT-based inversion is inherently required to compute $2^k$-th powers many times for large $k$, previous FLT-based inversion algorithms applied a circuit for computing squaring $k$ times for computing $2^k$-th power. In contrast, we analyze quantum circuits for computing $2^k$-th powers directly and find that much less depth is sufficient for any $n$. The circuits are effective for all FLT-based inversion algorithms and enable our algorithm to preserve the advantage of FLT-based inversion.

*Organization.* In Sect. 3, we present our FLT-based method. In Sect. 4, we analyze the quantum resource and compare it with previous ones.

## 2 Preliminaries

In Sect. 2.1, we explain binary elliptic curves and a binary elliptic curve discrete logarithm problem (binary ECDLP). In Sect. 2.2, we explain quantum computations and quantum basic arithmetics over $\mathbb{F}_{2^n}$. In Sect. 2.3, we describe Shor's algorithm for solving the binary ECDLP.

### 2.1 Binary Elliptic Curve Discrete Logarithm Problem

Let $n$ be a non-negative integer. A binary elliptic curve of degree $n$ is given by $y^2 + xy = x^3 + ax^2 + b$, where $a \in \mathbb{F}_{2^n}$ and $b \in \mathbb{F}_{2^n}^*$. The set of rational points on an elliptic curve and a special point $O$ form an abelian group under point addition, where $O$ is the identity element called a point at infinity. Let $P = (x_1, y_1)$ and $Q = (x_2, y_2)$ denote rational points on a binary elliptic curve. If $P \neq Q$, $P + Q = (x_3, y_3)$ is given by

$$x_3 = \lambda^2 + \lambda + x_1 + x_2 + a, \quad y_3 = (x_2 + x_3)\lambda + x_3 + y_2,$$

where $\lambda = (y_1 + y_2)/(x_1 + x_2)$. Otherwise, $P + P = (x_3, y_3)$ is given by

$$x_3 = \lambda^2 + \lambda + a, \quad y_3 = x_1^2 + (\lambda + 1)x_3,$$

where $\lambda = x_1 + y_1/x_1$. As the above formulas imply, we compute an inversion when we compute a point addition. Hereafter, $[k]P$ denotes a sum of $k$ $P$'s under point addition. The above two formulas indicate that we can compute $[k]P$ from $P$ and $k$ in polynomial time. However, there is no known polynomial time algorithm that computes $k$ from $P$ and $[k]P$. This problem over a binary field is called the binary elliptic curve discrete logarithm problem (binary ECDLP).

### 2.2 Quantum Computation in $\mathbb{F}_{2^n}$

In classical computation, we use a "bit" represented by 0 or 1. In contrast, in quantum computation, we use a "qubit" represented by $|0\rangle, |1\rangle$ and their superposition. Let $m(x)$ be an irreducible polynomial in $\mathbb{F}_2[x]$ of degree $n$ and $(m(x))$ be an ideal generated by $m(x)$ over $\mathbb{F}_2[x]$. To represent an element in $f \in \mathbb{F}_{2^n}$ by qubits, we use a polynomial representation based on a relation $\mathbb{F}_{2^n} \simeq \mathbb{F}_2[x]/(m(x))$. Since $f$ is represented by a polynomial of degree less than $n-1$, we represent it by $n$ qubits and corresponding coefficients of the polynomial as the quantum state of $|0\rangle$ or $|1\rangle$. Hereafter, we call the $n$ qubits representing an element in $\mathbb{F}_{2^n}$ a *register.*

We employs quantum circuits to describe quantum computations, where X gates, CNOT gates, Toffoli (TOF) gates, and SWAP gates are basic quantum gates. An X gate exchanges the coefficients of $|0\rangle$ and $|1\rangle$. Let $a, b$, and $c$ denote $|0\rangle$ or $|1\rangle$. Then, CNOT, TOF, and SWAP operations are given by $\text{CNOT}(a, b) = (a, a \oplus b)$, $\text{TOF}(a, b, c) = (a, b, c \oplus (a \cdot b))$, and $\text{SWAP}(a, b) = (b, a)$, respectively. A TOF gate is believed to be much more expensive than a CNOT gate. To explain our method in Sect. 3, we may use a SWAP gate; however, we do not use the gate actually by designing subsequent circuits appropriately.

Next, we explain quantum basic arithmetics. Let $f, g$, and $h$ denote quantum states of elements in $\mathbb{F}_{2^n}$. We use `ADD` (resp. `SQUARE` and `spSQUARE`) to denote Banegas et al.'s algorithm [1] for addition (resp. squaring) over $\mathbb{F}_{2^n}$, where $\texttt{ADD}\,(f, g) = (f, f+g)$, $\texttt{SQUARE}\,(f) = f^2$, and $\texttt{spSQUARE}\,(f, g) = (f, f^2+g)$. We can use `ADD` to compute a copy of a given element by $\texttt{ADD}(f, 0) = (f, f)$. We use $\texttt{SQUARE}^{-1}$ and $\texttt{spSQUARE}^{-1}$ to denote inverse operations of `SQUARE` and `spSQUARE`, respectively. Banegas et al.'s algorithms [1] for computing the operations are based only on CNOT gates, where `ADD`, `SQUARE`, and `spSQUARE` require $n$, at most $n^2 - n$, and at most $n^2$ CNOT gates, respectively. Circuits for computing $\texttt{SQUARE}^{-1}$ and $\texttt{spSQUARE}^{-1}$ are reversed circuits for computing `SQUARE` and `spSQUARE`, respectively. We use `MODMULT` to denote Kim et al.'s multiplication algorithm over $\mathbb{F}_{2^n}$ [7], where $\texttt{MODMULT}\,(f, g, h) = (f, g, f \cdot g + h)$ which requires TOF gates as well as CNOT gates. Indeed, we can compute multiplication of given two elements by $\texttt{MODMULT}\,(f, g, 0) = (f, g, f \cdot g)$. Since we consider the arithmetics over $\mathbb{F}_{2^n}$, it holds that $\texttt{ADD}\,(f, f) = (f, 0)$ and $\texttt{MODMULT}\,(f, g, f \cdot g) = (f, g, 0)$.

Finally, we describe `INV` which denotes the inversion computation over $\mathbb{F}_{2^n}$, where $\texttt{INV}\,(f, [0, \ldots, 0], 0) = (f, [r_1, \ldots, r_m], f^{-1})$. Observe that `INV` requires $m+2$ registers whose first one stores $f \in \mathbb{F}_{2^n}$. The other $m+1$ registers are ancillary registers that include the last one to store $f^{-1}$. We call the register for output and the $m$ registers enclosed by [ ] *inversion ancillary registers.* Moreover, we call an inversion ancillary register a *dirty ancillary register* if the output $r_i$ is non-zero. We use $\texttt{INV}^{-1}$ to denote an inverse operation of `INV`, where $\texttt{INV}^{-1}(f, [r_1, \ldots, r_m], f^{-1}) = (f, [0, \ldots, 0], 0)$. We use $\texttt{INV}^{-1}$ only when the input $[r_1, \ldots, r_m]$ in the inversion ancillary registers is the same as the output of `INV` in the same registers.

In this paper, the above quantum computations also take registers as input, e.g., $\texttt{ADD}(g_1, g_2)$, where $g_1$ and $g_2$ is a register which stores $f \in \mathbb{F}_{2^n}$ and 0, respectively. Then, $\texttt{ADD}(g_1, g_2)$ describes $\texttt{ADD}(f, 0) = (f, f)$.

### 2.3 Shor's Algorithm for Solving the Binary ECDLP

Shor's algorithm mainly consists of a point addition part and a quantum Fourier transform. Since the former and the latter require $O(n^3)$ and $O(n^2)$ quantum gates, respectively, the point addition part is relatively expensive. Banegas et al.'s point addition algorithm [1] consists of quantum arithmetics over $\mathbb{F}_{2^n}$ denoted by `MODMULT`, `INV`, `INV`$^{-1}$, `spSQUARE`, `const_ADD`, `ctrl_ADD`, and `ctrl_const_ADD`. Although we do not explain in detail, `const_ADD`, `ctrl_ADD`, and `ctrl_const_ADD` operate addition, where they require at most $n$ X gates, at most $n$ TOF gates, and at most $n$ CNOT gates, respectively. In this paper, we count the numbers of TOF and CNOT gates and ignore $X$ gates by following previous works [1]. Banegas et al.'s point addition algorithm requires $3n + 1$ qubits except inversion ancillary registers. More precisely, they require $2n + 1$ qubits for input and $n$ qubits for an ancillary register of point addition which we call a *point addition ancillary register.*

## 3 Our Method

In Sect. 3.1, we explain register-bounded addition chain. In Sect. 3.2, we propose a quantum point addition algorithm. In Sect. 3.3, we describe the depth reduction of squaring. In Sect. 3.4, we show our quantum FLT-based inversion algorithm.

### 3.1 Register-Bounded Addition Chain

Hereafter, we use a notation $\langle\alpha\rangle := f^{\alpha}$ for simplicity for $f \in \mathbb{F}^*_{2^n}$. Then, the FLT-based inversion computes $\langle -1\rangle = \langle 2^n - 2\rangle$. We focus on the computation of $\langle 2^{n-1} - 1\rangle$ hereafter since we can compute $\langle 2^n - 2\rangle$ by applying squaring to $\langle 2^{n-1} - 1\rangle$.

**Taguchi-Takayasu's FLT-Based Algorithm.** At first, we summarize overvie- ws of Taguchi-Takayasu's quantum FLT-based inversion algorithm [15]. To be precise, Taguchi and Takayasu proposed two algorithms, i.e., Basic algorithm and Extended algorithm. Hereafter, we only describe thier Extended algorithm since their Extended algorithm requires fewer qubits than their Basic algorithm. Therefore, we call their Extended algorithm simply Taguchi-Takayasu's FLT-based algorithm.

We review an addition chain that is Taguchi-Takayasu's FLT-based essential ingredient to improve previous FLT-based algorithms.

**Definition 1 (Addition chain).** *Let $\ell$ and $N$ denote non-negative integers. An addition chain for $N$ of length $\ell$ is a sequence $p_0 = 1, p_1, p_2, \ldots, p_\ell = N$ which satisfies the following condition:*

- *For all $s = 1, 2, \ldots, \ell$, there exist $i$ and $j$ which satisfy $p_s = p_i + p_j$, where $0 \le i, j < s$.*

We call each term $p_s$ of an addition chain a doubled term or an added term. In particular, if there are no $i$ and $j$ which satisfy $0 \leq i, j < s, p_s = p_i + p_j$, and $p_i \neq p_j$, and an added term otherwise. Taguchi-Takayasu's FLT-based algorithm takes $\langle 2^{p_0} - 1 \rangle = f \in \mathbb{F}_{2^n}^*$ and an addition chain $\{p_s\}_{s=0}^{\ell}$ for $n-1$ of length $\ell$ as inputs and computes $\langle 2^{p_1} - 1 \rangle, \langle 2^{p_2} - 1 \rangle, \ldots, \langle 2^{p_\ell} - 1 \rangle = \langle 2^{n-1} - 1 \rangle$ sequentially by the relation

$$\langle 2^\alpha - 1 \rangle^{2^\beta} \times \langle 2^\beta - 1 \rangle = \langle 2^{\alpha+\beta} - 1 \rangle. \tag{1}$$

Taguchi-Takayasu's FLT-based algorithm computes $\langle 2^{p_s} - 1 \rangle$ in two distinct ways for all $1 \leq s \leq \ell$ depending on whether $p_s$ is an added term or a doubled term. If $p_s$ is an added term, we compute $\langle 2^{p_s} - 1 \rangle = \langle 2^{p_i + p_j} - 1 \rangle$ from $\langle 2^{p_i} - 1 \rangle$ and $\langle 2^{p_j} - 1 \rangle$ which have been stored distinct registers. In particular, we first apply `SQUARE` $p_i$ times to $\langle 2^{p_j} - 1 \rangle$ and obtain $\langle 2^{p_i + p_j} - 2^{p_i} \rangle$. After that, we apply `MODMULT` to $\langle 2^{p_i + p_j} - 2^{p_i} \rangle$ and $\langle 2^{p_i} - 1 \rangle$ and obtain $\langle 2^{p_i + p_j} - 1 \rangle = \langle 2^{p_s} - 1 \rangle$. On the other hand, if $p_s$ is a doubled term, we first compute a copy of $\langle 2^{p_i} - 1 \rangle$ in another ancillary register by using `ADD`. Then, we apply `SQUARE` $p_i$ times to the copy and obtain $\langle 2^{p_i + p_i} - 2^{p_i} \rangle$. Finally, we apply `MODMULT` to $\langle 2^{p_i} - 1 \rangle$ and $\langle 2^{p_i + p_i} - 2^{p_i} \rangle$ and obtain $\langle 2^{p_i + p_i} - 1 \rangle = \langle 2^{p_s} - 1 \rangle$. To reduce the qubits, we uncompute the copy of $\langle 2^{p_i} - 1 \rangle$ by `ADD`. Theorem 1 describes the quantum resources for Taguchi-Takayasu's FLT-based algorithm.

**Theorem 1** ([15], **Theorem 2**). *Let $f$ be an element in $\mathbb{F}_{2^n}^*$ and $\{p_s\}_{s=0}^{\ell}$ be an addition chain for $n-1$ of length $\ell$ with $p_\ell$ is an added term. Taguchi-Takayasu's FLT-based algorithm takes $f = \langle 1 \rangle$ and $\{p_s\}_{s=0}^{\ell}$ as input and outputs $\langle -1 \rangle = \langle 2^n - 2 \rangle$ with $\ell$ ancillary registers and $\ell$ multiplications.*

Taguchi-Takayasu's FLT-based algorithm requires $\ell$ ancillary registers to store $\langle 2^{p_s} - 1 \rangle$ for all $s = 1, 2, \ldots, \ell$. Furthermore, every term of an addition chain for Taguchi-Takayasu's algorithm appears only once.

**Our Proposed Algorithm.** Now, we reduce even more qubits than Taguchi-Takayasu's FLT-based algorithm. Keen readers may notice that we can further reduce required qubits by uncomputing not only copied $\langle 2^{p_s} - 1 \rangle$ but also original $\langle 2^{p_s} - 1 \rangle$ itself. For an example of Taguchi-Takayasu's FLT-based algorithm with an addition chain $\{p_s\}_{s=0}^{9} = \{1, 2, 3, 6, 9, 18, 27, 54, 108, 162\}$, observe that $\{1, 2, 3, 6, 9, 18\}$ will not be used again after computing 27. In other words, after we compute 27, we can uncompute $\{2, 3, 6, 9, 18\}$ if possible. However, while an addition chain tells us a sequence of computation, it does not tell us which terms can be uncomputed and when. Therefore, we need another method to analyze our proposed algorithm. For this purpose, we introduce register-bounded addition chains.

**Definition 2 (Register-Bounded Addition Chain).** *Let $\tilde{\ell}$ and $N$ denote non-negative integers. A register-bounded addition chain for $N$ of length $\tilde{\ell}$ is a sequence $\tilde{p} := \{\tilde{p}_s\}_{s=0}^{\tilde{\ell}} = \tilde{p}_0 = 1, \tilde{p}_1, \tilde{p}_2, \ldots, \tilde{p}_{\tilde{\ell}}$ which satisfies following conditions:*

- *For all $s = 1, \ldots, \tilde{\ell}$, there exist $i$ and $j$ which satisfy $\tilde{p}_i + \tilde{p}_j = \tilde{p}_s$ and $\tilde{p}_i \in S(\tilde{p}, s-1), \tilde{p}_j \in S(\tilde{p}, s-1)$, where $S(\tilde{p}, t) := \{\tilde{p}_s \mid 0 \leq s \leq t$, there exists no $s'$ such that $0 \leq s' \leq t, s \neq s'$, and $\tilde{p}_s = \tilde{p}_{s'}\}$.*
- *There exists $\omega$ which satisfies $\tilde{p}_\omega = N$.*
- *Every term appears once or twice.*

Due to the first condition, a register-bounded addition chain $\{\tilde{p}_s\}_{s=0}^{\tilde{\ell}}$ is an addition chain. Therefore, we can also define doubled terms and added terms for a register-bounded addition chain. Furthermore, a sequence of different terms of $\{\tilde{p}_s\}_{s=0}^{\tilde{\ell}}$ is also an addition chain. A register-bounded addition chain explains both computations and uncomputations. Specifically, the first and second time each term $\tilde{p}_s$ appear, we compute and uncompute $f^{2^{\tilde{p}_s}-1}$, respectively. Briefly speaking, $S(\tilde{p}, t)$ is a set of $\tilde{p}_0, \tilde{p}_1, \ldots, \tilde{p}_t$ that appear only once. Thus, when we compute or uncompute $\tilde{p}_s$ for all $1 \leq s \leq \tilde{\ell}$, we choose former terms that appear once in $\tilde{p}_0, \tilde{p}_1, \ldots, \tilde{p}_{s-1}$, while there is no condition for an addition chain. Then, we define a function $C(\tilde{p}, t)$ by $C(\tilde{p}, t) := 1$ when $\tilde{p}_t$ is a doubled term and $C(\tilde{p}, t) := 0$ otherwise. We also define $r(\tilde{p}, t)$ which we call the *register counting function* given by $r(\tilde{p}, t) := \#S(\tilde{p}, t) + C(\tilde{p}, t) - 1$. Intuitively, $r(\tilde{p}, t)$ denotes the number of required ancillary registers when we compute or uncompute $\langle 2^{\tilde{p}_t} - 1 \rangle$. Moreover, we use the notation $R(\tilde{p}) := \max_{1 \leq t \leq \tilde{\ell}} r(\tilde{p}, t)$ hereafter. Thus, $R(\tilde{p})$ describes the number of required ancillary registers for a whole inversion computation. We explain quantum resources for a quantum FLT-based inversion algorithm which we compute and uncompute based on a register-bounded addition chain by Theorem 2.

**Theorem 2.** *Let $f$ be an element in $\mathbb{F}_{2^n}^*$, $\{\tilde{p}_s\}_{s=0}^{\tilde{\ell}}$ be a register-bounded addition chain for $n-1$ of length $\tilde{\ell}$, and $\ell$ denote the length of an addition chain which consists of different terms of $\{\tilde{p}_s\}_{s=0}^{\tilde{\ell}}$. There exists a quantum algorithm that takes $f = \langle 1 \rangle$ and $\{\tilde{p}_s\}_{s=0}^{\tilde{\ell}}$ as input and outputs $\langle -1 \rangle = \langle 2^n - 2 \rangle$ with $R(\tilde{p})$ ancillary registers, $\tilde{\ell}$ multiplications, and $2\ell - \tilde{\ell}$ dirty ancillary registers at the end of the algorithm.*

*Proof.* We compute or uncompute $\langle 2^{\tilde{p}_s} - 1 \rangle$ in the $s$-th procedure for all $s = 1, \ldots, \tilde{\ell}$. More precisely, we compute $\langle 2^{\tilde{p}_s} - 1 \rangle$ if $\tilde{p}_s$ appears for the first time in $\{\tilde{p}_s\}_{s=0}^{\tilde{\ell}}$ and uncompute $\langle 2^{\tilde{p}_s} - 1 \rangle$ if it is the second time to appear. By the second condition of Definition 2, we compute $\langle 2^{n-1} - 1 \rangle$ in the $\omega$-th procedure, where $0 \leq \omega \leq \tilde{\ell}$ in the same way as Taguchi-Takayasu's FLT-based algorithm. Then, we explain uncomputations of $\langle 2^{\tilde{p}_s} - 1 \rangle$. We only describe the case that $\tilde{p}_s$ is a doubled term.

**Uncomputation of** $\langle 2^{\tilde{p}_s} - 1 \rangle$: We have $\langle 2^{\tilde{p}_i} - 1 \rangle$ stored in the register $g_{k_1}$, 0 stored in the register $g_{k_2}$, and $\langle 2^{\tilde{p}_s} - 1 \rangle$ stored in the register $g_{k_3}$, where $\tilde{p}_s = \tilde{p}_i + \tilde{p}_i$ and $i \in S(\tilde{p}, s-1)$. At first, we apply `ADD` $(g_{k_1}, g_{k_2})$ and obtain $\langle 2^{\tilde{p}_i} - 1 \rangle$ in the $g_{k_2}$. Next, we apply `SQUARE` $\tilde{p}_i$ times to the $g_{k_2}$ and obtain $\langle 2^{\tilde{p}_i} - 1 \rangle^{2^{\tilde{p}_i}} = \langle 2^{\tilde{p}_i + \tilde{p}_i} - 2^{\tilde{p}_i} \rangle$. Then, we apply `MODMULT` $(g_{k_1}, g_{k_2}, g_{k_3})$ and obtain $\langle 2^{\tilde{p}_i + \tilde{p}_i} - 2^{\tilde{p}_i} \rangle \times \langle 2^{\tilde{p}_i} - 1 \rangle + \langle 2^{\tilde{p}_s} - 1 \rangle = \langle 2^{\tilde{p}_i + \tilde{p}_i} - 1 \rangle + \langle 2^{\tilde{p}_s} - 1 \rangle = \langle 2^{\tilde{p}_s} - 1 \rangle +$

$\langle 2^{\tilde{p}_s} - 1\rangle = 0$ in the $g_{k_3}$ by (1). By the same procedure as the uncomputation of copy in Taguchi-Takayasu's FLT-based algorithm, we uncompute the $g_{k_2}$.

Then, $\langle 2^{\tilde{p}_s} - 1\rangle$ is stored after the $t$-th procedure if and only if $s \in S(\tilde{p}, t)$. Therefore, we can always compute or uncompute $\langle 2^{\tilde{p}_s} - 1\rangle$ since there exist $\langle 2^{\tilde{p}_i} - 1\rangle$ and $\langle 2^{\tilde{p}_j} - 1\rangle$ in some registers such that $0 \leq i, j < s, \tilde{p}_s = \tilde{p}_i + \tilde{p}_j$ by the first condition of Definition 2. Furthermore, $\#S(\tilde{p}, t)$ describes the number of registers that store non-zero terms including input after the $t$-th procedure. However, we also require another register to copy $\langle 2^{\tilde{p}_t} - 1\rangle$ when $\tilde{p}_t$ is a doubled term. In other words, we use $\#S(\tilde{p}, t)+1$ registers when $\tilde{p}_t$ is a doubled term and $\#S(\tilde{p}, t)$ registers when $\tilde{p}_t$ is an added term for $t$-th procedure. Then, the number of required ancillary registers for $t$-th procedure is $\#S(\tilde{p}, t)+C(\tilde{p}, t)-1 = r(\tilde{p}, t)$. Therefore, we require $\max_{0 \leq t \leq \tilde{\ell}} r(\tilde{p}, t) = R(\tilde{p})$ ancillary registers. Moreover, each procedure requires a multiplication, in other words, we require $\tilde{\ell}$ multiplications in total. The third condition of Definition 2 ensures that we compute $\ell$ different terms only once, in other words, we do not compute $\langle 2^{\tilde{p}_s} - 1\rangle$ after we uncompute $\langle 2^{\tilde{p}_s} - 1\rangle$. We require $\ell$ registers to store them. However, there are $r(\tilde{p}, \tilde{\ell})$ non-zero ancillary registers at the end of the algorithm. Therefore, we uncompute $\ell - r(\tilde{p}, \tilde{\ell})$ times. Then, it holds that $\tilde{\ell} = \ell + (\ell - r(\tilde{p}, \tilde{\ell})) = 2\ell - r(\tilde{p}, \tilde{\ell})$. By this relation, it holds $r(\tilde{p}, \tilde{\ell}) = 2\ell - \tilde{\ell}$. □

By Theorem 2, we use $R(\tilde{p})n$ qubits except for $g_0$, and $\tilde{\ell} = 2\ell - r(\tilde{p}, \tilde{\ell})$ multiplications for our proposed inversion algorithm. Then, when we fix $\ell$ and $R(\tilde{p})$, larger $r(\tilde{p}, \tilde{\ell})$ is desired to reduce multiplications. On the other hand, it holds that $r(\tilde{p}, \tilde{\ell}) \leq R(\tilde{p})$ by the definition of $R(\tilde{p})$.

### 3.2 Modified Quantum Point Addition Algorithm

As we explained in Sect. 2.3, there are two types of ancillary registers, i.e., inversion ancillary registers and a point addition ancillary register to run Shor's algorithm. We modify Banegas et al.'s quantum point addition algorithm [1] described as Algorithm 1 to reduce required qubits by combining with our FLT-based inversion algorithm in Sect. 3.1, where we use $R := R(\tilde{p})$ to describe the number of inversion ancillary registers for simplicity. Intuitively, we delete the point addition ancillary register and perform point addition by using an inversion ancillary register. Briefly speaking, Algorithm 1 is the same as Banegas et al.'s algorithm by deleting `SWAP` operations in lines 6 and 16, exchanging line 5 and line 7, and exchanging line 15 and line 17. The modification changes the role of a register $\lambda$ which is a point addition ancillary register in Banegas et al.'s algorithm, while it is both a point addition ancillary register and an inversion ancillary register in Algorithm 1. In other words, all $R$ inversion ancillary registers are divided into the registers for only inversion computation, i.e., $g_1, \ldots, g_{R-1}$, and the register for both inversion computation and point addition computation, i.e., $\lambda$. Then, the number of qubits for Shor's algorithm with Algorithm 1 is $(2 + R)n + 1$ qubits, while $(3 + R)n + 1$ qubits with Banegas et al.'s point addition algorithm. We note that Algorithm 1 itself does not purely

**Algorithm 1.** Proposed quantum point addition algorithm

**Input:** An irreducible polynomial $m(x) \in \mathbb{F}_2[x]$ of degree $n$, a coefficient of an binary elliptic curve $a$, single qubit $q$, an elliptic curve point $P_1 = (x_1, y_1)$ stored in $x, y$, a fixed elliptic curve point $P_2 = (x_2, y_2)$, a non-negative integer $R$, registers $g_1, g_2, \ldots, g_{R-1}, g_R = \lambda$ initialized to an all-$|0\rangle$ state

**Output:** $(x, y) = P_1 + P_2 = P_3(x_3, y_3)$ if $q = 1$
$(x, y) = P_1 = (x_1, x_2)$ if $q = 0$

`const_ADD` $(x_2, x)$
`ctrl_const_ADD`$_q(y_2, y)$ // $\lambda = 0$
`INV` $(x, [g_2, \ldots, g_{R-1}, \lambda], g_1)$
`MODMULT` $(g_1, y, \lambda)$
`MODMULT` $(x, \lambda, y)$
`SWAP` $(y, \lambda)$ // $\lambda = 0$
`INV`$^{-1}(x, [g_2, \ldots, g_{R-1}, \lambda], g_1)$
`SWAP` $(y, \lambda)$
`spSQUARE` $(\lambda, y)$
`ctrl_const_ADD`$_q(a + x_2, x)$
`ctrl_ADD`$_q(\lambda, x)$
`ctrl_ADD`$_q(y, x)$
`spSQUARE` $(\lambda, y)$
`SWAP` $(y, \lambda)$ // $\lambda = 0$
`INV` $(x, [g_2, \ldots, g_{R-1}, \lambda], g_1)$
`SWAP` $(y, \lambda)$
`MODMULT` $(x, \lambda, y)$
`MODMULT` $(g_1, y, \lambda)$ // $\lambda = 0$
`INV`$^{-1}(x, [g_2, \ldots, g_{R-1}, \lambda], g_1)$
`const_ADD` $(x_2, x)$
`ctrl_ADD`$_q(x, y)$
`ctrl_const_ADD`$_q(y_2, y)$

improve Banegas et al.'s point addition algorithm since Algorithm 1 requires some conditions. Concretely, Algorithm 1 requires that `INV` and `INV`$^{-1}$ satisfy two conditions, i.e., (i) $\lambda$ store 0 at the end of `INV` and (ii) $x$ at the beginning of `INV` (`INV`$^{-1}$) and $x$ at the end of `INV` (`INV`$^{-1}$) must be the same state. Quantum FLT-based inversion algorithms always satisfy (ii). However, previous FLT-based inversion algorithms do not satisfy (i) since they fully use all registers at the end of algorihtm. Our proposed FLT-based inversion algorithm can prepare a clear register at the end of algorithm by choosing $\{\tilde{p}_s\}_{s=0}^{\ell}$ properly. We explain the detail in Sect. 3.4. On the other hand, previous quantum GCD-based inversion algorithms satisfy (i), while they do not satisfy (ii). GCD-based inversion algorithms apply Euclidean algorithm to $x$ and $m$, where $m$ is an irreducible polynomial in Sect. 2.2. In Euclidean algorithm, we compute $x \leftarrow x \mod m$ or $m \leftarrow m \mod x$ until it holds $x = 1$ or $m = 1$. Thus, $x$ at the end of quantum GCD-based inverion algorithms is different state to $x$ at the beginning.

### 3.3 Depth Reduction of Quantum Multiple Squaring Circuits

We explain how to reduce the depth of quantum circuits for computing $2^k$-th powers. Let $f = a_0 + a_1x + \cdots + a_{n-1}x^{n-1}$ be a polynomial which represents an element in $\mathbb{F}_{2^n}$ with coefficients $a_i \in \mathbb{F}_2$. For an irreducible polynomial $m(x) \in \mathbb{F}_2[x]$ of degree $n$, we have $f^2 = a_0 + a_1x^2 + \cdots + a_{n-1}x^{2n-2} \mod m(x) = a'_0 + a'_1x + \cdots + a'_{n-1}x^{n-1} \mod m(x)$. Since each $a'_i$ is a sum of $a_0, a_1, \ldots, a_{n-1}$, there exists a matrix $T_n = (t_{i,j}) \in GL_n(\mathbb{F}_2)$ which satisfies

$$[a'_0, a'_1, a'_2, \ldots, a'_{n-1}]^\top = T_n[a_0, a_1, a_2, \ldots, a_{n-1}]^\top, \tag{2}$$

where $t_{i,j} \in \mathbb{F}_2$ for all $1 \leq i, j \leq n$. The matrix $T_n$ is uniquely determined for $m(x)$; in other words, the relation (2) holds for any $f$.

**Banegas et al.'s Estimate.** We explain how Banegas et al. [1] constructed a quantum circuit of `SQUARE` and `spSQUARE` by using the above matrix $T_n$. We also review their quantum resource estimation of `SQUARE` and `spSQUARE`.

`SQUARE`. Let $T_n = L_nU_nP_n$ be an LUP decomposition, where $L_n$ and $U_n$ are lower and upper triangular matrices, respectively, and $P_n$ is a permutation matrix. The multiplication by matrices $U_n$ and $L_n$ (resp. $P_n$) can be performed by CNOT (resp. SWAP) gates. In particular, Banegas et al. showed that the numbers of CNOT gates are the number of ones in $L_n$ and $U_n$ except their diagonal entries; thus, the circuits require at most $n(n-1)/2$ CNOT gates and the depth is at most $n(n-1)/2$. In total, $\texttt{SQUARE}(f) = f^2$ requires at most $n^2 - n$ CNOT gates and the depth is at most $n^2 - n$. Since we can compute the concrete number of CNOT gates of `SQUARE` for every irreducible polynomial $m(x)$, we use $SQ_n$ to denote the number, where the depth is at most $SQ_n$.

`spSQUARE`. For the above matrix $T_n$ determined by an irreducible polynomial $m(x)$, let $spSQ_n \geq n$ denote the number of ones in $T_n$ including diagonal entries. Let $a_i$ and $b_i$ be coefficients of $f$ and $g$ for $x^i$, respectively. Then, we can describe a computation $\texttt{spSQUARE}(f, g) = (f, f^2 + g)$ by

$$\begin{bmatrix} I_n & O_n \\ T_n & I_n \end{bmatrix} [a_0, a_1, \ldots, a_{n-1}, b_0, b_1, \ldots, b_{n-1}]^\top, \tag{3}$$

where $I_n$ and $O_n$ are an identity matrix and a zero matrix, respectively. As `SQUARE`, we can compute `spSQUARE` with $spSQ_n$ CNOT gates and the upper bound of depth of the circuit is $spSQ_n$.

**Depth Reduction of `spSQUARE`.** Observe that $spSQ_n \geq n$ holds due to $T_n \in GL_n(\mathbb{F}_2)$. However, we show that a smaller depth is sufficient for computing `spSQUARE` with the following stronger claim.

**Theorem 3.** *For a matrix $H_n = (h_{i,j}) \in M_n(\mathbb{F}_2)$, there exists a quantum circuit for computing a multiplication by a matrix $\begin{bmatrix} I_n & O_n \\ H_n & I_n \end{bmatrix}$ with depth at most $n$.*

Before providing a proof, we show an example for $H_3 = \begin{bmatrix} 1\,1\,0 \\ 1\,0\,1 \\ 1\,1\,1 \end{bmatrix}$, where $spSQ_3 = 7$. In this case, we want to compute

$$\begin{bmatrix} I_3 & O_3 \\ H_3 & I_3 \end{bmatrix} [a_0, a_1, \dots, a_{n-1}, b_0, b_1, \dots, b_{n-1}]^\top$$
$$= [a_0, a_1, a_2, b_0 + a_0 + a_1, b_1 + a_0 + a_2, b_2 + a_0 + a_1 + a_2]^\top.$$

It is easy to check that $spSQ_3 = 7$ CNOT gates are sufficient for the purpose by adding $a_0$ to the fourth, fifth, and sixth bits, $a_1$ to the fourth and sixth bits, and $a_2$ to the fifth and sixth bits. We can design a circuit with depth $spSQ_3 = 7$ by applying the CNOT gates one by one. On the other hand, we find that the depth $n = 3$ is sufficient by applying several CNOT gates simultaneously. In particular, the following design of a circuit works with the claimed depth, while distinct CNOT gates do not share their working bits at the same time:

- Add $a_0$ and $a_2$ to the fourth and sixth bits, respectively.
- Add $a_0, a_1$, and $a_2$ to the sixth, fourth, and fifth bits, respectively.
- Add $a_0$ and $a_1$ to the fifth and sixth bits, respectively.

We express the design by matrices

$$\Gamma_0 = \begin{bmatrix} 1\,0\,0 \\ 0\,0\,0 \\ 0\,0\,1 \end{bmatrix}, \quad \Gamma_1 = \begin{bmatrix} 0\,1\,0 \\ 0\,0\,1 \\ 1\,0\,0 \end{bmatrix}, \quad \Gamma_2 = \begin{bmatrix} 0\,0\,0 \\ 1\,0\,0 \\ 0\,1\,0 \end{bmatrix}$$

such that $H_3 = \Gamma_0 + \Gamma_1 + \Gamma_2$ and every rows and columns have at most one 1. The three columns of the matrices correspond to the first, second, and third bits, while the three rows correspond to the fourth, fifth, and sixth bits. The condition $H_3 = \Gamma_0 + \Gamma_1 + \Gamma_2$ ensures that matrices $\Gamma_0, \Gamma_1$, and $\Gamma_2$ represent the computation by $H_3$, while the other condition ensures that distinct CNOT gates do not share their working bits at the same time. We show how to decompose $H_n$ to at most $n$ $\Gamma_i$'s in general and provide a proof of Theorem 3.

*Proof.* We define a matrix $\Gamma(H_n, \iota) = (c(\iota)_{i,j})$, where $c(\iota)_{i,j} = h_{i,j}$ if $h_{i,j} = 1$ and $j - i = \iota \mod n$ for $\iota = 0, 1, \dots, n-1$. Then, $H_n = \Gamma(H_n, 0) + \Gamma(H_n, 1) + \dots + \Gamma(H_n, n-1)$. We can compute $\mathrm{CNOT}(a_i, b_j)$ for $(i, j) \in \Gamma(H_n, \iota)$ simultaneously for each $\iota = 0, 1, \dots, n-1$. Therefore, the depth for computing $H_n$ is at most $n$. □

By Theorem 3, we reduce the depth for `spSQUARE` from $SQ_n$ to $n$. However, this is only a small contribution when we estimate the resources for Shor's algorithm since $H_n = T_n$ is a sparse matrix and $SQ_n$ is sufficiently close to $n$ for all NIST-recommended $n$. On the other hand, if $H_n$ is not sparse, we can drastically reduce the depth.

We consider quantum FLT-based inversion algorithms. Let $k$ be a non-negative integer. When we compute a doubled term, i.e., $\langle 2^{2k} - 1 \rangle$ by using a register $g_1$ which stores $\langle 2^k - 1 \rangle$ and $g_2$ which stores 0, we employ a quantum computation called `ADD-SQUARE`$^k$ given by

```
ADD (g_1, g_2)
for s = 1, ..., k do
    SQUARE (g_2)
```

Previous works estimated the depth for $\texttt{ADD-SQUARE}^k$ is $1 + kSQ_n$. We give a tighter upper bound for $\texttt{ADD-SQUARE}^k$.

Let $f$ in $\mathbb{F}_{2^n}$ and denote $f = a_0 + a_1 x + a_2 x^2 + \cdots + a_{n-1} x^{n-1}$, where $a_i \in \mathbb{F}_2$. By observing (2), $T_n^k$ satisfies

$$[a_0^{(k)}, a_1^{(k)}, a_2^{(k)}, \ldots, a_{n-1}^{(k)}]^\top = T_n^k [a_0, a_1, a_2, \ldots, a_{n-1}]^\top, \tag{4}$$

where $a_i^{(k)}$ is a coefficient of $x^i$ for $f^{2^k}$ for $i = 0, 1, \ldots, n-1$. Then, a quantum computation called $\texttt{spSQUARE}^k$ given by

$$\begin{bmatrix} I_n & O_n \\ T_n^k & I_n \end{bmatrix} [a_0, a_1, \ldots, a_{n-1}, 0, 0, \ldots, 0]^\top$$

also describes $\texttt{ADD-SQUARE}^k$. Thus, let $H_n = T_n^k$ in Theorem 3, the depth for $\texttt{spSQUARE}^k$ is at most $n$. This is a significantly large contribution since $T_n^k$ contains about $n^2/2$ ones for almost all $k$ for all $n$. In almost all $k$, the upper bound of the depth for $\texttt{spSQUARE}^k$ is much smaller than the upper bound of the depth for $\texttt{ADD-SQUARE}^k$ for all $n$, however, we choose the lesser way when we apply this in FLT-based inversion algorithms. We note that we use an inverse of $\texttt{spSQUARE}^k$ or $\texttt{ADD-SQUARE}^k$ written by $(\texttt{spSQUARE}^k)^{-1}$ or $(\texttt{ADD-SQUARE}^k)^{-1}$ when we uncompute $\langle 2^{2k} - 1 \rangle$. Then, we use a reversed circuit of $\texttt{spSQUARE}^k$ or $\texttt{ADD-SQUARE}^k$. We repeatedly claim that we can apply the above depth reduction to all quantum FLT-based inversion algorithms.

When we compute or uncompute an added term, we can use $\texttt{SQUARE}^k$ which is given by applying LUP decomposition to $T_n^k$. Let $SQ_n^{(k)}$ denote the upper bound of the CNOT gates and the depth for $\texttt{SQUARE}^k$. In FLT-based inversion algorithms, we compare the depth of applying $\texttt{SQUARE}$ $k$ times, i.e., $kSQ_n$, and the depth of $\texttt{SQUARE}^k$, i.e., $SQ_n^{(k)}$ and choose the lesser way.

### 3.4 Proposed Inversion Algorithm

In this section, we construct our proposed quantum inversion algorithm that is based on the idea in Sect. 3.1. As we described in Sect. 3.1, larger $r(\tilde{p}, \tilde{\ell})$ is desired to reduce multiplications and it follows $r(\tilde{p}, \tilde{\ell}) \leq R(\tilde{p})$. However, to apply our proposed quantum point addition algorithm in Sect. 3.2, conditions (i) and (ii) must be satisfied. Our proposed inversion algorithm always satisfies (ii). On the other hand, (i) is satisfied if and only if $r(\tilde{p}, \tilde{\ell}) < R(\tilde{p})$. For this reason, we consider the case of $r(\tilde{p}, \tilde{\ell}) = R(\tilde{p}) - 1$ hereafter. We apply the depth reduction in squaring described in Sect. 3.3. Then, we prepare several sequences that describe our proposed inversion algorithm. We define two sequences $\{\tilde{a}_s\}_{s=1}^{\tilde{\ell}}, \{\tilde{b}_s\}_{s=1}^{\tilde{\ell}}$ that satisfy $\tilde{p}_{\tilde{a}_s} \in S(\tilde{p}, s-1)$ and $\tilde{p}_{\tilde{b}_s} \in S(\tilde{p}, s-1)$, and $\tilde{p}_s = \tilde{p}_{\tilde{a}_s} + \tilde{p}_{\tilde{b}_s}$ for all $1 \leq s \leq \tilde{\ell}$, where $\{\tilde{p}_s\}_{s=0}^{\tilde{\ell}}$ is a register-bounded addition chain for $n-1$. We assume that

$\tilde{a}_s = \tilde{b}_s$ if and only if $\tilde{p}_s$ is a doubled term of $\{\tilde{p}_s\}_{s=0}^{\tilde{\ell}}$. For the register-bounded addition chain $\{\tilde{p}_s\}_{s=0}^{\tilde{\ell}}$, we define two sets

$$D := \{s \in \{1, 2, \ldots, \tilde{\ell}\} \mid \tilde{a}_s = \tilde{b}_s\},$$
$$M := \{s \in \{1, 2, \ldots, \tilde{\ell}\} \mid \tilde{a}_s \neq \tilde{b}_s\}.$$

Now, we consider the general case of computation or uncomputation of $\langle 2^{\tilde{p}_s} - 1\rangle$ by using $\langle 2^{\tilde{p}_{\tilde{a}_s}} - 1\rangle$ and $\langle 2^{\tilde{p}_{\tilde{b}_s}} - 1\rangle$ for all $1 \leq s \leq \tilde{\ell}$ since we explained only a simple case. More precisely, we compute or uncompute $\langle 2^{\tilde{p}_s} - 1\rangle^{2^{\gamma_s}}$ in the $h_3$-th register by using $\langle 2^{\tilde{p}_{\tilde{a}_s}} - 1\rangle^{2^{\alpha_s}}$ in the $h_1$-th register and $\langle 2^{\tilde{p}_{\tilde{b}_s}} - 1\rangle^{2^{\beta_s}}$ in the $h_2$-th register, where $\alpha_s, \beta_s, \gamma_s$ are integers for all $s = 1, \ldots, \tilde{\ell}$. We decide that $\gamma_s = 0$ when we compute $\langle 2^{\tilde{p}_s} - 1\rangle$ and $\alpha_s = \beta_s$ when $\tilde{p}_s$ is a doubled term. Then, we define the sequences $\{\tilde{Q}_s^{(a)}\}_{s=1}^{\tilde{\ell}}, \{\tilde{Q}_s^{(b)}\}_{s=1}^{\tilde{\ell}}, \{\tilde{Q}_s\}_{s=1}^{\tilde{\ell}}$ such that $\tilde{Q}_s^{(a)}, \tilde{Q}_s^{(b)}, \tilde{Q}_s$ describe the times to apply squaring or its inverse to the $h_1$-th register, the $h_2$-th register, $h_3$-th register in the $s$-th procedure, respectively. In this case, it holds that $\tilde{Q}_s^{(a)} = -\alpha_s, \tilde{Q}_s^{(b)} = \tilde{p}_{\tilde{a}_s} - \beta_s$, and $\tilde{Q}_s = -\gamma_s$ by observing

$$\left(\langle 2^{\tilde{p}_{\tilde{a}_s}} - 1\rangle^{2^{\alpha_s}}\right)^{2^{-\alpha_s}} \times \left(\langle 2^{\tilde{p}_{\tilde{b}_s}} - 1\rangle^{2^{\beta_s}}\right)^{2^{\tilde{p}_{\tilde{a}_s} - \beta_s}} = \langle 2^{\tilde{p}_{\tilde{a}_s} + \tilde{p}_{\tilde{b}_s}} - 1\rangle = \langle 2^{\tilde{p}_s} - 1\rangle,$$
$$\left(\langle 2^{\tilde{p}_s} - 1\rangle^{2^{\gamma_s}}\right)^{2^{-\gamma_s}} = \langle 2^{\tilde{p}_s} - 1\rangle.$$

As we described in a proof of Theorem 2, we can construct a quantum algorithm that computes or uncomputes by the above two relations based on a register-bounded addition chain $\{\tilde{p}_s\}_{s=0}^{\ell}$.

We describe our proposed algorithm in Algorithm 2 which takes a register-bounded addition chain $\{\tilde{p}_s\}_{s=0}^{\tilde{\ell}}$ for $n-1$ of length $\tilde{\ell}$ and sequences $\{\tilde{a}_s\}_{s=1}^{\tilde{\ell}}$, $\{\tilde{b}_s\}_{s=1}^{\tilde{\ell}}$, $\{\tilde{Q}_s^{(a)}\}_{s=1}^{\tilde{\ell}}$, $\{\tilde{Q}_s^{(b)}\}_{s=1}^{\tilde{\ell}}$, $\{\tilde{Q}_s\}_{s=1}^{\tilde{\ell}}$ as input. `caseOPTSQUARE`$(g, v)$ applies ca- `seSQUARE`$(g, v)$ if $|v|SQ_n < SQ_n^{(|v|)}$ and applies `caseSQUARE`$^v(g)$ otherwise, where `caseSQUARE`$(g, v)$ applies `SQUARE` $v$ times to $g$ when $v > 0$, applies `SQUARE`$^{-1}$ $-v$ times to $g$ when $v < 0$, and do nothing when $v = 0$ and `caseSQUARE`$^v(g)$ applies `SQUARE`$^v(g)$ when $v > 0$, applies $($`SQUARE`$^{-v})^{-1}(g)$ when $v < 0$, and do nothing when $v = 0$. `caseOPTspSQUARE`$(g_1, g_2, v)$ applies `ADD`$(g_1, g_2)$ and `caseSQUARE`$(g_2, v)$ if $1 + |v|SQ_n < n$ and applies `casespSQUARE`$^v(g_1, g_2)$ otherwise, where `casespSQUARE`$^v(g_1, g_2)$ applies `spSQUARE`$^v(g_1, g_2)$ when $v > 0$, applies $($`spSQUARE`$^{-v})^{-1}(g_1, g_2)$ when $v < 0$, and applies `ADD`$(g_1, g_2)$ when $v = 0$. We note that a $($`SQUARE`$^v)^{-1}$ circuit, a $($`spSQUARE`$^v)^{-1}$ circuit, and a `caseOPTspSQUA- RE`$^{-1}$ are a reversed circuit of `SQUARE`$^v$, a reversed circuit of `spSQUARE`$^v$, and a reversed circuit of `caseOPTspSQUARE`$^v$, respectively. pl[$s$] stores the register number which stores $f^{2^{\tilde{p}_s}-1}$ for all $1 \leq s \leq \tilde{\ell}$. pld[$s$] stores the register number which stores the copy of $f^{2^{\tilde{p}_{\tilde{a}_s}}-1}$ for all $s \in D$. The size of pld, i.e., $\tilde{d}$ equals $\#D$. We note that $\tilde{p}_{\tilde{\ell}}$ does not always equal $n-1$. In other words, $g_{\text{pl}[\tilde{\ell}]}$ does not always store $\langle 2^{n-1} - 1\rangle$. Then, we define the non-negative integer $\omega$ such that $g_{\text{pl}[\omega]}$ stores $\langle 2^{n-1} - 1\rangle$ at the end of the loop from line 2 to line 16. By `SWAP` procedure in line 18,

**Algorithm 2.** Proposed inversion algorithm

**Input:** An irreducible polynomial $m(x) \in \mathbb{F}_2[x]$ of degree $n$, a register-bounded addition chain $\{\tilde{p}_s\}_{s=0}^{\tilde{\ell}}$, sequences $\{\tilde{a}_s\}_{s=1}^{\tilde{\ell}}, \{\tilde{b}_s\}_{s=1}^{\tilde{\ell}}, \{\tilde{Q}_s^{(a)}\}_{s=1}^{\tilde{\ell}}, \{\tilde{Q}_s^{(b)}\}_{s=1}^{\tilde{\ell}}, \{\tilde{Q}_s\}_{s=1}^{\tilde{\ell}}$, a register $g_0$ which stores a polynomial $f \in \mathbb{F}_{2^n}^*$ of degree up to $n-1$, registers $g_1, \ldots, g_{R(\tilde{p})}$ initialized to an all-$|0\rangle$ state, arrays $\mathrm{pl}[\tilde{\ell}]$, $\mathrm{pld}[\tilde{d}]$, a non-negative integer $\omega$ which satisfies $\tilde{p}_\omega = n-1$

**Output:** $g_1 = f^{2^n-2}$

$dcount \leftarrow 0$
**for** $s = 1, \ldots, \tilde{\ell}$ **do**
  **if** $s \in D$ **then**
    caseOPTspSQUARE $(g_{\mathrm{pl}[\tilde{a}_s]}, g_{\mathrm{pld}[dcount]}, \tilde{Q}_s^{(b)})$
    caseOPTSQUARE $(g_{\mathrm{pl}[\tilde{a}_s]}, \tilde{Q}_s^{(a)})$
    caseOPTSQUARE $(g_{\mathrm{pl}[s]}, \tilde{Q}_s)$
    MODMULT $(g_{\mathrm{pl}[\tilde{a}_s]}, g_{\mathrm{pld}[dcount]}, g_{\mathrm{pl}[s]})$
    caseOPTspSQUARE$^{-1}$ $(g_{\mathrm{pl}[\tilde{a}_s]}, g_{\mathrm{pld}[dcount]}, \tilde{p}_{\tilde{a}_s})$
    $dcount \leftarrow dcount + 1$
  **else** // $s \in M$
    caseOPTSQUARE $(g_{\mathrm{pl}[\tilde{a}_s]}, \tilde{Q}_s^{(a)})$
    caseOPTSQUARE $(g_{\mathrm{pl}[\tilde{b}_s]}, \tilde{Q}_s^{(b)})$
    caseOPTSQUARE $(g_{\mathrm{pl}[s]}, \tilde{Q}_s)$
    MODMULT $(g_{\mathrm{pl}[\tilde{a}_s]}, g_{\mathrm{pl}[\tilde{b}_s]}, g_{\mathrm{pl}[s]})$
SQUARE $(g_{\mathrm{pl}[\omega]})$
SWAP $(g_{\mathrm{pl}[\omega]}, g_1)$

$\langle 2^n - 2 \rangle = \langle -1 \rangle$ is always stored in $g_1$. However, this procedure can be abbreviated because we can change the registers in advance such that $\mathrm{pl}[\omega] = 1$. In Sect. 4, we explain our choices of $\ell$ and $R(\tilde{p})$ and show $\{\tilde{p}_s\}_{s=0}^{\tilde{\ell}}$ for all $n$.

Finally, we describe the number of qubits of our method and Banegas et al.'s method for Shor's algorithm. Banegas et al. [1] showed the number of qubits for Shor's algorithm using their quantum point addition algorithm with their quantum GCD-based inversion algorithm is $7n + \lfloor \log n \rfloor + 9$ for all $n$. Then, we show the number of qubits for our method for Shor's algorithm in Theorem 4

**Theorem 4.** *The number of qubits for using Algorithm 1 as a point addition with Algorithm 2 as an inversion algorithm which takes* $\{\tilde{p}_s\}_{s=0}^{\tilde{\ell}}$ *as an input is given by* $(2 + R(\tilde{p}))n + 1$.

Therefore, if we find a register-bounded addition chain with $R(\tilde{p}) \le 5$, our method achieves fewer qubits than Banegas et al.'s GCD-based method.

## 4 Comparison

In Sect. 4.1, we explain our choice of register-bounded addition chains and compare the number of qubits for an inversion. In Sect. 4.2, we describe the trade-off

**Table 1.** Our choice of register-bounded addition chains $\{\tilde{p}_s\}_{s=0}^{\tilde{\ell}}$

| $n$ | Register-bounded addition chains |
|---|---|
| 163 | $\{\tilde{p}_s\}_{s=0}^{14} = \{1, 2, 3, 6, 9, 6, 3, 2, 18, 27, 54, 27, 18, 108, 162\}$ |
| 233 | $\{\tilde{p}_s\}_{s=0}^{16} = \{1, 2, 3, 4, 7, 4, 3, 2, 14, 28, 29, 28, 14, 58, 116, 58, 232\}$ |
| 283 | $\{\tilde{p}_s\}_{s=0}^{18} = \{1, 2, 3, 6, 9, 15, 9, 6, 3, 30, 45, 47, 45, 30, 2, 94, 141, 94, 282\}$ |
| 571 | $\{\tilde{p}_s\}_{s=0}^{20} = \{1, 2, 3, 4, 7, 4, 3, 2, 14, 28, 29, 57, 29, 28, 14, 114, 171, 285, 171, 114, 570\}$ |

for our proposed inversion algorithm. In Sect. 4.3, we compare the quantum resources in a whole Shor's algorithm between our proposed method and previous methods.

### 4.1 Our Choice of Register-Bounded Addition Chains

As we showed in Theorem 2, the number of ancillary registers and the number of multiplications for our proposed inversion algorithm depends on $\{\tilde{p}_s\}_{s=0}^{\tilde{\ell}}$ for $n-1$. In particular, the number of ancillary registers equals $R(\tilde{p})$, and the number of multiplications equal $\tilde{\ell}$, where $\ell$ is the length of an addition chain $\{p_s\}_{s=0}^{\ell}$ for $n-1$ which consists of the different terms in $\{\tilde{p}_s\}_{s=0}^{\tilde{\ell}}$. As we described in Sect. 3.1, we consider the case of $r(\tilde{p}, \tilde{\ell}) = 2\ell - \tilde{\ell} = R(\tilde{p}) - 1$. In this situation, we reduce the number of qubits as much as possible, in other words, we find register-bounded addition chains $\{\tilde{p}_s\}_{s=0}^{\tilde{\ell}}$ with as small $R(\tilde{p})$ as possible. For this purpose, we find the shortest addition chains for $n - 1$ at first. After that, we add some terms to the shortest addition chains and get register-bounded addition chains. Thus, we find some register-bounded addition chains with as small $R(\tilde{p})$ as possible.

In Table 1, we show our register-bounded addition chains $\{\tilde{p}_s\}_{s=0}^{\tilde{\ell}}$ for NIST-recommended degrees $n = 163, 233, 283$, and 571. In Table 2, we show $\ell, R$ and the number of qubits for our proposed inversion algorithm and previous quantum inversion algorithms, i.e., Banegas et al.'s quantum GCD-based inversion algorithm which we call BBHL21-GCD, Kim-Hong's quantum GCD-based inversion algorithm which we call KH23-GCD, and Taguchi-Takayasu's quantum FLT-based inversion algorithm which we call TT23-FLT for all $n$. $R$ for our proposed algorithm is minimum $R(\tilde{p})$. We do not compare quantum FLT-based inversion algorithms proposed by Putranto et al. [10] and Banegas et al. [1] since Taguchi-Takayasu's FLT-based Basic and Extended algorithm reduce all quantum resources compared to them. We also do not compare Taguchi-Takayasu's Basic algorithm since their Extended algorithm requires fewer qubits than Basic algorithm. The number of qubits in Table 2 includes an input $f \in \mathbb{F}_{2^n}^*$. Table 2 indicates the minimum $R = R(\tilde{p})$ of register-bounded addition chains for $n - 1$ is 5 for all NIST-recommended $n$ when we use shortest addition chains for $n - 1$. Then, our proposed algorithm achieves the fewest qubits compared to the previous quantum FLT-based inversion algorithms, however, it is still larger than the number of both GCD-based algorithms for all cases.

**Table 2.** Comparison of $\ell, R$ and the number of qubits for an inversion between ours and prior works

| $n$ | Proposed algorithm | | | BBHL21-GCD | | | KH23-GCD | | | TT23-FLT | | |
|---|---|---|---|---|---|---|---|---|---|---|---|---|
| | $\ell$ | $R$ | qubits | $\ell$ | $R$ | qubits | $\ell$ | $R$ | qubits | $\ell$ | $R$ | qubits |
| 163 | 9 | 5 | 978 | – | – | 830 | – | – | 690 | 9 | 9 | 1,630 |
| 233 | 10 | 5 | 1,398 | – | – | 1,180 | – | – | 970 | 10 | 10 | 2,563 |
| 283 | 11 | 5 | 1,698 | – | – | 1,431 | – | – | 1,174 | 11 | 11 | 3,396 |
| 571 | 12 | 5 | 3,426 | – | – | 2,872 | – | – | 2,330 | 12 | 12 | 7,423 |

### 4.2 Quantum Resources Trade-Off in Our Proposed Inversion Algorithm

In Sect. 4.1, we showed register-bounded addition chains with $R(\tilde{p}) = 5$ for all $n$, where $R(\tilde{p})$ describes the number of ancillary registers. On the other hand, TT23-FLT requires $\ell$ ancillary registers, where $\ell$ is the length of shortest addition chains for $n-1$. As we described in Table 2, $\ell = 9, 10, 11, 12$ when $n = 163, 233, 283, 571$, respectively. Then, we also consider all possible cases, i.e., $R(\tilde{p}) = 5, 6, \ldots, \ell$ for our proposed inversion algorithm for all $n$ and estimate the quantum resources. We note that $R(\tilde{p}) = \ell$ is not the case of TT23-FLT since $r(\tilde{p}, \tilde{\ell}) = R(\tilde{p})-1 = \ell-1$ for our proposed algorithm. In other words, our proposed algorithm has a clear ancillary register at the end of the algorithm, while TT23-FLT has no clear ancillary register at the end of the algorithm. In Sect. 4.3, we show which $R(\tilde{p})$ is preferable in some parameters.

### 4.3 Comparison with Previous Methods in Shor's Algorithm

In this section, we compare the quantum resources of our method for Shor's algorithm, i.e., our proposed quantum inversion algorithm in Sect. 3.3 with our proposed quantum point addition algorithm described in Algorithm 1 and previous methods, i.e., BBHL21-GCD, KH23-GCD, and TT23-FLT with Banegas et al.'s quantum point addition algorithm, since previous three algorithms do not satisfy the conditions (i) and (ii) in Sect. 3.2.

Here, we concretely estimate the quantum resources, i.e., the number of qubits, TOF gates, and depth of our method and previous methods for Shor's algorithm. We also compute the number of CNOT gates, however, we note that a CNOT gate is much cheaper than a TOF gate. We note that Shor's algorithm requires $2n+2$ point additions. As Roetteler et al. [12] mentioned, we can ignore the special cases of point addition since it does not affect quantum Fourier transform. Moreover, we apply semiclassical Fourier transform [4] in Shor's algorithm since it requires only 1 qubit. Our proposed inversion algorithm uses the register-bounded addition chains of Table 1. For estimating the resources of TT23-FLT, we use addition chains that Taguchi and Takayasu [15] used. Values of the depth are upper bounds because we do not completely consider parallel quantum computation. Moreover, we compute the concrete number of CNOT gates of `SQUARE`,

**Table 3.** Comparison of the number of qubits, TOF gates, depth, and CNOT gates for Shor's algorithm between ours and prior works

| $n$ | Proposed method | | | |
|---|---|---|---|---|
| | qubits | TOF | depth | CNOT |
| 163 | 1,142 | 19,682,952 | 233,563,552 | 1,672,852,808 |
| 233 | 1,632 | 46,185,516 | 536,005,548 | 5,556,172,752 |
| 283 | 1,982 | 77,493,944 | 1,170,486,688 | 10,840,880,376 |
| 571 | 3,998 | 368,373,720 | 9,751,547,520 | 95,224,517,960 |
| $n$ | BBHL21-GCD method | | | |
| | qubits | TOF | depth | CNOT |
| 163 | 1,157 | 288,641,640 | 341,963,616 | 322,348,232 |
| 233 | 1,647 | 772,092,828 | 945,129,276 | 926,188,848 |
| 283 | 1,998 | 1,359,458,584 | 1,672,107,936 | 1,644,678,648 |
| 571 | 4,015 | 10,156,396,536 | 12,962,714,336 | 13,091,280,488 |
| $n$ | KH23-GCD method | | | |
| | qubits | TOF | depth | CNOT |
| 163 | 1,017 | 243,048,328 | 319,284,384 | 391,632,328 |
| 233 | 1,437 | 694,262,556 | 898,421,004 | 1,128,567,024 |
| 283 | 1,741 | 1,237,627,128 | 1,594,550,944 | 2,006,665,048 |
| 571 | 3,473 | 9,942,884,952 | 12,608,046,880 | 16,064,737,832 |
| $n$ | TT23-FLT method | | | |
| | qubits | TOF | depth | CNOT |
| 163 | 1,957 | 13,175,432 | 159,675,648 | 1,130,020,680 |
| 233 | 3,030 | 30,000,204 | 345,703,644 | 3,604,728,816 |
| 283 | 3,963 | 49,121,208 | 708,332,352 | 6,782,597,624 |
| 571 | 8,566 | 228,787,416 | 5,143,602,464 | 57,782,226,216 |

$\texttt{SQUARE}^{-1}$, and `spSQUARE`, and assume that `const_ADD` requires $n/2$ X gates on average, `ctrl_ADD` requires $n/2$ TOF gates on average, and `ctrl_const_ADD` requires $n/2$ CNOT gates on average. We estimate the upper bound of the depth of `SQUARE` as the number of CNOT gates for `SQUARE`, while we estimate the depth of `spSQUARE` as described in Sect. 3.3. We also apply the depth reduction for `SQUARE` and `spSQUARE` described in Sect. 3.3 to the TT23-FLT method and estimate the quantum resources. When we estimate the upper bound of the depth for Shor's algorithm, we simply add the upper bound of the depth for each distinct quantum computation. Banegas et al. [1] applied windowing that reduces the number of TOF gates by using some lookups from a QROM and estimated the number of TOF gates. We note that we can also apply windowing our proposed method while we do not estimate the quantum resources. We provide a python code [14] for computing quantum resources.

**Table 4.** Comparison of QD = "the number of qubits" × "depth" in Shor's algorithm between ours and prior works

| $n$ | QD | | | |
|---|---|---|---|---|
| | Proposed method | BBHL21-GCD method | KH23-GCD method | TT23-FLT method |
| 163 | $2.67 \cdot 10^{11}$ | $3.96 \cdot 10^{11}$ | $3.25 \cdot 10^{11}$ | $3.12 \cdot 10^{11}$ |
| 233 | $8.75 \cdot 10^{11}$ | $1.56 \cdot 10^{12}$ | $1.29 \cdot 10^{12}$ | $1.05 \cdot 10^{12}$ |
| 283 | $2.32 \cdot 10^{12}$ | $3.34 \cdot 10^{12}$ | $2.78 \cdot 10^{12}$ | $2.81 \cdot 10^{12}$ |
| 571 | $3.89 \cdot 10^{13}$ | $5.20 \cdot 10^{13}$ | $4.38 \cdot 10^{13}$ | $4.41 \cdot 10^{13}$ |

**Table 5.** Comparison of QT = "the number of qubits" × "the number of TOF gates" in Shor's algorithm between ours and prior works

| $n$ | QT | | | |
|---|---|---|---|---|
| | Proposed method | BBHL21-GCD method | KH23-GCD method | TT23-FLT method |
| 163 | $2.25 \cdot 10^{10}$ | $3.34 \cdot 10^{11}$ | $2.47 \cdot 10^{11}$ | $2.58 \cdot 10^{10}$ |
| 233 | $7.54 \cdot 10^{10}$ | $1.27 \cdot 10^{12}$ | $9.98 \cdot 10^{11}$ | $9.09 \cdot 10^{10}$ |
| 283 | $1.54 \cdot 10^{11}$ | $2.72 \cdot 10^{12}$ | $2.15 \cdot 10^{12}$ | $1.95 \cdot 10^{11}$ |
| 571 | $1.47 \cdot 10^{12}$ | $4.08 \cdot 10^{13}$ | $3.45 \cdot 10^{13}$ | $1.96 \cdot 10^{12}$ |

Table 3 compares the number of qubits, TOF gates, depth, and CNOT gates in all cases for all $n$. We show the quantum resources in the case of $R(\tilde{p}) = 5$ for our proposed method. We compare our proposed method with the previous GCD-based methods and the FLT-based method.

**Comparison with the GCD-Based Methods.** The number of qubits for our proposed method is close to the GCD-based methods, i.e., the BBHL21-GCD method and the KH23-GCD method for all $n$. Especially, our proposed method achieves fewer qubits than the BBHL21-GCD method, while it does not for an inversion as shown in Table 2. As described in Sect. 3.2, our proposed method for Shor's algorithm requires $(2+R(\tilde{p}))n+1$ qubits. Furthermore, we found register-bounded addition chains with $R(\tilde{p}) = 5$ for all $n$. Then, the number of qubits is $7n + 1$ and it is smaller than the number of qubits for the BBHL21-GCD method, i.e., $7n + \lfloor \log n \rfloor + 9$. The KH23-GCD method requires fewer qubits than our proposed method, however, the difference is less than $n$. Precisely, the KH23-GCD method requires $6n + 4\lfloor \log n \rfloor + 11$ qubits and the difference to $7n + 1$ is $n - 4\lfloor \log n \rfloor - 10$. Furthermore, our proposed method still achieves much fewer TOF gates and less depth compared to the GCD-based methods while we halve the number of qubits from the TT23-FLT method. The number of TOF gates of our proposed method is from only 2% to 5% of the number of the GCD-based methods. As for the depth, the depth reduction of the squaring part in our algorithm in Sect. 3.3 contributes to keeping fewer than the GCD-based methods.

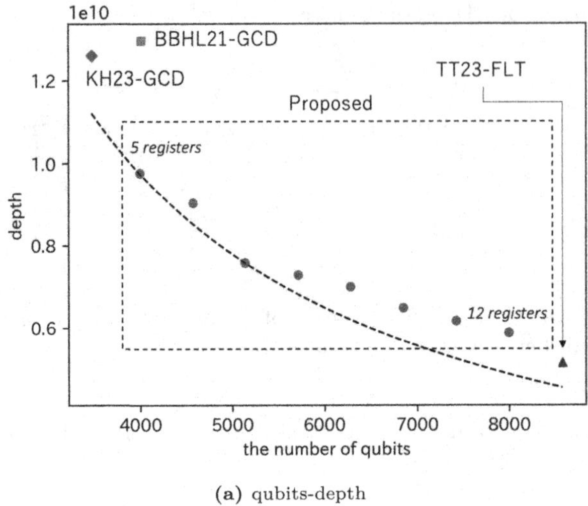


(a) qubits-depth

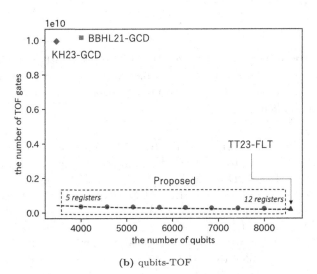

(b) qubits-TOF

**Fig. 1.** Quantum resources trade-off in all methods for $n = 571$

**Comparison with the TT23-FLT Method.** Our proposed method drastically reduces the number of qubits from the TT23-FLT method. Precisely, we halve the qubits for all $n$. Our proposed inversion algorithm applies additional procedures for uncomputations which require TOF gates, depth, and CNOT gates to TT23-FLT. When $n = 571$, our proposed inversion algorithm requires 8 additional procedures which is about 70% of the number of procedures for TT23-FLT. As you can see in Table 3, the number of TOF gates, depth, and CNOT gates for our proposed method is about 170% of the number for the TT23-FLT method.

By using the concrete number of quantum resources, we compute two values, i.e., "the number of qubits" × "depth" called QD and "the number of qubits" × "the number of TOF gates" called QT. QD is a same metric to "spacetime volume" by Gidney and Ekerå [3] and QT is a similar metric. Gidney and Ekerå used spacetime volume to evaluate Shor's algorithm for solving a factoring problem. Briefly speaking, QD and QT describe how a quantum algorithm works better on both the number of qubits and the number of TOF gates and both the number of qubits and depth, respectively. We show QD and QT for our proposed method and previous methods for all $n$ in Tables 4, 5, respectively. We also illustrate the relation between the number of qubits and depth and between the number of qubits and the number of TOF gates of our proposed method and the previous methods for $n = 571$ in Fig. 1. Blue lines in Fig. 1 describe the points that QD = const. and QT = const.

In Tables 4, 5, $R(\tilde{p}) = 5, 5, 5, 7$ and $R(\tilde{p}) = 5, 5, 5, 5$ for our proposed method for $n = 163, 233, 283, 571$, respectively. Our proposed method achieves the fewest QD and QT compared to the previous method for all $n$. Thus, our proposed algorithm gives good trade-offs between the number of qubits and depth and between the number of qubits and the number of TOF gates.

**Acknowledgements.** This research was in part conducted under a contract of "Research and Development for Expansion of Radio Wave Resources (JPJ000254)" the Ministry of Internal Affairs and Communications, Japan, and JSPS KAKENHI Grant Numbers JP19K20267 and JP21H03440, Japan.

## References

1. Banegas, G., Bernstein, D.J., van Hoof, I., Lange, T.: Concrete quantum cryptanalysis of binary elliptic curves. IACR Trans. CHES **2021**(1), 451–472 (2020)
2. Cameron, F., Patrick, D.: FIPS PUB 186-4 digital signature standard (DSS). In: NIST, pp. 92–101 (2013)
3. Gidney, C., Ekerå, M.: How to factor 2048 bit ch1RSA integers in 8 hours using 20 million noisy qubits. Quantum **5**, 433 (2021)
4. Griffiths, R.B., Niu, C.S.: Semiclassical Fourier transform for quantum computation. Phys. Rev. Lett. **76**(17), 3228–3231 (1996). https://doi.org/10.1103/physrevlett.76.3228
5. van Hoof, I.: Space-efficient quantum multiplication of polynomials for binary finite fields with sub-quadratic Toffoli gate count. Cryptology ePrint Archive, Paper 2019/1170 (2019)
6. Kim, H., Hong, S.: New space-efficient quantum algorithm for binary elliptic curves using the optimized division algorithm. Quant. Inf. Process. **22**(6), 237 (2023)
7. Kim, S., Kim, I., Kim, S., Hong, S.: Toffoli gate count optimized space-efficient quantum circuit for binary field multiplication. Cryptology ePrint Archive, Paper 2022/1095 (2022). https://eprint.iacr.org/2022/1095
8. Koblitz, N.: Elliptic curve cryptosystems. Math. Comput. **48**(177), 203–209 (1987)

9. Miller, V.S.: Use of elliptic curves in cryptography. In: Williams, H.C. (ed.) CRYPTO '85. Lecture Notes in Computer Science, vol. 218, pp. 417–426. Springer, Cham (1985)
10. Putranto, D.S.C., Wardhani, R.W., Larasati, H.T., Kim, H.: Another concrete quantum cryptanalysis of binary elliptic curves. Cryptology ePrint Archive, Paper 2022/501 (2022). https://eprint.iacr.org/2022/501
11. Rivest, R.L., Shamir, A., Adleman, L.M.: A method for obtaining digital signatures and public-key cryptosystems. Commun. ACM **21**(2), 120–126 (1978)
12. Roetteler, M., Naehrig, M., Svore, K.M., Lauter, K.: Quantum resource estimates for computing elliptic curve discrete logarithms. In: Takagi, T., Peyrin, T. (eds.) ASIACRYPT 2017. LNCS, vol. 10625, pp. 241–270. Springer, Heidelberg (2017). https://doi.org/10.1007/978-3-319-70697-9_9
13. Shor, P.: Algorithms for quantum computation: discrete logarithms and factoring. In: FOCS 1994, pp. 124–134 (1994)
14. Taguchi, R.: Quantum resource estimate for Shor's algorithm for solving binary ECDLP. Github (2023). https://github.com/RenTaguchi/Quantum-resource-estimate-for-Shor-s-algorithm
15. Taguchi, R., Takayasu, A.: Concrete quantum cryptanalysis of binary elliptic curves via addition chain. In: Rosulek, M. (ed.) CT-RSA 2023. LNCS, vol. 13871, pp. 57–83. Springer, Heidelberg (2023). https://doi.org/10.1007/978-3-031-30872-7_3

# Breaking DPA-Protected Kyber via the Pair-Pointwise Multiplication

Estuardo Alpirez Bock[1], Gustavo Banegas[2], Chris Brzuska[3], Łukasz Chmielewski[4(✉)], Kirthivaasan Puniamurthy[3], and Milan Šorf[4]

[1] Xiphera LTD, Espoo, Finland
estuardo.alpirezbock@xiphera.com
[2] Qualcomm France SARL, Valbonne, France
gustavo@cryptme.in
[3] Aalto University, Espoo, Finland
{chris.brzuska,kirthivaasan.puniamurthy}@aalto.fi
[4] Masaryk University, Brno, Czech Republic
{chmiel,xsorf}@fi.muni.cz

**Abstract.** We introduce a novel template attack for secret key recovery in Kyber, leveraging side-channel information from polynomial multiplication during decapsulation. Conceptually, our attack exploits that Kyber's incomplete number-theoretic transform (NTT) causes each secret coefficient to be used multiple times, unlike when performing a complete NTT.

Our attack is a single trace *known* ciphertext attack that avoids machine-learning techniques and instead relies on correlation-matching only. Additionally, our template generation method is very simple and easy to replicate, and we describe different attack strategies, varying on the number of templates required. Moreover, our attack applies to both masked implementations as well as designs with multiplication shuffling.

We demonstrate its effectiveness by targeting a masked implementation from the *mkm4* repository. We initially perform simulations in the noisy Hamming-Weight model and achieve high success rates with just 13 316 templates while tolerating noise values up to $\sigma = 0.3$. In a practical setup, we measure power consumption and notice that our attack falls short of expectations. However, we introduce an extension inspired by known online template attacks, enabling us to recover 128 coefficient pairs from a single polynomial multiplication. Our results provide evidence that the incomplete NTT, which is used in Kyber-768 and similar schemes, introduces an additional side-channel weakness worth further exploration.

**Keywords:** Post-quantum Cryptography · Template attack · Kyber · Side-channel Attack · Single Trace

Author list in alphabetical order; see https://www.ams.org/profession/leaders/CultureStatement04.pdf. Date of this document: 2024-02-20.


C. Pöpper and L. Batina (Eds.): ACNS 2024, LNCS 14584, pp. 101–130, 2024.
https://doi.org/10.1007/978-3-031-54773-7_5

# 1 Introduction

NIST selected Kyber [3,8] to be standardized as a post-quantum secure key encapsulation mechanism (KEM) after a rigorous competition. The primary security requirement of the NIST competition is achieving message confidentiality against chosen-plaintext (CPA) and chosen-ciphertext attacks (CCA) based on plausibly post-quantum hard problems. Additionally, the competition emphasizes the resistance of implementations to side-channel attacks. This paper builds upon the previous research exploiting differences in side-channel traces based on the chosen inputs [6,20,21] to design a new single-trace template attack against masked Kyber implementations. In particular, we target the decapsulation phase, leveraging templates to extract the long-term secret key from the polynomial multiplication process. Our goal is to show that in this context, masking is not sufficient protection, even considering relatively simple attacks.

Kyber's key encapsulation (encryption) performs a matrix-vector multiplication in the ring of polynomials $\mathcal{R}_q = \mathbb{Z}_q[x]/(x^{256}+1)$ and then adds a small noise vector to the result. In turn, Kyber's decapsulation (decryption), multiplies a ciphertext $\mathsf{b}$ and a secret $\mathsf{a}$, each of which corresponds to a polynomial. Polynomials in Kyber are of degree 255 and their coefficients are integers between 0 and $q-1$, with $q = 3329$. Kyber turns this core IND-CPA-secure scheme into IND-CCA-secure encryption using the Fujisaki-Okamoto (FO) transform [16]. Black-box security against IND-CCA security, however, does not protect against known/chosen ciphertext *side-channel* attacks, since the input ciphertext is always multiplied with the secret key right at the beginning of the decapsulation process, cf. [4,14,17,33].

**Number Theoretic Transform and Pair-Pointwise Multiplication.** Standard polynomial multiplication has a quadratic time complexity. Therefore, Kyber and similar lattice-based systems employ the Number Theoretic Transform (NTT) to convert polynomials into a representation where multiplication takes linear time. In the NTT domain, polynomial multiplications can be computed point-wise. Given polynomials $\hat{\mathsf{a}}$ and $\hat{\mathsf{b}}$ with coefficients $(a_0, a_1, \ldots, a_{n-1})$ and $(b_0, b_1, \ldots, b_{n-1})$ respectively, their point-wise multiplication is $\hat{\mathsf{a}} \circ \hat{\mathsf{b}} = (a_0 \cdot b_0, a_1 \cdot b_1, \ldots, a_{n-1} \cdot b_{n-1})$, whereby each pointwise multiplication is performed independently. Kyber uses a small modulus and thus applies the NTT *partially*, resulting in multiplications of polynomials *of degree 1*, e.g., $(a_0 + a_1X) \cdot (b_0 + b_1X)$ which we refer to as *pair-pointwise* multiplication.

## 1.1 Our Contribution

We propose an attack on the pair-pointwise multiplication of Kyber-like implementations and start by observing that Kyber executes more secret-dependent operations than lattice-based schemes, which perform a full NTT:

1. Instead of *one* multiplication (as in full NTT), in pair-point multiplications, *three* multiplications (cf. Eq. (3)) depend on the same coefficient pair.

2. Since multiplications are performed mod $q$, the code requires 3 additional operations to execute a *modulus* reduction after each multiplication.
3. While $a_i \in [0, \ldots, q-1]$ are 12-bit integers, the registers operate on 24-bit and 28-bit integers before the modulus reduction. Thus, in the Hamming weight model, the expected information per instruction is $H(24) \approx 3.34$ and $H(28) \approx 3.45$ bits of information rather than only $H(12) \approx 2.84$.

Starting from these observations, we devise an attack which extracts each coefficient from a pair-point multiplication individually and requires $q+q$ templates. We next explore an extension of our attack that extracts pairs of coefficients from each pair-point multiplication via $q^2$ templates, but has a much higher success probability given that the templates target complete regions of pair-point multiplications and thus have more samples for comparison with the target trace. Then we validate our attacks against the masked implementation of [2]. We first conduct simulations showing that a template attack with $100q$ templates succeeds with the probability $\geq 0.999$ even in the presence of Gaussian noise with standard deviation $\sigma \leq 0.87$. Our attack strategy requires a single target trace from a known ciphertext and avoids complex attack methods like machine learning, since it succeeds by performing simple correlation analysis. We refer the reader to Sect. 3 for the specific steps of our attack and its adaptations.

*Experimental Results.* We perform a power analysis attack also on the masked implementation of Kyber [2] using the ChipWhisperer Lite platform [30]. We detect leakage for both $q+q$ and $q^2$ attacks, but unfortunately it is not enough to recover a pair of coefficients from a pair-point multiplication. We show that the low success of these experiments is influenced by microarchitectural aspects and the implementation we target: essentially, the power profile of a pair-point multiplication is slightly influenced by the operations done before it started[1].

However, the success rate, especially for the $q^2$ attack, is quite promising and therefore, to make the attack work we come up with an extension inspired by the Online Template Attack (OTA), originally used to attack elliptic curve cryptography [5,6]. OTA is a powerful technique residing between horizontal and template attacks with the main distinctive characteristics of building the templates after capturing the target trace and not before. The combined attack works as follows: first we reduce the number of candidate templates using the $q^2$ attack and then we launch iteratively OTA to limit the microarchitectural noise. This way we are able to recover all the coefficients of 128 pair-pointwise multiplications. In particular, we completely recover all coefficients for 3 attacked target traces at the cost of maximum 43M templates. While these numbers are high, they are required to recover all the coefficients from a single trace.

We also estimated how many templates we need to attack masked Kyber768 with the order 2. Here we need more templates since such implementation uses 6 full polynomial multiplications. For such attack we would need 78M to achieve 43% success rate and to increase it to 90% we need approximately 105M traces.

[1] For details the attacks and the experiments see Sect. 5.

With respect to the experiments it is also an interesting question whether our experiments may provide better results if we use electro-magnetic emanations as the side-channel information instead of power consumption. It would be also interesting to see whether we can lower the number of used templates. We leave these investigations as future work.

### 1.2 State of the Art

Attacks on the polynomial multiplication of Kyber were successfully performed using correlation power analysis techniques [27]. However, early proposals recognized the need to apply masking to the polynomial multiplication in lattice-based schemes as a countermeasure against side-channel analysis [29,34,35]. Consequently, many research efforts have focused on attacking other components of the Kyber decapsulation process. Primas, Pessl, and Mangard introduced a template attack on the inverse NTT during decryption, enabling them to recover a decrypted message and subsequently extract the session key [32]. This attack leverages belief propagation for template matching and has since been extended and improved in subsequent works [17,31]. In a different approach, Dubrova, Ngo, and Gärtner propose the use of deep learning techniques to recover the message and subsequently extract the long-term secret key [15] from the re-encryption step of decapsulation. Notably, research in this area has demonstrated the success of deep learning in attacking lattice-based schemes [4,22,26,28]. Further SCA attacks on masked implementations of Kyber were presented on the message encoding [37] and on the arithmetic-to-boolean conversion step [38]. Note that all works cited above attack parts of Kyber other than the pointwise multiplication.

Our attack differs from the previous attacks in two significant ways when applied to masked implementations: we directly extract the long-term secret key from pointwise multiplication and we do not require deep learning or belief propagation for template construction and matching. Although machine learning (ML) techniques were shown to be particularly successful again post-quantum schemes, for example, in [15], we prefer a more classical approach based on Pearson correlation matching due to the following reasons: (1) the attack description is simpler, (2) the attack is easier to replicate since the adversary does not require the knowledge of ML, (3) it is easier to explain where the leakage comes from and thus come up with countermeasures, and (4) crucially we wanted to show that (even) classic side-channel methods effectively extract the key from masked Kyber.

In parallel to this work, the authors of [40] developed a single-trace template attack on Kyber's polynomial multiplication. Their successful experiments validate exploitable leakage in single traces, but their approach differs from ours. They focus on key generation and encryption, exploiting additional side-channel leakage due to the multiplication of secret polynomials with $k$ values in matrix

$A$. Their method employs Hamming Weight templates for multiple intermediates, using key enumeration akin to belief propagation. Notably, they target an unmasked implementation *pqm4* [1], while we target the optimized masked implementation *mkm4* [2], enhancing the practicality of our approach for protected libraries. See Appendix D for a detailed comparison.

## 2 Notation and Preliminaries

We represent matrices by bold capital letters $\mathbf{A}$, and vectors by bold small letters $\mathbf{b}$, $\mathsf{b}$. Given a polynomial $a = \sum_{i=0}^{n-1} a_i X^i$ of degree $n-1$, we usually write $a$ as a vector $a = (a_0, a_1, a_2, ..., a_{n-1})$. Also, the operation $\cdot$ represents standard multiplication between two integers, while $\circ$ represents point-wise multiplication between two polynomials in NTT domain (cf. Subsect. 2.2). When writing polynomial $a$ in NTT domain, we will often write $\hat{a}$ for clarity and also use the hat notation for matrices, e.g., $\hat{\mathbf{A}}$.

We next provide descriptions of Kyber. Our descriptions of the algorithms will be simplified and we will elaborate mostly on the parts of the KEM that are relevant to our attack. We refer the reader to the supporting documentation from Kyber for more details on the KEM [3].

### 2.1 Kyber

As previously mentioned, Kyber is a lattice-based KEM. It relies on the hardness of the Module-LWE problem. The latest parameters for Kyber are: $n = 256, q = 3329, \eta = 2$ and module dimension $k = 2$, 3, or 4. The security level of Kyber increases with its module dimension (in the case $k$).

Algorithm 1 gives the overview of the key generation. The private key of Kyber consists of a vector of polynomials of degree $n = 256$, and with coefficients in $R_q$ with $q = 3329$. The $k$ determines the dimension of the vector. The functions $\text{SAMPLE}_U$ and $\text{SAMPLE}_B$ are functions which uniformly sample values in the ring $R_q$ given a seed. The $\text{SAMPLE}_U$ provides a uniform random matrix, and $\text{SAMPLE}_B$ gives uniform random vectors. The function $\mathsf{H}$ is a secure hash function (SHA3 in Kyber).

Algorithm 2 shows the decapsulation algorithm. Note that the ciphertext is first decompressed into its standard form $\mathsf{b}$, and then in line 3 the ciphertext is transformed to its NTT domain. After this transformation, a pair-pointwise multiplication between $\hat{\mathsf{a}}$ and $\hat{\mathsf{b}}$. This operation will be the target of *our attack*.

**Alg. 1:** Kyber-CCA2-KEM Key Generation (simplified)

Public key $pk$, secret key $sk$ Choose uniform seeds $\rho, \sigma, z$;
$\hat{\mathbf{A}} \in R_q^{k \times k} \leftarrow \textsc{Sample}_U(\rho)$;
$\mathbf{a}, \mathbf{e} \in R_q^k \leftarrow \textsc{Sample}_B(\sigma)$;
$\hat{\mathbf{a}} \leftarrow \mathsf{NTT}(a)$;
$\hat{\mathbf{t}} \leftarrow \hat{\mathbf{A}} \circ \hat{\mathbf{a}} + \mathsf{NTT}(e)$;
$pk \leftarrow (\hat{\mathbf{t}}, \rho)$; $sk \leftarrow (\hat{\mathbf{a}}, pk, \mathsf{H}(pk), z)$;
**return** $pk, sk$;

**Alg. 2:** Kyber-CCA2-KEM Decryption (simplified)

secret key $sk = (\hat{\mathbf{a}}, pk, \mathsf{H}(pk), z)$, ciphertext $c = (\mathbf{c_1}, c_2)$
**Output:** Shared key $K$
$\mathbf{b}, v \leftarrow \textsc{Decompress}(\mathbf{c_1}, c_2)$;
$m \leftarrow \textsc{Decode}(v - \mathsf{NTT}^{-1}(\hat{\mathbf{a}})^T \circ \mathsf{NTT}(\mathbf{b})))$;
$(\bar{K}, \tau) \leftarrow \mathsf{H}(m || \mathsf{H}(pk))$;
$c' \leftarrow \text{PKE.}\textsc{Enc}(pk, m, \tau)$;
**if** $c = c'$ **then**
  $K \leftarrow \mathsf{KDF}(\bar{K} || \mathsf{H}(c))$;
**else**
  $K \leftarrow \mathsf{KDF}(z || \mathsf{H}(c))$;
**return** $K$;

We do not describe the encryption and encapsulation functions of Kyber since we do not attack these algorithms, for details, see Appendix A.

## 2.2 Number Theoretic Transform (NTT)

Kyber performs polynomial multiplications and speeds it up to *linear* time by transforming the polynomials into the NTT domain, allowing for a so-called *pointwise* multiplication between the polynomials. The NTT is a version of Fast Fourier Transform (FFT) over a finite ring. To perform the transformation, one evaluates the polynomial at powers of a primitive root of unity, which are usually represented by the symbol $\zeta$. We refer to [23] for details on how to implement the NTT (in Kyber and Dilithium) and cover relevant aspects of Kyber below. Kyber has dimension $k$, and each dimension has its own roots $\zeta_k^0, \zeta_k^1, \ldots, \zeta_k^{n-1}$. In the following, we focus on a single dimension for ease of presentation.

**The NTT on Kyber.** In Kyber, the $n$-th root of unity does not exist and therefore, the $2n$-th roots of unity are used so that modulus polynomial $X^n + 1$ is factored into polynomials of degree 2 rather, i.e., Kyber performs an *incomplete* NTT, where the last layer is not executed. Therefore, in Kyber, after the (incomplete) NTT transformation, a polynomial $a$ corresponds to 128 polynomials of degree 1 each. Polynomial $a$ is thus transformed to $\mathsf{NTT}(a) = a_0 + a_1 x, \ldots, a_{254} x + a_{255} x$. The incomplete transformation of the polynomials to their NTT domains has an impact on the way, multiplications are performed in Kyber. Namely, when computing the multiplication between two transformed polynomials, we are not computing a point-wise multiplication between the coefficients of the polynomials (i.e. $a \cdot b = (a_0 b_0 = c_0, a_1 b_1 = c_1, \ldots, a_n b_n = c_n))$. Instead, we multiply the coefficients pairwise and, for instance, the first two coefficients of the resulting polynomial are obtained as follows:

$$c_1 = a_0 b_1 + a_1 b_0, \quad c_0 = a_0 b_0 + a_1 b_1 \zeta. \tag{1}$$

We will denote the multiplication in Eq. (1) as *pair-pointwise*.

**Multiplication Optimizations.** In Eq. (1), we see a very straightforward way of calculating a pair-pointwise multiplication, and obtaining the resulting two adjacent coefficients of a polynomial. We see that a total of 5 multiplications are performed. This multiplication process can be optimized via the Karatsuba algorithm in such a way that we only need to perform 4 multiplications per each pair-pointwise multiplication:

$$\begin{aligned}&(a_0 + a_1x)(b_0 + b_1x) \bmod (x^2 - \zeta)\\&= a_0b_0 + ((a_0 + a_1)(b_0 + b_1) - a_0b_0 - a_1b_1)x + a_1b_1x^2\\&= a_0b_0 + a_1b_1\zeta + ((a_0 + a_1)(b_0 + b_1) - a_0b_0 - a_1b_1)x.\end{aligned} \tag{2}$$

Thus, we can obtain the resulting polynomial $c_0 + c_1x$ via

$$c_0 = a_0b_0 + a_1b_1\zeta, \qquad c_1 = (a_0 + a_1)(b_0 + b_1) - (a_0b_0 + a_1b_1). \tag{3}$$

Observe that Karatsuba multiplication is the most popular approach for implementing pair-pointwise multiplication in Kyber. It allows us to reduce the number of multiplications from five to four. The software implementation has adopted the approach we analyze in this paper; it was also used in public hardware implementations of Kyber such as [39].

**Masking Kyber.** There are several proposals to mask lattice-based schemes such as NTRU [29] and Saber [7], whereby the following works present concrete masking schemes for Kyber [10,18]. The masking of the schemes addresses various secret-dependent operations, such as computing inverse NTT, the key derivation function in the decapsulation process, or more commonly, masking polynomial multiplication with the long-term secret. The approach for masking polynomial multiplication in Kyber follows a similar pattern to other cryptographic schemes: the secret is divided into shares, and secret-dependent operations are performed on each share. The results are then combined. In the case of Kyber, this involves splitting the secret polynomials into shares and multiplying the input ciphertext separately with each share.

### 2.3 Online Template Attacks

*Online Template Attack (OTA)*, introduced in [5,6], is a powerful technique residing between horizontal and template attacks. The main distinctive characteristic is building the templates after capturing the target trace and not before like in classical template attacks [12]. In general, creating templates in advance is feasible when the number of possible templates is small, like for example, for a binary exponentiation algorithm, where templates need to distinguish a single branch result, which only requires two templates [12]. However, if the number of leaking features increases, the number of different templates could be infeasible to generate in advance. This scenario is where OTAs enter into play by capturing templates on-demand based on secret guesses [5,6].

In general, OTA works as follows: the attacker creates templates corresponding to partial guesses of the secret and then matches the templates to the target trace; the best matching indicates which guess was correct. The attacker continues by iteratively targeting new parts of the secret until it is fully recovered.

In recent years OTA was applied in many scenarios, most notably, against Frodo post-quantum proposal [9] and several crypto-libraries (`libgcrypt`, `mbedTLS`, and `wolfSSL`) using microarchitectural side-channels [11].

We will use OTA in our experiments to improve the success rate of our attacks to 100%, namely, we will first use attacks to learn the secret coefficients and the remaining entropy we will recover using OTA (for details see Sect. 5).

## 3 Our Attack

In this section, we detail our template attack on Kyber's decapsulation, extracting secret coefficients $\mathsf{a}$ during polynomial multiplication. We outline the attack steps, explore variations with fewer or more templates impacting key recovery success, and discuss its application to masked implementations. Additionally, we explain its extension to target implementations employing shuffling in polynomial multiplication.

### 3.1 Attack Steps—Extracting the Key via $q + q$ Templates

The ciphertexts which we use for creating our templates have a specific structure when represented in NTT (see below). Since the (incomplete) NTT is an efficiently computable bijection, we can create the desired structure by choosing a vector of which we set 128 polynomials of degree 1 (in NTT domain) and then compute the ciphertext by applying the inverse NTT (see Sect. 2.2) to this vector. Additionally, we also perform the compression since the input ciphertexts are provided to the decapsulation algorithm in compressed form (see Algorithm 2).

We recall that the compression and decompression algorithms may introduce some errors in the least significant bits of some coefficients of the polynomials. Thus, when setting a value $\hat{\mathsf{b}}$ with a desired structure, and then transforming it into its standard domain $\mathbf{b}$, we should check whether $\mathbf{b}$ can be compressed and decompressed such that $\textsc{Decompress}(\textsc{Compress}(\mathbf{b})) = \mathbf{b}$. If that holds, we ensure that on line 2 of Algorithm 2, $\mathsf{NTT}(\mathbf{b})$ is indeed transformed into a vector with the structure we initially desired. In [17], the authors deal with the same issue for their chosen ciphertext attack on the decapsulation process of Kyber. The authors need a ciphertext $\mathbf{b}$ which on NTT domain would be sparse, and they present two methods for generating such ciphertexts and ensuring that they would preserve the desired properties after compression and decompression. For our attack, it is much easier to deal with this issue since the structure we desire for the NTT-ed value is much more flexible as we explain below.

In essence, for our attack, we simply require a ciphertext vector which on NTT domain has either of the two following properties: (1) For each pair of coefficient values $b_0, b_1$, it holds that $b_0 \neq b_1$, or (2) For any two coefficients

$b_i, b_j$ in $\mathbf{b}$ it holds that $b_i \neq b_j$. The first property is enough for attacking unprotected and even masked implementations. The second property will be relevant for attacking designs that implement shuffling of the polynomial multiplication (see Subsect. 3.2). Naturally, vectors with the second property can also be used for attacking masked or unprotected implementations since the second property implies the first property. Our advantage is that there is no restriction with respect to the specific values these coefficients should have. Thus, when generating the inputs, we could simply set the desired vector $\hat{\mathsf{b}}$, run the inverse NTT on it and then check whether the result preserves its form after compression and decompression. Moreover, it is not even necessary that the vector in the standard domain preserves its original form. It is only important that the resulting vector can be transformed via NTT into a vector with any of the properties listed above. Therefore, it should be easy to just try out some values. Another simple strategy could be to set a vector in the standard domain $\mathbf{b}$ with small coefficients. The small values ensure that the coefficients will preserve their original values after compression and decompression. Then, we can simply apply NTT to $\mathbf{b}$ and check whether the resulting vector $\hat{\mathsf{b}}$ has the desired properties. Finally, we point out that finding input ciphertexts that achieve the second property can be done very easily and we may not even need to choose those ciphertexts ourselves. Thus, our attack can also be described as a *known* ciphertext attack.

We will now explain the attack that uses only $2q$ templates to recover $\mathsf{a}$.

**Step 1: Template Building.** We build our templates on a device identical to the device we are going to attack. In this device, we are able to set the value of the secret key. We start by building a template for the case that the secret $\hat{\mathsf{a}}$ consists only of zero coefficients: $\hat{\mathsf{a}} = (0_0, \ldots, 0_{255})$. For the input ciphertext, we can choose any ciphertext for which the coefficients corresponding to $b_0$ and $b_1$ are always different, i.e. $b_0 \neq b_1$. For example, we consider the following ciphertext: $\hat{\mathsf{b}} = (2649_0, 317_1, 2649_2, 317_3, \ldots, 2649_{254}, 317_{255})$. We record thus a power trace and obtain the template $T_0$. We repeat this process for all possible values between 0 and $q-1$ and obtain templates $T_1, T_2, \ldots, T_{q-1}$. For each new template, we change the value of $\hat{\mathsf{a}}$ accordingly (i.e. setting $\hat{\mathsf{a}} = (1_0, 1_1, 1_2, \ldots, 1_{255}), \hat{\mathsf{a}} = (2_0, 2_1, 2_2, \ldots, 2_{255})$, etc) and we always use the same ciphertext $\hat{\mathsf{b}}$.

**Step 2: Obtaining the Target Trace.** We now turn to the target device running a key decapsulation of Kyber and querying it using the same ciphertext $\mathsf{b}$, which on NTT domain maps to the ciphertext $\hat{\mathsf{b}}$ we used in **Step 1**. We record a power trace during execution and obtain our *target trace* $T_t$.

We now have our set of templates and our target trace and can perform template matching. The idea is that we will obtain enough information to identify good matches for operations involving the operands $a_1$, since this coefficient is used independently in several operations during each pair-point multiplication. We assume that it would be harder to identify any matches for coefficients $a_0$ since this coefficient is only used once during each pair-point multiplication.

**Step 3: Template Matching.** We match the target trace $T_t$ with each template $T_j$ and we expect to see no correlations between any regions of the traces, *unless* both the target trace and the template used the same operands $a_1, b_0, b_1$ within some pair-point multiplication. First, we compare the target trace with the template $T_0$. There are a total of 128 pair-point multiplications and, thus, a total of 128 regions corresponding to this operation in the power traces. We can numerate each region sequentially from 0 to 127. If we observe some correlations between the target $T_t$ and our template $T_0$ on region $i$, then we will know that the operand $a_{2i+1}$ has the value 0. We then repeat the process with all remaining templates, or until we have extracted all $a_1$ operands of the polynomial $\hat{\mathsf{a}}$.

**Step 4: Template Building with Extracted Coefficients.** We will now use the coefficient values extracted in the previous step to build a new set of templates. These templates will help us extract all operands corresponding to $a_0$ in each pair-point multiplication, i.e. all even coefficients.

Let us denote by $\psi$ an operand $a_1$ whose value was extracted in the previous step. In essence, we can now build templates in the same way as we did in **Step 1**, but the keys $\hat{\mathsf{a}}$ will now have the following structure. For each value $j \in [0, 1, \ldots, 3328]$ we construct a template for, i.e. each value we set for the key during each template generation, we set the key as follows: $\hat{\mathsf{a}} = (j_0, \psi_1, j_2, \psi_3, \ldots, j_{254}, \psi_{255})$. We will denote the templates generated during this step as $T_{j,\psi}$, and we will generate all of them the same way as described in **Step 1**, using the same input ciphertext $\hat{\mathsf{b}}$. We obtain a total of $q$ new templates $T_{j,\psi}$.

**Step 5: Template Matching.** We perform template matching in the exact same way as we did in **Step 3**, but using the templates $T_{j,\psi}$ obtained in **Step 4**. We now expect to see correlations, which will let us extract all $a_0$ values. As opposed to the template matching we performed on **Step 3**, we now will have more points of comparison for finding correlations between some template $T_{j,\psi}$ and the target trace $T_t$. Namely, for a template corresponding to the correct $j$ for some $a_0$, we now expect to find correlations not only on the single multiplication $a_0 \cdot b_0$, but also on all remaining operations dependent on $a_0$ and $a_1$, i.e. all operations within the pair-point multiplication. Since the value for $a_1$ has already been taken into consideration, a correct guess for $a_0$ will lead to a good match for the *complete* region corresponding to the whole pair-point multiplication.

Now, let us discuss how the above attack can be implemented using a smaller or a larger number of templates. The attack strategy remains the same, but varying the number of templates might affect our attack success rate.

**Attack Using $q$ Templates.** Ideally, a total of $q$ templates would be enough for extracting each coefficient in $\hat{\mathsf{a}}$ one by one. In that case, we would only need to perform the first three steps of the attack described above. Such an attack may work if we assume, for instance, that the pair-point multiplication is implemented according to Eq. (1) and not optimized via Karatsuba. In that case, we'd have more points of comparison for extracting $a_0$ and $a_1$ independently. $q$ templates may also be enough, for instance, if each integer multiplication requires several clock cycles, extending thus the points of comparison as well. If single integer multiplications are enough for successfully performing template matching, our attack could potentially generalize to implementations of Dilithium [25] as well, when collecting $q$ traces for the (larger) Dilithium modulus. Namely, Dilithium actually performs complete NTTs on its polynomials and, thus, multiplications are actually point-wise and not pair-pointwise. Thus, each secret coefficient is multiplied once, and then a modulus reduction is performed. In the Hamming weight model (see Sect. 4), this might not provide sufficient leakage (since Hamming leakage of $k$ bits scales with $\sqrt{k}$), but the real-life leakage might nevertheless suffice to attack also Dilithium.

**Attack Using $q^2$ Templates.** Each pair-point multiplication involves two adjacent coefficients of $\hat{\mathsf{a}}$, which we have referred so far as $a_0$ and $a_1$ (see Equation (1)). We could thus build templates for each possible *pair* of coefficients $a_0, a_1$. When performing template matching, we will be comparing regions corresponding to the *complete* pair-point multiplication (similar to **Step 5** in Sect. 3.1). This increases our chances of performing a key extraction.

Making templates for each possible pair of coefficients implies that we need a total of $q^2$ templates, which in Kyber translates to $3329^2 \approx 11M$ templates. While this number is much larger than what we considered initially, this attack strategy is very likely to work. Acquiring 11M traces may need a couple of days. However such an attack complexity is still considered a real threat.

**Improving Success Rates of the Attacks Using Online Template Attack.** We now consider the case where the success rate of an attack (either $q$ or $q^2$) is too low to recover all coefficients, e.g., when mounting a single-trace attack or when the attack is affected by noise. Then, in the $q^2$ attack, correlation analysis might not rank the template with the correct pair $(a_0, a_1)$ first, but rather as the $x$-th most likely template. To recover $(a_0, a_1)$, enumerating over all possible $x$ pairs is prohibitive for all 128 coefficient pairs since it would require $2^{128}$ trials.

In this case, it is worth to check whether the *first* pair of coefficients is always determined correctly. Indeed, this is the case in our experiments (Sect. 5). Our interpretation is that values in registers set by multiplications in previous iterations slightly affect the power consumption when the registers are overwritten. On the other hand, since there is no previous operation for the first multiplication, the initial register state is deterministic, and the attack is successful. Thus, the attack improves if we proceed *adaptively* and only attack the $y$-th pair after having correctly recovered the $y-1$ coefficient pairs before. Since all registers are now set correctly, the attack on the $y$-th multiplication should succeed similarly to the attack on the first multiplication. This attack creates template *online*, i.e., after obtaining the target power trace. Similarly to improving the $q^2$ attack, it can also improve the accuracy of the $q+q$ attack and all intermediate variants. For details about this method in practice, see Sect. 5.

## 3.2 Attack on DPA-Protected Kyber

We can apply the previously described attack analogously on masked implementations of Kyber. In this case, we recover each *share* of the secret key using our method and then add them to obtain the secret key.

Also in this case, one target trace suffices if each share is used independently and sequentially, which is the case in software implementations that first multiply the ciphertext with share one and then multiply the ciphertext with share two (and so on in case of higher-order masking). For hardware implementations, there exists the possibility of performing some multiplications in parallel as long as the Kyber module counts on more than one multiplier. However, not all designs of Kyber can afford to have several multiplier due to the costs in the area.

Let us assume that we are attacking a masked implementation that produces shares with all coefficients taking values between 0 and $q - 1 = 3328$. In this case, we will be able to perform a key extraction using the same number of templates as for an unmasked implementation. Namely, the templates we need for attacking such a masked implementation correspond to multiplications between known coefficients (for our chosen ciphertext), and unknown coefficients with values between 0 and $q - 1$. Thus, after obtaining all $q$ templates, we only need to perform the template matching twice with respect to an unmasked implementation (once for each share). The number of templates *matchings* we perform increases linearly with the masking degree. However, if we perform template matching over a power trace corresponding to the complete multiplication process involving both shares, we only need to perform the matching once for each template. For each $0 \leq j \leq q-1$, each match will reveal which coefficient in any of the two shares and has a value equal to $j$. Note, however, that if the masked implementation operates on a modulus notably larger than $q$, the complexity increases linearly, and the success probability is affected (see Sect. 6).

**Attack on Shuffled Implementations—Distinguishing via the Input Ciphertext.** A potential countermeasure against our attack might be randomizing the shuffling of pair-point multiplications. While a shuffled Kyber implementation would still allow us to correctly extract all coefficients, determining their original order in the resulting polynomial becomes challenging. However, we find that our attack can be adapted for effectiveness on shuffled implementations with just one target trace. Using a ciphertext with unique coefficient values for template generation, we obtain templates as before. During template matching, each template is attempted $\frac{n}{2}$ times, with varied pair-point multiplication positions. Successful matches reveal operand values and their original positions, exposing the secret coefficient's location. This attack initially focuses on extracting coefficients $a_{2i+1}$ (specifically, coefficient $a_1$ within each pair-point multiplication), akin to our approach in Subsect. 3.1.

**Generating the Inputs.** We choose an input ciphertext for which (in the NTT domain) each of its coefficients has a unique value, i.e., given the ciphertext $\hat{\mathsf{b}} =$

$b_0, b_1, b_2, \ldots, b_{255}$, it holds that for each $b_i, b_j$, with $i \neq j, b_i \neq b_j$. For illustration purposes, let us set $\hat{\mathfrak{b}}$ as follows: $\hat{\mathfrak{b}} = 9_0, 78_1, 1753_2, 7_3, \ldots, 17_{254}, 104_{255}$.

**Template Building.** We build templates like described in **Step 1** of Subsect. 3.1. Thus, we obtain a total of $q$ templates. For a coefficient $j$, the templates will be of the form: $T_j = (j_0 + j_1) \cdot (9_0 + 78_1), \ldots, (j_{254} + j_{255}) \cdot (17_{254} + 104_{255})$.

**Obtaining the Target Trace.** We obtain the target trace the same way as described in **Step 2** of Subsect. 3.1, i.e. by providing our chosen ciphertext $\hat{\mathfrak{b}}$ as input. Moreover, note that the resulting target trace corresponds to a shuffled evaluation of the pair-pointwise multiplication. For instance, the target trace might correspond to the following shuffled sequence of operations

$$T_t = (a_{22} + a_{23}) \cdot (b_{22} + b_{23}), (a_{104} + a_{105}) \cdot (b_{104} + b_{105}), \ldots, \\ (a_0 + a_1) \cdot (b_0 + b_1), (a_{56} + a_{57}) \cdot (b_{56} + b_{57}).$$

**Secret Coefficient Extraction and Location Identification via Template Matching.** Now, we match our templates with the target trace in a similar way as described in **Step 3** of Subsect. 3.1 with some additional steps. For each template $T_j$, we will perform a template matching with the target trace as follows.

(1) We first test a matching with the template $T_j$ and target $T_t$ the same way as in our original attack. Let us assume that we find a match at position $i$, revealing that the secret coefficient used at that position equals $j$, i.e. $a_{2i+1} = j$. Let us recall that at this point, the template $T_j$ corresponds to a non-shuffled sequence of pair-point multiplications and that for generating the template and the target traces, we used a ciphertext polynomial whose coefficients (in the NTT domain) are all different from each other. Finally, observe that for obtaining a match, *all* input operands used within the analyzed computations need to be the same, i.e., for a pair-point multiplication, the same $b_0, b_1$ and $a_1$ need to be used in the template *and* in the target. Given the observations above, we know that if now we obtain a match at position $i$, then the original, non-shuffled position of the extracted coefficient in the secret key is $i$. The coefficients of our input ciphertext serve as orientation since they are unique, and we know their positions in the templates.
(2) We will now try to find out whether a value $j$ appears in some shuffled pair-point multiplication, and we will also find out *where* in the non-shuffled key $j$ is located. For this, we start shifting the multiplication regions of our trace $T_j$. Concretely, we will shift the positions of all pair-point multiplications. Thus, for each template, there is a total of 128 shifts we can do since each template corresponds to 128 pair-point multiplications. Let $w$ denote the number of shifts we do on a template and let $T_j^{>w}$ denote the template built for the coefficient $j$ and shifted a total of $w$ times. For instance, if

we shift the multiplications once, we obtain the template with the following form: $T_j^{>1} = (j_{254} + j_{255}) \cdot (b_{254} + b_{255}), (j_0 + j_1) \cdot (b_0 + b_1), (j_2 + j_3) \cdot (b_2 + b_3), \ldots, (j_{252} + j_{253}) \cdot (b_{252} + b_{253})$.

(3) Next, we perform template matching with $T_j^{>w}$ and $T_t$. Let us assume that we find a match at position $i$. The match tells us that $a_{2i+1}$ in the target trace has the value $j$. However, since we know that $T_j^{>w}$ shifted the pair-point multiplications by $w$ positions, we know that it is actually the coefficient $a_{2(i-w)+1}$ in the (non-shuffled) secret key which equals $j$.

(4) We repeat the same matching + shifting process with all templates until we recover all coefficients. Recall that we are recovering all coefficients $a_1$ for each pair-point multiplication. Once we have recovered them, we can build a new set of $q$ templates by placing all recovered coefficients in their *shuffled* position and then just repeat the matching process from **Step 5** in Subsect. 3.1. This will let us recover all coefficients $a_0$ in each (shuffled) pair-point multiplication. In the previous step, we learnt the original (non-shuffled) position of each multiplication, we will also know the original position of the extracted $a_0$ coefficients in the non-shuffled secret key.

## 4 Simulations

This section presents simulations for the masked Kyber implementation [2,18].

### 4.1 Implementation of Pair-Point Multiplication

The code which we analyze implements the pair-pointwise multiplication as in Listing 1.1 and corresponds to the Karatsuba multiplication algorithm [24] (see Eq. (3) for reference). The procedure first loads a *pair* of secret coefficients $a_0||a_1$ into a 32-bit register poly0 and a pair of public coefficients $b_0||b_1$ into a 32-bit register poly1. The coefficients $a_0$, $a_1$, $b_0$, and $b_1$ are 12-bit integers in $\{0, \ldots, 3328\}$. In this overview, we skip over the instructions at lines 3 and 4 which are the analogous load operations for the next pair of coefficients in the key and in the ciphertext. Next, in line 8, we multiply the top parts of the registers poly0 and poly1, obtaining a product corresponding to $a_1 \cdot b_1$. This product is a 24-bit result and it is stored in **tmp**. The value in **tmp** is then reduced mod 3329 (line 9). Listing 1.2 gives the code of the Montgomery subroutine and Appendix B explains why the deployed *Montgomery*

**Listing 1.1.** Multiplication.

```
1  ldr poly0, [aptr], #4
2  ldr poly1, [bptr], #4
3  ldr poly2, [aptr], #4
4  ldr poly3, [bptr], #4
5
6  ldrh zeta, [zetaptr], #2
7
8  smultt tmp, poly0, poly1
9  montgomery q, qinv, tmp, tmp2
10 smultb tmp2, tmp2, zeta
11 smlabb tmp2, poly0, poly1, tmp2
12 montgomery q, qinv, tmp2, tmp
13
14 smuadx tmp2, poly0, poly1
15 montgomery q, qinv, tmp2, tmp3
```

**Listing 1.2.** Montgomery subroutine.

```
.macro montgomery q, qinv, a, tmp
  smulbt \tmp, \a, \qinv
  smlabb \tmp, \q, \tmp, \a
.endm
```

*reduction* algorithm for mod 3329 computation induces 3 further operations on 28-bit values. Next, the result is multiplied by $\zeta$ (line 10), added to $a_0 \cdot b_0$ (line 11) and reduced mod 3329 via Montgomery reduction (line 12), resulting in the term $a_1 \cdot b_1 \cdot \zeta + a_0 \cdot b_0$ (cf. Eq. (1)). Next, the code sums of the cross terms as $a_1 \cdot b_0 + a_0 \cdot b_1$ (line 14) and reduces it mod 3329 (line 15).

### 4.2 Hamming Weight Model

We analyze our attack in the *Hamming weight* model which leaks the number of ones in the processed values. We assume that the power consumption of a device correlates with the Hamming weights of the computed states. In our analysis, we will check whether each possible secret coefficient $a_i \in \{0, .., 3328\}$ (or each possible pair of coefficients) leads to a unique sequence of hamming weight values during the pair-point multiplication. If this is the case, then we expect that the leakage coming from a pair-point multiplication will allow us to identify the value of the secret coefficients used within that pair-point multiplication.

For the first heuristic estimate, let us compute an *upper bound* on the leaked information by assuming that all computations correspond to *independent* uniformly random $k$-bit strings. The *expected information* we obtain from the Hamming weight of a uniformly random $k$-bit string $|\log \Pr[\mathrm{HW} = i]|$ is the number of bits of information which we weigh by the probability of obtaining a state with hamming weight $i$, leading to the expected information (or *Shannon Entropy*)

$$H(k) := \sum_{i=0}^{k} \Pr[\text{ HW} = i] \cdot |\log(\Pr[\text{ HW} = i])| = \sum_{i=0}^{k} \frac{\binom{k}{i}}{2^k} \left|\log\left(\frac{\binom{k}{i}}{2^k}\right)\right|$$

for a uniformly random $k$-bitstring. Asymptotically, the expected information $H(k)$ grows linearly in $\sqrt{k}$. For example, we have $H(24)$=3.34 and $H(28)$=3.45.

Recall that our attack using $q$+$q$ templates (see Subsect. 3.1) first extracts $a_1$ before extracting $a_0$. Concretely, the five operations up to and including line 10 in Listing 1.1 only depend on $a_1$. They first write a 24-bit value for multiplication of $a_1$ and $b_1$, then three 28-bit values in the Montgomery reduction (cf. Appendix B) and then another 24-bit value for multiplication of $a_1 \cdot b_1 \cdot \zeta$. We obtain the overall expected information of $H(24) + 3 \cdot H(28) + H(24) \approx 13.69$ bits leakage about $a_1$ only. Since $a_1$ is a 12-bit value, it is plausible that we extract $a_1$ correctly with good probability from these five operations, even if not always, since 13.69 bits is only slightly above 12 bits and the random variable is concentrated around its expectation rather than exactly at its expectation.

To extract *both* values $a_0$ and $a_1$, we have two Montgomery reductions (line 12 and line 15), each resulting in 3 more operations, leaking together $6 \cdot H(28) \approx 20.7$ additional bits and the computation and addition of cross terms in line 14, which generate another H(24)-bit value, leading to an overall leakage of $13.69 + 20.7 + 3.34 = 37.73$ bits to extract a $12 + 12 = 24$-bit value $(a_0, a_1)$, suggesting that trying out all *pairs* should succeed with a high probability. Appendix C confirms our heuristic calculus with simulations. Additionally, the heuristic calculations and the simulations from the next section suggest that the $q + q$ attack and the $q^2$ attack are robust even when adding a certain amount of Gaussian noise.

### 4.3 Simulations of Gaussian Noise

We now simulate the aforementioned operations while adding a small Gaussian noise with standard deviation $\sigma$ to the simulated target trace. Subsequently, we list the best coefficient candidates according to the $L_2$-norm.

Using this method (see Appendix C for details), we analyze the probability of $a_{2i}$ being amongst the top 1, 2, 3, 10, 100 candidates (cf. Fig. 6) when analyzing only the operations that depend on $a_{2i}$ alone as well as the probability of $(a_{2i}, a_{2i+1})$ being amongst the top candidates (cf. Fig. 7) when analyzing all operations depending on $(a_{2i}, a_{2i+1})$. Since the probability of $a_{2i}$ being the top 1 candidate is only 0.9475 when no noise is added, the probability of obtaining all 128 correct $a_{2i}$ is $(0.9475)^{128} \approx 0.001$ and thus too low to be useful. However, up to $\sigma = 0.87$, the probability of $a_{2i}$ being amongst the top 100 candidates is $\geq 0.999$ and thus, up to a noise of $\sigma = 0.7$, with probability $0.99^{128} \approx 0.88$, we can significantly reduce the search space for the coefficient pairs from $q^2$ to $100q$.

For larger noise, we need to run the $q^2$ attack. The probability of $(a_{2i}, a_{2i+1})$ being the top 1 candidate drops below $\frac{15}{16}$ at $\sigma = 0.54$. In turn, the probability of $(a_{2i}, a_{2i+1})$ being amongst the top 100 candidates stays above 0.99 up to $\sigma = 0.72$. When aiming to brute-force the remaining uncertainty, in expectation, for $\sigma = 0.72$, we have $\frac{15}{16} \cdot 128 \approx 16$ positions where we need to try out 100 candidates yielding a computation cost of $100^{16} \leq 2^{20}$ times $\binom{128}{16} \approx 2^{128}$. The brute-forcing cost is thus dominated by the binomial coefficient $\binom{128}{\ell}$, determined by the number $\ell$ positions which we need to brute-force. $\binom{128}{\ell}$ remains below $2^{40}$ for $\ell \leq 5$. For each noise rate, we can now compute the probability of extracting all 128 coefficients if we brute-force only up to 5 positions as follows:

$$p_{100}^{128} \cdot \sum_{\ell=0}^{5} \binom{128}{\ell} \cdot (1 - p_1)^{\ell} \cdot p_1^{128-\ell},$$

where $p_{100}$ is the probability that $(a_{2i}, a_{2i+1})$ is amongst the top 100 candidates and $p_1$ is the probability that it is the top candidate. This probability is almost 1 when $\sigma \leq 0.4$ and then drops to almost 0 sharply for $0.4 \leq \sigma \leq 0.55$, also see the dashed line in Fig. 7.

## 5 Experimental Evidence

This section presents experimental results for three attack variations from Sect. 3: $q^2$, $q$, and an improved version using an online template attack (OTA)[2]. Similar to the original OTA [5,6], we calculate the correlation between the target trace and a template, resulting in a *matching trace* that indicates a match. If the secret coefficient pair in the template matches that used in *some* multiplication in the target trace, we observe a region in the matching trace with values close to one. We first describe our experimental setup and then discuss our results.

[2] Paper supplementary materials, the attack scripts in particular, are available at: https://github.com/crocs-muni/Attack_Kyber_ACNS2024.

We target the masked Kyber implementation from the mkm4 repository [18]. Our experiments use the same setup as described in that paper, utilizing the ChipWhisperer Lite platform with an STM32F303 target [30], featuring an Arm Cortex-M4 core. This setup ensures low noise and well-aligned traces. Our focus is the `poly_basemul` function, where we compute pair-pointwise multiplication.

In our experiments, we use the same physical instance of the ChipWhisperer device for profiling and attacking, which is the best scenario for an attacker. However, this might not reflect a real-world scenario and we leave investigating the portability of templates in our attack as future work.

Before launching the attack, we need to select relevant regions of the traces. After testing multiple methods and approaches, the Difference-of-Means approach described in [5] proved to be the best. We always select 33 points of interest per pair-pointwise multiplication for all our attacks.

In the $q + q$ attack, we observe a limited leakage and the results are rather modest. We obtain a more accurate success rate for the first pair-pointwise multiplication than the remaining ones. On average, the correct candidate for the first multiplication is ranked at 282, and for all multiplications, it is at 1623 (out of 3329). This is insufficient for the attack to succeed. Improving the success rate, possibly using deep learning, is left for future work.

Next, we attempt $q^2$ attack. We obtain the $q^2$ templates for all pairs of coefficients and each template is exactly *one trace.* Therefore, for this experiment, we use exactly 11082241 template traces to attack single target traces separately.

In Fig. 1, we illustrate our method for visualizing leakage, following the approach outlined in [21]. This approach involves calculating the difference between a template and our target trace, as depicted in Figures 3 and 4 of [21]. The top trace in Fig. 1 represents our target trace, with the highlighted area indicating the calculation of a pair-point multiplication. The middle trace shows the result when we subtract the target from a template that *does not* match the secret coefficients used in the highlighted pair-point multiplication. The bottom trace corresponds to the difference between the target and a template using the correct pair of secret coefficients. Notably, the highlighted region in this trace contains sample values very close to zero.

When comparing a target traces to the template corresponding to the pair of coefficients found in the secret key, our difference trace consistently contains a region with samples close to zero, as shown at the bottom of Fig. 1. However, when attempting to compare a template for a pair of coefficients that *do not* appear in the key, the difference trace does not exhibit such a low region.

In the $q^2$ attack, we compare each pair of coefficients with templates, resulting in an ordered list of candidate values. Notably, there is a significant difference in accuracy between the first pair of coefficients and the rest. As shown in Fig. 3, the first pair is correctly recovered in about 86% of cases, while the average success rate across all multiplications is 34%. This discrepancy is due to traces being influenced by previous multiplications, as illustrated in Fig. 2, where the coefficient from the first multiplication affects slightly the subsequent multiplica-

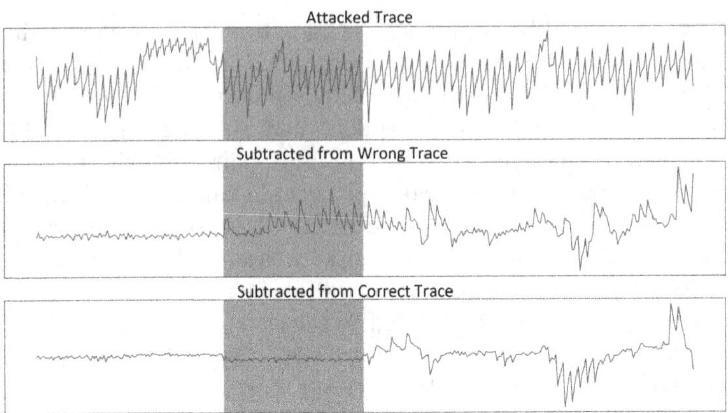


**Fig. 1.** Characterization: target trace (top), subtraction of the target trace from an incorrect template (middle) and from the correct template (bottom).

tion, too. The first multiplication is not affected by any previous multiplication and that is why the corresponding success rate is much better.

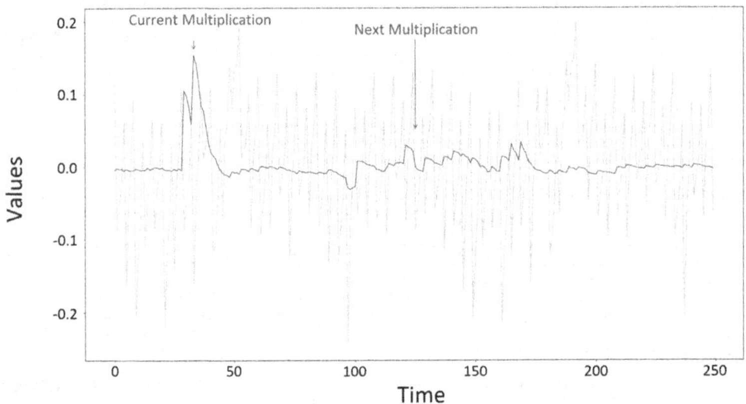


**Fig. 2.** The effect of previous multiplication on the following one: the correlation between the current multiplication value and the whole trace (in blue). (Color figure online)

Given the high success rates of the $q^2$ attack in recovering the first multiplication, we can reduce the number of candidate templates and initiate a combined attack using both $q^2$ and OTA. We begin with the $q^2$ attack. Assuming successful recovery of the first multiplication, we generate a new set of templates by combining the top two results for the first multiplication with a select number of top candidates for the second multiplication. These new templates cover a larger portion of the trace and are fewer in number, resulting in improved matching

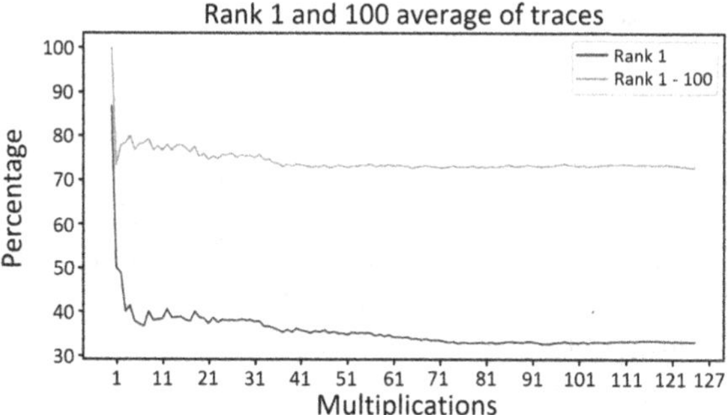


**Fig. 3.** $q^2$ attack success rate: blue line corresponds to the first candidate being correct and orange line to the correct candidate being in the top 100 results. (Color figure online)

rates. We now repeat this process, assuming the first two multiplication coefficients have been recovered correctly, iterating through the whole trace. The main downside of this approach is requiring additional templates.

We *successfully recover all coefficients* for 3 attacked traces with this approach, at the cost of the increased number of templates - 20 600 000, 43 000 000, and 20 600 000, respectively. These numbers can be lowered, as described in the analysis of the required number of traces in the following section. With our setup, gathering additional 15 000 templates per multiplication takes about 9 days[3] and cover 87% of attacked traces. The success rates for different amounts of templates for the full attack on masked Kyber768 are shown in Fig. 4.

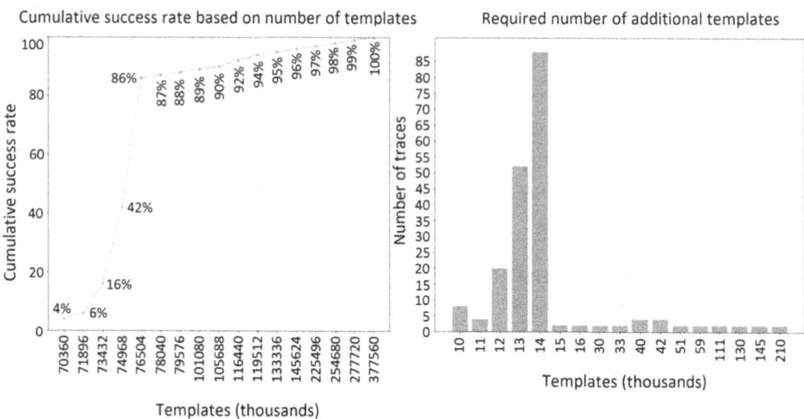


**Fig. 4.** *Left:* success rates of the full attack on masked Kyber768 wrt. the number of captured templates, estimated from 100 random target traces. *Right:* the extra number of templates required for the OTA attack (only non-zero values).

[3] Note, however, that we did not optimize our setup for the speed of acquisition.

### 5.1 Attack Analysis

In order to launch the $q^2$ + OTA attack, it is necessary to collect the 11M templates for the $q^2$ attack and the additional traces for each multiplication. Based on the analysis of 100 random traces, the additional requirement is, on average 13 000 - 15 000 per candidate for each multiplication, as shown in Fig. 4.

To successfully attack unmasked Kyber768, we need to repeat the attack 3 times, reducing the experimental success rate to 65%. Kyber768 performs three polynomial multiplications: the initial `poly_basemul` and two subsequent `poly_basemul_acc` operations. The `poly_basemul_acc` function is similar to operation `poly_basemul` but also accumulates its results into the previous multiplication, hence the name "accumulation."

The code of `poly_basemul_acc` mixes accumulation instructions with other multiplication instructions, necessitating separate template collection. These templates rely on results from previous multiplications. However, we already have these coefficients from previous attacks (notably, on `poly_basemul`). While the attack on `poly_basemul_acc` should perform better due to more leaking instructions, new templates must be collected for each execution, depending on the previously recovered coefficients.[4] For a complete attack on unmasked Kyber768, we would need approximately 44.5M templates: $3 \times 11$ million (for 3 executions) and $3 \times 15\,000 \times 2 \times 128$. Here, we assume that we need 15 000 additional templates per multiplication and a conservative estimate that we cannot reuse templates for `poly_basemul_acc` if accumulation inputs differ. Based on preliminary characterization, it seems that re-using templates for different inputs is challenging and we leave it to be investigated in future work.

To attack masked Kyber768 with order 2, we need to execute attack 6 times: 2 times for `poly_basemul` and 4 times for `poly_basemul_acc`. For `poly_basemul` we would need to collect templates once, but for `poly_basemul_acc` templates need to be collected each time. Therefore, we would need the following number of templates: $5 * 11\text{M} + 6 * 15000 * 2 * 128 \approx 78\text{M}$ to achieve 43% success rate; to increase it to 90% we need approximately 105M traces as shown in Fig. 4. At the time of writing, the current setup was able to capture 1 500 traces per minute. At this rate, gathering the full 78M templates would take about 45 days. In general, we leave improving the efficiency of this attack as future work.

## 6 Possible Countermeasures

One possible countermeasure against our attack may be the random shuffling of the operations *within* each pair-point multiplication (see the listings in Sect. 4). Moreover as discussed in Subsect. 3.2, masking schemes with coefficients with larger values would imply an increase in the number of templates needed for our attack and in the chances of getting false positive matches. There also exist

[4] Initial tests hint at a 30% acquisition reduction for the OTA step with a single `poly_basemul_acc` experiment. However, we exclude this result from our estimates, reserving exploration of this optimization for future work.

schemes which *blind* the secret coefficients [19,41] in a similar way as the blinding countermeasure for elliptic curve crypto [13] and schemes which mask the input ciphertext [34]. Parallelizing pair-point multiplications requires designs with spare multipliers, but it adds extra noise to computations, making our attack more difficult. Also, if Kyber employs a complete NTT and actual point multiplication between secret and known coefficients, our attack becomes more challenging given the reduced number of secret-dependent operations.

**Acknowledgements.** E. A. Bock conducted part of this research while at Aalto University. His work at Aalto and the work of K. Puniamurthy were supported by MATINE, Ministry of Defence of Finland. The work of Ł. Chmielewski and M. Šorf was supported by the Ai-SecTools (VJ02010010) project. Computational resources were provided by the e-INFRA CZ project (ID:90254), supported by the Ministry of Education, Youth and Sports of the Czech Republic.

# A Kyber Algorithms

Algorithms 3 and 4 describe the encryption and encapsulation functions in Kyber. The functions COMPRESS and DECOMPRESS are defined as $\text{COMPRESS}(u) := \lfloor u \cdot 2^d/q \rceil \bmod (2)^d$ and $\text{DECOMPRESS} := \lfloor q/2^d \cdot u \rceil$, with $d = 10$ if $k = 2$ or 3 and $d = 11$ if $k = 4$. Note that the output of the encryption corresponds to a ciphertext $c$, which consists of two *compressed* ciphertexts. This ciphertext $c$ will be the input to the decapsulation algorithm.

**Alg. 3:** Kyber-PKE Encryption (simplified)

Public key $pk = (\hat{\mathbf{t}}, \rho)$, message $m$, seed $\tau$ **Output:** Ciphertext $c$
$\hat{\mathbf{A}} \in R_q^{k \times k} \leftarrow \text{SAMPLE}_U(\rho)$;
$\mathbf{r}, \mathbf{e}_1 \in R_q^k, e_2 \in R_q \leftarrow \text{SAMPLE}_B(\tau)$;
$\mathbf{b} \leftarrow \mathsf{NTT}^{-1}(\hat{\mathbf{A}}^T \circ \mathsf{NTT}(\mathbf{r})) + \mathbf{e}_1$;
$v \leftarrow \mathsf{NTT}^{-1}(\hat{\mathbf{t}}^T \circ \mathsf{NTT}(\mathbf{r})) + e_2 + \text{ENCODE}(m)$;
$\mathbf{c}_1, c_2 \leftarrow \text{COMPRESS}(\mathbf{b}, v)$;
$c = (\mathbf{c}_1, c_2)$;
**return** $c$;

**Alg. 4:** Kyber-CCA2-KEM Encryption (simplified)

Public key $pk = (\hat{\mathbf{t}}, \rho)$ **Output:** Ciphertext $c$, shared key $K$
Choose uniform $m$;
$(\bar{K}, \tau) \leftarrow \mathsf{H}(m||\mathsf{H}(pk))$;
$c \leftarrow \text{PKE.ENC}(pk, m, \tau)$;
$K \leftarrow \mathsf{KDF}(\bar{K}||\mathsf{H}(c))$;
**return** $c, K$;

**Alg. 5:** Montgomery reduction

```
modulus q, R = 2^n > q, q^{-1} mod (R), a ∈ ℤ such that a < qR Output: t ≡ aR^{-1} (mod q), 0 ≤ t ≤ 2sq
t ← a(−q^{-1}) mod (R);
t ← (a + tq)/R;
s return t;
```

**Alg. 6:** Signed Montgomery reduction from [36]

```
modulus q, R = 2^n > q, q^{-1} mod^± (R), a ∈ ℤ such that a < qR Output: t ≡ aR^{-1} (mod q), |t| ≤ q
t ← aq^{-1} mod^± (R);
t ← (tq)/R;
t ← ⌊a/R⌋ − t;
return t;
```

## B Montgomery Reduction

Kyber represents elements in Montgomery representation in order to avoid expensive division by $q$ and computation mod $q$ and replace it by division by $2^{16}$ (taking the top half of a register) and computation mod $2^{16}$ (taking the bottom half of a register). In the following, we present the Montgomery reduction with general $R$ and $q$, but Kyber indeed uses $R = 2^{16}$.Consider $R = 2^k > q$, and an element $a < qR$. To reduce the memory footprint, we can store $a/R$ and this reduces the element $a$ by $k$ bits, and it can be efficiently implemented. In the Montgomery domain, the idea is to make sure that the element $a$ is a multiple of $R$ by introducing a correction step. More precisely, imagine that we want to find a value $t$, such that $a - tq$ is divisible by $R$. To bring the element to the Montgomery domain, one computes $t$ as $aq^{-1} \pmod R$ in a way that $a - aq^{-1}q \pmod R = 0$. Following closely Sect. 2.3.2 in [23], Algorithm 6 shows the case of signed Montgomery reduction from [36].

We now provide more details on how we determined the length of values for the Hamming weight that we use in our numerical estimates in Sect. 4.2:

1. $a_1 \cdot b_1$ — $12 + 12 = 24$ bits
   take bottom of register — 16 bits
   then multiply by $q_{inv}$ — $|q_{\text{inv}}| = 12$ bits
2. $(a_1 \cdot b_1)_B \cdot q_{\text{inv}}$ — $16 + 12 = 28$ bits
   take bottom of register — 16 bits
   then multiply by q — $|q| = 12$ bits
3. $((a_1 \cdot b_1)_B \cdot q_{\text{inv}})_B \cdot q$ — $16 + 12 = 28$ bits
   add $(a_1 \cdot b_1)$ — $|a_1 \cdot b_1| = 24$ bits
4. $((a_1 \cdot b_1)_B \cdot q_{\text{inv}})_B + (a_1 \cdot b_1)$ — $\max\{24, 48\} = 28$ bits
   take **top** of register and call it $c$ — $|c| = 12$ bits
5. $c \cdot \zeta$ — $12 + 12 = 28$ bits

# C Details on Noiseless and Noisy Simulations

We now discuss our simulations for noiseless operations within the pair-point multiplications comprehensively and additionally explain how we calculated probabilities in our noisy simulations. We first focus on the first 5 instructions of the pair-point multiplication, cf. Section 4.2. Our simulations calculate which coefficients $a_{2i+1} \in [0, \ldots, q-1]$ have *unique* combinations of hamming weight values (hamming weight tuples) during these instructions. Recall from Eq. 3 that pair-point multiplication also computes the term $a_1 b_1 \zeta$, where the value of $\zeta$ changes for each pair-point multiplication. So for our simulations, we initially fix $\zeta_0$ and try out all possible values for $a_1$ and all possible values $b_1$. We obtain the average probability that a value for $a_1$ leads to a unique hamming weight tuple. Then, we change to $\zeta_1$ and iterate over all possible values for $a_3$ and all possible values for $b_3$. We continue this process, obtaining the averages for all $a_{2i+1}$, given all $\zeta_i$. We thus obtain probabilities for extracting each odd coefficient, given a random ciphertext. Observe that in our simulations we do not consider micro-architectural aspects, like instruction pipelining, of our target.

As we show, most of the values for an odd coefficient indeed lead to unique hamming weight tuples. Only a small fraction of coefficients have collisions. On average, 3031 of these values have unique hamming weight tuples, i.e. there exist 3031 hamming weight tuples which map to exactly one coefficient value. 259 coefficients lead to 2-way collisions. This means that there exist $259/2 \approx 130$ hamming weight tuples which map to exactly two different coefficient values. Subsequently, there exist 34 coefficients which have 3-way collisions and 4 coefficients which have 4-way collisions each. On the average only a 0.03125 fraction of tuples maps to more than 4 different coefficient values. We now provide further details about the results of our simulations.

*Extracting Odd Coefficients ($a_{2i+1}$).* Our simulations show that for a uniformly *random* $b_{2i+1}$, the probability of extracting $a_{2i+1}$ from the first 5 instruction is $\approx 0.90$. This means that given a random ciphertext, we have good chances of extracting each odd coefficient. The probability of obtaining *two* possible candidates for each odd coefficient is $\approx 0.085$, and the probability of obtaining three possible candidates for each odd coefficient is $\approx 0.011$. Thus, taking a union bound, we obtain that the probability that a given $a_{2i+1}$ has either a unique hamming weight tuple, or a 2- or 3-way collision is $\approx 0.996$. For this reason in the rest of this analysis we only consider the case that we are dealing with coefficients with unique hamming weight tuples, or with 2- or 3-way collisions.

In the table under **Number of Matches (1)**, we see the probability that each odd coefficient $a_1, a_3, ..., a_{255}$ has a unique hamming weight tuple. We calculate this probability over all $b_1 \in [1, \ldots, q-1]$, and note that the probability is dependent on the value of $\zeta$. Thus, the probability that $a_1$ has a unique hamming weight tuple is different from that of $a_3, a_5$, etc., but the probability is always between 0.801 and 0.937, with an average of 0.90. Under **Number of Matches (2) and (3)**, we see the analogous probabilities that each odd coefficient $a_{2i+1}$ has a hamming weight tuple with a 2- and 3-way collision correspondingly.

We recall that in our attack using $q + q$ templates (cf Subsect. 3.1), we use the first set of $q$ templates for extracting the odd coefficients. According to our results, we should have a 90% chance of correctly extracting each odd coefficient - but we should recall that in Kyber, the secret keys consist of polynomials of degree 255. Thus, the probability of extracting *all* odd coefficients correctly is notably smaller. In fact, if we consider all probabilities of Fig. 5 for the chances that each odd coefficient has a unique hamming weight tuple, we obtain a probability of $\Pi_{i=0}^{127} p_i \approx 1.2967 \times 10^{-6}$ of extracting all odd coefficients from one polynomial, given only $q$ templates. We will explain later in this section how we can use the results of our simulations to outline an attack strategy that easily increases our success probabilities, with just a linear increase in the number of templates needed.

*Extracting Coefficient Pairs* $(a_{2i}, a_{2i+1})$. The lower part of Fig. 5 gives the probabilities that each secret coefficient pair leads to a unique hamming weight tuple. We obtain these probabilities in an analogous way as for the odd coefficients. Thus, the probabilities for each pair $(a_0, a_1), (a_2, a_3), (a_4, a_5), \ldots, (a_{254}, a_{255})$ are different as they are dependent on $\zeta$. Note that in this case, the hamming weight tuples consist of more values since we are considering *all instructions* within one pair-point multiplication. Hence, the very high probabilities under **Number of Matches (1)**. We can conclude from these results that if we create templates for all possible pairs of secret coefficients, our success probabilities are fairly high, while, on the other hand, it also requires creating a total of $q^2$ templates.

| Nr. of templates | Root | | Number of Matches | | |
|---|---|---|---|---|---|
| | | | 1 | 2 | 3 |
| $q$-templates | $\zeta_0$ | 2226 | 0.8696 | 0.108 | 0.018 |
| | $\zeta_1$ | −2226 | 0.9344 | 0.0603 | 0.0042 |
| | $\zeta_2$ | 430 | 0.8688 | 0.1087 | 0.0178 |
| | ⋮ | ⋮ | ⋮ | ⋮ | ⋮ |
| | $\zeta_{126}$ | 1628 | 0.8715 | 0.1067 | 0.0173 |
| | $\zeta_{127}$ | −1628 | 0.9329 | 0.0615 | 0.0044 |
| $q^2$-templates | $\zeta_0$ | 2226 | 0.9974 | 0.0025 | $1.01 \times 10^{-5}$ |
| | $\zeta_1$ | −2226 | 0.9973 | 0.0026 | $7.1474 \times 10^{-6}$ |
| | $\zeta_2$ | 430 | 0.9978 | 0.0021 | $4.6282 \times 10^{-6}$ |
| | ⋮ | ⋮ | ⋮ | ⋮ | ⋮ |
| | $\zeta_{126}$ | 1628 | 0.9973 | 0.0027 | $7.4805 \times 10^{-6}$ |
| | $\zeta_{127}$ | −1628 | 0.9976 | 0.0024 | $5.5263 \times 10^{-6}$ |

**Fig. 5.** Number of Matches: given $\zeta_i$, probability of a 1-, 2- or 3-way collision. Upper part: the probability of extracting odd coefficients with $q$ templates. Lower part: probability of extracting pairs of coefficients with $q^2$ templates.

*Efficiency Optimizations.* While $q^2$ is a reasonable number of template traces, collecting all of them is still quite consuming. Thus, we may indeed try extracting all odd coefficients first and then extracting all even coefficients with an additional set of templates. From the discussions above, we can conclude that our success probabilities of running a $q+q$ attack are not as high as we would originally hope (for the mkm4 implementation in the Hamming weight model). However, the simulation results suggest a natural and very simple way of optimizing the success of the attack. In the following, we outline an attack adaptation that increases the success probability of our attack and only requires a linear increase in the number of templates.

First, we can perform a template matching using $q$ templates (as originally done in Subsect. 3.1). For each coefficient we are trying to extract, we rank the top 3 candidate values for which we get the best matches. Now, we build templates for extracting the even coefficients. We will create 3 versions of these templates. In each version, we use a different top 3 candidate for each odd coefficient, creating an additional set of $3q$ templates. Thus, we first determine the top three candidates for each $a_{2i+1}$ (with high probability) and then try all three of them in combination with all possible $a_{2i}$, leading to an overall number of $q + 3q$ templates. When trying to extract the even coefficients, we get a very high success rate *iff* we are using the correct odd coefficient $a_{2i+1}$. Namely, as we see in Fig. 5, each secret coefficient pair has a very high probability of having a unique hamming weight tuple.

We can even optimize our attack further by considering the top 4 match candidates for each coefficient, generating an additional set of $4q$ templates. Concretely for the optimized attacks using $q+3q$ and $q+4q$ templates, we obtain success probabilities of $\Pi_{i=0}^{127} p_i \approx 0.6755$ and $\Pi_{i=0}^{127} p_i \approx 0.875$, respectively. With $6q = 19974$ templates, we have a very high success probability of 0.944, given a single target trace and a random ciphertext. Subsequently, we can use our analysis of the coefficients to determine the (expected) $\approx 0.875$ fraction of coefficients that are unique, given our list of coefficients that have a unique Hamming weight pattern. For the remaining $\approx 0.125$ coefficients, brute-forcing over $4^{0.125 \cdot 128} = 2^{32}$ coefficients is feasible (Table 1).

**Table 1.** Simulation results for noisy traces.

| # templates | $\sigma$ | Probability of being amongst top .. matches | | |
|---|---|---|---|---|
| | | 1 | 2 | 3 |
| **$q$-templates** | 0.3 | 0.8915 | 0.9775 | 0.9936 |
| | 0.4 | 0.7851 | 0.9205 | 0.9617 |
| | 0.5 | 0.6530 | 0.8231 | 0.8948 |
| | 0.6 | 0.5291 | 0.7027 | 0.7911 |
| | 0.7 | 0.4214 | 0.5860 | 0.6775 |
| **$q^2$-templates** | 0.5 | 0.9336 | 0.9788 | 0.9890 |
| | 0.6 | 0.8234 | 0.9112 | 0.9415 |
| | 0.7 | 0.6707 | 0.7906 | 0.8419 |
| | 0.8 | 0.4998 | 0.6310 | 0.7027 |
| | 0.9 | 0.3697 | 0.4839 | 0.5517 |
| | 1.0 | 0.2581 | 0.3559 | 0.4135 |

*Noise.* We now add Gaussian noise with standard deviation $\sigma$ to the target trace and see for which $\sigma$ we can still extract one or both coefficients. Instead of searching for perfect matchings, we minimize the $L_2$-norm of the *differences* between the simulated target trace and the template. Unfortunately, even for the $q^2$ attack, the best match under the $L_2$ norms provides the correct $(a_{2i}, a_{2i+1})$ value with probability $\leq 0.5$ when $\sigma \geq 0.8$. All probabilities are calculated via 10,000 samples and using a random root out of all possible 128 roots.

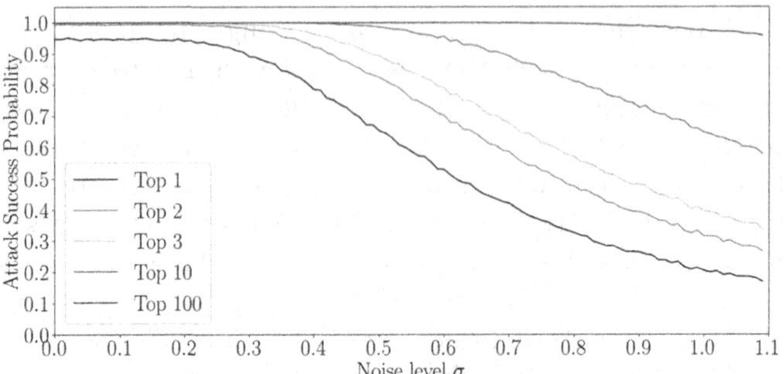


**Fig. 6.** Noisy $q + q$ attack simulations.

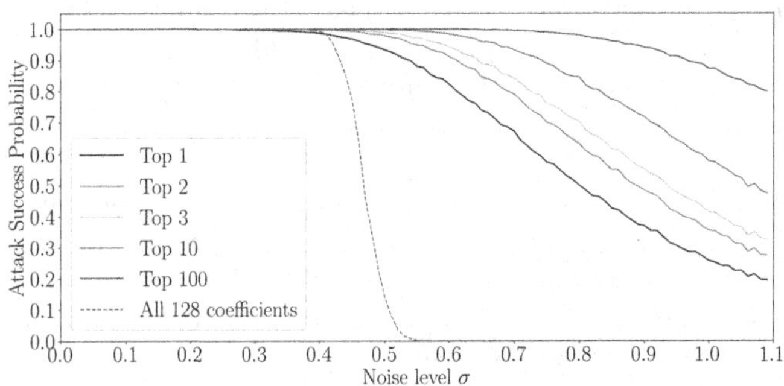


**Fig. 7.** Noisy $q^2$ attack simulations.

# D Comparison

To the best of our knowledge, there exist two other works in the literature that target polynomial multiplication in Kyber. In [27], the authors present a CPA attack on an unprotected polynomial multiplication implementation of Kyber. This attack led to the extraction of the long-term secret using approximately 200 traces. The main difference in comparison to our work is that the attack [27] requires multiple target traces and thus is not successful in the presence of a masking countermeasure. Our attack, on the other hand, requires a single target trace and, therefore, can successfully target masked implementations. The drawback of our approach is that we consider an adversary who can build template traces using a profiling device on which the secret can be freely changed. A classic CPA attack, as presented in [27], does not require any such profiling.

Another related work [40] presents a single-trace template attack on the polynomial multiplication of an unmasked implementation *pqm4* [1] during key generation[5]. There are several differences between this work and ours. First, note that they did not attack any masked implementation, but only argue about the attack's applicability to masking schemes since it attacks single traces. The attack is performed against a non-optimized implementation, utilizing straightforward polynomial multiplication without Karatsuba, leading to each secret coefficient being loaded twice, while our attack is on the *mkm4* masked implementation, which accesses the secret only once. Second, the attack [40] cannot be replicated on decapsulation since their template requires the leakage from the multiplication of $k$ different polynomial values in the matrix $A$ — which happens in the key generation. On the other hand, our attack can be applied to the key generation by utilizing the public polynomial values in $A$. Finally, their attack does not recover the full secret, but employs an extra key enumeration to finish the attack; as a result, their attack works for Kyber768 and Kyber1024, but not for Kyber512. Precise performance comparison is challenging due to uncertainties about the number of required templates in [40]. The authors mention using 500 traces to build templates for each intermediate, with approximately 14 attacked intermediates in each multiplication. This means that their attack would require only 7 000 templates if one template can be created for all pairwise multiplications or 896 000 if each multiplication needs to be templated separately. Consequently, it seems that the attack [40] requires fewer template traces for profiling than our approach, albeit with increased complexity and a lower success rate, necessitating final key enumeration.

Comparing our approach with [40] is intricate due to the mentioned differences. Foremost, [40] attacks key generation of the unprotected implementation, which involves a broader range of secret-dependent operations than our target. Therefore, we cannot estimate how well the attack from [40] would work against protected implementation like *mkm4*. In summary, the attack in [40] has advantages as it exploits various leaks and capitalizes on them. However, it is not easy to adapt to other procedures, such as the technique presented in this paper. Thus, this makes our attack more generic than the one presented in [40].

**Table 2.** Comparison of attacks on the long-term secret key from the polynomial multiplications; the analysis is made for Kyber768 unless stated otherwise.

| Work | Implementation | No. of target traces | No. of templates | Target algorithm | Remaining Brute-Force |
|---|---|---|---|---|---|
| [27] | Non-masked *pqm4* | 200 | 0 | Decapsulation | No |
| [40] | Non-masked reference and pqm4 implementations | 1 | *Not provided*, estimation: 7 000 or 896 000 | Key generation | For pqm4 Kyber: 512 – infeasible; 768 – $2^{40}$; 1024 – $2^5$. |
| This work (Simulation) | Optimized masked mkm4 imp. | 1 | 6 628 ($q+q$ attack), or 11 082 241 ($q^2$ attack) | Key generation *and* Decapsulation | No |
| This work (Experiment) | | | $q^2$+OTA attack: 78M (43% SR) or 105M (90% SR) | | |

[5] They also attack a reference implementation, but we do not concentrate on that since this implementation leaks much more than *pqm4* and the attacked by us *mkm4*. We are only looking at the long-term secret key and we do not consider the attacks on the encryption procedure.

In Table 2, we give a summary of the comparison with [27] and [40]. From our work, we present the two versions, i.e., "Simulation" refers to the numbers of the original introduction of our attack described in Sect. 3 and concerning the results obtained via simulations in Sect. 4. The "Experiment" work refers to the real-world attack from Sect. 5, where 78M traces give a 43% success of extracting the secret key, while 105M traces give over 90% success rate.

## References


1. Github repository: Collection of post-quantum cryptographic algorithms for the arm cortex-m4 (2023). https://github.com/mupq/pqm4
2. Github respository for masked Kyber presented in [18] (2022). https://github.com/masked-kyber-m4/mkm4
3. Avanzi, R., et al.: CRYSTALS-Kyber (version 3.0) - submission to round 3 of the NIST post-quantum project. submission to the NIST post-quantum cryptography standardization project (2020). https://pq-crystals.org/kyber/data/kyber-specification-round3-20210804.pdf
4. Backlund, L., Ngo, K., Gärtner, J., Dubrova, E.: Secret key recovery attacks on masked and shuffled implementations of CRYSTALS-Kyber and saber. Cryptology ePrint Archive, Paper 2022/1692 (2022). https://eprint.iacr.org/2022/1692
5. Batina, L., Chmielewski, Ł., Papachristodoulou, L., Schwabe, P., Tunstall, M.: Online template attacks. In: Meier, W., Mukhopadhyay, D. (eds.) Progress in Cryptology - INDOCRYPT 2014–15th International Conference on Cryptology in India, New Delhi, India, 14–17 December 2014, Proceedings, vol. 8885 of Lecture Notes in Computer Science, pp. 21–36. Springer, Heidelberg (2014). https://doi.org/10.1007/s13389-017-0171-8
6. Batina, L., Chmielewski, Ł, Papachristodoulou, L., Schwabe, P., Tunstall, M.: Online template attacks. J. Cryptogr. Eng. **9**, 1–16 (2019)
7. Van Beirendonck, M., D'Anvers, J.P., Karmakar, A., Balasch, J., Verbauwhede, I.: A side-channel-resistant implementation of SABER. ACM J. Emerg. Technol. Comput. Syst. **17**(2), 10:1–10:26 (2021)
8. Bos, J.W., et al.: CRYSTALS - kyber: a CCA-secure module-lattice-based KEM. In: 2018 IEEE European Symposium on Security and Privacy, EuroS&P 2018, London, United Kingdom, 24–26 April 2018, pp. 353–367. IEEE (2018)
9. Bos, J.W., Friedberger, S., Martinoli, M., Oswald, E., Stam, M.: Assessing the feasibility of single trace power analysis of frodo. In: Cid, C., Jacobson Jr., M.J. (eds.) Selected Areas in Cryptography - SAC 2018–25th International Conference, Calgary, AB, Canada, 15–17 August 2018, Revised Selected Papers, vol. 11349 of Lecture Notes in Computer Science, pp. 216–234. Springer, Heidelberg (2018). https://doi.org/10.1007/978-3-030-10970-7_10
10. Bos, J.W., Gourjon, M., Renes, J., Schneider, T., van Vredendaal, C.: Masking Kyber: first- and higher-order implementations. IACR Trans. Cryptogr. Hardw. Embed. Syst. **2021**(4), 173–214 (2021)
11. Aldaya, A.C., Brumley, B.B.: Online template attacks: revisited. IACR Trans. Cryptogr. Hardware Embed. Syst. **2021**(3), 28–59 (2021). https://artifacts.iacr.org/tches/2021/a11
12. Chari, S., Rao, J.R., Rohatgi, P.: Template attacks. In: Kaliski, B.S., Koç, Ç.K., Paar, C. (eds.) Cryptographic Hardware and Embedded Systems - CHES 2002, pp. 13–28. Springer, Heidelberg (2003). https://doi.org/10.1007/3-540-36400-5_3

13. Coron, J.S.: Resistance against differential power analysis for elliptic curve cryptosystems. In: Koç, Ç.K., Paar, C. (eds.) Cryptographic Hardware and Embedded Systems, pp. 292–302. Springer, Heidelberg (1999). https://doi.org/10.1007/3-540-48059-5_25
14. D'Anvers, J.P., Tiepelt, M., Vercauteren, F., Verbauwhede, I.: Timing attacks on error correcting codes in post-quantum schemes. In: Proceedings of ACM Workshop on Theory of Implementation Security Workshop, TIS 2019, pp. 2–9. Association for Computing Machinery, New York (2019)
15. Dubrova, E., Ngo, K., Gärtner, J., Wang, R.: Breaking a fifth-order masked implementation of crystals-kyber by copy-paste. In: Proceedings of the 10th ACM Asia Public-Key Cryptography Workshop, APKC 2023, pp. 10–20. Association for Computing Machinery, New York (2023)
16. Fujisaki, E., Okamoto, T.: Secure integration of asymmetric and symmetric encryption schemes. J. Cryptol. **26**(1), 80–101 (2013)
17. Hamburg, M.: Chosen ciphertext k-trace attacks on masked CCA2 secure Kyber. IACR Trans. Cryptogr. Hardw. Embed. Syst. **2021**(4), 88–113 (2021)
18. Heinz, D., Kannwischer, M.J., Land, G., Pöppelmann, T., Schwabe, P., Sprenkels, A.: First-order masked Kyber on ARM Cortex-M4. Cryptology ePrint Archive, Paper 2022/058 (2022). https://eprint.iacr.org/2022/058
19. Heinz, D., Pöppelmann, T.: Combined fault and DPA protection for lattice-based cryptography. IEEE Trans. Comput. **72**(4), 1055–1066 (2023)
20. Homma, N., Miyamoto, A., Aoki, T., Satoh, A., Shamir, A.: Collision-based power analysis of modular exponentiation using chosen-message pairs. In: Oswald, E., Rohatgi, P. (eds.) Cryptographic Hardware and Embedded Systems - CHES 2008, 10th International Workshop, Washington, D.C., USA, 10–13 August 2008. Proceedings, vol. 5154 of Lecture Notes in Computer Science, pp. 15–29. Springer, Heidelberg (2008). https://doi.org/10.1007/978-3-540-85053-3_2
21. Hutter, M., Kirschbaum, M., Plos, T., Schmidt, J.M., Mangard, S.: Exploiting the difference of side-channel leakages. In: Schindler, W., Huss, S.A., (eds.) Constructive Side-Channel Analysis and Secure Design - Third International Workshop, COSADE 2012, Darmstadt, Germany, 3–4 May 2012. Proceedings, vol. 7275 of Lecture Notes in Computer Science, pp. 1–16. Springer, Heidelberg (2012). https://doi.org/10.1007/978-3-642-29912-4_1
22. Ji, Y., Wang, R., Ngo, K., Dubrova, E., Backlund, L.: A side-channel attack on a hardware implementation of CRYSTALS-Kyber. Cryptology ePrint Archive, Paper 2022/1452 (2022). https://eprint.iacr.org/2022/1452
23. Kannwischer, M.J.: Polynomial Multiplication for Post-Quantum Cryptography. PhD thesis, Nijmegen U. (2022)
24. Karatsuba, A., Ofman, Yu.: Multiplication of multidigit numbers on automata. Soviet Physics Doklady **7**, 595 (1963)
25. Lyubashevsky, V., et al.: CRYSTALS-Dilithium (2020). https://csrc.nist.gov/projects/post-quantum-cryptography/round-3-submissions
26. Marzougui, S., Kabin, I., Krämer, J., Aulbach, T., Seifert, J.P.: On the feasibility of single-trace attacks on the Gaussian sampler using a CDT. In: Kavun, E.B., Pehl, M. (eds.) Constructive Side-Channel Analysis and Secure Design - 14th International Workshop, COSADE 2023, Munich, Germany, 3–4 April 2023, Proceedings, vol. 13979 of Lecture Notes in Computer Science, pp. 149–169. Springer, Heidelberg (2023). https://doi.org/10.1007/978-3-031-29497-6_8
27. Mujdei, C., Wouters, L., Karmakar, A., Beckers, A., Mera, J.M.B., Verbauwhede, I.: Side-channel analysis of lattice-based post-quantum cryptography: Exploiting polynomial multiplication. ACM Trans. Embed. Comput. Syst. (2022)

28. Ngo, K., Wang, R., Dubrova, E., Paulsrud, N.: Side-channel attacks on lattice-based kems are not prevented by higher-order masking. Cryptology ePrint Archive, Paper 2022/919 (2022). https://eprint.iacr.org/2022/919
29. Oder, T., Schneider, T., Pöppelmann, T., Güneysu, T.: Practical CCA2-secure and masked Ring-LWE implementation. IACR Trans. Cryptogr. Hardw. Embed. Syst. **2018**(1), 142–174 (2018)
30. O'Flynn, C., Chen, Z.D.: ChipWhisperer: an open-source platform for hardware embedded security research. In: Prouff, E. (ed.) Constructive Side-Channel Analysis and Secure Design - 5th International Workshop, COSADE 2014, Paris, France, 13–15 April 2014. Revised Selected Papers, vol. 8622 of Lecture Notes in Computer Science, pp. 243–260. Springer, Heidelberg (2014). https://doi.org/10.1007/978-3-319-10175-0_17
31. Pessl, P., Primas, R.: More practical single-trace attacks on the number theoretic transform. In: Schwabe, P., Thériault, N. (eds.) Progress in Cryptology - LATINCRYPT 2019–6th International Conference on Cryptology and Information Security in Latin America, Santiago de Chile, Chile, 2–4 October 2019, Proceedings, vol. 11774 of Lecture Notes in Computer Science, pp. 130–149. Springer, Heidelberg (2019). https://doi.org/10.1007/978-3-030-30530-7_7
32. Primas, R., Pessl, P., Mangard, S.: Single-trace side-channel attacks on masked lattice-based encryption. In: Fischer, W., Homma, N. (eds.) Cryptographic Hardware and Embedded Systems - CHES 2017–19th International Conference, Taipei, Taiwan, 25–28 September 2017, Proceedings, vol. 10529 of Lecture Notes in Computer Science, pp. 513–533. Springer, Heidelberg (2017). https://doi.org/10.1007/978-3-319-66787-4_25
33. Ravi, P., Roy, S.S., Chattopadhyay, A., Bhasin, S.: Generic side-channel attacks on CCA-secure lattice-based PKE and kems. IACR Trans. Cryptogr. Hardw. Embed. Syst. **2020**(3), 307–335 (2020)
34. Reparaz, O., de Clercq, R., Roy, S.S., Vercauteren, F., Verbauwhede, I.: Additively homomorphic ring-LWE masking. In: Takagi, T. (ed.) Post-Quantum Cryptography, pp. 233–244. Springer, Cham (2016). https://doi.org/10.1007/978-3-319-29360-8_15
35. Reparaz, O., Roy, S.S., de Clercq, R., Vercauteren, F., Verbauwhede, I.: Masking ring-LWE. J. Cryptogr. Eng. **6**(2), 139–153 (2016)
36. Seiler, G.: Faster AVX2 optimized NTT multiplication for Ring-LWE lattice cryptography. IACR Cryptol. ePrint Arch., 39 (2018)
37. Wang, J., Cao, W., Chen, H., Li, H.: Practical side-channel attack on masked message encoding in latticed-based kem. Cryptology ePrint Archive, Paper 2022/859 (2022). https://eprint.iacr.org/2022/859
38. Wang, R., Brisfors, M., Dubrova, E.: A side-channel attack on a bitsliced higher-order masked crystals-kyber implementation. IACR Cryptol. ePrint Arch. 1042 (2023)
39. Xing, Y., Li, S.: A compact hardware implementation of CCA-secure key exchange mechanism CRYSTALS-Kyber on FPGA. IACR Trans. Cryptogr. Hardware Embed. Syst. **2021**(2), 328–356 (2021)
40. Yang, B., Ravi, P., Zhang, F., Shen, A., Bhasin, S.: STAMP-single trace attack on M-LWE pointwise multiplication in Kyber. Cryptology ePrint Archive, Paper 2023/1184 (2023). https://eprint.iacr.org/2023/1184
41. Zijlstra, T., Bigou, K., Tisserand, A.: FPGA implementation and comparison of protections against SCAs for RLWE. In: Hao, F., Ruj, S., Gupta, S.S. (eds.) Progress in Cryptology - INDOCRYPT 2019, pp. 535–555. Springer, Cham (2019). https://doi.org/10.1007/978-3-030-35423-7_27

# Cryptographic Protocols II

# The Key Lattice Framework for Concurrent Group Messaging

Kelong Cong[3], Karim Eldefrawy[2], Nigel P. Smart[1,3](✉), and Ben Terner[2]

[1] COSIC, KU Leuven, Leuven, Belgium
nigel.smart@kuleuven.be
[2] SRI International, Menlo Park, USA
{karim.eldefrawy,ben.terner}@confidencial.io
[3] Zama Inc., Paris, France
kelong.cong@zama.ai

**Abstract.** Today, two-party secure messaging is well-understood and widely adopted, e.g., Signal and WhatsApp. Multiparty protocols for secure group messaging are less mature and many protocols with different tradeoffs exist. Generally, such protocols require parties to first agree on a shared secret group key and then periodically update it while preserving forward secrecy (FS) and post compromise security (PCS).

We present a new framework, called a *key lattice*, for managing keys in concurrent group messaging. Our framework can be seen as a "key management" layer that enables concurrent group messaging when secure pairwise channels are available. Security of group messaging protocols defined using the key lattice incorporates both FS and PCS simply and naturally. Our framework combines both FS and PCS into directional variants of the same abstraction, and additionally avoids dependence on time-based epochs.

## 1 Introduction

End-to-end encrypted secure messaging systems such as Signal and WhatsApp are widely deployed and used. The case of two-party protocols is well-understood, and has been extensively analyzed in the literature [3,8,18,20,26], but multiparty protocols (for group messaging) are still an active research area. At the moment, the Message Layer Security (MLS) IETF working group[1] is developing a standard to define an efficient and secure group messaging protocol. The key building block of MLS is continuous group key agreement (CGKA), which lets a group of users securely agree on a shared secret key [4], evolve it continuously while ensuring forward secrecy (FS) and post compromise security (PCS).

Many existing CGKA protocols, and their extension to group messaging protocols, require an additional infrastructure server that guarantees availability and orders messages. Recent work reduces dependence on the additional infrastructure, but still depends on a propose-and-commit paradigm [1,2,6] that

[1] https://messaginglayersecurity.rocks/.


C. Pöpper and L. Batina (Eds.): ACNS 2024, LNCS 14584, pp. 133–162, 2024.
https://doi.org/10.1007/978-3-031-54773-7_6

allows concurrent update proposals but requires serial commitments to accept the changes. This work develops abstractions and protocols to advance group messaging towards truly asynchronous channels and a decentralized environment where there is no central server to order messages. In such an environment, there may be a different "latest" group key in the view of every honest user—all of whom simultaneously encrypt messages, all of which must be decrypted.

Our main contribution is conceptual. We model the group keys used within the protocol via a key lattice, which can be seen as an $n$-dimensional grid if there are $n$ participants. The key lattice tracks all the group keys that will ever be used by the parties. Each key evolution travels along a path in the lattice. Every party uses the key lattice to track not only its own view of the current group key(s), but also the information it has about the other parties' views. To both permit concurrency (via the ability to swap the order of key updates) and to prevent the state space from exploding, we require that the key evolution functions are commutative.

By framing our (new) security definitions with respect to the key lattice, we intuitively find that the dual (and simultaneous) notions of FS and PCS become directional variants of the same simple notion, which states that the adversary cannot traverse the key lattice to learn keys which it has not yet compromised.[2] We also eliminate any dependence on epoch-based time from the analysis and solely focus on the keys' relationships to each other. To ensure PCS, parties evolve the group key with random updates and define new points on the key lattice. To ensure FS, each party tracks other parties' views of the group key, and deletes keys which it knows will never be used again. We also show how to trade FS for correctness when desired, since in a fully asynchronous network, the adversary may arbitrarily delay delivery of an encrypted application message in order to force one party to hold old keys.

Our secondary contribution is an instantiation of a novel group messaging protocol that uses the key lattice, and we prove its security.

**Group Key Agreement vs. Group Messaging:** It is not always straightforward to transform from group key agreement to group messaging. Key exchange protocols usually contain a key-confirmation step, but when the key exchange protocol is used as a building block in a larger protocol (e.g., secure messaging), this step breaks the key indistinguishability property of key exchange. This is a well known problem even for two-party key agreement followed by composition with a secure channel, see for example [15,16]. We avoid this definitional problem by treating key-agreement and messaging together and directly analyzing the scheme for group messaging.

**Asynchrony vs. Concurrency:** An *asynchronous* group messaging protocol means that the adversary can arbitrarily reorder messages that are sent, as long

[2] This approach bears some resemblance to the analysis of Fuchsbauer et al. [24] for public key re-encryption.

as all are eventually delivered. This models a highly adversarial network, and subsumes the scenario that some parties can temporarily "go offline" (if the adverary does not deliver messages to them) and then receive messages later when they come back online. A *concurrent* protocol allows messages, including update messages, to be sent and processed concurrently. But messages are delivered within some round of execution. The work by Bienstock, Dodis and Rösler [7] studied the trade-off between PCS, concurrency, and communication complexity. They show an upper-bound in terms of communication overhead that increases from $O(\log n)$ when there is no concurrency, to $O(n)$ when the update messages are fully concurrent.

Concurrent group messaging is suitable for the *decentralized* setting where there does not exist a central party to order messages. Nevertheless, it is possible to use a central server as a broadcast station to improve the communication cost, this way parties no longer need to broadcast messages to the group by themselves.

### 1.1 Related Work

Group key agreement and group messaging protocols have a long history. Early work focused on generalizing the Diffie-Hellman key exchange protocol [25,32]. Later work extended the security guarantees (e.g., by providing authentication, forward secrecy, and post-compromise security) [10,12–14], and improved performance and added new features (e.g., support for dynamic groups) [11]. This section outlines a few of the related work that are similar to our work. For the full details on the related work, please see the full version [21].

The closest work to ours is the recent paper by Weidner et al. [33], who introduced "decentralized" continuous group key agreement (DCGKA). DCGKA makes progress on the concurrency problems in ART and RTreeKEM so that all group members converge to the same view if they receive the same set of messages (possibly in different orders). The key primitive that enables concurrent updates is authenticated causal broadcast, defined in a similar way as Lamport's vector clocks [27]. Additionally, the authors made progress on how to manage group membership in an asynchronous network without a central server. However, their construction still requires a serial commitment.

In comparison to Weidner et al. [33], our construction does not require authenticated causal broadcast; we permit asynchronous messaging by buffering messages that are received out of order, and we authenticate via authenticated encryption. Our construction also does not require acknowledgements. This substantially reduces the cost of an update because DCGKA requires $n-1$ broadcast acknowledgements for an update.

Sender Keys, currently deployed by WhatsApp [35], also builds group messaging from pairwise Signal. During initialization, each party sends a symmetric "sender" key to all the group members using the pairwise Signal protocol. This key is used for encrypting payload messages by that party. Every party keeps $n$ "sender" keys in their state where $n-1$ keys are used for decryption and 1 is used for encryption. Sender Keys does not provide PCS since an adversary

**Table 1.** Comparing our work and existing work. PCS denotes post compromise security, and FS denotes forward secrecy. ROM stands for the random oracle model, StM denotes the standard model. (□) an update for DCGKA requires $n-1$ broadcast acknowledgements, so the total complexity is $O(n^2)$, although the sender's computational complexity is $O(n)$. (◇) These works use the propose-and-commit paradigm, where assumes the existence of epochs and allows concurrent proposals but a serial commitment is required. (†) $t$ is the number of corrupt parties. (‡) The server in CoCoA and SAIK processes an update to send an individual packet to each participant. They also order messages. (△) The SAIK server arbitrarily chooses one of concurrent updates to be processed. Our work is the only one which supports concurrent updates, does not require an active server, is PCS and FS and has a proof of security against adaptive adversaries. In this table desired features are highlighted in blue and those which negative impact security are in red.

| Protocol | Update Cost | | PCS | FS | Active Server | Concurrent Updates | Proof | Adaptive | |
|---|---|---|---|---|---|---|---|---|---|
| | Sender | Receiver | Healing Rounds | | | | | | |
| Original TreeKEM [30] | $O(\log n)$ | $O(1)$ | $n$ | yes | yes | Ordering | no | None | n/a |
| Causal TreeKEM [34] | $O(\log n)$ | $O(1)$ | $n$ | yes | yes | none | causal | StM | yes |
| RTreeKEM [4] | $O(\log n)$ | $O(1)$ | 2 | yes | yes | Ordering | no | ROM | yes |
| Concurrent TreeKEM [7] | $O(n)$ | $O(1)$ | 2 | yes | no | none | yes | StM | yes |
| Signal group [22,31] | $O(n)$ | $O(1)$ | 2 | yes | yes | Prekeys | yes | None | n/a |
| Sender Keys [31,35] | $O(n^2)$ | $O(n)$ | 2 | yes | yes | Prekeys | yes | None | n/a |
| DCGKA [33] | $O(n)$ (□) | $O(1)$ | 2 | yes | yes | none | yes (◇) | ROM | no |
| CoCoA [2] | $O(\log n)$ | $O(1)$ | $\log(n)$ | yes | yes | Process-Updates (‡) | yes (◇) | ROM | yes |
| SAIK [6] | $O(\log n)$ | $O(1)$ | 2 | yes | yes | Process-Updates (‡) | yes (△) | ROM | yes |
| DeCAF [1] | $O(\log t)$ (†) | $O(1)$ | $\log(t)$ | yes | yes | blockchain | yes (◇) | ROM | yes |
| Our work | $O(n)$ | $O(1)$ | 2 | yes | yes | none | yes | StM | yes |

who corrupts a party will learn all the symmetric keys and decrypt future messages sent to all parties. Fully healing the state therefore requires every party to update its symmetric key, which has a cost of $O(n^2)$.

Our work can be viewed as a generalization of Sender Keys with improved security and functionality, where parties update the key lattice instead of holding symmetric keys for each party. The group session heals once a corrupted party's pairwise channels heal because the next update it sends or receives is indecipherable to the adversary. This requires $O(n)$ public key operations (also $O(n)$ communication complexity) after one corruption.

**Summary:** Table 1 summarizes a representative sample of recent literature on group key agreement and group messaging. "Update Cost" gives the communication complexity to update a shared or pairwise key, for the sender and the receiver, and "Healing rounds" describes the round complexity of healing the session after a corruption. "Active Server" is a server that provides additional functionalities other than a PKI, such as ordering messages or post-processing updates. For example, the Signal servers need to store single-use pre-keys and the TreeKEM servers need to order messages. "Adaptive" means whether the adversary can adaptively pick which oracles to query during the security game.

Our work, on the last row, carves out a new trade-off in the group messaging design space. Specifically, we use pairwise channels which results in $O(n)$ update cost and, in contrast to prior work, maintain a set of evolving shared group key without compromising security, i.e., allowing adaptive queries.

### 1.2 Technical Overview

Our group messaging (GM) protocol consists of three building blocks: (1) an initial group key agreement (GKA) protocol, (2) a group randomness messaging (GRM) protocol used to transport key updates, and (3) a key lattice. We overview all blocks but focus on the key lattice as it is our primary contribution.

**Group Key Agreement (GKA):** Our GKA assumes existence of a public key infrastructure (PKI). In other words, each party knows the other party's long-term public key. The protocol takes as input the identities and public keys of the group members and outputs a symmetric key shared by those members. This symmetric key is used by the other two building blocks detailed below. We use the GKA as a black box and thus are not concerned with the exact construction in this work. Nevertheless, we require that it is forward secure, i.e., if the long-term secret key is compromised after agreeing on a shared key, the adversary still learns nothing about the shared key. Note that many GKA protocols exist in the literature [9,13,14,29]. In this work we use the definition from [14], which allows for asynchrony (as needed by our construction).

**Group Randomness Messaging (GRM):** GRM abstracts the transport mechanism used to communicate key updates and make our proof more modular. Because GRM requires pairwise channels with FS & PCS, it could be implemented using pairwise 2-party secure messaging e.g., pairwise Signal or another double-ratchet-based protocol. We provide a custom instantiation of GRM in Sect. 5 that better fits our assumptions (specifically, we assume only a public key infrastructure and do not require a server to distribute pre-key bundles), is conceptually simpler than a double-ratchet, and is easier to prove secure. Nevertheless, we give an outline of how to build a concurrent group messaging protocol from black-box primitives in Sect. 3.4.

Our GRM protocol is intuitively simple. Whenever a party $U$ sends a random message $x$ to party $V$, $U$ samples a fresh key pair $(\mathtt{pk}', \mathtt{sk}')$, and encrypts $(x, \mathtt{pk}')$ under the public key $\mathtt{pk}_V$ that $U$ holds for $V$. When $V$ receives $(x, \mathtt{pk}')$, it assigns $\mathtt{pk}'$ as its latest public key for $U$ and outputs $x$ as $U$'s message. Future messages sent by $V$ to $U$ must be encrypted under the latest ephemeral public key that $V$ holds for $U$. The scheme achieves both FS and PCS because all secret keys are independently sampled with every message sent, and therefore leaking one secret key never reveals information about another. The scheme uses a public key AEAD scheme for all encrypted messages, where the associated data are bookkeeping material on the order of updates.

**Key Lattice:** We now explain our key lattice framework, including our security game and its representation of FS and PCS.

*Framework:* Every group key in a group messaging protocol is associated with a coordinate in a discrete $n$-dimensional space, where $n$ is the number of players

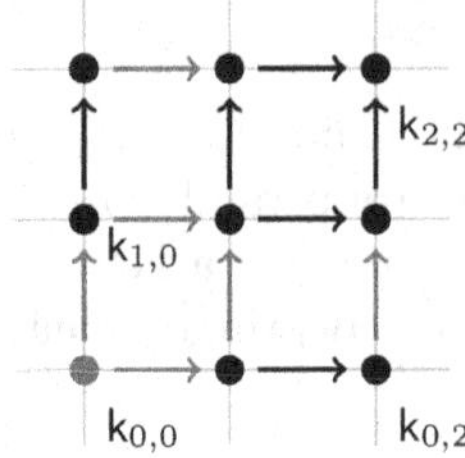


(a) The red vertices and edges are explicitly revealed to the adversary.

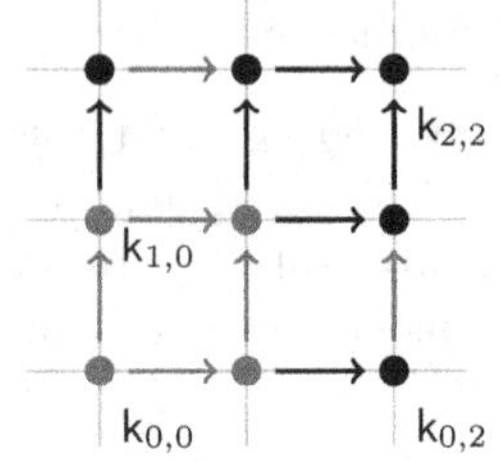


(b) The full set of information that an adversary can compute from 1a.

**Fig. 1.** In Fig. a, the red vertices and edges are explicitly revealed to the adversary. If PCS holds, then the adversary cannot compute the key $k_{2,2}$ because there is no path of red edges from a red vertex to $k_{2,2}$. In Fig. b, the adversary can compute the keys $k_{0,1}$, and $k_{0,1}$, and $k_{1,1}$ by starting at $k_{0,0}$ and following a path of red edges. FS can analogously be visualized by (preventing) traversing the directed graph "backwards" from a compromised vertex. (Color figure online)

in the group. When parties update the group key (at some index), the new key produced is mapped to a larger index. For example, for $n = 2$, a key $k_{1,0}$ at coordinate $(1, 0)$ may be updated to a new key with an associated coordinate $k_{1,1}$. We also provide a graphical explanation of a key lattice in which the indices in the discrete $n$-dimensional space are vertices, and each vertex is labeled with a key. In the graph, edges between vertices represent key updates.

*FS & PCS:* Our key lattice allows us to discuss FS & PCS in a unified and simple manner, as directional variants of the same abstraction. In Fig. 1, every key is mapped to a point on the graph, and updates are mapped to edges in the graph. Black vertices and edges are not revealed to the adversary, and red vertices and edges are revealed. A party that "knows" both the key corresponding to a vertex and an edge leaving that vertex will also "know" the vertex's neighbor. FS & PCS mean that the *only* way the adversary can learn a key $k^*$ at some target vertex $v^*$ is by starting with a red vertex on the graph and following a path of red edges to $v^*$. In the traditional definition of FS, this would mean that given a vertex $v$, without following (in reverse) a path of red edges, the adversary cannot learn a predecessor of $v$. In the traditional definition of PCS, this would mean that given a vertex $v$, without following a path of red edges, the adversary cannot learn a successor of $v$. The key lattice is described in full in Sect. 3.

*Security Game and Freshness:* Our security game is an oracle game in which the adversary activates oracles corresponding to parties running a polynomial number of protocol executions. The adversary plays a semantic security game against a "fresh" key on one of the lattices. A key is "fresh" precisely if the adversary cannot derive that key from its view of the execution thus far; graphically, this means that the key is black in the corresponding graph akin to Fig. 1b. The

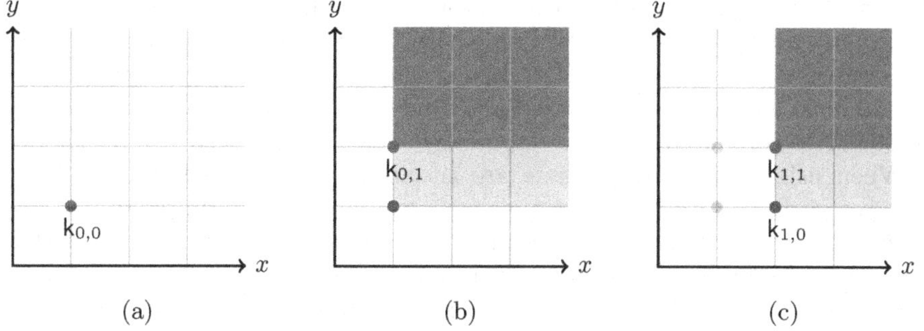


**Fig. 2.** An example of a local key lattice in an execution with two players (blue and red) from the perspective of the red party. (Color figure online)

adversary wins the semantic security game if it can distinguish two ciphertexts encrypted under a fresh key.

*Tracking Keys of Other Parties:* Each party maintains a local key lattice to track the group keys, but does not (necessarily) need to maintain a full view of the key lattice. Each party tracks only the keys it needs in order to decrypt a message that it has not yet received. This permits the construction to achieve the best possible FS while also achieving correctness; as soon as some party knows it no longer needs some key, it deletes the key from its view (in order to prevent an adversary from learning the key after it has become deprecated).

We illustrate our approach in Fig. 2. For simplicity, we only consider two parties labelled with the colors red and blue. The shaded regions, assigned by color, indicate the set of points towards which the corresponding party may define a new group key in the future. Any point in a totally unshaded region represents an index of a key that can be deleted. In our construction, when any party updates the key, it moves the latest group key towards a point in the n-dimensional space along an axis that has been assigned uniquely to it. Blue and red update the key towards higher indices on the $x$ axis and $y$ axis, respectively.

1. In Fig. 2a, the red and blue parties initialize their local lattices with $\mathsf{k}_{0,0}$.
2. In Fig. 2b, red evolves the group key, which moves red's latest key to $\mathsf{k}_{0,1}$.
3. In Fig. 2c, suppose red received an update message from blue. Red applies the update and evolves its own index from $\mathsf{k}_{0,1}$ to $\mathsf{k}_{1,1}$. Because red knows that blue evolved its key, red updates its view of blue's index $\mathsf{k}_{0,0}$ to $\mathsf{k}_{1,0}$. Specifically, red's perspective of the latest key for blue becomes $\mathsf{k}_{1,0}$. Since $\mathsf{k}_{0,0}$ and $\mathsf{k}_{0,1}$ are outside the shaded region, these keys are removed.

*Windowing to Limit State Expansion:* In addition to the state reduction described above, we also apply a state "window" that prevents the state from blowing up in case encrypted messages are delayed over the network, at the expense of the ability to decrypt long-delayed messages. Consider that if one party makes $m$ updates to the shared group key, resulting in $m$ possible different group keys, then parties must keep $O(m)$ states in case another party sends a message using one of those $m$ keys. In our windowing scheme, each party maintains *at most* the latest $w$ key evolutions from every other party, which provides the ability to compute at most $w^n$ total keys on the key lattice at any time.

When using this scheme, there are situations in which parties may send messages such that some application messages are not decryptable. Suppose sender $S$ sends an application message $m$ encrypted under key $k$, and then suppose $S$ updates the group key $w$ times starting with $k$. If $S$'s message $m$ is delayed until after receiver $R$ receives $S$'s key updates, then $R$ will delete the key material describing how to decrypt $m$. In synchronous networks, the window can be set such that parties update their keys once per epoch, and the window can be set large enough (by setting $w$ is equal to the number of epochs that measure the network delay) for sent messages to always be received in time to be decrypted. In the general asynchronous case, the window can be set to $\infty$ in order to always guarantee decryption, but this approach loses FS.[3] Thus, windowing allows us to trade between security and correctness.

**Group Messaging (GM):** In our construction, parties who wish to participate in a GM instance begin by running a GKA protocol to obtain a shared symmetric key $\mathsf{k}$. They use $\mathsf{k}$ to initialize their key lattice, and then use GRM to securely communicate update messages that can be applied to the key lattice to evolve the shared group key. When a party encrypts an application (payload) message, it always uses the latest key in its key lattice.

**Dynamic Membership:** We provide an informal extension of our framework that permits dynamic group membership "for free," and additionally handles simultaneous adds and removals with no additional effort, thus completely avoiding "splitting" [5] issues in synchronous protocols where multiple parties make competing simultaneous updates. The intuitive understanding is to view our representation of a key lattice as a lossless compression of an $n$-dimensional space in which only a finite number of points are defined, where $n$ is the number of all possible identities. Each dimension in the key lattice represents a party that belongs to the group, and all other dimensions in the lattice are defined to contain points set to $\perp$. When a party joins the group, points become defined in its corresponding dimension. When it leaves the group, its future group updates become invalid.

Treating dynamic membership in this way averts all of the problems of concurrency incurred by other works, including with respect to insider attacks, since groups including the new members are only defined in the lattice as successor points of the addition operation, and we incur no conflicts by maintaining multiple copies of the lattice that correspond to groups both with and without the

[3] This tradeoff was similarly explored by [28]; our asynchronous security model specifically accounts for the attacks they describe by withholding some ciphertexts and corrupting a party days later to recover the messages.

new member. Dynamic membership is not the main focus of our work and a formal definition and analysis is needed before it can be considered for practical use, which we leave for future work. Nevertheless, we provide more details of our dynamic group extension in the full version [21].

## 2 General Definitions and Notation

We denote by $\mathbb{N}$ the natural numbers. For a list $\ell$, $\ell[i]$ denotes the $i$th element of $\ell$. We write $[m] = \{1, \ldots, m\}$, and $[a, b] = \{a, a+1, \ldots, b-1, b\}$ where $b > a$. $\mathcal{P}$ is the set of all possible parties, and $n = |\mathcal{P}|$. We define a function $\phi : \mathcal{P} \to [n]$ that assigns a canonical ordering of $\mathcal{P}$, i.e., to each $U \in \mathcal{P}$, $\phi(U)$ assigns a unique index between 1 and $n$.

Let $\mathbf{i} \in \mathbb{N}^n$ denote an *index vector*. All keys will be indexed by index vectors, i.e., we will always write the secret keys as $\mathsf{k}_{\mathbf{i}}$. The $j$-th element of index vector $\mathbf{i}$ will be denoted by $\mathbf{i}^{(j)}$. We introduce a function $\mathsf{increment}(\mathbf{i}, j)$ with inputs an index vector $\mathbf{i}$ and an integer $j \in [n]$ and returns an index vector $\mathbf{i}'$ such that for $i \neq j$, $\mathbf{i}'^{(i)} = \mathbf{i}^{(i)}$, and $\mathbf{i}'^{(j)} = \mathbf{i}^{(j)} + 1$. Similarly, $\mathsf{decrement}(\mathbf{i}, j)$ returns an index vector $\mathbf{i}'$ such that for $i \neq j$, $\mathbf{i}'^{(i)} = \mathbf{i}^{(i)}$, and $\mathbf{i}'^{(j)} = \mathbf{i}^{(j)} - 1$. We define a partial ordering over index vectors by saying $\mathbf{i} \geq \mathbf{c}$ if $\mathbf{i}^{(j)} \geq \mathbf{c}^{(j)}$ for all $j$. $\mathcal{H}_{\geq \mathbf{c}}$ for a constant index vector $\mathbf{c} \in \mathbb{N}^n$ denotes the $n$-dimensional hyperplane of all index vectors $\mathbf{i}$ such that $\mathbf{i}^{(j)} \geq \mathbf{c}^{(j)}$ for all $j \in [n]$.

**Network Model:** Parties are connected via pairwise channels such that both parties know the identity of the party on the other end. A PKI provides a mapping between an identity $U \in \mathcal{P}$ and its long-term public key. Every $U \in \mathcal{P}$ also has its own long-term private key.

**Adversarial Model:** In our security game, the adversary is responsible for delivering all messages to its oracles. It may reorder messages arbitrarily, as per the definition of an asynchronous network [17]. Proper ordering of messages *within a subprotocol* is enforced by sequence numbers on our updates and encrypted messages, and therefore in the exposition we assume that each subprotocol's messages are ordered, but messages sent by different subprotocols (such as GKA, GRM, and GM application messages) are not ordered with respect to each other.

The adversary may call its oracles on messages that have not been sent by honest parties. This is an injection attack. However, because all messages in our constructions are authenticated, successfully changing the state of an oracle without knowledge of a party's underlying key would break the security of an authenticated cryptographic primitive (e.g., AEAD).

The adversary can corrupt parties to learn protocol keys, and in some cases may inject messages based on those keys. For example, learning a group key allows the adversary to inject application messages, but these injections do not affect the security of other keys.[4]

We defer a discussion of insider security in our model to the full version [21].

**Encryption:** In the full version [21] we give the standard definitions for encryption, key encapsulation mechanisms (KEMs) and authenticated encryption with associated data (AEAD) that we use in this paper. Notably, we use a variant of public key encryption—public key encryption with additional data (PKEAD). It is similar to an IND-CCA secure public key encryption scheme that allows additional plaintext data to be appended, where the additional data binds to the ciphertext.

## 3 Key Lattice

The key lattice is our central idea for managing concurrent key updates. Because the key lattice tracks the set of group keys generated during a group messaging execution, we additionally define security of group messaging with respect to the key lattice. We now formally define a key lattice.

**Definition 3.1 (Key Lattice).** *We define $\mathbb{K}$ to be the space of keys, and we define $\mathbb{L}$ to be the lattice of $\mathbb{N}^n$ where the ordering is defined by $\mathbf{i}_a \leq \mathbf{i}_b$ if all elements in $\mathbf{i}_a$ are less or equal to $\mathbf{i}_b$, and $\mathbf{i} \in \mathbb{N}^n$ denotes a point on the lattice. A* key lattice *$L = \{(\mathbf{i}, \mathsf{k}_\mathbf{i})\}_{\mathbf{i} \in \mathbb{L}}$ where $\mathsf{k}_\mathbf{i} \in \mathbb{K} \cup \{\perp\}$ is a discrete lattice for which every point $\mathbf{i} \in \mathbb{L}$ is associated with either a single key or $\perp$.*

We denote the association by letting $\mathsf{k}_\mathbf{i}$ be the key associated with $\mathbf{i}$. We also say that the key for an index $\mathbf{i}$ is *defined* if $\mathsf{k}_\mathbf{i} \neq \perp$. Intuitively, parties will compute and agree on many pairs $(\mathbf{i}, \mathsf{k}_\mathbf{i})$.

Given a key lattice, a key $\mathsf{k}_\mathbf{i}$ is $j$-maximal if there is no $\mathbf{j} \in \mathbb{N}^n$ for which $\mathbf{j}^{(j)} > \mathbf{i}^{(j)}$ and $\mathsf{k}_\mathbf{j} \neq \perp$. If a key is $j$ maximal for all $j \in [n]$, we say the key is maximal in the lattice. Looking ahead, in each party's local lattice there is always a maximal key, computed by all applying all updates that the party knows.

### 3.1 Key Evolution

When a party evolves the group key, it adds a new key (or, as in our construction in Sect. 3.3, a group of keys), to the key lattice. Key evolution is described by a function $\mathsf{KeyRoll} : \mathbb{K} \times \mathcal{X} \rightarrow \mathbb{K}$, where $\mathbb{K}$ is the key space and $\mathcal{X}$ is the *update space,* which encodes the data applied to the key during evolution. In our construction, we will require a few properties of the KeyRoll function. First, we require that KeyRoll is commutative, i.e. $\mathsf{KeyRoll}(\mathsf{KeyRoll}(\mathsf{k}, x), x') = \mathsf{KeyRoll}(\mathsf{KeyRoll}(\mathsf{k}, x'), x)$ for all $\mathsf{k} \in \mathbb{K}$ and $x, x' \in \mathcal{X}$.

[4] Some authentication schemes require parties to sign messages with their long-term keys [23] but adapting this to concurrent group messaging is non-trivial, and not the focus of this work.

In addition to commutativity, we require that $\mathsf{KeyRoll} : \mathbb{K} \times \mathcal{X} \rightarrow \mathbb{K}$ is *unpredictable* in its second input. Intuitively, knowing only the first input (a key from $\mathbb{K}$), no adversary can "predict" the output (another key from $\mathbb{K}$), if the second input (an update from $\mathcal{X}$) is sampled at random. Similarly, we say that KeyRoll's inverse is unpredictable if given only $\mathsf{k}' \leftarrow \mathsf{KeyRoll}(\mathsf{k}, x)$, no adversary can "guess" the input $\mathsf{k}$. More formally, we have the following.

**Definition 3.2 (Unpredictability).** *A family of functions $\mathcal{F} = \{F_\lambda\}_\lambda$ where $F_\lambda \colon \mathbb{K}_\lambda \times \mathcal{X}_\lambda \rightarrow \mathbb{K}_\lambda$ is* unpredictable *in its second input if there exists a negligible function* negl *such that for every probabilistic polynomial time adversary $\mathcal{A}$ and every $\lambda$:*

$$\Pr[y = F_\lambda(k, x) \colon k \leftarrow \mathbb{K}_\lambda, x \leftarrow \mathcal{X}_\lambda, y \leftarrow \mathcal{A}(1^\lambda, k)] \leq \mathsf{negl}(\lambda)$$

*$\mathcal{F}$'s inverse is unpredictable if there exists a negligible function* negl *such that for any polynomial time adversary $\mathcal{A}$ and every $\lambda$:*

$$\Pr[k' = k \colon k \leftarrow \mathbb{K}_\lambda, x \leftarrow \mathcal{X}_\lambda, k' \leftarrow \mathcal{A}(1^\lambda, F_\lambda(k, x))] \leq \mathsf{negl}(\lambda)$$

*where in each experiment, $k$ and $x$ are sampled uniformly at random from their respective domains.*

We remark that there are many families of unpredictable functions. For instance, $\mathsf{KeyRoll}(k, x) = k \oplus x$ satisfies the unpredictability definition, as well as $\mathsf{KeyRoll}(k, x) = \mathsf{PRF}_x(k)$[5]. In both cases, it is not possible to predict the output without knowing the key. The difference between the first construction and the second is that in the first case, knowing the first input and the output completely leaks the update material $x$. This property is not critical to our construction; we can prove security for our main protocol assuming only that KeyRoll is unpredictable. However, for completeness (and for situations where unpredictability is not enough), one can define a variant of one-wayness.

*One-Wayness.* We introduce a non-standard form of one-wayness to analyze the properties of our scheme. Intuitively, a function is one-way on a challenge (first or second) input if, given $F(k, x)$ and the other input, it is hard for any adversary to compute the challenge input. Below we provide definitions of one-wayness on the second input. Although we do not use it in our construction, it is also possible to define one-way-ness in the first input analogously to one-wayness in the second input. Intuitively, given $x$ and $F(k, x)$, it should be hard to compute $k$. If KeyRoll is one-way in the first input, then the construction inherits additional useful properties, which we describe in the full version [21]. We now present our definitions for one-wayness on the second input.[6]

[5] In practice we cannot use the PRF construction because it is not commutative.

[6] We remark that the standard definition of one-wayness requires the adversary to find an equivalent pre-image of the function, and not the exact same pre-image.

**Definition 3.3 (One-Wayness (on the Second Input)).** *A family of functions* $\mathcal{F} = \{F_\lambda\}_\lambda$ *where* $F_\lambda : \mathbb{K}_\lambda \times \mathcal{X}_\lambda \to \mathbb{K}_\lambda$ *is one-way on its second input if there exists a negligible function* negl *such that for every probabilistic polynomial-time adversary* $\mathcal{A}$ *and every* $\lambda$

$$\Pr[x' = x : k \leftarrow \mathbb{K}_\lambda, x \leftarrow \mathcal{X}_\lambda, x' \leftarrow \mathcal{A}(1^\lambda, k, F_\lambda(k, x))] \leq \mathsf{negl}(\lambda).$$

*where* $k$ *and* $x$ *are sampled randomly from their respective domains.*

*$\ell$-Point One-Wayness.* The definition above can be generalized to the setting where $\mathcal{A}$ obtains polynomially many (in the security parameter) samples of $(k, F_\lambda(k, x))$ pairs for different randomly sampled $k$ but the same $x$. This additional property allows us to further constrain the power of the adversary. We defer the definition and discussion to the full version [21].

### 3.2 The Key Graph

In our construction, parties track the group key(s) by assigning each key to a point on the lattice. When a party evolves the group key, it defines the transition from one point on the lattice to another. In fact, our construction defines the transitions from a family of points to another family of points. Therefore, it is useful to describe the key lattice as a directed acyclic graph, where the vertices are labeled with keys, and the edges encode key evolutions.[7] Specifically, we define a key graph $\mathcal{G}$, where each lattice point $\mathbf{i} \in \mathbb{N}^n$ is a vertex, and each vertex is labeled with a single key or with $\perp$. In our discussion, we refer to vertices by the lattice points they represent. There exists a directed edge from vertex $\mathbf{i}$ to $\mathbf{j}$ if $\mathbf{j} = \mathsf{increment}(\mathbf{i}, k)$ for some $k \in [n]$, and we say that $\mathbf{i}$ *precedes* $\mathbf{j}$, or $\mathbf{j}$ *succeeds* $\mathbf{i}$, if there is an edge from $\mathbf{i}$ to $\mathbf{j}$. Edges in a key graph are labeled with the key evolutions that they represent. We say there exists a *path* $\rho$ of length $\ell$ between two vertices $\mathbf{i}$ and $\mathbf{i}'$ if there exists a sequence of edges $(v_1, v_2), (v_2, v_3), \ldots, (v_{\ell-1}, v_\ell)$ such that (a) $v_1 = \mathbf{i}$, (b) $v_\ell = \mathbf{i}'$, and (c) $v_{j-1}$ precedes $v_j$ for all $j \in [2, \ell]$. The local state held by each party in our protocol is a pair $(L, E)$, where $L$ denotes the key lattice held by the party and $E$ represents the edges representing the transformation between keys.

### 3.3 Instantiation

We now describe how parties manipulate a key lattice.

*Generating a Set of Key Evolutions.* In our construction, each party updates the group key in its own "direction" in $L$; the $d$th party ($U \in \mathcal{P}$ for which $\phi(U) = d$) always updates the group key towards larger indices in the $d$th dimension on the lattice. A key update $\sigma \in \Sigma$ sent by one party to another is therefore a tuple $(d, j, x)$, where $d$ is a dimension in the key lattice (generated by the party

[7] In this work, every graph is a directed acyclic graph.

$U$ such that $\phi(U) = d$), $j \in \mathbb{N}$ is an index that annotates how many times the updating party has updated the group key, and $x \in \mathcal{X}$ is data that describes how to update the key (for $\mathsf{KeyRoll}$). In other words, $\Sigma = [n] \times \mathbb{N} \times \mathcal{X}$. The $j$th key evolution generated by any party therefore defines the transition from *every* index $\mathbf{i}$ to index $\mathbf{i}'$ such that $\mathbf{i}^{(d)} = j$ and $\mathbf{i}' = \mathsf{increment}(\mathbf{i}, d)$, and it defines the evolution to use update data $x$. In our construction, the space $\mathcal{X}$ is the same as described in Definitions 3.2 and 3.3.

Observe that each key update in our construction defines a group of key evolutions, which can be described in our graphical representation as a group of edges. We require commutativity of $\mathsf{KeyRoll}$ to guarantee that when transitioning from key $k$ to key $k'$ (over one or more edges), where $k$ is represented by vertex $u$, $k'$ is represented by vertex $v$, and there are multiple paths between $u$ and $v$ in some party's key lattice, it does not matter which path is taken.

*Our KeyRoll Function.* Our construction depends on the discrete logarithm assumption to instantiate $\mathsf{KeyRoll}(\mathsf{k}, x)$ as $\mathsf{k}^x$. That is to say, let key space $\mathbb{K}$ be a prime-order group $\mathsf{G}$ in which the discrete log problem is hard, and let update space $\mathcal{X}$ be $\mathbb{Z}_{|\mathsf{G}|-1}$. This construction easily satisfies our commutativity requirement since $(\mathsf{k}^x)^{x'} = (\mathsf{k}^{x'})^x$. For appropriately chosen parameters, the construction is trivially unpredictable. If the discrete logarithm problem is hard in $\mathsf{G}$, then $\mathsf{KeyRoll}$ is also one-way on its second input.

**Computable Lattice:** The description of a key lattice $L$ may not be "complete" in the sense that given a set $L = \{(\mathbf{i}, \mathsf{k})\}$ representing a key lattice, it may be possible to infer the keys assigned to other indices on the lattice (i.e., points not in $L$). Below we illustrate the possible inferences depend on the choice of the $\mathsf{KeyRoll}$ function. Consider the case where $\mathsf{KeyRoll}$ is defined using XOR, then knowing the key at $\mathbf{i}$ and a succeeding key at $\mathbf{i}' = \mathsf{increment}(\mathbf{i}, d)$ allows us to derive the update $\sigma$, which may allow us to derive the keys at other lattice points $\mathbf{j}$ such that $\mathbf{j}^{(d)} = \mathbf{i}^{(d)}$.

The function $\mathsf{Computable}(L, E) \rightarrow L'$ outputs all the computable lattice points $L'$ given the original lattice $L$ and a set of updates $E = \{(d, j, x)\}$, where $d \in [n]$ is the dimension, $j$ is an index and $x$ is the argument to $\mathsf{KeyRoll}$.

Two examples below illustrate the dependence of $\mathsf{Computable}$ on the properties of $\mathsf{KeyRoll}$. Figure 3 illustrates how $\mathsf{Computable}$ works if a $\mathsf{KeyRoll}$ function is not one-way. Figure 4 illustrates the difference when $\mathsf{KeyRoll}$ is one-way.

The function $\mathsf{Computable}(L, E)$ can be realized as follows:

1. Interpret the lattice $L$ as a directed graph $\mathcal{G}$. Initially this graph has no edges, only vertices from $L$.
2. Add every edge from $E$ to the graph. Recall that every edge in $E$ corresponds to multiple edges in $\mathcal{G}$. Specifically, $e = (d, j, x)$ describes all edges that begin with a vertex $(\ldots, j, \ldots)$ and end with a vertex $(\ldots, j+1, \ldots)$ where $j$ and $j+1$ are on the $d$th position, and each edge is labeled with the update $x$.

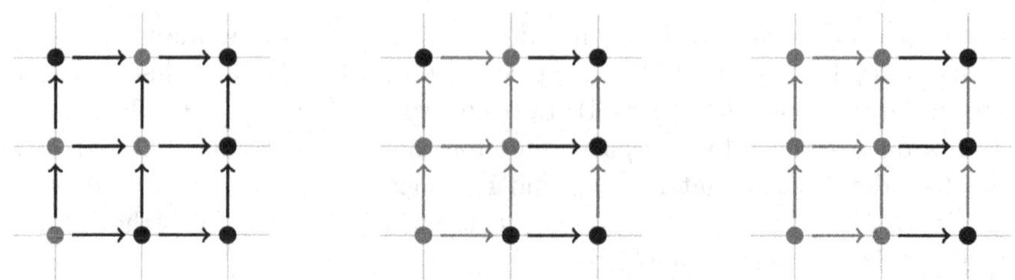

**Fig. 3.** Suppose the red keys in the figure on the left are revealed in a key lattice. If the KeyRoll function is unpredictable but not one-way, then knowledge of a pair of adjacent keys would reveal all edges (updates) in the corresponding row or column, as shown in the middle figure. These inferred edges lead to additional computable keys (colored in red) in the right figure. (Color figure online)

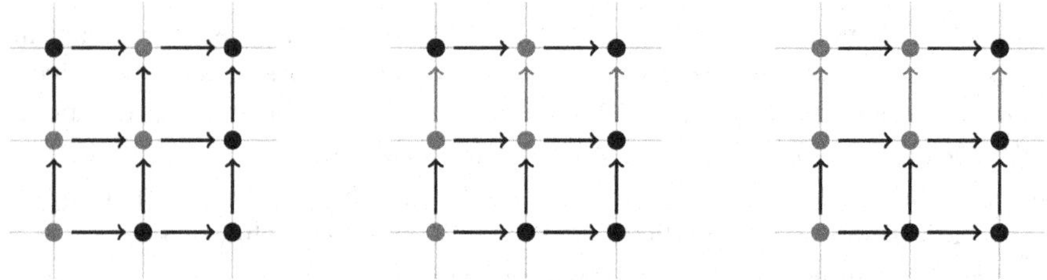

**Fig. 4.** Begin with the same lattice as in Fig. 3 but assume that KeyRoll is one-way. The lattice points in the left figure do not allow us to compute a new lattice with more keys. Given additional information on the edges in the middle figure, one additional lattice point is computable (top left in the right figure).

3. Traverse $\mathcal{G}$ from the origin. For every pair of predecessor-successor vertices $(u, v)$ where $u \neq \perp$ and $v = \perp$, if there exists an edge labeled with $x$ connecting $u$ to $v$, then compute $k_v \leftarrow \mathsf{KeyRoll}(k_u, x)$.
4. Similar as above, but traverse $\mathcal{G}$ backwards and if there exist two predecessor-successor vertices $(u, v)$ where $k_u = \perp$ and $k_v \neq \perp$ then compute $k_u \leftarrow \mathsf{KeyRoll}^{-1}(k_v, x)$, where $x$ is the label on the edge between $u$ and $v$. Note that, if KeyRoll is one-way on its first input, then this step is omitted, as it is hard to compute $u$ given $x$ and $v$.

**Adding Keys:** Parties may update the key lattice using $\mathsf{Update}(L, e) \rightarrow L'$ which takes a key lattice $L$ and an update $e = (d, j, x)$ and a returns a new key lattice $L'$ as follows:

- Let $D = \{\mathbf{i}_m\}$ be all $d$-maximal index vectors in $L$.
- Output a new lattice $L'$ with additional points defined by $(\mathsf{increment}(\mathbf{i}), \mathsf{KeyRoll}(\mathsf{k}_\mathbf{i}, x))$ for all $\mathbf{i} \in D$.

Note that since the lattice points included in D are $d$-maximal, all keys in $\mathsf{increment}(\mathbf{i}, d+1)$ are $\perp$ in the original lattice $L$. One can think of this operation as (possibly) adding keys to the lattice based on $e$.

In the key graph interpretation of the lattice, Update looks at the largest index $i$ for which a key is defined in dimension $d$, and labels every edge from $i$ to $i+1$ in dimension $d$ (holding every other dimension constant) with update $e$.

**Forgetting Keys:** A key lattice is an infinite object. To manage memory requirements, (and looking ahead, to provide FS) we remove keys from a party's local version of the key lattice. The function $\mathsf{Forget}(L, \mathbf{i}) \rightarrow L'$ takes a key lattice $L$ and an index vector $\mathbf{i}$, and returns a new lattice $L'$ such that all keys in index vectors $\mathbf{i}'$ such that $\mathbf{i}' < \mathbf{i}$, are set to $\perp$. Implicitly, Forget also deletes from a party's state all of the edges leading to vertices that have been forgotten.

We use windowing to limit state expansion and provide FS (Sect. 1.2). When we write $\mathsf{Forget}(L, w) \rightarrow L'$, then Forget works as follows, where $w$ is the window parameter. We call $\mathbf{i}_w$ below the *threshold index vector.*

- For every dimension $d \in [n]$, let $i_d$ the maximum $j$ such that there is a key defined in $L$ at index $j$ in dimension $d$.
- Let $\mathbf{i}_w$ be an index vector such that for every $d \in [n]$, $\mathbf{i}_w^{(d)} = \max(0, i_d - w)$.
- Execute $\mathsf{Forget}(L, \mathbf{i}_w)$ and return the new lattice $L'$.

### 3.4 Key Lattice as a Key Management Technique

The key lattice is enough to build a concurrent group messaging protocol from existing primitives such as pairwise channels. The following generic approach uses a key lattice to build concurrent group messaging using three building blocks: (1) an initial group key, (2) secure pairwise channels between all parties in a group and (3) an AEAD scheme for sending payload messages.

- Given the initial group key $\mathsf{k}_0$, the parties initialize their key lattice with $(\mathbf{0}, \mathsf{k}_0)$, and assign $\perp$ to the key at every other lattice point.
- If a party at index $d \in [n]$ updates the key for the $j$th time, it samples $x \xleftarrow{\$} \mathcal{X}$ and sends $(d, j, x)$ using the secure pairwise channels.
- Upon receiving $(d, j, x)$ the receiver adds key $\mathsf{k}' \leftarrow \mathsf{KeyRoll}(\mathsf{k}, x)$ to the lattice at point $\mathbf{i}'$, where $\mathsf{k}$ is the maximal key in the lattice and is located at point $\mathbf{i}$, and $\mathbf{i}' \leftarrow \mathsf{increment}(\mathbf{i}, d)$.
- When a party at index $d \in [n]$ sends an application message, it encrypts the message using the maximal key $\mathsf{k}$ in its local key lattice and sends the ciphertext to the group members (without using secure pairwise channels). The ciphertext is encrypted using AEAD where the associated data is the lattice index corresponding to the key used to encrypt the message.
- Upon receiving the ciphertext encrypting a payload message, the receiver checks whether it has the key in the key lattice required to decrypt. If so, then the receiver decrypts it immediately. Otherwise, the receiver buffers the message until it receives sufficient information to decrypt.

- Storing all the keys that are in the key lattice is expensive and trades off forward security. Every party runs $\mathsf{Forget}(L, w)$ for its lattice $L$ and the window parameter $w$ every time the party processes an update message.

## 4 Group Key Agreement

To agree on the very first shared key we use an existing group key agreement (GKA) protocol. There are many definitions of security of GKA protocols; for our purposes we adapt the one from [14] as it captures strong-forward secrecy and a strong corruption model. For our GM protocol to be asynchronous, the GKA subprotocol must also be asynchronous; this is true for the model of [14].

In this section, we reproduce the definition and introduce a few syntactic tweaks. For the full security definition we refer the reader to the full version [21]. The GKA will be used to construct our GM protocol in Sect. 6.

**Definition 4.1 (Group Key Agreement).** *We use $G \subseteq \mathcal{P}$ to denote some group of players that participate in the protocol. Each party $U \in \mathcal{P}$ is assumed to already have a long term public/private key pair $(\mathtt{pk}_U, \mathtt{sk}_U)$. We assume a PKI exists and the public keys are available to all parties.*

*The protocol consist of two stateful algorithms.*

- $\{m_V\}_{V \in G} \leftarrow \mathsf{GKA.Init}(G)$*: Initialize an instance of the GKA protocol for a group $G$ and return a set of responses, one for every party in $G$.*
- $\{m_V\}_{V \in G} \leftarrow \mathsf{GKA.Recv}(M)$*: Process message $M$ and return a set of responses.*

*The GKA outputs* done *with a key $k$ to notify that the protocol completed.*

## 5 Group Randomness Messaging

We present the group randomness messaging (GRM) abstraction through which the parties communicate update messages. The main functionality is to send authenticated data and a ciphertext encrypting a random key update to all members in the group using pairwise channels. We require the pairwise channels to have FS & PCS properties.

**Definition 5.1 (Group Randomness Messaging (GRM)).** *Consider the player executing the protocol is $U$, a GRM scheme consists of three stateful algorithms.*

- $\{c_{U,V}\}_{V \in G} \leftarrow \mathsf{GRM}_U.\mathsf{Init}(\mathsf{k}, w, G)$*: initialize the GRM instance using the initial key* $\mathsf{k}$*, the window size $w$, and the group members $G$.*
*This step initializes the internal state* $\mathsf{state}_{U,i}$*. The output is a set of ciphertexts, one for every player in $G$.*
- $\{c_{U,V}\}_{V \in G} \leftarrow \mathsf{GRM}_U.\mathsf{Evolve}()$*: output a ciphertext $c_{U,V}$ for every $V \in G$.*

- $\sigma_{V,U} \leftarrow \mathsf{GRM}_U.\mathsf{Recv}(c_{V,U})$: *process the ciphertext* $c_{V,U}$*, update the internal state and return the plaintext* $\sigma_{V,U}$ *if the decryption is successful. If decryption is unsuccessful, return* $\perp$.

In the above definition, $\sigma_{V,U}$ is a triple $(U, j, x)$ where $U$ is the identity of the sender, $j$ is a positive integer and $x \in \mathcal{X}$. The full version [21] discusses the correctness and security definitions for GRM.

### 5.1 Instantiation

We instantiate GRM using PKEAD. In essence, every party keeps a queue of $w$ public and secret key-pairs. This queue is updated every time the party calls Evolve by dropping the oldest keypair and adding a new one. Each party $U$ also maintains a public key for every other party $V$ which is updated whenever $U$ receives the output of $V$'s Evolve. $U$ uses this public key in order to encrypt messages to $V$. $U$ also maintains an integer $j_V$ that tracks the index of the latest public key $U$ has received from $V$.

This initial message sent by each party is a pair $(\mathbf{pk}_U^0, m)$, where $\mathbf{pk}_U^0$ is the party's initial ephemeral public key, $m$ is a MAC on the public key using the key k provided as input to Init. Where k is the key output by a GKA execution, this effectively "ties" a GRM to the GM application that uses it, as the MAC links the output k of a GKA session with the GRM session that will be used to evolve the key.

On a high level, the protocol achieves PCS because public keys are cycled over time and FS because old keys are dropped. Our construction is detailed below. Let the set $\mathcal{X}$ to be domain from which updates are randomly sampled.

- $\mathsf{GRM}_U.\mathsf{Init}(\mathsf{k}, w, G)$: Generate an ephemeral key pair $(\mathbf{pk}_U^0, \mathbf{sk}_U^0)$. Initialize $\mathsf{state}_U.\mathbf{sks} = \{\mathbf{sk}_U^0\}$ and $\mathsf{state}_U.\mathbf{pks} = \emptyset$, and save $w$ as the window parameter. Compute $m \leftarrow \mathsf{MAC}(\mathbf{pk}_U^0; \mathsf{k})$, where k is the input key, $\mathbf{pk}_U^0$ is the message and MAC is a cryptographic MAC scheme. Send the same message $(\mathbf{pk}_U^0, m)$ to every member in $G$.
- $\mathsf{GRM}_U.\mathsf{Evolve}()$:
  1. A new private key $\mathbf{sk}_U^{j+1}$ is generated, along with its public key $\mathbf{pk}_U^{j+1}$.
  2. Sample $x \xleftarrow{\$} \mathcal{X}$ and let $\sigma \leftarrow (U, j+1, x)$, where $j$ is the index of the latest secret key in $\mathsf{state}_U.\mathbf{sks}$.
  3. Repeat the steps below for every $V \in G$ (including $U$).
     - If the public key of the receiver $V$ is not known, abort.
     - Call $(c, t) \leftarrow \mathsf{PKEAD.Enc}(\mathbf{pk}_U^{j+1} \| \sigma, j_V; \mathbf{pk}_V^{j_V})$ and then set $c_{U,V} \leftarrow (c, t, j_V)$. Note that $\mathbf{pk}_V^{j_V}$ can be found in $\mathsf{state}_U.\mathbf{pks}$ and $j_V$ is the index of the public key associated with $V$.
  4. $\mathsf{state}_U$ is updated as follows.
     - Add $\mathbf{sk}_U^{j+1}$ to $\mathsf{state}_{U,i}.\mathbf{sks}$
     - If $|\mathsf{state}_U.\mathbf{sks}| > w$, remove the oldest one (i.e., $\mathbf{sk}_U^{j-w}$).

- $\mathsf{GRM}_U.\mathsf{Recv}(c_{V,U})$: There are two possible message formats. The message output by Init is an ephemeral public key $\mathbf{pk}_V^0$ with a Mac; if the message is this type, then verify the Mac using the key k provided to Init[8] and then set $V$'s public key in $\mathsf{state}_U.\mathbf{pks}$ to be $(0, \mathbf{pk}_V^0)$. All other messages are handled as follows.
  1. Parse the message $c_{V,U}$ as $(c, t, j)$, where $j$ is an index into the current user $U$'s secret key.
  2. Find secret key $\mathbf{sk}_U^j$. Abort the protocol if it does not exist.
  3. $\mathbf{pk}_V^{j_V} \| \sigma_{V,U} \leftarrow \mathsf{PKEAD.Dec}(c, t, j; \mathbf{sk}_U^j)$, abort if this step returns $\perp$.
  4. Add or update $V$'s public key in $\mathsf{state}_U.\mathbf{pks}$ to be $(j, \mathbf{pk}_V^{j_V})$.
  5. Let $j_{\mathsf{min}}$ be the smallest $j$ in $\{(j, \mathbf{pk}_V^{i_V}) : V \in G\}$.
  6. Delete all secret keys $\mathbf{sk}_U^j$ where $j < j_{\mathsf{min}}$.
  7. Return $\sigma_{V,U}$

**Theorem 5.1.** *Let $\mathcal{A}$ be an adversary against the GRM game, let $\mathcal{B}$ be an adversary against the PKEAD game, and let $\mathcal{C}$ be an adversary against the MAC EUF-CMA game. Then*

$$\mathsf{Adv}_{\mathcal{A}}^{\mathsf{grm}} \leq n_S \cdot \mathsf{Adv}_{\mathcal{C}}^{\mathsf{mac}} + 2 \cdot |Q|_{\mathsf{max}} \cdot n_Q \cdot \mathsf{Adv}_{\mathcal{B}}^{\mathsf{pkead}}.$$

*where $|Q|_{\mathsf{max}}$ is the upperbound for the number of oracles in a group, $n_Q$ is the upperbound of the number of queries to the encryption oracle that $\mathcal{B}$ makes on behalf of $\mathcal{A}$ for the instance under test, and $n_S = \mathsf{poly}(\lambda)$ is the maximum number of concurrent GRM sessions that $\mathcal{A}$ is allowed to invoke in its security game.*

For a proof of this theorem see the full version [21].

## 6 Group Messaging

We define group messaging as a protocol which establishes and evolves a lattice of keys. Parties may additionally send messages encrypted under the group keys, which must be decrypted successfully by the other group members.

Our definition of group messaging assumes the existence of a Group Key Agreement (GKA) primitive (Sect. 4).

**Definition 6.1 (Group Messaging).** *A group messaging protocol consists of five stateful algorithms defined as follows:*

- $\mathsf{GM.Init}(G, w)$: *Initialize the protocol with group $G \subseteq \mathcal{P}$ and the windows size $w$. Output a set of messages, one for each party in $G$.*
- $\mathsf{GM.Evolve}()$: *Outputs a set of update messages, one for each party in $G$.*
- $\mathsf{GM.Recv}(M)$: *Processes the message $M$ (e.g., from the network), and outputs a response.*
- $\mathsf{GM.Enc}(m)$: *Encrypts a plaintext $m$ and outputs a ciphertext.*
- $\mathsf{GM.Dec}(c)$: *Decrypts ciphertext $c$ and outputs a plaintext.*

8 If verification fails due to trying the wrong key from multiple concurrent sessions, return $\perp$ and process the incoming message via Recv of a different session.

### 6.1 Security Definition

The security of GM is modeled via a game between a challenger and an adversary, where the key lattice tracks the evolution of the group key(s) over time. Our freshness definition specifies the conditions under which a particular state (in our case the state is a key in the key lattice) is not compromised by the adversary. Contrary to the definitions of freshness in other key agreement works (e.g., [4, 19]), we state freshness below with respect to a specific lattice point.

The adversary invokes oracles $\Pi^{\mathsf{gm}}_{U,i}$ where $U$ is a group member and $i \in [1, \ldots, n_S]$, where the subscript $i$ denotes a specific instance of the oracle that belongs to party $U$. Different instances that belong to the same party may share long-term keys, e.g., identity keys. The adversary invokes the oracles arbitrarily as long as it follows the constraints described in Sect. 2.

We assume there is an instance of the GKA oracle running under every GM oracle. This method allows us to inherit the partnering definition and many oracle queries. Nevertheless, our description is self-contained since we reproduce the common oracle queries in the GM definition. Additional details of the GKA can be found in Sect. 4.

Each oracle $\Pi^{\mathsf{gm}}_{U,i}$ maintains internal variables to track each party's view of the key lattice and the group messages that have been received by that party. They also collectively maintain global state that tracks which elements of the key lattice and which key updates have been explicitly revealed to the adversary. We denote by $L^{\mathsf{rev}}_{\mathsf{sid}}$ the key lattice describing all keys (points on the lattice) which are revealed to the adversary, and we denote by $E^{\mathsf{rev}}_{\mathsf{sid}}$ the set of key updates, modeled as edges in the graphical interpretation of the key lattice, which are revealed to the adversary. $S^{\mathsf{rev}}_{\mathsf{sid}} = (L^{\mathsf{rev}}_{\mathsf{sid}}, E^{\mathsf{rev}}_{\mathsf{sid}})$ denotes all of the key material that is revealed to the adversary in some session $\mathsf{sid}$. The session ID $\mathsf{sid}$ is a unique identifier for the group members who have successfully completed the initial group key agreement and established a session (described in detail in Sect. 4 since it is a property inherited from GKA). Indeed, $\mathsf{sid}$ is not defined when a GKA session begins, but this is not an issue since the session's lattice is instantiated only after the session is established. The full information on the key lattice available to the adversary is given by $\mathsf{Computable}(L^{\mathsf{rev}}_{\mathsf{sid}}, E^{\mathsf{rev}}_{\mathsf{sid}})$. We remark that the session ID ($\mathsf{sid}$) is not the same as the instance ID. The instance of an oracle, e.g., $(U, i)$, is established when the oracles are initialized, but the session ID is only established some time later, after the oracles are ready to evolve keys.

Specifically, the oracles maintain the following state:

- $\delta_{U,i} \in \{\mathsf{pending}, \mathsf{accept}, \mathsf{abort}\}$ indicates whether the oracle is ready to start evolving keys.
- $L_{U,i}$ represents the key lattice maintained by oracle $\Pi^{\mathsf{gm}}_{U,i}$. We use the language from Sect. 3 to describe the key lattice.
- $\mathsf{state}_{U,i}$ is the remaining state that the implementation may keep. (For our protocol, this includes $E_{U,i}$, a set of edges between lattice points, as well as the state held by underlying subprotocols.)
- $S^{\mathsf{rev}}_{\mathsf{sid}} = (L^{\mathsf{rev}}_{\mathsf{sid}}, E^{\mathsf{rev}}_{\mathsf{sid}})$ represents the key lattice $L^{\mathsf{rev}}_{\mathsf{sid}}$ containing all the revealed keys by the adversary as well as the revealed updates $E^{\mathsf{rev}}_{\mathsf{sid}}$ in session $\mathsf{sid}$.

The full details of the GM oracles are specified below.

- $\Pi^{\mathsf{gm}}_{U,i}.\mathsf{Init}(G, w)$: Initialize an instance of the GM protocol for the group members in $G$ where $U \in G$ and $w$ is the window size. Set $\delta_{U,i} = \mathsf{pending}$ and return a hash function $\mathsf{H}$. The response is returned to the adversary.
- $\Pi^{\mathsf{gm}}_{U,i}.\mathsf{Corrupt}()$: Return the long-term secret to the adversary.
- $\Pi^{\mathsf{gm}}_{U,i}.\mathsf{Reveal}()$: If $\delta_{U,i} \neq \mathsf{accept}$ then return $\bot$. Otherwise, return the set of keys that are computable from $L_{U,i}$, and add these keys to $L^{\mathsf{rev}}_{\mathsf{sid}}$
- $\Pi^{\mathsf{gm}}_{U,i}.\mathsf{StateReveal}()$: If $\delta_{U,i} \neq \mathsf{accept}$ then return $\bot$. Else, return the internal state $\mathsf{state}_{U,i}$, excluding the computable keys $L_{U,i}$. [9]
- $\Pi^{\mathsf{gm}}_{U,i}.\mathsf{Evolve}()$: If $\delta_{U,i} = \mathsf{abort}$ then return $\bot$. Else, return a set of message $\{M_V\}_{V \in G}$.
- $\Pi^{\mathsf{gm}}_{U,i}.\mathsf{Recv}(M)$:
  - If $\delta_{U,i} = \mathsf{abort}$ then this call does nothing.
  - Otherwise process the message, optionally update the state $\mathsf{state}_{U,i}$ and the key lattice $L_{U,i}$. Return a set of messages $\{M_V\}_{V \in G}$. The input $M$ should be from either the output of $\mathsf{Recv}$ or $\mathsf{Evolve}$.
- $\Pi^{\mathsf{gm}}_{U,i}.\mathsf{Dec}(c)$: Use the available internal state to decrypt the ciphertext $c$ and output the plaintext. If the oracle does not have enough information to decrypt the message, then it is buffered.
- $\Pi^{\mathsf{gm}}_{U,i}.\mathsf{Enc}(m)$: Encrypts the plaintext $m$ using the maximal key in $L_{U,i}$ and returns a ciphertext.
- $\Pi^{\mathsf{gm}}_{U,i}.\mathsf{Test}(m_0, m_1)$: This is defined in the security game below.

By execution of Corrupt, Reveal and StateReveal queries the adversary can learn the entire secret internal state of the oracle $\Pi^{\mathsf{gm}}_{U,i}$. Specifically, Reveal gives the party's current group keys, and StateReveal gives the party's internal state except for what is provided by the former two queries. Corrupt gives the party's long-term public key and secret key (from the PKI); because this is only used for the GKA protocol, which we require to be forward secure, this reveals the initial group keys in *future* GKA executions. Also note that the above gives the adversary a decryption oracle via Dec.

**Modeling Pairwise Channels in the Oracle Game:** In our general oracle game, the adversary is permitted to invoke the oracles in any order, which models an asynchronous network. However, to describe the guarantees that the protocol achieves when windowing, we define a syntactic model to describe the messages sent "between parties" in the oracle game. Specifically, between every ordered pair of parties $(U, V)$ the adversary maintains a special buffer $\mathcal{C}_{U,V}$ called a *channel* representing the pairwise connection between $U$ and $V$. When an oracle query returns a message $c$ to be sent from $U$ to $V$, the adversary places $(c, n)$ into $\mathcal{C}_{U,V}$, where $n$ is an integer recording that $c$ is the $n$th message placed into the channel.

[9] For our construction, this adds all of the edges in $E_{U,i}$ to $E^{\mathsf{rev}}_{\mathsf{sid}}$.

In the above game description, each oracle provides three queries to generate messages to other parties. $\Pi^{\mathsf{gm}}_{U,i}.\mathsf{Enc}(m)$ encrypts a message using the oracle's latest key and returns a ciphertext which is forwarded to all other parties. Whenever a $\Pi^{\mathsf{gm}}_{U,i}.\mathsf{Enc}(m)$ query is made, the returned message $c$ is simultaneously put into the channels $\mathcal{C}_{U,V}$ for all $V \in G$. $\Pi^{\mathsf{gm}}_{U,i}.\mathsf{Evolve}()$ generates a key evolution, but returns *a different message* for each other party in the execution. Similarly, $\Pi^{\mathsf{gm}}_{U,i}.\mathsf{Recv}(M)$ may output a different message for every other party in the execution, but it may also output no messages. Whenever a $\Pi^{\mathsf{gm}}_{U,i}.\mathsf{Evolve}()$ or $\Pi^{\mathsf{gm}}_{U,i}.\mathsf{Recv}(M)$ query is made, the oracle returns a list of ciphertexts $c_V$, one for each $V \in G$. Each of these messages is immediately placed into the corresponding channel $\mathcal{C}_{U,V}$ along with its index.

A message $c$ generated by an Enc query is removed from its corresponding buffer only when it is input to a corresponding oracle $\Pi^{\mathsf{gm}}_{V,j}.\mathsf{Dec}(c)$. A message $c$ generated by an Recv or Evolve query is removed from its corresponding buffer only when it is input to a corresponding oracle $\Pi^{\mathsf{gm}}_{V,j}.\mathsf{Recv}(c)$. Note that if an oracle receives a message that it cannot yet process due to reordering of messages over a pairwise channel, then the oracle is expected to buffer the message until it can process the message, and return the result once it can process the message.

The adversary may additionally invoke Recv or Dec oracles on messages that have not been placed in channels but instead were adversarially generated. These actions do not affect the channels.

**Partnering:** For group messaging, *partnering* is analogous to the case for GKA. Intuitively, a group in a GKA protocol is partnered if the parties participate in the same session and agreed on the same group key. For group messaging, parties are partnered if they are running a protocol with each other to agree on a lattice of group keys.

**Definition 6.2 (Partnering).** *Given a group $G \subseteq \mathcal{P}$ and a set of pairs $Q = (U, i_U)_{U \in G}$ defining associated oracles $\Pi^{\mathsf{gm}}_{U,i_U}$, we say the oracles are* partnered *if the underlying GKA oracles $\Pi^{\mathsf{gka}}_{U,i_U}$ are partnered.*

For some security parameter $\lambda$ we define a security game for the adversary $\mathcal{A}$, this consists of the set of participants $\mathcal{P}$ where $n$ (the number of participants) is a polynomial function of $\lambda$, as is the maximum number of sessions per participant $n_S$. Thus the number of oracles $\Pi^{\mathsf{gm}}_{U,i}$ is also a polynomial function of $\lambda$. The adversary $\mathcal{A}$ is given at the start of the game all the public keys $\mathsf{pk}_U$ for $\mathsf{pk} \in \mathcal{P}$ and it interacts with the oracles $\Pi^{\mathsf{gm}}_{U,i}$ via the sequence of oracle queries as above.

**Freshness:** We now define freshness for our game. Intuitively, we say that a key is *fresh* if it has not been revealed to the adversary, either explicitly via Reveal queries, or implicitly, via a combination of Reveal and StateReveal queries. The global state $S^{\mathsf{rev}}_{\mathsf{sid}}$ tracks the keys computable by the adversary, and a key is fresh if and only if it is not computable from $S^{\mathsf{rev}}_{\mathsf{sid}}$.

**Definition 6.3 (Freshness).** *In a session* sid*, a key* $\mathsf{k}_{\mathsf{i}^*}$ *with at index* $\mathbf{i}^*$ *is fresh if and only if it is not computable from* $S_{\mathsf{sid}}^{\mathsf{rev}}$ *using the* Computable *function, as defined in the group messaging definition (Definition 6.1).*

Depending on when the adversary invokes Corrupt on a party and learns its long-term secret key, the adversary might learn *all* messages delivered to that party, and any such key or update material is included in $S_{\mathsf{sid}}^{\mathsf{rev}}$. Therefore, keys that the adversary can learn from messages delivered to this party are not fresh.

**Security Game:** The security game tries to break the semantic security of a message sent between the parties. It runs in two phases, the division between the two phases is given by the point in which the adversary executes a Test query.

- **Phase 1:** All queries can be executed without restriction.
- **Test Query:** $\Pi_{U,i}^{\mathsf{gm}}.\mathsf{Test}(m_0, m_1)$: Given two equal length messages $m_0$ and $m_1$, if $\mathsf{k}_U$ is fresh, where $\mathsf{k}_U$ is the maximal key of instance$(U, i)$, then the challenger selects a bit $b \in \{0, 1\}$ and applies $\Pi_{U,i}^{\mathsf{gm}}.\mathsf{Enc}(m_b)$, returning the output $\mathtt{ct}^*$ to the adversary. We denote the test oracle by $\Pi_{U^*,i^*}^{\mathsf{gm}}$. We call $\mathbf{i}^*$ the test index.
- **Phase 2:** All queries can be executed except for:
  1. Any query that would add $\mathsf{k}_{\mathsf{i}^*}$ to the set of keys computable from $S_{\mathsf{sid}}^{\mathsf{rev}}$.
  2. If $\mathtt{ct}^*$ is at any point processed by $\mathsf{Dec}(\mathtt{ct}^*)$, by the oracles, then the result is not returned to the adversary but the game still continues.

At the end of the game, the adversary $\mathcal{A}$ needs to output its guess $b'$, and wins the game if $b = b'$. We define $\mathsf{Adv}_{\mathcal{A}}(\lambda) = 2 \cdot |\Pr[b = b'] - 1/2|$.

**Definition 6.4 (Security of Group Messaging).** *A GM scheme is secure if for any probabilistic polynomial time adversary* $\mathcal{A}$ *the advantage* $\mathsf{Adv}_{\mathcal{A}}(\lambda)$ *is negligible in the security parameter* $\lambda$.

Thanks to the underlying key lattice, our security game captures FS and PCS at the same time in a natural way. Specifically, queries to Reveal, StateReveal or Corrupt during **Phase 1** are used for capturing PCS and queries to these oracles during **Phase 2** captures FS. Unlike prior definitions [4,33] we do not need to use epoches or separate definitions for PCS and FS.

**Correctness.** Intuitively, a GM protocol is correct if every message that is encrypted with the group key is correctly decrypted by every recipient. We write the formal definition with respect to the oracles defined for our security game. Our definition of correctness requires all encrypted messages must eventually be correctly decrypted under a property called "well-ordered execution" which we define as well.

**Definition 6.5 (Correctness of Group Messaging).** *A GM protocol is* correct *if in every infinite execution by every PPT adversary* $\mathcal{A}$ *who is allowed to query the GM oracles except* Corrupt, StateReveal, Reveal *and* Test *and must* *deliver all messages, for all* $U, i$*, for all* $c \leftarrow \Pi^{\mathsf{gm}}_{U,i}.\mathsf{Enc}(m)$*, and for all* $V \in G \backslash \{U\}$ *there exists a* $j$ *and an oracle call* $m' \leftarrow \Pi^{\mathsf{gm}}_{V,j}.\mathsf{Dec}(c)$ *such that* $(U, i)$ *is partnered with* $(V, j)$ *and* $m' = m$*.*

Recall that when we apply windowing, some party may be forced by the protocol to discard the group key used to decrypt a message that has still not been delivered to it. To facilitate our analysis of correctness when windowing, we define an ordering property of an execution that describes how many times a party may evolve the group key between the moment it sends a message and that message is delivered.

*$\omega$-Well-Ordered Execution.* Recall that our oracle game tracks the order in which messages are returned from oracles to be sent to other parties via our abstraction of pairwise channels, and that the adversary may delay and reorder messages sent via the pairwise channels. A channel is *$\omega$-well-ordered* if the $n$th message sent over $C$ is removed from the channel before the $(n + \omega)$th message (via delivery to the correct oracle), for all $n \in \mathbb{N}$. An execution is *$\omega$-well-ordered* if all pairwise channels are $\omega$ well-ordered.

We claim that when windowing with our protocol, for any $\omega$-well-ordered execution, if the window parameter $w$ is greater than or equal to $\omega$, then the protocol is correct. The proof is trivial by construction of the protocol. When $w < \omega$, windowing may force some decryption keys to be purged before the corresponding message is delivered.

*Remark 6.1 (Well Ordering and Network Synchrony).* Well-ordering is a strict relaxation of network synchrony that depends on ordering messages rather than on time. In a synchronous network, a delay parameter of $\Delta$ implies $\Delta$-well-ordered channels; therefore, setting $w = \Delta$ implies correctness. If the network is asynchronous, then $w$ must be set to $\infty$ to guarantee correctness. However, this sacrifices forward secrecy, as parties may store old group keys indefinitely.

### 6.2 GM from GRM and GKA

We first present our construction of GM from GKA, GRM, and a CCA-secure AEAD scheme; we then prove security of GM based on the underlying primitives.

**Protocol Overview.** In our construction of a group messaging protocol, parties maintain local versions of a global key lattice in order to track the group key. They then encrypt and decrypt messages using keys from the lattice, and they update the group key by adding new keys on the key lattice. Our protocol uses the above primitives to initialize their key lattices, encrypt and decrypt messages using the keys in the lattice, send updates to the group key, and remove keys from their lattices. Specifically, each party maintains a local key lattice $\mathcal{L}$, a local set of key updates $\mathcal{E}$, and a buffer $\mathtt{B}$ of unprocessed messages, which contains both GRM messages that it cannot yet process and application messages that it is not yet able to decrypt. Every update $e \in \mathcal{E}$ has the form $(d, i, x)$ where

$d \in [n]$ corresponds to the dimension of the party that generates the update, $i$ is an index and $x$ is key transformation data. Parties also maintain a list of index vectors $\mathcal{I} \in (\mathbb{N}^n)^n$ that tracks each party's view of the current key of every other party, which is used to optimistically exclude keys from its state.

*Message Headers and the* Recv *Subprotocol.* We make the distinction between *protocol messages* and *application messages*. Protocol messages in GM are either GKA messages (to agree on an initial group key) or GRM messages (to evolve the group key). Application messages are encryptions under some group key.

Our construction uses a single Recv function to process every incoming protocol message, provided in Fig. 7, which directs the incoming message to the appropriate subprotocol (either GKA or GRM). To help distinguish between GKA protocol messages and GRM protocol messages in the descriptions of the protocols and the proofs, we say that a message is a "GKA message" if it contains a prefix gka, and a message is a "GRM message" if it contains a prefix grm. In an implementation, these headers can be encoded as flags. Where the context is clear, we elide these prefixes from the exposition.

**Initialization:** When a group of parties begin a GM protocol, they initialize the execution via GM.Init(), which is described in Fig. 5. Each party saves the set of other parties in the protocol and the window parameter. They also agree on a hash function H described below, which is a public parameter. The parties then run GKA in order to agree on an initial group key. Note that the key lattice and GRM is *not* initialized yet; they can only be initialized after the GKA outputs the initial key as shown in Fig. 6.

**Sending and Receiving Key Updates:** Our GM construction uses GRM as a transport for generating and communicating random key updates. In Fig. 6 and Fig. 7 we specify how parties generate new key updates and process updates form other parties, respectively.

Specifically, parties invoke GRM.Evolve() to receive a random key update $\sigma$ along with an encryptions of the update to send to each other party via pairwise channel. The calling party adds $\sigma$ to its set of edges $\mathcal{E}$ and computes any possible new points in $\mathcal{L}$. When a party receives a key update, it calls GRM.Recv() on the update, and if a key update is returned then it adds the update as an edge in $\mathcal{E}$ and computes any possible new keys in $\mathcal{L}$. If it cannot yet decrypt the key update, it buffers the message.

**Encrypting and Decrypting a Message:** Whenever a party wishes to encrypt a message $m$ using the group key, it calls GM.Enc using the maximal key in its key store. Specifically, we require a hash function $\mathsf{H}\colon \mathbb{K} \to \mathsf{K}$, that maps from the keyspace of the key lattice to the keyspace for a CCA-secure

AEAD encryption scheme.[10] When a party encrypts a message, it provides the hashed key corresponding to the maximal index $\mathbf{i}$ in its key lattice $\mathcal{L}$ as input to $\mathsf{AEAD.Enc}$, and it includes the index $\mathbf{i}$ as associated data. The encrypting party then forwards the encrypted message to every other party.

When a party seeks to decrypt a message, it looks up the corresponding key (the index of which is found in associated data), and supplies the hashed key to $\mathsf{AEAD.Dec}$. When a party receives an encrypted message, it checks whether the index of the key used to encrypt is in $\mathsf{Computable}(\mathcal{L}, \mathcal{E})$. If so, it uses the key at that index to decrypt the message. If not, it adds the message to the buffer $\mathsf{B}$. The implementations of encryption and decryption in given in Fig. 8 and Fig. 9.

**Pruning the Key Lattice:** Parties continuously attempt to prune elements from their local state, both in order to manage the size of the state they keep, and also because deleting old keys facilitates forward secrecy. When a party knows that it will no longer receive any messages encrypted with keys below a particular key index $\mathbf{i}$, it optimistically prunes all such keys from its lattice via $\mathsf{Forget}(\mathcal{L}, \mathbf{i})$. Additionally, if ever a key index exceeds the key window (keys whose index vector that are less than the threshold index vector $\mathbf{i}_w$) it purges the key (and relevant updates) from $\mathcal{L}$ (and $\mathcal{E}$).

Whenever a party receives an encryption from a party $V$, it updates its index vector $\mathcal{I}[\phi(V)]$ tracking the keys used by $V$. Recall that because our construction requires key updates to move toward higher lattice indices, the set of future indices is the union of the $n$-dimensional hyperplanes $\mathcal{H}^* = \bigcup_{\mathbf{i}_V \in \mathcal{I}} \mathcal{H}_{\geq \mathbf{i}_V}$. Any index *outside* this union represents an obsolete key, and the related keys are deleted via $\mathsf{Forget}$ in Fig. 9.

In summary, keys and edges that fall outside the window parameter are deleted as specified in Fig. 7. Keys and edges that will not be used in the future are deleted as specified in Fig. 9. This is possible because parties also send their maximal lattice point along with their message (in Fig. 8) so that the receiving party can compute the minimum view (lattice point) of all parties and delete keys and edges that are smaller than the minimum view.

On execution of $\mathsf{GM.Init}()$, run $\mathsf{GKA.Init}(G)$ and output the result. Note that $U$ holds the long-term key pair $(\mathbf{pk}_U^{lt}, \mathbf{sk}_U^{lt})$.

**Fig. 5.** Algorithm for $\mathsf{GM.Init}(G, w)$

[10] This hash function's purpose is semantic to convert between types. We only require (informally) that if the adversary does not know $k$ then it does not know $\mathsf{H}(k)$. We elide discussion of $\mathsf{H}$ in the proof.

$U$ calls $\{c_{U,X}\}_{X \in G} \leftarrow \mathsf{GRM.Evolve}()$, and outputs $c_{U,X}$ to $X$ for $X \in G$.

**Fig. 6.** Algorithm for $\mathsf{GM.Evolve}()$

If $M$ is a GKA message:

- Compute $\{m_{U,V}\}_{V \in G} \leftarrow \mathsf{GKA.Recv}(M)$, and output $m_{U,V}$ to party $V$ for $V \in G$.
- If $\mathsf{GKA}$ outputs $\mathsf{done}$ with a key $\mathsf{k}$:
  - Initialize $\mathcal{L}$ with the point $(\mathbf{0}, \mathsf{k})$.
  - Initialize a GRM execution via $\{c_{U,V}\}_{V \in G} \leftarrow \mathsf{GRM.Init}(\mathsf{k}, w, G)$ and send $c_{U,V}$ to $V$ for $V \in G$.
  - Initialize an empty message buffer $\mathtt{B} \leftarrow \emptyset$.

If $M$ is a GRM message received from party $V$:

1. Compute $\sigma \leftarrow \mathsf{GRM.Recv}(M)$. If $\sigma = \perp$, then add $M$ to $\mathtt{B}$ and return. Otherwise, let $(d, j, x) \leftarrow \sigma$, add $(d, j, x)$ to the set of edges $\mathcal{E}$ and then compute $\mathcal{L} \leftarrow \mathsf{Computable}(\mathcal{L}, \mathcal{E})$.[a]
2. Delete deprecated keys using $\mathcal{L} \leftarrow \mathsf{Forget}(\mathcal{L}, w)$.
3. Delete deprecated edges from $\mathcal{E}$ that precede the corresponding index in the threshold index vector (see Section 3.3). Specifically, suppose the threshold index vector is $\mathbf{i}_w = (i_1, \ldots, i_{n_S})$ and $E = \{(d_k, j_k, x_k)\}_k$, then remove all edges $(d_k, j_k, x_k)$ where $j_k < i_{d_k}$.
4. While $\mathtt{B}$ is not empty or $\mathtt{B}$ has not changed from the previous iteration:
   - For every message $M \in \mathtt{B}$, execute $\mathsf{GM.Recv}(M)$

[a] A sanity check would be that $d = \phi(V)$ and $j$ should equal the $d$th element of the maximal index vector of $\mathcal{L}$.

**Fig. 7.** Algorithm for $\mathsf{GM.Recv}(M)$

Player $U$ finds the $\phi(U)$-maximal lattice point $\mathbf{i}$ in its local lattice $\mathcal{L}$, computes $(\mathtt{ct}, t) \leftarrow \mathsf{AEAD.Enc}(m, U \| \mathbf{i}; \mathsf{H}(k_{\mathbf{i}}))$, and then returns $(\mathtt{ct}, U \| \mathbf{i}, t)$.

**Fig. 8.** Algorithm for $\mathsf{GM.Enc}(M)$

### 6.3 Concrete Costs

We give an estimate of our concrete communication cost for 128-bit security. Since the payload ciphertext form is $(\mathtt{ct}, U \| i, t)$, the concrete communication cost for 32 bytes payload is $32 + 3 \cdot 16 = 80$ bytes, assuming the identity $U$, the lattice point $i$, and the AEAD tag $t$ are 128 bits. Additionally, the update ciphertext has the form $(c, t, j)$ where $c$ is a ciphertext encrypting $\mathsf{pk} \| U \| i \| x$, under a public key encryption scheme, where $\mathsf{pk}$ is assumed to be 32 bytes and

Parse $M$ as $(\mathsf{ct}, V\|\mathbf{i}, t)$. If $M$ is not of this form, return $\perp$. Then:

- If $\mathbf{i} < \mathbf{i}_w$, where $\mathbf{i}_w$ is the threshold index vector, or if $\mathbf{i} < \mathcal{I}[\phi(V)]$, return $\perp$.
- Update $\mathcal{I}[\phi(V)] \leftarrow \mathbf{i}$, compute $\mathbf{i}_{\mathsf{min}}$ as the index vector of the element-wise minimum of all $\mathbf{i} \in \mathcal{I}$, and then execute $\mathcal{L} \leftarrow \mathsf{Forget}(\mathcal{L}, \mathbf{i}_{\mathsf{min}})$.
- Find the key at $\mathbf{i}$ in $\mathcal{L}$ using $\mathsf{Computable}(\mathcal{L}, \mathcal{E})$, if $\mathsf{k}_{\mathbf{i}} = \perp$, then add $M$ to $\mathtt{B}$ and return $\perp$.
- If $\mathsf{k}_{\mathbf{i}} \neq \perp$, compute $m \leftarrow \mathsf{AEAD.Dec}(\mathsf{ct}, V\|\mathbf{i}, t; \mathsf{H}(k_{\mathbf{i}}))$. If $m = \perp$, abort the protocol. Otherwise, return $m$.

**Fig. 9.** Algorithm for $\mathsf{GM.Dec}(M)$

$x$ is from the update space assumed to be 16 bytes. One update message is needed for every party in the group, for a group size of 128, the update cost is $128 \cdot (32 + 5 \cdot 16) = 14.3$ KB. Our scheme uses less communication than Weidner et al. [33] which has a payload ciphertext cost of 139 bytes and an update cost of 39.6 KB in the same setting.

The storage overhead comes from the window parameter $w$ and the group size $N$. Specifically, we need to maintain at most $w$ update messages per party and only one key in the lattice at the minimum view. For a window size of $1,000$ and 128 parties, the storage requirement would be just over 14 MB in the worst case which is insignificant in today's devices.

### 6.4 Main Theorem

We now state our main theorem. The proof is in the full version [21].

**Theorem 6.1 (Security of Group Messaging).** *If $\mathcal{A}$ is an adversary against the GM game, then there exist adversaries $\mathcal{B}$, $\mathcal{C}$, and $\mathcal{D}$ such that*

$$\mathsf{Adv}^{\mathsf{gm}}(\mathcal{A}) \leq 2n_S \mathsf{Adv}^{\mathsf{gka}}(\mathcal{B}) + 2n_S n \mathsf{Adv}^{\mathsf{grm}}(\mathcal{C}) + n_S n_q \mathsf{Adv}^{\mathsf{cca}}(\mathcal{D}),$$

*where $n_S = \mathsf{poly}(\lambda)$ is the maximum the number of GM sessions $\mathcal{A}$ may invoke, and $n_q = \mathsf{poly}(\lambda)$ is the maximum number of keys that $\mathcal{A}$ may query in a session.*

**Acknowledgments.** This work was supported in part by the Defense Advanced Research Projects Agency (DARPA) and Space and Naval Warfare Systems Center, Pacific (SSC Pacific) under contract No. FA8750-19-C-0502 (Approved for Public Release, Distribution Unlimited). The first and third author would also like to thank the FWO under an Odysseus project GOH9718N, and by CyberSecurity Research Flanders with reference number VR20192203.

The work of the first author was conducted whilst he was at KU Leuven, the third author whilst he was at SRI International, and the fourth author whilst he was a student at UC Irvine.

Any opinions, findings and conclusions or recommendations expressed in this material are those of the author(s) and do not necessarily reflect the views of any of the funders. The U.S. Government is authorized to reproduce and distribute reprints for governmental purposes notwithstanding any copyright annotation therein.

## References


1. Alwen, J., Auerbach, B., Noval, M.C., Klein, K., Pascual-Perez, G., Pietrzak, K.: DeCAF: decentralizable continuous group key agreement with fast healing. Cryptology ePrint Archive, Report 2022/559 (2022). https://eprint.iacr.org/2022/559
2. Alwen, J., et al.: CoCoA: concurrent continuous group key agreement. In: Dunkelman, O., Dziembowski, S. (eds.) EUROCRYPT 2022, Part II. LNCS, May–June 2022, vol. 13276, pp. 815–844. Springer, Heidelberg (2022). https://doi.org/10.1007/978-3-031-07085-3_28
3. Alwen, J., Coretti, S., Dodis, Y.: The double ratchet: security notions, proofs, and modularization for the signal protocol. In: Ishai, Y., Rijmen, V. (eds.) EUROCRYPT 2019, Part I. LNCS, vol. 11476, pp. 129–158. Springer, Cham (2019). https://doi.org/10.1007/978-3-030-17653-2_5
4. Alwen, J., Coretti, S., Dodis, Y., Tselekounis, Y.: Security analysis and improvements for the IETF MLS standard for group messaging. In: Micciancio, D., Ristenpart, T. (eds.) CRYPTO 2020, Part I. LNCS, vol. 12170, pp. 248–277. Springer, Cham (2020). https://doi.org/10.1007/978-3-030-56784-2_9
5. Alwen, J., Coretti, S., Jost, D., Mularczyk, M.: Continuous group key agreement with active security. In: Pass, R., Pietrzak, K. (eds.) TCC 2020, Part II. LNCS, vol. 12551, pp. 261–290. Springer, Cham (2020). https://doi.org/10.1007/978-3-030-64378-2_10
6. Alwen, J., Hartmann, D., Kiltz, E., Mularczyk, M.: Server-aided continuous group key agreement. In: Yin, H., Stavrou, A., Cremers, C., Shi, E. (eds.) ACM CCS 2022, November 2022, pp. 69–82. ACM Press (2022). https://doi.org/10.1145/3548606.3560632
7. Bienstock, A., Dodis, Y., Rösler, P.: On the price of concurrency in group ratcheting protocols. In: Pass, R., Pietrzak, K. (eds.) TCC 2020, Part II. LNCS, vol. 12551, pp. 198–228. Springer, Cham (2020). https://doi.org/10.1007/978-3-030-64378-2_8
8. Borisov, N., Goldberg, I., Brewer, E.: Off-the-record communication, or, why not to use PGP. In: Proceedings of the 2004 ACM Workshop on Privacy in the Electronic Society, pp. 77–84 (2004)
9. Boyd, C., Mathuria, A., Stebila, D.: Protocols for Authentication and Key Establishment. Information Security and Cryptography. Springer, Heidelberg (2020). https://doi.org/10.1007/978-3-662-58146-9
10. Bresson, E., Chevassut, O., Pointcheval, D.: Provably authenticated group Diffie-Hellman key exchange—the dynamic case. In: Boyd, C. (ed.) ASIACRYPT 2001. LNCS, vol. 2248, pp. 290–309. Springer, Heidelberg (2001). https://doi.org/10.1007/3-540-45682-1_18
11. Bresson, E., Chevassut, O., Pointcheval, D.: Dynamic group Diffie-Hellman key exchange under standard assumptions. In: Knudsen, L.R. (ed.) EUROCRYPT 2002. LNCS, vol. 2332, pp. 321–336. Springer, Heidelberg (2002). https://doi.org/10.1007/3-540-46035-7_21
12. Bresson, E., Chevassut, O., Pointcheval, D., Quisquater, J.J.: Provably authenticated group Diffie-Hellman key exchange. In: Reiter, M.K., Samarati, P. (eds.) ACM CCS 2001, November 2001, pp. 255–264. ACM Press (2001). https://doi.org/10.1145/501983.502018
13. Bresson, E., Manulis, M.: Securing group key exchange against strong corruptions. In: Abe, M., Gligor, V. (eds.) ASIACCS 2008, March 2008. pp. 249–260. ACM Press (2008)

14. Bresson, E., Manulis, M., Schwenk, J.: On security models and compilers for group key exchange protocols. In: Miyaji, A., Kikuchi, H., Rannenberg, K. (eds.) IWSEC 2007. LNCS, vol. 4752, pp. 292–307. Springer, Heidelberg (2007). https://doi.org/10.1007/978-3-540-75651-4_20
15. Brzuska, C., Fischlin, M., Smart, N.P., Warinschi, B., Williams, S.C.: Less is more: relaxed yet composable security notions for key exchange. Int. J. Inf. Sec. **12**(4), 267–297 (2013). https://doi.org/10.1007/s10207-013-0192-y
16. Brzuska, C., Fischlin, M., Warinschi, B., Williams, S.C.: Composability of Bellare-Rogaway key exchange protocols. In: Chen, Y., Danezis, G., Shmatikov, V. (eds.) ACM CCS 2011, October 2011, pp. 51–62. ACM Press (2011). https://doi.org/10.1145/2046707.2046716
17. Cachin, C., Guerraoui, R., Rodrigues, L.: Introduction to Reliable and Secure Distributed Programming, 2nd edn. Springer, Heidelberg (2014). https://doi.org/10.1007/978-3-642-15260-3
18. Cohn-Gordon, K., Cremers, C., Dowling, B., Garratt, L., Stebila, D.: A formal security analysis of the signal messaging protocol. J. Cryptol. **33**(4), 1914–1983 (2020). https://doi.org/10.1007/s00145-020-09360-1
19. Cohn-Gordon, K., Cremers, C., Garratt, L., Millican, J., Milner, K.: On ends-to-ends encryption: asynchronous group messaging with strong security guarantees. In: Lie, D., Mannan, M., Backes, M., Wang, X. (eds.) ACM CCS 2018, October 2018, pp. 1802–1819. ACM Press (2018). https://doi.org/10.1145/3243734.3243747
20. Cohn-Gordon, K., Cremers, C.J.F., Garratt, L.: On post-compromise security. In: Hicks, M., Köpf, B. (eds.) Computer Security Foundations Symposium, CSF 2016, pp. 164–178. IEEE Computer Society Press (2016). https://doi.org/10.1109/CSF.2016.19
21. Cong, K., Eldefrawy, K., Smart, N.P., Terner, B.: The key lattice framework for concurrent group messaging. Cryptology ePrint Archive, Report 2022/1531 (2022). https://eprint.iacr.org/2022/1531
22. Cremers, C., Hale, B., Kohbrok, K.: The complexities of healing in secure group messaging: why cross-group effects matter. In: Bailey, M., Greenstadt, R. (eds.) USENIX Security 2021, August 2021, pp. 1847–1864. USENIX Association (2021)
23. Dowling, B., Günther, F., Poirrier, A.: Continuous authentication in secure messaging. In: Atluri, V., Di Pietro, R., Jensen, C.D., Meng, W. (eds.) ESORICS 2022, Part II. LNCS, September 2022, vol. 13555, pp. 361–381. Springer, Heidelberg (2022). https://doi.org/10.1007/978-3-031-17146-8_18
24. Fuchsbauer, G., Kamath, C., Klein, K., Pietrzak, K.: Adaptively secure proxy re-encryption. In: Lin, D., Sako, K. (eds.) PKC 2019. LNCS, vol. 11443, pp. 317–346. Springer, Cham (2019). https://doi.org/10.1007/978-3-030-17259-6_11
25. Ingemarsson, I., Tang, D.T., Wong, C.K.: A conference key distribution system. IEEE Trans. Inf. Theor. **28**(5), 714–719 (1982). https://doi.org/10.1109/TIT.1982.1056542
26. Kobeissi, N., Bhargavan, K., Blanchet, B.: Automated verification for secure messaging protocols and their implementations: a symbolic and computational approach. In: 2017 IEEE European Symposium on Security and Privacy (EuroS&P), pp. 435–450. IEEE (2017)
27. Lamport, L.: Time, clocks, and the ordering of events in a distributed system. Commun. ACM **21**(7), 558–565 (1978). https://doi.org/10.1145/359545.359563
28. Pijnenburg, J., Poettering, B.: On secure ratcheting with immediate decryption. In: Agrawal, S., Lin, D. (eds.) ASIACRYPT 2022, Part III. LNCS, December 2022, vol. 13793, pp. 89–118. Springer, Heidelberg (2022). https://doi.org/10.1007/978-3-031-22969-5_4

29. Poettering, B., Rösler, P., Schwenk, J., Stebila, D.: SoK: game-based security models for group key exchange. In: Paterson, K.G. (ed.) CT-RSA 2021. LNCS, May 2021, vol. 12704, pp. 148–176. Springer, Heidelberg (2021). https://doi.org/10.1007/978-3-030-75539-3_7
30. Rescorla, E.: Subject: [MLS] TreeKEM: an alternative to ART. MLS Mailing List (2019). https://mailarchive.ietf.org/arch/msg/mls/e3ZKNzPC7Gxrm3Wf0q96dsLZoD8/. Accessed 19 Jan 2022
31. Rösler, P., Mainka, C., Schwenk, J.: More is less: on the end-to-end security of group chats in Signal, Whatsapp, and Threema. In: 2018 IEEE European Symposium on Security and Privacy, EuroS&P 2018, 24–26 April 2018, London, United Kingdom, pp. 415–429. IEEE (2018). https://doi.org/10.1109/EuroSP.2018.00036
32. Steiner, M., Tsudik, G., Waidner, M.: Diffie-Hellman key distribution extended to group communication. In: Gong, L., Stern, J. (eds.) ACM CCS 1996, March 1996, pp. 31–37. ACM Press (1996). https://doi.org/10.1145/238168.238182
33. Weidner, M., Kleppmann, M., Hugenroth, D., Beresford, A.R.: Key agreement for decentralized secure group messaging with strong security guarantees. In: Vigna, G., Shi, E. (eds.) ACM CCS 2021, November 2021, pp. 2024–2045. ACM Press (2021). https://doi.org/10.1145/3460120.3484542
34. Weidner, M.A.: Group messaging for secure asynchronous collaboration. M. Phil thesis, University of Cambridge, June 2019. https://mattweidner.com/acs-dissertation.pdf
35. WhatsApp Inc.: Whatsapp encryption overview. Online, September 2021. https://www.whatsapp.com/security/WhatsApp-Security-Whitepaper.pdf. Accessed 19 Jan 2022

# Identity-Based Matchmaking Encryption from Standard Lattice Assumptions

Roberta Cimorelli Belfiore[1(✉)], Andrea De Cosmo[2], and Anna Lisa Ferrara[1]

[1] University of Molise, 86100 Campobasso, Italy
r.cimorellibelfio@studenti.unimol.it , annalisa.ferrara@unimol.it
[2] Leonardo S.p.A. Cyber and Security Solutions Division, Rome, Italy

**Abstract.** Identity-Based Matchmaking Encryption (IB-ME), initially proposed by Ateniese et al. (Crypto 2019), is an extension of Identity-Based Encryption (IBE) that emphasizes privacy and authenticity. It ensures that the content of a message is only revealed when the recipient's identity matches the intended recipient specified by the sender, and when the target sender's identity, chosen by the receiver during decryption, matches the actual sender's identity. In cases where there is a mismatch, no information about the sender, receiver, or message is disclosed.

Francati et al. (IndoCrypt 2021) observed that the privacy definition for IB-ME solely guarantees the concealment of the message and sender identity when the receiver's identity does not match the intended recipient specified by the sender. It does not consider whether the target sender's identity matches the actual sender's identity. To overcome this limitation, they proposed an *enhanced privacy* notion and developed an IB-ME scheme that achieves it in the plain model, even though relying on non-standard assumptions.

In this paper, we address the problem of constructing an IB-ME scheme that offers enhanced privacy under *standard assumptions* with particular emphasis on post *quantum security*. Specifically, we first show how to obtain an IB-ME that achieves the notion of enhanced privacy using as building blocks any anonymous IBE and reusable computational extractors. Next, we show how to construct an IB-ME starting from an IB-ME satisfying enhanced privacy and a context-hiding homomorphic signature, thereby ensuring not only enhanced privacy but also authenticity. Notably, our framework allows for secure IB-ME schemes to be instantiated in the standard model from lattice assumptions, thus providing also post-quantum security.

**Keywords:** Identity-based Anonymous Encryption · Lattice-based Cryptography · Identity-based Matchmaking Encryption


C. Pöpper and L. Batina (Eds.): ACNS 2024, LNCS 14584, pp. 163–188, 2024.
https://doi.org/10.1007/978-3-031-54773-7_7

# 1 Introduction

Matchmaking Encryption (ME), as introduced by Ateniese et al. in [4], enables the sender and receiver to establish policies that must be met for an encrypted message to be disclosed. ME schemes must guarantee two fundamental security properties: privacy and authenticity. Privacy ensures that the sender's private information, such as the selected policy and its attributes, as well as the confidentiality of the ciphertext, remain completely concealed from unintended receivers. Authenticity, on the other hand, guarantees that an adversarial sender cannot generate a valid ciphertext if it fails to satisfy the receiver's policy requirements.

The notions of privacy and authenticity make ME highly applicable in covert communication services. When both communicating parties are designated as intended targets by each other, the encrypted traffic can be correctly retrieved. However, if this is not the case, the decryption process fails without revealing the cause of failure. Furthermore, ME can find practical use in Internet of Things (IoT) applications and data sharing services [7,21].

Building upon the concept of matchmaking encryption in the identity-based context, Ateniese et al. [4] further developed and formalized the concept of *Identity-Based Matchmaking Encryption* (IB-ME) exploring its applications, particularly in the creation of an anonymous bulletin board operating over a Tor network.

In IB-ME, the receiver $\rho$ specifies a target sender's identity $\mathsf{snd}$ during decryption, while the sender $\sigma$ beside specifying the intended receiver's identity $\mathsf{rcv}$, must obtain an encryption key $\mathsf{ek}_\sigma$ from the authority to encrypt a message. Messages can be decrypted by a receiver only if its identity matches the sender's intended recipient, and the target sender's identity also matches the identity associated with the encryption key $\mathsf{ek}_\sigma$ used in the encryption process. In other words, the encrypted message can only be decrypted if there is a match in both directions (i.e., $\rho = \mathsf{rcv}$ and $\sigma = \mathsf{snd}$); otherwise, no information beyond the mismatch is leaked. Specifically, in IB-ME privacy ensures that unauthorized parties cannot access the plaintext or learn any additional information about the sender's or the receiver's identities, while authenticity guarantees that the ciphertext can only be generated by means of the actual sender's encryption key.

Francati et al. [12] observed that the privacy definition for IB-ME defined in [4] solely ensures the secrecy of the message and sender identity when the recipient's identity does not match the one specified by the sender. However, it does not take into account whether the actual sender's identity corresponds to the desired sender's identity. To overcome this limitation, they proposed an *enhanced privacy notion* which ensures that the identities $\sigma$ and $\mathsf{rcv}$, along with the message derived from the ciphertext, remain hidden even when $\rho = \mathsf{rcv}$ and $\sigma \neq \mathsf{snd}$. They also developed an IB-ME scheme that achieves enhanced privacy in the plain model, even though relying on non-standard assumptions.

*Our Contribution.* In this paper, we address the problem of designing an IB-ME scheme achieving both enhanced privacy and authenticity from standard assumptions by proposing a generic construction. Specifically, we first show how to obtain an IB-ME that achieves the notion of enhanced privacy using as building blocks any anonymous IBE and any reusable extractor. In particular, the scheme allows the recipient to only decrypt a ciphertext if it knows, or can guess, the sender's identity. This is done by adding an extra layer of encryption that uses a one-time pad generated from the sender's identity through a reusable computational extractor. Moreover, we show how to construct an IB-ME that satisfies both enhanced privacy and authenticity starting from any IB-ME that satisfies enhanced privacy and a context-hiding fully homomorphic signature. Given a Boolean circuit $C$, and a signature $\varsigma_{\mathsf{x}}$ that verifies the authenticity of a message $\mathsf{x}$, a fully homomorphic signature scheme allows to generate a signature $\varsigma_{C(\mathsf{x})}$ that certifies the value of $C(\mathsf{x})$. A homomorphic signature scheme, roughly speaking, is said to be context hiding if $\varsigma_{C(\mathsf{x})}$ does not contain any information on the original message $\mathsf{x}$. The main idea behind our construction is to let the sender's encryption key consist of a homomorphic signature $\varsigma_{\sigma}$ over the sender's identity $\sigma$ (computed during the setup by means of secret parameters). Moreover, we define a family of circuits $\mathsf{C}$ such that for each circuit $C \in \mathsf{C}$ it holds that $C(\sigma) = 1$ if and only if the sender identity $\sigma$ matches a target identity $\mathsf{snd}$ hard-wired in the circuit $C$ along with a message $\mathsf{m}$, a receiver identity $\mathsf{rcv}$ and the ciphertext $\mathsf{c}$ computed encrypting $\mathsf{m}$ for the receiver $\mathsf{rcv}$ with the underlying IB-ME. When the sender $\sigma$ encrypts $\mathsf{m}$ it produces a ciphertext $(\mathsf{c}, \varsigma_{C(\sigma)})$ where the signature $\varsigma_{C(\sigma)}$ certifies that $C(\sigma) = 1$ (i.e., it ensures that $\mathsf{snd}$ hard-wired in $C$ matches the sender's identity $\sigma$). Intuitively, the enhanced privacy follows by the privacy property of the underlying IB-ME along with the context-hiding property of the homomorphic signature scheme which ensures that, when homomorphically evaluating the pair $(\sigma, \varsigma_{\sigma})$ with respect to the circuit $C$, the resulting signature $\varsigma_{C(\sigma)}$ will not reveal anything about $\sigma$ making it difficult for an attacker to guess the sender's identity. On the other hand, authenticity follows by the unforgeability of the homomorphic signature scheme which ensures that, it is difficult for an adversary to produce a valid signature $\varsigma_{C(\sigma)}$ that verifies with respect to the circuit $C$ without knowing a signature on the identity $\sigma$.

Our framework leads to IB-ME schemes that achieve both enhanced privacy and authenticity. Moreover, since it allows for IB-ME schemes to be instantiated in the standard model from lattice assumptions (as discussed later in the paper), the framework yields constructions achieving both enhanced privacy and authenticity from standard lattice assumptions, thus also providing post-quantum security.

*Related Works.* IB-ME schemes have been introduced by Ateniese et al. in [4]. Specifically, they presented the more general concept of ME, where both the sender and receiver (each with their own attributes) can specify policies the other party must meet for the message to be revealed. The authors also designed an IB-ME scheme in the random oracle model from the bilinear Diffie-Hellman assumption. Francati et al. later showed the first construction for IB-ME without random oracles [12]. The construction uses as building block the anonymous IBE in [13] to achieve privacy and relies on a generic transform that uses a signature scheme and a multi-theorem Non-Interactive Zero Knowledge (NIZK) proof system for any NP language to achieve authenticity. Additionally, they defined the stronger security notion for privacy, known as *enhanced privacy.* Subsequently, Chen et al. [8] presented an IB-ME from symmetric external Diffie-Hellman assumption in the standard model. The scheme is proven to be secure under the weaker notion of privacy, but does not achieve enhanced privacy. Wang et al. in [20] proposed a different security model for IB-ME and showed a construction inspired by Chen's work [8] from lattice assumptions which, however, does not achieve enhanced privacy. Finally, we note that an IB-ME that achieves both enhanced privacy and authenticity based on lattice assumptions can be obtained by building upon the enhanced private IB-ME achieved through our construction that utilizes any anonymous IBE and reusable extractors from lattice assumptions. The addition of authenticity can be achieved through the transformation described by Francati et al. [12]. However, implementing this transformation needs the use of signature schemes and expensive multi-theorem NIZK proofs. Recently, Peikert et al. [18] instantiated NIZK proof systems for any NP language based on the plain Learning With Errors (LWE) problem, with polynomial approximation factors. The zero-knowledge property of such NIZK constructions holds for a single statement and proof. To achieve a multi-theorem NIZK, it must be combined with transformations described in [10,11] that generally turn single-theorem NIZK proofs into multi-theorem zero-knowledge protocols.

*Organization.* The remainder of this paper is organized as follows. In Sect. 2 we review some useful concepts. In Sect. 3, we present a generic construction for IB-ME that satisfies enhanced privacy. Then, we propose a generic transform that results in an IB-ME that also satisfies the authenticity security notion. In Sect. 4, we point out possible instantiations of our framework from lattice assumptions. We conclude the paper in Sect. 5.

## 2 Preliminaries

*Notation.* We denote by $\mathbb{N}$ the set of non-negative integers, by $\mathbb{Z}$ the set of integers, and by $\mathbb{R}$ the set of real numbers. For a positive integer $n$, we write $[n]$ to denote the set of integers $\{1, \ldots, n\}$.

Uppercase boldface letters (such as $\mathbf{X}$) are used to denote random variables, lowercase letters (such as $x$) to denote concrete values, and uppercase letters (such as $X$) to denote sets.

Vectors are denoted by lowercase boldface letters (such as $\boldsymbol{v}$), we refer to the $i$-th component of $\boldsymbol{v}$ as $v_i$. We use calligraphic letters (such as $\mathcal{A}$) to denote algorithms. When an algorithm $\mathcal{A}$ has access to an oracle $\mathcal{O}$, we define the set of queries that $\mathcal{A}$ issues to $\mathcal{O}$ as $Q_{\mathcal{O}}$, and the set of outputs that $\mathcal{O}$ provides to $\mathcal{A}$ as $O_{\mathcal{O}}$, respectively. Given a set $S$, the notation $x \leftarrow S$ means that $x$ is sampled from $S$, whereas $x \leftarrow\!\!\$\, S$ means that $x$ is chosen uniformly at random from $S$; if $\mathbf{D}$ is a distribution, we use the notation $x \leftarrow\!\!\$\, \mathbf{D}$ to mean that $x$ is chosen according to the distribution $\mathbf{D}$. A run of a PPT algorithm $\mathcal{A}$ having input $x$ and output $y$ is denoted as $y \leftarrow\!\!\$\, \mathcal{A}(x)$.

*Negligible Functions.* We denote by $\lambda \in \mathbb{N}$ the security parameter. We assume that every algorithm takes as input the security parameter, written in unary (i.e. $1^\lambda$). A function $\epsilon\colon \mathbb{N} \to [0,1]$ is *negligible* in the security parameter $\lambda$ if it is asymptotically smaller than any inverse polynomial function in $\lambda$ i.e. if $\epsilon(\lambda) \in O(1/p(\lambda))$. We refer to an unspecified negligible function in the security parameter as $\mathsf{negl}(\lambda)$. We say that an event occurs with overwhelming probability if it occurs with probability at least $1 - \epsilon(\lambda)$, for some negligible function $\epsilon(\lambda)$.

*Unpredictability and Indistinguishability.* The min-entropy of a random variable $\mathbf{X} \in X$ is $\mathbb{H}_\infty(\mathbf{X}) \stackrel{\text{def}}{=} -\log \max_{x \in X} \Pr[\mathbf{X} = x]$, and it measures the best chance to predict $\mathbf{X}$ (by a computationally unbounded algorithm).

Given two random variables $\mathbf{X}$ and $\mathbf{Y}$, we say that they are *computationally* indistinguishable ($\mathbf{X} \stackrel{c}{\approx} \mathbf{Y}$) if for all PPT distinguishers $\mathcal{D}$ it holds that the advantage $\mathrm{Adv}^{\mathsf{ind}}_{\mathbf{X},\mathbf{Y},\mathcal{D}}(\lambda) := \left|\Pr\left[\mathcal{D}(1^\lambda, \mathbf{X}) = 1\right] - \Pr\left[\mathcal{D}(1^\lambda, \mathbf{Y}) = 1\right]\right|$ is negligible.

## 2.1 Identity-Based Matchmaking Encryption

Let $\sigma$ and $\rho$ respectively denote the identities of the sender and the receiver, whereas let $\mathsf{rcv}$ and $\mathsf{snd}$ denote the target identities specified by the sender and the receiver, respectively. Thus, in order to encrypt a message using the sender's own encryption key $\mathsf{ek}_\sigma$, the sender $\sigma$ must specify the identity of the intended receiver $\mathsf{rcv}$. Similarly, when decrypting a ciphertext, the receiver $\rho$ specifies the identity of the sender $\mathsf{snd}$ and uses its own decryption key $\mathsf{dk}_\rho$ to decrypt the message. The original message is revealed only in case of a match, that is when $\sigma = \mathsf{snd}$ and $\rho = \mathsf{rcv}$. If $\sigma \neq \mathsf{snd}$ or $\rho \neq \mathsf{rcv}$ we say that a mismatch occurs.

Formally, an IB-ME [4,12] with message space $\mathcal{M}$, ciphertext space $\mathcal{C}$, and identity space $\mathcal{I}$, is a tuple of five probabilistic polynomial-time algorithms ($\mathsf{Setup}$, $\mathsf{SKGen}$, $\mathsf{RKGen}$, $\mathsf{Enc}$, $\mathsf{Dec}$) such that:

$\mathsf{Setup}(1^\lambda)$: On input the security parameter $1^\lambda$, the randomized setup algorithm returns as output a master public-key $\mathsf{mpk}$ and a master secret-key $\mathsf{msk}$. We assume that all the other algorithms take $\mathsf{mpk}$ as input.

$\mathsf{SKGen}(\mathsf{msk}, \sigma)$: On input the master secret-key $\mathsf{msk}$, and an identity $\sigma$, the randomized sender-key generator algorithm returns as output an encryption key $\mathsf{ek}_\sigma$ for the identity $\sigma$.

$\mathsf{RKGen}(\mathsf{msk}, \rho)$: On input the master secret-key $\mathsf{msk}$, and an identity $\rho$, the randomized receiver-key generator algorithm returns as output a decryption key $\mathsf{dk}_\rho$ for the identity $\rho$.

$\mathsf{Enc}(\mathsf{ek}_\sigma, \mathsf{rcv}, \mathsf{m})$: On input the encryption key $\mathsf{ek}_\sigma$ for identity $\sigma$, a target identity $\mathsf{rcv}$, and a message $\mathsf{m} \in \mathcal{M}$, the randomized encryption algorithm returns as output a ciphertext $\mathsf{c}$.

$\mathsf{Dec}(\mathsf{dk}_\rho, \mathsf{snd}, \mathsf{c})$: On input the decryption key $\mathsf{dk}_\rho$ for identity $\rho$, a target identity $\mathsf{snd}$, and a ciphertext $\mathsf{c}$, the deterministic decryption algorithm returns as output either a message $\mathsf{m}$ or a special symbol $\perp$ denoting a failure.

**Definition 1** (**[12] Correctness of IB-ME**). *An IB-ME scheme* $\Pi = (\mathsf{Setup}, \mathsf{SKGen}, \mathsf{RKGen}, \mathsf{Enc}, \mathsf{Dec})$ *is correct if* $\forall \lambda \in \mathbb{N}$, $\forall (\mathsf{mpk}, \mathsf{msk})$ *output by* $\mathsf{Setup}(1^\lambda)$, $\forall \mathsf{m} \in \mathcal{M}$, $\forall \sigma$, $\rho$, $\mathsf{rcv}$, $\mathsf{snd} \in \mathcal{I}$ *such that* $\sigma = \mathsf{snd}$ *and* $\rho = \mathsf{rcv}$ *it holds that*

$$Pr[\mathsf{Dec}(\mathsf{dk}_\rho, \mathsf{snd}, \mathsf{Enc}(\mathsf{ek}_\sigma, \mathsf{rcv}, \mathsf{m})) = \mathsf{m}] \geq 1 - \mathsf{negl}(\lambda)$$

*where* $\mathsf{ek}_\sigma \leftarrow\$ \mathsf{SKGen}(\mathsf{msk}, \sigma)$ *and* $\mathsf{dk}_\rho \leftarrow\$ \mathsf{RKGen}(\mathsf{msk}, \rho)$.

**Security Notions.** An IB-ME should satisfy two main security properties: *authenticity* and *enhanced privacy.*

*Authenticity.* Informally, the authenticity property requires that no PPT adversary can compute a valid ciphertext $\mathsf{c}$ under the identity $\sigma$ without holding the corresponding encryption key $\mathsf{ek}_\sigma$.

**Definition 2** ([12] **Authenticity of IB-ME).** *An IB-ME scheme* $\Pi = (\mathsf{Setup}, \mathsf{SKGen}, \mathsf{RKGen}, \mathsf{Enc}, \mathsf{Dec})$ *satisfies* authenticity *if for all PPT adversaries* $\mathcal{A}$ *it holds that*

$$\mathrm{Succ}^{\mathsf{ib\text{-}auth}}_{\Pi,\mathcal{A}}(\lambda) := \Pr\left[\mathsf{Game}^{\mathsf{ib\text{-}auth}}_{\Pi,\mathcal{A}}(\lambda) = 1\right] \leq \mathsf{negl}(\lambda)$$

*where* $\mathsf{Game}^{\mathsf{ib\text{-}auth}}_{\Pi,\mathcal{A}}(\lambda)$ *is defined in Fig. 1.*

$\mathsf{Game}^{\mathsf{ib\text{-}auth}}_{\Pi,\mathcal{A}}(\lambda)$

1. $(\mathsf{mpk}, \mathsf{msk}) \leftarrow\$ \mathsf{Setup}(1^\lambda)$
2. $(\mathsf{c}, \rho, \mathsf{snd}) \leftarrow\$ \mathcal{A}^{\mathcal{O}_1,\mathcal{O}_2}(1^\lambda, \mathsf{mpk})$
3. $\mathsf{dk}_\rho \leftarrow\$ \mathsf{RKGen}(\mathsf{msk}, \rho)$
4. $\mathsf{m} := \mathsf{Dec}(\mathsf{dk}_\rho, \mathsf{snd}, \mathsf{c})$
5. **if** $\forall \sigma \in Q_{\mathcal{O}_1} : (\sigma \neq \mathsf{snd}) \wedge (\mathsf{m} \neq \bot)$
   **return** 1
6. **else return** 0

**Fig. 1.** $\mathsf{Game}^{\mathsf{ib\text{-}auth}}_{\Pi,\mathcal{A}}(\lambda)$ defining authenticity. $\mathcal{O}_1$ and $\mathcal{O}_2$ are implemented respectively throughout the $\mathsf{SKGen}$ and $\mathsf{RKGen}$ algorithms and on input an arbitrary identity return respectively the corresponding encryption key and decryption key.

*Enhanced Privacy.* The original privacy definition in [4] captures the secrecy of the sender's inputs $(\sigma, \mathsf{rcv}, \mathsf{m})$ according to every possible mismatch condition for the receiver. However, given a known decryption key $\mathsf{dk}_\rho$ for an identity $\rho$, the adversary can always choose a target sender's identity $\mathsf{snd}$ on the fly and try to decrypt the ciphertext. To rule out this attack, the enhanced privacy defines a mismatch condition that hides the sender's identity $\sigma_0$ and $\sigma_1$ into two adversarial distributions $\mathbf{ID}_0$ and $\mathbf{ID}_1$, respectively, each having a non-trivial amount of min-entropy.

| $\mathsf{Game}^{\mathsf{ib\text{-}priv}^+}_{\Pi,\mathcal{A}}(\lambda)$ |
|---|
| 1. $(\mathsf{mpk}, \mathsf{msk}) \leftarrow\$ \mathsf{Setup}(1^\lambda)$ |
| 2. $(\mathsf{m}_0, \mathsf{m}_1, \mathsf{rcv}_0, \mathsf{rcv}_1, \mathbf{ID}_0, \mathbf{ID}_1) \leftarrow\$ \mathcal{A}_1^{\mathcal{O}_1,\mathcal{O}_2}(1^\lambda, \mathsf{mpk})$ |
| 3. $\sigma_0 \leftarrow\$ \mathbf{ID}_0$ |
| 4. $\sigma_1 \leftarrow\$ \mathbf{ID}_1$ |
| 5. $\mathsf{ek}_{\sigma_0} \leftarrow\$ \mathsf{SKGen}(\mathsf{msk}, \sigma_0)$ |
| 6. $\mathsf{ek}_{\sigma_1} \leftarrow\$ \mathsf{SKGen}(\mathsf{msk}, \sigma_1)$ |
| 7. $b \leftarrow\$ \{0,1\}$ |
| 8. $\mathsf{c} \leftarrow\$ \mathsf{Enc}(\mathsf{ek}_{\sigma_b}, \mathsf{rcv}_b, \mathsf{m}_b)$ |
| 9. $b' \leftarrow\$ \mathcal{A}_2^{\mathcal{O}_1,\mathcal{O}_2,\{\mathcal{O}_3^i\}_{i\in\{0,1\}}}(1^\lambda, \mathsf{c})$ |
| 10. **if** $(b' = b)$ **return** 1 |
| 11. **else return** 0 |

**Fig. 2.** $\mathsf{Game}^{\mathsf{ib\text{-}priv}^+}_{\Pi,\mathcal{A}}(\lambda)$ defining enhanced privacy. $\mathcal{O}_1$ and $\mathcal{O}_2$ are implemented respectively throughout the SKGen and RKGen algorithms and on input an arbitrary identity return respectively the corresponding encryption key and decryption key. $\mathcal{O}_3^i$ allows the adversary to obtain the ciphertexts of arbitrary $(\mathsf{m}, \mathsf{rcv})$ encrypted by sender $\sigma_i$.

**Definition 3** ([12] **Enhanced Privacy of IB-ME).** *An IB-ME scheme* $\Pi = (\mathsf{Setup}, \mathsf{SKGen}, \mathsf{RKGen}, \mathsf{Enc}, \mathsf{Dec})$ *satisfies* enhanced privacy *if for all valid PPT adversaries* $\mathcal{A} = (\mathcal{A}_1, \mathcal{A}_2)$ *it holds that*

$$\mathrm{Adv}^{\mathsf{ib\text{-}priv}^+}_{\Pi,\mathcal{A}}(\lambda) := \left|\Pr\left[\mathsf{Game}^{\mathsf{ib\text{-}priv}^+}_{\Pi,\mathcal{A}}(\lambda) = 1\right] - \frac{1}{2}\right| \leq \mathsf{negl}(\lambda)$$

*where* $\mathsf{Game}^{\mathsf{ib\text{-}priv}^+}_{\Pi,\mathcal{A}}(\lambda)$ *is defined in Fig. 2.*

An adversary is considered valid if for every identity $\rho$ for which it knows the corresponding decryption key $\mathsf{dk}_\rho$ either (i) $\rho \neq \mathsf{rcv}_0$ and $\rho \neq \mathsf{rcv}_1$, or (ii) the distributions $\mathbf{ID}_0$ and $\mathbf{ID}_1$ have a non-trivial amount of min-entropy $\mathbb{H}_\infty(\mathbf{ID}_i) \geq \omega(\log(\lambda))$, or (iii) $\rho \neq \mathsf{rcv}_0$ and $\mathbf{ID}_1$ has a non-trivial amount of min-entropy $\mathbb{H}_\infty(\mathbf{ID}_1) \geq \omega(\log(\lambda))$, or (iv) $\rho \neq \mathsf{rcv}_1$ and $\mathbf{ID}_0$ has a non-trivial amount of min-entropy $\mathbb{H}_\infty(\mathbf{ID}_0) \geq \omega(\log(\lambda))$.

## 2.2 Homomorphic Signatures

Homomorphic signature schemes allow to perform computations on data that have been signed. In particular, for a function $\mathsf{f}$ represented as a Boolean circuit $C$, and a signature $\varsigma_{\mathsf{x}}$ that verifies the authenticity of a message $\mathsf{x}$, it is possible to generate a signature $\varsigma_{\mathsf{f}(\mathsf{x})}$ that certifies the value of $\mathsf{f}(\mathsf{x})$ with respect to the function $\mathsf{f}$. We adapt the following definitions from [6,15,16].

**Definition 4 (Homomorphic Signatures).** *Let $X$ be the message space and $n \in \mathbb{N}$ be the maximum length of a dataset. Let $\mathsf{C}$ be a family of circuits such that each $C \in \mathsf{C}$ denote a circuit that implements a function from $X^n$ to $X$ (i.e., $C : X^n \rightarrow X$). A homomorphic signature scheme is a tuple of four PPT algorithms* (Setup, Sign, Eval, Verify) *with the following properties:*

$\mathsf{Setup}(1^\lambda, 1^n)$: On input the security parameter $1^\lambda$ and maximum dataset length $n$, the randomized setup algorithm outputs a public-key $\mathsf{pk}$ and a secret-key $\mathsf{sk}$.

$\mathsf{Sign}(\mathsf{sk}, \tau, \mathbf{x})$: On input the secret-key $\mathsf{sk}$, a tag $\tau \in \{0,1\}^\lambda$, and a dataset $\mathbf{x} = (\mathsf{x}_1, \ldots, \mathsf{x}_n)$, outputs a signature $\boldsymbol{\varsigma} = (\varsigma_1, \ldots, \varsigma_n)$.

$\mathsf{Eval}(\mathsf{pk}, \tau, \mathbf{x}, \boldsymbol{\varsigma}, C)$: On input the public-key $\mathsf{pk}$, a tag $\tau \in \{0,1\}^\lambda$, a dataset $\mathbf{x} = (\mathsf{x}_1, \ldots, \mathsf{x}_n)$ with corresponding signature $\boldsymbol{\varsigma} = (\varsigma_1, \ldots, \varsigma_n)$, and a circuit $C$, outputs a signature $\varsigma'$ on the value $\mathsf{x}' = C(\mathbf{x})$.

$\mathsf{Verify}(\mathsf{pk}, \tau, \mathsf{x}, \varsigma, C)$: On input the public-key $\mathsf{pk}$, a tag $\tau \in \{0,1\}^\lambda$, a message $\mathsf{x} \in X$ with signature $\varsigma$, outputs either 1 (accept) or 0 (reject).

*Note that the tags serve to distinguish between different datasets, with the intent being that only signatures with matching tags be combinable homomorphically. From the user's viewpoint, the tag is a bit-string of length $\lambda$ selected uniformly at random.*

**Definition 5 ([6,15] Correctness of Homomorphic Signatures).** *We say that a homomorphic signature scheme is correct if for any tag $\tau \in \{0,1\}^\lambda$, for any circuit $C : X^n \rightarrow X$, when $(\mathsf{pk}, \mathsf{sk})$ is output of $\mathsf{Setup}(1^\lambda, 1^n)$, and $\boldsymbol{\varsigma} \leftarrow \mathsf{Sign}(\mathsf{sk}, \tau, \mathbf{x})$, it holds that:*

1. *for any index $i \in [n]$, $\mathsf{Verify}(\mathsf{pk}, \tau, \mathsf{x}_i, \varsigma_i, C)$ returns 1*
2. *for any message $\mathsf{x}' \in X$, $\mathsf{Verify}(\mathsf{pk}, \tau, \mathsf{x}', \varsigma', C)$ returns 1 when $\varsigma' \leftarrow \mathsf{Eval}(\mathsf{pk}, \tau, \mathbf{x}, \boldsymbol{\varsigma}, C)$ and $\mathsf{x}' = C(\mathbf{x})$.*

The security of such schemes is ensured by two main properties: *unforgeability* and *context-hiding.*

**Definition 6 (Existential unforgeability against adaptive chosen-dataset attacks).** *A homomorphic signature scheme $\Sigma = (\mathsf{Setup}, \mathsf{Sign}, \mathsf{Eval}, \mathsf{Verify})$ is* fully unforgeable against adaptive chosen-dataset queries *if for all $n \in \mathbb{N}$ and for all PPT adversaries $\mathcal{A}$ it holds that*

$$\mathrm{Succ}^{\mathsf{EUF\text{-}FH\text{-}CDA}}_{\Sigma,\mathcal{A}}(\lambda) := \Pr\left[\mathsf{Game}^{\mathsf{EUF\text{-}FH\text{-}CDA}}_{\Sigma,\mathcal{A}}(\lambda) = 1\right] \leq \mathsf{negl}(\lambda)$$

*where $\mathsf{Game}^{\mathsf{EUF\text{-}FH\text{-}CDA}}_{\Sigma,\mathcal{A}}(\lambda)$ is defined in Fig. 3.*

Eventually, the attacker produces a forgery $(\tau^*, \mathsf{x}^*, \varsigma^*, C^*)$ and the winning condition captures two distinct types of forgeries. In a type 1 forgery, for any $\tau$ such that $(\tau, \varsigma_{\mathbf{x}}) \in O_{\mathcal{O}}$, $\tau^* \neq \tau$. In a type 2 forgery, there exist a pair $(\tau^*, \varsigma_x)$ in $O_{\mathcal{O}}$ for some dataset $\mathbf{x}$ (i.e. $\mathbf{x}$ is the dataset associated to tag $\tau^*$) but $\mathsf{x}^* \neq C(\mathbf{x})$.

$\mathsf{Game}^{\mathsf{EUF\text{-}FH\text{-}CDA}}_{\Sigma,\mathcal{A}}(\lambda)$

$(\mathsf{pk},\mathsf{sk}) \leftarrow\$ \mathsf{Setup}(1^\lambda, 1^n)$
$(\tau^*, \mathsf{x}^*, \varsigma^*, C^*) \leftarrow\$ \mathcal{A}^{\mathcal{O}}(1^\lambda, \mathsf{pk})$
**if** $\mathsf{Verify}(\mathsf{pk}, \tau^*, \mathsf{x}^*, \varsigma^*, C^*) = 1$ and either
  (1) $\tau^* \neq \tau$ for all $\tau$ s.t. $(\tau, \varsigma_{\mathbf{x}}) \in O_{\mathcal{O}}$, or
  (2) $\tau^* = \tau$ for some $\tau$ s.t. $(\tau, \varsigma_{\mathbf{x}}) \in O_{\mathcal{O}}$ but $\mathsf{x}^* \neq C(\mathbf{x})$ where $\mathbf{x}$ is the dataset associated to tag $\tau$;
  **return** 1
**else return** 0

**Fig. 3.** Unforgeability of homomorphic signatures. The oracle $\mathcal{O}$ on input $\mathbf{x} = (\mathsf{x}_1, \dots, \mathsf{x}_n)$, replies with a tag $\tau$ and a signature $\varsigma \leftarrow\$ \mathsf{Sign}(\mathsf{sk}, \tau, \mathbf{x})$.

The context-hiding requirement, roughly says that if a user evaluates a function $f$ on a dataset-signature pair $(\mathbf{x}, \varsigma)$ to obtain a signature $\varsigma$ on $C(\mathbf{x})$, and then runs the ReRand algorithm on $\varsigma$, the resulting signature does not contain any information about the dataset $\mathbf{x}$.

**Definition 7 (Context-hiding).** *A homomorphic signature scheme is* context hiding *if there exist two additional PPT algorithms:*

$\mathsf{ReRand}(\mathsf{pk}, \tau, \mathsf{x}, \varsigma, C)$ On input the public-key $\mathsf{pk}$, a tag $\tau \in \{0,1\}^\lambda$, a message $\mathsf{x}$ with signature $\varsigma$, a circuit $C$ returns as output $\varsigma'$;
$\mathsf{RVerify}(\mathsf{pk}, \tau, \mathsf{x}, \varsigma, C)$ On input the public-key $\mathsf{pk}$, a tag $\tau \in \{0,1\}^\lambda$, a message $\mathsf{x} \in X$ with signature $\varsigma$, outputs either 1 (accept) or 0 (reject);

*and it holds that:*

**Correctness:** *for any* $(\mathsf{pk}, \mathsf{sk}) \leftarrow \mathsf{Setup}(1^\lambda, 1^n)$, *and any tuple tag/message/signature* $(\tau, \mathsf{x}, \varsigma)$ *such that* $\mathsf{Verify}(\mathsf{pk}, \tau, \mathsf{x}, \varsigma) = 1$, $\mathsf{RVerify}(\mathsf{pk}, \tau, \mathsf{x}, \mathsf{ReRand}(\mathsf{pk}, \tau, \mathsf{x}, \varsigma, C), C) = 1$;
**Unforgeability:** *the unforgeability property still holds when replacing the original verify algorithm with* RVerify *in the security game;*
**Context-hiding:** *for any fixed* $(\mathsf{pk}, \mathsf{sk}) \leftarrow \mathsf{Setup}(1^\lambda, 1^n)$, *and any tuple tag/message/signature* $(\tau, \mathsf{x}, \varsigma)$ *for which* $\mathsf{RVerify}(\mathsf{pk}, \tau, \mathsf{x}, \varsigma, C) = 1$ *there exists a simulator* Sim *such that* $\mathsf{ReRand}(\mathsf{pk}, \tau, \mathsf{x}, \varsigma, C) \overset{c}{\approx} \mathsf{Sim}(\mathsf{sk}, \mathsf{x}, \tau)$.

## 3 IB-ME: Generic Construction

In this section, we first present a generic construction for IB-ME that satisfies enhanced privacy. Then, we propose a generic transform that, by combining any IB-ME achieving enhanced privacy and a context-hiding homomorphic signature, results in an IB-ME that also satisfies the authenticity security notion.

### 3.1 IB-ME Achieving Enhanced Privacy

In Fig. 4 we show an IB-ME achieving enhanced privacy. It uses a reusable computational extractor and any IBE achieving INDr-ID-CPA security. Formal definitions regarding IBE and reusable computational extractors can be find respectively in Appendix B and Appendix A.

Let $\lambda \in \mathbb{N}$ be the security parameter. Let $\Sigma = (\mathsf{Setup}, \mathsf{Extract}, \mathsf{Encrypt}, \mathsf{Decrypt})$ be an IBE with identity space $\mathcal{I} = \{0,1\}^\ell$, message space $\mathcal{M}$ and ciphertext space $\mathcal{C}$, satisfying INDr-ID-CPA security. Let $\mathsf{Ext}\colon S \times \mathcal{I} \to \mathcal{C}$ be a reusable computational extractor. We define an IB-ME as follows:

**Algorithm** $\mathsf{Setup}(1^\lambda)$
1. Execute $(\mathsf{mpk}, \mathsf{msk}) \leftarrow\$ \Sigma.\mathsf{Setup}(1^\lambda)$;
2. Output $(\mathsf{mpk}, \mathsf{msk})$.

**Algorithm** $\mathsf{SKGen}(\mathsf{msk}, \sigma)$
1. Output $\mathsf{ek}_\sigma := \sigma$.

**Algorithm** $\mathsf{RKGen}(\mathsf{msk}, \rho)$
1. Execute $\mathsf{dk}_\rho \leftarrow\$ \Sigma.\mathsf{Extract}(\mathsf{msk}, \rho)$;
2. Output $\mathsf{dk}_\rho$.

**Algorithm** $\mathsf{Enc}(\mathsf{ek}_\sigma, \mathsf{rcv}, \mathsf{m})$
1. Sample a seed $s \leftarrow\$ S$;
2. Compute $g_\sigma \leftarrow\$ \mathsf{Ext}_s(\mathsf{ek}_\sigma) = \mathsf{Ext}_s(\sigma)$;
3. Execute $c_1 \leftarrow\$ \Sigma.\mathsf{Encrypt}(\mathsf{rcv}, \mathsf{m})$;
4. Compute $c_2 := c_1 \oplus g_\sigma$;
5. Output $\mathsf{c} := (c_2, s)$.

**Algorithm** $\mathsf{Dec}(\mathsf{dk}_\rho, \mathsf{snd}, \mathsf{c})$
1. Parse $\mathsf{c} := (c_2, s)$
2. Compute $g_{\mathsf{snd}} \leftarrow\$ \mathsf{Ext}_s(\mathsf{snd})$;
3. Compute $c_1 := c_2 \oplus g_{\mathsf{snd}}$;
4. Execute $\mathsf{m} := \Sigma.\mathsf{Decrypt}(\mathsf{dk}_\rho, c_1)$;
5. Output $\mathsf{m}$.

**Fig. 4.** An IB-ME construction achieving enhanced privacy.

In this construction we let $\mathsf{ek}_\sigma$ be equal to the identity $\sigma$ obtained through $\mathsf{SKGen}(\mathsf{msk}, \sigma)$. Indeed, the secret encryption key $\mathsf{ek}_\sigma$ is needed only when authenticity is required.

It is straightforward to see that the correctness of the scheme follows from that of the underlying IBE. Indeed, it is correct if $\forall\lambda \in \mathbb{N}$, $\forall(\mathsf{mpk}, \mathsf{msk})$ output by $\mathsf{Setup}(1^\lambda)$, $\forall \mathsf{m} \in \mathcal{M}$, $\forall\sigma$, $\rho$, $\mathsf{rcv}$, $\mathsf{snd}$ in the identity space $\mathcal{I} = \{0,1\}^\ell$ such that $\sigma := \mathsf{snd}$ and $\rho := \mathsf{rcv}$, it holds that:

$$Pr[\mathsf{Dec}(\mathsf{dk}_\rho, \mathsf{snd}, \mathsf{Enc}(\mathsf{ek}_\sigma, \mathsf{rcv}, \mathsf{m})) = \mathsf{m}] \geq 1 - \mathsf{negl}(\lambda)$$

where $\mathsf{ek}_\sigma := \sigma$ and $\mathsf{dk}_\rho \leftarrow\$ \mathsf{Extract}(\mathsf{msk}, \rho)$.

In order to prove that the construction in Fig. 4 achieves enhanced privacy, we introduce a security game that captures a strong privacy property, that we dub *indistinguishable from random privacy*, in which the challenge ciphertext is indistinguishable from a uniform random string of equal length. Such a definition subsumes recipient's identity anonymity, meaning that even if the adversary presumes the identity of the actual receiver, it cannot confirm it. This definition is similar to the notion of *indistinguishable from random* for IBE [1].

$\mathsf{Game}^{\mathsf{ib\text{-}INDr\text{-}priv}}_{\Pi,\mathcal{A}}(\lambda)$

1. $(\mathsf{mpk}, \mathsf{msk}) \leftarrow\$ \mathsf{Setup}(1^\lambda)$
2. $(\mathsf{m}_0, \mathsf{rcv}_0, \mathbf{ID}_0) \leftarrow\$ \mathcal{A}_1^{\mathcal{O}_1,\mathcal{O}_2}(1^\lambda, \mathsf{mpk})$
3. $\sigma_0 \leftarrow\$ \mathbf{ID}_0$
4. $\mathsf{ek}_{\sigma_0} \leftarrow\$ \mathsf{SKGen}(\mathsf{msk}, \sigma_0)$
5. $\mathsf{c}_0 \leftarrow\$ \mathsf{Enc}(\mathsf{ek}_{\sigma_0}, \mathsf{rcv}_0, \mathsf{m}_0)$
6. $\mathsf{c}_1 \leftarrow\$ \mathcal{C}$
7. $b \leftarrow\$ \{0,1\}$
8. $b' \leftarrow\$ \mathcal{A}_2^{\mathcal{O}_1,\mathcal{O}_2,\mathcal{O}_3}(1^\lambda, \mathsf{c}_b)$
9. **if** $(b' = b)$ **return** 1
10. **else return** 0

**Fig. 5.** $\mathsf{Game}^{\mathsf{ib\text{-}INDr\text{-}priv}}_{\Pi,\mathcal{A}}(\lambda)$ defining the indistinguishable from random privacy.

Consider the game in Fig. 5. The adversary $\mathcal{A}$ selects a challenge tuple ($\mathsf{m}_0$, $\mathsf{rcv}_0$, $\mathbf{ID}_0$). The challenger samples an identity $\sigma_0$ from the distribution $\mathbf{ID}_0$ and randomly extracts a bit $b \leftarrow\$ \{0,1\}$ to determine whether to compute the challenge ciphertext $\mathsf{c}$ as $\mathsf{Enc}(\mathsf{ek}_{\sigma_0}, \mathsf{rcv}_0, \mathsf{m}_0)$ (if $b = 0$), or sample a random ciphertext $\mathsf{c}$ in the ciphertext space $\mathcal{C}$ (if $b = 1$).

Oracles $\mathcal{O}_1$ and $\mathcal{O}_2$ are implemented by $\mathsf{SKGen}(\mathsf{msk}, \cdot)$, and $\mathsf{RKGen}(\mathsf{msk}, \cdot)$, respectively. The oracle $\mathcal{O}_3$ allows the adversary to choose a message $\mathsf{m}$ and a target receiver's identity $\mathsf{rcv}$, and obtain the ciphertext $\mathsf{c}$ when $\mathsf{ek}_{\sigma_0}$ is unknown to $\mathcal{A}$. Specifically, if $b = 0$ then $\mathcal{O}_3$ will output the ciphertext $\mathsf{c}$ as $\mathsf{Enc}(\mathsf{ek}_{\sigma_0}, \mathsf{rcv}, \mathsf{m})$, otherwise $\mathsf{c}$ is randomly chosen in the ciphertext space $\mathcal{C}$.

**Definition 8 (Indistinguishable from random privacy).** *We say that an IB-ME scheme* $\Pi$ *satisfies* indistinguishable from random privacy *if for all valid PPT adversaries* $\mathcal{A} = (\mathcal{A}_1, \mathcal{A}_2)$:

$$\mathrm{Adv}^{\mathsf{ib\text{-}INDr\text{-}priv}}_{\Pi,\mathcal{A}}(\lambda) := \left|\Pr\left[\mathsf{Game}^{\mathsf{ib\text{-}INDr\text{-}priv}}_{\Pi,\mathcal{A}}(\lambda) = 1\right] - \frac{1}{2}\right| \leq \mathsf{negl}(\lambda)$$

*where* $\mathsf{Game}^{\text{ib-INDr-priv}}_{\Pi,\mathcal{A}}(\lambda)$ *is described in Fig. 5.*

*An adversary* $\mathcal{A} = (\mathcal{A}_1, \mathcal{A}_2)$ *is valid if* $\forall \rho \in Q_{\mathcal{O}_2}$ *the following invariant holds:*

$$(\rho \neq \mathsf{rcv}_0) \vee (\mathbb{H}_\infty(\mathbf{ID}_0) \geq \omega(\log(\lambda))) \tag{1}$$

An adversary is valid if for every identity $\rho$ for which it knows the corresponding decryption key $\mathsf{dk}_\rho$, either (i) $\rho \neq \mathsf{rcv}_0$ (i.e., the adversary does not know the decryption key for the challenge target receiver's identity), or (ii) the distribution $\mathbf{ID}_0$ has a non-trivial amount of min-entropy $\mathbb{H}_\infty(\mathbf{ID}_0) \geq \omega(\log(\lambda))$ (i.e., the adversary has the decryption key for the challenge target receiver's identity, but does not know the challenge sender's identity $\sigma_0$, so it can not set $\mathsf{snd} = \sigma_0$).

It is easy to see that indistinguishability from random privacy implies enhanced privacy, for completeness we include the proof in Appendix C. Thus, in order to prove that the construction in Fig. 4 achieves enhanced privacy, we show that it satisfies indistinguishable from random privacy. Specifically, we define the events corresponding to each mismatch conditions given in Eq. 1 as follows:

$\mathbf{Mismatch_1}$: $\forall \rho \in Q_{\mathcal{O}_2},\ \rho \neq \mathsf{rcv}_0$;
$\mathbf{Mismatch_2}$: $\mathbb{H}_\infty(\mathbf{ID}_0) \geq \omega(\log(\lambda))$.

Since the adversary $\mathcal{A}$ must satisfy at least one of the two mismatch conditions to be valid, we analyze these events separately. We begin by studying the advantage of the adversary in the $\mathsf{Game}^{\text{ib-INDr-priv}}_{\Pi,\mathcal{A}}(\lambda)$ when $\mathbf{Mismatch_1}$ occurs.

**Lemma 1.** *Let* $\Pi = (\mathsf{Setup}, \mathsf{SKGen}, \mathsf{RKGen}, \mathsf{Enc}, \mathsf{Dec})$ *be the IB-ME described in Fig. 4, and let* $\Sigma = (\mathsf{Setup}, \mathsf{Extract}, \mathsf{Encrypt}, \mathsf{Decrypt})$ *be the underlying IBE satisfying* INDr-ID-CPA *security. It holds that:*

$$\left| \Pr\left[ \mathsf{Game}^{\text{ib-INDr-priv}}_{\Pi,\mathcal{A}}(\lambda) = 1 \,\middle|\, \mathbf{Mismatch_1} \right] - \frac{1}{2} \right| \leq \mathsf{negl}(\lambda)$$

*Proof.* To prove the lemma, we need to show that, when $\mathbf{Mismatch_1}$ occurs, the adversary's view in the $\mathsf{Game}^{\text{ib-INDr-priv}}_{\Pi,\mathcal{A}}(\lambda)$ with challenge bit $b = 0$ is computationally indistinguishable from the adversary's view when the challenge bit is $b = 1$. We consider a sequence of hybrid experiments $\mathbf{H}_i(\lambda)$, for $i \in 1, \ldots, 3$. For the remainder of this proof, these experiments will assume that the event $\mathbf{Mismatch_1}$ has occurred.

$\mathbf{H}_1(\lambda)$: This experiment is identical to $\mathsf{Game}^{\text{ib-INDr-priv}}_{\Pi,\mathcal{A}}(\lambda)$ with challenge bit $b = 1$;

$\mathbf{H}_2(\lambda)$: This experiment is identical to $\mathbf{H}_1(\lambda)$, except that the challenge ciphertext $\mathsf{c}$ is not chosen completely at random in the ciphertext space but it is computed as $\mathsf{c} = \mathsf{c}' \oplus g_{\sigma_0}$ where $\mathsf{c}'$ is randomly chosen in $\mathcal{C}$ and $g_{\sigma_0} \leftarrow\!\!\$\ \mathsf{Ext}_s(\sigma_0)$ for some seed $s$ chosen at random.

$\mathbf{H}_3(\lambda)$: This is identical to $\mathsf{Game}^{\text{ib-INDr-priv}}_{\Pi,\mathcal{A}}(\lambda)$ with challenge bit $b = 0$.

It is easy to see that $\mathbf{H}_1(\lambda)$ and $\mathbf{H}_2(\lambda)$ are identically distributed, as the only difference between the two experiments is that the ciphertext in $\mathbf{H}_1(\lambda)$ is a random element in $\mathcal{C}$, while in $\mathbf{H}_2(\lambda)$ it is computed by xoring a random element in $\mathcal{C}$ to the extractor $g_{\sigma_0}$.

We now prove that the adversary's views in the experiments $\mathbf{H}_2(\lambda)$ and $\mathbf{H}_3(\lambda)$ are computationally indistinguishable. In particular, we show that if there exists a PPT algorithm $\mathcal{D}$ which is able to distinguish between experiments $\mathbf{H}_2(\lambda)$ and $\mathbf{H}_3(\lambda)$ with non-negligible probability then it is possible to construct a PPT adversary $\mathcal{B} = (\mathcal{B}_1, \mathcal{B}_2)$ that running $\mathcal{D}$ as a sub-routine has a non-negligible advantage in the $\mathsf{Game}^{\mathsf{INDr\text{-}ID\text{-}CPA}}_{\Sigma,\mathcal{B}}(\lambda)$ against the underlying IBE $\Sigma$.

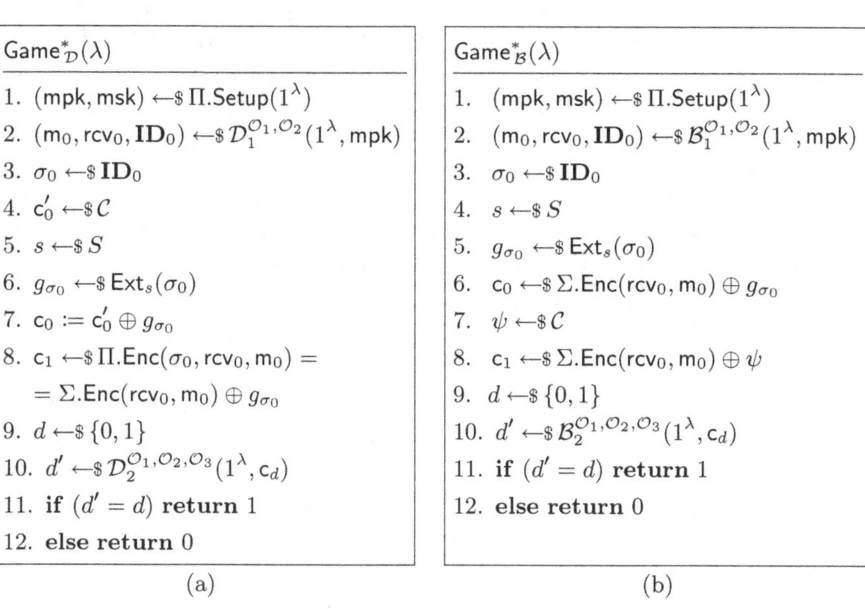

$\mathsf{Game}^*_{\mathcal{D}}(\lambda)$
$(\mathsf{mpk}, \mathsf{msk}) \leftarrow\$ \Pi.\mathsf{Setup}(1^\lambda)$
$(\mathsf{m}_0, \mathsf{rcv}_0, \mathbf{ID}_0) \leftarrow\$ \mathcal{D}_1^{\mathcal{O}_1,\mathcal{O}_2}(1^\lambda, \mathsf{mpk})$
$\sigma_0 \leftarrow\$ \mathbf{ID}_0$
$\mathsf{c}'_0 \leftarrow\$ \mathcal{C}$
$s \leftarrow\$ S$
$g_{\sigma_0} \leftarrow\$ \mathsf{Ext}_s(\sigma_0)$
$\mathsf{c}_0 := \mathsf{c}'_0 \oplus g_{\sigma_0}$
$\mathsf{c}_1 \leftarrow\$ \Pi.\mathsf{Enc}(\sigma_0, \mathsf{rcv}_0, \mathsf{m}_0) =$
$= \Sigma.\mathsf{Enc}(\mathsf{rcv}_0, \mathsf{m}_0) \oplus g_{\sigma_0}$
$d \leftarrow\$ \{0,1\}$
$d' \leftarrow\$ \mathcal{D}_2^{\mathcal{O}_1,\mathcal{O}_2,\mathcal{O}_3}(1^\lambda, \mathsf{c}_d)$
**if** $(d' = d)$ **return** 1
**else return** 0
(a)
$\mathsf{Game}^*_{\mathcal{B}}(\lambda)$
$(\mathsf{mpk}, \mathsf{msk}) \leftarrow\$ \Pi.\mathsf{Setup}(1^\lambda)$
$(\mathsf{m}_0, \mathsf{rcv}_0, \mathbf{ID}_0) \leftarrow\$ \mathcal{B}_1^{\mathcal{O}_1,\mathcal{O}_2}(1^\lambda, \mathsf{mpk})$
$\sigma_0 \leftarrow\$ \mathbf{ID}_0$
$s \leftarrow\$ S$
$g_{\sigma_0} \leftarrow\$ \mathsf{Ext}_s(\sigma_0)$
$\mathsf{c}_0 \leftarrow\$ \Sigma.\mathsf{Enc}(\mathsf{rcv}_0, \mathsf{m}_0) \oplus g_{\sigma_0}$
$\psi \leftarrow\$ \mathcal{C}$
$\mathsf{c}_1 \leftarrow\$ \Sigma.\mathsf{Enc}(\mathsf{rcv}_0, \mathsf{m}_0) \oplus \psi$
$d \leftarrow\$ \{0,1\}$
$d' \leftarrow\$ \mathcal{B}_2^{\mathcal{O}_1,\mathcal{O}_2,\mathcal{O}_3}(1^\lambda, \mathsf{c}_d)$
**if** $(d' = d)$ **return** 1
**else return** 0
(b)


**Fig. 6.** Auxiliary games. Oracles $\mathcal{O}_1$ and $\mathcal{O}_2$ on input an identity return respectively the corresponding encryption key and decryption key. Oracle $\mathcal{O}_3$ on input a message and a receiver return a ciphertexts encrypted under the encryption key of sender $\sigma_0$.

Consider the game $\mathsf{Game}^*_{\mathcal{D}}(\lambda)$ in Fig. 6(a). Notice that $\mathsf{Game}^*_{\mathcal{D}}(\lambda)$ with challenge bit $d = 0$ corresponds to experiment $\mathbf{H}_2(\lambda)$, whereas $\mathsf{Game}^*_{\mathcal{D}}(\lambda)$ with challenge bit $d = 1$ corresponds to experiment $\mathbf{H}_3(\lambda)$. The algorithm $\mathcal{B}_1$, on input the security parameter $1^\lambda$ and the master public-key $\mathsf{mpk}$, runs $\mathcal{D}_1$ on input $1^\lambda$ and $\mathsf{mpk}$. The oracles $\mathcal{O}_1$ and $\mathcal{O}_2$ for $\mathcal{D}_1$ can be implemented by $\mathcal{B}_1$; in particular, when $\mathcal{D}_1$ asks for the encryption key for a sender's identity $\sigma$, $\mathcal{B}_1$ returns $\mathsf{ek}_\sigma = \sigma$, whereas when $\mathcal{D}_1$ asks for the decryption key for a receiver's identity $\rho$ where $\rho \neq \mathsf{rcv}_0$, $\mathcal{B}_1$ issues the same query to its decryption key oracle. We are assuming that $\mathcal{D}_1$ will not ask for the decryption key of the identity $\mathsf{rcv}_0$ because we are operating under the assumption that $\mathbf{Mismatch}_1$ event occurs.

When the adversary $\mathcal{D}_1$ outputs its challenge tuple $(\mathsf{m}_0, \mathsf{rcv}_0, \mathbf{ID}_0)$, $\mathcal{B}_1$ sets its challenge tuple $(\mathsf{m}_0, \mathsf{id}_0) := (\mathsf{m}_0, \mathsf{rcv}_0)$. Then, the adversary $\mathcal{B}_2$, on input a ciphertext $\mathsf{c}$, randomly samples $\sigma_0 \leftarrow\!\$\, \mathbf{ID}_0$ and a seed $s \leftarrow\!\$\, S$. Next it computes $g_{\sigma_0} = \mathsf{Ext}_s(\sigma_0)$ and sets the challenge ciphertext $\mathsf{c}_d$ for $\mathcal{D}_2$, where $\mathsf{c}_1 := \Pi.\mathsf{Enc}(\sigma_0, \mathsf{rcv}_0, \mathsf{m}_0) \oplus g_{\sigma_0}$ and $\mathsf{c}_0 = \mathsf{c}_0' \oplus g_{\sigma_0}$ such that $\mathsf{c}_0' \leftarrow\!\$\, \mathcal{C}$. Notice that $\mathcal{D}_2$'s queries to oracles $\mathcal{O}_1$ and $\mathcal{O}_2$ can be implemented by $\mathcal{B}_2$ as in the first phase of the game. Moreover, $\mathcal{B}_2$ is able to answer to $\mathcal{D}_2$'s queries to oracle $\mathcal{O}_3$ regarding a message $\mathsf{m}$ and a receiver $\mathsf{rcv}$, if $d = 1$ by running the algorithm $\Sigma.\mathsf{Enc}(\mathsf{rcv}, \mathsf{m}) \oplus g_{\sigma_0}$ on input the sender key $\mathsf{ek}_{\sigma_0} = \sigma_0$. If $d = 0$, $\mathsf{c}_0 = \mathsf{c}_0' \oplus g_{\sigma_0}$ such that $\mathsf{c}_0' \leftarrow\!\$\, \mathcal{C}$. Eventually, the adversary $\mathcal{D}_2$ outputs its answer $d'$, if $d' = d$ then $\mathcal{B}_2$ outputs 1. Otherwise, $\mathcal{B}_2$ outputs 0. It is easy to see that the advantage $\mathrm{Adv}^{\mathsf{INDr\text{-}ID\text{-}CPA}}_{\Sigma,\mathcal{B}}(\lambda)$ of $\mathcal{B}$ in the $\mathsf{Game}^{\mathsf{INDr\text{-}ID\text{-}CPA}}_{\Sigma,\mathcal{B}}(\lambda)$ is the same that $\mathcal{D}$ has in $\mathsf{Game}^{*}_{\mathcal{D}}(\lambda)$. Thus, assuming the existence of a distinguisher $\mathcal{D}$ whose advantage is non-negligible leads to a contradiction because it also implies that $\mathrm{Adv}^{\mathsf{INDr\text{-}ID\text{-}CPA}}_{\Sigma,\mathcal{B}}(\lambda)$ is non-negligible. Since we have reached a contradiction, we can conclude that the experiments $\mathbf{H}_2(\lambda)$ and $\mathbf{H}_3(\lambda)$ are computationally indistinguishable.

Finally, since $\mathbf{H}_1(\lambda)$ and $\mathbf{H}_3(\lambda)$ correspond to $\mathsf{Game}^{\mathsf{ib\text{-}INDr\text{-}priv}}_{\Pi,\mathcal{A}}(\lambda)$ when the challenge bit $b = 1$ and $b = 0$, respectively, we can conclude that when the $\mathbf{Mismatch_1}$ event occurs the advantage $\mathrm{Adv}^{\mathsf{ib\text{-}INDr\text{-}priv}}_{\Pi,\mathcal{A}}(\lambda)$ of an adversary $\mathcal{A}$ in the $\mathsf{Game}^{\mathsf{ib\text{-}INDr\text{-}priv}}_{\Pi,\mathcal{A}}(\lambda)$ is negligible in $\lambda$. □

Now, we analyze the $\mathbf{Mismatch_2}$ event.

**Lemma 2.** *Let* $\Pi = (\mathsf{Setup}, \mathsf{SKGen}, \mathsf{RKGen}, \mathsf{Enc}, \mathsf{Dec})$ *be the IB-ME described in Fig. 4 and let* $\Sigma = (\mathsf{Setup}, \mathsf{Extract}, \mathsf{Encrypt}, \mathsf{Decrypt})$ *the underlying IBE satisfying* INDr-ID-CPA *security.*

*Let* $\mathsf{Ext}\colon S \times X \to \mathcal{C}$ *be an* $(\omega(\log(\lambda)), q_{\mathcal{O}_3})$*-reusable extractor (where* $q_{\mathcal{O}_3}$ *is the number of queries submitted to oracle* $O_3$ *in the game* $\mathsf{Game}^{\mathsf{ib\text{-}INDr\text{-}priv}}_{\Pi,\mathcal{A}}(\lambda)$*), it holds that:*

$$\left|\Pr\left[\mathsf{Game}^{\mathsf{ib\text{-}INDr\text{-}priv}}_{\Pi,\mathcal{A}}(\lambda) = 1 \middle| \mathbf{Mismatch_2}\right] - \frac{1}{2}\right| \leq \mathsf{negl}(\lambda).$$

*Proof.* To prove the lemma, we need to show that, when $\mathbf{Mismatch_2}$ occurs, the adversary's view in the game $\mathsf{Game}^{\mathsf{ib\text{-}INDr\text{-}priv}}_{\Pi,\mathcal{A}}(\lambda)$ with challenge bit $b = 0$ is computationally indistinguishable from the adversary's view when the challenge bit is $b = 1$. We consider a sequence of hybrid experiments $\mathbf{H}_i(\lambda)$, for $i, \ldots, 3$. For the remainder of this proof, these experiments will assume that the event $\mathbf{Mismatch_2}$ has occurred.

$\mathbf{H}_1(\lambda)$: This experiment is identical to $\mathsf{Game}^{\mathsf{ib\text{-}INDr\text{-}priv}}_{\Pi,\mathcal{A}}(\lambda)$ with challenge bit $b = 0$;

$\mathbf{H}_2(\lambda)$: This experiment is identical to $\mathbf{H}_1(\lambda)$, except that the challenge ciphertext is computed as $\mathsf{c} \leftarrow\!\$\, \Sigma.\mathsf{Enc}(\mathsf{rcv}, \mathsf{m}) \oplus \psi$ where $\psi \leftarrow\!\$\, \mathcal{C}$, see lines 7–8 of Fig. 6(b).

$\mathbf{H}_3(\lambda)$: This is identical to $\mathbf{H}_2(\lambda)$ except that the challenge ciphertext is computed as $\mathsf{c} = \mathsf{c}' \oplus \psi$ where both $\mathsf{c}'$ and $\psi$ are randomly chosen in $\mathcal{C}$.

We first prove the following claim:

**Claim 1.** Experiments $\mathbf{H}_1(\lambda)$ and $\mathbf{H}_2(\lambda)$ are computationally indistinguishable.

We will show that if there exists a PPT algorithm $\mathcal{B} = (\mathcal{B}_1, \mathcal{B}_2)$ which is able to distinguish between experiments $\mathbf{H}_1(\lambda)$ and $\mathbf{H}_2(\lambda)$ with non-negligible probability then there exists an $\mathbf{id} \in \mathcal{I}$ such that $\mathbb{H}_\infty(\mathbf{id}) \geq \omega(\log(\lambda))$ and a PPT adversary $\mathcal{D}$ that running $\mathcal{B}$ as a sub-routine has a non-negligible advantage in breaking the security of the $(\omega(\log(\lambda)), q_{\mathcal{O}_3})$-reusable extractor $\mathsf{Ext}\colon S \times \mathcal{I} \to \mathcal{C}$.

Consider the auxiliary game $\mathsf{Game}^*_{\mathcal{B}}(\lambda)$ in Fig. 6(b). Notice that $\mathsf{Game}^*_{\mathcal{B}}(\lambda)$ with challenge bit $d = 0$ corresponds to experiment $\mathbf{H}_1(\lambda)$, whereas $\mathsf{Game}^*_{\mathcal{B}}(\lambda)$ with challenge bit $d = 1$ corresponds to experiment $\mathbf{H}_2(\lambda)$.

The distinguisher $\mathcal{D}$ instantiates the scheme $\Pi$ by running the $\Pi.\mathsf{Setup}$ algorithm and runs the algorithm $\mathcal{B}_1$ on input the security parameter $1^\lambda$ and the master public-key $\mathsf{mpk}$. The distinguisher $\mathcal{D}$ is able to implement $\mathcal{B}_1$'s oracles $\mathcal{O}_1$ and $\mathcal{O}_2$ by simply running $\mathsf{SKGen}(\mathsf{msk}, \cdot)$ and $\mathsf{RKGen}(\mathsf{msk}, \cdot)$, respectively. Eventually, $\mathcal{B}_1$ outputs the challenge tuple $(\mathsf{m}_0, \mathsf{rcv}_0, \mathbf{ID}_0)$. Let the random variable $\mathbf{X}$ of Definition 9, be $\mathbf{ID}_0$. The distinguisher $\mathcal{D}$ randomly samples an identity $\sigma_0$ from $\mathbf{ID}_0$ and on input the tuple $(s_0, \ldots, s_{q_{\mathcal{O}_3}}, g_0, \ldots, g_{q_{\mathcal{O}_3}})$ computes the challenge ciphertext $\mathsf{c}_d$ for $\mathcal{B}_2$. Specifically, if $d = 0$, samples $g_{\sigma_0} \leftarrow\$ \mathsf{Ext}_s(\sigma_0)$, where $s = s_0$ and $\mathsf{c}_d \leftarrow\$ \Sigma.\mathsf{Enc}(\mathsf{rcv}_0, \mathsf{m}_0) \oplus g_{\sigma_0}$. If $d = 1$, $\psi \leftarrow\$ \mathcal{C}$ and $\mathsf{c}_d \leftarrow\$ \Sigma.\mathsf{Enc}(\mathsf{rcv}_0, \mathsf{m}_0) \oplus \psi$;

The distinguisher $\mathcal{D}$ works similarly according to the value of the bit $d$, when responding to each query $i \in [q_{\mathcal{O}_3}]$ to the oracle $\mathcal{O}_3$ made by $\mathcal{B}_2$.

Eventually, $\mathcal{B}$ will output its guess about whether it is interacting with $\mathbf{H}_1(\lambda)$ or $\mathbf{H}_2(\lambda)$. If $\mathcal{B}$ believes it is interacting with $\mathbf{H}_1(\lambda)$, the distinguisher $\mathcal{D}$ will conclude that the tuple $(g_0, \ldots, g_{q_{\mathcal{O}_3}})$ is the output of the extractor $\mathsf{Ext}$. Otherwise, $\mathcal{D}$ will conclude that the tuple was randomly chosen.

It is easy to see that the advantage $\mathrm{Adv}^{\mathsf{ind}}_{\mathsf{Ext},\mathcal{D}}(\lambda)$ of $\mathcal{D}$ is the same as the one of adversary $\mathcal{B}$. Since we assumed by contradiction that the advantage of $\mathcal{B}$ in non-negligible, this leads to the contradiction that $\mathrm{Adv}^{\mathsf{ind}}_{\mathsf{Ext},\mathcal{D}}(\lambda)$ is also non-negligible. Thus, we can conclude that the experiments $\mathbf{H}_1(\lambda)$ and $\mathbf{H}_2(\lambda)$ are computationally indistinguishable.

Next, we prove the following claim:

**Claim 2.** Experiments $\mathbf{H}_2(\lambda)$ and $\mathbf{H}_3(\lambda)$ are computationally indistinguishable.

We now prove that the adversary's views in the experiments $\mathbf{H}_2(\lambda)$ and $\mathbf{H}_3(\lambda)$ are computationally indistinguishable. In particular, we show that if there exists a PPT algorithm $\mathcal{D}$ which is able to distinguish between experiments $\mathbf{H}_2(\lambda)$ and $\mathbf{H}_3(\lambda)$ with non-negligible probability then it is possible to construct a PPT adversary $\mathcal{B} = (\mathcal{B}_1, \mathcal{B}_2)$ that running $\mathcal{D}$ as a sub-routine has a non-negligible advantage in the $\mathsf{Game}^{\mathsf{INDr\text{-}ID\text{-}CPA}}_{\Sigma,\mathcal{B}}(\lambda)$ against the underlying IBE $\Sigma$.

Consider the game $\mathsf{Game}^*_{\mathcal{D}}(\lambda)$ in Fig. 7. Notice that $\mathsf{Game}^*_{\mathcal{D}}(\lambda)$ with challenge bit $d = 1$ corresponds to experiment $\mathbf{H}_2(\lambda)$, whereas $\mathsf{Game}^*_{\mathcal{D}}(\lambda)$ with challenge bit $d = 0$ corresponds to experiment $\mathbf{H}_3(\lambda)$. The algorithm $\mathcal{B}_1$, on input the

| $\mathsf{Game}^*_{\mathcal{D}}(\lambda)$ |
|---|
| 1. $(\mathsf{mpk}, \mathsf{msk}) \leftarrow\$ \Pi.\mathsf{Setup}(1^\lambda)$ |
| 2. $(\mathsf{m}_0, \mathsf{rcv}_0, \mathbf{ID}_0) \leftarrow\$ \mathcal{D}_1^{\mathcal{O}_1,\mathcal{O}_2}(1^\lambda, \mathsf{mpk})$ |
| 3. $\sigma_0 \leftarrow\$ \mathbf{ID}_0$ |
| 4. $\mathsf{c}'_0 \leftarrow\$ \mathcal{C}$ |
| 5. $\psi \leftarrow\$ \mathcal{C};$ |
| 6. $\mathsf{c}_0 := \mathsf{c}'_0 \oplus \psi.$ |
| 7. $\mathsf{c}_1 \leftarrow\$ \Pi.\mathsf{Enc}(\sigma_0, \mathsf{rcv}_0, \mathsf{m}_0) =$ $= \Sigma.\mathsf{Enc}(\mathsf{rcv}_0, \mathsf{m}_0) \oplus \psi$ |
| 8. $d \leftarrow\$ \{0, 1\}$ |
| 9. $d' \leftarrow\$ \mathcal{D}_2^{\mathcal{O}_1,\mathcal{O}_2,\mathcal{O}_3}(1^\lambda, \mathsf{c}_d)$ |
| 10. **if** $(d' = d)$ **return** 1 |
| 11. **else return** 0 |

**Fig. 7.** Auxiliary game. $\mathcal{O}_1$ and $\mathcal{O}_2$ on input an arbitrary identity return respectively the corresponding encryption key and decryption key. $\mathcal{O}_3$ allows the adversary to obtain the ciphertexts of arbitrary $(\mathsf{m}, \mathsf{rcv})$ encrypted by the sender $\sigma$.

security parameter $1^\lambda$ and the master public-key $\mathsf{mpk}$, runs $\mathcal{D}_1$ on input $1^\lambda$ and $\mathsf{mpk}$. The oracles $\mathcal{O}_1$ and $\mathcal{O}_2$ for $\mathcal{D}_1$ can be implemented by $\mathcal{B}_1$; in particular, when $\mathcal{D}_1$ asks for the encryption key for a sender's identity $\sigma$, $\mathcal{B}_1$ returns $\mathsf{ek}_\sigma = \sigma$, whereas when $\mathcal{D}_1$ asks for the decryption key for a receiver's identity $\rho$, $\mathcal{B}_1$ issues the same query to its decryption key oracle. When the adversary $\mathcal{D}_1$ outputs its challenge tuple $(\mathsf{m}_0, \mathsf{rcv}_0, \mathbf{ID}_0)$, $\mathcal{B}_1$ outputs $(\mathsf{m}_0, \mathsf{id}_0)$ where $\mathsf{id}_0 = \mathsf{rcv}_0$. Then, the adversary $\mathcal{B}_2$, on input a challenge ciphertext $\mathsf{c}$, randomly samples a value $\psi \leftarrow\$ \mathcal{C}$. Next it sets the challenge ciphertext $\mathsf{c}_d$ for $\mathcal{D}_2$, as $\mathsf{c}_d = \mathsf{c} \oplus \psi$. Notice that $\mathcal{D}_2$'s queries to oracles $\mathcal{O}_1$ and $\mathcal{O}_2$ can be implemented by $\mathcal{B}_2$ as in the first phase of the game. Moreover, $\mathcal{B}_2$ is able to answer to $\mathcal{D}_2$'s queries to oracle $\mathcal{O}_3$ regarding a message $\mathsf{m}$ and a receiver $\mathsf{rcv}$, by first sampling a random $\psi \leftarrow\$ \mathcal{C}$, if $d = 1$ $\mathcal{B}$ runs the algorithm $\Sigma.\mathsf{Enc}(\mathsf{rcv}, \mathsf{m}) \oplus \psi$. If $d = 0$, $\mathsf{c}_d = \mathsf{c}'_0 \oplus \psi$ such that $\mathsf{c}'_0 \leftarrow\$ \mathcal{C}$. Eventually, the adversary $\mathcal{D}_2$ outputs its answer $d'$. If $d' = d$ then $\mathcal{B}_2$ outputs 1. Otherwise, $\mathcal{B}_2$ outputs 0. It is easy to see that the advantage $\mathrm{Adv}^{\mathsf{INDr\text{-}ID\text{-}CPA}}_{\Sigma,\mathcal{B}}(\lambda)$ of $\mathcal{B}$ in the $\mathsf{Game}^{\mathsf{INDr\text{-}ID\text{-}CPA}}_{\Sigma,\mathcal{B}}(\lambda)$ is the same that $\mathcal{D}$ has in $\mathsf{Game}^*_{\mathcal{D}}(\lambda)$ in Fig. 7. Thus, assuming the existence of a distinguisher $\mathcal{D}$ whose advantage is non-negligible leads to a contradiction because it also implies that $\mathrm{Adv}^{\mathsf{INDr\text{-}ID\text{-}CPA}}_{\Sigma,\mathcal{B}}(\lambda)$ is non-negligible. Since we have reached a contradiction, we can conclude that the experiments $\mathbf{H}_2(\lambda)$ and $\mathbf{H}_3(\lambda)$ are computationally indistinguishable.

Finally, since $\mathbf{H}_1(\lambda)$ and $\mathbf{H}_3(\lambda)$ correspond to $\mathsf{Game}^{\mathsf{ib\text{-}INDr\text{-}priv}}_{\Pi,\mathcal{A}}(\lambda)$ respectively with the challenge bit $b = 0$ and $b = 1$, we can conclude that the advantage $\mathrm{Adv}^{\mathsf{ib\text{-}INDr\text{-}priv}}_{\Pi,\mathcal{A}}(\lambda)$ of any adversary $\mathcal{A}$ in the game $\mathsf{Game}^{\mathsf{ib\text{-}INDr\text{-}priv}}_{\Pi,\mathcal{A}}(\lambda)$ when $\mathbf{Mismatch_2}$ occurs is negligible in $\lambda$. □

From Lemma 1 and Lemma 2 the following result holds:

**Theorem 1.** *The IB-ME construction of Fig. 4 achieves* indistinguishable from random privacy.

Since indistinguishable from random privacy implies enhanced privacy (see Appendix C), from Theorem 1 it holds that:

**Corollary 1.** *The IB-ME construction of Fig. 4 satisfies enhanced privacy.*

### 3.2 Achieving Authenticity

In this section we show how to build an IB-ME which achieves both authenticity and enhanced privacy by using as building blocks any IB-ME satisfying enhanced privacy and a context-hiding homomorphic signature scheme. Figure 8 shows our generic construction. In our construction the sender's encryption key consist of a homomorphic signature $\varsigma_\sigma$ over the sender's identity $\sigma$. We define a family of circuits $\mathsf{C}$ such that for each circuit $C \in \mathsf{C}$ it holds that $C[\mathsf{m}, \mathsf{rcv}, \mathsf{snd}, \mathsf{c}](\sigma) = 1$ if and only if the sender identity $\sigma$ matches a target identity $\mathsf{snd}$ hard-wired in the circuit $C$ along with a message $\mathsf{m}$, a receiver identity $\mathsf{rcv}$ and the ciphertext $\mathsf{c}$ which is computed encrypting $\mathsf{m}$ for the receiver $\mathsf{rcv}$ with the underlying IB-ME. When the sender $\sigma$ encrypts $\mathsf{m}$ it produces a ciphertext $(\mathsf{c}, \varsigma_{C(\sigma)})$ [1] where the signature $\varsigma_{C[\mathsf{m},\mathsf{rcv},\mathsf{snd},\mathsf{c}](\sigma)}$ certifies that $C[\mathsf{m}, \mathsf{rcv}, \mathsf{snd}, \mathsf{c}](\sigma) = 1$ (i.e., given that $\mathsf{snd} = \sigma$, the signature $\varsigma_{C[\mathsf{m},\mathsf{rcv},\mathsf{snd},\mathsf{c}](\sigma)}$ certifies that $\mathsf{snd}$ hard-wired in $C$ matches the sender's identity $\sigma$) and that $\mathsf{c}$ decrypts to $\mathsf{m}$ when using the decryption key associated to the receiver $\rho$. Notice that a receiver $\rho$ will successfully decrypt a ciphertext only if $C[\mathsf{m}, \mathsf{rcv}, \mathsf{snd}, \mathsf{c}](\sigma) = 1$, otherwise the verification procedure of the underlying signature scheme will not succeed (see line 4 of Algorithm $\mathsf{Dec}$ in Fig. 8). Thus, it is easy to see that the correctness of the IB-ME of Fig. 8 follows by the correctness of both the underlying IB-ME achieving enhanced privacy and the homomorphic signature scheme.

### 3.3 Security Analysis

Next, we show that the construction of Fig. 8 satisfies the security notions of authenticity and enhanced privacy. Informally, the enhanced privacy follows by the privacy property of the underlying IB-ME along with the context-hiding property of the homomorphic signature scheme which ensures that, when homomorphically evaluating the pair $(\sigma, \varsigma_\sigma)$ with respect to the circuit $C[\mathsf{m}, \mathsf{rcv}, \mathsf{snd}, \mathsf{c}]$, the resulting signature $\varsigma_{C[\mathsf{m},\mathsf{rcv},\mathsf{snd},\mathsf{c}](\sigma)}$ will not reveal anything about $\sigma$ making it difficult for an attacker to guess the sender's identity. On the other hand, authenticity follows by the unforgeability of the homomorphic signature scheme which ensures that, it is difficult for an adversary to produce a valid signature $\varsigma_{C[\mathsf{m},\mathsf{rcv},\mathsf{snd},\mathsf{c}](\sigma)}$ that verifies with respect to the circuit $C[\mathsf{m}, \mathsf{rcv}, \mathsf{snd}, \mathsf{c}]$.

[1] Notice that in the construction the ciphertext also contains a tag, this is included only for consistency with the definition of homomorphic signatures.

Let $\Pi = (\mathsf{Setup}, \mathsf{SKGen}, \mathsf{RKGen}, \mathsf{Enc}, \mathsf{Dec})$ be an IB-ME, with message space $\mathcal{M}$, ciphertext space $\mathcal{C}$, and identity space $\mathcal{I} = \{0,1\}^{\ell}$ which achieves enhanced privacy. Let $\Sigma = (\mathsf{Setup}, \mathsf{Sign}, \mathsf{Eval}, \mathsf{Verify}, \mathsf{ReRand}, \mathsf{RVerify})$ be a homomorphic signature scheme with message space $\{0,1\}$ and maximum dataset length $\ell$. **Define a family of circuits** $\mathsf{C}$ such that each $C[\mathsf{m}, \mathsf{rcv}, \mathsf{snd}, \mathsf{c}] \in \mathsf{C}$ denote a circuit that implements a function from $\{0,1\}^{\ell}$ to $\{0,1\}$ such that:

$$C[\mathsf{m}, \rho, \mathsf{snd}, \mathsf{c}](\sigma) := \begin{cases} 1 & \text{iff } \mathsf{snd} = \sigma \text{ and } \mathsf{m} = \Pi.\mathsf{Dec}(\mathsf{dk}'_{\rho}, \mathsf{snd}, \mathsf{c}'), \text{ where} \\ & \mathsf{dk}'_{\rho} \leftarrow\!\$\, \Pi.\mathsf{RKGen}(\mathsf{msk}', \rho); \\ 0 & \text{otherwise} \end{cases}$$

where $\mathsf{m} \in \mathcal{M}, \mathsf{rcv} \in \mathcal{I},\ \mathsf{snd} \in \mathcal{I},\ \mathsf{c} \in \mathcal{C}$ are hard-weired in the circuit.

We design an IB-ME as follows:

**Algorithm** $\mathsf{Setup}(1^{\lambda})$
1. Execute $(\mathsf{mpk}', \mathsf{msk}') \leftarrow\!\$\, \Pi.\mathsf{Setup}(1^{\lambda})$;
2. Execute $(\mathsf{pk}, \mathsf{sk}) \leftarrow\!\$\, \Sigma.\mathsf{Setup}(1^{\lambda}, 1^{n})$;
3. Set $\mathsf{mpk} = (\mathsf{mpk}', \mathsf{pk})$ and $\mathsf{msk} = (\mathsf{msk}', \mathsf{sk}, \mathsf{pk})$;
4. Output $(\mathsf{mpk}, \mathsf{msk})$.

**Algorithm** $\mathsf{SKGen}(\mathsf{msk}, \sigma)$
1. Parse $\mathsf{msk}$ as $(\mathsf{msk}', \mathsf{sk}, \mathsf{pk})$;
2. Execute $\mathsf{ek}'_{\sigma} \leftarrow\!\$\, \Pi.\mathsf{SKGen}(\mathsf{msk}', \sigma)$;
3. Pick random $\tau_{\sigma} \in \{0,1\}^{\lambda}$
4. Execute $\varsigma_{\sigma} \leftarrow\!\$\, \Sigma.\mathsf{Sign}(\mathsf{sk}, \tau_{\sigma}, \sigma)$;
5. Set $\mathsf{ek}_{\sigma} = (\sigma, \mathsf{ek}'_{\sigma}, \varsigma_{\sigma}, \tau_{\sigma})$;
6. Output $\mathsf{ek}_{\sigma}$.

**Algorithm** $\mathsf{RKGen}(\mathsf{msk}, \rho)$
1. Parse $\mathsf{msk}$ as $(\mathsf{msk}', \mathsf{sk}, \mathsf{pk})$;
2. Execute $\mathsf{dk}'_{\rho} \leftarrow\!\$\, \Pi.\mathsf{RKGen}(\mathsf{msk}', \rho)$;
3. Output $\mathsf{dk}_{\rho} = (\mathsf{dk}'_{\rho}, \mathsf{pk})$.

**Algorithm** $\mathsf{Enc}(\mathsf{mpk}, \mathsf{ek}_{\sigma}, \mathsf{rcv}, \mathsf{m})$
1. Parse $\mathsf{mpk}$ as $(\mathsf{mpk}', \mathsf{pk})$;
2. Parse $\mathsf{ek}_{\sigma}$ as $(\sigma, \mathsf{ek}'_{\sigma}, \varsigma_{\sigma}, \tau_{\sigma})$;
3. Execute $\mathsf{c}' \leftarrow\!\$\, \Pi.\mathsf{Enc}(\mathsf{mpk}', \mathsf{ek}'_{\sigma}, \mathsf{rcv}, \mathsf{m})$;
4. Let the circuit $C[\mathsf{m}, \mathsf{rcv}, \sigma, \mathsf{c}']$ defined as above.
   Execute $\varsigma' \leftarrow\!\$\, \Sigma.\mathsf{Eval}(\mathsf{pk}, \tau_{\sigma}, \sigma, \varsigma_{\sigma}, C[\mathsf{m}, \mathsf{rcv}, \sigma, \mathsf{c}'])$;
5. Execute $\varsigma \leftarrow\!\$\, \Sigma.\mathsf{ReRand}(\mathsf{pk}, \tau_{\sigma}, C[\mathsf{m}, \mathsf{rcv}, \sigma, \mathsf{c}'](\sigma), \varsigma', C[\mathsf{m}, \mathsf{rcv}, \sigma, \mathsf{c}'])$
6. Set $\mathsf{c} = (\mathsf{c}', \varsigma, \tau_{\sigma})$;
7. Output $\mathsf{c}$.

**Algorithm** $\mathsf{Dec}(\mathsf{dk}_{\rho}, \mathsf{snd}, \mathsf{c})$
1. Parse $\mathsf{c}$ as $(\mathsf{c}', \varsigma, \tau_{\sigma})$;
2. Parse $\mathsf{dk}_{\rho}$ as $(\mathsf{dk}'_{\rho}, \mathsf{pk})$;
3. Execute $\mathsf{m} := \Pi.\mathsf{Dec}(\mathsf{dk}'_{\rho}, \mathsf{snd}, \mathsf{c}')$;
4. Let the circuit $C[\mathsf{m}, \rho, \mathsf{snd}, \mathsf{c}']$ be defined as above.
   If $\Sigma.\mathsf{RVerify}(\mathsf{pk}, \tau_{\sigma}, 1, \varsigma, C[\mathsf{m}, \rho, \mathsf{snd}, \mathsf{c}']) = 0$ then output $\bot$.
5. Otherwise, output $\mathsf{m}$.

**Fig. 8.** An IB-ME Generic Construction.

**Theorem 2.** *Let* $\Sigma = (\mathsf{Setup}, \mathsf{Sign}, \mathsf{Eval}, \mathsf{RVerify}, \mathsf{ReRand}, \mathsf{RVerify})$ *be a homomorphic signature scheme fully unforgeable against adaptive chosen-dataset attacks. The IB-ME* $\Gamma = (\mathsf{Setup}, \mathsf{SKGen}, \mathsf{RKGen}, \mathsf{Enc}, \mathsf{Dec})$ *obtained from the construction of Fig. 8 achieves the security notion of* authenticity.

*Proof.* Assume by contradiction that $\Gamma$ does not achieve authenticity. In other words there exists a PPT adversary $\mathcal{A}$ whose advantage $\mathrm{Succ}^{\mathsf{ib\text{-}auth}}_{\Gamma,\mathcal{A}}(\lambda)$ in the game of Fig. 1 is non-negligible in $\lambda$. Next, we show that there exists a PPT adversary $\mathcal{B}$ that by using $\mathcal{A}$ will produce a forgery for the homomorphic signature scheme $\Sigma$ (see $\mathsf{Game}^{\mathsf{EUF\text{-}FH\text{-}CDA}}_{\Sigma,\mathcal{B}}(\lambda)$ in Fig. 3).

The adversary $\mathcal{B}$, on input the public key $\mathsf{pk}$, runs $\Pi.\mathsf{Setup}$ to obtain ($\mathsf{msk}'$, $\mathsf{mpk}'$) and set $\mathsf{mpk} = (\mathsf{mpk}', \mathsf{pk})$. Then, $\mathcal{B}$ runs the algorithm $\mathcal{A}$ on input $\mathsf{mpk}$.

Notice that $\mathcal{B}$ is able to implement the interactions between $\mathcal{A}$ and its oracles $\mathcal{O}_1$ and $\mathcal{O}_2$. Specifically, in order to produce an answer to an $\mathcal{O}_1$'s query regarding a sender identity $\sigma$, $\mathcal{B}$, first execute $\mathsf{ek}'_\sigma \leftarrow\!\!\$\ \Pi.\mathsf{SKGen}(\mathsf{msk}', \sigma)$ and then calls its signing oracle $\mathcal{O}$ to obtain a signature $\varsigma_\sigma$ on $\sigma$ and a tag $\tau_\sigma$. Thus, $\mathcal{B}$ generates the response from $\mathcal{O}_1$ as $\mathsf{ek}_\sigma = (\sigma, \mathsf{ek}'_\sigma, \varsigma_\sigma, \tau_\sigma)$ and stores $(\tau_\sigma, \sigma)$ in $\mathcal{O}_O$. On the other hand, $\mathcal{B}$ can easily implement $\mathcal{O}_2$ when queried on a receiver identity $\rho$ by running $\Pi.\mathsf{RKGen}(\mathsf{msk}', \rho)$. Eventually, $\mathcal{A}$ outputs $(\mathsf{c}, \rho, \mathsf{snd})$ where $\mathsf{c} = (\mathsf{c}', \varsigma, \tau^*)$. Since $\mathcal{A}$ wins the game $\mathsf{Game}^{\mathsf{ib\text{-}auth}}_{\Gamma,\mathcal{A}}(\lambda)$ it holds that $\Gamma.\mathsf{Dec}(\mathsf{dk}_\rho, \mathsf{snd}, \mathsf{c}) \neq \perp$ meaning that $\Gamma.\mathsf{RVerify}(\mathsf{pk}, \tau^*, 1, \varsigma, C[\mathsf{m}, \rho, \mathsf{snd}, \mathsf{c}']) = 1$ where $\mathsf{m} := \Pi.\mathsf{Dec}(\mathsf{dk}'_\rho, \mathsf{snd}, \mathsf{c}')$. Then, $\mathcal{B}$ returns $(\tau^*, \mathsf{x}^*, \varsigma^*, C^*)$ where $\mathsf{x}^* = 1$, $\varsigma^* = \varsigma$ and $C^* = C[\mathsf{m}, \rho, \mathsf{snd}, \mathsf{c}']$. We distinguish two cases:

[$\tau^* \neq \tau$ for all $\tau$ s.t. $(\tau, \sigma) \in \mathcal{O}_O$]. This is a Type (1) forgery for the signature scheme.

[$\tau^* = \tau$ for some $\tau$ s.t. $(\tau, \sigma) \in \mathcal{O}_O$]. Notice that if $(\tau, \sigma) \in \mathcal{O}_O$ then $\sigma \in Q_{\mathcal{O}_1}$. Since $\mathcal{A}$ wins the game $\mathsf{Game}^{\mathsf{ib\text{-}auth}}_{\Gamma,\mathcal{A}}(\lambda)$, $\mathsf{snd}$ cannot be equal to $\sigma$ (see Fig. 1). Then, it must be the case that $\mathcal{A}$ gave as output $\tau^*$ and $\mathsf{snd}$ such that $\tau^* = \tau$ for some $\tau$ s.t. $(\tau, \sigma) \in \mathcal{O}_O$ but $\sigma \neq \mathsf{snd}$. However, when $\sigma \neq \mathsf{snd}$ it holds that $C[\mathsf{m}, \mathsf{rcv}, \mathsf{snd}, \mathsf{c}'](\sigma) = 0 \neq \mathsf{x}^*$. Since $\sigma$ is the dataset associated to $\tau$, the tuple $(\tau^*, \mathsf{x}^*, \varsigma^*, C^*)$ is a type (2) forgery for the signature scheme.

Thus, if $\mathrm{Succ}^{\mathsf{ib\text{-}auth}}_{\Gamma,\mathcal{A}}(\lambda)$ in the game of Fig. 1 is non-negligible then $\mathcal{B}$ wins the game $\mathsf{Game}^{\mathsf{EUF\text{-}FH\text{-}CDA}}_{\Sigma,\mathcal{B}}(\lambda)$ with non-negligible probability in $\lambda$. Contradiction. □

**Theorem 3.** *Let* $\Pi$ *be an IB-ME that achieves the notion of enhanced privacy and let* $\Sigma$ *be a context-hiding homomorphic signature scheme. The IB-ME* $\Gamma = (\mathsf{Setup}, \mathsf{SKGen}, \mathsf{RKGen}, \mathsf{Enc}, \mathsf{Dec})$ *obtained from the construction of Fig. 8 satisfies* enhanced privacy.

*Proof.* Consider the following hybrid experiments:

$\mathbf{H}_1(\lambda)$: This is identical to the game $\mathsf{Game}^{\mathsf{ib\text{-}priv}^+}_{\Gamma,\mathcal{A}}(\lambda)$ defined in Fig. 2.

$\mathbf{H}_2(\lambda)$: Same as $\mathbf{H}_1(\lambda)$, but now the challenger uses the simulator $\mathsf{Sim}$ to generate the signature belonging to the challenge ciphertext. Formally, when the adversary $\mathcal{A}$ outputs the challenge $(\mathsf{m}_0, \mathsf{m}_1, \mathsf{rcv}_0, \mathsf{rcv}_1, \mathbf{ID}_0, \mathbf{ID}_1)$, the challenger generates the ciphertext $\mathsf{c}^* = (\mathsf{c}', \varsigma, \tau_\sigma)$, where $\mathsf{c}' \leftarrow\!\!\$\ \Pi.\mathsf{Enc}(\mathsf{mpk}', \sigma_b,$

$\mathsf{rcv}_b, \mathsf{m}_b)$, $\sigma_b \leftarrow\!\!\$\, \mathbf{ID}_b$, $(\mathsf{mpk}', \mathsf{msk}') \leftarrow\!\!\$\, \Pi.\mathsf{Setup}(1^\lambda)$, and $\varsigma \leftarrow\!\!\$\, \mathsf{Sim}(\mathsf{sk}, C[\mathsf{m}, \mathsf{rcv}_b, \sigma_b, \mathsf{c}'](\sigma_b), \tau_\sigma)$, where $b \in \{0,1\}$.

It is easy to see that $\mathbf{H}_1(\lambda)$ and $\mathbf{H}_2(\lambda)$ are computationally indistinguishable, given the context hiding property of the homomorphic signature scheme $\Sigma$. Thus, the proof follows by proving the next claim:

**[Claim 3.]** $\left|\Pr[\mathbf{H}_2(\lambda) = 1] - \frac{1}{2}\right| \leq \mathsf{negl}(\lambda)$.

We now prove Claim 3. Assume by contradiction that $\Gamma$ does not achieve enhanced privacy. In other words there exists a PPT adversary $\mathcal{A}$ whose advantage in the game $\mathbf{H}_2(\lambda)$ is non-negligible in $\lambda$. Next, we show that there exists a PPT adversary $\mathcal{B}$ for the game $\mathsf{Game}^{\mathsf{ib\text{-}priv}^+}_{\Pi,\mathcal{B}}(\lambda)$ that by using $\mathcal{A}$ has non-negligible advantage in breaking the game of Fig. 2 with respect to the underlying IB-ME. The adversary $\mathcal{B}$, on input the public key $\mathsf{mpk}'$, runs $\Sigma.\mathsf{Setup}$ to obtain $(\mathsf{pk}, \mathsf{sk})$ and set $\mathsf{mpk} = (\mathsf{mpk}', \mathsf{pk})$. Then, $\mathcal{B}$ runs the algorithm $\mathcal{A}$ on input $\mathsf{mpk}$.

Notice that $\mathcal{B}$ is able to implement the interactions between $\mathcal{A}$ and its oracles $\mathcal{O}_1$, $\mathcal{O}_2$. Specifically, in order to produce an answer to an $\mathcal{O}_1$'s query regarding a sender identity $\sigma$, $\mathcal{B}$ calls its oracle $\mathcal{O}_1$ to obtain $\mathsf{ek}'_\sigma$, then it simply generates a signature on the sender identity to obtain a signature on $\sigma$ and a tag $\tau_\sigma$. On the other hand, $\mathcal{B}$ can easily implement $\mathcal{O}_2$ when queried on a receiver identity $\rho$ by using his oracle $\mathcal{O}_2$. The adversary $\mathcal{A}_1$ outputs a challenge tuple $(\mathsf{m}_0, \mathsf{m}_1, \mathsf{rcv}_0, \mathsf{rcv}_1, \mathsf{ID}_0, \mathsf{ID}_1)$, and then $\mathcal{B}$ also chooses the same challenge. In order to compute the challenge ciphertext $\mathsf{c} = (\mathsf{c}', \varsigma, \tau_\sigma)$ for $\mathcal{A}$, $\mathcal{B}_2$ on input its challenge ciphertext $\mathsf{c}'$ picks a random tag $\tau_\sigma$ and runs $\varsigma \leftarrow\!\!\$\, \mathsf{Sim}(\mathsf{sk}, 1, \tau_\sigma)$. $\mathcal{A}_2$'s queries to oracles $\mathcal{O}_1$ and $\mathcal{O}_2$ can be implemented by $\mathcal{B}_2$ as in the first phase of the game. Moreover, $\mathcal{B}$ is able to answer to $\mathcal{A}_2$'s queries to oracle $\mathcal{O}_3^i$ by first running its own oracle $\mathcal{O}_3^i$ to get the ciphertext $\mathsf{c}'$, then picking a random tag $\tau_\sigma$ and executing $\varsigma \leftarrow\!\!\$\, \mathsf{Sim}(\mathsf{sk}, 1, \tau_\sigma)$. When $\mathcal{A}_2$ outputs its answer $b$, $\mathcal{B}$ output $b$. Since $\mathcal{A}$ wins its game in experiment $\mathbf{H}_2(\lambda)$ with non negligible probability, then $\mathcal{B}$ also wins the game $\mathsf{Game}^{\mathsf{ib\text{-}priv}^+}_{\Pi,\mathcal{B}}(\lambda)$ with non-negligible probability in $\lambda$. Contradiction.

□

## 4 Instantiations from Lattice Assumptions

Our framework enables instantiations in the standard model based on lattice assumptions. Specifically, in order to achieve enhanced privacy, it requires reusable extractors and anonymous IBE meeting INDr-ID-CPA security. Reusable extractors can be efficiently built from LWE as shown by Alwen et al. in [3]. Examples of anonymous IBE achieving INDr-ID-CPA based on the LWE problem include the IBE proposed by Agrawal et al. [2], and the construction by Gentry et al. [14] in the random oracle model. Agrawal et al. provide detailed parameter choices for their IBE scheme, which are essential for its security and efficiency. Notably, Agrawal et al.'s IBE scheme has the advantage of maintaining a compact ciphertext size. Let $q$ be a prime, $n$ a positive integer and $m > n$. Specifically, the total ciphertext size using this technique amounts to 1 element of $\mathbb{Z}_q$ for each bit of the message, along with a constant $2m$ elements of $\mathbb{Z}_q$, irrespective of the message length. This results in a ciphertext size of $(N + 2m)$ elements of $\mathbb{Z}_q$, where $N$ represents the number of bits in the message [2]. The public parameters in Agrawal et al.'s IBE scheme consist of three $n \times m$ matrices in $\mathbb{Z}_q$ and a vector in $\mathbb{Z}_q^n$. On the other hand Gentry et al.'s scheme security is based on the Learning With Errors (LWE) problem in the random oracle model. The scheme is asymptotically highly efficient, where the master public key and individual secret keys are $O(\lambda^2)$ bits in size, where $\lambda$ is the security parameter.

To achieve authenticity our construction needs adaptively unforgeable fully homomorphic signatures also meeting the context hiding property. Efficient solutions based on the hardness of the Small Integer Solution (SIS) problem in standard lattices include the fully homomorphic signatures by Boyen et al. [6], and the construction by Luo et al. [17]. In Boyen et al.'s construction [6], the size of signatures is proportional to that of the data being signed. Signature are elements in $Z_q^{2m \times m}$. Let $\lambda$ be the security parameter, $l$ be the maximum number of inputs for the circuit family, and $|\tau|$ be the number of bits for the tag (where $|\tau| = |t| + |b|$, typically $|\tau| = \lambda + l$). The public key $pk$ consists of a total of $3 + 2l + \lambda$ matrices, each of size $n \times m$, where each element is in $Z_q$. Luo et al.'s [17] construction has similar features of that of Boyen's with respect of public key and signature sizes while improving the efficiency of generating signatures.

## 5 Conclusions

In this paper, we focused on the design of IB-ME schemes from lattice assumptions. To begin, we built upon an anonymous IBE to produce an IB-ME that ensured enhanced privacy. Additionally, we presented a generic method that, by using any IB-ME achieving enhanced privacy and a context-hiding homomorphic signature scheme as building blocks, resulted in an IB-ME that guarantees both enhanced privacy and authenticity. By appropriately instantiating the underlying components, our framework yields secure IB-ME schemes from lattice assumptions in the standard model.

**Acknowledgements.** This work was partially supported by projects *VITALITY Ecosystem, Spoke 1 MEGHALITIC* (E13C22001060006) under the NRRP MUR program funded by the EU - NGEU and *Verifica di proprietà di sicurezza nello sviluppo del software* under the Start-up 2022 program funded by the Computer Science Division, UNIMOL and by INDAM-GNCS 2023.

## A Reusable Computational Extractors

A computational extractor is a polynomial-time algorithm $\mathsf{Ext}\colon S \times X \to Y$ that on input a seed $s \in S$ and a value $x \in X$ outputs $\mathsf{Ext}_s(x) = y \in Y$. The security of a computational extractor guarantees that $y \in Y$ is pseudorandom when the seed is sampled at random from $S$ and $x$ is sampled from an input distribution

$\mathbf{X}$ (defined over the input space $X$) of min-entropy $\mathbb{H}_\infty(\mathbf{X}) \geq k$, even if the seed is made public. We will rely on so-called *reusable* [9] computational extractors, that produce random looking outputs even if evaluated multiple times on the same input.

**Definition 9 (Reusable computational extractor).** *An algorithm* $\mathsf{Ext} : S \times X \to Y$ *is a* $(k, q)$*-reusable extractor if for all random variables* $\mathbf{X} \in X$ *such that* $\mathbb{H}_\infty(\mathbf{X}) \geq k$*, and for all PPT distinguishers* $\mathcal{D}$*, the advantage* $\mathrm{Adv}^{\mathsf{ind}}_{\mathsf{Ext},\mathcal{D}}(\lambda)$ *defined as*

$$\left|\Pr\left[\mathcal{D}(s_1, \ldots, s_q, \mathsf{Ext}_{s_1}(x), \ldots, \mathsf{Ext}_{s_q}(x)) = 1\right] - \Pr[\mathcal{D}(s_1, \ldots, s_q, y_1, \ldots, y_q) = 1]\right|$$

*where* $x \leftarrow\$ \mathbf{X}$*,* $s_i \leftarrow\$ S$*, and* $y_i \leftarrow\$ Y$ *(for all* $i \in [q]$*), is negligible in* $\lambda$*.*

## B Identity-Based Encryption

In IBE, each user has as a public-key an arbitrary string representing its identity (e.g. its email address). In order to encrypt a message, the sender only has to specify the identity $\mathsf{rcv}$ of the receiver. The user whose identity $\rho = \mathsf{rcv}$ is the only one that holds the decryption key to correctly reveal the message.

An Identity-Based Encryption (IBE) scheme [5,19] with message space $\mathcal{M}$ and ciphertext space $\mathcal{C}$, is a tuple of four probabilistic polynomial-time algorithms (Setup, Extract, Encrypt, Decrypt) such that:

$\mathsf{Setup}(1^\lambda)$: On input the security parameter $1^\lambda$, the randomized setup algorithm returns as output a master public-key $\mathsf{mpk}$ (i.e. the system parameters) and a master secret-key $\mathsf{msk}$. We assume that all the algorithms of the tuple take $\mathsf{mpk}$ as input.

$\mathsf{Extract}(\mathsf{msk}, \mathsf{id})$: On input the master secret-key $\mathsf{msk}$, and an identity $\mathsf{id}$, the randomized extract algorithm returns as output a secret-key (or private-key) $\mathsf{sk}_{\mathsf{id}}$ for the identity $\mathsf{id}$.

$\mathsf{Encrypt}(\mathsf{id}, \mathsf{m})$: On input an identity $\mathsf{id}$ and a message $\mathsf{m} \in \mathcal{M}$, the randomized encryption algorithm returns as output a ciphertext $\mathsf{c} \in \mathcal{C}$.

$\mathsf{Decrypt}(\mathsf{sk}_{\mathsf{id}}, \mathsf{c})$: On input the secret-key $\mathsf{sk}_{\mathsf{id}}$ for identity $\mathsf{id}$, and a ciphertext $\mathsf{c}$, the deterministic decryption algorithm returns as output either a message $\mathsf{m}$ or a special symbol $\perp$ denoting a failure.

**Definition 10 ([1] Correctness of IBE).** *An IBE scheme* $\Pi$ = (Setup, Extract, Encrypt, Decrypt) *is correct if* $\forall \lambda \in \mathbb{N}$, $\forall (\mathsf{mpk}, \mathsf{msk})$ *output by* $\mathsf{Setup}(1^\lambda)$*, and* $\forall \mathsf{m} \in \mathcal{M}$*:*

$$\Pr[\mathsf{Decrypt}\,(\mathsf{sk}_{\mathsf{id}}, \mathsf{Encrypt}(\mathsf{id}, \mathsf{m})) = \mathsf{m}] \geq 1 - \mathsf{negl}(\lambda)$$

*where* $\mathsf{sk}_{\mathsf{id}} \leftarrow\$ \mathsf{Extract}(\mathsf{msk}, \mathsf{id})$.

**Security.** To define IBE adaptive security, in [1] Agrawal et al. introduce a security game that captures a strong privacy property known as *indistinguishable from random*, see Fig. 9. Such a property requires that the challenge ciphertext is indistinguishable from a random element in the ciphertext space. This definition, dubbed as INDr-ID-CPA, implies semantic security, recipient anonymity.

**Definition 11** ([1] **INDr-ID-CPA**). *We say that an IBE scheme* $\Pi$ *satisfies* indistinguishable from random under an adaptive chosen-identity and chosen-plaintext attack *if for all PPT adversaries* $\mathcal{A} = (\mathcal{A}_1, \mathcal{A}_2)$:

$$\mathrm{Adv}_{\Pi,\mathcal{A}}^{\mathsf{INDr\text{-}ID\text{-}CPA}}(\lambda) := \left|\Pr\left[\mathsf{Game}_{\Pi,\mathcal{A}}^{\mathsf{INDr\text{-}ID\text{-}CPA}}(\lambda) = 1\right] - \frac{1}{2}\right| \leq \mathsf{negl}(\lambda)$$

*where* $\mathsf{Game}_{\Pi,\mathcal{A}}^{\mathsf{INDr\text{-}ID\text{-}CPA}}(\lambda)$ *is defined in Fig. 9.*

$\mathsf{Game}_{\Pi,\mathcal{A}}^{\mathsf{INDr\text{-}ID\text{-}CPA}}(\lambda)$

1. $(\mathsf{mpk}, \mathsf{msk}) \leftarrow\$ \mathsf{Setup}(1^\lambda)$
2. $(\mathsf{m}_0, \mathsf{id}_0) \leftarrow\$ \mathcal{A}_1^{\mathcal{O}_1}(1^\lambda, \mathsf{mpk})$
3. $\mathsf{c}_0 \leftarrow\$ \mathsf{Encrypt}(\mathsf{id}_0, \mathsf{m}_0)$
4. $\mathsf{c}_1 \leftarrow\$ \mathcal{C}$
5. $b \leftarrow\$ \{0, 1\}$
6. $b' \leftarrow\$ \mathcal{A}_2^{\mathcal{O}_1}(1^\lambda, \mathsf{c}_b)$
7. **if** $(b' = b)$ **return** 1
8. **else return** 0

**Fig. 9.** Game defining the INDr-ID-CPA for IBE.

$\mathcal{A}$ has access to an oracle $\mathcal{O}_1$ that, given an identity $\mathsf{id}$, returns as output the corresponding secret-key $\mathsf{sk}_{\mathsf{id}}$. In order to be valid, $\mathcal{A}$ cannot set as the challenge identity $\mathsf{id}_0$ an identity $\mathsf{id}$ for which it has issued a private-key query (i.e. $\mathsf{id}_0 \notin Q_{\mathcal{O}_1}$).

# C Indistinguishable from Random Privacy vs Enhanced Privacy

**Theorem 4.** *Let* $\Pi = (\mathsf{Setup}, \mathsf{SKGen}, \mathsf{RKGen}, \mathsf{Enc}, \mathsf{Dec})$ *be an IB-ME scheme. If* $\Pi$ *satisfies* indistinguishable from random privacy *then* $\Pi$ *achieves also* enhanced privacy.

*Proof.* Assume, by contradiction, that $\Pi$ achieves indistinguishability from random privacy but it does *not* satisfy enhanced privacy; this means that there exists a PPT adversary $\mathcal{B} = (\mathcal{B}_1, \mathcal{B}_2)$ whose advantage in the $\mathsf{Game}^{\text{ib-priv}^+}_{\Pi,\mathcal{B}}(\lambda)$ of Fig. 2 is non-negligible. We show how to construct a PPT adversary $\mathcal{A} = (\mathcal{A}_1, \mathcal{A}_2)$ that running $\mathcal{B}$ as a sub-routine has a non-negligible advantage in winning the $\mathsf{Game}^{\text{ib-INDr-priv}}_{\Pi,\mathcal{A}}(\lambda)$ of Fig. 5.

The algorithm $\mathcal{A}_1$, on input the security parameter $1^\lambda$ and the master public-key $\mathsf{mpk}$, runs the algorithm $\mathcal{B}_1$ on the same inputs (i.e., $1^\lambda$ and $\mathsf{mpk}$). The adversary $\mathcal{A}_1$ will answer to any oracle call that $\mathcal{B}_1$ issues to its oracles $\mathcal{O}'_1$ and $\mathcal{O}'_2$ by calling its own corresponding oracles. When $\mathcal{B}_1$ outputs the tuple ($\mathsf{m}_0$, $\mathsf{m}_1$, $\mathsf{rcv}_0$, $\mathsf{rcv}_1$, $\mathbf{ID}_0$, $\mathbf{ID}_1$), the algorithm $\mathcal{A}_1$ randomly samples a bit $b \leftarrow\$ \{0,1\}$ and outputs the tuple ($\mathsf{m}_b$, $\mathsf{rcv}_b$, $\mathbf{ID}_b$).
The challenger for $\mathcal{A}$ samples an identity $\sigma_b \leftarrow\$ \mathbf{ID}_b$.
The challenger for $\mathcal{A}$ then randomly samples a bit $b_\mathcal{A} \leftarrow\$ \{0,1\}$ and sets the challenge ciphertext $\mathsf{c}$ in such a way that $\mathsf{c} \leftarrow\$ \mathsf{Enc}(\mathsf{ek}_{\sigma_b}, \mathsf{rcv}_b, \mathsf{m}_b)$ when $b_\mathcal{A} = 0$, or $\mathsf{c}$ is a randomly generated ciphertext when $b_\mathcal{A} = 1$.
$\mathcal{A}_2$ randomly samples an identity $\sigma_{1-b} \leftarrow\$ \mathbf{ID}_{1-b}$ and queries its oracle $\mathcal{O}_2$ for the corresponding encryption key $\mathsf{ek}_{\sigma_{(1-b)}}$. This is necessary to allow $\mathcal{A}_2$ to answer the queries of $\mathcal{B}_2$ to $\mathcal{O}_3^{1-b}$ for ciphertexts generated by the sender's identity $\sigma_{1-b}$. On the other hand, when $\mathcal{B}_2$ asks to $\mathcal{O}_3^b$ the ciphertexts generated by the sender's identity $\sigma_b$, $\mathcal{A}_2$ calls its oracle $\mathcal{O}_3$. Finally, $\mathcal{A}_2$ sets as a challenge for $\mathcal{B}_2$ the challenge ciphertext $\mathsf{c}$ received from its own challenger.

Eventually, $\mathcal{B}_2$ outputs a bit $b'$. If $b' = b$, then $\mathcal{A}_2$ return $b'_\mathcal{A} = 0$, otherwise $\mathcal{A}_2$ return $b'_\mathcal{A} = 1$.

From Definition 3 the advantage of $\mathcal{B}$ is:

$$\mathrm{Adv}^{\text{ib-priv}^+}_{\Pi,\mathcal{B}}(\lambda) := \left|\Pr\left[\mathsf{Game}^{\text{ib-priv}^+}_{\Pi,\mathcal{B}}(\lambda) = 1\right] - \frac{1}{2}\right| = \left|\Pr[b' = b] - \frac{1}{2}\right|$$

As stated in Definition 8, the advantage of $\mathcal{A}$ is:

$$\begin{aligned}
\mathrm{Adv}^{\text{ib-INDr-priv}}_{\Pi,\mathcal{A}}(\lambda) &:= \left|\Pr\left[\mathsf{Game}^{\text{ib-INDr-priv}}_{\Pi,\mathcal{A}}(\lambda) = 1\right] - \frac{1}{2}\right| \\
&= \left|\Pr[b_\mathcal{A} = b'_\mathcal{A}] - \frac{1}{2}\right| \\
&= \left|\Pr[b_\mathcal{A} = b'_\mathcal{A} = 0] + \Pr[b_\mathcal{A} = b'_\mathcal{A} = 1] - \frac{1}{2}\right| \\
&= \left|\Pr[b = b'] + \Pr[b_\mathcal{A} = b'_\mathcal{A} = 1] - \frac{1}{2}\right| \\
&\geq \left|\Pr[b = b'] - \frac{1}{2}\right| = \mathrm{Adv}^{\text{ib-priv}^+}_{\Pi,\mathcal{B}}(\lambda)
\end{aligned}$$

Since, by assumption, $\mathrm{Adv}^{\text{ib-priv}^+}_{\Pi,\mathcal{B}}(\lambda)$ is non-negligible, the advantage of $\mathcal{A}$ is also non-negligible. Contradiction.

We can therefore conclude that such an adversary $\mathcal{B}$ cannot exist and thus a scheme that satisfies indistinguishable from random privacy also satisfies enhanced privacy. □

## References


1. Agrawal, S., Boneh, D., Boyen, X.: Efficient lattice (H)IBE in the standard model. In: Gilbert, H. (ed.) EUROCRYPT 2010. LNCS, vol. 6110, pp. 553–572. Springer, Heidelberg (2010). https://doi.org/10.1007/978-3-642-13190-5_28
2. Agrawal, S., Boneh, D., Boyen, X.: Lattice basis delegation in fixed dimension and shorter-ciphertext hierarchical IBE. In: Rabin, T. (ed.) CRYPTO 2010. LNCS, vol. 6223, pp. 98–115. Springer, Heidelberg (2010). https://doi.org/10.1007/978-3-642-14623-7_6
3. Alwen, J., Krenn, S., Pietrzak, K., Wichs, D.: Learning with rounding, revisited. In: Canetti, R., Garay, J.A. (eds.) CRYPTO 2013. LNCS, vol. 8042, pp. 57–74. Springer, Heidelberg (2013). https://doi.org/10.1007/978-3-642-40041-4_4
4. Ateniese, G., Francati, D., Nuñez, D., Venturi, D.: Match me if you can: matchmaking encryption and its applications. J. Cryptol. **34**(3), 1–50 (2021). https://doi.org/10.1007/s00145-021-09381-4
5. Boneh, D., Franklin, M.: Identity-based encryption from the weil pairing. In: Kilian, J. (ed.) CRYPTO 2001. LNCS, vol. 2139, pp. 213–229. Springer, Heidelberg (2001). https://doi.org/10.1007/3-540-44647-8_13
6. Boyen, X., Fan, X., Shi, E.: Adaptively secure fully homomorphic signatures based on lattices. Cryptology ePrint Archive, Paper 2014/916 (2014). https://eprint.iacr.org/2014/916
7. Chen, B., Xiang, T., Ma, M., He, D., Liao, X.: CL-ME: efficient certificateless matchmaking encryption for internet of things. IEEE Internet Things J. **8**(19), 15010–15023 (2021). https://doi.org/10.1109/JIOT.2021.3073008
8. Chen, J., Li, Y., Wen, J., Weng, J.: Identity-based matchmaking encryption from standard assumptions. In: Agrawal, S., Lin, D. (eds.) Advances in Cryptology, ASIACRYPT 2022. LNCS, vol. 13793, pp. 394–422. Springer, Cham (2022). https://doi.org/10.1007/978-3-031-22969-5_14
9. Dodis, Y., Kalai, Y.T., Lovett, S.: On cryptography with auxiliary input. In: Mitzenmacher, M. (ed.) Proceedings of the 41st Annual ACM Symposium on Theory of Computing, STOC 2009, May–June 2009, pp. 621–630. ACM (2009)
10. Feige, U., Lapidot, D., Shamir, A.: Multiple noninteractive zero knowledge proofs under general assumptions. SIAM J. Comput. **29**(1), 1–28 (1999). https://doi.org/10.1137/S0097539792230010
11. Fischlin, M., Rohrbach, F.: Single-to-multi-theorem transformations for non-interactive statistical zero-knowledge. In: Garay, J.A. (ed.) PKC 2021. LNCS, vol. 12711, pp. 205–234. Springer, Cham (2021). https://doi.org/10.1007/978-3-030-75248-4_8
12. Francati, D., Guidi, A., Russo, L., Venturi, D.: Identity-based matchmaking encryption without Random Oracles. In: Adhikari, A., Küsters, R., Preneel, B. (eds.) INDOCRYPT 2021. LNCS, vol. 13143, pp. 415–435. Springer, Cham (2021). https://doi.org/10.1007/978-3-030-92518-5_19
13. Gentry, C.: Practical identity-based encryption without Random Oracles. In: Vaudenay, S. (ed.) EUROCRYPT 2006. LNCS, vol. 4004, pp. 445–464. Springer, Heidelberg (2006). https://doi.org/10.1007/11761679_27

14. Gentry, C., Peikert, C., Vaikuntanathan, V.: Trapdoors for hard lattices and new cryptographic constructions. In: Proceedings of the Fortieth Annual ACM Symposium on Theory of Computing, STOC 2008, pp. 197–206. Association for Computing Machinery, New York (2008). https://doi.org/10.1145/1374376.1374407
15. Gorbunov, S., Vaikuntanathan, V., Wichs, D.: Leveled fully homomorphic signatures from standard lattices. In: Servedio, R.A., Rubinfeld, R. (eds.) Proceedings of the Forty-Seventh Annual ACM on Symposium on Theory of Computing, STOC 2015, pp. 469–477. ACM (2015)
16. Kim, S., Wu, D.J.: Multi-theorem preprocessing NIZKs from lattices. In: Shacham, H., Boldyreva, A. (eds.) CRYPTO 2018. LNCS, vol. 10992, pp. 733–765. Springer, Cham (2018). https://doi.org/10.1007/978-3-319-96881-0_25
17. Luo, F., Wang, F., Wang, K., Chen, K.: A more efficient leveled strongly-unforgeable fully homomorphic signature scheme. Inf. Sci. **480**, 70–89 (2019). https://doi.org/10.1016/j.ins.2018.12.025. https://www.sciencedirect.com/science/article/pii/S002002551830971X
18. Peikert, C., Shiehian, S.: Noninteractive zero knowledge for np from (plain) learning with errors. In: Boldyreva, A., Micciancio, D. (eds.) CRYPTO 2019. LNCS, vol. 11692, pp. 89–114. Springer, Cham (2019). https://doi.org/10.1007/978-3-030-26948-7_4
19. Shamir, A.: Identity-based cryptosystems and signature schemes. In: Blakley, G.R., Chaum, D. (eds.) CRYPTO 1984. LNCS, vol. 196, pp. 47–53. Springer, Heidelberg (1985). https://doi.org/10.1007/3-540-39568-7_5
20. Wang, Y., Wang, B., Lai, Q., Zhan, Y.: Identity-based matchmaking encryption with stronger security and instantiation on lattices. Cryptology ePrint Archive, Paper 2022/1718 (2022). https://eprint.iacr.org/2022/1718
21. Xu, S., Ning, J., Huang, X., Zhou, J., Deng, R.H.: Server-aided bilateral access control for secure data sharing with dynamic user groups. IEEE Trans. Inf. Forensics Secur. **16**, 4746–4761 (2021). https://doi.org/10.1109/TIFS.2021.3113516

# Decentralized Private Stream Aggregation from Lattices

Uddipana Dowerah[1,2(✉)] and Aikaterini Mitrokotsa[2]

[1] Chalmers University of Technology, Gothenburg, Sweden
[2] University of St. Gallen, St. Gallen, Switzerland
{uddipana.dowerah,katerina.mitrokotsa}@unisg.ch

**Abstract.** As various industries and government agencies increasingly seek to build quantum computers, the development of post-quantum constructions for different primitives becomes crucial. Lattice-based cryptography is one of the top candidates for constructing quantum-resistant primitives. In this paper, we propose a decentralized Private Stream Aggregation (PSA) protocol based on the Learning with Errors (LWE) problem. PSA allows secure aggregation of time-series data over multiple users without compromising the privacy of the individual data. In almost all previous constructions, a trusted entity is used for the generation of keys. We consider a scenario where the users do not want to rely on a trusted authority. We, therefore, propose a decentralized PSA (DPSA) scheme where each user generates their own keys without the need for a trusted setup. We give a concrete construction based on the hardness of the LWE problem both in the random oracle model and in the standard model.

**Keywords:** Private Stream Aggregation · Learning with Errors · Post-quantum cryptography · Decentralized

## 1 Introduction

The growing interest in building quantum computers has led to a widespread need for the development of post-quantum cryptographic protocols. Lattice-based cryptography is among the best candidates for post-quantum cryptography due to its versatility and resistance to quantum attacks. The hardness of lattice-based cryptographic algorithms is based on the assumed worst-case hardness of lattice problems. A well-known computational problem based on lattices is the Learning with Errors (LWE) problem introduced in [19]. In this paper, we focus on constructing a Private Stream Aggregation (PSA) protocol based on the LWE problem.

In various real-world scenarios, a data aggregator may seek to collect data from multiple organizations or individuals to compute various statistics over the data. However, a significant challenge in such applications is to ensure the privacy of the participants, particularly when the aggregator is not trusted. Certain


C. Pöpper and L. Batina (Eds.): ACNS 2024, LNCS 14584, pp. 189–214, 2024.
https://doi.org/10.1007/978-3-031-54773-7_8

examples of such applications include personal identifiable information such as social security numbers, financial data such as credit card details, medical data such as health records, or educational data such as transcripts, etc. This motivated the construction of private stream aggregation protocols that preserves individual data privacy and enables secure aggregation of time-series data across multiple users.

In a PSA protocol, there are multiple clients and one untrusted aggregator. Each client sends an encrypted message over a time period, usually called a timestamp (also called a label in some papers [15]), to the aggregator and the aggregator decrypts the sum of the messages over that time period without the knowledge of the individual messages. Timestamps are used to prevent the aggregator from mixing ciphertexts with different timestamps which in turn prevents the leakage of information about the values of individual clients. The security of a PSA protocol is captured by the notion of *aggregator obliviousness* which requires that the aggregator learns nothing more than the aggregated sum. A PSA protocol remains secure even in situations where the aggregator colludes with a subset of clients. In this case, the aggregator can only learn the sum of the messages from the non-colluding clients. A possible application scenario for PSA is Smart Grids where PSA can be used to collect and analyze real-time energy consumption data from different households or businesses for load balancing, energy management, or renewable energy integration, while maintaining the privacy of the customers. Another possible application is Traffic Management where it can be used to collect and analyze real-time traffic data from different sensors or vehicles for traffic prediction, route optimization, or accident prevention, while preserving the privacy of individuals. Private stream aggregation can also be applied in federated learning to enable the aggregation of locally trained models from multiple devices, while preserving privacy. In federated learning, each device trains a model on its local data and sends the updated model to a centralized server for aggregation. However, the privacy of local data is a major concern in this process.

Furthermore, to provide an additional layer of privacy protection, differential privacy can be used with PSA [21]. Private stream aggregation with differential privacy involves the addition of noise to the data prior to aggregation. The amount of noise added is defined by a privacy budget that limits the amount of information that can be revealed about an individual. Various PSA constructions consider the distributed model of differential privacy, where the clients add differentially private noise to their data [21,24] before encryption. In this paper, we do not explicitly consider differential privacy in our construction. However, similar procedures can be adopted as in previous works [21] to add differentially private noise to the inputs.

A closely related notion to private stream aggregation is Multi-Client Functional Encryption (MCFE) for inner products. In contrast to traditional public key encryption that either decrypts the entire message or nothing, Functional Encryption (FE) allows a user to learn specific functions of the encrypted data without disclosing any other information. More specifically, in FE, a secret key

$\mathsf{sk}_f$ is associated to a function $f$ and the ciphertext $\mathsf{ct}_{\mathbf{x}}$ encrypts a message $\mathbf{x}$ and decrypting $\mathsf{ct}_{\mathbf{x}}$ with $\mathsf{sk}_f$ reveals $f(\mathbf{x})$ and nothing else. In Inner Product Functional Encryption (IPFE), the ciphertext $\mathsf{ct}_{\mathbf{x}}$ is associated to a message vector $\mathbf{x}$ and the secret keys $\mathsf{sk}_{\mathbf{y}}$ can be generated with respect to some vector $\mathbf{y}$, while the decryption of $\mathsf{ct}_{\mathbf{x}}$ with $\mathsf{sk}_{\mathbf{y}}$ recovers the inner product $\langle \mathbf{x}, \mathbf{y} \rangle$. In inner product MCFE, there are multiple clients and one or more aggregators. Each user encrypts their input $x_i$ using a secret key $\mathsf{sk}_i$ and sends the ciphertext $\mathsf{ct}_{x_i}$ to the aggregator. Using the functional key $\mathsf{sk}_{\mathbf{y}}$, the aggregator recovers the inner product $\langle \mathbf{x}, \mathbf{y} \rangle = \sum_i x_i y_i$ where $\mathbf{x} := (x_1, x_2, \ldots)$ and $\mathbf{y} := (y_1, y_2, \ldots)$. Observe that for the all ones vector $\mathbf{y} = (1, \ldots, 1)$, this is exactly a PSA scheme. Therefore, PSA can be seen as a specific case of MCFE for the evaluation of inner products where only a single key corresponding to the vector $\mathbf{y} = (1, \ldots, 1)$ is revealed to the aggregator.

## 1.1 Our Contributions

Almost all known PSA schemes [4,7,13,15,21,23,24,27] use a trusted authority for key generation that generates the client keys for encryption and aggregator key for decryption. However, since the main goal of PSA is to allow an untrusted aggregator to perform aggregate statistics without compromising individual data, the use of a trusted authority is not aligned with the objectives of PSA. The use of a trusted authority can be avoided by decentralizing the setup and key generation procedure.

In this paper, we propose a decentralized private stream aggregation (DPSA) protocol that does not rely on a trusted authority for key generation. We take inspiration from the decentralized multi-client functional encryption scheme proposed in [12]. In the DPSA scheme, the clients generate their own keys and share it with the aggregator in a secure way such that the aggregator does not learn the individual client keys and only learns the aggregator decryption key which is equal to the sum of the client keys. We first give a construction in the random oracle model using a hash function modeled as a random oracle. We then show how to modify it into a construction in the standard model using a weak pseudorandom function (PRF). For the standard model we modify the ideas from [26] to achieve a construction with unbounded timestamps. Our scheme achieves aggregator oblivious security with *static corruptions* based on the LWE problem. If instantiated with a trusted setup, the protocol achieves aggregator obliviousness with *adaptive corruptions.* We also discuss possible solutions for practical deployments such as clients joining and leaving the system. Further, we provide example parameter choices for the proposed scheme based on the LWE assumption and show that our scheme achieves competitive ciphertext sizes to that of SLAP [24] for equivalent plaintext spaces.

## 1.2 Related Work

The notion of PSA was introduced by Shi et al. in [21]. They proposed a construction based on the Decisional Diffie-Hellman (DDH) assumption. The decryption procedure is inefficient due to its requirement for computing a discrete logarithm. Subsequent works [7,14,17] focused on constructing PSA with better efficiency and larger plaintext space. Leontiadis et al. introduced PSA with verifiability of the aggregated sum [18] followed by a construction by Emura [13]. These works are not post-quantum secure and can be broken easily by a quantum computer using Shor's algorithm [22].

A number of post-quantum PSA constructions have been proposed in previous works. Valovich proposed a PSA scheme from key homomorphic weak PRFs and gave an instantiation based on the LWE problem [26]. Their construction achieves a weaker variant of aggregator obliviousness (AO) called non-adaptive AO in the standard model. Further, the set of timestamps needs to be fixed at the setup and therefore their scheme only supports a bounded number of timestamps. Our scheme in the standard model follows a similar design policy as Valovich but we show how to get unbounded number of timestamps using a PRF. Becker et al. proposed a generic PSA scheme called LaPS [4] based on the LWE problem. Their construction can be instantiated using any additively homomorphic encryption scheme. However, their scheme uses two layers of encryption where the homomorphically encrypted input is encoded again using an Augmented-LWE (A-LWE) term. Further, their construction does not rely on timestamps directly and they only give a brief description on how to extend the scheme to work with timestamps. Takeshita et al. proposed two PSA schemes called SLAP [24] using two different fully homomorphic encryption schemes. Their schemes achieve aggregator obliviousness based on the RLWE problem in the random oracle model. The authors also implement their scheme and show their improvements over the LaPS protocol. In a subsequent work [23], Takeshita et al. proposed a variant of their SLAP protocol with better efficiency.

Other post-quantum secure works that do not use the RLWE problem include [15,27]. Ernst et al. proposed a PSA scheme using key-homomorphic PRFs [15] based on the Learning with Rounding (LWR) problem. Currently, this is one of the most efficient schemes that achieve smaller ciphertexts compared to previous works. Another efficient PSA scheme using labeled secret sharing schemes (LaSS) was proposed in [27]. However, it is not efficient for a large number of users due to multiple rounds of communication to generate shared keys among the users which leads to key sizes quadratic in the number of users.

All of these schemes rely on a trusted setup for key generation. There are brief discussions in [15,27] on how to modify their schemes to avoid a central authority. Recently, Brorsson et al. proposed a distributed setup PSA protocol called DIPSAUCE [10] that does not rely on a trusted party. Their protocol is a distributed setup variant of the protocol in [27]. In contrast to the other PSA schemes, no key is required for aggregating the sum of the inputs. However, their distributed key generation procedure relies on a Public Key Infrastructure (PKI) to provide the keys to each user which in turn is usually implemented as a central authority. Further DIPSAUCE relies on a randomness beacon and care should be taken not to introduce a trusted party to realize the beacon.

Another line of work focuses on constructing secure aggregation protocols for the aggregation of model updates in distributed machine learning [5,6,8,16,25]. These works are not directly comparable to ours as their work has a distinct focus, specifically designed to meet the requirements of distributed machine learning.

We give a comparison of the various PSA schemes described in this section with respect to different characteristics in Table 1.

**Table 1.** Comparison of different PSA schemes with respect to different characteristics

| Scheme | Decentralized Setup | Timestamps | Assumption | Post-quantum security |
|---|---|---|---|---|
| Shi et al. [21] | ✗ | unbounded | DDH | ✗ |
| Valovich [26] | ✗ | bounded | LWE | ✓ |
| LaPS [4] | ✗ | none | (R)LWE | ✓ |
| SLAP [24] | ✗ | unbounded | RLWE | ✓ |
| Ernst et al. [15] | ✗ | unbounded | LWR | ✓ |
| Waldner et al. [27] | ✗ | unbounded | security of LaSS | ✓ |
| DIPSAUCE [10] | ✓ | unbounded | security of LaSS | ✓ |
| Our Scheme | ✓ | unbounded | LWE | ✓ |

### 1.3 Organization

We organize the paper as follows. Section 2 contains some necessary background and definitions. In Sect. 3, we formally define the DPSA protocol and give a concrete construction based on the LWE problem in the ROM. In Sect. 4, we give a construction in the standard model based on LWE.

## 2 Preliminaries

**Notation**: $\lambda$ denotes the security parameter. For a set $S$, $a \leftarrow_{\$} S$ means that $a$ is sampled uniformly at random from $S$. For a probability distribution $\mathcal{X}$ over a set $S$, $x \leftarrow \mathcal{X}$ means that $x$ is sampled from $S$ according to the distribution $\mathcal{X}$. A distribution $\mathcal{X}$ over the set of integers is said to be $B$-bounded if it is supported on $[-B, B]$. For a number $x$, $\lceil x \rceil$, $\lfloor x \rfloor$ and $\lfloor x \rceil$ denotes the rounding $x$ up, down and to the closest integer respectively. We use 'log' to denote a logarithm to the base 2. For a prime $q$, $\mathbb{Z}_q$ denotes the set of integers in the interval $(-q/2, q/2] \cap \mathbb{Z}$. For some $a \in \mathbb{Z}$, we use $(a \bmod q)$ and $[a]_q$ interchangeably to denote the modular reduction of $a$ by $q$ into the interval $(-q/2, q/2] \cap \mathbb{Z}$. We use lowercase boldface letters (e.g., $\mathbf{a}$) to denote row vectors and uppercase boldface letters (e.g., $\mathbf{A}$) to denote matrices. The notation $[n]$ denotes the set of integers $\{1, 2, \ldots, n\}$. An arbitrary negligible function is denoted by $\mathsf{negl}(\cdot)$ where the function $\mathsf{negl}(x) : \mathbb{N} \rightarrow \mathbb{R}$ is called negligible if for every $c \in \mathbb{N}$, there exists an integer $\eta_c$ such that $|\mathsf{negl}(x)| < \frac{1}{x^c}$ for all $x > \eta_c$.

### 2.1 Lattices

A $k$ dimensional lattice $\Lambda$ is a discrete additive subgroup of $\mathbb{R}^k$ given by the set of all integer linear combinations of $l \leq k$ linearly independent vectors in $\mathbb{R}^k$ where $l$ is called the rank of $\Lambda$. We are interested in $q$-ary integer lattices. A $q$-ary lattice can be thought of as a discrete additive subgroup of $\mathbb{Z}_q^k$. A vector $\mathbf{v}$ is in the lattice $\Lambda$ if $\mathbf{v}$ mod $q \in \Lambda$. Given a matrix $\mathbf{B} \in \mathbb{Z}_q^{l \times k}$, the following are two $k$ dimensional $q$-ary lattices.

$$\Lambda_q(\mathbf{B}) = \{\mathbf{v} \in \mathbb{Z}_q^k \mid \mathbf{v} = \mathbf{w} \cdot \mathbf{B} \bmod q \text{ for some } \mathbf{w} \in \mathbb{Z}_q^l\}$$
$$\Lambda_q^{\perp}(\mathbf{B}) = \left\{\mathbf{v} \in \mathbb{Z}_q^k \mid \mathbf{v} \cdot \mathbf{B}^T = \mathbf{0} \bmod q\right\}$$

### 2.2 Learning with Errors

Learning with Errors is the problem of solving a system of noisy linear equations over $\mathbb{Z}_q$ [19]. It can be defined as follows.

**Definition 1 (Learning with errors).** *Let $\mathcal{X}$ be a probability distribution on $\mathbb{Z}$ and $\mathbf{s}$ be a secret vector chosen uniformly at random from $\mathbb{Z}_q^n$ for some $n, q \in \mathbb{N}$. Let $\mathcal{A}_{\mathbf{s},\mathcal{X}}$ be the distribution that generates a pair $(\mathbf{a}, b = \langle \mathbf{a}, \mathbf{s} \rangle + e) \in \mathbb{Z}_q^n \times \mathbb{Z}_q$ obtained by choosing a vector $\mathbf{a} \leftarrow_\$ \mathbb{Z}_q^n$ and an error $e \leftarrow \mathcal{X}$. Given polynomially many samples from $\mathcal{A}_{\mathbf{s},\mathcal{X}}$, the learning with errors problem is to output the vector $\mathbf{s} \in \mathbb{Z}_q^n$ with overwhelming probability.*

*The decisional LWE problem is to distinguish the distribution $\mathcal{A}_{\mathbf{s},\mathcal{X}}$ from the uniform distribution over $\mathbb{Z}_q^n \times \mathbb{Z}_q$. We use $\mathrm{LWE}_{n,q,\mathcal{X}}$ to denote the LWE problem with parameters $n, q, \mathcal{X}$.*

The decisional LWE problem has been shown to be at least as hard as the LWE search problem [19,20]. There are known quantum and classical reductions of LWE to approximating short vector problems in lattices [9,20]. In these reductions, the noise distribution $\mathcal{X}$ is usually considered to be a discretized Gaussian distribution that is indistinguishable from a $B$-bounded distribution for some appropriate $B$.

The security of our protocol is based on a variant of the decisional LWE problem where along with the noise, the secret $\mathbf{s}$ is chosen from the distribution $\mathcal{X}$.

**Definition 2 (LWE problem with short secrets).** *Let $\mathcal{X}$ be a probability distribution on $\mathbb{Z}$ and $\mathbf{s}$ be a secret vector chosen from the distribution $\mathcal{X}$ over $\mathbb{Z}_q^n$ for some $n, q \in \mathbb{N}$. Let $\mathcal{A}_{\mathbf{s},\mathcal{X}}$ be the distribution defined in Definition 1. Then, the decision LWE problem with short secrets is to distinguish the distribution $\mathcal{A}_{\mathbf{s},\mathcal{X}}$ from the uniform distribution over $\mathbb{Z}_q^n \times \mathbb{Z}_q$. We use $\text{ss-LWE}_{n,q,\mathcal{X}}$ to denote the LWE problem with short secrets.*

A reduction from the short secret variant exists to the decisional LWE problem as shown in [2].

**Lemma 1** ([2]). *Let $n, q, \mathcal{X}$ be as described above. If there exists a distinguishing algorithm $\mathcal{A}$ for the decision LWE problem with short secrets, then there exists a distinguishing algorithm $\mathcal{B}$ for the decision LWE problem that runs in roughly the same time as $\mathcal{A}$, with $\mathcal{B}$ making $\mathcal{O}(n^2)$ calls to its oracle and satisfying $Adv_{\mathcal{B}}^{\mathsf{LWE}}(\lambda) = Adv_{\mathcal{A}}^{\mathsf{ss\text{-}LWE}}(\lambda)$.*

In this paper, we consider an extended form of the problem where the secret is a matrix. We consider the LWE distribution with $N \geq 1$ secrets $\mathbf{s}_1, \ldots, \mathbf{s}_N$ for some $N = poly(n)$. Then $\mathcal{A}_{\mathbf{S},\mathcal{X}}$ is defined as the distribution that generates a pair $(\mathbf{a}, \mathbf{b} := \mathbf{a} \cdot \mathbf{S}^\top + \mathbf{e})$ obtained by choosing $\mathbf{a} \leftarrow_\$ \mathbb{Z}_q^n$ and an error vector $\mathbf{e} \leftarrow_\$ \mathcal{X}^N$ where the $i$-th row of $\mathbf{S} \in \mathbb{Z}_q^{N \times n}$ is the secret $\mathbf{s}_i$. Using a standard hybrid argument, it can be shown that distinguishing $\mathbf{S}$ from uniformly random is as hard as the $\mathrm{LWE}_{n,q,\mathcal{X}}$ problem.

### 2.3 Pseudorandom Functions

A pseudorandom function (PRF) is an efficiently computable deterministic function that is computationally indistinguishable from a truly random function.

**Definition 3 (PRF).** *A pseudorandom function family $\mathcal{F} = \{F_K\}_{K \in \mathcal{K}_\lambda}$ with keyspace $\mathcal{K}_\lambda$ is a family of functions $F_K : \mathcal{X} \to \mathcal{Y}$ such that $F_K$ can be computed in $poly(\lambda)$ time and for any $x \in \mathcal{X}$, $F_K(x)$ cannot be distinguished from a random function (RF) in polynomial time. For all PPT adversaries $\mathcal{A}$, the advantage of $\mathcal{A}$ in distinguishing a PRF from a RF is given by*

$$Adv_{\mathcal{A}}^{\mathsf{PRF}}(\lambda) = \left| Pr[\mathcal{A}^{F_K(\cdot)}(\lambda) = 1] - Pr[\mathcal{A}^{\mathsf{RF}(\cdot)}(\lambda) = 1] \right| \leq \mathsf{negl}(\lambda)$$

## 3 Decentralized Private Stream Aggregation

In this section, we formally define a decentralized PSA (DPSA) scheme and give a concrete construction based on the LWE problem. Consider a scenario with $\ell$ users for some $\ell \in \mathbb{N}$ and an untrusted aggregator. We consider the users to be semi honest, i.e., honest but curious. Each user generates private data $\mathbf{x}_{i,t}$ with respect to some time stamp $t$ and wishes to compute the sum $\sum_{i=1}^{\ell} \mathbf{x}_{i,t}$ securely and privately. In Private Stream Aggregation (PSA) the sum can be computed by the aggregator given only the encrypted values of the user's data while preserving the user's privacy. The users encrypt their data $\mathbf{x}_{i,t}$ using a user specific secret key $\mathsf{sk}_i$ before sending it to the aggregator. The aggregator then performs the aggregating function on the encrypted data and recovers the sum of the input data using an aggregator decryption key $\mathsf{dk}_0$. In a centralized PSA scheme, the encryption and decryption keys are generated by a trusted setup. Since the setup in DPSA is decentralized, the users need to generate the aggregator decryption key themselves apart from their own encryption keys. Each user generates a share of the aggregator key and sends it to the aggregator in a secure way without revealing their individual keys. Upon receiving the partial keys from all the users, the aggregator can recover its decryption key for aggregation.

**Definition 4 (Decentralized Private Stream Aggregation).** *A decentralized private stream aggregation scheme over a message space $\mathcal{M}$ consists of the following PPT algorithms:*

$\mathsf{Setup}(1^\lambda, 1^\ell)$: *This is a procedure between the users. It takes the security parameter $\lambda$ and the number of users $\ell$ and generates the public parameters* $\mathsf{pp}$ *and their own secret keys $\mathsf{sk}_i$ for $i \in [\ell]$. The public parameters* $\mathsf{pp}$ *is an implicit input to the rest of the algorithms.*

$\mathsf{AggKeyGenShare}(i, \mathsf{sk}_i)$: *It takes user index $i$ and secret key $\mathsf{sk}_i$ and outputs the partial aggregator key $\mathsf{dk}_i$.*

$\mathsf{AggKeyGen}(\{\mathsf{dk}_i\}_{i\in[\ell]})$: *It takes the partial aggregator keys $\mathsf{dk}_i$ for $i \in [\ell]$ and computes aggregator decryption key $\mathsf{dk}_0 = \sum_{i=1}^{\ell} \mathsf{dk}_i$.*

$\mathsf{Enc}(i, \mathsf{sk}_i, \mathbf{x}_{i,t}, t)$: *It takes as input the user index $i$, the secret key $\mathsf{sk}_i$, timestamp $t$ and input data $\mathbf{x}_{i,t} \in \mathcal{M}$ and outputs a ciphertext $\mathsf{ct}_{i,t}$.*

$\mathsf{AggDec}(\mathsf{dk}_0, \{\mathsf{ct}_{i,t}\}_{i\in[\ell]}, t)$: *It outputs the aggregated sum $\mathbf{x}_t = \sum_{i=1}^{\ell} \mathbf{x}_{i,t}$ from the ciphertexts $\{\mathsf{ct}_{i,t}\}_{i\in[\ell]}$ using $\mathsf{dk}_0$ for the time period $t$.*

Here, the $\mathsf{Setup}$ algorithm is run between the users to generate the public parameters $\mathsf{pp}$ and their secret keys $\mathsf{sk}_i$. The users compute partial aggregator keys $\mathsf{dk}_i$ using $\mathsf{AggKeyGenShare}$ and sends $\mathsf{dk}_i$ to the aggregator. The aggregator computes its decryption key $\mathsf{dk}_0$ using $\mathsf{dk}_0 \leftarrow \mathsf{AggKeyGen}(\{\mathsf{dk}_i\}_{i\in[\ell]})$. Each user $i$ then encrypts their input $\mathbf{x}_{i,t}$ at timestamp $t$ such that $\mathsf{ct}_{i,t} \leftarrow \mathsf{Enc}(i, \mathsf{sk}_i, \mathbf{x}_{i,t}, t)$. The aggregator outputs $\mathbf{x}_t \leftarrow \mathsf{AggDec}(\mathsf{dk}_0, \{\mathsf{ct}_{i,t}\}_{i\in[\ell]}, t)$. The algorithms $\mathsf{Setup}$, $\mathsf{AggKeyGenShare}$ and $\mathsf{AggKeyGen}$ are run only once in the beginning of the protocol.

**Correctness**: The above DPSA scheme $\mathsf{DPSA}=(\mathsf{Setup}, \mathsf{AggKeyGenShare}, \mathsf{AggKeyGen}, \mathsf{Enc}, \mathsf{AggDec})$ is said to be correct if for any $\lambda, \ell \in \mathbb{N}$, any message $\mathbf{x}_{i,t} \in \mathcal{M}$, it holds that

$$\Pr\left[\mathsf{AggDec}(\mathsf{dk}_0, \{\mathsf{ct}_{i,t}\}_{i\in[\ell]}, t) = \sum_{i=1}^{\ell} \mathbf{x}_{i,t} : \begin{array}{l} (\mathsf{pp}, \{\mathsf{sk}_i\}_{i\in[\ell]}) \leftarrow \mathsf{Setup}(1^\lambda, 1^\ell) \\ \{\mathsf{dk}_i\}_{i\in[\ell]} \leftarrow \mathsf{AggKeyGenShare}(i, \mathsf{sk}_i) \\ \mathsf{dk}_0 \leftarrow \mathsf{AggKeyGen}(\{\mathsf{dk}_i\}_{i\in[\ell]}) \\ \mathsf{ct}_{i,t} \leftarrow \mathsf{Enc}(i, \mathsf{sk}_i, \mathbf{x}_{i,t}, t) \end{array}\right] = 1$$

**Security**: The security of a private stream aggregation scheme is captured by the notion of *aggregator obliviousness.* It requires that the aggregator does not learn anything more than the aggregated value of their input values at each time period. If some parties collude with the aggregator then it requires that the aggregator only learns the aggregated value of the honest users and nothing more. Further, each user encrypts their data only once every time period.

**Definition 5 (Aggregator Obliviousness for DPSA).** *The aggregator obliviousness security for a DPSA scheme can be defined in terms of the security experiment* $\mathsf{AO}_\beta(\lambda, \ell, \mathcal{A})$ *given in Fig. 1. No adversary* $\mathcal{A}$ *should be able to win this game with non-negligible advantage.*

```
AO_β(λ, ℓ, A)
(pp, {sk_i}_{i∈[ℓ]}) ← Setup(1^λ, 1^ℓ)
β ← A^{QCorr(·),QEnc(·,·,·),QChallenge(·,·,·,·)}(pp)
if condition (∗) is satisfied then
    output β
else
    output 0
```

**Fig. 1.** Aggregator Obliviousness experiment for DPSA

*The challenger first runs the* $\mathsf{Setup}$ *algorithm and returns the public parameters* $\mathsf{pp}$ *to the adversary. The adversary makes queries to the following oracles:*

- ***Corruption oracle*** $\mathsf{QCorr}(i)$*: The adversary submits an integer* $i \in \{1, \ldots, \ell\}$ *and gets back the i-th user's secret key* $\mathsf{sk}_i$*. If the adversary submits* $i = 0$*, then it gets* $\mathsf{dk}_j \leftarrow \mathsf{AggKeyGenShare}(j, \mathsf{sk}_j)$ *for all* $j \in [\ell]$*.*
- ***Encryption oracle*** $\mathsf{QEnc}(i, \mathbf{x}_{i,t}, t)$*: The adversary submits* $(i, \mathbf{x}_{i,t}, t)$ *and receives* $\mathsf{ct}_{i,t}, \leftarrow \mathsf{Enc}(i, \mathsf{sk}_i, \mathbf{x}_{i,t}, t)$ *from the challenger.*
- ***Challenge oracle*** $\mathsf{QChallenge}(\mathcal{U}, \{\mathbf{x}^0_{i,t^*}\}_{i\in\mathcal{U}}, \{\mathbf{x}^1_{i,t^*}\}_{i\in\mathcal{U}}, t^*)$*: This query can be made only once by the adversary. The adversary selects a set of users* $\mathcal{U}$ *and time period* $t^*$ *and for each* $i \in \mathcal{U}$*, the adversary chooses two sets of inputs* $\mathbf{x}^0_{i,t^*}$*,* $\mathbf{x}^1_{i,t^*}$*. The challenger randomly samples* $b \leftarrow \{0, 1\}$ *and returns* $\mathsf{ct}_{i,t^*} \leftarrow \mathsf{Enc}(\mathsf{sk}_i, \mathbf{x}^0_{i,t^*}, t^*)$ *for all* $i \in \mathcal{U}$ *if* $b = 0$ *and* $\mathsf{ct}_{i,t^*} \leftarrow \mathsf{Enc}(\mathsf{sk}_i, \mathbf{x}^1_{i,t^*}, t^*)$ *for all* $i \in \mathcal{U}$ *if* $b = 1$*.*

*Finally, the adversary outputs a guess* $b'$ *for the value of* $b$ *and the experiment outputs* $\beta$ *depending on the following conditions.*

*Let* $\mathcal{CS}$ *be the set of corrupted users,* $\mathcal{HS}$ *be the set of honest users at the end of the game and let* $\mathcal{E}_{t^*}$ *be the set of users for which an encryption query has been made at time* $t^*$*. Let* $\mathcal{Q}_{t^*} := \mathcal{U} \cup \mathcal{E}_{t^*}$ *be the set of users for which* $\mathcal{A}$ *receives an encryption or a challenge ciphertext at timestamp* $t^*$*. The condition* $(*)$ *is satisfied if all of the following conditions hold:*

- $\mathcal{U} \cap \mathcal{CS} = \emptyset$*: The set of users specified during the* $\mathsf{Challenge}$ *phase must be uncorrupted at the end of the game.*
- *Adversary* $\mathcal{A}$ *has not queried* $\mathsf{QEnc}(i, \mathbf{x}_{i,t}, t^*)$ *for the same* $i$ *and* $t^*$*. Otherwise, this would violate the encrypt-once policy.*
- $\mathcal{U} \cap \mathcal{E}_{t^*} = \emptyset$*: The adversary cannot query challenge ciphertexts to the users in* $\mathcal{E}_{t^*}$*. In other words, the adversary cannot get a challenge ciphertext from users for which it has queried the encryption oracle at time* $t^*$*.*

– *If the adversary has compromised the aggregator and* $\mathcal{Q}_{t^*} \cup \mathcal{CS} = [\ell]$, *then the following condition must be satisfied.*

$$\sum_{i \in \mathcal{U}} \boldsymbol{x}_{i,t^*}^0 = \sum_{i \in \mathcal{U}} \boldsymbol{x}_{i,t^*}^1$$

*We set* $\beta \leftarrow b'$ *if the above conditions are satisfied, otherwise we set* $\beta = 0$.

*A DPSA scheme is said to be aggregator oblivious if for any PPT adversary* $\mathcal{A}$, *there exists a negligible function* $\mathsf{negl}$ *such that*

$$\mathsf{Adv}_{\mathcal{A},\mathsf{DPSA}}^{\mathsf{AO}}(\lambda, \ell) = |Pr[\mathsf{AO}_0(\lambda, \ell, \mathcal{A}) = 1] - Pr[\mathsf{AO}_1(\lambda, \ell, \mathcal{A}) = 1]| \leq \mathsf{negl}(\lambda)$$

If an adversary can corrupt the parties only at the beginning of the protocol, then we say that the scheme is secure against *static corruptions*. On the other hand, if an adversary can corrupt the parties dynamically during the execution of the protocol, then we say that the scheme is secure against adaptive corruptions. For static security, the corruption queries are sent by the adversary before obtaining the public parameters.

### 3.1 Our Construction

Our concrete DPSA scheme over the plaintext space $\mathcal{M} := \mathbb{Z}_p^n$ can be described in terms of the following PPT algorithms.

$\mathsf{Setup}(1^\lambda, 1^\ell)$: This is a protocol between the users. Let $H$ be a hash function mapping from the domain of all timestamps onto $\mathbb{Z}_q^n$. Let $\mathcal{X}$ be a $B$-bounded distribution over $\mathbb{Z}$. Each user generates a matrix $\mathbf{S}_i \leftarrow_\$ \mathcal{X}^{n \times n}$ and interactively generates secret shares $\mathbf{V}_i \leftarrow \mathbb{Z}_q^{n \times n}$ of 0 such that $\sum_{i=1}^{\ell} \mathbf{V}_i = 0 \bmod q$. Output public parameters $\mathsf{pp} = (p, q, n, \ell, H, \mathcal{X})$ and user secret keys $\mathsf{sk}_i = (\mathbf{S}_i, \mathbf{V}_i)$ for $i \in [\ell]$. The public parameters $\mathsf{pp}$ is an implicit input to all the algorithms.

$\mathsf{AggKeyGenShare}(i, \mathsf{sk}_i)$: Given user index $i$ and secret key $\mathsf{sk}_i = (\mathbf{S}_i, \mathbf{V}_i)$, compute partial aggregator key $\mathsf{dk}_i = \mathbf{S}_i + \mathbf{V}_i \pmod q$.

$\mathsf{AggKeygen}(\{\mathsf{dk}_i\}_{i \in [\ell]})$: Given $\{\mathsf{dk}_i\}_{i \in [\ell]}$, compute aggregator decryption key

$$\mathsf{dk}_0 := \sum_{i=1}^{\ell} \mathsf{dk}_i = \sum_{i=1}^{\ell} (\mathbf{S}_i + \mathbf{V}_i) = \sum_{i=1}^{\ell} \mathbf{S}_i \pmod q = \mathbf{S}_0 \tag{1}$$

$\mathsf{Enc}(i, \mathsf{sk}_i, \mathbf{x}_{i,t}, t)$: Given input $\mathbf{x}_{i,t} \in \mathbb{Z}_p^n$ and timestamp $t$, sample $\mathbf{e}_{i,t} \leftarrow \mathcal{X}^n$. Set $\mathbf{y}_t := H(t) \in \mathbb{Z}_q^n$ and compute the ciphertext $\mathsf{ct}_{i,t}$ as

$$\mathsf{ct}_{i,t} = \mathbf{x}_{i,t} + \mathbf{y}_t \cdot \mathbf{S}_i^\top + p \cdot \mathbf{e}_{i,t} \pmod q \tag{2}$$

$\mathsf{AggDec}(\mathsf{dk}_0, \{\mathsf{ct}_{i,t}\}_{i \in [\ell]}, t)$: Compute $\mathbf{y}_t = H(t)$ and output the aggregated sum

$$\mathbf{x}_t = \left[ \left( \sum_{i=1}^{\ell} \mathsf{ct}_{i,t} - \mathbf{y}_t \cdot \mathbf{S}_0^\top \pmod q \right) \right]_p \tag{3}$$

**Correctness**: The correctness of the sum can be verified as follows:

$$\sum_{i=1}^{\ell} \mathsf{ct}_{i,t} - \mathbf{y}_t \cdot \mathbf{S}_0^\top \pmod q = \sum_{i=1}^{\ell} \mathbf{x}_{i,t} + p \cdot \sum_{i=1}^{\ell} \mathbf{e}_{i,t} \pmod q \tag{4}$$

The magnitude of the sum of the errors is bounded by $\ell \cdot p \cdot B$ where $B$ is the maximum bound on the error distribution $\mathcal{X}$. The magnitude of the sum of the inputs is bounded by $\ell \cdot \frac{p}{2}$. If $\frac{\ell \cdot p}{2}(1 + 2B) < \frac{q}{2}$, then $\sum_{i=1}^{\ell} \mathbf{x}_{i,t} + p \cdot \sum_{i=1}^{\ell} \mathbf{e}_{i,t} \pmod q = \sum_{i=1}^{\ell} \mathbf{x}_{i,t} + p \cdot \sum_{i=1}^{\ell} \mathbf{e}_{i,t}$ and reducing it modulo $p$ removes the error and recovers the sum $\sum_{i=1}^{\ell} \mathbf{x}_{i,t}$.

### 3.2 Aggregator Obliviousness

We show that the proposed construction achieves aggregator obliviousness with static corruptions in the encrypt-once security model under the hardness of the LWE problem.

**Theorem 1.** *For any PPT adversary $\mathcal{A}$ against the aggregator obliviousness game, there exists a PPT adversary $\mathcal{B}$ against the LWE problem such that*

$$\mathsf{Adv}_{\mathcal{A}}^{\mathsf{AO}}(\lambda, \ell) \leq (8\ell^3 + 4\ell^2) \cdot \mathsf{Adv}_{\mathcal{B}}^{\mathsf{LWE}}(\lambda)$$

*Proof.* We use similar ideas from [15] to prove this Theorem. WLOG, we assume that the adversary queries the QChallenge oracle only at one timestamp $t^*$ that has not been queried to the QEnc oracle.

We proceed via a series of Games $\mathsf{G}_i$ for $i \in \{0, 1, 2, 3\}$ described in Fig. 4 of Appendix B. A summary of the transitions is provided in Table 2. We denote the advantage of $\mathcal{A}$ in game $\mathsf{G}_i$ using $\mathsf{Adv}_{\mathcal{A}}(\mathsf{G}_i)$. Similar to [15], we consider two cases. I) *When the adversary corrupts the aggregator*: The adversary can decrypt the sum in this case and therefore, we need to make sure that the sum remains unchanged throughout the games. II) *When the adversary does not corrupt the aggregator*: In this case we can directly go from game $\mathsf{G}_0$ to $\mathsf{G}_3$ using a hybrid argument over all the users.

**Game** $\mathsf{G}_0$: This is the $\mathsf{AO}_0$ game where the challenge query is answered with the encryption of $\mathbf{x}_{i,t}^0$.

**Game** $\mathsf{G}_1$: In Game $\mathsf{G}_1$, we change the way the vectors $\mathbf{c}_{i,t}$ in QChallenge are generated. The challenge query is still answered with encryptions of $\mathbf{x}_{i,t}^0$ but we add a share of a perfect $\mu$-out-of-$\mu$ secret sharing of zero denoted by $\mathbf{r}_i \leftarrow SS(0)$ to $\mathbf{c}_{i,t}$s where $\mu$ is the number of users in the challenge query. We need to make this change in such a way that the aggregate sum on decryption remains the same. The transition from $\mathsf{G}_0$ to $\mathsf{G}_1$ can be proved via a hybrid argument over the $\ell$ users relying on the LWE assumption.

**Lemma 2 (Transition from $\mathbf{G}_0$ to $\mathbf{G}_1$).** *For all PPT adversary $\mathcal{A}$, that corrupts the aggregator, there exists a PPT adversary $\mathcal{B}$ such that*

$$|\mathsf{Adv}_{\mathcal{A}}(\mathsf{G}_0) - \mathsf{Adv}_{\mathcal{A}}(\mathsf{G}_1)| \leq 2\ell h(h-1) \cdot \mathsf{Adv}_{\mathcal{B}}^{\mathsf{LWE}}(\lambda)$$

**Table 2.** A summary of the games used in the proof of Theorem 1. Change in each game is highlighted with a square box

| Game | $\mathsf{ct}_{i,t}$ | Justification |
|---|---|---|
| $\mathsf{G}_0$ | $\mathbf{c}_{i,t} \leftarrow \mathbf{y}_t \cdot \mathbf{S}_i + p \cdot \mathbf{e}_{i,t}$ <br> $\mathsf{ct}_{i,t} \leftarrow \mathbf{x}^0_{i,t} + \mathbf{c}_{i,t}$ | $\mathsf{AO}_0$ game |
| $\mathsf{G}_1$ | $\mathbf{c}'_{i,t} \leftarrow \mathbf{y}_t \cdot \mathbf{S}_i + p \cdot \mathbf{e}_{i,t}$ <br> $\boxed{\mathbf{c}_{i,t} \leftarrow \mathbf{c}'_{i,t} + \mathbf{r}_i}$, $\mathbf{r}_i \leftarrow SS(0)$ <br> $\mathsf{ct}_{i,t} \leftarrow \mathbf{x}^0_{i,t} + \mathbf{c}_{i,t}$ | LWE assumption |
| $\mathsf{G}_2$ | $\mathbf{c}'_{i,t} \leftarrow \mathbf{y}_t \cdot \mathbf{S}_i + p \cdot \mathbf{e}_{i,t}$ <br> $\mathbf{c}_{i,t} \leftarrow \mathbf{c}'_{i,t} + \mathbf{r}_i$, $\mathbf{r}_i \leftarrow SS(0)$ <br> $\boxed{\mathsf{ct}_{i,t} \leftarrow \mathbf{x}^1_{i,t} + \mathbf{c}_{i,t}}$ | information-theoretic |
| $\mathsf{G}_3$ | $\boxed{\mathbf{c}_{i,t} \leftarrow \mathbf{y}_t \cdot \mathbf{S}_i + p \cdot \mathbf{e}_{i,t}}$ <br> $\mathsf{ct}_{i,t} \leftarrow \mathbf{x}^1_{i,t} + \mathbf{c}_{i,t}$ | LWE assumption |

*Proof.* To prove this transition, we use a sequence of hybrid games $\mathsf{G}_{0.l}$ for $l \in [\ell]$ defined in Fig. 5 of Appendix B. Note that, $\mathsf{G}_0 := \mathsf{G}_{0.1}$ and $\mathsf{G}_1 := \mathsf{G}_{0.\ell}$. The goal in each hybrid game is to add a perfect secret share of 0 to the LWE mask $\mathbf{c}_{i,t} := \mathbf{y}_t \cdot \mathbf{S}_i^\top + p \cdot \mathbf{e}_{i,t}$ of one more user. Let $\mu := |\mathcal{U}|$ where $\mathcal{U} := \{i_1, \ldots, i_\mu\}$ is the set of users specified by $\mathcal{A}$ during $\mathsf{QChallenge}$. Let $K := min(\mu, l)$. If $K \geq 2$ in hybrid step $l$, then a share of a perfect $K$-out-of-$K$ secret sharing of 0 is added to the LWE masks of the first $K$ users in $\mathcal{U}$. This can be done using two users at a time and the condition $K \geq 2$ is needed to go from one hybrid to another. To prove the indistinguishability of $\mathsf{G}_1$ from $\mathsf{G}_0$, it suffices to show that the adjacent games $\mathsf{G}_{0.l-1}$ and $\mathsf{G}_{0.l}$ are computationally indistinguishable. Precisely, we have

$$|\mathsf{Adv}_{\mathcal{A}}(\mathsf{G}_0) - \mathsf{Adv}_{\mathcal{A}}(\mathsf{G}_1)| = \sum_{l=1}^{\ell} |\mathsf{Adv}_{\mathcal{A}}(\mathsf{G}_{0.l-1}) - \mathsf{Adv}_{\mathcal{A}}(\mathsf{G}_{0.l})|$$

If there is an adversary $\mathcal{A}$ that can distinguish $\mathsf{G}_{0.l-1}$ from $\mathsf{G}_{0.l}$, then there exists an adversary $\mathcal{B}$ against the $\mathrm{LWE}_{n,q,\mathcal{X}}$ assumption. We consider the case $K \geq 2$. In $\mathsf{G}_{0.l-1}$, we have secret shares added to $\mathbf{c}_{i,t} = \mathbf{y}_t \cdot \mathbf{S}_i^\top + p \cdot \mathbf{e}_{i,t}$ of the first $K-1$ users in $\mathcal{U}$. To add a share of a perfect $K$-out-of-$K$ secret sharing of 0 to the $K$-th user in $\mathcal{U}$, $\mathcal{B}$ first guesses the first and the $K$-th users of $\mathcal{U}$ such that $i_1^* \leftarrow_\$ [\mathcal{HS}]$, $i_K^* \leftarrow_\$ [\mathcal{HS}] \setminus \{i_1^*\}$ where $\mathcal{HS} = [\ell] \setminus \mathcal{CS}$ is the set of honest users. $\mathcal{B}$ then samples $\mathbf{S}_i \leftarrow_\$ \mathcal{X}^{n \times n}$ and $\mathbf{V}_i \leftarrow_\$ \mathbb{Z}_q^{n \times n}$ for $i \in [\ell] \setminus \{i_1^*, i_K^*\}$. It can therefore set $\mathsf{sk}_i := (\mathbf{S}_i, \mathbf{V}_i)$ for $i \in \mathcal{CS}$ and send them to $\mathcal{A}$. It also samples aggregator key $\mathbf{S}_0 \leftarrow \mathcal{X}^{n \times n}$ uniformly at random. If the guess is incorrect, the simulation aborts the game and outputs 0. If the guess is correct then it replaces $\mathbf{c}_{i_1^*,t}$ with a random vector $\mathbf{b}_t \leftarrow_\$ \mathbb{Z}_q^n$ using the LWE assumption on $\mathbf{S}_{i_1^*}$. To make sure that the sum $\mathbf{S}_0 = \sum_{i=1}^{\ell} \mathbf{S}_i$ is satisfied, we need to modify $\mathbf{c}_{i_K^*,t}$ as $\mathbf{c}_{i_K^*,t} := H(t) \cdot \mathbf{S}_0 - H(t) \sum_{j \in [\ell] \setminus \{i_1^*, i_K^*\}} \mathbf{S}_j - \mathbf{b}_t$. Then $\mathbf{c}_{i_1^*,t}$ and $\mathbf{c}_{i_1^*,t} + \mathbf{u}_K$ are indistinguishable where $\mathbf{u}_K \leftarrow_{\$} \mathbb{Z}_q^n$. Then, replace $\mathbf{c}_{i_1^*,t}$ back with $\mathbf{y}_t \cdot \mathbf{S}_{i_1^*}^\top + p \cdot \mathbf{e}_{i_1^*,t}$ using the LWE assumption on $\mathbf{S}_{i_1^*}$.

The guessing of the users $i_1^*$ and $i_K^*$ incurs a security loss of $h(h-1)$ where $h$ is the number of users in $\mathcal{HS}$. Therefore for all $l \in \{2, \ldots, \ell]$ there exists a PPT adversary $\mathcal{B}$ such that

$$|\mathsf{Adv}_{\mathcal{A}}(\mathsf{G}_{0.l-1}) - \mathsf{Adv}_{\mathcal{A}}(\mathsf{G}_{0.l})| \leq h(h-1) \cdot \mathsf{Adv}_{\mathcal{B}}^{\mathsf{LWE}}$$

Summing up for all the hybrid games, it leads to a security loss of $\ell h(h-1)$. Since the reduction is applied twice, total loss is $2\ell h(h-1)$. Therefore, we obtain a PPT adversary $\mathcal{B}$ such that

$$|\mathsf{Adv}_{\mathcal{A}}(\mathsf{G}_0) - \mathsf{Adv}_{\mathcal{A}}(\mathsf{G}_1)| \leq 2\ell h(h-1) \cdot \mathsf{Adv}_{\mathcal{B}}^{\mathsf{LWE}}$$

□

Now, we are in game $\mathsf{G}_1$ and $\mathsf{QChallenge}(\mathcal{U}, \{\mathbf{x}_{i,t^*}^0\}_{i\in\mathcal{U}}, \{\mathbf{x}_{i,t^*}^1\}_{i\in\mathcal{U}}, t^*)$ in $\mathsf{G}_1$ is answered with $\mathbf{x}_{i,t^*}^0 + \mathbf{c}_{i,t^*} + \sum_{j\in\mathcal{U}\setminus\{i_1\}} \mathbf{u}_j$ for $i = i_1$ and $\mathbf{x}_{i,t^*}^0 + \mathbf{c}_{i,t^*} - \mathbf{u}_i$ for $i \in \mathcal{U} \setminus \{i_1\}$. This is clear that these shares form a perfect $\mu$ out of $\mu$ secret sharing of 0. Further, the corruption queries in $\mathsf{G}_1$ are answered as follows. On input $i \in [\mathcal{CS}]$, $\mathcal{B}$ returns the key $\mathsf{sk}_i$ to $\mathcal{A}$. If the adversary corrupts the aggregator, then $\mathsf{QCorr}$ queries are answered with partial decryption keys for the honest users because the keys for the corrupted users can be generated by the adversary itself. To answer $\mathsf{QCorr}(0)$, $\mathcal{B}$ first generates secret shares of 0 for all the honest users, $\mathbf{R}_i \leftarrow SS(0)$ and computes

$$\begin{aligned} \mathsf{dk}_i &= \mathbf{S}_i + \mathbf{V}_i + \mathbf{R}_i \quad \text{for } i \in \mathcal{HS} \setminus \{i_1^*, i_K^*\} \\ \mathsf{dk}_{i_1^*} &= \mathbf{S}_0 - \sum_{j\in[\mathcal{CS}]} (\mathbf{S}_j + \mathbf{V}_j) + \mathbf{R}_{i_1*} \\ \mathsf{dk}_{i_K^*} &= - \sum_{j\in\mathcal{HS}\setminus\{i_1^*, i_K^*\}} (\mathbf{S}_j + \mathbf{V}_j) + \mathbf{R}_{i_K^*} \end{aligned}$$

**Game** $\mathsf{G}_2$: In this game, all the challenge queries are answered with encryptions of $\mathbf{x}_{i,t}^1$ instead of $\mathbf{x}_{i,t}^0$. This is possible because the secret shares hide all the information on the individual ciphertexts.

**Lemma 3 (Transition from $\mathbf{G}_1$ to $\mathbf{G}_2$).** *For all PPT adversary $\mathcal{A}$, that corrupts the aggregator, there exists a PPT adversary $\mathcal{B}$ such that*

$$|\mathsf{Adv}_{\mathcal{A}}(\mathsf{G}_1) - \mathsf{Adv}_{\mathcal{A}}(\mathsf{G}_2)| \leq 2 \cdot \mathsf{Adv}_{\mathcal{B}}^{\mathsf{LWE}}(\lambda)$$

*Proof.* Let $\mathcal{Q}_{t^*}$ be the set of users for which $\mathcal{A}$ has a ciphertext at timestamp $t^*$ and let $\mathcal{HS}$ be the set of honest users. We consider the following two cases here.

**Case 1** ($\mathcal{Q}_{t^*} = \mathcal{HS}$): In this case, the adversary receives a ciphertext for all the honest users at timestamp $t^*$ either from the encryption oracle or from the challenge oracle. Then $\mathcal{Q}_{t^*} \cup \mathcal{CS} = [\ell]$ and the condition $\sum_{i\in\mathcal{U}} \mathbf{x}_{i,t^*}^0 = \sum_{i\in\mathcal{U}} \mathbf{x}_{i,t^*}^1$

must be satisfied. Let $\mathbf{r}_i$ be the pads added to the ciphertexts of the users in $\mathcal{U}$ at the end of game $\mathsf{G}_1$, where

$$\mathbf{r}_i = \begin{cases} \sum_{i \in \mathcal{U} \setminus \{i_1\}} \mathbf{u}_i & \text{if } i = i_1 \\ -\mathbf{u}_i & \text{if } i \in \mathcal{U} \setminus \{i_1\} \end{cases} \tag{5}$$

These $\mathbf{r}_i$'s are perfect secret shares of 0. Therefore $\{\mathbf{x}_{i,t}^0 + \mathbf{c}_{i,t} + \mathbf{r}_i\}_{i \in \mathcal{U}}$ and $\{\mathbf{x}_{i,t}^1 + \mathbf{c}_{i,t} + \mathbf{r}_i\}_{i \in \mathcal{U}}$ are perfect secret shares of $\sum_{i \in \mathcal{U}}(\mathbf{x}_{i,t}^0 + \mathbf{c}_{i,t})$ and $\sum_{i \in \mathcal{U}}(\mathbf{x}_{i,t}^1 + \mathbf{c}_{i,t})$ respectively. Since, $\sum_{i \in \mathcal{U}} \mathbf{x}_{i,t^*}^0 = \sum_{i \in \mathcal{U}} \mathbf{x}_{i,t^*}^1$, $\{\mathbf{x}_{i,t}^0 + \mathbf{c}_{i,t} + \mathbf{r}_i\}_{i \in \mathcal{U}}$ and $\{\mathbf{x}_{i,t}^1 + \mathbf{c}_{i,t} + \mathbf{r}_i\}_{i \in \mathcal{U}}$ are perfect secret shares of the same secret and are therefore perfectly indistinguishable from each other.

**Case 2** ($\mathcal{Q}_{t^*} \neq \mathcal{HS}$): In this case, there exists an honest user from which the adversary does not get a ciphertext at timestamp $t^*$. Therefore the condition $\sum_{i \in \mathcal{U}} \mathbf{x}_{i,t^*}^0 = \sum_{i \in \mathcal{U}} \mathbf{x}_{i,t^*}^1$ does not hold in this case. Since $\mathcal{HS}$ is known in advance, it is possible to identify an user in $\mathcal{HS} \setminus \mathcal{Q}_{t^*}$ that is not in $\mathcal{U}$. $\mathcal{B}$ then chooses two such users $i_h \in \mathcal{HS} \setminus \mathcal{Q}_{t^*}$ and $i_u \in \mathcal{U}$ and simulates the ciphertexts as follows. For $i = i_u$, $\mathcal{B}$ sets $\mathbf{c}_{i,t} = \mathbf{b}_t$ where $\mathbf{b}_t$ is a random vector in $\mathbb{Z}_q^n$. For $i = i_h$, $\mathcal{B}$ sets $\mathbf{c}_{i,t} = H(t) \cdot \mathbf{S}_0 - \sum_{i \in [\ell] \setminus i_h} H(t) \cdot \mathbf{S}_i + \mathbf{e}_{i,t}$. Next, we change the challenge queries from encryption of $\mathbf{x}_{i,t}^0$ to encryptions of $\mathbf{x}_{i,t}^1$. For $b \in \{0,1\}$, we have $\sum_{i \in \mathcal{U}}(\mathbf{x}_{i,t}^b + \mathbf{c}_{i,t}) = \sum_{i \in \mathcal{U} \setminus i_u}(\mathbf{x}_{i,t}^b + \mathbf{c}_{i,t}) + \mathbf{x}_{i_u,t}^b + \mathbf{c}_{i_u,t}$. Since $\mathbf{c}_{i_u,t}$ is a random vector in $\mathbb{Z}_q^n$, $\{\mathbf{x}_{i,t}^0 + \mathbf{c}_{i,t} + \mathbf{r}_i\}_{i \in \mathcal{U}}$ and $\{\mathbf{x}_{i,t}^1 + \mathbf{c}_{i,t} + \mathbf{r}_i\}_{i \in \mathcal{U}}$ are secret shares of a random value. Therefore, they are indistinguishable from each other. Finally, we change the random vector with an LWE mask again.

**Game** $\mathsf{G}_3$: In this game we remove the secret shares from the challenge ciphertexts. Therefore, this game is identical to $\mathsf{AO}_1$ where the challenge queries are answered with encryptions of $\mathbf{x}_{i,t}^1$.

**Lemma 4 (Transition from $\mathsf{G}_2$ to $\mathsf{G}_3$).** *For all PPT adversary $\mathcal{A}$, that corrupts the aggregator, there exists a PPT adversary $\mathcal{B}$ such that*

$$|\mathsf{Adv}_{\mathcal{A}}(\mathsf{G}_2) - \mathsf{Adv}_{\mathcal{A}}(\mathsf{G}_3)| \leq 2\ell h(h-1) \cdot \mathsf{Adv}_{\mathcal{B}}^{\mathsf{LWE}}(\lambda)$$

*Proof.* This is symmetric to the transition from $\mathsf{G}_0$ to $\mathsf{G}_1$ applying the changes backwards.

For the case when the adversary does not corrupt the aggregator, we can directly go from $\mathsf{G}_0$ to $\mathsf{G}_3$.

**Lemma 5 (Transition from $\mathsf{G}_0$ to $\mathsf{G}_3$).** *For all PPT adversaries $\mathcal{A}$, that do not corrupt the aggregator, there exists a PPT adversary $\mathcal{B}$ such that*

$$|\mathsf{Adv}_{\mathcal{A}}(\mathsf{G}_0) - \mathsf{Adv}_{\mathcal{A}}(\mathsf{G}_3)| \leq 2\ell h \cdot \mathsf{Adv}_{\mathcal{B}}^{\mathsf{LWE}}(\lambda)$$

*Proof.* In this case, the adversary does not corrupt the aggregator and we can directly go from $\mathsf{G}_0$ to $\mathsf{G}_3$ using a hybrid argument over all the users. Let $\mathcal{U} := \{i_1, \ldots, i_\mu\}$ be the set of users specified in the challenge phase. The hybrid game $\mathsf{H}_l$ is given by

$$\mathsf{H}_l: \quad \mathbf{c}_{i,t^*} = \begin{cases} \mathsf{Enc}(i, \mathbf{x}^0_{i,t^*}, t^*) & \text{if } i = i_\tau \text{ for } \tau > l \\ \mathsf{Enc}(i, \mathbf{x}^1_{i,t^*}, t^*) & \text{if } i = i_\tau \text{ for } \tau \le l \end{cases}$$

In other words, in $\mathsf{H}_l$, the challenge query is answered with encryptions of $\mathbf{x}^1_{i,t^*}$ for $i \in \{i_1, \ldots, i_l\}$ and with encryptions of $\mathbf{x}^0_{i,t^*}$ for the rest of the users. Note that $\mathsf{G}_0 = \mathsf{H}_0$ and $\mathsf{G}_3 = \mathsf{H}_\ell$. It suffices to show that the adjacent games $\mathsf{H}_{l-1}$ and $\mathsf{H}_l$ are computationally indistinguishable. Let $\mathcal{A}$ be an adversary that can distinguish $\mathsf{H}_{l-1}$ and $\mathsf{H}_l$. Then there exists an adversary $\mathcal{B}$ against the LWE problem. In $\mathsf{H}_{l-1}$, the challenge query for users $i_\tau$ with $\tau \le l-1$ is answered with encryptions of $\mathbf{x}^1_{i_\tau,t^*}$ and for users $i_\tau$ with $\tau > l-1$, it is answered with encryptions of $\mathbf{x}^0_{i_\tau,t^*}$. The simulation $\mathcal{B}$ first guesses the user $i_l \leftarrow_\$ [\mathcal{HS}]$ and replaces $\mathbf{c}_{i,t^*} = H(t^*) \cdot \mathbf{S}_i^\top + p \cdot \mathbf{e}_{i,t^*}$ for $i = i_l$ with a random vector $\mathbf{b}_{t^*}$ using the LWE assumption on $\mathbf{S}_i$. Then $\mathbf{x}^0_{i,t^*} + \mathbf{c}_{i,t^*}$ is computationally indistinguishable from $\mathbf{x}^1_{i,t^*} + \mathbf{c}_{i,t^*}$ for $i = i_l$. Then, change $\mathbf{c}_{i,t^*}$ back to $\mathbf{c}_{i,t^*} = H(t^*) \cdot \mathbf{S}_i^\top + p \cdot \mathbf{e}_{i,t^*}$ for $i = i_l$.

The guessing of the user $i_l$ incurs a loss of $h$ where $h$ is the number of uncompromised users and this leads to $\ell h$ for $\ell$ hybrid games. Total loss in this case is $2\ell h$. Therefore, there is a PPT adversary $\mathcal{B}$ such that

$$|\mathsf{Adv}_{\mathcal{A}}(\mathsf{G}_0) - \mathsf{Adv}_{\mathcal{A}}(\mathsf{G}_3)| \le 2\ell h \cdot \mathsf{Adv}^{\mathsf{LWE}}_{\mathcal{B}}(\lambda)$$

□

□

### 3.3 Parameters

In this section, we describe how to choose parameters for the proposed scheme for correctness and security. The LWE problem is parameterised by $n, q, \mathcal{X}$ where $\mathcal{X}$ is a discrete Gaussian distribution with mean 0 and standard deviation $\sigma$. The choice of $n, q, \sigma$ determines the security level of the scheme. For correctness, we need $\frac{\ell \cdot p}{2}(1 + 2B) < \frac{q}{2}$.

We use the LWE estimator [1] and the condition for correctness to determine parameters for a security level of 128 bits. Given $n$, modulus $q$ is determined for an error distribution with standard deviation $\sigma = 3.2$. We give example parameters for 128 bit security level in Table 3 when the secret is sampled from the error distribution.

Further, we compare the size of the ciphertexts between our DPSA scheme and the noise scaled version of SLAP as shown in Table 4. For a smaller number of users, the ciphertext size of the proposed DPSA scheme is either the same as or smaller than that of the SLAP scheme. However, for a larger number of users, the SLAP scheme has a slightly better ciphertext size compared to the proposed DPSA scheme.

**Table 3.** Example parameters for the DPSA scheme with LWE dimension $n$, modulus $q$ and noise distribution with standard deviation $\sigma = 3.2$ for 128-bit security level for varying number of users $\ell$ and plaintext modulus $p$

| No. of users | $\log p$ | $n$ | $\log q$ | Ciphertext bytes |
|---|---|---|---|---|
| 100 | 16 | 1200 | 29 | 4350 |
| 1000 | 16 | 1400 | 31 | 5425 |
| 10000 | 32 | 2510 | 51 | 16001 |
| $10^{13}$ | 32 | 4892 | 80 | 48920 |
| $10^{15}$ | 128 | 13800 | 183 | 315675 |
| $10^{21}$ | 128 | 17300 | 203 | 438987 |

**Table 4.** Comparison of ciphertext size between SLAP and our DPSA scheme

| No. of users | $\log p$ | $\log q$ | | Ciphertext bytes | |
|---|---|---|---|---|---|
| | | $\text{SLAP}_{NS}$ | DPSA | $\text{SLAP}_{NS}$ | DPSA |
| 1000 | 16 | 28 | 31 | 16384 | 5425 |
| 10000 | 32 | 48 | 51 | 16384 | 16001 |
| $10^{15}$ | 128 | 184 | 183 | 196608 | 315675 |
| $10^{21}$ | 128 | 204 | 203 | 262144 | 438987 |

### 3.4 Decentralized Setup

In the proposed DPSA construction, the setup is an interactive protocol between the users who generate their own keys and share it with the aggregator in a secure way. The aggregator then recovers the aggregate key for decryption which is the sum of the user keys. The users can generate their keys by sampling $\mathbf{S}_i$ uniformly at random from $\mathcal{X}^{n\times n}(\mathbb{Z}_q)$ and setting $\mathsf{sk}_i = \mathbf{S}_i$ for $i \in [\ell]$. To share the key with the aggregator, each user adds a random pad to their key which when added sums to zero. These random pads can be generated using a secret sharing protocol among the users. Each user $U_i$ generates secret shares $\{\mathbf{V}_{i,1}, \ldots, \mathbf{V}_{i,\ell}\}$ of 0 and shares $\mathbf{V}_{i,j}$ with user $U_j$ for $j \in [\ell] \setminus \{i\}$. User $U_i$ then generates its pad as $\mathbf{V}_i = \sum_{j=1}^{\ell} \mathbf{V}_{j,i}$ for $i \in [\ell]$ which is added to its secret key and the partial key $\mathbf{S}_i + \mathbf{V}_i$ is sent to the aggregator. When these partial keys are added together, the $\mathbf{V}_i$s sum to zero and the aggregator recovers $\mathbf{S}_0 = \sum_{i=1}^{\ell} \mathbf{S}_i$.

The communication cost per client during setup is sending one share to every other user and sending the partial key to the aggregator. The computational cost involves generating its share $\mathbf{V}_i$ and computing the partial aggregator key $\mathsf{dk}_i$. The setup is executed only once in the beginning of the protocol and does not affect the overall performance of the scheme.

### 3.5 Client Failures

If a client fails to submit its input message, then the aggregator cannot evaluate the sum because the equation $\mathbf{S}_0 = \sum_{i=1}^{\ell} \mathbf{S}_i$ does not satisfy (because of the missing ciphertext) and the decryption outputs a random value. Chan et al. [11] proposed a generic solution to deal with this problem and it is applicable to all PSA schemes. They use differential privacy and allow the aggregator to learn partial sums of the user's inputs such that the total sum can always be computed for the non-failing clients.

Their idea is to use a binary tree where the leaf nodes represent the clients and the intermediate nodes represent the partial sums of the clients beneath that node. Technically, the aggregator and the clients run an instance of the PSA protocol for each intermediate node. Therefore, each client generates $\log \ell$ ciphertexts using $\log \ell$ secret keys corresponding to the number of nodes from the client to the root of the binary tree. The aggregator is given an aggregator key for each intermediate node. The aggregator will always be able to compute the sum for the non-failing clients, albeit with an increase in noise in the overall sum. For example, consider the binary tree in Fig. 2 [11] for $\ell = 8$. The notation $[i, j]$ denotes the sum of the inputs of clients $\{i, \ldots, j\}$. If client 4 fails, the aggregator fails to obtain the sums $[4, 4]$, $[3, 4]$ and $[1, 4]$. The aggregator then uses the blocks corresponding to the black nodes in the tree to compute the sum of the remaining clients.

### 3.6 Optimizing Peer-to-Peer Communication

As a byproduct of the fault tolerance technique, we can also use the binary tree to reduce peer-to-peer communication among the clients during the setup phase. Instead of generating secret shares for all the $\ell - 1$ clients, each client can now generate shares only for those clients with whom they share an intermediate node. This will reduce the communication cost per client during the setup phase.

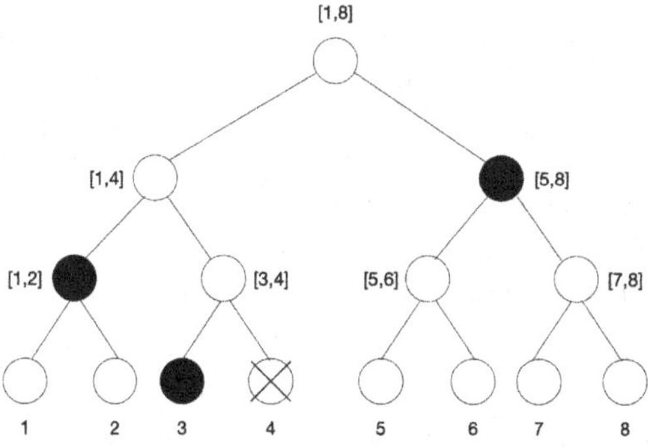


**Fig. 2.** When client 4 fails, the aggregator uses the partial sums corresponding to the black nodes (Color figure online)

### 3.7 Dynamic Join and Leave

Dynamic Join: Chan et al. [11] proposed the idea to create a tree with more leaf nodes than the number of clients to accommodate future client joining. In a centralized scheme, the trusted setup generates secret keys for every leaf node. The additional clients that have not joined the protocol yet are considered as failed until they join. Once a new client joins it receives a secret key from the setup. However, the trusted party needs to be present when a new client joins. In our DPSA scheme, we can use this technique as follows. When a new client $U_{\ell+1}$ joins the protocol before the computation of a new sum, the client first generates a uniformly random $\mathbf{S}_{\ell+1} \in \mathcal{X}^{n\times n}$ and sets $\mathbf{S}_{\ell+1}$ as its secret key. The client can broadcast its joining to the other clients through a bulletin board. Then each client that shares an intermediate node with the new client, chooses a new secret key and generates secret shares of zero and send these shares to the other clients that they share a node with. Using these shares, the clients then generate new aggregator keys and shares them with the aggregator. This is done for all the $\log \ell$ nodes.

*Dynamic Leave:* If some clients leave the protocol before the evaluation of a new sum, we can consider them as permanently failed. For the remaining clients, one possible solution is to run the Setup again. This will update their pads $\mathbf{V}_i$, which now consist of shares from the remaining users. Similarly, the aggregator receives a new key consisting of partial keys from the remaining users. Since the setup is decentralized, the users do not need to depend on a trusted entity to generate the updated pads or the updated aggregator key which makes it more practical than having a centralized setup.

## 4 DPSA in the Standard Model

In this section, we give a possible construction of a DPSA scheme in the standard model. We use similar ideas from [26] that uses a weak PRF to construct a PSA scheme based on the LWE problem. However, in [26], the number of timestamps is bounded as it needs to be fixed in the setup phase. We show how to get unbounded timestamps using a PRF. Let $\mathcal{F}_1 := \{F_{\mathbf{S}} \mid F_{\mathbf{S}} : \mathbb{Z}_q^n \to \mathbb{Z}_q^n, \mathbf{S} \in \mathbb{Z}_q^{n\times n}\}$ such that $F_{\mathbf{S}}(\mathbf{t}) = \mathbf{t} \cdot \mathbf{S}^\top + \mathbf{e}$. Here $\mathcal{F}_1$ is a randomized weak pseudorandom function family as described in [2,3]. Let $\mathcal{F}_2 = \{F_K \mid F_K : \mathbb{Z} \to \mathbb{Z}_q^n, K \in \mathcal{K}_\lambda\}$ be a PRF family such that $F_K(i) = \mathbf{t}_i \in \mathbb{Z}_q^n$. Then, a DPSA scheme in the standard model can be described in terms of the following algorithms.

$\mathsf{Setup}(1^\lambda, 1^\ell)$: This is a protocol between the users. Each user generates a matrix $\mathbf{S}_i \leftarrow_\$ \mathbb{Z}_q^{n\times n}$ and interactively generates $\mathbf{V}_i \leftarrow \mathbb{Z}_q^{n\times n}$ such that $\sum_{i=1}^{\ell} \mathbf{V}_i = 0 \bmod q$. Choose PRF key $K \leftarrow \mathcal{K}_\lambda$ and output public parameters $\mathsf{pp} = (p, q, n, \ell, K, \mathcal{X})$ and each user's secret key $\mathsf{sk}_i = (\mathbf{S}_i, \mathbf{V}_i)$. Since the PRF key is a public information, one of the clients can choose this key and broadcast it to the other clients.

$\mathsf{AggKeyGenShare}(i, \mathsf{sk}_i)$: Given user index $i$ and secret key $\mathsf{sk}_i = (\mathbf{S}_i, \mathbf{V}_i)$, compute partial aggregator key $\mathsf{dk}_i = \mathbf{S}_i + \mathbf{V}_i \pmod q$.

$\mathsf{AggKeygen}(\{\mathsf{dk}_i\}_{i\in[\ell]})$: Given $\{\mathsf{dk}_i\}_{i\in[\ell]}$, compute aggregator decryption key

$$\mathsf{dk}_0 := \sum_{i=1}^{\ell} \mathsf{dk}_i = \sum_{i=1}^{\ell} (\mathbf{S}_i + \mathbf{V}_i) = \sum_{i=1}^{\ell} \mathbf{S}_i \pmod q = \mathbf{S}_0 \tag{6}$$

$\mathsf{Enc}(i, \mathsf{sk}_i, \mathbf{x}_{i,t}, t)$: Given input $\mathbf{x}_{i,t} \in \mathbb{Z}_p^n$ and a timestamp $t = t_j$, generate a vector $\mathbf{t}_j = F_K(j) \in \mathbb{Z}_q^n$. Sample $\mathbf{e}_{i,t} \leftarrow \mathcal{X}^n$ and compute the ciphertext $\mathsf{ct}_{i,t}$ as

$$\mathsf{ct}_{i,t} = \left\lfloor \frac{q}{p} \right\rfloor \cdot \mathbf{x}_{i,t} + \mathbf{t}_j \cdot \mathbf{S}_i^\top + \mathbf{e}_{i,t} \pmod q \tag{7}$$

$\mathsf{AggDec}(\mathsf{dk}_0, \{\mathsf{ct}_{i,t}\}_{i\in[\ell]}, t)$: Given timestamp $t = t_j$, generate the vector $\mathbf{t}_j = F_K(j) \in \mathbb{Z}_q^n$ and compute the aggregated sum as

$$\mathbf{x}_t = \left[\left\lfloor \frac{p}{q} \left( \sum_{i=1}^{\ell} \mathsf{ct}_{i,t} - \mathbf{t}_j \cdot \mathbf{S}_0^\top \pmod q \right) \right\rceil\right]_p \tag{8}$$

**Correctness:** Correctness follows similarly as described in Sect. 3.1. At timestamp $t = t_j$, we have

$$\sum_{i=1}^{\ell} \mathsf{ct}_{i,t} - \mathbf{t}_j \cdot \mathbf{S}_0^\top \pmod q = \sum_{i=1}^{\ell} \left\lfloor \frac{q}{p} \right\rfloor \cdot \mathbf{x}_{i,t} + \sum_{i=1}^{\ell} \mathbf{e}_{i,t} \pmod q \tag{9}$$

Observe that for an odd prime $q$,

$$\sum_{i=1}^{\ell} \left\lfloor \frac{q}{p} \right\rfloor \cdot \mathbf{x}_{i,t} = \left\lfloor \frac{q}{p} \right\rfloor \cdot \sum_{i=1}^{\ell} [\mathbf{x}_{i,t}]_p - \frac{1}{2} \left( \sum_{i=1}^{\ell} \mathbf{x}_{i,t} - \sum_{i=1}^{\ell} [\mathbf{x}_{i,t}]_p \right) \tag{10}$$

To make sure that $\left\lfloor \frac{q}{p} \right\rfloor \cdot \sum_{i=1}^{\ell} \mathbf{x}_{i,t} + \sum_{i=1}^{\ell} \mathbf{e}_{i,t}$ does not flow over the modulus $q$, we need to ensure that

$$\left\| \sum_{i=1}^{\ell} \mathbf{e}_{i,t} - \frac{1}{2} \left( \sum_{i=1}^{\ell} \mathbf{x}_{i,t} - \sum_{i=1}^{\ell} [\mathbf{x}_{i,t}]_p \right) \right\|_\infty < \frac{q}{2} \tag{11}$$

This is satisfied when $\frac{\ell}{2}(p + 2B) < \frac{q}{2}$.

**Security:** The security of the above DPSA scheme can be proved using the same proof strategy as described in Sect. 3.2. It can be proved using a hybrid argument consisting of the games outlined in Table 5. Here $\mathsf{G}_0$ corresponds to the $\mathsf{AO}_0$ game where $\mathsf{QChallenge}$ queries are answered with an encryption of $\mathbf{x}_{i,t}^0$

and $\mathsf{G}_3$ corresponds to the $\mathsf{AO}_1$ game where the challenge queries are answered with an encryption of $\mathbf{x}_{i,t}^1$.

The transition from $\mathsf{G}_0$ to $\mathsf{G}_1$ consists of adding perfect secret shares of 0 denoted by $\mathbf{r}_i \leftarrow SS(0)$ to the challenge ciphertexts. It can be achieved by replacing the PRF $F_{\mathbf{S}_i}(\mathbf{t}_j)$ with a random function (RF) and using a sequence of hybrid games as described in Lemma 2. Transition from $\mathsf{G}_1$ to $\mathsf{G}_2$ can be done similarly by changing the PRF with an RF for the two users as described in Case 2 of Lemma 3. Case 1 follows directly from Lemma 3. Finally, transition from $\mathsf{G}_2$ to $\mathsf{G}_3$ consists of making the changes backwards.

**Table 5.** Hybrid games for the AO security of the DPSA scheme in the standard model. Change in each games is highlighted with a square box

| Game | $\mathsf{ct}_{i,t}$ | Justification |
|---|---|---|
| $\mathsf{G}_0$ | $\mathbf{c}_{i,t} \leftarrow F_{\mathbf{S}_i}(\mathbf{t}_j)$<br>$\mathsf{ct}_{i,t} \leftarrow \mathbf{c}_{i,t} + \lfloor q/p \rfloor \cdot \mathbf{x}_{i,t}^0$ | $\mathsf{AO}_0$ game |
| $\mathsf{G}_1$ | $\mathbf{c}'_{i,t} \leftarrow F_{\mathbf{S}_i}(\mathbf{t}_j)$<br>$\boxed{\mathbf{c}_{i,t} \leftarrow \mathbf{c}'_{i,t} + \mathbf{r}_i}, \quad \mathbf{r}_i \leftarrow SS(0)$<br>$\mathsf{ct}_{i,t} \leftarrow \mathbf{c}_{i,t} + \lfloor q/p \rfloor \cdot \mathbf{x}_{i,t}^0$ | $\mathbf{c}_{i,t}$ indistinguishable from random |
| $\mathsf{G}_2$ | $\mathbf{c}'_{i,t} \leftarrow F_{\mathbf{S}_i}(\mathbf{t}_j)$<br>$\mathbf{c}_{i,t} \leftarrow \mathbf{c}'_{i,t} + \mathbf{r}_i, \quad \mathbf{r}_i \leftarrow SS(0)$<br>$\boxed{\mathsf{ct}_{i,t} \leftarrow \mathbf{c}_{i,t} + \lfloor q/p \rfloor \cdot \mathbf{x}_{i,t}^1}$ | information-theoretic |
| $\mathsf{G}_3$ | $\boxed{\mathbf{c}_{i,t} \leftarrow F_{\mathbf{S}_i}(\mathbf{t}_j)}$<br>$\mathsf{ct}_{i,t} \leftarrow \mathbf{c}_{i,t} + \lfloor q/p \rfloor \cdot \mathbf{x}_{i,t}^1$ | $\mathbf{c}_{i,t}$ indistinguishable from random |

## 5 Conclusion

In this paper, we presented a decentralized private stream aggregation (DPSA) protocol that does not rely on a trusted authority for key generation. We gave a formal definition of a DPSA scheme and presented a concrete construction based on the LWE problem both in the random oracle model as well as the standard model. We proved the security of the DPSA scheme under the aggregator obliviousness notion with static corruptions. Further, we discussed possible solutions for practical deployments such as clients joining and leaving the system. In addition, we provided sample parameters for the concrete construction based on the LWE assumption, and demonstrated that our scheme achieves comparable ciphertext sizes to that of SLAP [24] for equivalent plaintext spaces.

**Acknowledgements.** This work was partially supported by the Wallenberg AI, Autonomous Systems and Software Program (WASP) funded by the Knut and Alice Wallenberg Foundation.

# Appendix

## A Private Stream Aggregation

**Definition 6 (Private Stream Aggregation** [21]**).** *A private stream aggregation scheme over an input space $\mathcal{M}$ consists of the following PPT algorithms:*

$\mathsf{Setup}(1^\lambda, 1^\ell)$: *Takes as input the security parameter $\lambda$ and number of users $\ell$ and generates public parameters $\mathsf{pp}$, user secret keys $\mathsf{sk}_i$ and aggregator decryption key $\mathsf{dk}_0$. Each user gets the corresponding secret key $\mathsf{sk}_i$ for $i \in [\ell]$ and the aggregator receives the decryption key $\mathsf{dk}_0$. The public parameters $\mathsf{pp}$ is implicitly an input to all the algorithms.*

$\mathsf{Enc}(i, \mathsf{sk}_i, \mathbf{x}_{i,t}, t)$: *Takes as input the user index $i$, the secret key $\mathsf{sk}_i$, the input $\mathbf{x}_{i,t} \in \mathcal{M}$ and generates an encryption of $\mathbf{x}_{i,t}$ using $\mathsf{sk}_i$. Outputs the ciphertext $\mathsf{ct}_{i,t}$.*

$\mathsf{AggDec}(\mathsf{dk}_0, \{\mathsf{ct}_{i,t}\}_{i\in[\ell]}, t)$: *Takes the aggregator decryption key $\mathsf{dk}_0$ and ciphertexts $\{\mathsf{ct}_{i,t}\}_{i\in[\ell]}$ for the time period $t$ and outputs the aggregated sum $\mathbf{x}_t = \sum_{i=1}^{\ell} \mathbf{x}_{i,t}$.*

**Correctness**: The above PSA scheme $\mathsf{PSA} = (\mathsf{Setup}, \mathsf{Enc}, \mathsf{AggDec})$ is said to be correct if for any $\lambda, \ell \in \mathbb{N}$, any message $\mathbf{x}_{i,t} \in \mathcal{M}$, it holds that

$$\Pr\left[\mathsf{AggDec}(\mathsf{dk}_0, \{\mathsf{ct}_{i,t}\}_{i\in[\ell]}, t) = \sum_{i=1}^{\ell} \mathbf{x}_{i,t} : \begin{array}{l} (\mathsf{pp}, \{\mathsf{sk}_i\}_{i\in[\ell]}, \mathsf{dk}_0) \leftarrow \mathsf{Setup}(1^\lambda, 1^\ell) \\ \mathsf{ct}_{i,t} \leftarrow \mathsf{Enc}(i, \mathsf{sk}_i, \mathbf{x}_{i,t}, t) \end{array}\right] = 1$$

**Definition 7 (Aggregator Obliviousness for PSA).** *The aggregator obliviousness security for a PSA scheme can be defined in terms of the security experiment $\mathsf{AO}_\beta(\lambda, \ell, \mathcal{A})$ given in Fig. 3. No adversary $\mathcal{A}$ should be able to win this game with non-negligible advantage.*

$\mathsf{AO}_\beta(\lambda, \ell, \mathcal{A})$

$(\mathsf{pp}, \{\mathsf{sk}_i\}_{i\in[\ell]}, \mathsf{dk}_0) \leftarrow \mathsf{Setup}(1^\lambda, 1^\ell)$.
$\beta \leftarrow \mathcal{A}^{\mathsf{QCorr}(\cdot), \mathsf{QEnc}(\cdot,\cdot,\cdot,\cdot), \mathsf{QChallenge}(\cdot,\cdot,\cdot,\cdot)}(\mathsf{pp})$
**if** condition $(*)$ is satisfied **then**
  output $\beta$
**else**
  output 0

**Fig. 3.** Aggregator Obliviousness experiment for PSA

*The challenger first runs the $\mathsf{Setup}$ algorithm and returns the public parameters $\mathsf{pp}$ to the adversary. The adversary makes queries to the following oracles:*

- ***Corruption oracle*** $\mathsf{QCorr}(i)$*: The adversary submits an integer* $i \in \{1, \ldots, \ell\}$ *and gets back the* $i$*-th user's secret key* $\mathsf{sk}_i$*. If the adversary submits* $i = 0$*, then it gets the aggregator decryption key* $\mathsf{dk}_0$.
- ***Encryption oracle*** $\mathsf{QEnc}(i, \mathbf{x}_{i,t}, t)$*: The adversary submits* $(i, \mathbf{x}_{i,t}, t)$ *and receives* $\mathsf{ct}_{i,t}, \leftarrow \mathit{Enc}(i, \mathsf{sk}_i, \mathbf{x}_{i,t}, t)$ *from the challenger.*
- ***Challenge oracle*** $\mathsf{QChallenge}(\mathcal{U}, \{\mathbf{x}^0_{i,t^*}\}_{i\in\mathcal{U}}, \{\mathbf{x}^1_{i,t^*}\}_{i\in\mathcal{U}}, t^*)$*: This query can be made only once by the adversary. The adversary selects a set of users* $\mathcal{U}$ *and time period* $t^*$ *and for each* $i \in \mathcal{U}$*, the adversary chooses two sets of inputs* $\mathbf{x}^0_{i,t^*}$*,* $\mathbf{x}^1_{i,t^*}$*. The challenger randomly samples* $b \leftarrow \{0, 1\}$ *and returns* $\mathsf{ct}_{i,t^*} \leftarrow \mathit{Enc}(\mathsf{sk}_i, \mathbf{x}^0_{i,t^*}, t^*)$ *for all* $i \in \mathcal{U}$ *if* $b = 0$ *and* $\mathsf{ct}_{i,t^*} \leftarrow \mathit{Enc}(\mathsf{sk}_i, \mathbf{x}^1_{i,t^*}, t^*)$ *for all* $i \in \mathcal{U}$ *if* $b = 1$.

*Finally, the adversary outputs a guess* $b'$ *for the value of* $b$ *and the experiment outputs* $\beta$ *depending on the following conditions.*

*Let* $\mathcal{CS}$ *be the set of corrupted users,* $\mathcal{HS}$ *be the set of honest users at the end of the game and let* $\mathcal{E}_{t^*}$ *be the set of users for which an encryption query has been made at time* $t^*$*. Let* $\mathcal{Q}_{t^*} := \mathcal{U} \cup \mathcal{E}_{t^*}$ *be the set of users for which* $\mathcal{A}$ *receives an encryption or a challenge ciphertext at timestamp* $t^*$*. The condition* $(*)$ *is satisfied if all of the following conditions hold:*

- $\mathcal{U} \cap \mathcal{CS} = \emptyset$*: The set of users specified during the* Challenge *phase must be uncorrupted at the end of the game.*
- *Adversary* $\mathcal{A}$ *has not queried* $\mathsf{QEnc}(i, \mathbf{x}_{i,t}, t^*)$ *for the same* $i$ *and* $t^*$*. Otherwise, this would violate the encrypt-once policy.*
- $\mathcal{U} \cap \mathcal{E}_{t^*} = \emptyset$*: The adversary cannot query challenge ciphertexts to the users in* $\mathcal{E}_{t^*}$*. In other words, the adversary cannot get a challenge ciphertext from users for which it has queried the encryption oracle at time* $t^*$.
- *If the adversary has compromised the aggregator and* $\mathcal{Q}_{t^*} \cup \mathcal{CS} = [\ell]$*, then the following condition must be satisfied.*

$$\sum_{i\in\mathcal{U}} \boldsymbol{x}^0_{i,t^*} = \sum_{i\in\mathcal{U}} \boldsymbol{x}^1_{i,t^*}$$

*We set* $\beta \leftarrow b'$ *if the above conditions are satisfied, otherwise we set* $\beta = 0$.

*A PSA scheme is said to be aggregator oblivious if for any PPT adversary* $\mathcal{A}$*, there exists a negligible function* $\mathsf{negl}$ *such that*

$$\mathsf{Adv}^{\mathsf{AO}}_{\mathcal{A},\mathsf{PSA}}(\lambda, \ell) = |Pr[\mathsf{AO}_0(\lambda, \ell, \mathcal{A}) = 1] - Pr[\mathsf{AO}_1(\lambda, \ell, \mathcal{A}) = 1]| \leq \mathsf{negl}(\lambda)$$

# B Games for the Proof of Theorem 1

G₀ | G₁ G₂ | G₃

$\mathcal{CS} \leftarrow \mathcal{A}(1^\lambda, 1^\ell)$
$(\mathsf{pp}, \{\mathsf{sk}_i\}_{i\in[\ell]}) \leftarrow \mathsf{Setup}(1^\lambda, 1^\ell)$.
$\beta \leftarrow \mathcal{A}^{\mathsf{QCor}(\cdot),\mathsf{QEnc}(\cdot,\cdot,\cdot,\cdot),\mathsf{QChallenge}(\cdot,\cdot,\cdot,\cdot)}(\mathsf{pp}, \{\mathsf{sk}_i\}_{i\in\mathcal{CS}})$
Output $\beta$ if condition $(*)$ is satisfied; otherwise output 0

QCorr(i)

**if** $i \in [\mathcal{CS}]$ **then**
**return** $\mathsf{sk}_i$
**if** $i = 0$ **then**
  $\mathsf{dk}_j \leftarrow \mathsf{AggKeyGenShare}(j, \mathsf{sk}_j)\ \forall j \in \mathcal{HS}$
  **for all** $j \in [\mathcal{HS}]$ **do** $\mathbf{R}_j \leftarrow_\$ \mathbb{Z}_q^{n\times n}$ s.t. $\sum_{j\in[\mathcal{HS}]} \mathbf{R}_j = 0$

  if $j = i_1$, $\mathsf{dk}_j = \mathbf{S}_0 - \sum_{i\in\mathcal{CS}}(\mathbf{S}_i + \mathbf{V}_i) + \mathbf{R}_j$
  if $j = i_K$, $\mathsf{dk}_j = -\sum_{i\in\mathcal{HS}\setminus\{i_1,i_K\}}(\mathbf{S}_i + \mathbf{V}_i) + \mathbf{R}_j$
  if $j = i_\tau$ for $\tau \in \mathcal{HS} \setminus \{i_1, i_K\}$, $\mathsf{dk}_j = \mathbf{S}_j + \mathbf{V}_j + \mathbf{R}_j$

**return** $\{\mathsf{dk}_j\}_{j\in\mathcal{HS}}$

$\mathsf{QEnc}(i, \mathbf{x}_{i,t}, t)$

$\mathsf{ct}_{i,t} \leftarrow \mathsf{Enc}(\mathsf{pp}, \mathsf{sk}_i, \mathbf{x}_{i,t}, t)$
**return** $\mathsf{ct}_{i,t}$

$\mathsf{QChallenge}(\mathcal{U}, \{\mathbf{x}^0_{i,t^*}\}_{i\in\mathcal{U}}, \{\mathbf{x}^1_{i,t^*}\}_{i\in\mathcal{U}}, t^*)$

Let $\mathcal{U} := \{i_1, \ldots, i_\mu\}$
**for all** $\tau \in \{2, \ldots, \mu\}$ **do** $\mathbf{u}_\tau \leftarrow_\$ \mathbb{Z}_q^n$
  **for all** $i \in \mathcal{U}$ **do**
    $\mathbf{c}_{i,t^*} := \mathbf{y}_{t^*} \cdot \mathbf{S}_i^\top + p \cdot \mathbf{e}_{i,t^*} \in \mathbb{Z}_q^n$; $\mathbf{e}_{i,t^*} \leftarrow \mathcal{X}^n$

    **if** $\mu \geq 2$ **then**
      if $i = i_1$, $\mathbf{c}_{i,t^*} = \mathbf{c}_{i,t^*} + \sum_{\tau=2}^{\mu} \mathbf{u}_\tau$
      if $i = i_\tau$ for $\tau \in \{2, \ldots, \mu\}$, $\mathbf{c}_{i,t^*} = \mathbf{c}_{i,t^*} - \mathbf{u}_\tau$

  $\mathsf{ct}_{i,t} := \mathbf{x}^0_{i,t^*} + \mathbf{c}_{i,t^*} \pmod q$
  $\mathsf{ct}_{i,t} := \mathbf{x}^1_{i,t^*} + \mathbf{c}_{i,t^*} \pmod q$

**return** $\mathsf{ct}_{i,t}$

**Fig. 4.** Games for the proof of Theorem 1. Here $\mathcal{HS} := [\ell] \setminus \mathcal{CS}$. Condition $(*)$ is given in Definition 5.

$\mathsf{G}_{0.l-1}$ for $l \in \{1, \ldots, \ell\}$:

$\mathcal{CS} \leftarrow \mathcal{A}(1^\lambda, 1^\ell)$
$i_1^* \leftarrow_\$ [\mathcal{HS}]$, $i_K^* \leftarrow_\$ [\mathcal{HS}] \setminus \{i_1^*\}$
$(\mathsf{pp}, \{\mathsf{sk}_i\}_{i\in[\ell]}) \leftarrow \mathsf{Setup}(1^\lambda, 1^\ell)$
$\beta \leftarrow \mathcal{A}^{\mathsf{QCor}(\cdot),\mathsf{QEnc}(\cdot,\cdot,\cdot,\cdot),\mathsf{QChallenge}(\cdot,\cdot,\cdot,\cdot)}(\mathsf{pp}, \{\mathsf{sk}_i\}_{i\in\mathcal{CS}})$
Output $\beta$ if condition $(*)$ is satisfied AND the game was not aborted; otherwise output 0

QCorr(i)

**if** $i \in [\mathcal{CS}]$ **then**
**return** $\mathsf{sk}_i$
**if** $i = 0$ **then**
$\mathsf{dk}_j \leftarrow \mathsf{AggKeyGenShare}(j, \mathsf{sk}_j)\ \forall j \in \mathcal{HS}$
**for all** $j \in [\mathcal{HS}]$ **do** $\mathbf{R}_j \leftarrow_\$ \mathbb{Z}_q^{n\times n}$ s.t. $\sum_{j\in[\mathcal{HS}]} \mathbf{R}_j = 0$

if $j = i_1$, $\mathsf{dk}_j = \mathbf{S}_0 - \sum_{i\in\mathcal{CS}}(\mathbf{S}_i + \mathbf{V}_i) + \mathbf{R}_j$
if $j = i_K$, $\mathsf{dk}_j = -\sum_{i\in\mathcal{HS}\setminus\{i_1,i_K\}}(\mathbf{S}_i + \mathbf{V}_i) + \mathbf{R}_j$
if $j = i_\tau$ for $\tau \in \mathcal{HS} \setminus \{i_1, i_K\}$, $\mathsf{dk}_j = \mathbf{S}_j + \mathbf{V}_j + \mathbf{R}_j$

**return** $\{\mathsf{dk}_j\}_{j\in\mathcal{HS}}$

$\mathsf{QEnc}(i, \mathbf{x}_{i,t}, t)$

$\mathbf{c}_{i,t} = \mathbf{y}_t \cdot \mathbf{S}_i^\top + p \cdot \mathbf{e}_{i,t}$
If $i = i_1^*$, $\mathbf{c}_{i,t} = \mathbf{b}_t$, $\mathbf{b}_t \leftarrow_\$ \mathbb{Z}_q^n$
If $i = i_K^*$, $\mathbf{c}_{i,t} = H(t) \cdot \mathbf{S}_0 - H(t) \sum_{j\in[\ell]\setminus\{i_1^*,i_K^*\}} \mathbf{S}_j - \mathbf{b}_t$

$\mathsf{ct}_{i,t} = \mathbf{x}_{i,t} + \mathbf{c}_{i,t}$
**return** $\mathsf{ct}_{i,t}$

$\mathsf{QChallenge}(\mathcal{U}, \{\mathbf{x}^0_{i,t^*}\}_{i\in\mathcal{U}}, \{\mathbf{x}^1_{i,t^*}\}_{i\in\mathcal{U}}, t^*)$

Let $\mathcal{U} := \{i_1, \ldots, i_\mu\}$ and $K = min(\mu, l)$
**for all** $\tau \in \{2, \ldots, K\}$ **do** $\mathbf{u}_\tau \leftarrow_\$ \mathbb{Z}_q^n$
**for all** $i \in \mathcal{U}$ **do**
$\mathbf{c}_{i,t^*} := \mathbf{y}_{t^*} \cdot \mathbf{S}_i^\top + p \cdot \mathbf{e}_{i,t^*}$
**if** $K \geq 2$ **then**
if $i_1 \neq i_1^*$ and $i_K \neq i_K^*$ then abort game
if $i = i_1$, $\mathbf{c}_{i,t^*} = \mathbf{c}_{i,t^*} + \sum_{\tau=2}^K \mathbf{u}_\tau$
if $i = i_\tau$ for $\tau \in \{2, \ldots, K\}$, $\mathbf{c}_{i,t^*} = \mathbf{c}_{i,t^*} - \mathbf{u}_\tau$
$\mathsf{ct}_{i,t^*} := \mathbf{x}^0_{i,t^*} + \mathbf{c}_{i,t^*} \pmod{q}$
**return** $\mathsf{ct}_{i,t}$

**Fig. 5.** Games for the proof of Lemma 2

## References


1. Albrecht, M.R., Player, R., Scott, S.: On the concrete hardness of learning with errors. J. Math. Cryptol. **9**(3), 169–203 (2015)
2. Applebaum, B., Cash, D., Peikert, C., Sahai, A.: Fast cryptographic primitives and circular-secure encryption based on hard learning problems. In: Halevi, S. (ed.) CRYPTO 2009. LNCS, vol. 5677, pp. 595–618. Springer, Heidelberg (2009). https://doi.org/10.1007/978-3-642-03356-8_35
3. Banerjee, A., Peikert, C., Rosen, A.: Pseudorandom functions and lattices. In: Pointcheval, D., Johansson, T. (eds.) EUROCRYPT 2012. LNCS, vol. 7237, pp. 719–737. Springer, Heidelberg (2012). https://doi.org/10.1007/978-3-642-29011-4_42
4. Becker, D., Guajardo, J., Zimmermann, K.H.: Revisiting private stream aggregation: lattice-based PSA. In: NDSS 2018. The Internet Society, 2018, vol. 2, p. 5 (2018)
5. Bell, J., et al.: {ACORN}: input validation for secure aggregation. In: 32nd USENIX Security Symposium (USENIX Security 2023), pp. 4805–4822 (2023)
6. Bell, J.H., Bonawitz, K.A., Gascón, A., Lepoint, T., Raykova, M.: Secure single-server aggregation with (poly) logarithmic overhead. In: Proceedings of the 2020 ACM SIGSAC Conference on Computer and Communications Security, pp. 1253–1269 (2020)
7. Benhamouda, F., Joye, M., Libert, B.: A new framework for privacy-preserving aggregation of time-series data. ACM Trans. Inf. Syst. Secur. (TISSEC) **18**(3), 1–21 (2016)
8. Bonawitz, K., et al.: Practical secure aggregation for privacy-preserving machine learning. In: Proceedings of the 2017 ACM SIGSAC Conference on Computer and Communications Security, pp. 1175–1191 (2017)
9. Brakerski, Z., Langlois, A., Peikert, C., Regev, O., Stehlé, D.: Classical hardness of learning with errors. In: Proceedings of the Forty-Fifth Annual ACM Symposium on Theory of Computing, pp. 575–584 (2013)
10. Brorsson, J., Gunnarsson, M.: Dipsauce: efficient private stream aggregation without trusted parties. IACR Cryptology ePrint Archive (2023). https://eprint.iacr.org/2023/214
11. Chan, T.H.H., Shi, E., Song, D.: Privacy-preserving stream aggregation with fault tolerance. In: Keromytis, A.D. (ed.) FC 2012. LNCS, vol. 7397, pp. 200–214. Springer, Heidelberg (2012). https://doi.org/10.1007/978-3-642-32946-3_15
12. Chotard, J., Dufour Sans, E., Gay, R., Phan, D.H., Pointcheval, D.: Decentralized multi-client functional encryption for inner product. In: Peyrin, T., Galbraith, S. (eds.) ASIACRYPT 2018, Part II. LNCS, vol. 11273, pp. 703–732. Springer, Cham (2018). https://doi.org/10.1007/978-3-030-03329-3_24
13. Emura, K.: Privacy-preserving aggregation of time-series data with public verifiability from simple assumptions. In: Pieprzyk, J., Suriadi, S. (eds.) ACISP 2017, Part II. LNCS, vol. 10343, pp. 193–213. Springer, Cham (2017). https://doi.org/10.1007/978-3-319-59870-3_11
14. Erkin, Z., Tsudik, G.: Private computation of spatial and temporal power consumption with smart meters. In: Bao, F., Samarati, P., Zhou, J. (eds.) ACNS 2012. LNCS, vol. 7341, pp. 561–577. Springer, Heidelberg (2012). https://doi.org/10.1007/978-3-642-31284-7_33
15. Ernst, J., Koch, A.: Private stream aggregation with labels in the standard model. In: Proceedings on Privacy Enhancing Technologies, vol. 2021, no. 4, pp. 117–138 (2021)

16. Fereidooni, H., et al.: Safelearn: secure aggregation for private federated learning. In: 2021 IEEE Security and Privacy Workshops (SPW), pp. 56–62. IEEE (2021)
17. Joye, M., Libert, B.: A scalable scheme for privacy-preserving aggregation of time-series data. In: Sadeghi, A.R. (ed.) FC 2013. LNCS, vol. 7859, pp. 111–125. Springer, Heidelberg (2013). https://doi.org/10.1007/978-3-642-39884-1_10
18. Leontiadis, I., Elkhiyaoui, K., Önen, M., Molva, R.: PUDA-privacy and unforgeability for data aggregation. In: Reiter, M., Naccache, D. (eds.) CANS 2015. LNCS, vol. 9476, pp. 3–18. Springer, Cham (2015). https://doi.org/10.1007/978-3-319-26823-1_1
19. Regev, O.: On lattices, learning with errors, random linear codes, and cryptography. In: 37th Annual ACM Symposium on Theory of Computing, pp. 84–93 (2005)
20. Regev, O.: On lattices, learning with errors, random linear codes, and cryptography. J. ACM (JACM) **56**(6), 1–40 (2009)
21. Shi, E., Chan, H., Rieffel, E., Chow, R., Song, D.: Privacy-preserving aggregation of time-series data. In: Annual Network & Distributed System Security Symposium (NDSS). Internet Society (2011)
22. Shor, P.W.: Algorithms for quantum computation: discrete logarithms and factoring. In: Proceedings 35th Annual Symposium on Foundations of Computer Science, pp. 124–134. IEEE (1994)
23. Takeshita, J., Carmichael, Z., Karl, R., Jung, T.: Terse: tiny encryptions and really speedy execution for post-quantum private stream aggregation. In: Li, F., Liang, K., Lin, Z., Katsikas, S.K. (eds.) SecureComm 2022, pp. 331–352. Springer, Cham (2023). https://doi.org/10.1007/978-3-031-25538-0_18
24. Takeshita, J., Karl, R., Gong, T., Jung, T.: Slap: simpler, improved private stream aggregation from ring learning with errors. J. Cryptol. **36**(2), 8 (2023)
25. Tsaloli, G., Liang, B., Brunetta, C., Banegas, G., Mitrokotsa, A.: Deva: Decentralized, verifiable secure aggregation for privacy-preserving learning. In: Liu, J.K., Katsikas, S., Meng, W., Susilo, W., Intan, R. (eds.) ISC 2021. LNCS, vol. 13118, pp. 296–319. Springer, Cham (2021). https://doi.org/10.1007/978-3-030-91356-4_16
26. Valovich, F.: Aggregation of time-series data under differential privacy. In: Lange, T., Dunkelman, O. (eds.) LATINCRYPT 2017. LNCS, vol. 11368, pp. 249–270. Springer, Cham (2019). https://doi.org/10.1007/978-3-030-25283-0_14
27. Waldner, H., Marc, T., Stopar, M., Abdalla, M.: Private stream aggregation from labeled secret sharing schemes. IACR Cryptology ePrint Archive 2021, 81 (2021). https://eprint.iacr.org/2021/081

# Wireless and Networks

# A Security Analysis of WPA3-PK: Implementation and Precomputation Attacks

Mathy Vanhoef(✉) and Jeroen Robben

DistriNet, KU Leuven, 3001 Leuven, Belgium
{mathy.vanhoef,jeroen.robben}@kuleuven.be

**Abstract.** Creating secure Wi-Fi hotspots has historically been challenging: when using an open network it is trivial for an adversary to eavesdrop traffic. Alternatively, when using a password-protected network and sharing the password publicly, anyone who knows the password can create a rogue clone of the network to intercept traffic. To overcome this problem, the Wi-Fi Alliance released SAE-PK as part of an update to WPA3, which we will call WPA3-PK. In this protocol, a public key is used to verify the hotspot's authenticity, and the password of the network encodes a fingerprint of this public key. As a result, someone who knows the password can no longer clone the network, because they do not know the corresponding private key.

In this paper, we systematically analyze the security of WPA3-PK. We first study implementations, where we show that the private WPA3-PK password gets leaked when using a flawed random number generator, and confirm that this may indeed happen in practice. We then study network aspects, where we show how a malicious insider can intercept the traffic of others. Our third focus is cryptographic attacks, where we perform an evaluation of time-memory trade-off attacks against WPA3-PK, and we optimize these attacks by combining the technique of rainbow tables with distinguished points. Additionally, we construct multi-network password collisions that allow an adversary to build a single rainbow table that can be used to attack multiple networks. Finally, we discuss defenses against our attacks and propose updates to the WPA3-PK standard.

**Keywords:** WPA3-PK · Rainbow table · Time-memory trade-off

## 1 Introduction

Securing Wi-Fi hotspots has historically been a daunting task. Using an open, unsecured, Wi-Fi network makes it trivial for an adversary to read and intercept any user's traffic. A password-protected network, where the password is shared publicly, is not much better: anyone who knows the password can create a rogue clone of the network to intercept all traffic. Previous works tried to improve this situation by creating a new enterprise authentication method, where the public


C. Pöpper and L. Batina (Eds.): ACNS 2024, LNCS 14584, pp. 217–240, 2024.
https://doi.org/10.1007/978-3-031-54773-7_9

key of the network is pinned and used to authenticate the hotspot, and where the client is not authenticated [11,14]. Unfortunately, these proposals never gained widespread adoption, and could still be attacked when a client connects to the network for the first time. To remedy this situation, and better protect Wi-Fi hotspots, the Wi-Fi Alliance released the Simultaneous Authentication of Equals Public Key (SAE-PK) protocol in December 2020 as part of an update to the WPA3 specification. We will refer to this protocol as WPA3-PK.

The goal of WPA3-PK is to strengthen the security of password-protected Wi-Fi hotspots by preventing an adversary from creating a rogue clone of the hotspot, even when that adversary possesses the pre-shared password. This is achieved by authenticating the hotspot with a public key and by verifying the authenticity of this public key using a password. The idea is that the password is derived from the hotspot's public key, meaning the password effectively contains a trusted fingerprint of the public key. When a user connects to the hotspot, the fingerprint encoded in the password can then be used to verify the hotspot's public key. An adversary cannot create a rogue clone of the hotspot as long as it is infeasible to generate a private and public key that results in the same fingerprint and WPA3-PK password.

In this paper, we systematically analyze the security of WPA3-PK. We first investigate existing deployments of WPA3-PK, where we analyze implementation and network-related aspects. Doing so, we discover that using a bad random number generator will cause the hotspot's password to be leaked. Additionally, because WPA3-PK does not mandate client isolation, we found that network-layer attacks can still be abused to intercept the traffic of other users.

Our second focus is time-memory trade-off attacks against WPA3-PK. In these attacks, the goal is to find a private and public key that result in a given WPA3-PK password, i.e., to perform a second preimage attack. We first evaluate the technique of distinguished points, and confirm that a precomputation attack reduces the time to find a second preimage of a WPA3-PK password from 48 CPU years to an amortized time of fewer than 12 d. We then combine this approach with rainbow tables to increase the success rate of the attack. To evaluate our rainbow table attack, we create a proof-of-concept tool that can generate the precomputed rainbow tables. These experiments confirm that using rainbow tables improves the performance of time-memory trade-off attacks against WPA3-PK. We also show how to construct multi-network WPA3-PK password collisions. These allow an adversary to attack multiple networks using a single precomputed table.

Finally, we propose improvements to the design of WPA3-PK that prevent our newly discovered attacks. We also discuss backward-compatible mitigations that either prevent or reduce the impact of our attacks.

To summarize, our contributions are:

- We analyze implementation and network aspects of WPA3-PK, such as random number generation, client isolation, and shared group keys (Sect. 3).
- We empirically evaluate time-memory trade-off attacks against WPA3-PK. We also show how to construct rainbow tables to more efficiently invert a WPA3-PK password into a public and private key pair (Sect. 4).

- We construct multi-network WPA3-PK password collisions that allow an adversary to attack multiple networks using a single rainbow table (Sect. 5).
- We discuss defenses against the identified design and implementation issues and suggest updates to the WPA3-PK standard (Sect. 6).

**Disclosure.** We reported our security analysis of WPA3-PK to the Wi-Fi Alliance. Our code to construct and analyze rainbow tables, and our multi-network WPA3-PK password collisions code, are both available online [1].

## 2 Background

In this section, we introduce the SAE handshake, how WPA3-PK extends SAE, and explain the generation of WPA3-PK passwords and their security properties.

### 2.1 Simultaneous Authentication of Equals (SAE)

The Simultaneous Authentication of Equals (SAE) handshake, also called Dragonfly, lies at the basis of WPA3 and provides forward secrecy and resistance against offline dictionary attacks. This handshake was first introduced in 2008 by Harkins [12] and in 2018 became mandatory in home WPA3 networks [29].

A client can discover nearby Wi-Fi networks that support SAE by sending a broadcast probe request (see Fig. 1). Nearby Access Points (APs) will reply with probe responses. These responses contain various properties of the network, including the name of the network, which is commonly also called the SSID (Service Set Identifier), and whether the network supports SAE.

Once the client finds a network to connect to, it can initiate the SAE handshake. This handshake consists of two phases, called the commit and confirm phase, and these are illustrated in Fig. 1. The first phase can be viewed as a variation of a Diffie-Hellman key exchange, except that the generator used for exponentiation is derived from a pre-shared password instead of being a fixed value [19]. In other words, the first phase negotiates a shared key between the client and AP using Auth-Commit frames. The second phase is used to confirm that the Access Point (AP) and client derived the same keys in the commit phase. More precisely, the confirm element in the Auth-Confirm frame is used to verify that the other party negotiated the same keys. After the SAE handshake, the client associates to the AP, and finally performs a 4-way handshake to derive pairwise transient keys that can be used to protect data frames.

The SAE password can only be shared with trusted individuals. This is because anyone that possesses the password can create a rogue clone of the network with the same SSID and password, and can then trick victims into connecting to this rogue clone. This makes SAE unsuitable for hotspots, since in that case the password is shared publicly, meaning adversaries will also possess the password.

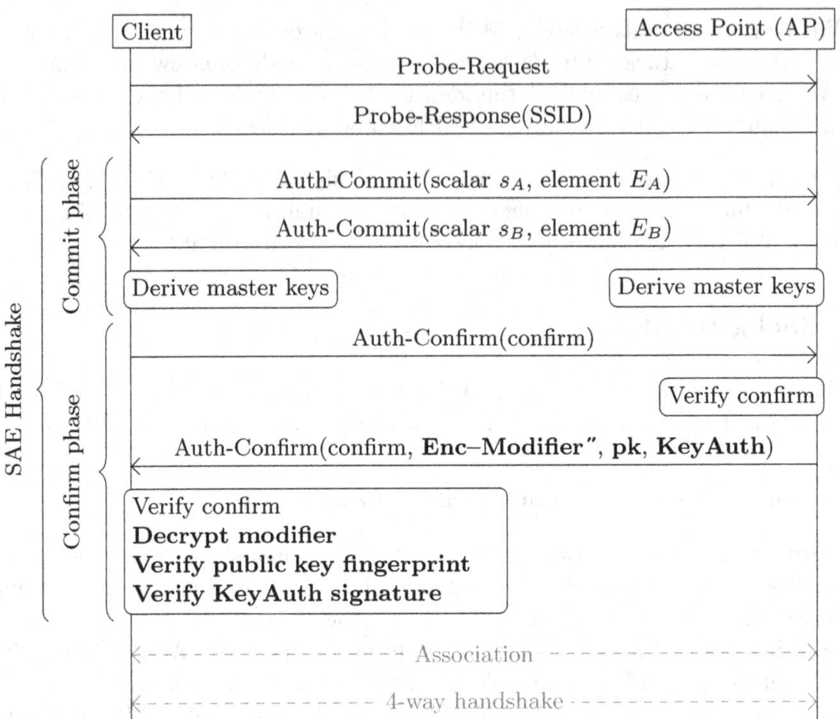


**Fig. 1.** Diagram of the SAE handshake and the extensions added by WPA3-PK. The parameters and actions shown in bold are unique to SAE-PK: these additions allow the client to verify the authenticity of the AP and assure the AP is not a rogue clone.

## 2.2 WPA3 Public Key (WPA3-PK)

In December 2020, the Wi-Fi Alliance released the SAE Public Key protocol as part of an update to the WPA3 certification [29]. We will use WPA3-PK to refer to this protocol. This protocol has as goal to improve the security of password-protected Wi-Fi hotspots and makes it infeasible for a malicious insider to create a rogue clone of a hotspot. In other words, even if an attacker has the hotspot's password, it would be infeasible to create a rogue clone of the network. The WPA3-PK protocol accomplishes this by authenticating the network using a public key and by making the password encode a fingerprint of this public key. When a client connects to the network, the AP transmits its public key $pk$ to the client in the confirm frame (see Fig. 1), and the authenticity of this public key is verified using the pre-shared WPA3-PK password. Once the public key is verified, it is used to authenticate the AP. Concretely, the AP will authenticate itself by signing the following data using its private key:

$$\text{KeyAuth} = \text{Sig}_{sk}(E_B \parallel E_A \parallel s_B \parallel s_A \parallel M \parallel pk \parallel \text{AP}_{\text{MAC}} \parallel \text{STA}_{\text{MAC}})$$

**Algorithm 1:** Create a fingerprint of an SSID and public key *pk*. We use $\text{PKHash}_{\theta,\ell}(pk, \text{SSID}, M)$ to denote the algorithm. The parameters $\theta$ and $\ell$ are dropped when clear from context.

**Input**: *pk*: Public key of the hotspot to calculate a fingerprint for.
SSID: Network name to calculate a fingerprint for.
$M$: Starting modifier, this is by default a random value.
$\theta$ : Number of internal digest bits that must be zero.
$\ell$: Fingerprint length in bits (excluding removed leading zeros).
**Returns**: Fingerprint of the given SSID and public key.

```
for i = 0 to 2^128 − 1 do
    m_i ← (M + i) mod 2^128              ▷ The modifier consists of 128 bits
    h ← Hash(SSID || m_i || pk)          ▷ m is encoded in big-endian
    if log_2(h) < 128 − θ then           ▷ Check whether the first θ bits are zero
        return L(h, θ, θ + ℓ)            ▷ Remove first θ zero bits and return result
    i ← i + 1
return false                             ▷ We should never get here in practice
```

Here *sk* represents the hotspot's private key. For our purposes, the parameters $E_A$, $E_B$, $s_A$, and $s_B$, can be treated as random values in the commit phase of the handshake. Including these parameters in the signed data ensures that the KeyAuth signature is unique for each execution of the handshake. The signature is also computed over the public key *pk*, over the MAC addresses of the AP and client, and over a modifier value $M$ that is used to generate the WPA3-PK password (see Sect. 2.3). The Elliptic Curve Digital Signature Algorithm (ECDSA) algorithm is used to create the signature, which implies that the public key *pk* must be based on elliptic curves. The client can verify the KeyAuth value using the public key *pk*, and in the next section, we describe how in turn the authenticity of the public key *pk* can be checked based on the WPA3-PK password.

### 2.3 Generation of the WPA3-PK Password

The WPA3-PK password is generated so that it can act as a secure and user-friendly fingerprint of the hotspot's public key. Note that simply using the normal fingerprint of a public key as the password would not be user-friendly, since a traditional fingerprint is the hash of the public key and this is too long. Instead, to balance security and usability, WPA3-PK generates a fingerprint of a public key as shown in Algorithm 1: The public key, along with the SSID of the hotspot, is combined with a random modifier $M$ such that the first $\theta$ bits of the following hash are zero:

$$\text{Hash}(\text{SSID} \parallel M \parallel pk) \tag{1}$$

Here $\parallel$ denotes concatenation of binary strings. Variable $M$ denotes a 32-byte integer which is incremented until this hash function returns an output whose first $\theta$ bits are zero. The modifier $M$ is encoded in big-endian, and SSID represents the binary encoding of the network name. Including the SSID in the hash input ensures that each network has a different fingerprint even when they use the same public key. The argument $pk$ represents the public key of the network and is encoded according to RFC 5480 [23]. Once a modifier has been found that results in $\theta$ leading zero bits, these first $\theta$ bits are dropped, and the next $\ell$ bits are returned. In other words, the function $L(h, \theta, N)$ in Algorithm 1 extracts bits $\theta$ to $N$ of the binary string $h$ starting from the left. The length of the public key influences the hash function that is used [29]. At the time of writing, this is either SHA2-256, SHA2-384, or SHA2-512 [3, §Table 12-1]. Algorithm 1 shows the resulting algorithm and we will represent it using the function $\text{PKHash}_{\theta,\ell}(pk, SSID, M)$.

The output from PKHash acts as a fingerprint of the public key, where the parameters $\theta$ and $\ell$ control the fingerprint's security. The values for both these parameters are derived from the parameters *Sec* and $\lambda$ as follows [29]:

$$\theta = 8 \cdot Sec \tag{2}$$

$$\ell = 19 \cdot \frac{\lambda}{4} - 5 \tag{3}$$

Allowed values for *Sec* are 3 or 5, and allowed values for $\lambda$ are 12, 16, 20, and so on [29]. For instance, when picking $Sec = 3$, the output of the hash operation in Eq. (1) must start with 24 zero bits, while with $Sec = 5$, the hash output must start with 40 zero bits. This fingerprint is then encoded into a human-readable password, where the parameter $\lambda$ corresponds to the number of characters that are required to encode the resulting password. The human-readable password also encodes the security parameter *Sec*. For the remainder of the paper, we will use the terms fingerprint and password as synonyms.

The AP will transmit the modifier $M$ and public key $pk$ to any client that connects using WPA3-PK (see Fig. 1). This allows the client to recompute the fingerprint of the given public key, SSID, and modifier, and compare the resulting fingerprint with the one encoded by the WPA3-PK password. In case these fingerprints do not match, the handshake is aborted. Note that the modifier value is encrypted with the negotiated key to ensure that the modifier remains unknown to outsiders. This is important, because if the modifier gets leaked to outsiders, then the WPA3-PK password of the network will leak (see Sect. 3.1).

### 2.4 Security Guarantees Provided by WPA3-PK

It is important that WPA3-PK is sufficiently resistant to second preimage attacks. That is, given a WPA3-PK password, it must be infeasible to find a modifier $M$ and public key $pk$ (for which the private key is known) that results in the given WPA3-PK password. To estimate the resistance against such attacks, the WPA3 specification calculates the cost of a brute-force preimage search for various security parameters $\lambda$ and *Sec*. This analysis indicates that, when targeting a network that uses the lowest allowed security setting of $\lambda = 12$ and $Sec = 3$, and when using a single hash miner capable of 50 TeraHashes per second, it would take roughly 48 CPU years to attack a WPA3-PK password [29].

**Table 1.** Different implementations of PKHash and whether they let the modifier $M$ start from a random value, and if so, which source is used to generate random numbers.

| Password generation tool | Start value of $M$ | Source of randomness |
|---|---|---|
| Hostap's sae-pk-gen | Random | Linux's `/dev/urandom/` |
| OpenSSL-based tool | Random | Router's MAC address |
| Python3 implementation | Zero | — |

We also remark that WPA3-PK can be used to secure private Wi-Fi networks. Compared to plain WPA3, using WPA3-PK has the advantage that, if an internal device is compromised, this compromised device cannot abuse the pre-shared password to create a rogue clone of the network to attack other devices.

## 3 Implementation and Network-Based Attacks

In this section, we investigate implementation risks of WPA3-PK. That is, we analyze the impact of bad randomness and study network-layer security aspects.

### 3.1 Bad Randomness Leaks the Password

**Threat Model.** In this subsection, we will assume that the adversary does not know the password of the WPA3-PK network, but wants to obtain it. This threat model corresponds to one of the design goals of WPA3-PK, namely, that the password should remain secret if it is not shared publicly. This means that in this subsection, WPA3-PK is not used to secure a hotspot, but we instead assume that WPA3-PK is used to secure a private home network.

**Flawed Randomness Risk.** To ensure that the WPA3-PK password stays secret, the modifier $M$ should start from an unpredictable value when generating the password (see Algorithm 1). In fact, the WPA3 specification states: "the Modifier is generated using a random number generator with high entropy" [29]. Using high entropy is essential because, due to the design of WPA3-PK, using low entropy randomness risks leaking the WPA3-PK password. In particular, when an adversary does not know the password of a WPA3-PK network, they can monitor the network until a legitimate client tries to connect. The adversary can then capture the public key $pk$ that is sent in plaintext in the last Auth-Confirm frame (see Fig. 1). Once the adversary has obtained the public key, the initial value of the modifier $M$ can be guessed, and the PKHash algorithm can be executed to find the WPA3-PK password of the network. It is therefore essential that a cryptographically strong random number generator is used to initialize the modifier $M$ in the PKHash algorithm, since that will prevent an adversary from guessing the (initial) value of the modifier.

**Implementation Analysis.** To investigate whether WPA3-PK implementations securely initialize the modifier $M$, we searched for open-source implementations of PKHash and studied those. More precisely, we analyzed: (1) the sae-pk-gen password generation tool included in Linux's hostap daemon; (2) an implementation of PKHash based on OpenSSL that is part of a modified dd-wrt release; and (3) a Python3 implementation of PKHash. The analyzed source code snapshots of these three tools are available on our repository [1]. Table 1 gives an overview of these three implementations and their properties.

We found that hostap's sae-pk-gen uses `/dev/urandom` to generate an initial value of $M$. Although researchers have previously identified weaknesses in older Linux implementations of `/dev/urandom` [15], it is believed to be a secure source of randomness in newer kernels. In contrast, we found that the PKHash implementation based on OpenSSL, and used in a dd-wrt fork, was using an insecure method to initialize the modifier. In particular, it used the MAC address of the router as the argument to `srand`, and then used libc's `rand` function to initialize the modifier. This means that the initial value of $M$ can be inferred by an adversary and that the resulting WPA3-PK password can be derived from the hotspot's public key. Finally, the Python3 implementation of PKHash always initialized the modifier $M$ to zero and incremented it until a valid modifier was found. This makes it trivial for an adversary to derive the WPA3-PK password when only knowing the public key of the network.

**Evaluation.** To evaluate our attack, and confirm that an adversary can infer the WPA3-PK password generated by vulnerable implementations, we generated WPA3-PK passwords using the three implementations in Table 1. The generated passwords and private keys were used to create a WPA3-PK hotspot using Linux's `hostapd` daemon. To then perform the attack and infer the network's password, we created a Python script that uses the `Scapy` library to monitor Wi-Fi frames sent by the AP. When a legitimate client connects, and the Auth-Confirm frame sent by the AP is detected, our script will extract the AP's public key from this frame (recall Fig. 1).

Once the AP's public key has been intercepted, our script runs the PKHash algorithm locally with the captured public key as input. In a first run of PKHash, the initial value of the modifier value $M$ is set to zero, to simulate the Python3 implementation. In a second run, the initial value is set based on the MAC address of the AP. All combined, this results in two potential WPA3-PK passwords. To determine whether one of these passwords is correct, we use `wpa_supplicant` to try to connect to the AP using these passwords. If one of the connections is successful, we know that the password is correct. We repeated this experiment 10 times, where each time new WPA3-PK passwords and public keys were generated, and each time our script was able to derive the password generated by the OpenSSL-based and Python3 implementation of PKHash.

### 3.2 Network-Based Attacks

**Client-to-client Attacks.** With WPA3-PK, an adversary cannot set up a rogue AP to intercept the traffic of clients. However, by default, it remains possible to intercept a victim's traffic using network-based attacks. In particular, an attacker can connect as a client and then use ARP poisoning to redirect and intercept the traffic of other users that are connected to the hotspot. To perform an ARP poisoning attack, the adversary must know the IP address of the victim, but that info can be determined by scanning the network using tools such as `nmap`.

We confirmed this attack in practice against a Linux AP running hostapd 2.10 that was configured as a WPA3-PK network, connecting to the AP using two Linux laptops, and using Scapy to perform an ARP poisoning attack. This successfully poisoned the ARP cache of both the victim client and the AP, and caused the attacker to intercept all traffic to and from the victim.

**Abusing Group Keys.** When using WPA3-PK, the group key that is used to protect broadcast and multicast Wi-Fi traffic is shared between all clients. This means that an adversary can connect to an WPA3-PK hotspot, learn the group key, and abuse this key to spoof broadcast and multicast traffic to all clients. More worrisome, previous work has shown that against many devices, it is possible to inject unicast traffic using the group key [27], worsening the impact of such an attack. Overall, we found that an adversary can abuse the group key in a WPA3-PK network to send arbitrary traffic to other clients even if client-to-client traffic was blocked by the network.

We confirmed the above attack against a Linux client that was using version 2.10 of `wpa_supplicant`. In our attack, we connected ourselves to the WPA3-PK network using a modified `wpa_supplicant` that outputs the group key. This group key was then used to inject both broadcast and unicast frames towards the victim, even though client-to-client traffic was disabled by the AP.

## 4 Precomputation Attacks and Rainbow Tables

In this section, we study improved time-memory trade-off attacks against WPA3's SAE-PK protocol, i.e., against WPA3-PK. We analyze the expected performance of a baseline attack, improve this attack using rainbow tables, and evaluate a proof-of-concept implementation of the rainbow table attack.

### 4.1 Background on Time-Memory Trade-Off Attacks

**Precomputation Attacks.** Our goal is to find a modifier $M$ and public key $pk$ that results in a given password, i.e., to perform a preimage attack. That is, we want to invert $\mathrm{PKHash}_{\theta,\ell}(pk, \mathrm{SSID}, M)$ when given a SSID, public key $pk$, and security parameters $\theta$ and $\ell$. One option is doing a brute-force search for a value $M$ that results in the desired output, but that requires either a large amount of computational power or takes a huge amount of time. When performing a preimage attack multiple times, it is typically possible to precompute information so that subsequent attacks can be carried out faster. Such time-memory trade-off attacks were first introduced by Hellman in 1980: he proposed a probabilistic method to break a block cipher that supports $2^n$ possible keys by precomputing a lookup table of $2^{2/3n}$ elements, after which recovering the key from a known plaintext takes $2^{2/3n}$ operations [13]. Another common use case for time-memory trade-off attacks is to invert a hash function.

In a time-memory trade-off attack, intermediate results are saved so that subsequent attacks are more efficient. For instance, assume we want to invert a hash function $H$, i.e., given a hash output $C$ we want to find an input $P$ such that $C = H(P)$. A naive idea is to iterate over all inputs and save *all* input and hash output pairs. However, this requires a large amount of storage. Instead, in a time-memory trade-off attack, the inputs and hash outputs are organized in chains, and only the first and last elements of each chain are saved. The chains are created by defining a reduction function $R$ that transforms a hash output into a new candidate hash input. We then define the function $f(p) = R(H(p))$ that maps an input $p$ to another input, and use this to construct a chain of inputs:

$$p_1 \xrightarrow{f(p_1)} p_2 \xrightarrow{f(p_2)} \dots \xrightarrow{f(p_{t-1})} p_t \tag{4}$$

For every chain only the first input $p_1$ and last input $p_t$ are stored. These two points are commonly called the starting point and endpoint, respectively. By changing the length $t$ of chains we will be able to trade lookup time with memory.

To find an input that results in a given hash output $C$, we first create a new (temporary) chain of inputs of length $t$ starting with $R(C)$. For every output in this temporary chain, we look up whether this input occurs as an endpoint in the precomputed table. Once an endpoint has been found, the entire chain in the precomputed table is reconstructed, which is possible since the precomputed table contains the starting input of each chain. If the recreated chain contains an input that results in the given hash output $C$, then the lookup was successful, since that means we found an input that results in the given hash output $C$. If the recreated chain does not contain the hash output $C$, then we say that a false alarm has occurred, and we continue the search until $t$ applications of $f$ are applied to $R(C)$.

**Chain Collisions.** Time-memory trade-off attacks are probabilistic: there is no guarantee that all hash inputs of a given length are contained in the table. The success probability of a preimage attack will therefore depend on the size of the precomputed table and how the table is constructed. Additionally, chains may collide with each other, meaning at some point they both generate the same (partial) chain of inputs. We call this a chain collision. To increase the success rate, and reduce the number of collisions, a common strategy is to create multiple smaller subtables that each use a (slightly) different reduction function $R$.

**Rainbow Tables and Distinguished Points.** Various improvements to time-memory trade-off attacks have been proposed over time. Two important ones are Distinguished Points (DP) and rainbow tables. The idea behind distinguished points was first mentioned by Rivest [9, p.100] and was later investigated in detail by Borst et al [7]. When using distinguished points, the number of table lookups is reduced, which is important when working with slow storage mediums or large lookup tables. Arguably the most well-known improvement is the technique of rainbow tables, which was proposed by Oechslin in 2003 [22]. The advantage of this technique is that the number of chain collisions is reduced, and that there is a reduction in the expected number of table lookups compared to the classical method of Hellman.

### 4.2 Motivation: SSID Reuse

The network's SSID influences the WPA3-PK password and thereby acts as a salt to mitigate precomputation and time-memory trade-off attacks. However, SSIDs are frequently reused by different networks, meaning it still is beneficial to perform precomputation attacks against WPA3-PK. To investigate how common SSID reuse is, we analyzed the SSID statistics provided by WiGLE [2], which at the time of our analysis contained 884 396 925 Access Points (APs). Based on this data, Fig. 2 shows how many Wi-Fi networks are represented by the most common 100 SSIDs. We can see that the most common 100 SSIDs represent almost 10% of all Wi-Fi networks worldwide. The most common SSID, `xfinitywifi`, represents 2,03% of all APs, and the top 10 SSIDs represent 5,02% of all APs. This shows that SSIDs are frequently reused and motivates our research into precomputation and time-memory trade-off attacks, since the reuse of SSIDs enables the use of a single precomputed table to attack multiple networks.

### 4.3 Baseline Precomputation Attack Against WPA3-PK

Our rainbow attack extends the time-memory trade-off attack of [26]. We therefore first introduce this baseline attack and perform a more extensive evaluation of its performance. Both attacks have as input a public key $pk$ for which we know the private key and a WPA3-PK password with parameters $\ell$ and $\theta$, i.e., a fingerprint, and then find a modifier $M$ such that $\text{PKHash}_{\theta,\ell}(pk, \text{SSID}, M)$ has as output the given fingerprint. The baseline time-memory trade-off attack works as follows [26]:

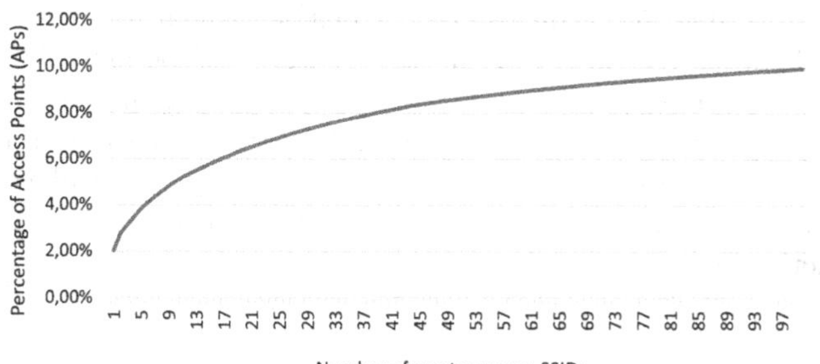


**Fig. 2.** Percentage of Access Points (APs) on WiGLE that are represented by the top most common SSIDs [2]. This excludes the empty SSID that is used to hide networks.

**Reduction Function.** The reduction function takes a fingerprint, i.e., an output of PKHash, and converts it to a modifier value $M$. The function takes the given fingerprint of $\ell$ bits, and appends it with zero bits until it has a total length of 16 bytes. With this construction, the chance of chain collisions is reduced, because the counter $m_i$ inside PKHash will then be unlikely to ever equal another fingerprint.

**Constructing Chains and Tables.** The baseline attack uses distinguished points to construct chains, which makes handling large tables more efficient [6,22]. That is, it keeps applying the reduction and PKHash function until a fingerprint with a given number of leading zero bits is encountered. This fingerprint is called a distinguished endpoint or distinguished fingerprint. The number of leading zeros of a distinguished fingerprint is represented by $d$. This implies that the internal hash output in Algorithm 1 must start with $\theta + d$ zero bits.

To construct one table, $m$ random fingerprints are picked as starting points, denoted by $p_1$ to $p_m$. For each starting point, the reduction and PKHash function, which corresponds to function $f$ in Sect. 4.1, is executed until we get a distinguished fingerprint. Function $f$ can now be written as follows:

$$p_{i,j+1} = \text{PKHash}_{\theta,\ell}\,(pk,\ \text{SSID},\ p_{i,j} \ll (32 \cdot 8 - \ell)) \tag{5}$$

Here $p_{i,j}$ is the $j$-th point in chain $i$. Each chain $i$ starts with fingerprint $p_{i,1} = p_i$. The operator $\ll$ denotes a binary left shift, and the constant $32 \cdot 8$ corresponds to the length of the modifier $M$. To detect loops in a chain, the length of a chain is limited to $t_{max}$ elements. If no distinguished fingerprint was found after $t_{max}$ applications of the function $f$, the chain is discarded.

**Storage.** For every chain $i$ we store the starting fingerprint $p_i$, the distinguished endpoint $p_{i,t}$, and the chain length $t$. By storing the chain length we can merge chain collisions and only keep the longest chain. To allow lookups of an endpoint in logarithmic time, the table is sorted based on the distinguished endpoints.

**Multiple Tables.** Using multiple smaller subtables, where each table uses a unique reduction function, reduces chain collisions which improves the success rate of table lookups and makes it easier to parallelize lookups [6,25]. One can construct a unique reduction function per table by encoding the index of the subtable into the high-order bits of the modifier $M$. After the bits that encode the table's index, the output of the previous PKHash call is placed. In other words, for subtable $r$ out of $T$ in total, the combination of the reduction and PKHash function becomes:

$$s_{table} = 32 \cdot 8 - \lceil \log_2(T) \rceil \tag{6}$$

$$s_{mod} = s_{table} - \ell \tag{7}$$

$$p_{i,j+1} = \text{PKHash}_{\theta,\ell}\,(pk,\ \text{SSID},\ (r \ll s_{table}) \mid (p_{i,j} \ll s_{mod})) \tag{8}$$

Operator $\mid$ denotes the binary OR operation and $T$ is the number of subtables.

### 4.4 Improved Analysis of the Baseline Precomputation Attack

**Table 2.** Symbols used in this paper and their meaning.

| Symbol | Description |
|---|---|
| $\lambda$ | Length of the SAE-PK password (defined by WPA3) |
| $Sec$ | Security level of the fingerprint (defined by WPA3) |
| $pk$ | Public key |
| $sk$ | Private key |
| $M$ | Modifier value used to calculate a fingerprint |
| $m$ | Number of starting points in one table |
| $r$ | Table index |
| $T$ | Number of tables |
| $B$ | Number of colors used in a table |
| $c$ | Current color |
| $\theta$ | Number of SHA2 output bits that must be zero |
| $\ell$ | Length in bits of the desired fingerprint |
| $d$ | Number of leading zeros in distinguished fingerprints |
| $t$ | Represents the (average) length of a chain |

To determine the performance of the above baseline time-memory trade-off attack, we improve its proof-of-concept implementation, evaluate its resulting performance, and compare this more thorough experimental evaluation with the theoretical estimates of [26]. Note that in the theoretical analysis, chain merges are ignored to simplify the analysis at the cost of some reduction in precision [25, §8].

**Experiments.** We started with the proof-of-concept implementation of [26] and carried out a more extensive evaluation over more parameters. While doing so, we fixed a bug in the lookup function in the proof-of-concept implementation that caused the endpoint in a chain to be overwritten, which caused the success rate of table lookups to be underestimated. When then ran simulations with the WPA3-PK security parameters $\theta = 8$ and $\ell = 24$, used $d = 8$ for distinguished fingerprints, $t_{max} = 2^{11}$ as the maximum chain length, used $m = 2^8$ starting points per table, and $T = 2^8$ individual tables. Based on a simulation of 400 password lookups, on average one lookup required $2^{16.42}$ calls to PKHash, and the success rate of a password lookup was 46.5%. This is a substantially higher success rate compared to the analysis in [26], which we attribute to the bug fix in the proof-of-concept implementation.

We also further improved the proof-of-concept code to support arbitrary bit lengths for the parameters $\theta$, $\ell$, and $d$. This enabled a more thorough performance

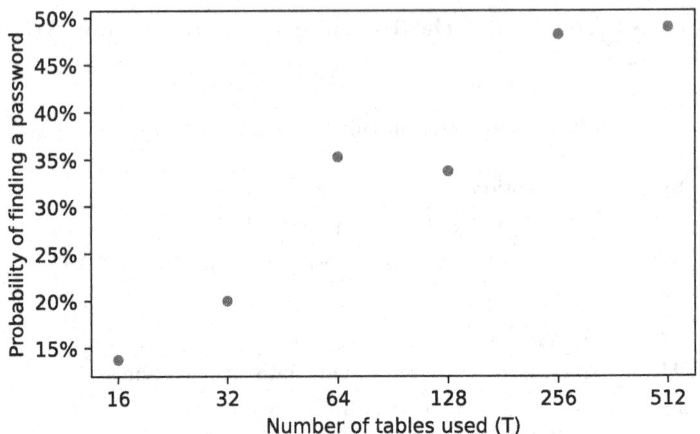


**Fig. 3.** Performance of lookup tables for the baseline time-memory trade-off attack. The x-axis denotes the number of subtables T. The total number of starting points across all subtables is identical in each experiment. In other words, when employing fewer subtables, each one contains a higher number of chains, i.e., starting points.

evaluation while still ensuring that simulations terminate within practical time. In particular, in our second set of experiments, we set $\theta = 0$, $\ell = 24$, and $d = 8$. The number of subtables $T$ was set to 16, 32, ..., 512. The number of chains $m$ was chosen so the table generation covered on average $2^\ell$ hash inputs. That is, $T = \frac{2^\ell}{2^d \cdot m}$, which ensures the generation time of the table is equal under all parameter combinations, and ensures that all subtables combined have the same size, resulting in a fair comparison between the different tables. For every generated table, we looked up 400 random passwords, and measured how many lookups were successful. The results of this experiment are shown in Fig. 3. We can clearly see that using different smaller subtables, each with their own unique reduction function, improves the performance of the time-memory trade-off attack.

**Precomputation Complexity.** We can compare our observed performance with the predicted theoretic performance calculated in [25,26]:

1. **Success rate.** The success rate of finding an WPA3-PK passphrase in a single table equals $SR \approx \frac{s(\gamma m)}{2^\ell}$ [25,26]. In case we use $T$ different tables, where each table has a different reduction function, the probability of a successful lookup is $PS(T) = 1 - (1 - SR)^T$ [25].

   For example, when using $T = 2^8$ tables, the expected success rate is 50%. In practice, we saw a success rate of 46.5% in the first experiment and 48.25% in the second experiment. As another example, for $T = 2^4$ tables the predicted success rate is 16%, and the observed success rate is 13.75% (see Fig. 3). Overall, the observed success rates are in line with the predicted rates.

2. **Lookup cost.** The processing complexity, i.e., the expected number of calls to PKHash when looking up an element over all $T$ subtables, can be estimated using $T \cdot \beta$. Here $\beta$ is the average length of a chain, which can be approximated by $2^d$. This assumes that there are no false alarms when looking up a password [25].

   For example, when using $T = 2^8$ tables, the expected lookup cost consists of $2^{16}$ calls to PKHash. In practice, we observe $2^{16.42}$ calls to PKHash in the first experiment, and $2^{16.44}$ in the second experiment. When using $T = 2^4$ tables, we would expect $2^{12}$ calls to PKHash, and in practice we observe $2^{13.28}$ calls per lookup. We conjecture that this higher time complexity is due to false alarms during a password lookup, e.g., with $T = 2^4$, on average there were 12 false alarms per lookup.

All combined, the results of our experiments are in line with the predicted success rates. The above also confirms the prediction of [26] that breaking WPA3-PK under its lowest security setting, namely when $Sec = 3$ and $\lambda = 12$, would require an amortized computational cost of less than 12 d, where a lookup in the precomputed table would have a success rate of close to 50%.

### 4.5 Rainbow Tables for WPA3-PK

To increase the success rate of a password lookup, we will combine the above table construction with rainbow tables. In a traditional rainbow table, the reduction function $R$ is (slightly) changed at every point in the chain to reduce chain collisions [16,22]. In our approach, we will change the reduction function once a distinguished fingerprint is encountered:

$$p_{1,1} \xrightarrow{f_1(p_{1,1})} \dots \xrightarrow{f_1(p_{1,t-1})} p_{1,t} \xrightarrow{f_2(p_{1,t})} p_{2,1} \xrightarrow{f_2(p_{2,1})} \dots \xrightarrow{f_2(p_{2,t-1})} p_{2,t} \quad (9)$$

Here function $f_1(p) = R_1(H(p))$ is applied until we get a fingerprint that starts with $d$ zero bits, which is the same as a distinguished fingerprint in our previous table. Once a distinguished fingerprint $p_{1,t}$ is found, we switch to a different reduction function $R_2$ meaning we apply the function $f_2 = R_2(H(p))$, until we obtain another fingerprint with $d$ leading zero bits, and so on. We say that each reduction function $R_c$ uses a different color $c$. The total number of colors $B$ used in a chain is a parameter of the table. Analogous to changing the reduction function for every table $r$, we create a new reduction function per color by encoding the color $c$ in the modifier $M$. All combined, the function $f_{c,r}(p_{i,j})$ for color $c$ in subtable $r$ becomes:

$$s_{color} = 32 \cdot 8 - \lceil \log_2(B) \rceil \quad (10)$$

$$s_{table} = s_{color} - \lceil \log_2(T) \rceil \quad (11)$$

$$s_{mod} = s_{table} - \ell \quad (12)$$

$$p_i^{j+1} = \text{PKHash}_{\theta,\ell}(pk, \text{SSID}, (c \ll s_{color}) \mid (r \ll s_{table}) \mid (p_{i,j} \ll s_{mod})) \quad (13)$$

Here $c$ represents the current color used in the reduction function, $B$ the number of colors used, $r$ the table index, and $T$ the number of tables. To detect possible loops in a chain, we discard a chain if no distinguished point was found after $2^{d+3}$ applications of $f_{c,r}$.

### 4.6 Rainbow Table: Performance Experiments

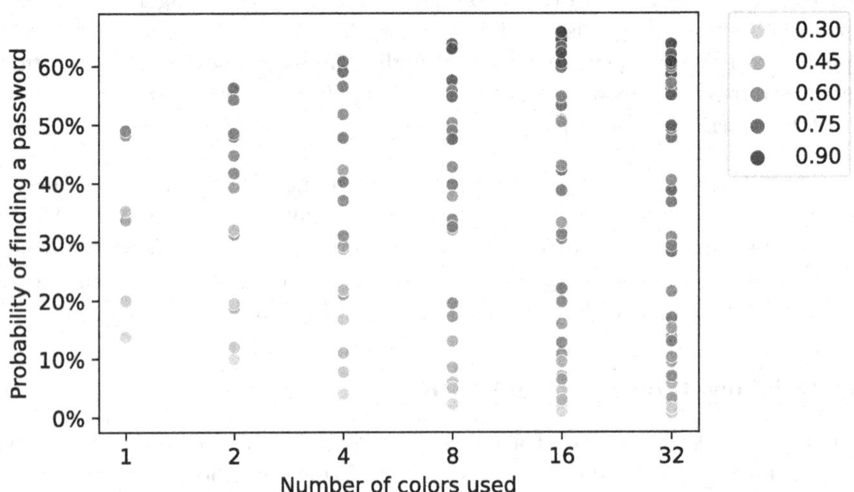


**Fig. 4.** Performance of lookup tables in function of the number of colors used, number of subtables, and the number of chains in a subtable (see Sect. 4.6 for details). Each point represents a lookup table containing at most $2^{16}$ chains. The x-axis denotes the number of colors in a table and the y-axis the resulting password lookup success. The hue of the point represents the normalized, in log scale, average number of table accesses when looking up a password, where the maximum number of table lookups was 10659.

We implemented a proof-of-concept of our rainbow table technique to estimate the success probability of password lookups. To ensure simulations finish within practical time, we set $\theta = 0$ and $\ell = 24$. Our tool has as parameters the number of leading bits $d$ of a distinguished point, the number of colors $B$, the number of subtables $T$, and the number of chains $m$ in a subtable. Note that when using $B = 1$, meaning only one color is used, the resulting table is equivalent to the tables constructed in the previous two sections.

We did simulations with $B \in \{1, 2, 4, 8, 2^4, 2^5\}$, $d$ ranging from 0 to 8, and $m \in \{2^7, \ldots, 2^{12}, 2^{13}\}$. The number of subtables $T$ was chosen so the table generation covered on average $2^\ell$ hashes. That is, $T = \frac{2^\ell}{2^d \cdot B \cdot m}$, which ensures the generation time is equal under all parameter combinations, ensuring a fair comparison between the created tables. Note that depending on the values for

$T$ and $m$ the resulting tables may be of different size. For every combination of parameters, our tool created the rainbow table, then performed 400 random lookups in the table, and finally wrote the resulting statistics to a JSON file. Figure 4 shows the performance of the resulting lookup tables for tables that store $2^{16}$ chains or less. This limit for the number of chains over all subtables effectively puts a limit on the size of the lookup table, further ensuring a fair comparison. We observe that for tables of similar size, and with a fixed table generation time, the usage of colors increases the attack success probability. For instance, the highest success probability over all parameter combinations with one color is 49%, with two colors this increases to 56%, and with 16 colors it reaches its maximum of 65%.

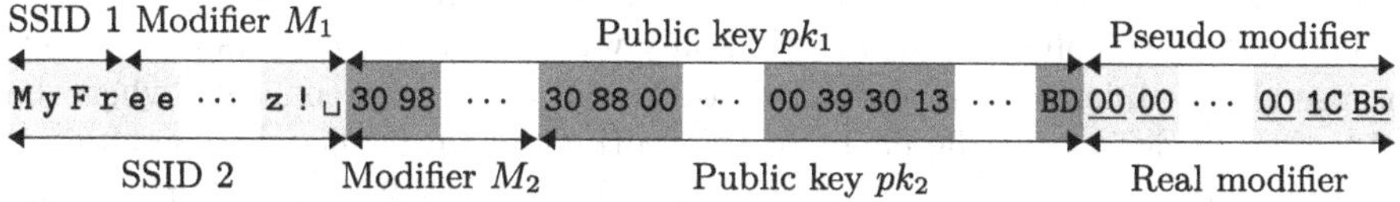


**Fig. 5.** Input given to PKHash such that the SAE-PK password for both SSIDs is identical. The top shows how this input is split into the SSID, modifier, and public key for the first network. The bottom shows how this input is mapped to the SSID, modifier, and public key for the second network.

The increased success probability of using different colors comes at the cost of more table accesses during the lookup of a password. For instance, for the highest success probability for each color, the number of table accesses equal 370 for 1 color, 706 for 2 colors, and 5091 for 16 colors.

# 5 Multi-network Password Collisions

In this section, we propose a new method to create password collisions, that is, we create networks with different SSIDs that have the same WPA3-PK password. This is non-trivial because the SSID acts as a salt when calculating the password. We also create multi-network password collisions, where multiple SSIDs have the same WPA3-PK password. These password collisions allow an attacker to create a single precomputed table that can be used to attack multiple networks.

## 5.1 Constructing Password Collisions

To create WPA3-PK password collisions, we ensure that the input to the underlying hash function of PKHash, i.e., Eq. 1 in Algorithm 1, is identical for different SSIDs [26]. The core idea to achieve this is that an attacker can still change the length of the SSID *after* the password has already been generated [26]. This idea is illustrated in Fig. 5, where the input to PKHash is given two interpretations. In the first interpretation, the SSID equals `MyFr`, the modifier equals the binary encoding of `eeWifi␣2.4␣GHz!␣`, and the public key starts with the bytes `30 90` and ends with the byte `BD`. In the second interpretation, the SSID equals `MyFreeWifi␣2.4␣GHz!␣`, the modifier equals the first 16 bytes of the public key $pk_1$, and the public key starts in the middle of $pk_1$ with the bytes `30 88` and ends with the byte `BD` (more on this later).

To create a valid WPA3-PK password, we need to be able to freely modify certain bytes to ensure that the internal hash operation in PKHash starts with enough zeros. However, as shown in Fig. 5, the modifier $M$ cannot be freely changed anymore because it now overlaps with the SSID or public key of the other network. To still be able to freely change bytes in the input of PKHash, we will not change the encoding of the public key as in [26], but we will instead include a pseudo modifier after the public key. This pseudo modifier can be changed until the hash output starts with sufficiently many zeros.

Our password collision construction only works if the client does not remove the pseudo modifier that is appended to the public key. Fortunately, when the public key $pk$ is sent to the client in the Auth-Confirm frame, the encoding of the public key is treated as an opaque data blob [3, §9.4.2.180]. This means we can add trailing data after the public key without the client noticing this.

We tested whether `wpa_supplicant`, which is the only open-source Wi-Fi client that supports WPA3-PK, accepts trailing data after the public key. This client supports two crypto libraries when using WPA3-PK, namely OpenSSL and WolfSSL, and in both cases trailing data *after* the public key was accepted and included in the input given to PKHash. This confirms that we can use the structure in Fig. 5 to build password collisions, where the pseudo modifier can be changed until the hash output starts with sufficiently many zero bits.

All combined, we can now build a precomputed table where the construction in Fig. 5 is used as the input to the internal hash function in PKHash. Here the pseudo modifier contains the argument $M$ of PKHash. An adversary can then use the resulting table to attack both SSIDs.

### 5.2 Public Key Embedding and Trailing Data

One obstacle when creating a password collision is that public key $pk_1$ must be constructed so that public key $pk_2$ starts in the middle of it, i.e., we must be able to embed one public key into another. To achieve this, we exploit a similar parsing vulnerability as the one in [18,26], namely that arbitrary data can be encoded in variable length fields. In particular, when encoding a length field, if the length is smaller or equal to 127, the length is directly encoded as a byte. For example, the byte `0x10` encodes the length 16. Otherwise, if the length is 128 or higher, the high-order bit of the first byte is set, and the other low-order bits denote how many subsequent bytes encode the actual length. For example, the two bytes `0x81 0xFF` represent the length 255. We can embed arbitrary data inside this variable length encoding by using the following construction:

```
8C XX XX XX XX 00 00 00 00 00 00 00 39
```

The first byte denotes that the next 12 bytes will be used to encode the length field. However, most implementations can handle at most 64-bit integers. As a result, only the last 8 bytes of the length field matter, and the 4 bytes represented by `XX` are effectively ignored due to an integer overflow.

We can now encode the *start* of a public key into the variable length field of another public key. In particular, we can put the bytes `30 88` in place of the last two `XX` bytes in our example. Here `30` encodes the start of the public key and `88` denotes a variable length field where the length is represented using the next 8 bytes. After this length field in the byte sequence, both public keys are aligned, meaning that the remaining bytes will encode the same public key.

### 5.3 Accepting Trailing Data Inside the Public Key

**Table 3.** Behavior of crypto libraries regarding the parsing of public keys. The second column contains the tested function, the third whether it returns the number of bytes read, and the fourth column whether trailing data is allowed in the ASN.1 sequence.

| Library | SubjectPublicKeyInfo parser | Bytes read | Extra data |
|---|---|---|---|
| OpenSSL | `d2i_PUBKEY` | Yes | Rejected |
| WolfSSL | `wc_EccPublicKeyDecode` | Yes | Accepted |
| GnuTLS | `gnutls_pubkey_import` | No | Rejected |
| MatrixSSL | `psParseSubjectPublicKeyInfo` | No | Accepted |

An alternative to putting the pseudo modifier as trailing data *after* the public key, is to put it in the *end* of the public key itself. More precisely, the encoding of the public key is defined using ASN.1 as follows:

```
SubjectPublicKeyInfo  ::=  SEQUENCE  {
   algorithm           AlgorithmIdentifier,
   subjectPublicKey  BIT STRING
   // Add trailing data, i.e., the pseudo modifier M, here  }
```

The idea is that we add trailing data after the subjectPublicKey, but inside the SubjectPublicKeyInfo sequence. Out of the 4 TLS libraries we tested, WolfSSL and MatrixSSL accepted trailing data in this location, and this did not interfere with the parsing of the public key. This was tested by calling the public key parsing functions shown in Table 3, where for MatrixSSL the functions `getEcPubKey` and `PsParseSubjectPublicKeyInfo` were combined to parse the public key.

### 5.4 Multi-network Password Collisions

Apart from creating a WPA3-PK password collision for two SSIDs, we can also create a collision for multiple SSIDs. To accomplish this, we assume that every SSID is a prefix or extension of another SSID, and that each SSID differs in length from all other SSIDs by at least two characters. This, for instance, allows us to construct collisions for the following sets of SSIDs:

$$\{ \texttt{MyFreeWifi␣2.4␣GHz!␣}, \texttt{MyFreeWifi␣2.4␣GHz}, \ldots, \texttt{MyFree}, \texttt{MyFr} \}$$

The maximum difference in length between the longest and shortest SSID is 16 characters. This limitation is a result of having to use the 16-byte modifier $M$ to ensure that different SSIDs still result in the same hash input (recall Fig. 5).

When constructing the collision, we use the same format as in Fig. 5 where a pseudo modifier $M$ is placed after the public key. However, the variable length fields of the public keys are now constructed as shown in Fig. 6. The idea is that, as long as the public key starts on one of the underlined bytes, then all the remaining bytes will be ignored until the actual public key starts. This means a valid public key can start at multiple locations, which in turn means multiple SSID lengths will result in a valid starting position of the public key.

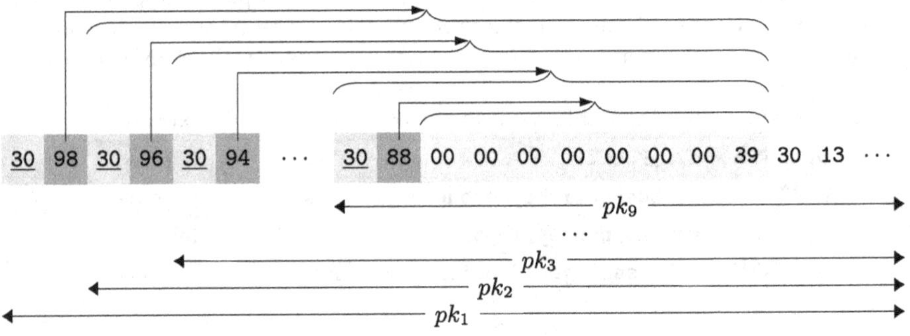


**Fig. 6.** Structure of the variable length fields in a multi-network password collision. The underlined bytes represent the start of a public key. The red bytes encode the size of the variable length field. The green bytes encode the actual length of the remaining public key bytes, and all preceding length bytes are ignored due to integer overflows. (Color figure online)

We created a script to create multi-network password collisions [1]. It takes as input a private key, the longest SSID that we want to be part of the collision, and the security parameter *Sec* of the resulting WPA3-PK password. The tool will then create collisions for all shorter SSIDs in steps of two characters.

We also created a modified AP that advertises our constructed public key along with the given SSID. When tested against a client that is vulnerable to the same parsing flexibility as in [18,26], the public key was accepted, and the client could use the same WPA3-PK password to connect to all the different SSIDs.

## 6 Defenses and Discussion

In this section, we discuss possible defenses against all our attacks and propose updates to the WPA3-PK standard.

### 6.1 Handling Bad Randomness: Encrypting the Public Key

To prevent bad randomness from leaking the password, the AP should send the public key to the client in an encrypted manner. This can easily be done: the AP already encrypts the modifier $M$ when sending it to the client (recall Fig. 1). The AP can use the same encryption operation to also encrypt the public key.

When the client uses the correct password to connect, they can decrypt and obtain the public key, and then verify the authenticity of the public key. In case the client is not using the correct key, the confirm message in the Auth-Confirm frame is invalid, and the client will drop the frame before trying to decrypt the public key. All combined, a legitimate client will still be able to obtain the public key, while it will remain hidden from an adversary. When adopting this approach, it is no longer possible for an adversary to derive the WPA3-PK password, even when the modifier $M$ was initialized in a predictable manner.

### 6.2 Preventing Network-Layer Attacks

Our network-based attacks can be prevented by: (1) blocking all types of client-to-client communication [4, §5.1]; and by (2) using the Downstream Group-Addressed Forwarding (DGAF) Disable feature of Passpoint [4, §5.2], which effectively disables the use of the group key in Wi-Fi networks.

### 6.3 Mitigating Time-Memory Trade-Off Attacks

To mitigate time-memory trade-off attacks in a backwards-compatible manner, networks can use a WPA3-PK password of at least $\lambda = 16$ characters or use a security parameter of $Sec = 5$. This makes it too costly to construct a precomputed table. Alternatively, to prevent time-memory trade-off attacks, the user can scan a QR code to learn the precise public key instead of only its fingerprint. Additionally, network administrators can decide to use a unique SSID, since adversaries are less likely to create a precomputed table for unique SSIDs.

### 6.4 Preventing Password Collisions: Committing to an SSID Length

To prevent an adversary from constructing password collisions, the input given to the hash function inside PKHash should be updated to start with a single byte that represents the length of the SSID. This forces an attacker to commit to a specific SSID length when constructing the precomputed time-memory trade-off table, or the rainbow table, and thereby prevents our WPA3-PK password collision attacks. Unfortunately, this change requires a modification to the protocol. A backwards-compatible mitigation is to more strictly parse the public key and to only allow a single possible encoding of the public key.

## 7 Related Work

This paper builds upon our previous preliminary analysis of WPA3-PK [26], and also investigates network-based attacks, studies practical implementation risks of the password generation algorithm, more accurately evaluates the baseline time-memory trade-off attack, proposes rainbow table attacks, and explores new techniques to construct multi-network password collisions.

The predecessor of WPA3, namely WPA2, was quickly shown to be susceptible to offline dictionary attacks [20]. Internally, WPA2 employs the PBKDF2 algorithm to derive a Pairwise Master Key (PMK) from the combination of the password and SSID. This resulting PMK serves as the input for the WPA2 4-way handshake, where the PMK, along with two random nonces, are mixed to generate a fresh session key. An adversary can intercept the 4-way handshake and then perform a brute-force attack to determine the password that results in the correct session key. However, due to the inclusion of two randomly generated 32-byte nonces in the session key derivation, performing a time-memory trade-off attack against the 4-way handshake is not possible. Nonetheless, given the slow nature of offline brute-forcing attempts on personal computers, lookup tables were generated to speed up the brute-force attacks against WPA2's 4-way handshake [24]. By using these precomputed tables, one can avoid executing the computationally intensive PBKDF2 hash that maps an SSID and password to the corresponding PMK. Initially, these tables covered the top 1 000 SSIDs using a dictionary of 172 000 possible passwords, which was subsequently expanded to a dictionary containing one million words. The resulting lookup tables occupied 7 GB and 33 GB of storage space. Due to the increased adoption of GPU-based password-cracking methods, the demand for such lookup tables has waned.

Regarding the security of WPA3, researchers quickly showed that it was vulnerable to timing attacks [28]. Although backwards-compatible defenses were proposed, not all implementations properly implemented these defenses [5].

Flexibilities in parsing public keys were previously abused to attack RSA [10]. Related to this, it was also discovered that some libraries accept arbitrary parameters in the algorithm identifier [8].

Hellman introduced time-memory trade-off attacks [13] and Oechslin improved them using the rainbow construction [22]. Using distinguished points to perform time-memory trade-off attacks was first proposed by Rivest [9] and later worked out by Borst et al. [7]. Nohl combined the technique of rainbow tables with distinguished points to break the GSM A5/1 cipher, where this combination was important to handle large lookup tables in practice [21], and the generation of these tables was later improved by using FPGAs [17].

## 8 Conclusion

Our security analysis of WPA3-PK revealed that, when using this protocol in practice, it is important to also consider implementation and network-layer attacks. In particular, implementations must use a secure random number generator and clients must be properly isolated from each other at the network layer.

When using the weakest allowed WPA3-PK password, we demonstrated that time-memory trade-off attacks, including the creation of rainbow tables, are on the verge of practicality. These attacks enable an adversary to perform a preimage attack, i.e., to find a public and private key that result in a given WPA3-PK password. To mitigate these attacks, we recommend setting the parameter *Sec* to 5, or using a WPA3-PK password of at least $\lambda = 16$ characters. This is especially important when using a common SSID name for the network.

**Acknowledgements.** This research is partially funded by the Research Fund KU Leuven and by the Flemish Research Programme Cybersecurity.

## References


1. https://github.com/vanhoefm/acns-wpa3-pk-sae
2. WiGLE: Statistics: SSID/manufacturer. https://web.archive.org/web/20220520222830/wigle.net/csv/ssid.csv (Accessed 20 May 2022 )
3. 802.11, I.S: Wireless LAN Medium Access Control (MAC) and Physical Layer (PHY) Spec (2020)
4. Alliance, W.F.: Hotspot 2.0 Specification Ver. 3.1 (2019)
5. de Almeida Braga, D., Fouque, P.A., Sabt, M.: Dragonblood is still leaking: practical cache-based side-channel in the wild. In: ACSAC (2020)
6. Borst, J.: Block ciphers: design, analysis and side-channel analysis. Ph.D. thesis, KU Leuven, Leuven, Belgium (2001)
7. Borst, J., Preneel, B., Vandewalle, J.: On the time-memory tradeoff between exhaustive key search and table precomputation. In: Symposium on Information Theory in the Benelux, pp. 111–118. Technische Universiteit Delft (1998)
8. Chau, S.Y., Yahyazadeh, M., Chowdhury, O., Kate, A., Li, N.: Analyzing semantic correctness with symbolic execution: a case study on PKCS# 1 v1.5 signature verification. In: NDSS (2019)
9. Denning, D.E., Denning, P.J.: Data security. ACM Comput. Surv. (CSUR) **11**(3), 227–249 (1979)
10. Finney, H.: Bleichenbacher's RSA signature forgery based on implementation error (2006). https://mailarchive.ietf.org/arch/msg/openpgp/5rnE9ZRN1AokBVj3VqblGlP63QE/ (Accessed 21 November 2021 )
11. Gonzales, H., Bauer, K., Lindqvist, J., McCoy, D., Sicker, D.: Practical defenses for evil twin attacks in 802.11. In: GLOBECOM (2010)
12. Harkins, D.: Simultaneous authentication of equals: a secure, password-based key exchange for mesh networks. In: The Second International Conference on Sensor Technologies and Applications (SENSORCOMM), pp. 839–844 (Aug 2008)
13. Hellman, M.: A cryptanalytic time-memory trade-off. IEEE Trans. Inf. Theory **26**(4), 401–406 (1980)
14. Hendershot, T.S.: Towards Using Certificate-Based Authentication as a Defense Against Evil Twins in 802.11 Networks. Master's thesis, Brigham Young University (2016)
15. Heninger, N., Durumeric, Z., Wustrow, E., Halderman, J.A.: Mining your Ps and Qs: detection of widespread weak keys in network devices. In: USENIX Security, pp. 205–220 (2012)

16. Hong, J., Jeong, K.C., Kwon, E.Y., Lee, I.S., Ma, D.: Variants of the distinguished point method for cryptanalytic time memory trade-offs. In: International Conference on Information Security Practice and Experience (2008)
17. Kalenderi, M., Pnevmatikatos, D., Papaefstathiou, I., Manifavas, C.: Breaking the GSM A5/1 cryptography algorithm with rainbow tables and high-end FPGAS. In: FPL (2012)
18. Langley, A.: PKCS# 1 signature validation (Sep 2014). https://www.imperialviolet.org/2014/09/26/pkcs1.html (Accessed 21 November 2021 )
19. Lee, H., Won, D.: Prevention of exponential equivalence in simple password exponential key exchange (speke). Symmetry **7**(3), 1587–1594 (2015)
20. Moskowitz, R.: Weakness in passphrase choice in WPA interface (2003). https://wifinetnews.com/archives/2003/11/weakness_in_passphrase_choice_in_wpa_interface.html (Accessed 26 December 2021)
21. Nohl, K.: Attacking phone privacy, pp. 1–6. Black Hat, USA (2010)
22. Oechslin, P.: Making a faster cryptanalytic time-memory trade-off. In: Boneh, D. (ed.) CRYPTO 2003. LNCS, vol. 2729, pp. 617–630. Springer, Heidelberg (2003). https://doi.org/10.1007/978-3-540-45146-4_36
23. Polk, T., Housley, R., Turner, S., Brown, D.R.L., Yiu, K.: Elliptic Curve Cryptography Subject Public Key Information. RFC 5480 (Mar 2009). https://doi.org/10.17487/RFC5480,https://rfc-editor.org/rfc/rfc5480.txt
24. RenderMan, Wright, J., Thorn, D., H1kari, T.: Church of wifi WPA-PSK lookup tables (2006). https://www.renderlab.net/projects/WPA-tables/ (Accessed 26 December 2021)
25. Standaert, F.-X., Rouvroy, G., Quisquater, J.-J., Legat, J.-D.: A time-memory tradeo. using distinguished points: new analysis & FPGA results. In: Kaliski, B.S., Koç, K., Paar, C. (eds.) CHES 2002. LNCS, vol. 2523, pp. 593–609. Springer, Heidelberg (2003). https://doi.org/10.1007/3-540-36400-5_43
26. Vanhoef, M.: A time-memory trade-off attack on WPA3's SAE-PK. In: Proceedings of the 9th ACM ASIA Public-Key Cryptography Workshop. ACM (2022)
27. Vanhoef, M., Piessens, F.: Predicting, decrypting, and abusing WPA2/802.11 group keys. In: USENIX Security, pp. 673–688 (2016)
28. Vanhoef, M., Ronen, E.: Dragonblood: analyzing the Dragonfly handshake of WPA3 and EAP-pwd. In: IEEE Security & Privacy (SP). IEEE (2020)
29. Wi-Fi Alliance: WPA3 specification version 3.0 (Dec 2020). https://www.wi-fi.org/file/wpa3-specification (Accessed 20 November 2021)

# When and How to Aggregate Message Authentication Codes on Lossy Channels?

Eric Wagner[1,2(✉)], Martin Serror[1], Klaus Wehrle[2], and Martin Henze[3,1]

[1] Cyber Analysis and Defense, Fraunhofer FKIE, Wachtberg, Germany
{eric.wagner,martin.serror}@fkie.fraunhofer.de

[2] Communication and Distributed Systems, RWTH Aachen University, Aachen, Germany
wehrle@comsys.rwth-aachen.de

[3] Security and Privacy in Industrial Cooperation, RWTH Aachen University, Aachen, Germany
henze@spice.rwth-aachen.de

**Abstract.** Aggregation of message authentication codes (MACs) is a proven and efficient method to preserve valuable bandwidth in resource-constrained environments: Instead of appending a long authentication tag to each message, the integrity protection of multiple messages is aggregated into a single tag. However, while such aggregation saves bandwidth, a single lost message typically means that authentication information for multiple messages cannot be verified anymore. With the significant increase of bandwidth-constrained lossy communication, as applications shift towards wireless channels, it thus becomes paramount to study the impact of packet loss on the diverse MAC aggregation schemes proposed over the past 15 years to assess when and how to aggregate message authentication. Therefore, we empirically study all relevant MAC aggregation schemes in the context of lossy channels, investigating achievable goodput improvements, the resulting verification delays, processing overhead, and resilience to denial-of-service attacks. Our analysis shows the importance of carefully choosing and configuring MAC aggregation, as selecting and correctly parameterizing the right scheme can, e.g., improve goodput by 39% to 444%, depending on the scenario. However, since no aggregation scheme performs best in all scenarios, we provide guidelines for network operators to select optimal schemes and parameterizations suiting specific network settings.

**Keywords:** Message Authentication Code · MAC Aggregation · IoT

## 1 Introduction

With the proliferation of the (industrial) Internet of Things (IoT), more and more battery-operated devices, such as sensors and actuators, rely on wireless communications. Consequently, the number of devices sharing the same transmission medium (with a fixed capacity) is growing, imposing increasingly


C. Pöpper and L. Batina (Eds.): ACNS 2024, LNCS 14584, pp. 241–264, 2024.
https://doi.org/10.1007/978-3-031-54773-7_10

stringent bandwidth constraints on IoT applications [29]. At the same time, wireless communication further amplifies the need to adequately secure transmitted messages [26], most notably to ensure the integrity of transmitted critical information [8], which would have prevented *e.g.*, the 2015 and 2016 cyberattacks on the Ukrainian power grid [33]. However, establishing integrity protection requires additional bandwidth to transmit authentication tags, thus conflicting with the already hard-to-reach constraints of IoT communication. Therefore, a vital research topic for industry and academia centers around the question of how to use the shared limited transmission resources efficiently and still provide adequate security [25].

As a result, many efforts across protocol stacks have been proposed to reduce bandwidth overhead. Prominent examples include 6LoWPAN header compression [20] or, more recently, the record layer headers of DTLS 1.3 [22] and Compact TLS 1.3 [21]. Such protocol improvements can however not address the inherent overhead necessary to provide integrity protection. Considering, *e.g.*, desirable 128-bit security requires the integration of a 16-byte authentication tag into the message's payload. Moreover, since (industrial) IoT protocols such as IEEE 802.15.4, LoRaWAN, or Bluetooth Low Energy often rely on short messages, such Message Authentication Codes (MACs) typically occupy a significant portion of each message and, in some cases, do not even fit [18].

For at least 15 years, the well-established and time-proven concept of MAC aggregation has been known to alleviate these limitations [14]. The idea is simple yet effective: Instead of protecting the integrity of each message individually, a single authentication tag is responsible for protecting the integrity of multiple messages. Given a reliable channel, this approach works flawlessly and can be reduced to a trade-off between saved bandwidth and the verification delay for received messages: Aggregating integrity protection of more and more messages reduces the induced overhead until it becomes negligible but implies that the receiver has to wait for the reception of all messages affected by the aggregation before being able to check their integrity, resulting in significant delays if too many authentication tags are aggregated.

Over the years, different MAC aggregation schemes have been proposed to address weaknesses [11,13,15], split authentication tags over multiple messages [18], or provide progressive security guarantees [3,17,31]. And while various implementations of security concepts, such as message authentication [28], have been evaluated and compared by literature, such analyses of MAC aggregation schemes in realistic wireless, and thus lossy, settings are practically nonexistent. Most importantly, current evaluations of MAC aggregation schemes neglect that losing a single message from a set of messages with aggregated authentication tags may have cascading effects depending on the chosen MAC aggregation scheme. This phenomenon becomes increasingly relevant as more and more communication transitions to low-bandwidth wireless, and thus lossy, channels in a diverse set of applications such as smart cities, underwater communication, or the (industrial) IoT [9]. Thus, MAC aggregation is arguably becoming even more critical for lossy channels than for its initial setting of reliable communication. However, research, thus far, did not provide sufficient address under which circumstances MAC aggregation on lossy channels is sensible and how to unlock its full potential. This knowledge is, however, crucial to optimally utilize scarce bandwidth in wireless scenarios with an ever-growing number of participating devices.

To address these shortcomings, this paper addresses the hitherto neglected analysis of the performance of relevant MAC aggregation schemes in the presence of lossy channels. We consider realistic wireless (industrial) IoT communication scenarios, which suffer from scarce transmission resources and significant packet losses, where we compare the performance of existing MAC aggregation schemes. Our analysis is thus a valuable contribution for security practitioners and researchers: On the one hand, it allows identifying suitable aggregation schemes depending on the considered scenario, and on the other hand, it reveals current shortcomings, which lay the foundation for identifying more effective approaches. Ultimately, we want to answer the questions of when MAC aggregation is sensible on lossy channels and how this aggregation should be performed by making the following contributions:

- We investigate the achievable goodput improvements of all MAC aggregation scheme known to us under various parameterizations in synthetic and real-world scenarios (Sect. 3 and Sect. 4);
- We further analyze the impact of MAC aggregation on decisive factors such as verification delay, processing times, memory cost, and the susceptibility to denial-of-service attacks (Sect. 5); and
- Finally, we provide actionable guidelines to help in deciding when and how current MAC aggregation schemes are best deployed (Sect. 6).

**Availability Statement.** To help in the decision process of which, if any, MAC aggregation scheme should be deployed in a concrete scenario, our tool to compare MAC aggregations schemes in concrete scenarios is available at: https://github.com/fkie-cad/mac-aggregation-analysis-tool.

## 2 MAC Aggregation on Lossy Channels

Achieving integrity protection is a significant challenge in bandwidth-constrained environments. Even the tiniest message requires an authentication tag of several bytes (e.g., 16 bytes for 128-bit security), thus occupying considerable space in each message. MAC aggregation schemes, as presented in this section, try to alleviate this overhead by distributing the burden of authentication over multiple messages. In the following, we first define MACs (Sect. 2.1) before formally introducing the concept of MAC aggregation (Sect. 2.2). To conclude, we introduce the existing MAC aggregation schemes (Sect. 2.3) and motivate research into their applicability in lossy conditions (Sect. 2.4).

### 2.1 Message Authentication Codes

Message Authentication Codes (MACs) allow two communication partners to verify the integrity of exchanged messages using a pre-shared secret $k$ [7]. This key $k$ can be derived dynamically through a key exchange protocol or hardcoded at both communicating entities. To authenticate a message $m$, the sender uses the tag generation algorithm $Sig_k(m)$ to generate the corresponding authentication tag $t$. Upon reception of a message, the verification algorithm $Vrfy_k(m, t)$ enables the recipient to evaluate whether the received tag is valid. Typically, this verification is done by computing the tag $t^* = Sig_k(m^*)$ for the received message $m^*$ and comparing it to the received tag $t$. A MAC scheme is considered secure if it is computationally infeasible to generate a $(m,t)$-pair that $Vrfy_k(\cdot)$ would accept without knowing the secret $k$. This requirement can be achieved by, *e.g.*, using keyed hash functions such as `HMAC-SHA256` to compute $t$. Thus, MACs provide integrity protection for communication channels, where they prevent any attacker not knowing $k$ from undetectably manipulating the content of transmitted messages.

### 2.2 MAC Aggregation to Combat Bandwidth Scarcity

Traditional MAC schemes consume significant bandwidth in constrained environments. Over 15 years ago, the concept of MAC aggregation was promoted to combat these limitations [14]. The idea is elegant and effective: Instead of authenticating each message individually, a single tag is responsible for protecting the integrity of multiple messages. Thus, the overhead of each tag is distributed over multiple messages, saving valuable bandwidth.

Formally, MAC aggregation schemes can be defined as an extension of traditional MAC schemes. In a traditional MAC scheme, the tag $t_i$ is computed over and transmitted alongside message $m_i$. For MAC aggregation schemes, the aggregated tag $t_i^{\text{agg}}$, which is transmitted alongside $m_i$, is computed by aggregating the integrity protection of multiple messages $m_{i-d}(d \in \mathcal{D})$ with an additional keyless function $Agg(\cdot)$, such that $t_i^{\text{agg}} = Agg(t_{i-d} | d \in \mathcal{D})$. We say that $\mathcal{D} \subset \mathbb{N}_0$ is the set of dependencies of a MAC aggregation scheme and, *e.g.*, $2 \in \mathcal{D}$ means that the tag $t_{i-2}$ is included in the computation of the aggregated tag $t_i^{\text{agg}}$. Vice versa, the integrity of message $m_{i-2}$ is protected by tags $t_i$.

Thus, aggregated authentication tags protect multiple messages. At the same time, each message is potentially protected by multiple tags as each (potentially shortened) tag may only be responsible for providing a fraction of the overall targeted security level. Since each tag aggregates integrity protection for multiple messages, aggregated MAC schemes result in, on average, shorter tags. In this context, the dependencies $\mathcal{D}$ describe how the reception of one message influences the verifiability of tags and the authenticity of surrounding messages. We say that if an aggregated MAC scheme has the dependencies $\mathcal{D}$, the generation and verification of tag $t_i$ require knowledge of $\{m_{i-d} | d \in \mathcal{D}\}$, as $t_{i-d} = Sig_k(m_{i-d})$. Consequently, a message $m_i$ blends into all tags $\{t_{i+d} | d \in \mathcal{D}\}$, and a tag $t_i$ protects the integrity of all messages $\{m_{i-d} | d \in \mathcal{D}\}$.

A specific MAC aggregation scheme defines the underlying MAC scheme, the dependencies $\mathcal{D}$, and the aggregation function $Agg(\cdot)$. In the following, we consider a simple XOR of authentication tags for the aggregation function, *i.e.*, $t_i^{\text{agg}} = Agg(t_{i-d}|d \in \mathcal{D}) = \bigoplus_{d\in\mathcal{D}} t_{i-d}$. This aggregation of tags is efficient and has been shown to be secure [4]. If, for example, $t_i$ and $t_j$ provide 128-bit integrity protection for $m_i$ and $m_j$, then $t^{\text{agg}} = t_i \oplus t_j$ provides 128-bit integrity protection for both messages $m_i$ and $m_j$. However, the security of this aggregation function requires that the chosen MAC function is pseudorandom and includes a nonce for replay protection to prevent mix-and-match attacks within one set of jointly authenticated messages [11]. Consequently, MAC schemes based on universal hashing, such as UMAC [6], should not be used in combination with XOR-based MAC aggregation[1]. Most prominent MAC schemes, such as `HMAC-SHA256`, can, however, be securely used with XOR-based MAC aggregation if used in combination with nonce-based replay protection.

### 2.3 Introducing Existing MAC Aggregation Schemes

After formalizing the concept of MAC aggregation in Sect. 2.2, we now introduce the different sets of MAC aggregation schemes, grouped by their choice of dependencies $\mathcal{D}$ and computation of $t^{\text{agg}}$. We do, however, not focus on the exact aggregation function or the underlying MAC scheme, as those choices do not impact the scheme's susceptibility to packet loss. Under these aspects, we present all four classes of aggregation that cover, to the best of our knowledge, all proposed schemes. For this presentation, we assume XOR-based aggregation with `HMAC-SHA256` as a suitable MAC scheme (including an appended nonce for replay protection).

**Traditional (Trad.):** To quantify the performance of existing MAC aggregation schemes, we compare them to the baseline performance of traditional MAC schemes. Therefore, we consider a traditional MAC scheme that authenticates each message $m_i$ with an individual tag $t_i$. This computation thus solely depends on $m_i$, *i.e.*, $\mathcal{D} = \{0\}$. As we target 128-bit security, the HMAC-SHA256 is truncated to 16B.

**Aggregated MAC (Agg(n)):** The most prominent scheme is aggregated MAC as introduced in 2008 [14] and later extended to prevent reordering attacks [11], allow messages to occur multiple times [15], and identify faulty messages in an aggregate [13]. For these schemes, a tag $t^{\text{agg}}$ is only appended to each n-th message, where $n$ is the parameter for how many messages' authentication tags are aggregated together. For our evaluation, we consider the aggregation of two,

[1] BP-MAC [32] (based on a Carter-Wegman construction), for example, is insecure if used in combination with XOR-based MAC aggregation. As each bit is authenticated individually and replay protection is only provided through a blinding tag, an attack can undetectably swap the x-th bits' values of two messages.

four, eight, and sixteen tags, *i.e.*, $n \in 2, 4, 8, 16$ to cover a range of different parameterizations. For every n-th message, a tag is then computed by XORing the authentication tags of all considered messages, as formalized in the following:

$$t_i^{\text{agg}} = \bigoplus_{i-n<k\leq i} t_k \quad \text{for } i \equiv 0 \pmod{n}$$

**Compound MAC (Comp(n)):** As the tags computed by `Agg`$(\cdot)$ are too long for some applications, Compound MAC is proposed that splits across multiple messages [18]. Thus, each message carries a shortened authentication tag, the length of which is inversely proportional to the number of aggregated messages, *i.e.*,$|t| = {}^{128}/{n}$. For our analysis, we again consider $n \in 2, 4, 8, 16$. We formalize `Comp`$(\cdot)$ in the following, where $t[a : b]$ means the chunk from the a-th to the b-th bit of tag $t$:

$$t_i^{\text{agg}} = \bigoplus_{\lfloor \frac{i}{n} \rfloor \cdot (n-1) \leq k < \lfloor \frac{i}{n} \rfloor \cdot n} t_k[(k \bmod n) \cdot |t| : ((k+1) \bmod n) \cdot |t|]$$

**Sliding Window-Based Progressive MACs (SW(n,o)):** Progressive MAC has been introduced to provide initially reduced security that is improved eventually upon message reception [3,17,24]. Therefore, each message is protected by a shortened tag that also verifies the integrity of the previous $n$ messages. As `SW`$(\cdot)$ is not equipped to provide full security under packet loss, it can be compensated by additionally considering an overprovisioning factor $o$. This factor defines in percent how much security may be extended beyond the target, *i.e.*, $o = 100$ means that messages may have 256-security at the expense of longer tags as $|t^{\text{agg}}| = {}^{128}/{n} \cdot (1 + {}^{o}/{100})$. Here, we select a number of parameter combinations that perform best under various scenarios. The tag computation of `SW`$(\cdot)$ can be formalized as follows:

$$t_i^{\text{agg}} = \bigoplus_{i-n<k\leq i} t_k[k \cdot |t| : (k+1) \cdot |t|]$$

**Randomized and Resilient Dependency Distribution (R2D2(n,g,o)):** To address weaknesses of `SW`$(\cdot)$ in the presence of packet loss, `R2D2`$(\cdot)$ introduces dependencies that bound the effect a dropped packet can have on the verifiability of any other message [31]. Therefore, the parameter $g$ is introduced, which defines how much security any message loses at most if a surrounding packet is lost, *i.e.*, $g = 1$ in combination with 2 B long packets means that any message can lose at most 16 bit of security. Furthermore, `R2D2`$(\cdot)$ randomizes the concrete dependency set $\mathcal{D}$ and assigns a different set to each bit of a tag. The final aggregate tag $t^{\text{agg}}$ is thus a juxtaposition of bit-long tags $t_j^{\text{agg}}$ and is defined as:

$$t_j^{\text{agg}} = \bigoplus_{0\leq k<|\mathcal{D}_j|} t_{i-\mathcal{D}_j[k]}[k * |t| + i]$$

with $\mathcal{D}_j[n]$ representing the $n$-th entry of j-th bit dependency set $\mathcal{D}_j$.

### 2.4 Interplay of Lossy Channels and MAC Aggregation

MAC aggregation can bring benefits to a wide range of constrained environments, such as Industrial Control Systems (ICSs), smart homes, smart city, or underwater networks. However, we see these targeted environments quickly shifting towards more and more lossy communication with protocols such as ZigBee, Sigfox, Bluetooth Low Energy, or LoRaWAN, to name only a few. This shift can significantly impact the performance of MAC aggregation schemes, especially considering Packet Error Rates (PERs) that can rise to 10% and above for certain scenarios [31]. With MAC aggregation, a lost packet means that the receiver cannot authenticate the initially transmitted message and all other messages that depend on it. Arguably, MAC aggregation has become even more critical in the lossy settings than for reliable communications since these networks more often expose bandwidth constraints due to the high number of nodes sharing the same transmission medium. LoRaWAN, for example, is often limited to less than 10 KB or even 1 KB of throughput per hour per device. Despite this stringent requirement of conserving bandwidth in lossy networks, no accurate performance analysis of MAC aggregation in this context has been conducted thus far to the best of our knowledge. In the following section, we provide the first such analyses for the different MAC aggregation schemes presented in Sect. 2.3.

## 3 Synthetic Measurements

We begin our analyses of MAC aggregations schemes by looking at synthetic measurements of simulated wireless channels. These measurements give us fine control over channel quality and payload length to investigate how these parameters influence the different MAC aggregation schemes. In Sect. 3.1, we first describe our setup before diving into the influence of channel quality and payload lengths in Sects. 3.2 and 3.3, respectively. Finally, we look at the established challenge of determining optimal payload lengths for given channel qualities under the additional constraint that the received data must be authenticated.

### 3.1 Simulation Setup

For our synthetic measurements, we use the network simulator `ns-3` (version 3.37), giving us fine-grained control over the underlying communication channel. As communication protocol, we choose the IEEE 802.15.4 protocol commonly used in constrained wireless environments and included in `ns-3`, where we consider the most compact header of 5 B. For payload lengths varying between 1 B and the maximum supported 115 B, we simulate the communication between two static antennas placed 25 m apart and extract binary loss traces of which transmitted packets have been correctly received or not. We additionally vary the transmit power varying between –21 dBm and –16 dBm using 0.1 dBm steps to increase the signal-to-noise ratio progressively, thus improving the channel quality and reducing PER. We only transmit each message once and do implement acknowledgments or retransmission, as these features are not always

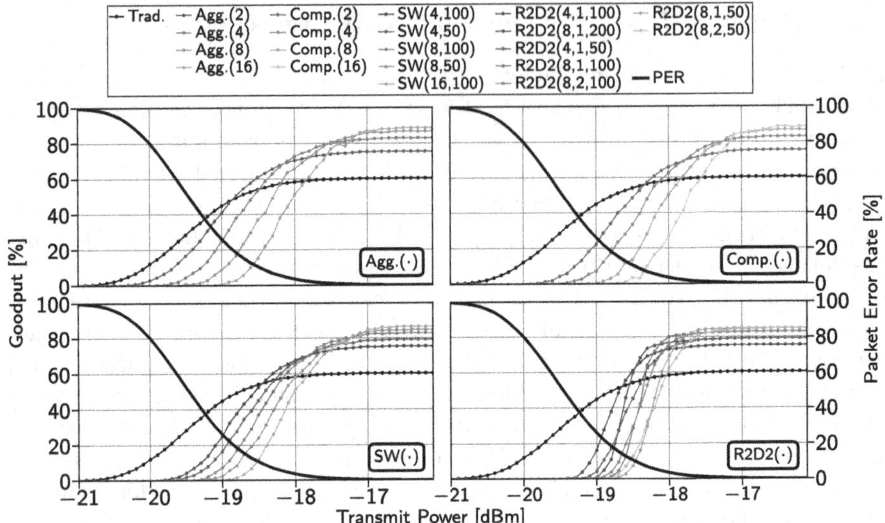


**Fig. 1.** Traditional MAC performs best with high packet error as all received data can be verified. For medium PERs, the aggregation of two tags with Agg(·) and various R2D2(·) parameterizations are preferable, while the aggregation of more messages with the simpler Agg(·) and Comp(·) scheme are is desirable with low PERs.

available. For all combinations of transmit power and payload length, we simulated the transmission of 10 000 packets, of which we selected a random sequence of 5000 packets for each of the following analyses. In a standalone simulation, we then implement the behavior of the different classes of MAC aggregation schemes and their selected parameterizations to extract which messages eventually become authenticated for a given binary loss trace. Our measurements focus on the achieved goodput by the different MAC aggregation schemes, where goodput is the ratio of received (and authenticated) payload bytes (*i.e.*, excluding header and authentication tag) to the number of transmitted bytes. We initially focus on goodput as performance metrics as it directly measures how efficient the transmission channel is utilized, the improvement of which is the main goal of MAC aggregation.

### 3.2 Influence of Channel Quality on Goodput

For an initial understanding of the different MAC aggregation schemes, we fixed the payload length to 48 B and gradually increased the transmission power, resulting in a slowly decreasing PER from 100% to 0%. Figure 1 shows our results.

We observe that all aggregation schemes exhibit the same general sigmoidal behavior: As the PER decreases, the achieved goodput increases slowly before increasing quickly and then leveling off. This behavior can be explained by the behavior of the packet delivery ratio (*i.e.*, the opposite of the packet error rate), which also increases first slowly and then rapidly as the channel quality improves. The interesting differences between the schemes and their parameterizations are thus defined by when and how goodput increases as the channel improves.

For the different aggregation schemes, we see that the maximally achieved goodput correlates inversely with the number of aggregated tags (parameter $n$). As a higher $n$ results in, on average, shorter tags, a better maximal goodput can be achieved due to less overhead. Similarly, the transmit power where the goodput of the different schemes starts to take off also correlates with $n$. The increasing likelihood can explain this observation that at least one of the tags in an aggregate cannot be computed as the set of aggregated messages becomes larger. Thus, the parameterizations with the higher bandwidth saving potential also require a better channel (*i.e.*, lower PER) to be beneficial over more conservative parameterizations. Consequently, traditional MACs perform best with high PERs while exposing the overall worst goodput as PER approaches 0%.

Comparing the performance of the different aggregation schemes, we observe that all schemes tend towards the same discrete goodput dictated by their average tag length. However, the goodput provided by `Agg`$(\cdot)$, `Comp`$(\cdot)$, and `SW`$(\cdot)$ increases earlier but more slowly with increasing transmit power in contrast to `R2D2`$(\cdot)$, which suddenly jumps up once the channel is good enough. The behavior of `R2D2`$(\cdot)$ can be explained by ideally distributing the effects of packet loss to surrounding messages, such that if security levels for a few messages become good enough to consider the message authenticated, surrounding messages are close to the threshold as well. Overall, for transmit powers up –18.9 dBm (PER=18.5%), traditional MACs perform best as they are not handicapped by the many lost packets. Then, the aggregation of two messages with `Agg`$(\cdot)$ is best until, between –18.3 dBm (PER=8.5%) and –17.1 dBm (PER=0.4%), there are different parameterizations of `R2D2`$(\cdot)$ that perform best. As the PER reduces further, the selected scheme becomes, however, less critical, and the differences for the same average tag length are marginal. Here, simpler schemes with no overprovisioning, such as `Agg`$(\cdot)$ and `Comp`$(\cdot)$, are usually preferable. Consequently, it mostly depends on the channel quality, which aggregation scheme and parameterization achieve the best goodput.

### 3.3 Influence of Payload Length on Goodput

In Sect. 3.2, we consider a fixed payload length and slowly increase the transmit power to improve the signal-to-noise ratio. To better understand the behavior of the different MAC aggregation schemes, we now vary the payload length for a fixed transmit power of –18.3 dBm, where we have realistic PER between 1.5 and 10.9% across the payload length range. We show our results in Fig. 2.

With changing transmit power, we observe the same characteristics in the goodput curves of all aggregation schemes. Goodput first quickly increases before slowly dropping after reaching a maximum. This phenomenon can be explained by the overlapping effects of reduced relative overhead of authentication tags and growing numbers of unverifiable tags due to raised PERs with increased payload lengths. Thus, selecting the best MAC aggregation scheme depends on the underlying channel quality, packet lengths, and resulting variable PERs.

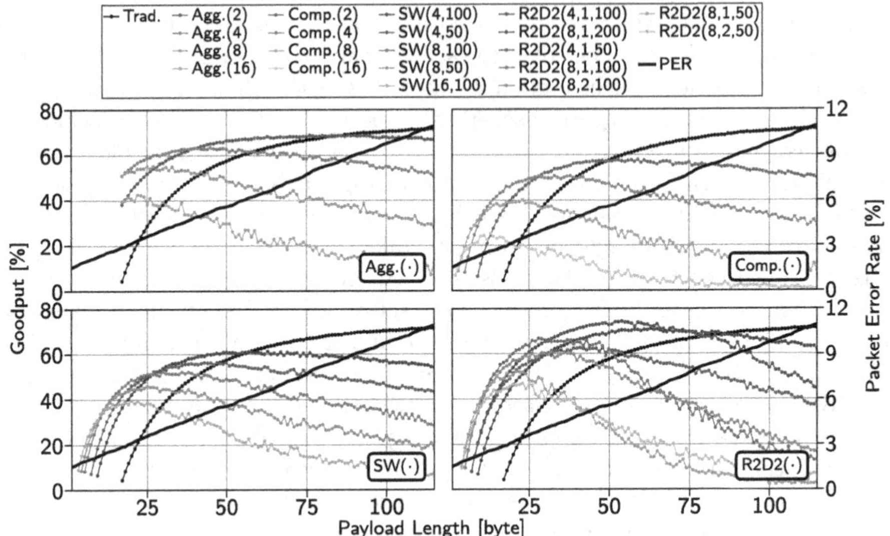


**Fig. 2.** For larger payloads, the PER increases and the relative overhead of authentication tags decrease. Therefore, different schemes and parameterizations are optimal depending on payload lengths.

Furthermore, we can see that not all aggregation schemes can be employed for short payload lengths. Traditional MAC and Agg(·) append 16-byte authentication tags (to a fraction of all) messages and thus require payload lengths of at least 17 B. The other aggregation schemes append a shortened tag to all messages, but the size of these tags also dictates how small messages can be. Thus, if transmitted packets can only carry a few bytes of payload, such as the unreliable CAN bus protocol, which supports at most 8-byte payloads and has no header fields intended for integrity protection, the choice of available MAC aggregation scheme shrinks.

Moreover, we observe different optimal payload lengths w.r.t. to goodput for the distinct schemes and parameterizations. While using the maximal payload length of 114 B yields the optimal goodput of 71.7% for traditional MACs, the overall maximal goodput of 74.4% is achieved by R2D2(8,1,200) with a payload length of 54 B. Hence, investigating the combined impact of packet lengths and MAC aggregation under varying conditions is essential to determine optimal network configurations in novel deployments.

### 3.4 Optimal Packet Lengths for Authenticated Data

Prior results indicate that considering the MAC aggregation scheme is crucial when optimizing packet lengths for a given channel. This search for optimal payload length gathered interest in the past [1,16,23,30] to make use of limited bandwidth availability or optimize the lifetimes of battery-powered devices. As resource-constrained devices consume most of their power for wireless transmis-

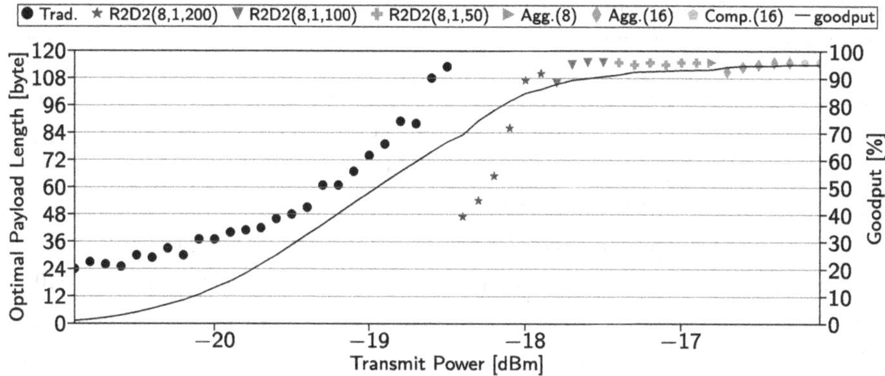


**Fig. 3.** Different MAC (aggregation) schemes achieve a higher goodput as channel quality improves under optimal payload lengths. Unintuitively, changing a scheme can result in a reduced optimal payload length even if the channel improves.

sions [27], optimizing goodput is essential for improving device lifetimes. Assuming constant energy consumption for each transmitted bit at a given transmit power, the optimal combination of payload lengths and MAC aggregation scheme also optimizes device lifetimes. These packet length optimizations, thus far, only looked at received data and not received *and authenticated* data. Assuming the imperative requirement of authenticated data, we search for the optimal payload lengths to optimize goodput across varying channel qualities, considering the different MAC aggregation schemes. Our results are shown in Fig. 3.

For low transmission powers, *i.e.*, low signal-to-noise ratio, we see that traditional MACs,*i.e.*, no aggregation, perform best. This behavior can be explained by the initially high PER, even for small messages, such that aggregated tags have a high risk of being composed of at least one message that did not arrive. Here, the behavior observed in our setup matches related work [1,16,23,30] in that optimal payload lengths are initially short and then slowly increase as the transmit power is increased.

As the transmission channel improves, message aggregation starts to pay off since the benefits of shorter tags outweigh the risk of received data that cannot be authenticated. Here, initially, between -18.4 and –17.2 dBM, R2D2(·) under various parameterizations performs best. However, the best MAC aggregation scheme does not only change with better channels; the optimal payload also decreases on each change before slowly increasing again. Therefore, the optimal payload length for a transmit power of –18.5 dBM is 113 B (with traditional MACs), but for a slightly higher transmit power of –18.4 dBM, it drops down to 47 B (for R2D2(8,1,100)). We can observe this same phenomenon for other changes between MAC aggregation schemes, and it is more or less pronounced depending on the header sizes, where the static overhead of larger packet headers dampens the drop in optimal packet sizes.

**Table 1.** Limited bandwidth availability for integrity protection is a serious challenge across a wide range of lossy environments.

| Scenario | Duration | Protocol | Header | Data | #pkts | PER | Src |
|---|---|---|---|---|---|---|---|
| ICS | 8 h | IEEE 802.15.4 | 11 B | 20 B | 57648 | 4.79% | [12] |
| Office | 22 h | BLE | 10 B | 32 B | 79032 | 3.22% | [12] |
| Smart City (sta.) | 131 days | LoRaWAN | 13 B | 16 B | 18790 | 1.97% | [5] |
| Smart City (mob.) | 250 days | LoRaWAN | 13 B | 24 B | 17415 | 7.09% | [19] |
| Underwater | 327 min | GUWMANET | 31 bit | 16 B | 334 | 16.46% | [10] |

Overall, we can see that the average tag lengths of the optimal schemes shrink for higher transmission power. Looking at the achieved goodput by the respective optimal scheme, we see a sigmoid curve that instead of leveling off at 82.5% if only using traditional MACs, the different MAC aggregation schemes boosts this achievable goodput to 95.0% as the PER approaches 0. However, it must also be understood that transmitting with optimal payload lengths is often not an option in practice. Here, the (established) applications and protocols often dictate the payload lengths, *e.g.*, a sensor may only have a single reading that should be transmitted quickly and thus has no other data to fill into the payload. Therefore, and because real wireless channels change over time, it is necessary to investigate MAC aggregation in real-world scenarios.

## 4 MAC Aggregation in Real-World Scenarios

Thus far, we have analyzed MAC aggregation schemes in controlled synthetic environments. While these analyses gave us insights into the behavior and nuances of the different schemes, they do not necessarily represent the entire story for realistic deployments. Here, we often have predetermined payload lengths dictated by available data or protocol specifications. Also, channel qualities vary dynamically over time, especially if some communication partners are mobile. In the following subsection, we first introduce distinct real-world scenarios, which we subsequently use to evaluate and compare the performance of the MAC aggregation schemes (*cf.* Sect. 2.3) under realistic conditions.

### 4.1 Description of the Scenarios

For our realistic measurements, we rely on network traces collected from real-world scenarios. Each trace has constant payload lengths and transmission configurations, and we extract a binary loss trace of which transmitted packets have been correctly received or not. This trace is then fed into our simulation to analyze the MAC aggregation schemes. We summarize the scenarios in Table 1 and briefly introduce them in the following subsections.

**Industrial Control System (ICS) Scenario.** For the first scenario, we look at a measurement campaign of wireless communication in a 3600 $m^2$ production hall with nearly a billion transmitted packets [12]. We select a single representative link from the various configurations using the IEEE 802.15.4 protocol with a payload length of 20 B. Our trace covers a total of 8 h of traffic on a typical workday with an overall PER of 4.79%. In this scenario, we observe primarily short bursts of packet loss with channel quality changing mostly over longer time windows (hours), while phases of high error rates (upwards of 50%) are possible for several minutes.

**Office Scenario.** With the same measurement setup as for the ICS scenario, wireless links between nodes placed in various office rooms on a single floor have been measured [12]. Here, we select a Bluetooth Low Energy (BLE) communication link with 32 B payloads over a 22 h window during a workday. We observe a relatively constant error distribution with short error bursts of a few packets each and an overall PER of 3.22%.

**Smart City (Stationary) Scenario.** Our first smart city scenario is based on the LoED dataset [5], where nine LoRaWAN gateways were placed in central London. We focus on the 18790 packets transmitted by a single stationary sender and received by any of the gateways. With an overall PER of 1.97%, we see primarily isolated packet loss due to long idle times between two transmissions, and the channel only experiences long-term changes in quality over several days, potentially due to altering weather conditions.

**Smart City (Mobile) Scenario.** In this scenario, mobile LoRaWAN senders transmit to a total of nine stationary gateways for 250 days. Specifically, the sender was mounted to the top of a garbage truck driving through a 200 $km^2$ area in the city of Bonn [19]. We observe burstier errors and overall channel qualities changing significantly over days and weeks. The burstiness is likely due to the sender quickly entering and exiting the line of sight of a gateway, while the long-term changes changing presumably again relate to the weather conditions.

**Underwater Scenario.** Finally, we consider acoustic underwater communication, with a trace of 334 16-byte messages being transmitted over 327 m between two stationary nodes placed in the sea [10]. The measurements were conducted during moderately rough weather conditions. Despite an overall high PER of 16.46%, most of these errors occurred during long bursts interspersed with periods of high packet delivery rates.

### 4.2 Evaluating MAC Aggregation in Realistic Scenarios

We now analyze MAC aggregation schemes in the different realistic scenarios introduced in the previous section. These scenarios are characterized by dynamic

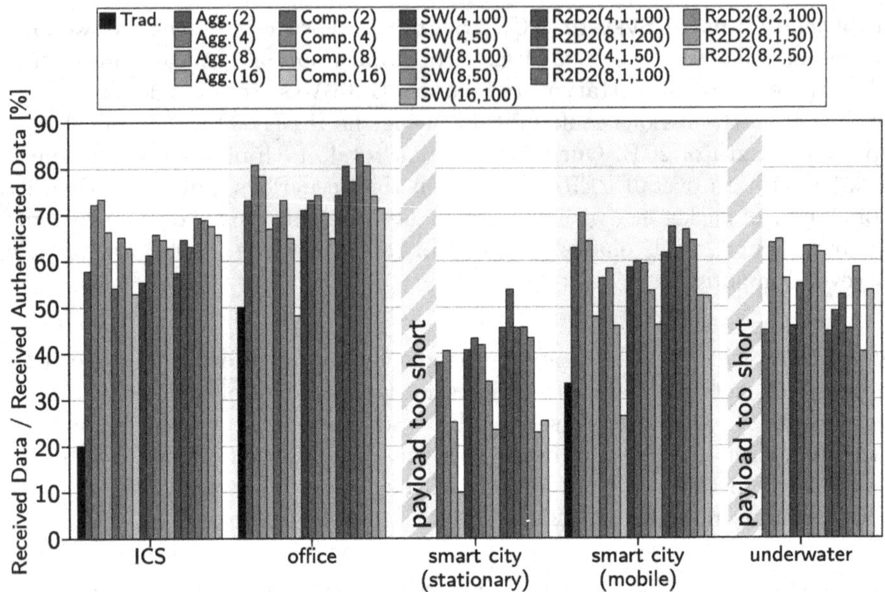


**Fig. 4.** Different MAC aggregation schemes and parameterizations perform best, depending on the payload lengths, error burstiness, and overall PERs, such that the right scheme selection is non-trivial but crucial for the optimal use of constrained channels.

channels, differing communication protocols, and prespecified header and payload lengths. For each scenario, we analyze the goodput (*i.e.*, the amount of received and authenticated data) in Fig. 4. We express the goodput as a percentage of the total amount of received payload data if no integrity protection was used. For the urban (static) and underwater scenarios, traditional MACs and Agg(·) cannot be included since the tags do not fit into the available payload.

We see different MAC aggregation schemes performing best in the synthetic measurements, depending on the investigated scenario. Payload lengths influence the concrete parameterization but do not directly correlate with which scheme performs best under the relatively small variations observed across the different scenarios. The best-performing MAC aggregation scheme thus depends primarily on two factors: overall PER and burstiness.

For the industry and urban (mobile) scenario, where overall PER is low and burstiness relatively high, Agg(·) performs best. During a burst, most packets in one set of aggregated messages are lost, while otherwise, most sets are received entirely and can be authenticated. For the office and urban (static) scenarios, R2D2(·) performs best due to the high PER and the short error bursts, where often only a single packet is lost. However, higher PERs do not immediately mean that R2D2(·) performs best (until traditional MACs are more favorable), as suggested by the synthetic scenarios. The long burst, where no traffic passes, in combination with a relatively good delivery ratio otherwise mean that SW(·)

and `Comp(·)` perform best in the underwater scenario. Overall, the best MAC aggregation scheme can achieve relative improvements of up to 24.2% better goodput compared to the second best scheme.

However, more important than selecting the scheme is using the correct parameterization. If the wrong parameters are used for the best-performing MAC aggregation scheme, performance can drop by an average between 14.0 and 57.4% in the worst case. With the PER of the different scenarios ranging between 1.97 and 16.46%, we have parameterizations that result in average tag lengths of 4 B performing best, which is more or less in line with the synthetic measurements from Sect. 3.2.

Overall, we see that PER and error burstiness play a significant role in finding the best scheme and parameterizations. Due to relatively small variance in payload lengths across the scenarios, we, however, cannot confirm its low impact in selecting the best schemes. Nevertheless, we know that the potential gains achieved through MAC aggregation shrink with larger payloads. Most importantly, we can conclude that adequate parameterization is more important than finding the best MAC aggregation scheme. Ultimately, both optimizations have a non-negligible effect on the achievable goodput.

## 5 Beyond Goodput as Evaluation Metric

Optimizing the goodput of MAC aggregation is the main goal for most scenarios. However, other effects must also be considered when choosing the MAC aggregation scheme, such as verification delay, processing overhead, and susceptibility to jamming attacks. In the following subsections, we compare the different MAC aggregation schemes (*cf.* Sec. 2.3) w.r.t. these effects.

### 5.1 Average Delay Until Authentication

First, we look at the authentication delay for the different MAC aggregation schemes. Traditional authentication tags can be verified immediately upon message reception, so no delay occurs due to waiting for additional data. With MAC aggregation, on the other hand, we need to wait until all messages depending on a specific tag have been received to verify it, which might introduce significant delays. To analyze these effects, we plotted the delay from the measurements on all traces from Sect. 4.1 as a CDF in Fig. 5.

We see major differences in the behavior of the different aggregation schemes for these measurements. `Agg(·)` and `Comp(·)` periodically verify a set of prior messages together, such that a range of different delays occur with the same frequency. The concrete span of possible delay is then proportional to the parameter $n$ of how many tags are aggregated together.

`SW(·)`, on the other hand, verifies messages continuously with an almost constant delay. This delay only varies if some messages get lost, which incurs a verification delay for surrounding messages. This behavior is beneficial for applications requiring periodic messages with practically no jitter, *e.g.*, control algorithms in ICSs relying on a constant delay of the received information. `R2D2(·)`

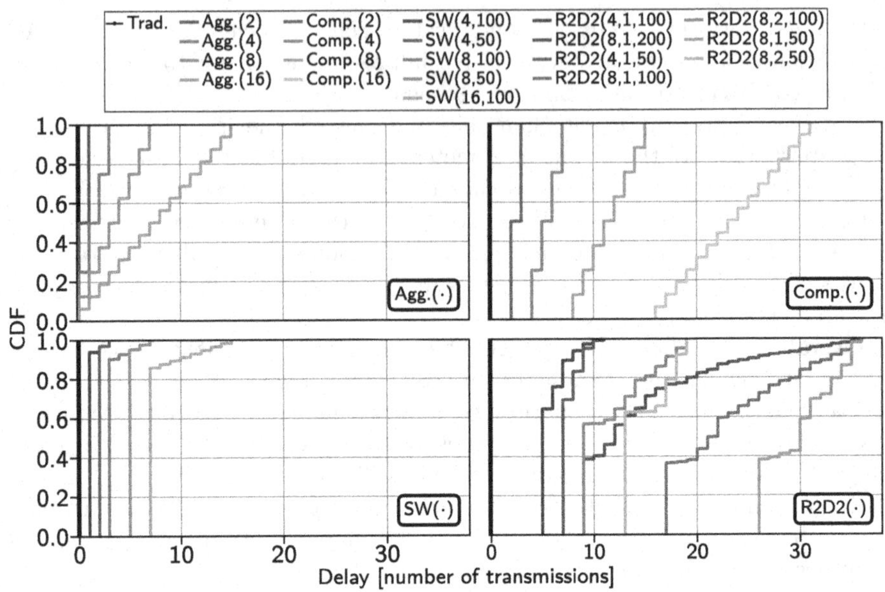


**Fig. 5.** Verification delay is an inherent drawback of MAC aggregation. For scenarios where verification delay is critical, SW(·) does, however, provide highly consistent delays which control algorithms can thus anticipate.

shows similar behavior for about half of all the received messages, while the rest have increasing delays. Again, the packet loss is responsible for higher delays, but since R2D2(·) distributed the effects of packet losses over multiple packets, more of them experience delayed verification. Moreover, the magnitude of these delays correlated with the overprovisioning factor $o$, allowing late authentication for messages that could otherwise not be authenticated.

In summary, the average delay until authentication of the different authentication schemes strongly differs. While Agg(·) offers, on average, the lowest delays, SW(·) has the most constant delays. On the other hand, R2D2(·) offers the best goodput for many scenarios with higher PER while messages have higher and more varying verification delays. Selecting the best aggregation scheme according to this delay thus depends on which balance the concrete application scenario demands between the goodput reduction and the type of verification delay.

### 5.2 Performance and Memory Overhead

Many of the considered scenarios involve resource-constrained IoT devices where substantial additional processing and memory overhead from the MAC aggregation scheme could significantly impact performance. Hence, we measure and compare the processing delay and memory overhead for tag computation and buffering by the different schemes. We conducted the analysis on the Arm Cortex M3 processor of a Zolertia RE-Mote board, a common choice to evaluate realistic

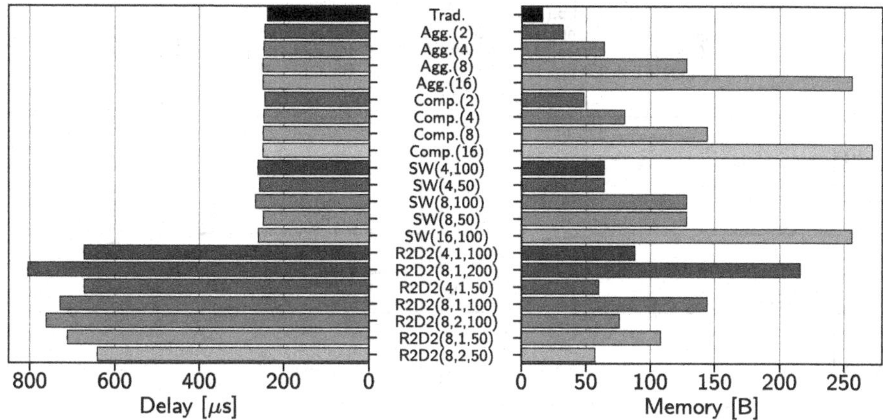


**Fig. 6.** Only R2D2(·) introduces significant processing overhead over traditional MACs. Memory overhead, on the other hand, is mostly dependent on how many tags are aggregated together but so small that it should rarely be a decisive factor.

resource-constrained hardware. As a baseline, we capture the time to authenticate a single 32 B message with hardware-accelerated HMAC-SHA256, which is the underlying MAC scheme used for the aggregation schemes as well. We averaged the average processing times over 16 tag generations (not all schemes do the same computations for each message) and repeated this measurement 30 times. For the memory overhead, we measure the memory necessary to buffer tags before their aggregation, as all other memory overhead is implementation-dependent and is mostly optimized away by the compiler. The results of both measurements are presented in Fig. 6.

Regarding processing times, we see only marginal overhead for all aggregation schemes except `R2D2`(·). There, we have a 168 to 237% increase in processing times compared to the baseline, where the differences across parameterizations are mostly insignificant. This overhead stems from the bitwise processing of `R2D2`(·), which requires a significant amount of XOR and bitshift operations. This processing overhead is, however, mostly only impactful for applications that run on slower hardware and have tight latency requirements, especially considering that the sender *and* receiver must conduct this additional processing.

We see a different picture across the MAC aggregation schemes for the memory overhead. For `Agg`(·), `Comp`(·), and `SW`(·), the needed memory depends on the message history. More tags must be stored concurrently for shorter aggregated tags, resulting in higher memory overhead. Here, the bitwise processing of `R2D2`(·) helps to partially process tags when new messages arise. Consequently, the memory depends mainly on the overprovisioning factor and less on the number of aggregated tags. The magnitude of the required additional memory for MAC aggregation schemes is, however, small enough that it should rarely influence the decision on which scheme should be deployed.

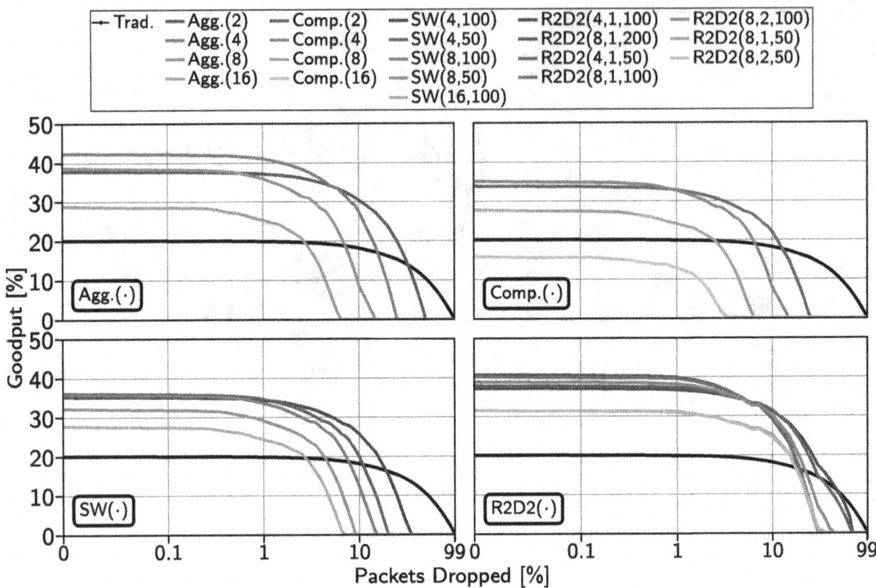


**Fig. 7.** R2D2(·) shows significantly increased resilience to denial-of-service attacks through selective jamming, especially if an attacker jams less than 10% of messages to remain stealthy or conserve energy.

### 5.3 Resilience to Adversarial Interference

In our final analysis, we compare the resilience of MAC aggregation schemes to selective jamming attacks. Selective jamming refers to jamming specific messages to prevent their correct reception which enables stealthy and energy-saving attacks as dropped packets are hardly distinguishable from random packet loss [2,34]. In the context of MAC aggregation schemes, a sophisticated attacker can amplify the effects of a denial-of-service attack due to the employed MAC aggregation. For example, for Agg(16), it suffices to jam every $16^{\text{th}}$ packet to reduce the (authenticated) goodput of the channel to zero.

For our measurements, we considered the trace from the urban (mobile) scenario introduced previously, as its payload is large enough for all schemes, and urban settings provide easy access to potential attackers. For each aggregation scheme, we developed the optimal jamming attack strategy to minimize the goodput at the receiver. In Fig. 7, we show how the achieved goodput of the different aggregation schemes is impacted by increased attacking capabilities.

The x-axis represents the number of overall dropped packets in percent on a logarithmic scale. For traditional authentication, we see, as expected, that the channel can still transmit authenticated data as long as not the entire channel is jammed. In general, we note that shorter average tags are more susceptible to selective jamming attacks, as each tag requires many received messages to become verifiable. Considering the shortest tags (n=16) for Agg(·), Comp(·), and

SW(·), we see that dropping between 27 and 29% targeted packet already suffices to prevent all data transmission over the channel.

The behavior of R2D2(·) requires, however, a separate analysis since one of the protocol's design goals is resilience against jamming attacks. Therefore, the exact dependencies between tags and messages are kept secret, such that attackers can only design their strategy to inflict the most damage for the average dependency selection. Furthermore, the design of R2D2(·) explicitly distributes the effects of packet losses (malicious or not) over many packets, thus cushioning the impact of selective jamming. Hence, up to 15% of packets need to be dropped to reduce goodput by even 20%. However, once a critical mass of packet loss occurs, such distribution no longer suffices for compensation, and the goodput quickly drops.

Overall, we can say that R2D2(·) is the most resilient scheme in the presence of a selective jammer. Considering our entire analysis, no scheme is an outright winner, and each scheme has its benefits. To summarize these findings, guide operators toward the right MAC aggregation scheme, and identify open research questions, we provide general recommendations in the following section.

# 6 Guidelines on Employing MAC Aggregation

In general, MAC aggregation shows promising potential to boost available bandwidth on lossy channels for various scenarios. However, not every scenario benefits from MAC aggregation compared to traditional MACs. More importantly, choosing the correct scheme and parameters is decisive in answering the questions of *when* and *how* to use MAC aggregation. Therefore, in the following, we deepen this discussion towards providing general guidelines on employing MAC aggregation based on our empirical measurements.

## 6.1 When to Use MAC Aggregation on Lossy Channels?

From our analysis, it is evident that MAC aggregation reliably improves goodput for relatively high PERs of 10% or below. In cases where the PER is higher, it is often more beneficial to rely on traditional MACs or, at most, aggregate MACs for no more than two messages (*i.e.*, setting the parameter $n$ to 2). However, for high PERs due to long error bursts where hardly any traffic arrives, MAC aggregation can still be beneficial (*cf.* Sect. 4.2).

Furthermore, we investigated the relationship between payload lengths and the resulting benefits of MAC aggregation. For instance, in scenarios involving 200 B payloads and minimalistic 5 B headers, a MAC aggregation scheme aggregating 16 tags (*i.e.*, $n = 16$) could still generate a 7.3% goodput improvement. Consequently, we conclude that MAC aggregation, in general, offers the most substantial benefits for short payload lengths, up to a few hundred bytes, and moderate PERs of up to 10%. As substantiated by the real-world scenarios (*cf.* Sect. 4.1), this is precisely the kind of communication that occurs in many (industrial) IoT scenarios, leading to the question of how to use MAC aggregation in such scenarios to gain the most benefit.

### 6.2 How to Employ MAC Aggregation on Lossy Channels?

In our evaluations of the goodput improvements that different MAC aggregation schemes and parameterizations can bring in real-world scenarios (*cf.* Sect. 4.2), we have seen that no aggregation scheme is a clear-cut winner (even when solely focusing on goodput as an evaluation metric). Moreover, we have seen that the correct parameterization for a given scenario is crucial to achieving optimal performance. These observations thus warrant a more nuanced discussion of when to use which MAC aggregation scheme and with which parameters.

Focusing solely on goodput, we see that generally `R2D2(·)` achieves the highest performance for PER between 0.4 and 8.5%, especially when packet errors occur as short bursts. For lower PERs and traffic with longer error bursts, the better performance and simplicity of `Agg(·)` is often preferable. If the periodic 16-byte tags for `Agg(·)` are not supported by the application (*e.g.*, due to fixed message sizes), `Comp(·)` is a good alternative to realize a constant tag size across all messages. Considering the parameterizations, a high $n$ has the potential to realize better goodput, but only if the PER is relatively low. For the overprovisioning factor $o$ of `SW(·)` and `R2D2(·)`, 100 is usually the best or least a decent choice. `R2D2(·)`'s $g$-factor is best set to 1 in those scenarios where `R2D2(·)` achieves the best goodput. Overall, `SW(·)` rarely outperforms the other schemes if only considering goodput since it is not designed for lossy communication [31]. Nevertheless, it can still be a sensitive choice when also considering *e.g.*, verification delays.

One disadvantage of MAC aggregation compared to traditional MACs is the inherent verification delay which we investigated in Sect. 5.1. This delay occurs as most messages cannot be verified directly upon reception and thus need to be buffered or processed optimistically [31], *i.e.*, processed under the assumption of being genuine before full integrity verification. This risk can be reduced by the two progressive schemes `SW(·)` and `R2D2(·)`, already providing some, yet reduced, security guarantees immediately upon message reception. Furthermore, if an application requires complete message verification, `SW(·)` provides deterministic verification delays, beneficial for real-time control.

Concerning other potential dimensions for selecting the best MAC aggregation scheme for a given scenario, memory overhead is so small that it should rarely be a decisive factor. When interested in optimizing processing overhead, only `R2D2(·)` shows a clear disadvantage (*cf.* Sect. 5.2) compared to the other aggregation schemes. Finally, if resilience to denial-of-service attacks through selective jamming is essential, `R2D2(·)` shows clear advantages over the other schemes. However, if another scheme must be used (*e.g.*, due to the excessive processing overhead of `R2D2(·)`), then lowering the parameter $n$ can reduce the effects of attacks at the cost of reduced goodput under normal operation.

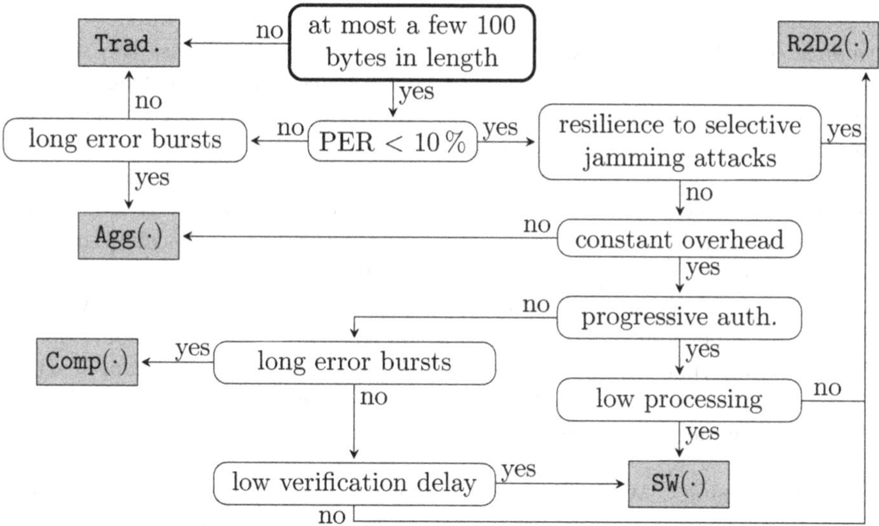


**Fig. 8.** The optimal MAC aggregation scheme depends on many different characteristics. This decision diagram assists in this selection process.

### 6.3 Selecting an MAC Aggregation Scheme

We observe that often many dimensions must be considered to decide when and how to perform MAC aggregation. To help operators in their decision process, we provide two forms of assistance. First, we provide a decision diagram to select the right MAC aggregation scheme in Fig. 8 based on basic network characteristics and feature demands. Secondly, and for more detailed analysis, we provide an evaluation tool[2] to aid further in this decision process. Our evaluation tool takes as input the header and payload lengths as well as an example binary loss trace, *i.e.*, a series of 1 s and 0 s for received and dropped packets, respectively. It provides a comparison of all MAC aggregation schemes and their parameterizations (as analyzed in this paper) for the given scenario. In combination with these tools, our guidelines support operators in deciding when and how to employ MAC aggregation and help researchers to identify further opportunities to optimize existing MAC aggregation schemes.

## 7 Conclusion

MAC aggregation effectively saves valuable bandwidth in resource-constrained networks by shifting integrity protection from single to multiple packets. However, as shown in this paper, the potential benefits of MAC aggregation strongly depend on the individual network scenario. In particular, the effects of (bursty)

[2] https://github.com/fkie-cad/mac-aggregation-analysis-tool.

packet losses, as experienced in wireless communication, severely impact the performance of MAC aggregation. Therefore, we specifically address the research question of *when* and *how* to aggregate MACs by comparing existing aggregation schemes in synthetic and real-world scenarios. Our empirical results indicate that, in general, MAC aggregation is particularly effective in scenarios with relatively reliable communication (*i.e.*, with PERs below 10%) and for short payload lengths (*i.e.*, below a few hundred bytes). Most importantly, however, correctly parameterizing MAC aggregation is even more critical than choosing the right scheme. Moreover, other optimization metrics than goodput may limit the choice of applicable MAC aggregation schemes and thus need to be considered. With our detailed guidelines and our public evaluation tool, we intend to support operators in deciding when and how to employ MAC aggregation for their applications and researchers to improve MAC aggregation further, ultimately strengthening security even under adverse networking conditions.

**Acknowledgements.** We thank Thomas Hänel, Michael Rademacher, and Michael Goetz for providing access to their datasets. We thank Jan Bauer, Michael Rademacher, and our anonymous reviewers for valuable feedback that improved this paper. This work is partially funded by the project MUM2, partially funded by the German Federal Ministry of Economic Affairs and Climate Action (BMWK) with contract number 03SX543B managed by the Project Management Jülich (PTJ), and by the Deutsche Forschungsgemeinschaft (DFG, German Research Foundation) under Germany's Excellence Strategy – EXC-2023 Internet of Production – 390621612. The authors are responsible for the contents of this work.

## References

1. Akbas, A., Yildiz, H.U., Tavli, B., Uludag, S.: Joint Optimization of transmission power level and packet size for WSN lifetime maximization. IEEE Sensors J. **16**(12) (2016). https://doi.org/10.1109/JSEN.2016.2548661
2. Aras, E., Small, N., Ramachandran, G.S., Delbruel, S., Joosen, W., Hughes, D.: Selective jamming of LoRaWAN using commodity hardware. In: Proceedings of the 14th EAI International Conference on Mobile and Ubiquitous Systems: Computing, Networking and Services (MobiQuitous). ACM (2017). https://doi.org/10.1145/3144457.3144478
3. Armknecht, F., Walther, P., Tsudik, G., Beck, M., Strufe, T.: ProMACs: progressive and resynchronizing macs for continuous efficient authentication of message streams. In: Proceedings of the Conference on Computer and Communications Security (CCS). ACM (2020). https://doi.org/10.1145/3372297.3423349
4. Bellare, M., Guérin, R., Rogaway, P.: XOR MACs: new methods for message authentication using finite pseudorandom functions. In: Coppersmith, D. (ed.) CRYPTO 1995. LNCS, vol. 963, pp. 15–28. Springer, Heidelberg (1995). https://doi.org/10.1007/3-540-44750-4_2
5. Bhatia, L., Breza, M., Marfievici, R., McCann, J.A.: Dataset: LoED: The LoRaWAN at the edge dataset. In: Proceedings of the Third Workshop on Data: Acquisition to Analysis (2020)

6. Black, J., Halevi, S., Krawczyk, H., Krovetz, T., Rogaway, P.: UMAC: fast and secure message authentication. In: Wiener, M. (ed.) CRYPTO 1999. LNCS, vol. 1666, pp. 216–233. Springer, Heidelberg (1999). https://doi.org/10.1007/3-540-48405-1_14
7. Boneh, D., Shoup, V.: A graduate course in applied cryptography (2023)
8. Castellanos, J.H., Antonioli, D., Tippenhauer, N.O., Ochoa, M.: Legacy-compliant data authentication for industrial control system traffic. In: Gollmann, D., Miyaji, A., Kikuchi, H. (eds.) ACNS 2017. LNCS, vol. 10355, pp. 665–685. Springer, Cham (2017). https://doi.org/10.1007/978-3-319-61204-1_33
9. Chen, Y., Kunz, T.: Performance evaluation of iot protocols under a constrained wireless access network. In: Proceedings of International Conf. on Selected Topics in Mobile & Wireless Networking (MoWNeT). IEEE (2016). https://doi.org/10.1109/MoWNet.2016.7496622
10. Dol, H., et al.: EDA-SALSA: development of a self-reconfigurable protocol stack for robust underwater acoustic networking. In: IEEE/MTS Oceans (2023). https://doi.org/10.1109/OCEANSLimerick52467.2023.10244330
11. Eikemeier, O., et al.: History-free aggregate message authentication codes. In: Garay, J.A., De Prisco, R. (eds.) SCN 2010. LNCS, vol. 6280, pp. 309–328. Springer, Heidelberg (2010). https://doi.org/10.1007/978-3-642-15317-4_20
12. Hänel, T., Brüggemann, L., Loske, F., Aschenbruck, N.: Long-term wireless sensor network deployments in industry and office scenarios. In: Proceedings of the 22nd International Symposium on a World of Wireless, Mobile and Multimedia Networks (WoWMoM). IEEE (2021). https://doi.org/10.1109/WoWMoM51794.2021.00024
13. Hirose, S., Shikata, J.: Non-adaptive group-testing aggregate MAC scheme. In: Su, C., Kikuchi, H. (eds.) ISPEC 2018. LNCS, vol. 11125, pp. 357–372. Springer, Cham (2018). https://doi.org/10.1007/978-3-319-99807-7_22
14. Katz, J., Lindell, A.Y.: Aggregate message authentication codes. In: Malkin, T. (ed.) CT-RSA 2008. LNCS, vol. 4964, pp. 155–169. Springer, Heidelberg (2008). https://doi.org/10.1007/978-3-540-79263-5_10
15. Kolesnikov, V.: MAC aggregation with message multiplicity. In: Visconti, I., De Prisco, R. (eds.) SCN 2012. LNCS, vol. 7485, pp. 445–460. Springer, Heidelberg (2012). https://doi.org/10.1007/978-3-642-32928-9_25
16. Kurt, S., Yildiz, H.U., Yigit, M., Tavli, B., Gungor, V.C.: Packet size optimization in wireless sensor networks for smart grid applications. IEEE Trans. Indus. Elect. **64**(3) (2016). https://doi.org/10.1109/TIE.2016.2619319
17. Li, H., Kumar, V., Park, J.M., Yang, Y.: Cumulative message authentication codes for resource-constrained IoT networks. IEEE Internet Things J. (2021). https://doi.org/10.1109/JIOT.2021.3074054
18. Nilsson, D.K., Larson, U.E., Jonsson, E.: Efficient in-vehicle delayed data authentication based on compound message authentication codes. In: Proceedings of the 68th Vehicular Technology Conference (VTC-Fall). IEEE (2008). https://doi.org/10.1109/VETECF.2008.259
19. Rademacher, M., Linka, H., Horstmann, T., Henze, M.: Path loss in urban LoRa networks: a large-scale measurement study. In: Proceedings of the 94th Vehicular Technology Conference (VTC-Fall). IEEE (2021). https://doi.org/10.1109/VTC2021-Fall52928.2021.9625531.
20. Raza, S., Trabalza, D., Voigt, T.: 6LoWPAN compressed DTLS for CoAP. In: Proceedings of the 8th International Conference on Distributed Computing in Sensor Systems (DCOSS). IEEE (2012). https://doi.org/10.1109/DCOSS.2012.55
21. Rescorla, E., Barnes, R., Tschofenig, H., Schwartz, B.: Compact TLS 1.3. Internet-Draft, IETF (2023)

22. Rescorla, E., Tschofenig, H., Modadugu, N.: The Datagram Transport Layer Security (DTLS) Protocol Version 1.3. RFC 9147, IETF (2022)
23. Sankarasubramaniam, Y., Akyildiz, I.F., McLaughlin, S.: Energy efficiency based packet size optimization in wireless sensor networks. In: Proceedings of the First International Workshop on Sensor Network Protocols and Applications (SNPA). IEEE (2003). https://doi.org/10.1109/SNPA.2003.1203351
24. Schmandt, J., Sherman, A.T., Banerjee, N.: Mini-MAC: Raising the bar for vehicular security with a lightweight message authentication protocol. Veh. Commun. **9** (2017). https://doi.org/10.1016/j.vehcom.2017.07.002
25. Seferagić, A., Famaey, J., De Poorter, E., Hoebeke, J.: Survey on wireless technology trade-offs for the industrial Internet of Things. Sensors **20**(2) (2020). https://doi.org/10.3390/s20020488
26. Serror, M., Hack, S., Henze, M., Schuba, M., Wehrle, K.: challenges and opportunities in securing the industrial Internet of Things. IEEE Trans. Indus. Inform. **17**(5) (2021). https://doi.org/10.1109/TII.2020.3023507
27. Shaikh, F.K., Zeadally, S.: Energy harvesting in wireless sensor networks: a comprehensive review. Renewable and Sustainable Energy Rev. **55** (2016). https://doi.org/10.1016/j.rser.2015.11.010
28. Simplicio Jr, M.A., De Oliveira, B.T., Margi, C.B., Barreto, P.S., Carvalho, T.C., Näslund, M.: Survey and comparison of message authentication solutions on wireless sensor networks. Ad Hoc Netw. **11**(3) (2013)
29. Vitturi, S., Zunino, C., Sauter, T.: Industrial communication systems and their future challenges: next-generation ethernet, IIoT, and 5G. Proc. IEEE **107**(6) (2019). https://doi.org/10.1109/JPROC.2019.2913443
30. Vuran, M.C., Akyildiz, I.F.: Cross-layer packet size optimization for wireless terrestrial, underwater, and underground sensor networks. In: Proceedings of the Conference on Computer Communications (INFOCOM). IEEE (2008). https://doi.org/10.1109/INFOCOM.2008.54
31. Wagner, E., Bauer, J., Henze, M.: Take a bite of the reality sandwich: revisiting the security of progressive message authentication codes. In: Proceedings of the 15th ACM Conference on Security and Privacy in Wireless and Mobile Networks. ACM (2022). https://doi.org/10.1145/3507657.3528539
32. Wagner, E., Serror, M., Wehrle, K., Henze, M.: BP-MAC: fast authentication for short messages. In: Proceedings of the 15th ACM Conference on Security and Privacy in Wireless and Mobile Networks (WiSec). ACM (2022). https://doi.org/10.1145/3507657.3528554
33. Whitehead, D.E., Owens, K., Gammel, D., Smith, J.: Ukraine cyber-induced power outage: analysis and practical mitigation strategies. In: Proceedings of the Conference for Protective Relay Engineers (CPRE). IEEE (2017). https://doi.org/10.1109/CPRE.2017.8090056
34. Wilhelm, M., Martinovic, I., Schmitt, J.B., Lenders, V.: Short paper: reactive jamming in wireless networks: how realistic is the threat? In: Proceedings of the fourth ACM conference on Wireless network security (WiSec). ACM (2011). https://doi.org/10.1145/1998412.1998422

# DoSat: A DDoS Attack on the Vulnerable Time-Varying Topology of LEO Satellite Networks

Tianbo Lu[1,2(✉)], Xia Ding[1,2], Jiaze Shang[1,2], Pengfei Zhao[1,2], and Han Zhang[1,2]

[1] School of Computer Science (National Pilot Software Engineering School), Beijing University of Posts and Telecommunications, Beijing, China
{lutb,smiling,sjz,pengfeizhao316,zh309}@bupt.edu.cn

[2] Key Laboratory of Trustworthy Distributed Computing and Service (BUPT), Ministry of Education, Beijing, China

**Abstract.** Low Earth orbit (LEO) satellite networks, which feature low-latency and full-coverage connectivity, promise to revolutionize the Internet and become an indispensable part of the next-generation communications network. However, due to the limited bandwidth and processing resources available on board, LEO satellite networks are susceptible to network attacks, especially link flooding attacks (LFAs). LFAs are a specific type of the notorious DoS attack where the attacker tries to cut off critical network links using seemingly legitimate traffic. Unlike attacks targeted directly on servers, LFAs undermine networks in a more insidious manner. In this paper, we present *DoSat* (DDoS on Satellites), an LFA attack model that focuses on the time-varying topology of satellite networks. The model takes advantage of such an opportunity to concentrate attack traffic: the traffic having been sent out during the process of path delay switching will reach the destination in tandem. We demonstrate through simulation experiments that *DoSat* can reduce the cost of LFAs by approximately 20% without any tradeoffs of attack's undetectability.

**Keywords:** LEO satellite network · Network topology · Link flooding attack · DDoS

## 1 Introduction

In the early days, satellite communications served as a supplement to the land-based communications technologies, relaying mostly low-frequency, narrowband signals that carry audio and video information. Nowadays, SpaceX, OneWeb and other companies are launching thousands of artificial satellites into space with the ultimate goal of building satellite internet constellations that provide low-latency, broadband global internet service.

Security is a constant topic of discussion. As the reliance on satellite communications keeps expanding, the protection of satellite networks from sabotage


C. Pöpper and L. Batina (Eds.): ACNS 2024, LNCS 14584, pp. 265–282, 2024.
https://doi.org/10.1007/978-3-031-54773-7_11

has become of significance. As for the emerging LEO satellite networks (LSNs), researchers today focus most of their attention on reducing communications delay [1,9], improving network topology [2] and designing new routing strategies [7,10]. The security issues of LSNs, however, are often overlooked.

In this paper, we propose *DoSat* (the abbreviation for DDoS on Satellites), a DDoS attack model against LSNs. DoSat fully leverages the topological characteristics of LSNs to concentrate the attack traffic on a small set of carefully chosen links, thereby congesting the target network. In addition, traffic of DoSat is generated only by bots (i.e. compromised satellite-enabled terminals) sending data to each other, which makes it less probable for the attack to be detected.

Our main contributions are:

- We develop a formal model of LSNs, based on which a vulnerability to DDoS caused by the time-varying property of dynamic networks is spotted and thoroughly analyzed.
- We present the DoSat attack and the pseudo-code for its core steps. It mainly consists of three steps: scheduling bot pairs, constructing cooperative flows and calculating the sent traffic.
- We implement the attack model in a simulation environment. Experiments suggest that our attack can be carried out with little risk of being detected, and its bandwidth costs are about 20% less than other similar work.

The remainder of this work is structured as follows. Section 2 gives necessary background knowledge about LSN and DoS, on which we base our discussion of DoSat. Section 3 analyzes the feasibility of DoSat attack, followed by a detailed description of the workflow of the proposed model. The simulation setup and performance evaluation are given in Sect. 4. Section 5 discusses how some of the existing countermeasures may be applied to mitigate DoSat. Finally, Sect. 6 concludes this paper.

## 2 Background and Related Work

### 2.1 LEO Satellite Network

The incorporation of satellites into Internet connections is not a new topic, but it's not until recent years that the exciting prospect of LSNs has started to reveal. Prior to 2015, two major satellite telecommunications companies, Globalstar and Iridium, had offered mobile-satellite service that relayed voice and data through LSNs. But they struggled to compete with terrestrial cellular networks due to high operating costs. Globalstar eventually repositioned itself as an emergency messaging service provider, while Iridium unfortunately went bankrupt. Later, SpaceX and Amazon have proven that it is commercially feasible to provide global coverage of high-speed Internet access to the entire Earth using satellite constellations.

LSNs are not just a complement to terrestrial networks, as demonstrated by the following three factors: (1) Scale: the current LSN is planned to have hundreds or thousands of satellites, providing sufficient access bandwidth, compared

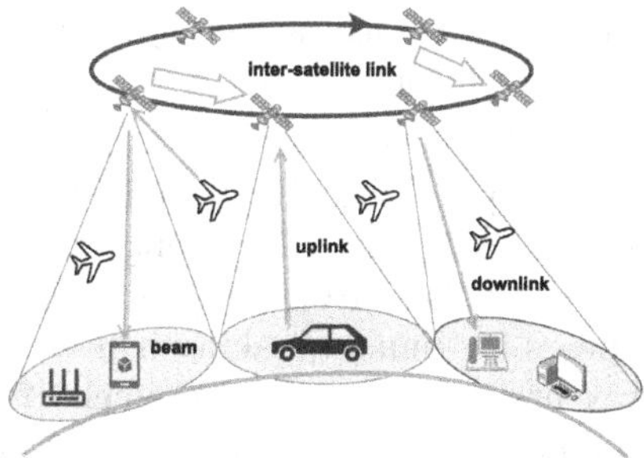


**Fig. 1.** A typical LEO satellite network.

to the previous dozens of satellites; (2) Frequency band: satellites use higher frequency bands simultaneously, mainly Ku-band (12–18 GHz) and Ka-band (26.5–40 GHz), to obtain greater bandwidth with rich frequency resources; (3) Orbital height: LSNs operate in low-Earth orbit, which is situated at most 2,000 km above the Earth's surface. The low-Earth orbit is at most 2,000 km above the Earth surface, and the transmission delay is less than 10ms. This kind of special network has aroused wide attention in the academic community. The main research challenge is that each satellite moves at a speed of about 27,000 km per hour, and this high speed motion poses difficulties for link switching, dynamic routing strategies, network security and so on.

The high motion of the satellite makes the network topology show dynamic changes, so that the inter-satellite links are constantly disconnected and reconnected. At present, there are two kinds of modeling methods. One is virtual topology, also known as snapshot, which was first proposed by [5], referring to the discretization of time domain into several time slices, in which a dynamic topology can be regarded as a static snapshot. The other is virtual node, which was first proposed by [19]. The earth surface is divided into several geographic regions, and the satellite is bound to the geographic region through which it passes, so as to obtain logical addresses. Both of the two modeling methods have their own advantages and disadvantages. Both are used to model LEO satellite networks, so as to shield network dynamics and facilitate research. As shown in Fig. 1, traffic of user terminals is transmitted to the satellite network through uplinks, then routed through the inter-satellite links (ISLs) between satellites, and finally transmitted back to user terminals through downlinks. In this way, the satellite provides services for the equipment on the ground, achieving full coverage.

### 2.2 Denial-of-Service Attack

Denial-of-service (DoS) attack is a notorious form of cyber-attack, in which the attacker attempts to make a service degraded or even unavailable to its legitimate users by overloading the servers or the routers that the servers connect to. And the distributed denial-of-service (DDoS) attack is a distributed augmentation of DoS. In DDoS, the attacker floods the targeted service with the help of a botnet containing typically thousands of bots. More sophisticated strategies are required to mitigate this type of attack, as simply attempting to block one or two IP addresses would be insufficient.

**Link Flooding Attack.** Our proposed DoSat originates from a specific type of DDoS called link flooding attack (LFA), which congests a target link by coordinating traffic through it. Unlike DDoS attacks that directly attack endpoints, the attack traffic of LFA appears legitimate, making it more challenging to detect. The concept of LFA was first proposed by Coremelt [22], in which $N$ compromised bots send seemingly legitimate traffic to each other to overload the core network with $\binom{N}{2}$ connections. Crossfire [13] extended this idea by flooding a small set of carefully chosen links, effectively cutting off the connection of the selected region from the Internet. In 2019, CrossPath [3] adopted LFA in software-defined networks (SDNs) to disrupt the SDN control channel by using the shared links in control traffic and data traffic.

In 2021, ICARUS [6] proposed to turn the key benefits of LSNs into vulnerabilities to launch LFA attacks, which represents, to the best of our knowledge, the only instance of an LFA attack model specifically designed for LSNs. The paper presented as an open problem to employ the "pulsing attack" technique to temporarily increase the intensity of the attack traffic. Our work is inspired by ICARUS and extends the LFA attack on LSNs with temporal lensing.

**Temporal Lensing Attack.** Temporal lensing, a form of amplification DDoS, is inspired by a military tactic known as TOT (Time-On-Target). TOT involves synchronizing clocks and estimating projectile flight times to ensure that multiple guns fire at different locations and times, but converge their shells to hit the target simultaneously, maximizing the damage inflicted. In 2015, Rasti et al.'s Temporal Lensing [21] utilized DNS infrastructure as reflectors to create delay differences in paths so as to concentrate attack traffic. They suggested that "the temporal lensing can be combined with LFA because the amplified attack flows can better reduce throughput on the target link". In 2016, the authors of Coremelt proposed a temporal lensing enhancement called Cicadas [15], which used congestion as an implicit signal, combined with Kalman filter to achieve accurate synchronization.

**Our DoSat Attack.** Now, LFA is no longer simply used, but the infrastructure in the network is used to enhance the effect. However, the attack of LSN still stays in primitive LFA, which can be solved by some defense strategies [11,17]. We mainly consider the scenario where temporal lensing strengthens LFA in LSN, because the delay difference required by the temporal lensing can naturally be provided by the time-varying topology of LEO satellite network itself. When the network switches from a snapshot to the next, the network topology changes, including path delays. We propose an attack model based on this, due to the limited bandwidth resources on the satellite, such attacks will be more severe.

As shown in Fig. 2, LSN is modeled for each individual snapshot. A period of motion of satellites is divided into $n$ time slots, which is called a cycle. The

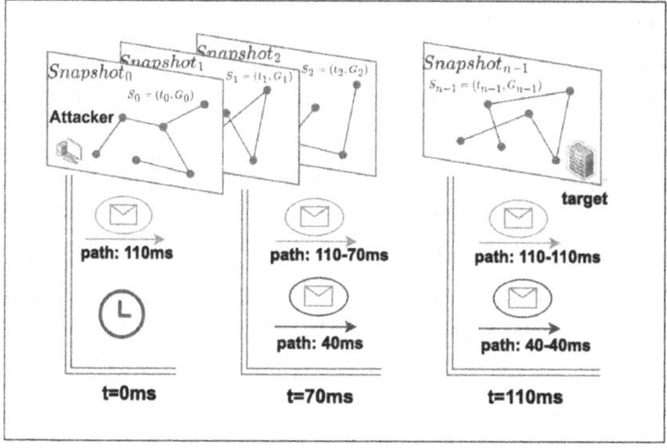


**Fig. 2.** Temporal lens in snapshots.

network topology is treated as a static snapshot in each time slot. At the 0 ms, the attacker sends a packet to the victim along the 110 ms path along the routing algorithm in $Snapshot_0$, and sends another packet at 70 ms. At this time, due to the change of the satellite position, the $Snapshot_1$ path has become 40 ms, while the previous packet is still along the original path, which is demonstrated in [14]. Finally, at 110 ms, both packets arrive at the destination at the same time, doubling the attack bandwidth.

### 2.3 LSN Simulation

LSNs possess distinctive characteristics that set them apart from terrestrial networks, presenting new challenges for network modeling. With the aim of facilitating research on LSNs, Simon Kassing et al. [14] proposed Hypatia in 2020, a framework for simulating and visualizing the network behavior of satellite constellations. Based on publicly available design details for commercial constellations like StarLink, Hypatia is able to capture the unique dynamics of these satellite networks.

In our work, we rely on Hypatia to setup the simulation environment for StarLink S1 to evaluate the performance of DoSat.

## 3 DoSat Attack

### 3.1 Threat Model

We consider a rational adversary that seeks to strategically inflict as much damage as possible on the target LSN while keeping the cost and detectability minimal. More specifically, the adversary has the following objectives in mind while launching an attack.

- **Minimize cost.** Cost represents the amount of resources (i.e. the computing power, bandwidth and number of satellite-enabled bots) an adversary has to

invest for a successful attack. A rational adversary would seek to minimize the cost of the attack, because it would be less demanding to construct and maintain a botnet of a smaller scale. The way we quantify cost will be described in Sect. 4.3.
- **Hamper detection.** Oftentimes, an adversary would keep the attack covert to avoid the detection of malicious traffic and protect the bots. To evade detection, the attack must mimic legitimate traffic patterns, a task at which our proposed DoSat excels, as it relies solely on communication traffic between bot pairs. The way we quantify detectability will also be described in Sect. 4.3.

### 3.2 Feasibility Analysis

**Table 1.** Notations

| | |
|---|---|
| **Network Topologies** | |
| Nodes | $N = n_1, n_2, ..., n_N$ |
| Links | $L \subseteq N \times N$ |
| Latency | $Lat \approx RTT/2$ |
| Topologies | $G = (N, L)$ |
| Time period | $T = t_1, t_2, ..., t_T$ |
| Time slots | $ST = \{t \in T \| t' \leq t \leq t'', t' \leq t''\}$ |
| Transition set | $I \subseteq T$ |
| Snapshots | $S = (t, G)$ |
| **Attack Components** | |
| Bot nodes | $B \subseteq N$ |
| Cooperative flows | $f = (t_i, (s, d), L_f, Lat_i)$ |
| Cooperative flows set | $F = f_1, f_2, ..., f_F$ |
| Link Capacity | $C = \{c_l \| l \in L\}$ |
| Bot bandwidth | $R = \{r_f \| f = (s, d) \in B\}$ |
| Attack window | $W \subseteq T$ |
| **Attack Parameters** | |
| Failure probability | $w_1$ |
| Risk of self-congestion | $w_2$ |
| Amplification factor | $\epsilon$ |

A summary of symbols and notations that will be used is given in Table 1 beforehand for the sake of readability.

We take a snapshot-based approach, which slices the time into consecutive time slots during which the network topology is considered static. The snapshot corresponding to $t_i$ is $(t_i, G_i)$, where $G = (N, L)$ is the network connectivity graph, $N$ is the node set, and $L$ is the link set. The snapshot was originally formalized by [5], for a time period $T$, given such $t', t'' \in T$ that $t' < t''$, a time slot $ST$ is defined by $\{t \in T | t' \leq t < t''\}$. If for any $t \in T$, $t$ falls into $[t', t'']$, and $t', t'' \in I$, then $I$ is defined as transition set. It's apparent that $I$ is a countably finite subset of $T$.

LFA [22] refers to the flow sent by the attacker between bots $s$ and $d$ as cooperative flow $f = ((s, d), L_f)$, $(s, d) \in B$ is the pair of bots, $L_f$ is the forwarding path that flow $f$ passes through. We assume that all messages in the flow between source and destination propagate on the same path, specifically, it is a set of inter-satellite links. It is verified experimentally in the temporal lensing [21] that the latency of the forwarding path can be estimated by Round-Trip Time (RTT), i.e. $Lat = RTT/2 + \omega$, where $\omega$ is an error constant. Even though halving the $RTT$ value does not actually give an accurate result of the delay due to the existence of asymmetric routing protocols on the Internet, it is still possible to get an estimate of the delay within the margin of error.

We measure latency for each cooperative flow and define it as

$$f = (t_i, (s, d), L_f, Lat_i) \tag{1}$$

For $t_i$ in each time slot, the attacker needs to construct a cooperative flow set $F = \{f_1, f_2, ...f_F\}$, set the bandwidth of each flow as $r_f$, then the condition for successful LFA attack is that the sum of bandwidth of $n$ flows is greater than the capacity $C$ of the target link, $n \cdot r_f > C$. Target link is the concept of LFA, which refers to inter-satellite link in LSN.

The introduction of temporal lensing into snapshots of satellite networks relies on two key operations: estimating attack path delay, and establishing optimal send scheduling. Temporal lensing also proposed the concept of attack window $W$, which refers to the duration of an attack. If the flow $f$ in the attack window $W$ is superimposed to $\epsilon$ times after send scheduling, then the number $n$ of flows in the attack flow set $F$ in DoSat should be satisfied

$$n > C/(r_f \cdot \epsilon) \tag{2}$$

Typical values are $W = 200s$ and $C$ is 20 Gbps according to Starlink's files [14]. In order to obtain the forwarding path $L_f$ of cooperation flow $f$, the attacker needs to know the routing policy in the network. The routing strategy in LEO satellite network is a widely discussed topic. The current research on satellite network simulation adopts the shortest path algorithm (Dijkstra) to realize the routing simulation [2]. In ICARUS [6], the author considers the case of single shortest path and multi-path, divides multi-path into four categories, namely $k$ shortest intersection path, $k$ Earth-earth intersection path, $k$ satellite intersection path and $k$ minimum coverage shortest path, and proposes a probabilistic routing strategy, that is, based on the idea of equal-cost multi-path routing (ECMP). From a group of $k$ pre-calculated shortest paths, one is randomly selected as the forwarding path. Compared with the traditional Dijkstra algorithm, this setting makes the attacker face a greater challenge, because the routing situation of the network is not completely transparent, in order to successfully congest the target, the attacker needs to make more sophisticated planning.

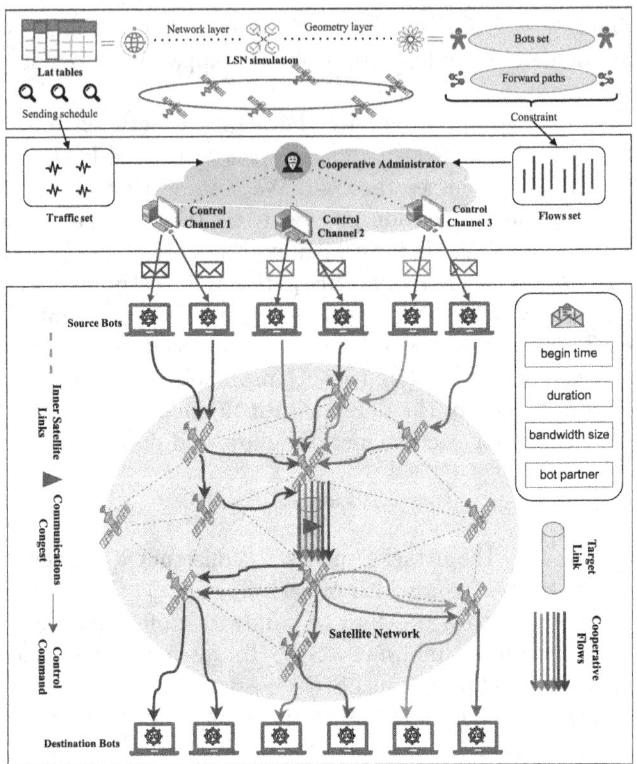


**Fig. 3.** An overview of DoSat.

The probability of success has been analyzed by ICARUS, given that the attacker does not know exactly which particular path the cooperation flow will take. However, it only considers the distribution of the attack flow in one snapshot, and its probability constraint is only for the original attack flow. In this paper, all the snapshots in a time cycle are calculated, and a set of cooperative flows is generated for each snapshot. Finally, the attack success probability of the amplified flow is deduced. Suppose that a pair of bot nodes $(s, d)$ selected by the attacker cooperate on a path, where $m$ crosses the target link. In probabilistic routing of ICARUS, the event "Cooperative flow across the target link" can be described as Bernoulli random variable $X_f$, and the probability that $f$ crosses the target link is $p_f = m/k'$, and $k' \leq k$ because there may not be enough paths between the source and the destination. Then, the random variable $\delta$ of the whole set $F$ should satisfy

$$\delta = \sum_{f \in F} X_f \geq C/(r_f \cdot \epsilon) \tag{3}$$

Assuming the configuration failure probability is $w_1$, the attacker is targeting $P\left[\delta < C/(r_f \cdot \epsilon)\right] \leq w_1$. The attacker also needs to consider that the sent traffic will not self-congestion before reaching the target, so for non-target link $l$, $m_l < c_l$. Let $w_2$ be the acceptable risk of self-congestion, then $P\left[m_l \geq c_l\right] \leq w_2$.

For target $P\left[\delta < C/(r_f \cdot \epsilon)\right] \leq w_1$, the expectation of $\delta$ is $\mu = E[\delta] = \sum_{f\in F} p_f$. Then the Chernoff bound [20] can be used in the approximate calculation. We get $P[\delta < C/(r_f \cdot \epsilon)] \leq exp(-\mu(1 - C/r_f \cdot \epsilon \cdot \mu)^2/2) \leq w_1$, where $w_1 \in (0,1)$ and $r_f \in [1, \mu]$, we can obtain

$$\mu > \sqrt{\ln w_1 \cdot (\ln w_1 - 2 \cdot r_f \cdot \epsilon)} + r_f \cdot \epsilon - \ln w_1 \tag{4}$$

For the attack target $P[m_l \geq c_l] \leq w_2$, there is $\mu_l = \sum_{f\in F} p_f$ similarly. Here considering the Chernoff upper-tail bound, we have $P[m_l \geq c_l] \leq \exp(-\mu_l(c_l/\mu_l - 1)^2/(2 + c_l/\mu_l - 1))) \leq w_2$, finally we get

$$\mu_l < 1/2(-\sqrt{\ln w_2 \cdot (\ln w_2 - 8c_l)} - \ln w_2 + 2c_l) \tag{5}$$

then the success probability is $P_{success} \geq 1 - (P[\delta < C/r_f \cdot \epsilon] + \sum_{l=1}^{|L|-1} P[m_l \geq c_l]) \geq 1 - [w_1 + (|L| - 1)w_2]$.

Based on the preceding analysis, we only need to construct an $F$ that meets the constraint Eqs. 4 & 5 to achieve a success probability of $P_{success}$, whose minimum value is $1 - [w_1 + (|L| - 1)w_2]$. Meanwhile, the smaller the failure probability and self-congestion risk are, the higher the success probability will be, aligning with common intuition. Although the conclusions are consistent with ICARUS, we have derived a new probabilistic constraint that guides the adversary's traffic sending behavior.

### 3.3 DoSat Overview

Figure 3 illustrates schematically the overview of our DoSat attack model, which involves three different roles.

**Cooperative Administrator.** It is responsible for the global orchestration of the attack, selecting target links and pairing up bots whose communication traffic can effectively congest these links. Actually, the fact that the information on satellites' position is publicly available makes the orchestration much easier, as the cooperative administrator gets to predict the network topology in the upcoming time slots with high accuracy.

**Control Channels.** They are normally servers scattering around the Internet whose IP addresses or domain names can be hidden in the bots' code or passed on later through updates. They act as brokers that relay commands from the cooperative administrator to the bots. Communications between control channels and bots are often encapsulated into various secure network protocols to make their actions covert.

**Bots.** Bots, in this context, are subverted satellite-enabled terminals that have legitimate access to the target LSN. According to speedtest results from SpaceX, the capacity of an ISL is 20 Gbps, which means that it only takes 500 bots each sending data at a rate of 40 Mbps to launch a brute-force DDoS attack. For comparison, SpaceX has licensed 5 million terminals as of 2020 in the United States.

### 3.4 Attack Mechanism

The deployment of DoSat attack relies on two intermediate artifacts: the flow set $F$ and the traffic set $T$. $F$ stores the paths between the source and destination bots, while $T$ indicates the timings and bandwidth of attack traffic. The attack can be divided into three core steps: Scheduling bot pairs, constructing cooperative flows and calculating the sent traffic.

**Scheduling Bot Pairs.** This step is aimed at cherry-picking a set of bot pairs whose transmission paths will cross the target link, as described in Algorithm 1. The attack window is evenly sliced into time slots $ST$ of size $slot\_size$ (line 3). Then, the topology snapshot is constructed for each $ST$ (lines 5–6) by calculating each satellite's position and constructing ISLs. For $N$ bots, there are $\binom{N}{2}$ possible bot pairs (line 7). We select the bot pairs so that their flows cross the target link (lines 9–11).

In the $G = (N, L)$ of each time slot, each bot is bound to the reachable satellite. For Starlink, the satellite-enabled terminal will establish uplink and downlink to the nearest satellite when the user accesses the network. We record the bot pairs crossing the target link and their flows for subsequent steps.

**Algorithm 1.** Scheduling bots for the target link

```
Input: W (attack window size), slot_size (time slot size), bot_pool (candidate bots
    set) and l (target link)
 1: var Snaps <t, G> // hashmap of t_i and G_i
 2: var bots_selected // the selected bot pairs
 3: cnt ← TimeSharding(W, slot_size)
 4: for all t = 0 to cnt do
 5:     G_t ← PositionOffset(t)
 6:     Snaps_t ← ISLBuild(G_t)
 7:     bot_pair_list ← BotWithBot(bot_pool)
 8:     for all pair in bot_pair_list do
 9:         bot_flow ← DijksKRoute(Snaps_t, pair)
10:         if IsCrossTarget(bot_flow, l) then
11:             Add pair to bots_selected.
12:         end if
13:     end for
14: end for
```

**Constructing Cooperative Flows.** For the scheduled bot pairs, we use *DijksKRoute* to calculate $k$ shortest paths, in which $m$ cross through the target link. Recall the analysis in §3.2, in the cooperative flow set $F$, $\mu = E[\delta] =$

$\sum_{f \in F} p_f$ satisfies the constraint, the attack succeeds with probability of $P_{success}$. The construction process of the cooperative flows is described by Algorithm 2. Since $\mu$ is cumulative, a pair of bots is iteratively added to $F$, and removed if Eq. 5 is not satisfied (lines 5–8). If the addition is complete, consider reducing $p_f$ (line 11) and continue the above process until Eq. 4 is met (lines 3–4).

**Calculating the Sent Traffic.** This step is adopted to make the traffic sent by the bot pairs on the cooperative flows exactly congested the target link, as shown in Algorithm 3.

The bandwidth of each bot is greedily initialized to the uplink capacity to obtain a maximum attack effect (line 2), and then the traffic is iteratively reduced until it is exactly greater than the bandwidth required to successfully launch the attack (lines 10–12). (lines 3–6) is the amplification factor calculation, if flow's probability meets the temporal lens, $\epsilon$ increase by one (lines 13–14). Finally, the bandwidth of traffic sent by each bot is $r_f$, and the sum of traffic sent by bots is $\sum_{f \in F} r_{uplink}/\epsilon_f$, which is optimized compared with the previous work $r_{uplink} \cdot |F|$ proposed by ICARUS.

**Algorithm 2.** Construct cooperative flows for bots_selected

**Input:** *bots_flows_list* (flows set), $w_1$ (failure probability) and $w_2$ (acceptance risk of self-congestion)

```
1:  var F ← ∅ // set of cooperative flows
2:  var m ← k // k paths in the routing policy
3:  while F not satify Equation 4 do
4:      SortByM(bots_selected, m)
5:      for all pair in bots_selected do
6:          Add pair to F.
7:          if F not satify Equation 5 then
8:              Remove pair in F.
9:          end if
10:     end for
11:     m decrease by 1
12: end while
```

In line 5, $IsPulseArrive()$ relies on two key operations: estimated path delay and flows send scheduling. In order to construct the attack path delay table, we measured the RTT through the network layer simulation of Hypatia platform [14]. In the 200 s time cycle, the bot source $s$ sent a Packet Internet Groper (ping) to the bot destination $d$ every $1ms$, and recorded the response time. Measure the RTT of all bot pairs and record the result in a *txt* file, the first column contains the packet sending time, and the second column contains the RTT value, in nanoseconds (ns).

Process all files, each pair of endpoints with 50 ms slot size, numbered from 0. A record is stored in the delay table: lat=(source $s$, destination $d$, slot number $i$, $latency$), where path latency is estimated by RTT/2. Iterate over the records in the table, when

$$((ST_j - ST_i) \times slot\_size = latency_j - latency_i \tag{6}$$

The two flows in slots $i$ and $j$ will arrive at their destinations at the same time in a small time range, doubling the bandwidth pressure on the target link, where $slot\_size$ is the size of the slot. For example, RTT in slot 0 is 140 ms, RTT in slot 2 is 40 ms, and slot size is 50 ms. When the flow in slot 0 has passed 100 ms after being sent, it still has a 40 ms path, which happens to arrive at the same time as the flow in slot 2. Add the slot number to the $ST$ set, and recording it in $T$.

Finally, the update of $T$ for $\epsilon = |ST|$, because when there are $\epsilon$ flows to arrive at the same time, equivalent to amplify the bandwidth of a bot to $\epsilon$ times.

**Algorithm 3.** Send traffic for each bot_pair

**Input:** $Snaps$, $F$, $C$ (capacity of target link)<br>
**var** $\epsilon_f$ // the amplification factor<br>
**var** $r_f \leftarrow R_{uplink}$ // initial to the capacity of uplink<br>
**for all** $f$ in $F$ **do**<br>
    **for all** $t$ in $Snaps$ **do**<br>
        **if** IsPulseArrive($f$) **then**<br>
            $\epsilon_f$ increase by 1<br>
        **end if**<br>
    **end for**<br>
**end for**<br>
**while** $R_{uplink} \times |F| > C$ **do**<br>
    $R_{uplink}$ decrease by 1<br>
**end while**<br>
**for all** $f$ in $F$ **do**<br>
    $r_f \leftarrow R_{uplink}/\epsilon_f$<br>
**end for**

# 4 Simulation and Evaluation

## 4.1 Simulation Setup

In order to verify the effect of the proposed attack model, we built an experimental system based on Hypatia [14], the satellite visualization framework proposed by kassing. The experimental environment was Linux Ubuntu 20.04 LTS system with 20 processors: 12th Gen Intel(R) Core(TM) i7-12700H, 2.30 GHz and 16 GBRAM. The simulation is based on the largest LEO constellation in existence: SpaceX's Starlink. According to the regulatory information submitted by SpaceX to the US Federal Communications Commission (FCC) and the International Telecommunication Union (ITU) and other regulatory bodies [16], orbital

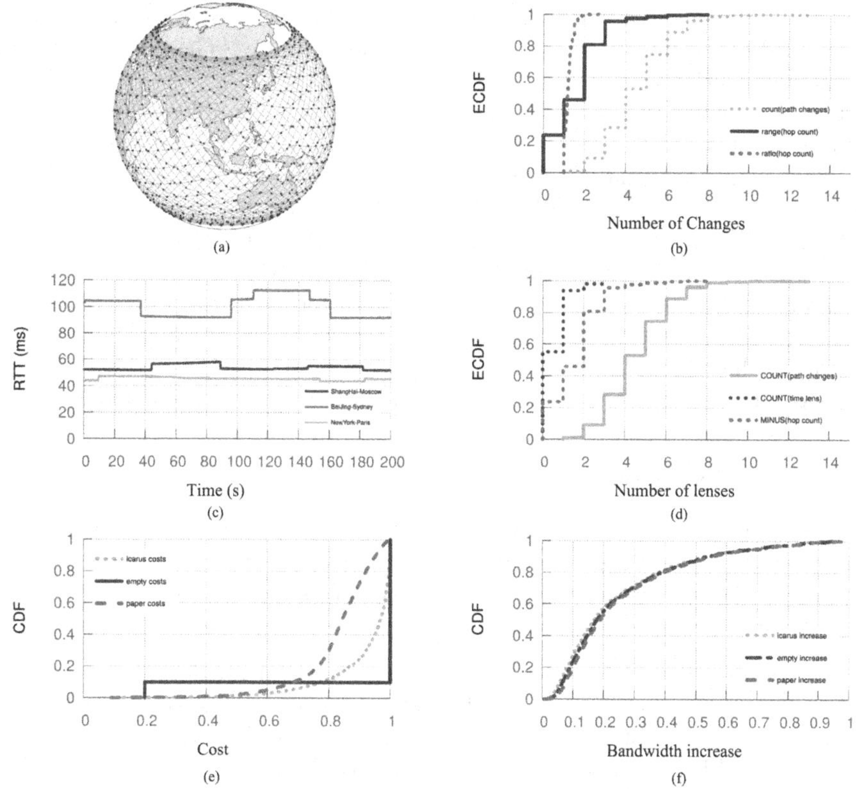


**Fig. 4.** Simulation results.

parameters of the constellation structure can be obtained, in which each shell constitutes a different constellation and is evenly distributed in different orbital space.

SpaceX is currently deploying shell S1, which is composed of 1,584 satellites with an altitude of $h$=550 km and an orbital inclination angle of $i = 53°$. S1 is a Walker delta constellation with 72 orbits, each with 22 satellites. S1 will cover most of the world's population, but will not extend the service to less populated areas in high latitudes, as will be the case with the high-inclination shell S3-S5. We takes Starlink S1 as LEO satellite network environment, firstly studies the visualization of satellite network topology, then studies the dynamic changes of network structure over time, and finally analyzes the effect and evaluates the performance of the DoSat attack scheme.

## 4.2 Network Setup

The simulation of LEO satellite network Starlink is demonstrated in Fig. 4 (a). The inter-satellite links adopt the classic mode of four ISLs: a link between satellites in one orbit and two satellites in two orbits. Recent work has referred to this grid-like connectivity as "+Grid" [2], and we use +Grid as the default ISL interconnection.

The top 1000 most populous cities are set as the terminals which connect to the nearest satellite. Each satellite can be connected to multiple terminals with multi-beam antennas. A single satellite covers an area of about 3.53 million $km^2$, about ten times the size of a city, this setup helps observe differences in the location of different terminals. For the traffic distribution, [10] means that it's difficult to evaluate matrix traffic in a topology, as it will be driven by market, regulatory, geographic changes and so on. Therefore, We use Gross Domestic Product (GDP) dataset traffic to simulate the legitimate traffic between two terminals. The higher the GDP is, the darker the link color is, indicating that bandwidth resources are more scarce, which is consistent with ICARUS.

### 4.3 Evaluation Metrics

As discussed in Sect. 3.1, the adversary strives to inflict as much damage as possible on the target LSN using minimal resources while remaining covert. Thus, we evaluate the performance of DoSat in terms of its *cost* and *detectability*. And the cost and detectabiliy are defined similarly to ICARUS [6].

**Cost:** The cost of a DDoS attack can be intuitively defined as the aggregate traffic volume (measured in Gbps) a botnet has to generate for the attack to be successful. A lower cost translates to smaller botnet scale and lighter stress on each individual bot, thus making it easier to launch an attack.

**Detectability:** Anomalies in traffic patterns detected on uplinks are more likely to lead to the identification of the compromised bots compared to ISLs and downlinks. The adversary, aware of this, will attempt to avoid abnormal surge in traffic volume on the uplinks by scheduling tasks to geographically dispersed bots. Therefore, the *maximum absolute increase of uplink bandwidth* caused by attack traffic is chosen to be the measurement of detectability.

For result demonstration as in Fig. 4, we employ cumulative distribution function (CDF) and empirical CDF (ECDF) from probability theory to portray the distribution of random variables representing certain properties of the traffic, CDF for continuous ones while ECDF for discrete ones. Formally, the CDF and ECDF of a real-valued random variable $X$ is given by

$$F_X(x) = P(X \leq x) \tag{7}$$

where the right-hand side represents the probability that the random variable $X$ takes on a value less than or equal to $x$.

### 4.4 Results

We analyze the above attack with Starlink shell S1 constellation.

The opportunity of attack lies in the dynamic nature of satellite network, so the changes of the path structure of Starlink are studied. Figure 4 (b) shows the

ECDF of the number of dynamic changes of the whole Starlink in the simulation for 200 s, and ECDF represents the cumulative proportion of values. The green line is the number of path changes, with four changes at the median; The blue line shows the difference in the number of hops, with more than a third of the connections exceeding two hops; The yellow line shows the ratio of maximum hops to minimum hops, and you can see that more than 10% of connections see a change in hops of more than 50%. Obviously, LEO network paths change many times per minute, which provides a opportunity for the attacks proposed.

For each bot pair, we study the change of its RTT over time, measured by the source bot sending a ping to the destination every 1ms and recording the response time. Figure 4 (c) shows the results for three pairs of endpoints as an example. We take 50 ms as time slot, and take 200 s as the attack window $W$ to observe the distribution of attack flows in snapshots. The path from Beijing to Sydney has the biggest change, with t = 95.9 s and two switches of 110.6 s, resulting in the RTT rising from 93 ms to 112 ms. For the other two paths, the minimum RTT of the Shanghai-Moscow route is 52.1 ms and the maximum RTT is 57 ms. For the New York-Paris route, this RTT ranges from 43.7–47.2 ms. The last two changes are small but still show regularity.

We take 200 s as the attack window to observe the amplification of the flow. Figure 4 (d), in the simulation for 200 s, compared with the path changes of Starlink as a whole, about 47% of the flows have one or more amplified flows, and the distribution ratio is similar to the hop number change. This fits intuitively, since a necessary condition for a time lens is that the path delay changes from large to small, which is satisfied when the path switches from a high-hop path to a low-hop path. The results show that about half of the flow can be amplified when the path RTT changes from long to short.

We launch attacks for ISLs, calculate the bandwidth uploaded and normalize the cost to the capacity of a single ISL (i.e. uplinks/downlinks cost 0.2 and an ISL cost 1 to fully congest). In Fig. 4 (e), the blue line is the empty network with no traffic within, there are only two situations: congesting the uplink/downlink and ISLs. The capacity of the uplink/downlink is 1/5 of that of the ISL [14], and the congesting of the ISLs must fill the links. The green line is the result in ICARUS [6]. The figure demonstrates that the presence of legitimate traffic reduces the cost, albeit with a negligible effect. The orange line is our setting, and the median cost is reduced by about 20%. For bot pairs with large path changes, the profit of temporal lensing is about half, about $(0.82 - 0.96) \cdot 20\,Gbps$. This is because a bot pair with a large path change will receive about half of the amplification flow revenue, while the median path switching in Starlink is four times. After obtaining the amplification revenue, the cost can be reduced by halving the bandwidth without affecting the blocking of the target link.

Figure 4 (f) shows that both ICARUS and DoSat cause approximately the same bandwidth increase as in the empty network. It can be speculated that the exist of bots cannot be detected on the traffic, especially when the bots send legitimate requests.

## 5 Mitigations

There has been extensive research on defending against traditional DDoS attacks and several effective countermeasures have been proposed. Here we discuss the possibility to adapt them to mitigate the DoSat attack.

**Attack Detection and Malicious Node Identification.** There arise some open problems when it comes to deploying attack detection onto LSNs: (1) traditional DDoS detection mechanisms assume abundant computing power and bandwidth while satellites have limited resources on board; (2) It is challenging to identify abnormal characteristics within traffic generated by valid user terminals communicating through legitimate protocols. Although recent work [8,12] has proposed a few lightweight detection procedures for satellite networks, it is still unclear how to distinguish malicious traffic from the benign one.

**Congestion management schemes.** As RFC 3272 [4] suggests, the network may try to address existing and/or anticipated congestion problems by provisioning additional bandwidth resources. It is, however, a palliative instead of a cure for ever-expanding botnets the adversary may gain, not to mention that it would be highly expensive to increase ISL capacity.

**Dynamic routing.** The fairly fixed ISL topology and routing algorithm are exposing current LSNs to various forms of attacks. The obfuscation of network topology and forwarding path seems to be a promising approach to thwarting DoSat. Bhattacherjee et al. [2] suggested a rearrangement of ISLs and Liu et al. [18] proposed a multi-path transmission algorithm based on fountain codes. The underlying idea is to minimize the path similarity, thereby reducing the probability of the adversary successfully creating temporal lenses. However, the tradeoffs of security and latency must be carefully balanced.

## 6 Conclusion

This paper mainly studies DDoS attacks in LEO satellite networks. In order to achieve lower cost and better concealment, we propose DoSat, which focuses on the time-varying topology of satellite networks. By dispatching bots in all snapshots in a time period, traffic is sent between bots. When the traffic passes through the same link, the target link is congested, so as to achieve the effect of link flooding. Through theoretical analysis and simulation, we take Starlink, the largest LEO satellite network, as an example to prove that DoSat is practically feasible. The experimental results show that this attack can reduce the cost of attack while maintaining the concealment, compared with the advanced ICARUS attack.

**Acknowledgements.** We would like to thank the anonymous reviewers and our shepherd for their helpful comments on our paper. Tianbo Lu is the corresponding author. This work is supported by the National Natural Science Foundation of China (No. 62162060) and the National Key Research and Development Program of China (No. 2023YFB3105902).

## References

1. Bhattacherjee, D., et al.: Gearing up for the 21st century space race. In: Proceedings of the 17th ACM Workshop on Hot Topics in Networks, pp. 113–119 (2018)
2. Bhattacherjee, D., Singla, A.: Network topology design at 27,000 km/hour. In: Proceedings of the 15th International Conference on Emerging Networking Experiments And Technologies, pp. 341–354 (2019)
3. Cao, J., et al.: The crosspath attack: Disrupting the sdn control channel via shared links. In: 28th USENIX Security Symposium (USENIX Security 19), pp. 19–36 (2019)
4. Elwalid, A., Chiu, A., Xiao, X., Awduche, D.O.: Overview and Principles of Internet Traffic Engineering. RFC 3272 (May 2002)
5. Fischer, D., Basin, D., Engel, T.: Topology dynamics and routing for predictable mobile networks. In: 2008 IEEE International Conference on Network Protocols, pp. 207–217. IEEE (2008)
6. Giuliari, G., Ciussani, T., Perrig, A., Singla, A.: Icarus: attacking low earth orbit satellite networks. In: 2021 USENIX Annual Technical Conference (USENIX ATC 21), pp. 317–331 (2021)
7. Giuliari, G., Klenze, T., Legner, M., Basin, D., Perrig, A., Singla, A.: Internet backbones in space. ACM SIGCOMM Comput. Commun. Rev. **50**(1), 25–37 (2020)
8. Guo, W., Xu, J., Pei, Y., Yin, L., Jiang, C., Ge, N.: A distributed collaborative entrance defense framework against ddos attacks on satellite internet. IEEE Internet Things J. **9**(17), 15497–15510 (2022)
9. Handley, M.: Delay is not an option: Low latency routing in space. In: Proceedings of the 17th ACM Workshop on Hot Topics in Networks, pp. 85–91 (2018)
10. Handley, M.: Using ground relays for low-latency wide-area routing in megaconstellations. In: Proceedings of the 18th ACM Workshop on Hot Topics in Networks, pp. 125–132 (2019)
11. Hsiao, H.C., et al.: Stride: sanctuary trail-refuge from internet ddos entrapment. In: Proceedings of the 8th ACM SIGSAC Symposium on Information, Computer and Communications Security, pp. 415–426 (2013)
12. Jiang, C., Wang, X., Wang, J., Chen, H.H., Ren, Y.: Security in space information networks. IEEE Commun. Mag. **53**(8), 82–88 (2015)
13. Kang, M.S., Lee, S.B., Gligor, V.D.: The crossfire attack. In: 2013 IEEE Symposium on Security and Privacy, pp. 127–141. IEEE (2013)
14. Kassing, S., Bhattacherjee, D., Águas, A.B., Saethre, J.E., Singla, A.: Exploring the "internet from space" with hypatia. In: Proceedings of the ACM Internet Measurement Conference, pp. 214–229 (2020)
15. Ke, Y.M., Chen, C.W., Hsiao, H.C., Perrig, A., Sekar, V.: Cicadas: Congesting the internet with coordinated and decentralized pulsating attacks. In: Proceedings of the 11th ACM on Asia Conference on Computer and Communications Security, pp. 699–710 (2016)
16. Kelso, T.: Celestrak: Current norad two-line element sets (2020)
17. Lee, S.B., Kang, M.S., Gligor, V.D.: Codef: collaborative defense against large-scale link-flooding attacks. In: Proceedings of the Ninth ACM Conference on Emerging Networking Experiments and Technologies, pp. 417–428 (2013)
18. Liu, J., Xu, J., Li, S., Cui, X., Zhang, Y.: A secure multi-path transmission algorithm based on fountain codes. Trans. Emerg. Telecommun. Technol. **33**(5), e4450 (2022)

19. Mauger, R., Rosenberg, C.: Qos guarantees for multimedia services on a tdma-based satellite network. IEEE Commun. Mag. **35**(7), 56–65 (1997)
20. Mitzenmacher, M., Upfal, E.: Probability and computing: Randomization and probabilistic techniques in algorithms and data analysis. Cambridge University Press (2017)
21. Rasti, R., Murthy, M., Weaver, N., Paxson, V.: Temporal lensing and its application in pulsing denial-of-service attacks. In: 2015 IEEE Symposium on Security and Privacy, pp. 187–198. IEEE (2015)
22. Studer, A., Perrig, A.: The coremelt attack. In: Backes, M., Ning, P. (eds.) ESORICS 2009. LNCS, vol. 5789, pp. 37–52. Springer, Heidelberg (2009). https://doi.org/10.1007/978-3-642-04444-1_3

# DDoSMiner: An Automated Framework for DDoS Attack Characterization and Vulnerability Mining

Xi Ling[1], Jiongchi Yu[2], Ziming Zhao[1], Zhihao Zhou[1], Haitao Xu[1], Binbin Chen[3], and Fan Zhang[1,4(✉)]

[1] College of Computer Science and Technology, Zhejiang University, Hangzhou, China

[2] School of Computing and Information Systems, Singapore Management University, Singapore, Singapore

[3] Information Systems Technology and Design, Singapore University of Technology and Design, Singapore, Singapore

[4] Zhengzhou Xinda Institute of Advanced Technology, Zhengzhou, China

fanzhang@zju.edu.cn

**Abstract.** With the proliferation of Internet development, Distributed Denial of Service (DDoS) attacks are on the rise. As rule-based traffic analysis frameworks and Deep Packet Inspection (DPI) defense measures can effectively thwart many DDoS attacks, attackers keep exploring various attack surfaces and traffic amplification strategies to nullify the defense. In this paper, we propose DDoSMiner, an automated framework for DDoS attack characterization and vulnerability mining. DDoSMiner analyzes system call patterns of the TCP-based DDoS attack family, then generates Attack Call Flow Graph (ACFG) by discerning the differences between DDoS attack traffic and benign traffic. Furthermore, DDoSMiner identifies and extracts drop nodes and pivotal TCP states from the distinctive characteristics of attack traffic, then passes to the symbolic execution framework for exploring variants of the DDoS attack. We collectively analyze six types of TCP-based DDoS attacks, construct the corresponding ACFG, and identify a set of attack traffic variants. The attack traffic variants are evaluated on the widely used Network Intrusion Detection System (NIDS) Snort with three popular rule sets. The result shows that DDoSMiner indeed discovers the new DDoS attack trace, and the corresponding attack traffic can bypass all three defense toolkits.

**Keywords:** TCP-based DDoS attacks · Attack Call Flow Graph · Symbolic execution

## 1 Introduction

With the evolution of the Internet, the security issues of the Internet have garnered increasing attention. Among the various threats to networks, Distributed


C. Pöpper and L. Batina (Eds.): ACNS 2024, LNCS 14584, pp. 283–309, 2024.
https://doi.org/10.1007/978-3-031-54773-7_12

Denial of Service (DDoS) attacks are regarded as one of the most serious and commonly employed attack methods in practice [16,35,37,56,61]. For instance, Cloudflare has reported a DDoS attack which is launched by a botnet comprising approximately 11,000 IP addresses, peaking at an alarming 1.4 Tbps of attack traffic [55].

Although there are various detection and defense techniques for DDoS attacks [9,29,59], the main defense methods rely on traffic scrubbing [50], which requires expensive dedicated hardware. The core idea of this approach is redirecting the traffic of the target to the scrubbing centers of the Internet security service providers, where malicious traffic is identified and filtered. To be more effective, traffic scrubbing has evolved from centralized single-point detection to distributed detection solutions [31]. However, these methods still face challenges, specifically in terms of flexibility. On one hand, these detection methods heavily depends on filtering strategies crafted from known attacks, making it vulnerable to zero-day threats. [23]. On the other hand, middle-box-based detection and defense systems rely on hardware devices [13,22] and lack adaptability to various attack scenarios and network configurations. In addition, these methods increase the cost for transmission and storage, and bring more attack surfaces targeting middleware and cloud platforms [1,12].

Fortunately, with the emergence of Software-Defined Networking (SDN) [15] and Network Function Virtualization (NFV) [19] technologies, research on defense systems based on programmable networks has also pointed out new directions for DDoS detection and defense [54]. Bohatei *et al.* [14] is the first to design a flexible and resilient DDoS detection and mitigation system based on SDN. Although, subsequent studies based on this new network paradigm and network devices (e.g., programmable switches and smart NICs) have improved the flexibility and scalability of defense systems [28,52,57], the real-time response speed and performance overhead need to be further improved.

Despite defense research efforts, the development of new DDoS attacks continues. Conversely, more and more diverse strategies have been shown in DDoS attacks [30,34,43]. Firstly, emergent malware [39,45,46], such as Mirai [2], has notably bolstered the potency of DDoS attacks by rapidly commandeering the ever-increasing Internet of Things devices [33], leading to increased peak traffic and diversified attack vectors. Secondly, many vulnerabilities are constantly being exploited in network protocols, especially those based on the TCP protocol. Bock *et al.* [6] show that attackers exploiting vulnerabilities in the TCP protocol for reflection amplification attacks is a potential new attack way, and the amplification effect produced surpasses that of UDP-based attacks. TCP-based DDoS attacks exploit the inherent characteristics of the TCP protocol. Attackers employ a myriad of strategies and techniques to implement these attacks and evolve them to evade detection. Thus, excavating attack patterns and identifying vulnerabilities in existing protocols and systems is imperative for effective detection.

Symbolic execution has been wilde used for is vulnerability exploitation and patching [4,42]. Its prowess in navigating through intricate branch conditions can achieve a deeper path execution. Further, Selective symbolic execution improves it, as it can analyze multiple execution paths of a program and switch modes between symbolic execution and concrete execution. Its flexibility in testing large and complex systems, such as operating system kernels, gives it superior performance in detecting bugs and vulnerabilities in binary-based projects [47]. Therefore, in this work, we adopt selective symbolic execution to discover more variants of TCP-based DDoS Attacks and recognize the different categories of attack methods at the system level, observing the depth of system calls and the behavior of the TCP protocol during the attack.

In this work, we propose an automated framework termed DDoSMiner, which can characterize DDoS attack patterns and explore variants of DDoS attack traffic. Specifically, DDoSMiner would initially record TCP traffic and generate the corresponding Attack Call Flow Graph (ACFG) for further recognition of the DDoS attack patterns. The key nodes of the ACFG are extracted by differentiating between benign and attack traffic for subsequent symbolic execution analysis. For the symbolic execution module, DDoSMiner explores potential attack traces within the TCP protocol based on reachable path termination key states from the ACFG, generating various reachable candidate attack packet sequences. Based on our experiments, we identify a new attack traffic, which is a variant of SYN Flood Attack related to timestamp obfuscation. The evaluation of the results on three popular rule sets of Snort demonstrates the new attack could bypass all defense rule sets, while traditional DDoS attacks cannot.

In summary, the contributions are as follows:

- We propose an automated framework DDoSMiner for characterizing the system control flow behavior of DDoS attacks and exploring new DDoS attacks.
- We gather 6 TCP-based DDoS attacks and adopt DDoSMiner to generate ACFG for analyzers. Furthermore, we discover a new DDoS attack trace and collect corresponding attack traffic.
- Empirical results show that the attack generated by DDoSMiner successfully evades three popular detection rule sets on NIDS.

## 2 Background and Related Work

In this section, we provide a brief background for TCP-based DDoS attack detection and defense. Subsequently, we summarize existing DDoS mining/exploit schemes. Finally, we introduce symbolic execution technology, which is used to construct DDoSMiner.

### 2.1 TCP-Based DDoS Attacks

DDoS attacks refer to attackers control devices on the Internet to generate massive malicious or useless packets to disrupt the target network services. Most DDoS attacks are developed based on TCP [32], and typical categories involve bandwidth attacks and resource exhaustion attacks [16]. This is because the characteristics of the TCP protocol could be exploited by adversaries to transport-layer paralyze target systems or services. For example, a series of TCP-based

DDoS attacks lies in exploiting TCP control packets by deceiving the three-way handshake between the source and target servers, exhausting the resources of the target server, eventually resulting in unavailable services. To resist these attacks, defenders typically adopt various strategies, such as IP address-based access control [21,48,49,53], intrusion detection system (IDS) [5,44,51,60,62], and distributed firewalls [3,24], to filter out forged connection requests and mitigate the impact of attacks.

### 2.2 DDoS Mining/Exploit Schemes

To mine more DDoS attack strategies, existing solutions mainly involve manual schemes and fuzzing-based. The former mainly mines emerging attacks in a manual manner and requires domain-specific expert experience. Rossow *et al.* [38] propose 14 types of reflective DDoS attacks based on features including protocols, payload sizes, and packet transmission frequency. Hong *et al.* [20] propose two attacks against network topologies by finding that most mainstream SDN controllers are vulnerable to network visibility poisoning. These works rely on expert knowledge and cannot be automatically conducted/explored.

The latter mainly leverages fuzzing to discover new DDoS strategies. Among them, AMPFUZZ [25] introduces a protocol-agnostic approach for UDP vulnerability, significantly enhancing the fuzzing performance of AMPFUZZ with UDP awareness. However, this work only covers states while ignoring state transitions, which has a significant impact on TCP implementation (compared with stateless UDP). For instance, TCP-Fuzz [63] proposes a new strategy for generating effective test cases for TCP stacks by considering the dependencies between inputs. TCP-Fuzz only tests TCP stacks in user space and does not check kernel-level TCP stacks, thus it cannot obtain coverage of their branches and branch transitions. StateDiver [58] is based on fuzzing and uses the discrepancy between the two inputs in the protocol stack as feedback to explore abnormal nodes in TCP implementations (on DPI). While there is a lack of relevant feedback for DDoS. Our work is based on the TCP stack at the Linux kernel level, allowing more precise analysis of TCP's state transitions and using symbolic execution to explore the TCP stack at the source code level.

### 2.3 Exploration TCP Stack with Symbolic Execution

Symbolic execution is a white-box program analysis technique. It explores multiple possible execution paths by adopting symbolic input values instead of concrete input values. This allows the exploration of various paths a program might take under different inputs, achieving good performance on program analysis/vulnerability detection. However, it has some problems regarding the explosion of path state space.

With the development of constraint satisfaction problems and the emergence of more scalable dynamic methods that combine concrete and symbolic execution [8], concolic testing merges symbolic execution with concrete execution, aiming to automatically discover vulnerabilities and errors in programs. Selective symbolic execution [10] further extends concolic execution, enabling program analysis in real software stacks (user programs, libraries, kernels, drivers, etc.) rather than using abstract models of these layers, and directly operating on binary files.

As a leading work, SYMTCP [51] uses symbolic execution technology to construct adversarial packets targeting TCP implementations. These packets are designed to leverage the discrepancies between Deep Packet Inspection (DPI) middleboxes and end hosts, to achieve eluding attacks. However, this requires the manual review of the TCP stack's source code and manual marking of drop points (serve as termination points) in the Linux kernel.

Based on these studies, we intend to utilize symbolic execution to analyze TCP-based DDoS attack patterns. Different from SYMTCP, our pipeline involves establishing and analyzing the ACFG by tracking TCP behavior on a white-box target. By comparing normal traffic with various categories of attack traffic, we identify drop nodes in the attack and generate related constraints for symbolic execution.

## 3 Threat Model and Problem Definition

In this section, we describe the threat model in the context of DDoS attacks and defense. We will provide a detailed definition of the ACFG in the following sections, which will be used to outline path constraints.

### 3.1 Threat Model

Consider the DDoS Attack Defense Architecture as illustrated in Fig. 1. Attackers send a large number of bogus TCP connection requests to the target system through infected computers or devices, aiming to exhaust the resources of the target server and thus prevent legitimate users from accessing the target service. The IDS acts as a middlebox to monitor and report the traffic.

Actually, the TCP protocol on the server can be regarded as a discrete state transition process, and the attack on the transmission protocol can be regarded as a process of finite state machine state transitions. The execution of the TCP protocol on the server can be modeled as a TCP finite state machine for program analysis. The attackers aim to change the state of the TCP state machine by sending probing attack packets and altering the response of the server to these probing packets.

We adopt the TCP stack of the Linux kernel for system-level program analysis. Furthermore, to expand attack scenarios, we assume that attackers can spoof addresses, which means they can disguise the source IP address of their attack traffic. This assumption increases the diversity and applicability of the attacks. Through comparative experiments between attack traffic and benign traffic, we ensure that the anomalies observed on the server side after an attack

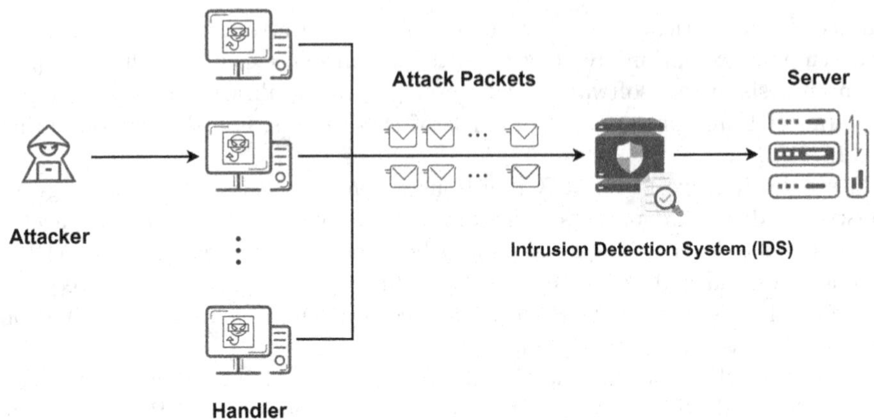


**Fig. 1.** Illustration of DDoS attack pipeline and IDS.

are due to resource exhaustion attacks caused by the TCP protocol, not bandwidth attacks overwhelmed by high traffic volume, because the server system will not be destroyed by benign packets under the equivalent traffic loads.

### 3.2 Problem Definition

In this section, we provide a detailed definition of this work and offer a characterization of the ACFG and its elements.

**Definition 1: TCP State Machine.** Based on the TCP protocol specifications, the Mealy TCP state machine [27,51] can be described as follows,

$$M = (S, I, O, \Sigma, Z), \tag{1}$$

$S$: The finite non-empty set of states. For instance, the typical set of TCP states includes LISTEN, SYN_RCVD, ESTABLISHED states. $s_0 \in S$ represents the initial state.

$I$: The input symbol set, representing input events of the state machine, i.e., TCP packets.

$O$: The output symbol set, represents the output actions of the state machine. For example, sending SYN packets, sending ACK packets, closing connections, etc.

$\Sigma$: The state transition function, which defines the transition rules between states, denoted as $S \times I \rightarrow S$. It specifies the next state the state machine will move to, given a certain state and input event.

$Z$: Output function, which defines the relationship between the output symbol, state, and input event, denoted as $S \times I \rightarrow O$. It specifies which output action the state machine should perform, given a state and input event.

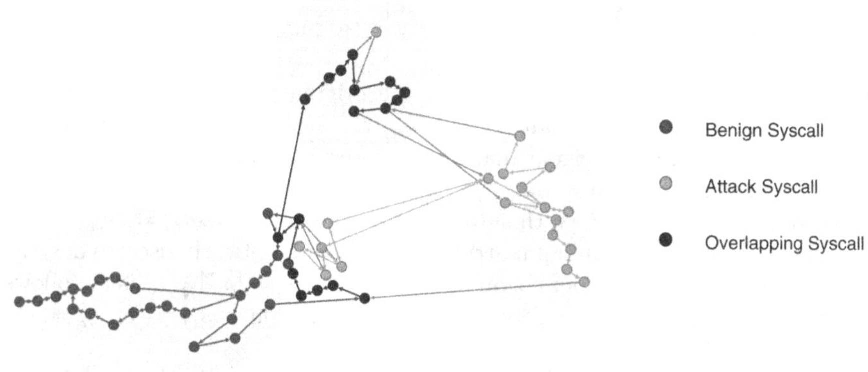


**Fig. 2.** Syscall interaction analysis based on categories and connectivity.

**Definition 2: Attack Call Flow Graph.** The ACFG is a directed weighted graph $G = (V, E)$, where each node in the set of vertices represents a function of the TCP stack. The call relationships between functions are represented by directed edges. We extract different classes of ACFGs based on the characteristics of benign traffic and attack traffic.

**Definition 3: Malicious Nodes.** Malicious nodes represent the function nodes involved in the attack. These nodes are typically the functions abused by attackers in the target system to initiate attacks or bypass security mechanisms. The set of malicious nodes is denoted as $V_M$.

**Definition 4: Critical Nodes.** Critical nodes represent important functional nodes in the TCP stack, and their stability and correctness are crucial for the operation of the entire system. Attackers may attempt to destroy the target system through these nodes. After visualizing the system calls of benign and attack traffic, we discover both of them rely on a specific node in a chained call process. These malicious nodes resemble nodes in the normal traffic. While there may be recursive calls within the path, such patterns often accompany the presence of a critical node. Therefore, we further extract the critical nodes from the ACFG.

As shown in Fig. 2, after clustering network nodes based on connectivity and categories, we find that some nodes have an impact on the network's cluster structure. The key to defining critical nodes is to find an optimal subset of nodes in the graph, denoted as $V_C \subseteq V_M$, such that the removal of these nodes has the maximum impact on the network's connectivity [26]. Let the set of critical nodes be denoted as $V_C = \{v_1, v_2, ..., v_l\}$,

$$\lambda_1 = \lambda_{N-1}, \tag{2}$$

$$\lambda_2 = \lambda_{N-l}, \tag{3}$$

$$\lambda_1\left[-c_0P_{(0)N-l}+\frac{\lambda_\tau}{2}\sum_{r=1}^{k}c_rP_{(r)N-l}^2\right]\geq\lambda_2\left[-c_0P_{(0)N}+\frac{\lambda_\tau}{2}\sum_{r=1}^{k}c_rP_{(r)N}^2\right], \quad (4)$$

where $\lambda_{N-1}$ represents the eigenvalue of the original matrix, $\lambda_{N-l}$ represents the eigenvalue of the matrix after removing the set of critical nodes, and $\lambda_\tau$ represents the maximum eigenvalue of the internal coupling matrix between the state variables of each node. The values $c_r > 0, r = 1, ..., k$ represent the connectivity strengths of the $r$-th sub-network. The matrix $P_{N(r)} = \left[p_{(r)ij}\right]_{N\times N}$ represents the external coupling matrix of the $r$-th sub-network, used to describe the network topology. The definition of the matrix $P_N = \left[p_{ij}\right]_{N\times N}$ is as follows: if there is an edge connecting node $i$ and node $j$, then $p_{(r)ij} = p_{(r)ji} = -1$, otherwise, it is 0.

The set of critical nodes should also satisfy that the nodes in $V_C$ have the maximum total weighted sum, where $f(v_i)$ represents the attribute value of node $v_i$,

$$\max\sum f\left(v_i\right), v_i\in V_C. \quad (5)$$

According to Definition 2 and Definition 4, we generate the critical nodes as described in Algorithm 1.

**Definition 5: Pivotal Nodes.** Pivotal nodes represent the distinctive nodes that cause a change of the TCP state. The set of pivotal nodes is denoted as $V_P$.

**Definition 6: Drop Nodes.** We focus primarily on nodes that not only have malicious behavior but also play a crucial role in the network. These types of nodes are not just potentially malicious in intent but also have a significant impact due to their critical position in the network structure. In addition, we consider those nodes that represent state transitions in TCP connections because they play an important role in determining the TCP state machine.

Thus, drop nodes are defined as the intersection of malicious nodes and critical nodes union with pivotal nodes, represented as,

$$V_D = V_M \cap V_C \cup V_P. \quad (6)$$

**Definition 7: Candidate Attack Sequence.** When exploring the TCP state machine $M$, if the TCP packet $Packet_i \in I$ either reaches our defined termination point or neither causes a change in the TCP state machine's state nor generates any output, then that packet belongs to the candidate attack sequence, as follows,

$$\varSigma(s, Packet_i) = s \wedge Z(s, Packet_i) = \varepsilon. \quad (7)$$

**Algorithm 1:** Critical Nodes Algorithm

**Input**: Directed graph $G$, node attribute value $f$, eigenvalues of the original matrix $\lambda_{N-1}$, maximum eigenvalue of inner coupling matrix $\lambda_\tau$, external coupling matrix of $r$th subnetwork $P_{N(r)}$.

**Output**: *criticalNodes*

```
// Step 1: Initialize criticalNodes and maxImpact
criticalNodes ← ∅, maxImpact ← −∞;
// Step 2: Traverse each node in the graph G
for node in G.nodes do
    // Step 3: Remove the current node, create graph G'
    G' ← G.removeNode(node);
    // Step 4: Initialize the impact of cluster C
    C.impact.init();
    // Step 5: Traverse each cluster in graph G
    for C in G.clusters do
        // Step 6: Traverse each node in the cluster C
        for node in C.nodes do
            // Step 7: The dependency of current and next node
            C.conn ← any(G.hasEdge(node, node.next) ∧ node ≠ node.next);
            C'.conn ← ¬all(G'.hasEdge(node, node.next) ∧ node ≠ node.next);
            if C.conn ∧ C'.conn then
                // Step 8: Calculate the sum of attribute value and
                update the impact of cluster C
                Σ f_C ← Σ(f_node for node in C);
                C.impact ← C.impact + P_{N(r)}^2 · (λ_{N−1} − λ_τ) · Σ f_C;
            end
        end
    end
    if C.impact > G.initImpact and C.impact > maxImpact then
        // Step 9: Update maxImpact, add node to criticalNode
        maxImpact ← C.impact;
        criticalNodes.add(node);
    end
end
```

## 4 Workflow of DDoSMiner

The overview of the DDoSMiner workflow is illustrated in Fig. 3, which consists of three modules. In Module 1, DDoSMiner traces the kernel for both benign and attack packets, and modeling attacks to generate a visual ACFG. In this stage, we aim to collect all attack paths and critical nodes under different TCP states when attacks occur. Module 2 refers to the symbolic execution phase. The inputs consist of a set of TCP seed packets that drive the selective symbolic execution engine to explore the TCP stack based on the drop nodes. Module 3 is the online verification phase, launching the generated candidate attack sequence to bypass the existing IDS.

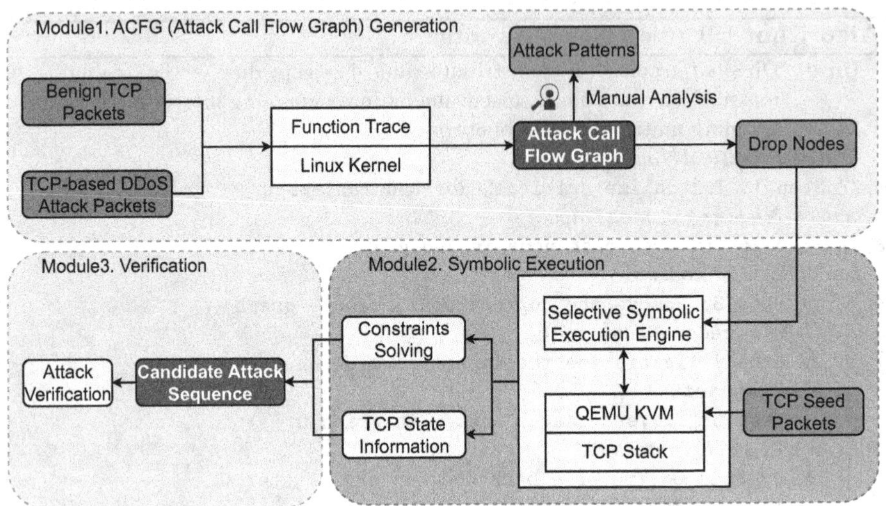


**Fig. 3.** Workflow of DDoSMiner.

### 4.1 Generation of Attack Call Flow Graph

The complete TCP state transition involves 11 states [18], and we simplify the states of the TCP finite state machine as shown in Fig. 4. When a TCP connection is established, both the client and server are in the CLOSED state. The server creates a socket and begins listening for incoming remote requests, at which point it enters the LISTEN state. The client initiates a connection by sending a SYN segment (SYN=1) to the server, requesting to establish a connection. Upon receiving the segment, the server responds by sending an ACK and SYN segment (SYN=1, ACK=1) to the client. Meanwhile, the server's state transitions to SYN_RCVD. After receiving the segment, the client sends an ACK to the server. Upon receiving the ACK, the server's state transitions to ESTABLISHED. Then the three-way handshake is completed, and the TCP connection is established.

We establish an experimental environment running on a standard Linux operating system, designed to collect kernel information and recreate TCP-based DDoS attacks from datasets [40,41] for kernel tracing and analysis.

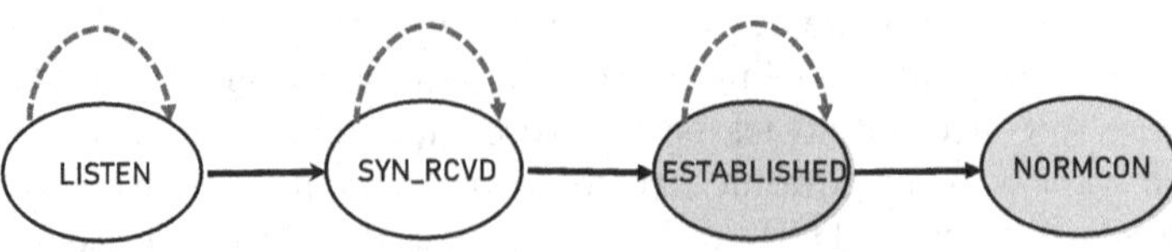


**Fig. 4.** Simplified TCP states.

Specifically, six categories of attacks are considered, including TCP Connect Flood, TCP SYN Flood, TCP ACK Flood, TCP RST Flood, ACK-PSH Flood, and SYN-RST-ACK Flood attacks. Each attack class abuses TCP connections consumes resources of the target server, or obfuscates network traffic in its unique way. Learning from these categories of attacks allows us to gain a more comprehensive understanding of the DDoS threats based on the TCP protocol and how to effectively identify and respond to these threats.

According to the definitions provided in Sect. 3.2, we generate ACFGs associated with different attack categories and present them through visualization. In Fig. 5, we use different colors to represent different classes of nodes. Blue nodes represent malicious nodes, orange nodes represent critical nodes, and red nodes represent pivotal nodes. The radius of each node reflects the size of its attribute value, with larger nodes indicating higher importance. Directed edges in the graph represent the call relationships between functions, and the edge weights indicate the level of dependence between different functions under the same traffic conditions.

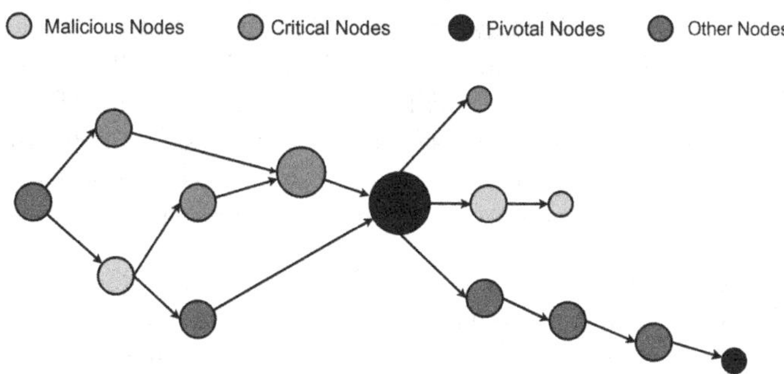


**Fig. 5.** Diagram depicting paths for benign and attack TCP packets.

### 4.2 Selective Symbolic Execution

S2E utilizes the symbolic execution engine KLEE [7] and conducts kernel testing through the QEMU simulation system. It also offers an API interface [11] that enables users to customize the scope of symbolic execution, facilitating a seamless transition between symbolic execution and concrete execution modes. Firstly, the symbolic execution engine initiates the running Linux kernel using a TCP socket in the LISTEN state. Subsequently, it provides multiple symbolized TCP packets to the kernel to comprehensively explore the server's TCP stack. The generation of symbolized data packets is divided into two parts:

(i) Generating TCP header packets with various combinations. During the subsequent symbolic execution process, we focus on how changes in TCP header fields such as sequence number, acknowledgment number, data offset, flags,

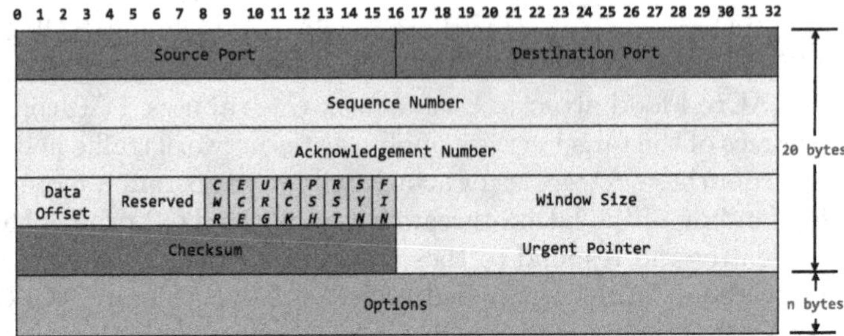


**Fig. 6.** Symbolized TCP header and options [51].

window size, and urgent pointer affect path exploration. We automatically generate various TCP header segments using script files, combine them with other components, and create TCP seed packets.

(ii) Symbolizing data packets. The input for symbolic execution is not concrete data, it requires symbolizing data values. A TCP header consists of a minimum of 20 bytes of fixed data (as shown in Fig. 6), storing the necessary information for the packet transmission. The 20-byte TCP header does not include options or data. Symbolizing TCP packets is one of the essential tasks in symbolic execution analysis. It allows analysis tools to use symbolic variables instead of concrete data values. This helps simulate various TCP packet transmission paths, identifying potential vulnerabilities or issues.

Consider DDoS attackers typically deliberately mask their source IP addresses and send a large number of false or invalid requests to the target port. Therefore, we do not symbolize the source port and destination port to avoid impacting the performance of symbolic execution. Symbolized fields include sequence number, acknowledgment number, data offset, flags, window size, urgent pointer, and TCP options. Changes in these fields can involve alterations in the TCP state. After constructing the TCP seed packets sent to the Linux host in S2E, we call the symbolization module for processing.

All execution paths for symbolic execution form a tree-like structure known as the symbolic execution tree. We convert the directed weighted graph $G$ corresponding to the ACFG into a directed spanning tree. We utilize a recursive depth-first search (DFS) to explore the graph $G$ and construct a directed spanning tree $T$, ensuring that no cycles are encountered during the analysis process. This way, we can define symbolic execution path constraints through the generated tree $T$.

Through symbolic execution, we are able to identify a candidate attack sequence that satisfies the branch termination conditions, and record the path selections and symbolic constraints from the path exploration process in an output document. This enables us to obtain attack patterns on the white-box system, allowing for a detailed analysis of the attacks and the discovery of new attack sequences.

# 5 Evaluation

In this section, we first introduce the environment and configuration of our experiment. We list the packet variants found by symbolic execution and check whether IDS can prevent the corresponding attack behavior. After that, we in-depth analyze the details of packet variants that can successfully bypass the defense of IDS, while others can not.

## 5.1 Experiment Configuration

**Testbed.** We develop the prototype of DDoSMiner based on S2E 2.0 and Linux kernel with S2E extension. The host operating system is Ubuntu 22.04, 64-bit, with a 12-core CPU, specifically the 12-*th* Gen Intel(R) Core(TM) i5-12400, and the GUEST operating system is Debian 11.3, 64-bit, with a 12-core CPU, specifically the 12-*th* Gen Intel(R) Core(TM) i5-12400. Both systems are all running based on Linux kernel v4.9.3. We run S2E in parallel mode with 48 cores, which is the maximum number of processes supported at present.

We use S2E to test the TCP stack implementation in the Linux kernel and switch between the concrete mode and symbolic execution mode. When the program reaches the `tcp_v4_rcv()` code segment, we switch to symbolic execution mode, while the rest of the code segments on the kernel remain in concrete execution mode. Test cases and symbolic constraints are generated when we reach the code segment where our marked drop nodes are located.

**IDS and Rule Sets.** For evaluation, we use Snort 3 [36] as the deployed IDS by the victim. Given Snort is the foremost open-source NIDS in the world, and it employs a set of defined rules to identify harmful network activities and alerts. In high-speed bandwidth environments, different rule sets vary in detection performance [17]. We evaluate the performance using Snort Registered (SR), Snort Community (SC), and Emerging Threats (ET) rule sets.

## 5.2 Attack Call Flow Graph Analysis

To better understand the attack patterns and find the key point, we construct ACFG to assist in identifying and analyzing existing DDoS attacks, especially for the difference of distinctive paths between attack and benign traffic. We conduct kernel tracing on benign TCP traffic, which amounts to approximately 30GB in total. This benign flow serves as a reference baseline and assists us in gaining a deeper understanding of the impact of DDoS attacks on the kernel and in identifying characteristics of abnormal behavior.

Take TCP Connect Flood attack and the TCP SYN Flood attack as examples, as shown in Fig. 12 in Appendix. TCP Connect Flood attack potentially triggers several TCP connection management functions within the kernel, such as `tcp_rcv_established()` and `tcp_time_wait()`, among others. This class of attack results in a large influx of connection requests, causing the server to

**Table 1.** Drop nodes counts in various states

| TCP-based DDoS Attacks | State | Count | TCP-based DDoS Attacks | State | Count |
|---|---|---|---|---|---|
| TCP Connect Flood | LISTEN | 1 | TCP SYN Flood | LISTEN | 7 |
| | SYN_RCVD | 2 | | SYN_RCVD | 12 |
| | ESTABLISHED | 5 | | ESTABLISHED | 44 |
| | ALL STATES | - | | ALL STATES | 3 |
| TCP ACK Flood | LISTEN | 6 | TCP RST Flood | LISTEN | 2 |
| | SYN_RCVD | 11 | | SYN_RCVD | 1 |
| | ESTABLISHED | 18 | | ESTABLISHED | 10 |
| | ALL STATES | 3 | | ALL STATES | 1 |
| ACK-PSH Flood | LISTEN | 6 | SYN-RST-ACK Flood | LISTEN | 2 |
| | SYN_RCVD | 11 | | SYN_RCVD | 4 |
| | ESTABLISHED | 21 | | ESTABLISHED | 2 |
| | ALL STATES | 2 | | ALL STATES | - |

continuously attempt to allocate resources to handle these requests, ultimately leading to resource exhaustion. TCP SYN Flood attacks trigger a large number of invocations of the `tcp_syn_ack_timeout()` function within the TCP stack. This function defines the timeout period during which the server waits for the client to respond with an ACK after sending a SYN-ACK response. In TCP SYN Flood attack scenario, the TCP state machine remains in the SYN_RCVD state and cannot progress to the next state.

We consider resolve oracle in the TCP LISTEN, SYN_RCVD, and ESTABLISHED states, given these states cover the complete window of the server side in the TCP three-way handshake. Such a way of focusing on core state transitions simplifies the state machine, making symbolic execution more efficient. Thus, in other TCP states, such as CLOSE_WAIT, the server will not accept any further packets. For different attacks, we mark different drop nodes in the source code. S2E symbolically executes Linux binary files, so these points will be mapped to the binary level. The number of drop nodes corresponding to different attacks is shown in Table 1. Due to space limitations, we have placed the original address table of drop nodes in Table 2 of the Appendix.

### 5.3 Symbol Execution Experiment Setup

Symbolic execution may get stuck at the beginning of execution and hard to reach deep paths, which is caused by path selection heuristic methods. Therefore, the key of the symbolic execution phase lies in the construction of TCP seed packets and the definition of pruning strategies. TCP seed packets guide the program along the path to the parts of the kernel and create side branches. Once construction process of the main path is completed, S2E explores side branches in depth. The promising seed packets help us penetrate deeper into the TCP stack quickly.

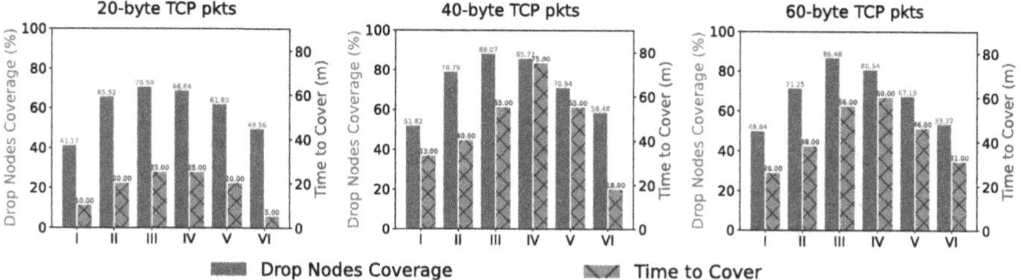


**Fig. 7.** Time costs and drop nodes coverage in symbolic execution.

In symbolic execution, we discard uninteresting paths, including: (i) Redundant paths that re-explore the same parts of the kernel code, *i.e.*, if a program path is identified to a previously explored path and reaches the same address with the same symbolic constraints, it will continue executing the same next branch. As a result, it can be discarded. (ii) Error detection path branches caused by incorrect concrete values generated by the solver. (iii) Path branches caused by Linux kernel check failures. (iv) Path branches leading to drop nodes. These strategies help us reduce the symbolic state space.

Although we generate specific TCP seed packets to reach drop nodes' addresses and employ optimization strategies to narrow down the search space for solutions, the complexity of the TCP stack makes it challenging for symbolic execution to provide comprehensive coverage. We examine the path coverage of the stack and track the accessed drop nodes, which can ensure critical nodes associated with potential attack paths have been checked.

In experiments, we send three types of symbolic data packets: 20-byte packets, 40-byte packets, and 60-byte packets, each of which includes a TCP header and payload. We observe that the composition of seed packet fields significantly affects the time cost of symbolic execution, especially when handling 40-byte and 60-byte packets, as shown in Fig. 7. We label six categories of attacks using Roman numerals: TCP Connect Flood (I), TCP SYN Flood (II), TCP ACK Flood (III), TCP RST Flood (IV), ACK-PSH Flood (V), and SYN-RST-ACK Flood (VI).

Large seed packets contain more variables and data to be symbolized, resulting in a significant increase in the number of paths that the symbolic execution engine needs to explore. This is because every possible branch of each conditional statement needs to be considered. It needs to backtrack to a previous branching point and reselect a path when the constraint is unsatisfied. These packets not only introduce more code blocks, increasing the time cost of symbolic execution but also imply exploring more paths to achieve higher code coverage.

After approximately 20 h of symbolic execution exploration, we utilize six instances to explore over 100,000 execution paths. During this process, more than 4,000 state transitions were triggered. Due to the server-side TCP state machine experiencing numerous repetitive cycles of state sequence (such as LISTEN → SYN_RCVD → SYN_RCVD), these transitions include repeated states, covering approximately 2,000 lines of code. Subsequently, we conduct further analysis of

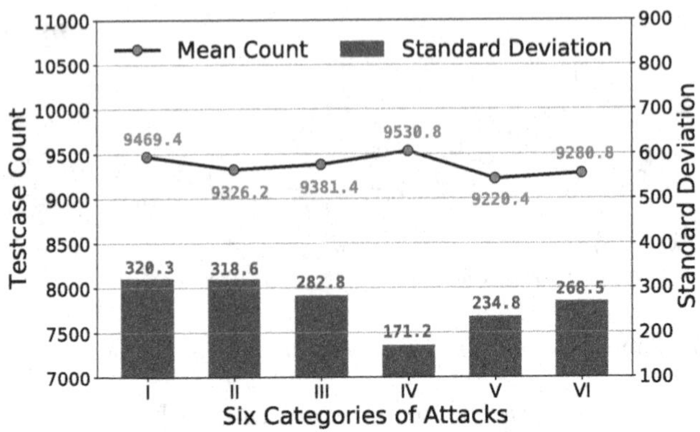


**Fig. 8.** Analysis of Testcase under various attacks.

the test cases associated with these newly discovered attack paths and perform kernel tracing. In subsequent experiments, we assess these new potential threats to better understand their potential risks and the impact of attacks.

## 5.4 Symbolic Execution Results

We solve the test cases for candidate attack sequences to generate specific values for TCP header fields and perform field padding and validation for the packets. Although selective symbolic execution explores paths close to the seed packets, the randomness of paths due to the complexity of the TCP protocol stack may lead to differences in path search results. Therefore, with the same configuration, we conduct five sets of experiments (labeled A to E) for six categories of attacks and record the following metrics:

**Testcase Count.** This metric represents the number of generated test cases. It demonstrates the exploration of potential attack paths by the symbolic execution engine and the quantity of generated attack samples.

**Attack Success Rate.** This metric reflects the ratio of actual successful attack attempts. It helps evaluate the effectiveness of the generated test cases in simulating real attacks.

**CPU Utilization.** By monitoring CPU utilization, we understand the system resource load during the attack.

**Connection Queueing Rate.** This metric shows the situation where TCP connection requests are forced to queue for processing due to the attack. This metric helps evaluate the performance of the system's responsiveness to service requests.

For the candidate attack sequence of each class attack, we conduct five independent simulations to observe the impact of different factors under the above metrics, as shown in Fig. 8 and 9. Actual data may varies due to network devices, configurations, and defense strategies in place traffic patterns can also influence the results. By monitoring and analyzing these metrics, we can more accurately assess the actual performance and effectiveness of the test cases generated by symbolic execution in the context of DDoS attack and defense.

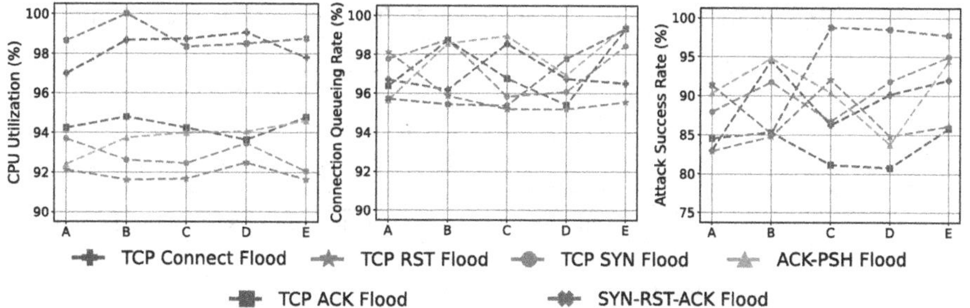


**Fig. 9.** Comparative metrics and impact of various attacks.

For the Testcase Count, the average number of Testcase Count is around 9300 for each type of attack, indicating that the symbolic execution engine explored attack paths to a similar extent across various types of attacks. The curves in Fig. 8 represent the average of five independent experiments for each type of attack, and the bars represent the standard deviation for each type of attack. From the averages, ACK-PSH Flood attack (V) and SYN-RST-ACK Flood attack (VI) had fewer test cases, indicating that the symbolic execution engine encountered fewer variants when exploring paths for these two types of attacks. The standard deviation indicates that the TCP RST Flood attack (IV) has the minimum fluctuation in test case count across different experiments.

Under different attacks, CPU utilization, connection queueing rate, and attack success rate show different performances as shown in Fig. 9. TCP Connect Flood and SYN-RST-ACK Flood attacks generally introduced more computation and connection requests, leading to higher CPU utilization, which was above 96% in experiments, even reaching 100%. Although TCP SYN Flood and TCP RST Flood attacks involve a large number of connection requests, their attack processes are simpler, thus requiring less CPU resources. TCP ACK Flood and ACK-PSH Flood attacks show moderate CPU utilization.

For the Connection Queueing Rate, the six attacks do not show significant differences. Effective test cases in most evaluations cause system capacity insufficiency and queuing of connection requests. This indicates that categories of attacks effectively exhaust server resources.

For the Attack Success Rate, TCP ACK Flood and TCP RST Flood attacks show lower success rates because these two types of attacks require matching valid connection states to deceive the TCP protocol stack, otherwise they would not affect the establishment of new connections or the continuation of existing ones. In contrast, attacks like TCP SYN Flood or TCP Connect Flood directly target the initialization process of connections, quickly filling the server's half-open connection queue and preventing the establishment of new legitimate connections. This directly affects server availability, hence they have higher attack success rates. ACK-PSH Flood and SYN-RST-ACK Flood attacks increase server processing load, leading to connection interruptions or service delays.

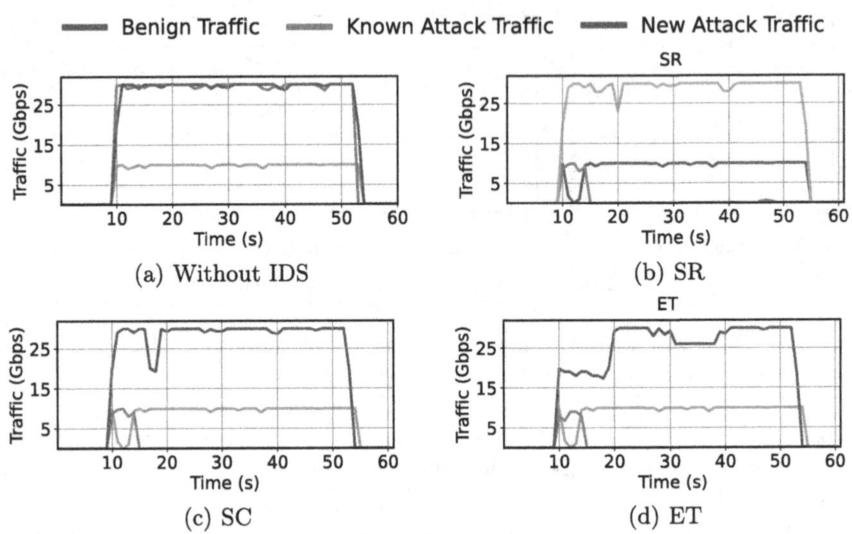


(a) Without IDS (b) SR

(c) SC (d) ET

**Fig. 10.** Analysis of Benign vs. Known attack vs. New attack TCP traffic.

### 5.5 Evasion Evaluation Against IDS

We utilize three rule sets compatible with the Snort: SR, SC, and ET, and evaluate about 10,000 candidate attack sequences generated by symbolic execution.

We analyze the network traffic without IDS and then apply the SR, SC, and ET rule sets for attack detection. To better understand this detection and filtering process, we visualize this process, as shown in Fig. 10. The Fig. 10(a) shows the states of benign traffic, known attack traffic, and new attack traffic when no IDS checks are enabled. The other three figures in Fig. 10 are the traffic conditions using the SR, SC, and ET rule sets. It shows that the ET rule set has better detection performance than the other two.

Under baseline conditions without IDS inspection enabled, we first verify known attack traffic, which mainly consists of traffic in public datasets. The results show that when rule inspection is enabled, the defense system can effectively mark and filter known attack traffic. However, for new attack traffic generated by candidate attack sequences through symbolic execution, although Snort successfully detects and blocks some attacks, a significant amount of traffic bypasses Snort's detection and successfully reaches its intended victim.

We evaluate CPU Utilization and Connection Queueing Rate as mentioned above, confirming they indeed caused resource occupancy and TCP connection queue congestion. Figure 11 shows the state of system resources is saturated during new attacks and queuing of TCP connection requests caused by the limitation of CPU capacity.

In the first 15 s, CPU occupancy is low, maintaining around 20%, and the message queuing rate is nearly zero, indicating the system is operating normally without significant load or congestion. However, after 15 s, CPU occupancy

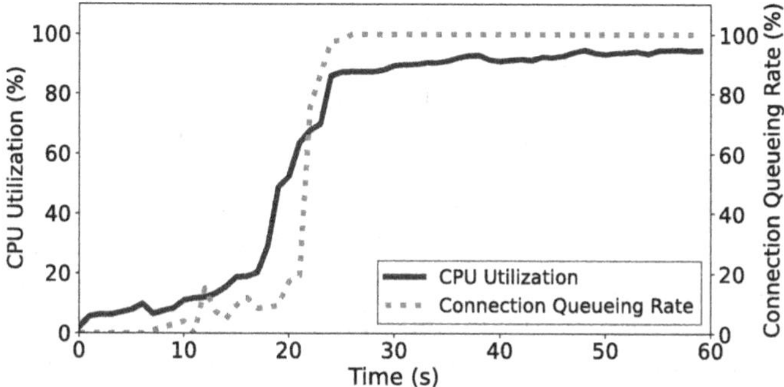


**Fig. 11.** Changes in CPU Utilization and Connection Queueing Rate over time.

began to rise sharply, quickly approaching 100%, indicating the attack started to cause significant processing pressure.

Meanwhile, the queuing rate of TCP connections began to rise slowly. After the CPU utilization reaches its peak, the message queuing rate gradually increases and reaches 100% at around 25 s. This means all new TCP connection requests are queuing up for processing, *i.e.,* unable to handle any TCP connection immediately. In this state, the system could not handle more load, and new requests could only wait, leading to service timeouts.

We found despite setting defense levels for the known six categories of attacks in the IDS, attackers can evade detection by adopting various attack variants, aiming to increase attack success or reduce detection risk. These variants include parameter randomization, attack mixing, malware use, IP address spoofing, attack segmentation, and evasion of known rules.

Further, we discover that successful evasion strategies are related to TCP timestamp option verification. Packets with time stamp echo reply (TSecr) not matching timestamp value (TSval) are usually detected and reported by rules, but successful IDS evasion cases with timestamped packet sequences include:

**Insert Invalid Values.** Randomizing Flag fields and TSval not conforming to the normal time progression pattern (e.g., echoing a value in the TSecr field that was never sent before in TSval), making packets appear as benign, delayed arrivals.

**Imitate Normal Communication.** Attackers observe normal TCP traffic timestamp patterns and imitate these patterns, using specific modes (e.g., adding extra microseconds every few packets) to alter the normal progression of timestamps.

**Timestamp Obfuscation.** Some sequence timestamps are abnormal, with their parsing observed to be incorrect on target servers. Compared to known attack traffic, IDS does not report these packets, but their TIME_WAIT state often last twice as long as the Maximum Segment Lifetime (MSL). Also, part of the timestamp confusion packets lead to abnormal transitions in the TCP state machine.

These attacks affect the TCP Retransmission Queue, with abnormal TSval causing the TCP stack to misjudge network conditions, affecting the calculation of retransmission timeouts. Multiple timers and timeout mechanisms in the TCP stack, like Keepalive timers and TIME_WAIT state processing, are also disrupted, affecting the TCP states.

Attackers could exploit flaws in TCP timestamp verification to disguise attack traffic as normal, avoiding detection by IDS. This camouflage method tampers with timestamps or inserts erroneous ones in attack packets, further increasing detection complexity and reducing accuracy. Although attacks using TCP timestamp options are not common, they are significantly effective. Developing IDS capable of deep analysis will help increase detection accuracy and reduce false positives.

## 6 Conclusion

In this work, we introduce DDoSMiner, an automated framework which utilizes the ACFG to extract critical attack points. In addition, we explore the system-level performance of an attack and provide visualization results. DDoSMiner integrates symbolic execution to systematically explore DDoS traffic variants with the guidance of identified key states in the TCP state machine. Our experiments generate a total of 9,741 candidate attack traffic variants, which are evaluated on the popular NIDS Snort with three main defense rule set toolkits. The result identifies one new attack traffic which is capable of bypassing all three defense measures, demonstrating the effectiveness of DDoSMiner in uncovering TCP-based DDoS attacks. Our work not only reveals potential security threats in the TCP protocol but also provides a new perspective on attack methodology, assisting researchers in better understanding and preventing network attacks.

## 7 Limitations and Future Work

Due to the complexity of the Linux kernel, exploration based on white-box strategies still has the problem of inefficiency. Distributed strategies can be considered to improve the efficiency of system operation. In addition, we chose a specific version of the Linux kernel v4.9.3 to evaluate our system. TCP state machines for other kernel versions and categories of attacks can be built through patch installation and other methods. Moreover, although we choose three widely covered and mature IDS rule sets for verification against new threats, specific subsequent defensive strategies and measures still need further research and exploration. In the future, we plan to improve DDoSMiner by increasing the path coverage of detection and applying DDoSMiner to other TCP stacks. Furthermore, DDoSMiner could be extended to explore more protocols. For different protocols, different drop nodes can be designed for expansion.

**Acknowledgements.** This work was supported in part by National Natural Science Foundation of China (62227805, 62072398 and 62172405), by SUTD-ZJU IDEA

Grant for visiting professors (SUTD-ZJUVP201901), by the Natural Science Foundation of Jiangsu Province (BK20220075), by the Fok Ying-Tung Education Foundation for Young Teachers in the Higher Education Institutions of China (20193218210004), by State Key Laboratory of Mathematical Engineering and Advanced Computing, and by Key Laboratory of Cyberspace Situation Awareness of Henan Province (HNTS2022001).

## A Visualization and Analysis of System Calls

The ACFG extracted from the TCP Connect Flood and TCP SYN Flood attacks are shown in Fig. 12. The nodes and edges of ACFG are highlighted in different colors to represent the corresponding types of packets (benign or attack). In the figure, green-colored elements represent syscalls triggered by benign packets, orange-colored elements represent syscalls triggered by attack packets, and blue elements represent syscalls triggered by both types of packets. The red colored nodes are identified as Pivotal Nodes. According to the definition in Sect. 3.2, the following nodes represent the change of TCP state:

(i) `tcp_v4_syn_recv_sock`: This is a critical function for handling client SYN packets. This function checks the current TCP state (for example, whether it is in LISTEN state) to determine if the connection can be established.
(ii) `tcp_check_req`: This function checks whether the SYN packet is valid and whether there are resources available to handle this new connection request. If the SYN packet is invalid, a RST packet will be sent to refuse the connection.
(iii) `tcp_v4_do_rcv`: When the client sends an ACK packet in response to the server's SYN and ACK, this function processes the ACK packet, thereby advancing the connection state transition process.
(iv) `tcp_rcv_state_process`: This function is crucial in the TCP state machine. Within this function, if the current connection state is SYN_RCVD and an appropriate ACK segment is received, the state transitions to ESTABLISHED. Other state transitions in the TCP connection and the processing of related packets also call this function.
(v) `tcp_rcv_established`: This function handles inputs in the ESTABLISHED state.
(vi) `tcp_close`: This function is used to close a TCP connection. It releases the resources occupied by the connection and changes the connection state.

By comparing the orange nodes in the syscall of TCP Connect Flood and TCP SYN Flood attacks, we can see that the two attacks have different characteristics (detailed analysis in Sect. 5.2).

## B The Kernel Address Corresponding to the Full Drop Nodes for Six Categories of Attacks

We extract the potential drop nodes from the ACFG and then indexed the corresponding addresses in the kernel. These addresses serve as path termination

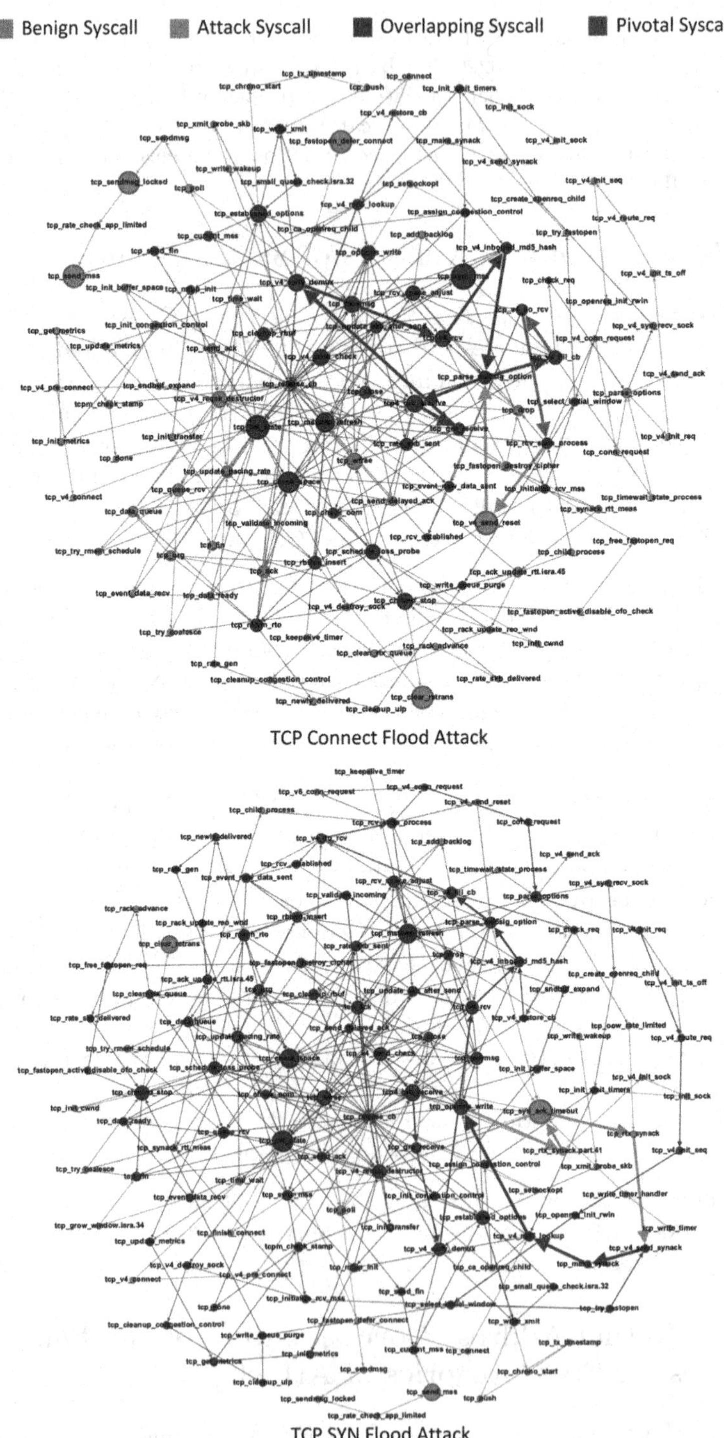


**Fig. 12.** Visualization of system calls for TCP Connect Flood Attack and TCP SYN Flood Attack.

**Table 2.** Kernel addresses associated with drop nodes for different attacks

| TCP-based DDoS Attacks | Address | | | |
|---|---|---|---|---|
| TCP Connect Flood | ffffffff819dc550 | ffffffff819d93d0 | ffffffff819e04d0 | ffffffff819e9bf0 |
| | ffffffff819dc3a0 | ffffffff819f1910 | ffffffff819ef4d0 | |
| TCP SYN Flood | ffffffff819f63b0 | ffffffff819e5410 | ffffffff819eaee0 | ffffffff819eda80 |
| | ffffffff819d9ce0 | ffffffff819de910 | ffffffff819ead60 | ffffffff819de6e0 |
| | ffffffff819d9e30 | ffffffff819e63d0 | ffffffff819de950 | ffffffff819d2250 |
| | ffffffff819d5010 | ffffffff819e4dd0 | ffffffff819f5720 | ffffffff819eb9d0 |
| | ffffffff819f6330 | ffffffff819d1830 | ffffffff819f5790 | ffffffff819d3290 |
| | ffffffff819dc3a0 | ffffffff819d9ef0 | ffffffff819e91a0 | ffffffff819e2a70 |
| | ffffffff819da3e0 | ffffffff819f5a90 | ffffffff819eafe0 | ffffffff819ebbf0 |
| | ffffffff819de6a0 | ffffffff819d38d0 | ffffffff819e4600 | ffffffff819ea720 |
| | ffffffff819d9e60 | ffffffff819d19d0 | ffffffff819e4550 | ffffffff819dee80 |
| | ffffffff819d9f50 | ffffffff819eca70 | ffffffff819d1c00 | ffffffff819ea5d0 |
| | ffffffff819dbee0 | ffffffff819ed670 | ffffffff819d7890 | ffffffff819d1790 |
| | ffffffff819d3490 | ffffffff81a87d40 | ffffffff819d6af0 | ffffffff819f5440 |
| | ffffffff819f25c0 | | | |
| TCP ACK Flood | ffffffff819e5410 | ffffffff819de6a0 | ffffffff819d19d0 | ffffffff819eca70 |
| | ffffffff819de910 | ffffffff819d1830 | ffffffff819f5790 | ffffffff819ef4d0 |
| | ffffffff819e63d0 | ffffffff819d38d0 | ffffffff819d1c00 | ffffffff819ed670 |
| | ffffffff819f5440 | ffffffff819d3490 | ffffffff819eda80 | ffffffff819d3290 |
| | ffffffff819d7890 | ffffffff819d6af0 | | |
| TCP RST Flood | ffffffff819d9470 | ffffffff819d9080 | ffffffff819efb70 | ffffffff819f06c0 |
| | ffffffff819f6a30 | ffffffff819e2b60 | ffffffff819f0560 | ffffffff819f6d10 |
| | ffffffff819ebfe0 | ffffffff819ee750 | | |
| ACK-PSH Flood | ffffffff819e5410 | ffffffff819e2a70 | ffffffff819d38d0 | ffffffff819eb9d0 |
| | ffffffff819de910 | ffffffff819dc3a0 | ffffffff819d19d0 | ffffffff819ef4d0 |
| | ffffffff819e63d0 | ffffffff819de6a0 | ffffffff819f5790 | ffffffff819eda80 |
| | ffffffff819f5440 | ffffffff819d1830 | ffffffff819e4600 | ffffffff819ebbf0 |
| | ffffffff819d3290 | ffffffff819e0460 | ffffffff819eca70 | ffffffff819d6af0 |
| | ffffffff819ea5d0 | ffffffff819d3490 | ffffffff819ed670 | ffffffff819d1c00 |
| | ffffffff819e4550 | ffffffff819d7890 | ffffffff81a87d40 | |
| SYN-RST-ACK Flood | ffffffff819e0460 | ffffffff819ea5d0 | ffffffff819ef4d0 | ffffffff81a87d40 |
| | ffffffff819e4600 | ffffffff819e4550 | | |

points for symbolic execution. The detailed attack types and the corresponding address we extracted for the experiment are listed in Table 2.

## References


1. Agrawal, N., Tapaswi, S.: Defense mechanisms against ddos attacks in a cloud computing environment: state-of-the-art and research challenges. IEEE Commun. Surv. Tutorials **21**(4), 3769–3795 (2019)
2. Antonakakis, M., April, T., et al.: Understanding the mirai botnet. In: 26th USENIX Security Symposium (USENIX Security 17), pp. 1093–1110 (2017)
3. Baig, Z.A., et al.: Controlled access to cloud resources for mitigating economic denial of sustainability (edos) attacks. Comput. Netw. **97**, 31–47 (2016)
4. Baldoni, R., Coppa, E., et al.: A survey of symbolic execution techniques. ACM Comput. Surv. (CSUR) **51**(3), 1–39 (2018)
5. Bhale, P., Chowdhury, D.R., Biswas, S., Nandi, S.: Optimist: Lightweight and transparent ids with optimum placement strategy to mitigate mixed-rate ddos attacks in iot networks. IEEE Internet of Things Journal (2023)
6. Bock, K., et al.: Weaponizing middleboxes for {TCP} reflected amplification. In: 30th USENIX Security Symposium (USENIX Security 21), pp. 3345–3361 (2021)
7. Cadar, C., Dunbar, D., Klee, D.E.: Unassisted and automatic generation of high-coverage tests for complex systems programs. In: Proceedings of Operating System Design and Implementation, pp. 209–224
8. Cadar, C., Sen, K.: Symbolic execution for software testing: three decades later. Commun. ACM **56**(2), 82–90 (2013)
9. Chang, R.K.: Defending against flooding-based distributed denial-of-service attacks: a tutorial. IEEE Commun. Mag. **40**(10), 42–51 (2002)
10. Chipounov, V., Kuznetsov, V., Candea, G.: S2e: a platform for in-vivo multi-path analysis of software systems. Acm Sigplan Notices **46**(3), 265–278 (2011)
11. Chipounov, V., et al.: The s2e platform: design, implementation, and applications. ACM Trans. Comput. Syst. (TOCS) **30**(1), 1–49 (2012)
12. Deshmukh, R.V., Devadkar, K.K.: Understanding ddos attack & its effect in cloud environment. Proc. Comput. Sci. **49**, 202–210 (2015)
13. Doshi, R., Apthorpe, N., Feamster, N.: Machine learning ddos detection for consumer internet of things devices. In: 2018 IEEE Security and Privacy Workshops (SPW), pp. 29–35. IEEE (2018)
14. Fayaz, S.K., Tobioka, Y., et al.: Bohatei: Flexible and elastic {DDoS} defense. In: 24th USENIX Security Symposium (USENIX Security 15), pp. 817–832 (2015)
15. Feamster, N., et al.: The road to sdn: an intellectual history of programmable networks. ACM SIGCOMM Comput. Commun. Rev. **44**(2), 87–98 (2014)
16. Gaurav, A., Gupta, B.B., Alhalabi, W., Visvizi, A., Asiri, Y.: A comprehensive survey on ddos attacks on various intelligent systems and it's defense techniques. Int. J. Intell. Syst. **37**(12), 11407–11431 (2022)
17. Granberg, N.: Evaluating the effectiveness of free rule sets for snort (2022)
18. Guha, B., Mukherjee, B.: Network security via reverse engineering of tcp code: vulnerability analysis and proposed solutions. IEEE Netw. **11**(4), 40–48 (1997)
19. Herrera, J.G., Botero, J.F.: Resource allocation in nfv: a comprehensive survey. IEEE Trans. Netw. Serv. Manage. **13**(3), 518–532 (2016)
20. Hong, S., Xu, L., et al.: Poisoning network visibility in software-defined networks: New attacks and countermeasures. In: Network and Distributed System Security Symposium (2015). https://api.semanticscholar.org/CorpusID:12312831
21. Jin, C., Wang, H., Shin, K.G.: Hop-count filtering: an effective defense against spoofed ddos traffic. In: Proceedings of the 10th ACM Conference on Computer and Communications Security, pp. 30–41 (2003)

22. Joseph, D.A., et al.: A policy-aware switching layer for data centers. In: Proceedings of the ACM SIGCOMM 2008 Conference On Data Communication, pp. 51–62 (2008)
23. Kaur, R., Singh, M.: A survey on zero-day polymorphic worm detection techniques. IEEE Commun. Surv. Tutorials **16**(3), 1520–1549 (2014)
24. Keromytis, A.D., et al.: Sos: an architecture for mitigating ddos attacks. IEEE J. Sel. Areas Commun. **22**(1), 176–188 (2004)
25. Krupp, J., Grishchenko, I., Rossow, C.: {AmpFuzz}: Fuzzing for amplification {DDoS} vulnerabilities. In: 31st USENIX Security Symposium (USENIX Security 22), pp. 1043–1060 (2022)
26. Lalou, M., Tahraoui, M.A., Kheddouci, H.: The critical node detection problem in networks: a survey. Comput. Sci. Rev. **28**, 92–117 (2018)
27. Lee, D., Yannakakis, M.: Principles and methods of testing finite state machines-a survey. Proc. IEEE **84**(8), 1090–1123 (1996)
28. Liu, Z., et al.: Jaqen: A {High-Performance}{Switch-Native} approach for detecting and mitigating volumetric {DDoS} attacks with programmable switches. In: 30th USENIX Security Symposium (USENIX Security 21), pp. 3829–3846 (2021)
29. Liu, Z., Jin, H., Hu, Y.C., Bailey, M.: Practical proactive ddos-attack mitigation via endpoint-driven in-network traffic control. IEEE/ACM Trans. Network. **26**(4), 1948–1961 (2018)
30. Mirsky, Y., Guri, M.: Ddos attacks on 9-1-1 emergency services. IEEE Trans. Dependable Secure Comput. **18**(6), 2767–2786 (2020)
31. Mizrak, A.T., Savage, S., Marzullo, K.: Detecting compromised routers via packet forwarding behavior. IEEE Netw. **22**(2), 34–39 (2008)
32. Moore, D., Shannon, C., Brown, D.J., Voelker, G.M., Savage, S.: Inferring internet denial-of-service activity. ACM Trans. Comput. Syst. (TOCS) **24**(2), 115–139 (2006)
33. Mosenia, A., Jha, N.K.: A comprehensive study of security of internet-of-things. IEEE Trans. Emerg. Top. Comput. **5**(4), 586–602 (2016)
34. Nayak, J., Meher, S.K., Souri, A., Naik, B., Vimal, S.: Extreme learning machine and bayesian optimization-driven intelligent framework for iomt cyber-attack detection. J. Supercomput. **78**(13), 14866–14891 (2022)
35. Nazario, J.: Ddos attack evolution. Netw. Secur. **2008**(7), 7–10 (2008)
36. O'Leary, M., O'Leary, M.: Snort. Cyber Operations: Building, Defending, and Attacking Modern Computer Networks, pp. 605–641 (2015)
37. Praseed, A., Thilagam, P.S.: Multiplexed asymmetric attacks: Next-generation ddos on http/2 servers. IEEE Trans. Inf. Forensics Secur. **15**, 1790–1800 (2019)
38. Rossow, C.: Amplification hell: Revisiting network protocols for ddos abuse. In: 2014 Network and Distributed System Security Symposium (2014)
39. Santanna, J.J., van Rijswijk-Deij, R., et al.: Booters-an analysis of ddos-as-a-service attacks. In: 2015 IFIP/IEEE International Symposium on Integrated Network Management (IM), pp. 243–251. IEEE (2015)
40. Sharafaldin, I., Lashkari, A.H., Hakak, S., Ghorbani, A.A.: Developing realistic distributed denial of service (ddos) attack dataset and taxonomy. In: 2019 International Carnahan Conference on Security Technology (ICCST), pp. 1–8. IEEE (2019)
41. Shiravi, A., Shiravi, H., Tavallaee, M., Ghorbani, A.A.: Toward developing a systematic approach to generate benchmark datasets for intrusion detection. Comput. Secur. **31**(3), 357–374 (2012)

42. Shoshitaishvili, Y., Wang, R., et al.: Sok:(state of) the art of war: offensive techniques in binary analysis. In: 2016 IEEE Symposium on Security and Privacy (SP), pp. 138–157. IEEE (2016)
43. Song, H., Liu, J., Yang, J., Lei, X., Xue, G.: Two types of novel dos attacks against cdns based on http/2 flow control mechanism. In: European Symposium on Research in Computer Security, pp. 467–487. Springer (2022)
44. Song, Z., Zhao, Z., Zhang, F., et al.: I2RNN: An incremental and interpretable recurrent neural network for encrypted traffic classification. IEEE Transactions on Dependable and Secure Computing (2023)
45. Specht, S., Lee, R.: Taxonomies of distributed denial of service networks, attacks, tools and countermeasures. CEL2003-03, Princeton University, Princeton, NJ, USA (2003)
46. Srivastava, A., Gupta, B.B., Tyagi, A., Sharma, A., Mishra, A.: A recent survey on ddos attacks and defense mechanisms. In: Nagamalai, D., Renault, E., Dhanuskodi, M. (eds.) Advances in Parallel Distributed Computing: First International Conference on Parallel, Distributed Computing Technologies and Applications, PDCTA 2011, Tirunelveli, India, September 23-25, 2011. Proceedings, pp. 570–580. Springer Berlin Heidelberg, Berlin, Heidelberg (2011). https://doi.org/10.1007/978-3-642-24037-9_57
47. Stephens, N., Grosen, J., et al.: Driller: Augmenting fuzzing through selective symbolic execution. In: NDSS. vol. 16, pp. 1–16 (2016)
48. Sung, M., Xu, J.: Ip traceback-based intelligent packet filtering: a novel technique for defending against internet ddos attacks. IEEE Trans. Parallel Distrib. Syst. **14**(9), 861–872 (2003)
49. Thing, V.L., Sloman, M., Dulay, N.: Non-intrusive ip traceback for ddos attacks. In: Proceedings of the 2nd ACM Symposium On Information, Computer and Communications Security, pp. 371–373 (2007)
50. Wagner, D., Kopp, D., et al.: United we stand: Collaborative detection and mitigation of amplification ddos attacks at scale. In: Proceedings of the 2021 ACM SIGSAC Conference on Computer and Communications Security, pp. 970–987 (2021)
51. Wang, Z., Zhu, S.: Symtcp: Eluding stateful deep packet inspection with automated discrepancy discovery. In: Network and Distributed System Security Symposium (NDSS) (2020)
52. Xing, J., Wu, W., Chen, A.: Ripple: A programmable, decentralized {Link-Flooding} defense against adaptive adversaries. In: 30th USENIX Security Symposium (USENIX Security 21), pp. 3865–3881 (2021)
53. Yaar, A., Perrig, A., Song, D.: Stackpi: new packet marking and filtering mechanisms for ddos and ip spoofing defense. IEEE J. Sel. Areas Commun. **24**(10), 1853–1863 (2006)
54. Yan, Q., et al.: Software-defined networking (sdn) and distributed denial of service (ddos) attacks in cloud computing environments: A survey, some research issues, and challenges. IEEE Commun. Surv. Tutorials **18**(1), 602–622 (2015)
55. Yoachimik, O., Pacheco, J.: DDoS threat report for 2023 q2 (2023). https://blog.cloudflare.com/ddos-threat-report-2023-q2/ Accessed 20 Sept 2023
56. Zargar, S.T., Joshi, J., Tipper, D.: A survey of defense mechanisms against distributed denial of service (ddos) flooding attacks. IEEE Commun. Surv. Tutorials **15**(4), 2046–2069 (2013)
57. Zhang, M., Li, G., et al.: Poseidon: mitigating volumetric ddos attacks with programmable switches. In: the 27th Network and Distributed System Security Symposium (NDSS 2020) (2020)

58. Zhang, Z., Yuan, B., Yang, K., Zou, D., Jin, H.: Statediver: Testing deep packet inspection systems with state-discrepancy guidance. In: Proceedings of the 38th Annual Computer Security Applications Conference, pp. 756–768 (2022)
59. Zhao, Z., Li, Z., et al.: DDoS Family: A Novel Perspective for Massive Types of DDoS Attacks. Comput, Secur (2023)
60. Zhao, Z., Li, Z., et al.: ERNN: error-resilient RNN for encrypted traffic detection towards network-induced phenomena. IEEE Transactions on Dependable and Secure Computing (2023)
61. Zhao, Z., Liu, Z., et al.: Effective DDoS mitigation via ML-driven in-network traffic shaping. IEEE Transactions on Dependable and Secure Computing (2024)
62. Zhao, Z., et al.: CMD: co-analyzed iot malware detection and forensics via network and hardware domains. IEEE Transactions on Mobile Computing (2023)
63. Zou, Y.H., Bai, J.J., et al.: {TCP-Fuzz}: Detecting memory and semantic bugs in {TCP} stacks with fuzzing. In: 2021 USENIX Annual Technical Conference (USENIX ATC 21), pp. 489–502 (2021)

# Privacy and Homomorphic Encryption

# Memory Efficient Privacy-Preserving Machine Learning Based on Homomorphic Encryption

Robert Podschwadt[1(✉)], Parsa Ghazvinian[1], Mohammad GhasemiGol[2], and Daniel Takabi[2]

[1] Georgia State University, Atlanta, GA 30303, USA
{rpodschwadt1,pghazvinian1}@student.gsu.edu
[2] Old Dominion University, Norfolk, VA 23529, USA
{mghasemi,takabi}@odu.edu

**Abstract.** Fully Homomorphic Encryption (FHE) enables computation on encrypted data and can be used to provide privacy-preserving computation for machine learning models. However, FHE is computationally expensive and requires significant memory. Single instruction multiple data (SIMD) can offset this cost. Batch-packing, an SIMD technique that packs data along the batch dimension, requires significant memory. In convolutional neural networks, we can exploit their regular and repeating structure to reduce the memory cost by caching recurring values. In this paper, we investigate strategies for dynamically loading data from persistent storage and how to cache it effectively. We propose a method that reorders operations inside the convectional layer to increase caching effectiveness and reduce memory requirements. We achieve up to 50x reduction in memory requirements with only a 13% increase in runtime compared to keeping the data in memory during the entire computation. Our method is up to 38% faster at no significant memory difference compared to not using caching. We also show that our approach is up to 4.5x faster than the operating system's swapping technique. These improvements allow us to run the models on less powerful and cheaper hardware.

**Keywords:** neural networks · homomorphic encryption · privacy · privacy-preserving machine learning

## 1 Introduction

Machine learning (ML) and neural networks specifically are widely deployed in many different scenarios, from voice assistants like Siri [27], Alexa [6], and Google Assistant [21] over writing assistants like Grammarly [22], and chatbots like Bard [20] and ChatGPT [39], to medical diagnostic systems [16,30]. Many of these systems deal with privacy-sensitive data, some of which enjoy special legal protections, e.g., medical data. These systems send the data to a server,


C. Pöpper and L. Batina (Eds.): ACNS 2024, LNCS 14584, pp. 313–339, 2024.
https://doi.org/10.1007/978-3-031-54773-7_13

which runs it through its model and returns the result to the client. Since the server needs access to the unencrypted client data to perform the computation, the client's privacy is at risk. The server might use the data to train further ML models, which could expose the data to privacy attacks, or the server itself could be breached and the data stolen. Researchers have recently proposed solutions to protect user data privacy in ML applications using different methods. Differential Privacy [18] solutions preserve the privacy of the training data in the trained model [1,40]. To protect the data during inference, solutions commonly use Secure Multiparty Computation (SMC) [12,14,36,37], Fully Homomorphic Encryption (FHE) [31,33,34] or a mixture between the two [7,38]. SMC allows multiple parties to jointly evaluate a function without revealing their private inputs; however, it requires all parties to stay online during the computation. FHE, on the other hand, can be used entirely offline. FHE is a type of encryption that allows computation on encrypted data without exposing any inputs, intermediate, or final results. Neural networks are a popular choice for privacy-preserving ML models since most operations, like fully connected layers or convolutions, can be performed easily using FHE. Additionally, neural networks perform very well on a wide range of tasks. However, FHE introduces significant time and memory overhead. Some FHE schemes support single instruction multiple data (SIMD) processing, which can offset some time and memory overhead. FHE ciphertexts can be thought of as fixed-sized encrypted vectors containing thousands of elements, called slots. Two approaches for filling the slots have been used for ML. 1.) Pack all the features of an instance into as few ciphertexts as possible and perform convolutions and dot products with the help of rotations [2,9,34], called inter-axis packing. This has the advantage that the number of ciphertexts and total operations is relatively small, making it fast for a small number of instances. However, this approach often requires large rotation keys, and the rotations require additional time. 2.) Pack multiple instances' features into a single ciphertext [17,25,42], called batch-packing. This produces as many ciphertexts as the data has features. Batch-packing allows us to simultaneously compute results for many instances, leading to low amortized per-instance cost and high throughput. However, it suffers from high latency and memory requirements. Batch-packing is beneficial when many instances need to be processed, and low latency is not essential. For example, in a medical image diagnostic system, where images are collected throughout the day, and an ML system analyzes them overnight. This work focuses on convolutional neural networks (CNN), specifically. We address the memory requirements for convolutional layers by trading disc space for main memory. Disc space is typically orders of magnitude cheaper. However, it is also slower. We dynamically load ciphertexts and plaintexts and clear them from memory when no longer needed. We present and compare different strategies and their impact on memory and runtime. Prior work focuses primarily on latency reduction; reduction in memory is often a side effect of inter-axis packing. To the best of our knowledge, this is the first study that performs an in-depth analysis of caching strategies and memory reduction for batch-packed inference. Brutzkus et al. [9] or Lee et al. [34] propose input packing techniques, which reduce the number of ciphertexts and thereby memory requirements. However, these approaches require additional operations like masking and rotation, which lower the overall throughput. Boemer et al. [7] present a complex encoding, allowing them to fit more values into a ciphertext. This can reduce the number of ciphertexts and plaintext when using inter-axis packing. However, for batch-packing, it only affects the batch size. Approaches that use client interaction, such as Boemer et al. [7], Podschwadt et al. [41], and Cai et al. [10] can often use smaller crypto parameters, since the client interaction resets the noise level, allowing for further computation. However, these approaches require the client to be online during the computation. We make the following main contributions:

- We propose a schedule representation for convolutions that allows us to reorder its fundamental operations to achieve increased caching performance.
- We propose a memory estimation algorithm for schedules.
- We propose an algorithm for executing a schedule using multiple threads.
- We propose multiple strategies for creating schedules, which we analyze and experimentally evaluate with regard to their time and memory requirements.

The paper is organized as follows: in Sect. 2, we discuss the theoretical background and notation. In Sect. 3, we discuss related work before we describe our proposed approach in detail in Sect. 4. Section 5 describes ways to reorder the computation to reduce memory requirements, which we experimentally evaluate in Sect. 6. We conclude the paper in Sect. 7.

## 2 Background

Here, we consider 2-D convolutional layers since they are commonly used in image classification, a prevalent ML task. However, our proposed approach is not limited to 2-D and can easily be transferred to convolutions in other dimensions. We consider convolutions with inputs $X$, weights $W$, and outputs $Y$, where $X$, $W$, and $Y$ are tensors all four-dimensional tensors. The first dimension of $X$ and $Y$ is the batch dimension, and $|\cdot|$ denotes the number of elements in a tensor. Lowercase bold letters, e.g., $\mathbf{x}$, indicate elements of a tensor.

### 2.1 Fully Homomorphic Encryption

FHE schemes are public key crypto schemes that can evaluate addition and multiplication on encrypted data without decrypting it at any point. The result of the computation is also encrypted. After decryption, the result is as if the computation was performed on plain data. In this paper, we use the Residue Number System (RNS) version of the Cheon-Kim-Kim-Song (CKKS) scheme [13]. Unlike most other schemes, CKKS supports real numbers. However, it performs encrypted computation only approximately, leading to approximation errors. The error appears first in the least significant bits of the result, keeping the error small. We can think of CKKS plain- and ciphertexts as one-dimensional vectors containing multiple values offering vectorized, element-wise SIMD computation

[44]. The maximum number of values, typically called slots, is determined by the security parameters, which is a power of two. The number of filled slots in ciphertext does not impact the performance of the operation, allowing us to perform addition or multiplication of thousands of values at once.

## 2.2 Batch Packing

We consider $n_s$ to be the number of slots in a ciphertext. For simplicity, we assume that the batch size is equal to $n_s$. Otherwise, we would need to split the data into multiple batches or pad it. We partially flatten all dimensions in $X$ except the batch dimension to encrypt the inputs. We take each column from the resulting two-dimensional matrix and encrypt that into a ciphertext, leaving us with a vector of ciphertexts. We need to encode the weights as well. Each weight value in $W$ is encoded into its own plaintext. Before encoding, we turn each value into a vector by repeating it $n_s$ times. This produces $|X|/n_s$ ciphertexts and $|W|$ plaintexts. If the model needs to be encrypted as well, we can encrypt the encoded plaintext weights. Similarly, the encoding of $W$ contains $|W|/n_s$ ciphertexts. We can think of the encoding as setting the batch axis to one. The issue that arises is that FHE ciphertexts and plaintexts require a substantial amount of memory. A single ciphertext can be between a few hundred kilobytes to multiple megabytes, depending on the crypto parameters; a plaintext is half the size of a ciphertext. We refer to the encoded and/or encrypted inputs, weights, and outputs as $X'$, $W'$, and $Y'$, respectively, and values taken from them as $\mathbf{x}'$, $\mathbf{w}'$ and $\mathbf{y}'$.

## 2.3 Convolutional Layers

Here, we consider two-dimensional convolutions commonly used in neural networks; however, other dimensionalities work fundamentally the same. Goodfellow et al. [19] define the operation as follows: given the inputs $X$,$W$, and the output $Y$, which are all tensors, we can define the two-dimensional convolution as:

$$Y_{b,m,n,c_{\text{out}}} = \sum_{j} \sum_{k} \sum_{c_{\text{in}}} X_{b,m-j,n-k,c_{\text{in}}} W_{j,k,c_{\text{in}},c_{\text{out}}} \tag{1}$$

We use the subscript to indicate a single element in the tensor, where $b$ is the batch index, $c_{\text{in}}$ the input channel index, and $c_{\text{out}}$, the output channel index. Eq 1 needs to be computed for all values in $Y$.

## 2.4 Lock-Free Multi-threaded Convolution

The most straightforward way to compute a convolution with multiple threads is to have each $\mathbf{y}$ computed by a thread; Eq. 1 is computed by a separated thread for each unique $(b, m, n, c_{\text{out}})$. For $s = |Y|$, we can use at most $n_t = s$ parallel threads without requiring some synchronization between the threads since all threads read from the shared resources $X$ and $W$ but do not modify them; every $Y_{b,m,n,c_{\text{out}}}$ is only modified by one thread, ruling out any race conditions that could lead to lost updates. With fewer than $s$ threads, threads can compute multiple $Y_{b,m,n,c_{\text{out}}}$. With more than $s$ threads, we either need synchronization or can not use these threads. Generally, given $n_t$ threads where each thread is assigned a unique integer $i \in [1, n_t]$, we can use Algorithm 1.

---

**Algorithm 1.** Lock-free multi-threaded Convolution

---

**Inputs:** input tensor $X$, weight tensor $W$, output tensor $Y$, number of threads $n_t$
**Outpus:** output tensor $Y$ containing the result of the convolution

1: **while** $t \leq n_t$ **and** $t \leq |Y|$ **do**
2:     **Start Thread** $t$ and execute:
3:         $q := t$
4:         **while** $q \leq |Y|$ **do**
5:             convert $q$ to multi-dimensional index $b, m, n, c_{\text{out}}$
6:             $Y_{b,m,n,c_o} := \sum_j \sum_k \sum_{c_i} X_{b,m-j,n-k,c_i} W_{j,k,c_i,c_o}$
7:             $q := q + n_t$
8:         **end while**
9:     **End Thread**
10: **end while**

---

We assume that inputs are stored on a disk (the term disk refers to any persistent storage, i.e., a hard disk drive or solid-state drive) and must be loaded into memory. With the Algorithm 1, we have two options to keep it lock-free. 1.) Load $X$ and $Y$ before we start the computation, or 2.) Each thread loads the $\mathbf{x}$ and $\mathbf{y}$ as needed. 1.) has the upside in that we only need to load each value once and can reuse them at no additional cost. However, the downside is that we need to keep them in memory for the entirety of the computation. 2.) On the other hand, needs to keep much fewer objects in memory. Each thread has only three objects in memory: one $\mathbf{x}$, one weight $\mathbf{w}$, and the output $\mathbf{y}$. However, each thread must perform two loads for each iteration of the nested sums in line 6. Furthermore, multiple threads may load the same $\mathbf{x}$ and $\mathbf{w}$, causing redundant loads. A further issue with this algorithm arises when $|Y|$ is not divisible by $n_t$. In this case, $|Y| - |Y| \mod n_t$ threads finish one iteration, line 4, early and are idle for the rest of the computation, leading to unused computational resources. However, this impact is small if $|Y|$ is large compared to $n_t$. Performing the second option on plain data will lead to slower results since arithmetic operations are much faster than data loading. Additionally, single $\mathbf{x}$ and $\mathbf{w}$ are so small that we can not save significant memory by loading them on demand.

Running Algorithm 1 on encrypted data is straightforward using batch-packing described earlier. To do this, we replace $X$ with $X'$, $W$ with $W'$, and $Y$ with $Y'$. This replacement sets the batch dimension to one, allowing us to remove it from consideration. For the algorithm, it does not matter if $W'$ is encoded FHE plaintexts or ciphertexts if the model is encrypted. In the case of the plaintext model, we assume that unencoded weights $W$ are loaded into memory before the computation starts and are encoded when needed; therefore, we don't need to load them strictly speaking. However, we call this operation loading for simplicity in this context.

## 3 Related Work

Akavia et al. [3] focus on reducing the storage footprint of FHE ciphertext rather than the in-memory size during computation. They design a protocol that allows multiple data producers to upload and store data in the cloud with no overhead compared to storing AES (Advanced Encryption Standard) encrypted data. Storing AES encrypted on an untrusted server and using secret sharing, a computing server can use the data for HE computation with the help of an auxiliary server. In contrast, our proposed solution reduces the memory footprint at computation rather than the encrypted storage size.

Jiang et al. [28], Brutzukus et al. [9], Lee et al. [34], Dathathri et al. [15], and Lee et al. [33] are conceptually similar works, who all reduce the number of ciphertexts required by using inter-axis packing. While all these approaches reduce the inference latency, they require expensive rotations, lowering the throughput compared to batch-packed solutions. Additionally, they often rely on designing the packing strategy for the specific network architecture.

Other studies rely on interactive solutions for privacy preservation. Hao et al. [23] and Huang et al. [26] both propose efficient matrix multiplications in a two-party setting. Both studies propose rotation-free matrix multiplication over polynomial encoded ciphertexts. However, both require interactive phases where one party must extract specific polynomial coefficients and mask the result. Zheng et al. [46] propose a method for fast private inference using transformers and SMC. The authors use a similar protocol to the one proposed by Juvekar et al. [29], where the server performs much of the expensive matrix multiplication computation in an offline phase. Zheng et al. [46] reduce the number of ciphertext rotations required by packing the same feature of different tokens into the same ciphertext, similar to the batch-packing we use in our approach. However, we compute the intermediate terms in a less memory-consuming way.

Prior work on batch-packed PPML using FHE [8,11,17,24] does not explicitly state how they perform matrix multiplication or convolutions. They focus on other improvements like better polynomial approximation [11,24], or parameter fusion and special value bypass [8]. We believe most of these solutions could decrease memory requirements using our proposed algorithm. Another work that addresses memory limitations is Badawi et al. [4], which implements a CNN over FHE data using GPU acceleration for the basic ciphertext operation. To fit the input to the convolution into GPU memory, they split it into multiple blocks of the same size as the filter. The filter and as many of these blocks as possible are loaded into GPU memory, where the convolution is performed. Compared to our proposed approach, this process only reduces the memory requirement on the GPU. The input and weights still need to be present in the main memory. Shivdikar et al. [43] also present techniques aimed at GPUs. They aim to reduce the repeated memory reads inside the GPU when performing polynomial multiplication for HE primitives. While this speeds up the low-level operations underpinning most HE schemes, unlike our work, it does not address the issue of requiring a large number of plaintexts or ciphertexts in memory.

# 4 Our Proposed Approach

To address the issues of memory consumption and unused resources, we model the convolutional layer as a schedule, which determines the order of operations. We present and compare multiple schedule construction strategies based on the computation and available resources. We further present an algorithm to execute a schedule. From now on, we assume that all tensors are flattened.

## 4.1 Modeling the Problem as a Schedule

We can write each element $\mathbf{y}$ as a sum of products of $\mathbf{x}$ and $\mathbf{w}$. We denote a product of two elements of $\mathbf{x}$ and $\mathbf{w}$ as the triple $t = (\mathbf{x}, \mathbf{w}, \mathbf{y})$, where $\mathbf{y}$ is the result that holds the sum that the product $\mathbf{xw}$ is a part of. To refer to an element in a triple $t$, we use the following notation $t^i; i \in \{x, w, y\}$.

---

**Algorithm 2.** Generating a schedule from a 2D Convolution

---

**Inputs:** Output shape $h_{\text{out}}, w_{\text{out}}, c_{\text{out}}$, Input shape $h_{\text{in}}, w_{\text{in}}c_{\text{in}}$, Filter size $w_h, w_w$
**Output:** The schedule $S$

1: $S := [\,]$
2: **for each** $i \in [1, \ldots, h_{\text{out}}w_{\text{out}}c_{\text{out}}]$ **do**
3:     convert $i$ to multi-dimensional index $(m, n, t^y)$
4:     **for each** $j \in [1, \ldots, w_h w_w c_{\text{in}}]$ **do**
5:         convert $j$ to multi-dimensional index $(p, q, r)$
6:         $t^x := m - p + ((n - q)w_{\text{in}} + (rh_{\text{in}}w_{\text{in}})$
7:         $t^w := p + (qw_h) + (rw_w w_h) + (rw_w w_h c_{\text{in}}))$
8:         append $(t^x, t^w, t^y)$ to $S$
9:     **end for**
10: **end for**

---

**Definition 1 (Schedule).** *Let $f$ be a convolutional layer; we say $t_i \in f$ iff the sum to compute $t_i^y$ contains the product $t_i^x t_i^w$. A schedule is an ordered list of triples $t_i$ that contains all $t_i \in f$ exactly once.*

In other words, we represent $f$ as a sequence of all its element-wise products. To compute the function $f$, we need to compute all products given in the schedule. Additionally, we must sum all products with the same value for $\mathbf{y}$. We call the number of triples in a schedule the length or steps of a schedule, denoted by $|S|$. Algorithm 2 shows how to generate a schedule for two-dimensional convolutions. Higher dimensional convolutions work analogously by expanding the iteration bounds in lines 2 and 4, the decomposition of $i$ and $j$ in lines 3 and 5, and the formula for $t^x$ and $t^w$ by the extra dimensions. In addition to the computation steps, we also insert load instructions into the schedule. Load instructions specify which elements to load into memory, discard from memory, or write back to disk in case they were updated.

### 4.2 Executing a Schedule

To execute a schedule, we evaluate all triples in order. To evaluate a triple $t$ we multiply the input $X_{t^x}$ with the weight $W_{t^w}$ and add the result to $Y_{t^y}$; $Y_{t^t} = Y_{t^y} + X_{t^x} W_{t^w}$. We assume that all $\mathbf{y}$ are 0 at the beginning. We parallelize the execution of the schedule across multiple threads. Each repeatedly evaluates the first unevaluated triple. This requires synchronization at two points. 1.) We must ensure that every triple is evaluated exactly once. 2.) Unlike in Algorithm 1, we cannot guarantee that multiple threads do not write to the same output; therefore, we need locking to prevent race conditions. We use the following algorithm to ensure all values are correctly summed into the output value. We show our proposed algorithm in Algorithm 3. The parts that must be protected from concurrent access are marked as Critical Section.

**Algorithm 3.** Executing a schedule

**Inputs:** inputs $X$, weights $W$, output $Y$, number of threads $n_t$, schedule $S$
**Outputs:** $Y$ containing the result of the convolution

1: ensure $Y_i = \varnothing; \forall i \in [1, |Y|]$
2: $i_s := 1$
3: **while** $i \leq n_t$ **and** $i \leq |S|$ **do**
4:     **Start Thread** $i$ and execute:
5:         **while** $i_s \leq |S|$ **do** } Critical Section
6:             $j := i_s$
7:             $i_s := i_s + 1$
8:             perform load instructions
9:             $t := S_j$
10:             $r := X_{t^c} \cdot W_{t^p}$ ▷ HE multiplication
11:             **if** $Y_{t^o} = \varnothing$ **then** } Critical Section (lines 11–15)
12:                 $Y_{t^o} := r$
13:             **else**
14:                 $v := Y_{t^o}$
15:                 $Y_{t^o} := \varnothing$
16:                 $r := v + r$ ▷ HE addition
17:                 **goto** line 11
18:             **end if**
19:         **end while**
20:     **End Thread**
21: **end while**

We indicate where in the algorithm process load instructions in line 8. A load instruction has three attributes: 1.) the step that is executed on, 2.) the type of instruction, load or unload, and 3.) the object to load. Every iteration, each thread checks if there is an unprocessed load instruction with a step equal to or lower than the step the thread is executing. If there is, the thread marks it complete and executes it. Again, we must ensure that only one thread updates the load instructions at any time. Each thread tries to execute any outstanding load instructions before moving on. Objects loaded through load instructions stay cached until explicitly unloaded through another load instruction or until the computation is complete. If a thread requires values not loaded by any load instructions, it loads them on demand and does not cache them.

### 4.3 Cost of a Schedule

We can use the schedule to estimate the maximum memory required on encrypted data. Maximum memory is important since we cannot execute the schedule if it requires more than the available memory. Most of the memory required during execution stems from the ciphertexts and plaintexts; therefore, we ignore additional objects like keys, the schedule, and other data in our estimation. To estimate the cost, we look at the load instructions, the number of threads, and the objects loaded on demand. We first examine the simpler case with only one thread and extend it to multiple threads later. Let $s_x$ be the size of a single $\mathbf{x}'$, $s_w$ the size of a single $\mathbf{w}'$, and $s_y$ the size of a single $\mathbf{y}'$. To estimate the memory requirement of a schedule, we need to perform the following steps:

1. Split the schedule into parts at the load instructions so that each part begins with load instructions and contains no other load instructions except those at the beginning. A part must not only contain load instructions.
2. For each part, count how many $\mathbf{x}'$, $\mathbf{w}'$, and $\mathbf{y}'$ are loaded and unloaded.
3. Weight the count of $\mathbf{x}'$, $\mathbf{w}'$, and $\mathbf{y}'$ by $s_x$, $s_w$, and $s_p$, respectively.
4. For every step, weigh the on-demand loaded objects and add them.
5. For each part, add the weighted counts from step 3 and the maximum from step 4. The maximum of all the parts is our estimate for the schedule.

We now extend the estimation to multiple threads. The estimate for multiple threads is less precise than that for a single thread since we can only make assumptions about how multiple threads will interact. We make the following simplifying assumptions: 1.) threads execute schedule steps at the same speed, and 2.) a continuous block of load instructions is executed simultaneously, no matter how many instructions are in that block. The main ideas are that if we have split the schedule into parts that contain fewer steps than we have threads $n_t$, we merge adjacent parts until all parts contain at least as many steps as we have threads available. Then we identifiy the $n_t$ steps that require the most memory in each part. To do this we start as we did in the single thread case above. Next, we look at the number of steps in each part. If the part has fewer steps than the number of threads $n_t$, we combine it with the next part to form a new part by adding the cost of the load instructions. We repeat this until the new combined part has more steps than threads. We repeat this for all parts of the schedule. To estimate the cost of the on-demand loaded objects, we assume that $n_t$ schedule steps are executed at the same time. In the final step, we handle the cost of the schedule steps. We compute the on-demand cost for all steps in the schedule parts created in the previous step. The computation happens the same way as described in the single-threaded case above. However, now we not only add the step with the highest cost; we add the $n_t$ steps with the highest costs. This method provides a reasonable estimate for the memory cost of a schedule with multi-threaded execution.

### 4.4 Threat Model

In this work, we assume that all parties are honest but curious. They follow all protocols and algorithms without deviation. However, they do try to learn as much information as they can. The server offers private inference to the client. Only the dimensions of the data and the data domain need to be shared between the client and server in plaintext. The actual instances and the inference result are only ever shared in encrypted form. Besides the input and output dimensions of the model, the client gains no additional information about the model. However, model extraction attacks by the client, as described by Tramer et al. [45], can still threaten the server-side model. Additionally, since we rely on the CKKS scheme, the client needs to make sure not to share decrypted inference results with the server since this can be used to compromise the security of the client's secret key [35]. Our proposed approach reorders the operation the server performs of the encrypted data, which is not observable by the client. The client can only observe the time the server needs to perform the computation. Without knowing the server's hardware configuration, this does not provide any useful information to the client. Even if the client knows the exact hardware configuration, it can not learn any other information than it would learn if the server used a different computational model.

## 5 Reduced Memory Schedules

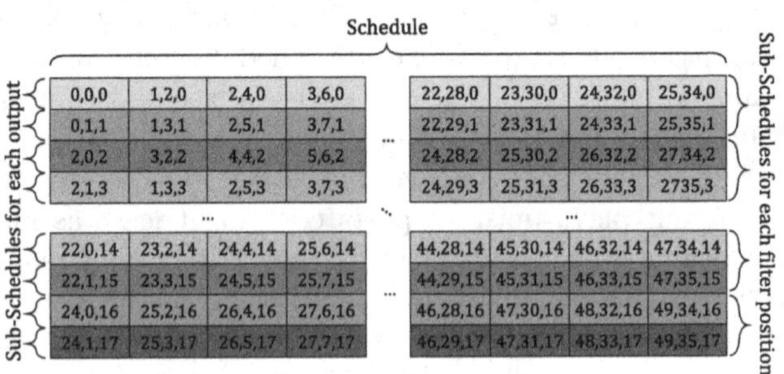


**Fig. 1.** Breaking an example base schedule down into multiple sub-schedules. This schedule is executed row-wise.

In this section, we propose different ways to construct schedules. These schedules provide trade-offs between runtime and memory. The fastest we can execute a schedule is by loading all data at the beginning of the computation and then using the lock-free Algorithm 1. However, this requires a large amount of memory. We can reduce the memory footprint by loading everything on demand. However, this increases runtime significantly.

We can transform the computation performed by Algorithm 1 into a schedule. Again, consider $n_t$ to be the number of threads, $n_o$ the number of outputs of the computation, and $n_f$ the number of products that sum up into a single output. In Algorithm 1, every thread executes a subschedule where all $t^y \mod i = 0; t \in S$, where $i$ is the thread id. We can obtain the combined schedule by taking all subschedules and interleaving them elementwise. See Fig. 2 for an example with three threads.

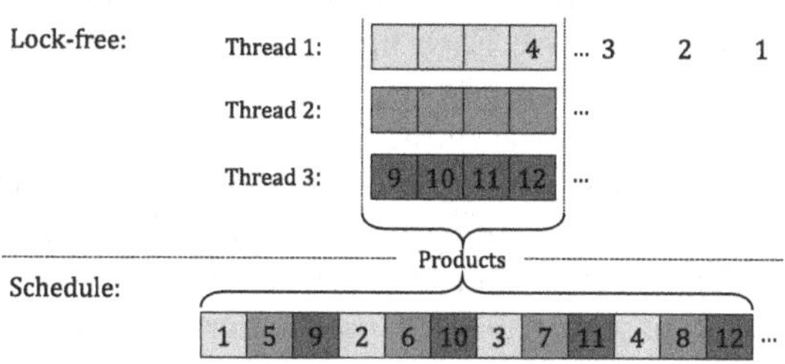


**Fig. 2.** Example of how to turn a lock-free execution with three threads into a schedule

The lock-free algorithm computes and needs to keep in memory $n_t$ outputs simultaneously. The base schedule, on the other hand, fully computes a single output before moving on to the next one. This allows us to keep fewer outputs in memory. This is the lowest amount of memory we can achieve. However, we need to load objects from disk frequently and are not using any caching. Caching aims to reduce the number of loading operations as much as possible. We can exploit the regular structure of convolutions to find the best values for caching. We can split a schedule into a regular, repeating pattern defined by the size and number of filters and input channels. In two-dimensional convolutions, as used in neural networks, we have a four-dimensional filter volume, $W$, where the dimensions are in order: $i$, $j$ the position in the filter, $c_{\text{in}}$ the input channel, and $c_{\text{out}}$ the output channel. We move $W$ across the entire input, creating $c_{\text{out}}$ outputs at every position. Note how far $W$ we move the filter is given by the stride, which we assume to be one here. However, our method remains applicable to other stride values. Each output, at a given position of $W$, uses the same values from $X$. We call each unique position of the filter on the inputs the filter position or window.

We need to keep three kinds of objects in memory during the computation. Inputs $\mathbf{x}$, weights $\mathbf{w}$ and, outputs $\mathbf{y}$. We design multiple caching strategies based on the memory available. We will not go over the trivial case that we can fit all values of $\mathbf{x}$ and $\mathbf{w}$ into memory.

### 5.1 Caching by Object Type

The simplest caching strategy, is to load either all values from $X'$ or $W'$ at the beginning of the computation and load the other values on demand as needed. This strategy creates very simple schedules; however, it underutilizes caching. If we preload all $\mathbf{x}'$, we load too many values much earlier than needed in the computation, and if we preload all $\mathbf{y}'$ we need to load $\mathbf{x}'$ values frequently.

### 5.2 Full Window Caching

We can improve the caching by object type strategy by utilizing the underlying structure of the convolution operation. To obtain the output values we move the filter across the input values. Each filter channel creates one output value. The filter values at every position are the same. Therefore, if we can load them only once and cache them for the duration of the computation we can save a significant amount of load operations. However, for each position the input values change. Each position of $W$ requires only $|W'|/c_{\text{out}}$ $\mathbf{x}'$. If we can fit these objects and all $\mathbf{y}'$ into memory, we only load $W'$ once. Since $W'$ usually moves over the inputs with some overlap, i.e., the stride is smaller than the width and height of the filter, we can reuse many $\mathbf{x}'$ and only need to unload and reload a small amount. We start at the top left and move $W$ from left to right. Once we reach the end on the right, we move down and start over on the right, repeating until we reach the bottom right. If the filter size or stride is not symmetrical, it is beneficial to change the behavior to first move in the direction that has the most overlap, reducing the number of values that need to be loaded and increasing the number of values that can be reused.

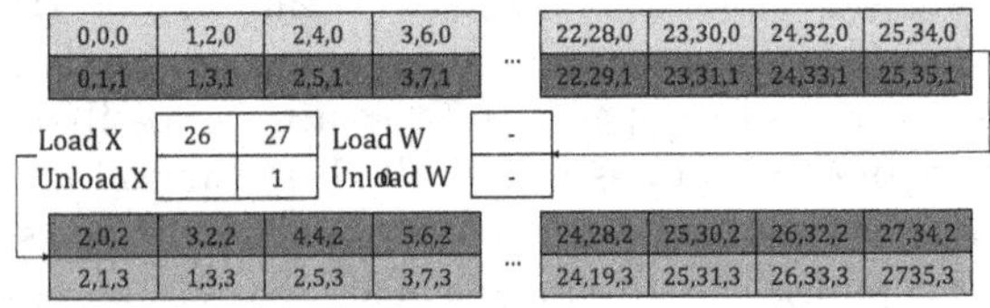


**Fig. 3.** Load instructions that are necessary when moving from the first window to the second using window caching with a $5 \times 5x2$ input and a $3 \times 3x2 \times 2$ kernel.

### 5.3 Partial Window Caching

If we can fit $|W'|/c_{\text{out}}$ $\mathbf{x}'$ but not all of $W'$ into memory, we can modify the full window caching strategy to reduce the number of loads. Let $n$ be the number of $\mathbf{w}'$ that we can fit into memory in addition to all the $\mathbf{x}'$ in the window. We then split the schedule into sub-schedules for every position of $W$. To reorder the sub-schedules to increase caching potential we reverse every second sub-schedule; see Fig. 4. This reordering makes it so that $i$ values to the left and right of the sub-schedule boundary are the same for all $i \in [1, |W|]$. This allows us to cache $n$ values before the sub-schedule boundary and reuse them in the next one.

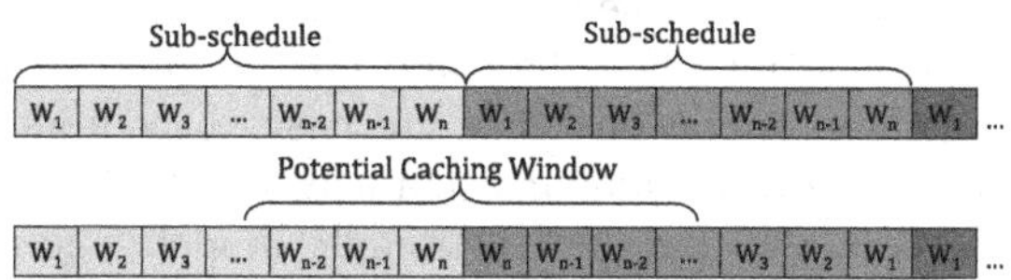


**Fig. 4.** Weights $W_i$ only in Sub-Schedules that correspond to individual filter positions and how they can be reordered to increase caching potential.

## 5.4 Column-Wise Caching

If we cannot fit $|W|/c_{\text{out}}$ $\mathbf{x}'$ or $W'$ into memory, we cannot use any of the caching methods described above. However, we can construct a different schedule that allows us to cache $\mathbf{x}'$ values. For this schedule, we need to be able to fit $c_{\text{out}}$ $\mathbf{y}'$ into memory. By taking each window sub schedule and reordering it column-major instead of row-major, see Fig. 5, we can reuse the same $\mathbf{x}'$ multiple times before we unload it. This ordering requires us to keep $c_{\text{out}}$ $\mathbf{y}'$ in memory. This ordering is most beneficial when the number of input channels is much larger than the output channels or the filter is relatively large. Both scenarios lead to a large number of $\mathbf{x}'$ in a window. Depending on how much memory is available, we can cache multiple columns. Additionally, we can combine this with the idea from partial window caching of reordering the computation to generate adjacent window subschedules that end and start with the same $X$ values.

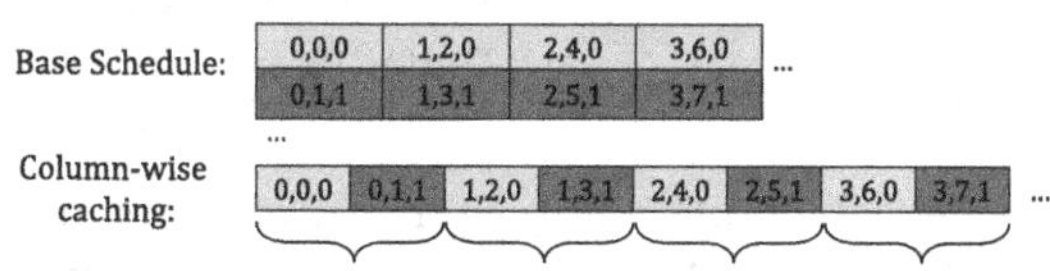


**Fig. 5.** Transforming the base schedule into a column-wise caching schedule

A downside of the proposed approach is that in order to achieve any benefits, we require the data to be batch-packed and a convolutional layer. Only batch-packing allows us to reorder the computation on a granular level. If this approach provides any benefits with inter-axis packing strategies is beyond the scope of this work. We need a convolutional layer to exploit its repeating weight structure. It is possible that we could use similar optimizations with recurrent layers since they also have repeating weights. However, recurrent layers impose additional challenges when used with HE [42].

## 6 Experimental Evaluation

We evaluate our proposed solution on the layers of a convolutional neural network (CNN) trained on the CIFAR-10 [32] dataset. We first estimate the memory requirements and then compare them to the measurements we obtain by running the model on encrypted data. Table 1 shows the model's architecture. We have two different models. One for plain data and one adapted to be HE-friendly, meaning it only contains operations that are easy to compute on encrypted data. Both models achieve very similar accuracies on the test data, 70.9% for the original model and 69.7% for the HE-friendly model. The main interest of this paper is not to propose new models or techniques that increase the accuracy of models on encrypted data but to analyze and reduce the memory consumption of these models.

**Table 1.** Architecture of the evaluation model with the layer parameters showing the filter size (FS), stride (S), number of filters (NF), and the activation or pooling function used on plain text (PT) and on encrypted data (HE).

| Layer | Input Shape | Output Shape | Parameters |
|---|---|---|---|
| Conv 2D (1) | $32 \times 32 \times 3$ | $30 \times 30 \times 32$ | FS: $3 \times 3$, S: $1 \times 1$, NF: 32, PT: ReLU, HE: $x^2$ |
| Pooling | $30 \times 30 \times 32$ | $15 \times 15 \times 32$ | FS: $2 \times 2$, S: $2 \times 2$, PT: Max, HE: Average |
| Conv 2D (2) | $15 \times 15 \times 32$ | $13 \times 13 \times 64$ | FS: $3 \times 3$, S: $1 \times 1$, NF: 64, PT: ReLU, HE: $x^2$ |
| Pooling | $13 \times 13 \times 64$ | $6 \times 6 \times 64$ | FS: $2 \times 2$, S: $2 \times 2$, PT: Max, HE: Average |
| Conv 2D (3) | $6 \times 6 \times 64$ | $4 \times 4 \times 64$ | FS: $3 \times 3$, S: $1 \times 1$, NF: 64, PT: ReLU, HE: $x^2$ |
| Flatten | $4 \times 4 \times 64$ | 1024 | - |
| Dense | 1024 | 64 | Units: 64, PT: ReLU, HE: $x^2$ |
| Dense | 64 | 10 | Units: 10 |

We define three sets of crypto parameters: small, medium, and large. All parameters guarantee at least 128-bit security. We use OpenFHE [5] as the underlying crypto library in our implementation. The small parameters have a ring dimension of $2^{14}$ and a multiplicative depth of 2. The medium parameters have a ring dimension of $2^{14}$ and a multiplicative depth of 8. And the large parameters have a ring dimension of $2^{15}$ and a multiplicative depth of 19. This results in a ciphertext size of 0.75 MB, 2.225 MB, and 10 MB for the small, medium, and large parameters respectively. A plaintext is always half the size of a ciphertext. We have two machines. One with 16 cores, 20 GB of memory, and 32 GB of operating system (OS) swap space, and another with 104 cores and 768 GB of memory. Both machines have two TB solid-state drives. We define different schedules, then estimate the required memory using the technique described in Sect. 4.3, and finally execute the schedules to obtain real measurements.

We define several schedules that we estimate and measure the memory requirements for. The names of the schedules are given italicized. We use the Lock-free algorithm (Algorithm 1) as our baselines once we load all values on demand (*Lock-free on demand*) and once we preload all values before execution *Lock-free Preload.* We compare these baselines to their direct equivalent using our proposed algorithm (Algorithm 3), where we preload all values (*Preload everything*). Next, we investigate the behavior when we either preload all of $X'$, *Preload* $X'$, or all $W'$ values *Preload* $W'$, $x'$ *on demand.* Finally, we look closer at the window, partial window, and column-wise caching. For (partial) window caching, we always load all of $\mathbf{x}'$ in the window and investigate the following strategies for loading $\mathbf{w}'$s:

- load all of $W'$, *Load* $X'$ *window* $W'$
- load $\mathbf{w}'$s on demand, *Load* $X'$ *window,* $w'$ *on demand*
- load half of $W'$ values, *Load* $X'$ *window,* $W'/2$
- load a quarter of $W'$, *Load* $X'$ *window,* $W'/4$

We only cache one $\mathbf{x}'X$, *Column Major* for column-wise caching. For all schedules, we cache the $y'$s from their first appearance in the schedule to their last.

### 6.1 Memory Estimate

To demonstrate that our proposed solution is scalable from large servers to consumer hardware, we run the selected schedules on two different machines. A desktop PC with a 16-core AMD Ryzen CPU, 20 GB of RAM, 32 GB of swap space, and a large server with two Intel 54-core CPUs and 756 GB of RAM. Both machines have a 2 TB solid-state drive and run Ubuntu Linux 20.04 LTS. In the tables and figures throughout this paper, we refer to the server and PC by their number of threads: 104 and 16, respectively.

We use the algorithm described in Sect. 4.3 to estimate the cost of all convolutional layers for small, medium, and large parameters and 16 and 104 threads. We need to estimate the memory requirements based on the number of threads that are used during execution since that can influence the number of objects in memory. The estimate column in Table 2, 3, and 4 shows the estimates for each layer and schedule for large parameters (for the small parameters see the appendix). We can see that, especially for the large parameters, the estimate frequently goes beyond the 20 GB of the PC. The estimate also often exceeds the 52 GB of memory and swap space combined. The estimate never exceeds the 756 GB of the server. For the estimate and following experiments, we assume the input $X'$ is encrypted while the model $W'$ is in plain.

Unsurprisingly, the schedules that preload all objects, *Preload everything* and *Lock-free Preload*, have the highest memory estimate. On the other hand, schedules that load most objects on demand and cache very little, *Lock-Free on demand* and *Column Major* have the lowest memory estimate. For the Conv 2d (1) layer, the estimates range from 380 MB to about 35 GB. Schedules that do not load all of $X'$ are significantly below that value, estimated at most 6193 MB. For the second layer, Conv 2D (2), both the number of $\mathbf{x}'$ and $\mathbf{w}'$ is significantly larger. This, however, does not significantly change the estimate for the *Lock-Free on demand* schedule. This observation also holds for the next layer, Conv 2D (3). The estimation aligns with the insights of a theoretical analysis of the execution. As discussed earlier, during runtime, this schedule has at most $n_t$ of each $\mathbf{x}'$, $\mathbf{w}'$, and $\mathbf{y}'$ in memory, where $n_t$ is the number of threads. Therefore, the memory consumption of the schedule is only influenced by the number of threads and independent of the layer. For the Conv 2D (2) layer, we also encounter values outside the PC's available memory, ranging from 400 MB to 164 GB. We see a similar picture for the last convolutional layer, Conv 2d (3). Large estimates of up to 208 GB, especially for layers that load and cache $W'$ values.

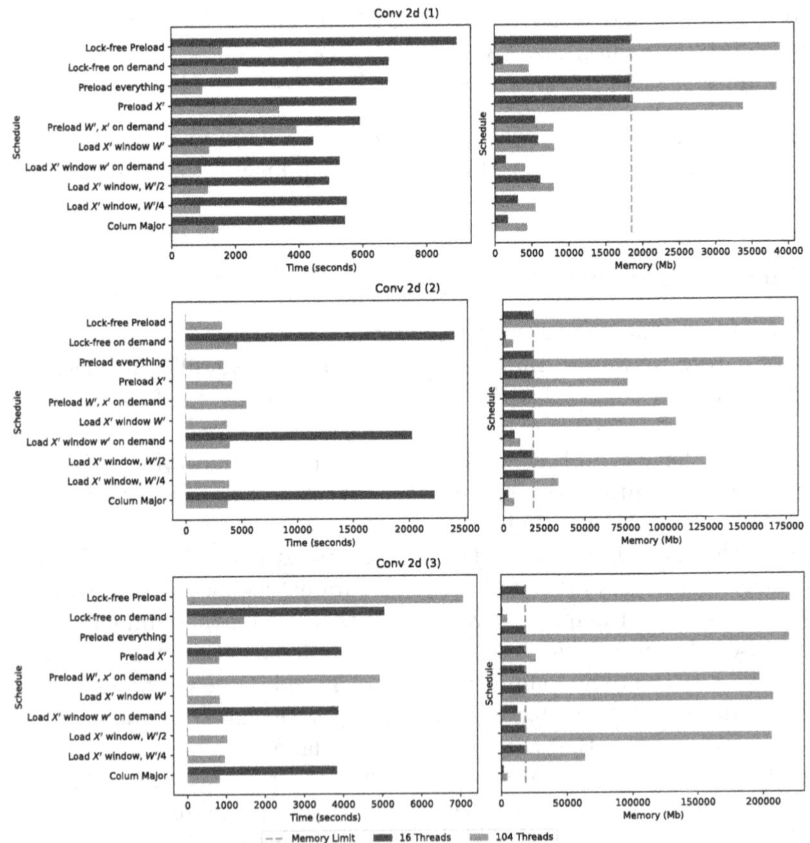


**Fig. 6.** Time and Memory requirements schedules, run with large parameters, on the 104 threads servers and the 16 threads PC. The memory graphs also include the PC's memory limit of 18000 MB.

### 6.2 Measurements

After obtaining the estimates, we execute the schedules on both the server and the PC. We measure the time it takes to execute the schedules, and the memory the process requires. For the memory measurement, it is important to note that it does include swap memory and only measures actual main memory usage. The PC has 20 GB of memory, about 1.5 GB of which the OS uses, leaving about 18.5 GB for the execution of the schedule. Therefore, measurements in the range of 18.5 GB on the PC will likely have used the OS's swapping mechanism, especially if the estimated value is much larger. As mentioned in the previous section, for some schedules, the memory available is insufficient, even with swapping. In these cases, the execution is terminated by the OS, yielding no result. We deliberately leave the OS swapping mechanism on to test if our implementation is faster than simply relying on the in-built OS methods. We further assign each schedule a score combining time and memory requirements. To calculate the score, we compute the geometric mean of the time $t$ and $m$ as $\sqrt{tm}$. The lower the score, the better. However, the schedule with the lowest score is automatically the best schedule on a given machine. The best schedule is typically the schedule that executes the fastest on the machine. It is possible for a slower schedule to achieve a lower score due to it requiring less memory. This, however, indicates that we could perform the computation on a machine with less memory.

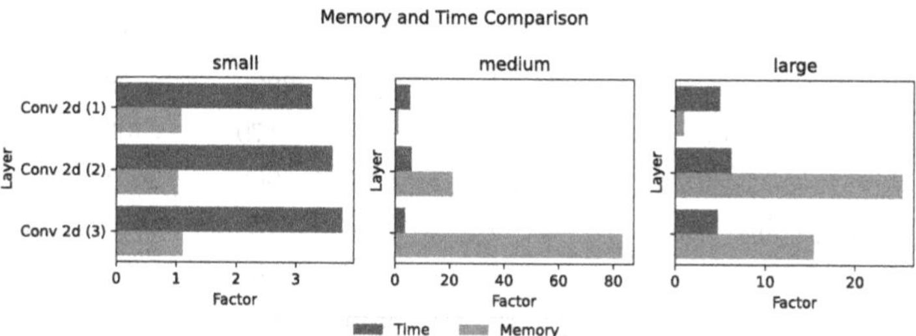


**Fig. 7.** Comparison of the fastest schedule for each layer with 16 and 104 threads. For each layer, the Figure shows the increase factor in runtime from 104 to 16 threads and the increase factor in memory from 16 to 104 threads for the fastest schedule

Tables 2, 3, and 4 list the time and memory requirements and the score, using the large crypto parameters (for medium and small, see the Appendix). The first important observation is the accuracy of the estimation algorithm. We expect the memory measurements to be larger than the estimate since there is runtime overhead, like the schedule itself, key material, and other data structures that the estimation does not take into account. However, in some cases, the estimate is off by a factor of 4–5. This is especially true for smaller values. An explanation for the discrepancy in estimate and measurements most likely lies in how we process cache instructions that drop data from memory. To ensure that we do not delete data that other threads still need, we only execute the delete instructions once all threads have passed the point for which the instructions are scheduled. During execution, we have little control over how fast threads advance. It is certainly possible for some threads to fall far behind, waiting for locks or input/output operations, thereby preventing the deletion of objects from memory. We have no way of predicting how the threads will interact at runtime and, therefore, need to make simplifying assumptions that can cause the differences in estimated and measured values. Overall, the estimate can still provide us with a useful tool to understand the schedule's memory requirements without running it.

The most important metric is time. The schedule that executes the fastest is typically the schedule that uses the available resources the most efficiently. Figure 6 shows the time and memory requirement for large parameters and all schedules. Note that the OS terminated schedules that do not display a time for 16 Threads (the PC) for running out of memory. For Conv 2d (2) and Conv 2d (3) we can see multiple schedules that reach the critical limit of 18000 GB memory, after which the OS's swapping system kicks in. On the medium parameters and Conv 2d (2) (complete Figures and Table in the Appendix), we observe that *Load*

**Table 2. Time** in s, **Memory** in MB requirements, for all Schedules on Conv 2d (1) with large parameters on the PC with 16 and the server with 104 Threads. Additionally, shown are memory **Estimate** in MB and **Score**.

| Schedule | Threads | Time | Memory | Estimate | Score |
|---|---|---|---|---|---|
| Lock-free Preload | 16 | 8952 | 18432 | 35215 | 12845 |
| | 104 | 1600 | 38839 | 36095 | 7883 |
| Lock-free on demand | 16 | 6830 | 1179 | 400 | 2838 |
| | 104 | 2091 | 4662 | 2601 | 3123 |
| Preload everything | 16 | 6805 | 18408 | 35075 | 11192 |
| | 104 | 973 | 38365 | 35885 | 6109 |
| Preload $X'$ | 16 | 5812 | 18680 | 30833 | 10420 |
| | 104 | 3379 | 33826 | 32084 | 10691 |
| Preload $W'$, $x'$ on demand | 16 | 5911 | 5459 | 4502 | 5681 |
| | 104 | 3925 | 7965 | 6193 | 5591 |
| Load $X'$ window $W'$ | 16 | 4458 | 5857 | 4622 | 5110 |
| | 104 | 1183 | 8036 | 5432 | 3083 |
| Load $X'$ window $w'$ on demand | 16 | 5278 | 1486 | 380 | 2801 |
| | 104 | 933 | 4074 | 1631 | 1950 |
| Load $X'$ window, $W'/2$ | 16 | 4955 | 6104 | 2461 | 5499 |
| | 104 | 1144 | 7972 | 3271 | 3021 |
| Load $X'$ window, $W'/4$ | 16 | 5498 | 3061 | 1451 | 4102 |
| | 104 | 899 | 5504 | 2701 | 2225 |
| Colum Major | 16 | 5442 | 1736 | 410 | 3074 |
| | 104 | 1452 | 4363 | 2531 | 2517 |

**Table 3.** textbfTime in s, **Memory** in MB requirements, for all Schedules on Conv 2d (2) with large parameters on the PC with 16 and the server with 104 Threads. Additionally, shown are memory **Estimate** in MB and **Score.*** indicate out of memory.

| Schedule | Threads | Time | Memory (MB) | Estimate | Score |
|---|---|---|---|---|---|
| Lock-free Preload | 16 | * | 18875 | 164390 | |
| | 104 | 3257 | 173712 | 165270 | 23787 |
| Lock-free on demand | 16 | 24060 | 1531 | 400 | 6069 |
| | 104 | 4599 | 6016 | 2601 | 5260 |
| Preload everything | 16 | * | 18819 | 164250 | |
| | 104 | 3364 | 173326 | 164250 | 24146 |
| Preload $X'$ | 16 | * | 18949 | 72131 | |
| | 104 | 4138 | 76506 | 72571 | 17792 |
| Preload $W'$, $x'$ on demand | 16 | * | 18816 | 92379 | |
| | 104 | 5416 | 101272 | 93260 | 23419 |
| Load $X'$ window $W'$ | 16 | * | 18754 | 95110 | |
| | 104 | 3662 | 106345 | 95110 | 19735 |
| Load $X'$ window $w'$ on demand | 16 | 20246 | 6888 | 2991 | 11809 |
| | 104 | 3914 | 10203 | 3431 | 6319 |
| Load $X'$ window, $W'/2$ | 16 | * | 18839 | 49011 | |
| | 104 | 4003 | 125113 | 49011 | 22379 |
| Load $X'$ window, $W'/4$ | 16 | * | 18871 | 26031 | |
| | 104 | 3843 | 33731 | 26471 | 11385 |
| Colum Major | 16 | 22251 | 2809 | 730 | 7906 |
| | 104 | 3724 | 6516 | 2291 | 4926 |

*$X'$ window $W'$* schedule reaches the swapping limit and takes 10675 s. The *Load $X'$ window $w'$ on demand* schedule does not reach that limit needing ~2 GB. However, despite needing to encode data more often, it is faster at 3885 s. This strongly suggests that our algorithm is more efficient than relying on the OS's swapping mechanism.

Table 5 and Fig. 7 compare the fastest schedule for each layer and set of parameters. We are most interested in the increase in runtime and the reduction in memory when running on the 16-thread PC as compared to running on the 104-thread server. For the small parameters, the fastest schedule is either the *Lock-free Preload* or *Preload everything* schedule. Since these schedules have very similar memory requirements, there is no significant reduction in memory. The time, however, increases by a factor of 3.3–3.8. We start to see a much bigger difference when moving to the medium parameters. For the Conv 2d (1) layer, the time increases by a factor of 5.4 while the memory usage stays almost the same between PC and server. For this layer, both systems can still use the *Lock-free Preload* schedule, which explains the negligible reduction in memory. The

**Table 4. Time** in s, **Memory** in MB requirements, for all Schedules on Conv 2d (3) with large parameters on the PC with 16 and the server with 104 Threads. Additionally, shown are memory **Estimate** in MB and **Score.*** indicate out of memory.

| Schedule | Threads | Time | Memory (MB) | Estimate | Score |
|---|---|---|---|---|---|
| Lock-free Preload | 16 | * | 18788 | 207608 | |
| | 104 | 7074 | 220310 | 208489 | 39479 |
| Lock-free on demand | 16 | 5054 | 1133 | 400 | 2393 |
| | 104 | 1469 | 4823 | 2601 | 2662 |
| Preload everything | 16 | * | 18838 | 207468 | |
| | 104 | 855 | 219812 | 207468 | 13709 |
| Preload $X'$ | 16 | 3955 | 18910 | 23150 | 8648 |
| | 104 | 815 | 26310 | 23590 | 4631 |
| Preload $W'$, $x'$ on demand | 16 | * | 18859 | 184578 | |
| | 104 | 4935 | 196842 | 185459 | 31168 |
| Load $X'$ window $W'$ | 16 | * | 18775 | 190191 | |
| | 104 | 831 | 207599 | 190191 | 13134 |
| Load $X'$ window $w'$ on demand | 16 | 3876 | 12218 | 5872 | 6881 |
| | 104 | 913 | 14437 | 6313 | 3631 |
| Load $X'$ window, $W'/2$ | 16 | * | 18860 | 97992 | |
| | 104 | 1024 | 206385 | 97992 | 14539 |
| Load $X'$ window, $W'/4$ | 16 | * | 18871 | 51962 | |
| | 104 | 955 | 63491 | 52402 | 7788 |
| Colum Major | 16 | 3834 | 1714 | 730 | 2564 |
| | 104 | 825 | 4609 | 2291 | 1950 |

time increase for the next two layers is 5.9 and 3.5, respectively; however, the memory reduction is significant and a factor of 21 and 83.3. While the server still uses the *Lock-free Preload* schedule the PC is forced to use window caching and column-wise window caching to fit the objects into memory. The picture repeats for the large parameters. Except that now the server uses a more memory-efficient schedule for Conv 2d (3), which leads to only 15.3 times memory reduction and an increase in runtime by 4.7. An interesting observation: on the small parameters, the PC seems to have a higher per-thread performance as the time increase is only around 3.5 for all layers despite the number of threads on the server being 6.5 more. As the parameters get larger, the time increase seems to approach 6.5 as expected.

Additionally, we compare the time and memory of the different schedules run on the large crypto parameters executed on the server. For the Conv 2d (1) layer the fastest schedule is *Load $X'$ window, $W'/4$*. It is 74 s, 8%, faster than the *Preload everything schedule.* The *Preload everything schedule*, in turn, is much

**Table 5.** Fastest Schedule for each layer and parameter size (Param.) on the server, 104 Threads (T), and PC, 16 Threads. As well as the increase (Inc.) in time and reduction (Red.) of memory.

| Param | Layer | T | Time | Inc. | Memory | Red | Schedule |
|---|---|---|---|---|---|---|---|
| small | Conv 2d (1) | 16 | 135 | 3.3 | 3084 | 1.1 | Lock-free Preload |
| | | 104 | 41 | | 3319 | | Lock-free Preload |
| | Conv 2d (2) | 16 | 580 | 3.6 | 15164 | 1.0 | Preload everything |
| | | 104 | 160 | | 15570 | | Lock-free Preload |
| | Conv 2d (3) | 16 | 116 | 3.8 | 18699 | 1.1 | Lock-free Preload |
| | | 104 | 30 | | 20727 | | Lock-free Preload |
| medium | Conv 2d (1) | 16 | 859 | 5.4 | 8447 | 1.1 | Lock-free Preload |
| | | 104 | 159 | | 9141 | | Lock-free Preload |
| | Conv 2d (2) | 16 | 3885 | 5.9 | 1939 | 21.0 | Load $X'$ window $w'$ on demand |
| | | 104 | 653 | | 40775 | | Lock-free Preload |
| | Conv 2d (3) | 16 | 743 | 3.5 | 629 | 83.3 | Colum Major |
| | | 104 | 211 | | 52415 | | Lock-free Preload |
| large | Conv 2d (1) | 16 | 4457 | 5.0 | 5857 | 0.9 | Load $X'$ window $W'$ |
| | | 104 | 899 | | 5504 | | Load $X'$ window, $W'/4$ |
| | Conv 2d (2) | 16 | 20246 | 6.2 | 6887 | 25.2 | Load $X'$ window $w'$ on demand |
| | | 104 | 3257 | | 173712 | | Lock-free Preload |
| | Conv 2d (3) | 16 | 3834 | 4.7 | 1714 | 15.3 | Colum Major |
| | | 104 | 815 | | 26309 | | Preload $X'$ |

faster, 627 s (64%), than the *Lock-free Preload* schedule. However, both preload schedules require 38 GB of memory, compared to the 5.4 GB of the *Load $X'$ window,* $W'/4$ schedule. For the second layer, Conv 2d (2), the *Lock-free Preload* schedule is the fastest at 3257 s. The *Preload every* is marginally slower at 3364 s. Both schedules require 170 GB of memory. Schedules that require significantly less memory *Load $X'$ window,* $W'/4$ (33 GB) and *Column Major* (6.3 GB) are only slightly slower at 3662 s and 3843 s. For the Conv 2d (3) layer the *Lock-free Preload* schedule is the slowest and consumes the most memory at 7074 s and 215 GB. The comparable *Preload everything* schedule requires approximately the same amount of memory, but only 12.5% of the time, 855 s. Interestingly, schedules that cache very little *Preload* $X'$ and *Column Major* are faster than the *Preload everything* at 815 s and 825 s. Both of these schedules also require significantly less memory, at 25.7 GB and 4.5 GB. This is a reduction factor of 47.8 between *Lock-free Preload* and *Column Major.*

Interestingly, schedules with minimal caching of $w$'s are often faster than schedules that substantially cache these values. A potential explanation could be the cache locality inside the CPU. Values that are not cached by our method and are loaded on demand could be accessed faster because they are placed inside the CPU cache. Alternatively, locking that is required for processing the load instructions could introduce additional slowdowns that are not present when values are loaded on demand. Another interesting observation is the poor performance of the *Lock-free Preload* schedule in the Conv 2d (3) layer. It is eight times slower than *Preload everything* schedule. Both schedules load all the required data at the start of the computation and do not need to load any values during. Where they differ is the points at which they write the results to disk. If we assume that all threads advance in lockstep, in the *Lock-free Preload* schedule, all threads want to write to disk at once. In *Preload everything* schedule, the write operations are more spaced out. It could be that the large number of simultaneous writes slows the schedule down significantly.

## 7 Conclusion

In this paper, we present ways of reordering the computation to tailor the memory requirements to the hardware available while executing as fast as possible. We further present a technique to estimate the required memory of convolutions over batch-packed, encrypted data. We show that our proposed caching mechanism is faster than relying on the OS's swapping mechanism. The method proposed in this paper is especially suited for ML workloads with thousands of instances that can run longer, i.e., overnight or over the weekend, and don't need a fast turnaround. Since our method can reduce the memory requirements for inference, it opens up the potential to save on hardware costs.

# Appendix

**Table 6.** Measurements for **Time** in seconds, Memory (**Mem**) in MB, for all Schedules with small parameters on the PC with 16 and the server with 104 Threads. Additionally, the table shows the memory Estimate in MB and **Score**.

| Layer | Schedule | Threads | Time | Memory (MB) | Estimate | Score |
|---|---|---|---|---|---|---|
| Conv 2d (1) | Lock-free Preload | 16 | 136 | 3084 | 2645 | 648 |
| | | 104 | 42 | 3319 | 2711 | 372 |
| | Lock-free on demand | 16 | 433 | 290 | 30 | 354 |
| | | 104 | 131 | 652 | 195 | 292 |
| | Preload everything | 16 | 142 | 3024 | 2634 | 656 |
| | | 104 | 45 | 3316 | 2695 | 387 |
| | Preload $X'$ | 16 | 184 | 2593 | 2316 | 691 |
| | | 104 | 52 | 2872 | 2409 | 385 |
| | Preload $W'$, $x'$ on demand | 16 | 333 | 724 | 338 | 491 |
| | | 104 | 108 | 1027 | 465 | 333 |
| | Load $X'$ window $W'$ | 16 | 143 | 771 | 347 | 332 |
| | | 104 | 46 | 1186 | 408 | 234 |
| | Load $X'$ window $w'$ on demand | 16 | 182 | 325 | 29 | 243 |
| | | 104 | 56 | 717 | 122 | 199 |
| | Load $X'$ window, $W'/2$ | 16 | 201 | 818 | 185 | 405 |
| | | 104 | 57 | 1197 | 246 | 261 |
| | Load $X'$ window, $W'/4$ | 16 | 190 | 450 | 109 | 293 |
| | | 104 | 74 | 972 | 203 | 268 |
| | Colum Major | 16 | 233 | 599 | 31 | 373 |
| | | 104 | 131 | 891 | 190 | 342 |
| Conv 2d (2) | Lock-free Preload | 16 | 583 | 15327 | 12346 | 2990 |
| | | 104 | 161 | 15570 | 12412 | 1583 |
| | Lock-free on demand | 16 | 1708 | 529 | 30 | 951 |
| | | 104 | 524 | 892 | 195 | 683 |
| | Preload everything | 16 | 581 | 15165 | 12335 | 2968 |
| | | 104 | 187 | 15446 | 12335 | 1700 |
| | Preload $X'$ | 16 | 727 | 5930 | 5417 | 2076 |
| | | 104 | 205 | 6187 | 5450 | 1127 |
| | Preload $W'$, $x'$ on demand | 16 | 1341 | 9729 | 6938 | 3613 |
| | | 104 | 449 | 10054 | 7004 | 2126 |
| | Load $X'$ window $W'$ | 16 | 609 | 10180 | 7143 | 2490 |
| | | 104 | 194 | 10427 | 7143 | 1423 |
| | Load $X'$ window $w'$ on demand | 16 | 765 | 934 | 225 | 845 |
| | | 104 | 210 | 1176 | 258 | 497 |
| | Load $X'$ window, $W'/2$ | 16 | 816 | 10281 | 3681 | 2896 |
| | | 104 | 239 | 11778 | 3681 | 1679 |
| | Load $X'$ window, $W'/4$ | 16 | 796 | 3257 | 1955 | 1610 |
| | | 104 | 223 | 3770 | 1988 | 917 |
| | Colum Major | 16 | 853 | 1099 | 55 | 968 |
| | | 104 | 492 | 1434 | 172 | 840 |
| Conv 2d (3) | Lock-free Preload | 16 | 117 | 18700 | 15591 | 1477 |
| | | 104 | 31 | 20728 | 15657 | 800 |
| | Lock-free on demand | 16 | 329 | 254 | 30 | 289 |
| | | 104 | 101 | 614 | 195 | 249 |
| | Preload everything | 16 | 132 | 19362 | 15581 | 1601 |
| | | 104 | 45 | 20710 | 15581 | 970 |
| | Preload $X'$ | 16 | 141 | 1980 | 1739 | 528 |
| | | 104 | 39 | 2221 | 1772 | 292 |
| | Preload $W'$, $x'$ on demand | 16 | 278 | 18688 | 13862 | 2281 |
| | | 104 | 95 | 18975 | 13928 | 1346 |
| | Load $X'$ window $W'$ | 16 | 134 | 19276 | 14283 | 1605 |
| | | 104 | 48 | 19769 | 14283 | 972 |
| | Load $X'$ window $w'$ on demand | 16 | 146 | 1085 | 441 | 399 |
| | | 104 | 43 | 1330 | 474 | 239 |
| | Load $X'$ window, $W'/2$ | 16 | 167 | 19254 | 7359 | 1792 |
| | | 104 | 56 | 20839 | 7359 | 1081 |
| | Load $X'$ window, $W'/4$ | 16 | 152 | 5781 | 3902 | 938 |
| | | 104 | 45 | 6374 | 3935 | 539 |
| | Colum Major | 16 | 160 | 416 | 55 | 258 |
| | | 104 | 94 | 787 | 172 | 272 |

**Table 7.** Measurements for **Time** in seconds, Memory (**Mem**) in MB, for all Schedules with medium parameters on the PC with 16 and the server with 104 Threads. Additionally, the table shows the memory Estimate in MB and **Score**. * values are unavailable because the execution ran out of memory.

| Layer | Schedule | Threads | Time | Memory (MB) | Estimate | Score |
|---|---|---|---|---|---|---|
| Conv 2d (1) | Lock-free Preload | 16 | 859 | 8448 | 7928 | 2695 |
| | | 104 | 160 | 9142 | 8126 | 1208 |
| | Lock-free on demand | 16 | 1120 | 409 | 90 | 676 |
| | | 104 | 233 | 1428 | 586 | 576 |
| | Preload everything | 16 | 873 | 8422 | 7897 | 2712 |
| | | 104 | 171 | 9286 | 8079 | 1258 |
| | Preload $X'$ | 16 | 1014 | 7304 | 6942 | 2721 |
| | | 104 | 215 | 8182 | 7223 | 1327 |
| | Preload $W'$, $x'$ on demand | 16 | 973 | 1472 | 1014 | 1197 |
| | | 104 | 188 | 2375 | 1394 | 669 |
| | Load $X'$ window $W'$ | 16 | 891 | 1600 | 1041 | 1194 |
| | | 104 | 174 | 2634 | 1223 | 677 |
| | Load $X'$ window $w'$ on demand | 16 | 1023 | 519 | 86 | 729 |
| | | 104 | 188 | 1600 | 367 | 548 |
| | Load $X'$ window, $W'/2$ | 16 | 988 | 1651 | 554 | 1277 |
| | | 104 | 194 | 2439 | 737 | 688 |
| | Load $X'$ window, $W'/4$ | 16 | 993 | 797 | 327 | 889 |
| | | 104 | 185 | 1732 | 608 | 567 |
| | Colum Major | 16 | 1177 | 751 | 92 | 940 |
| | | 104 | 242 | 1726 | 570 | 646 |
| Conv 2d (1) | Lock-free Preload | 16 | 17154 | 18531 | 37011 | 17829 |
| | | 104 | 654 | 40776 | 37209 | 5162 |
| | Lock-free on demand | 16 | 4636 | 631 | 90 | 1710 |
| | | 104 | 944 | 1668 | 586 | 1255 |
| | Preload everything | 16 | 16589 | 18764 | 36979 | 17643 |
| | | 104 | 769 | 40970 | 36979 | 5612 |
| | Preload $X'$ | 16 | 3946 | 16852 | 16239 | 8155 |
| | | 104 | 881 | 17736 | 16339 | 3952 |
| | Preload $W'$, $x'$ on demand | 16 | 12054 | 19356 | 20798 | 15275 |
| | | 104 | 955 | 24631 | 20996 | 4850 |
| | Load $X'$ window $W'$ | 16 | 10675 | 19036 | 21413 | 14255 |
| | | 104 | 803 | 25897 | 21413 | 4561 |
| | Load $X'$ window $w'$ on demand | 16 | 3885 | 1939 | 673 | 2745 |
| | | 104 | 958 | 2864 | 773 | 1656 |
| | Load $X'$ window, $W'/2$ | 16 | 11570 | 18950 | 11034 | 14807 |
| | | 104 | 1069 | 29330 | 11034 | 5598 |
| | Load $X'$ window, $W'/4$ | 16 | 3989 | 8043 | 5861 | 5664 |
| | | 104 | 1438 | 10983 | 5960 | 3974 |
| | Colum Major | 16 | 3933 | 1395 | 164 | 2342 |
| | | 104 | 1759 | 2758 | 516 | 2203 |
| Conv 2d (1) | Lock-free Preload | 16 | * | 18640 | 46741 | |
| | | 104 | 212 | 52416 | 46939 | 3331 |
| | Lock-free on demand | 16 | 817 | 387 | 90 | 562 |
| | | 104 | 329 | 1396 | 586 | 677 |
| | Preload everything | 16 | * | 18971 | 46709 | |
| | | 104 | 325 | 52493 | 46709 | 4131 |
| | Preload $X'$ | 16 | 748 | 5552 | 5212 | 2038 |
| | | 104 | 283 | 6296 | 5311 | 1336 |
| | Preload $W'$, $x'$ on demand | 16 | 5237 | 18853 | 41556 | 9936 |
| | | 104 | 547 | 47242 | 41754 | 5083 |
| | Load $X'$ window $W'$ | 16 | * | 18821 | 42819 | |
| | | 104 | 347 | 49830 | 42819 | 4159 |
| | Load $X'$ window $w'$ on demand | 16 | 753 | 2950 | 1322 | 1491 |
| | | 104 | 263 | 3475 | 1421 | 956 |
| | Load $X'$ window, $W'/2$ | 16 | * | 19015 | 22062 | |
| | | 104 | 441 | 52804 | 22062 | 4826 |
| | Load $X'$ window, $W'/4$ | 16 | 752 | 15296 | 11699 | 3392 |
| | | 104 | 354 | 17400 | 11798 | 2482 |
| | Colum Major | 16 | 744 | 630 | 164 | 684 |
| | | 104 | 323 | 1715 | 516 | 745 |

## References


1. Abadi, M., et al.: Deep learning with differential privacy. In: Proceedings of the 2016 ACM SIGSAC Conference on Computer and Communications Security, pp. 308–318 (2016)
2. Aharoni, E., et al.: HeLayers: A Tile Tensors Framework for Large Neural Networks on Encrypted Data. Proceedings on Privacy Enhancing Technologies 2023(1), 325–342 (Jan 2023). https://doi.org/10.56553/popets-2023-0020, http://arxiv.org/abs/2011.01805, arXiv:2011.01805 [cs]
3. Akavia, A., Oren, N., Sapir, B., Vald, M.: Compact storage for homomorphic encryption. Cryptology ePrint Archive (2022)
4. Al Badawi, A., et al.: Towards the AlexNet Moment for Homomorphic Encryption: HCNN, the First Homomorphic CNN on Encrypted Data with GPUs. IEEE Trans. Emerg. Topics Comput. (2020). https://doi.org/10.1109/TETC.2020.3014636, conference Name: IEEE Transactions on Emerging Topics in Computing
5. Al Badawi, A., et al.: OpenFHE: open-source fully homomorphic encryption library. in: proceedings of the 10th workshop on encrypted computing & applied homomorphic cryptography, pp. 53–63. WAHC'22, Association for Computing Machinery, New York, NY, USA (2022). https://doi.org/10.1145/3560827.3563379 event-place: Los Angeles, CA, USA
6. Amazon.com, I.: Amazon alexa voice ai, alexa developer offical site. https://developer.amazon.com/en-US/alexa Accessed 17 Oct 2023
7. Boemer, F., Costache, A., Cammarota, R., Wierzynski, C.: ngraph-he2: A high-throughput framework for neural network inference on encrypted data. In: Proceedings of the 7th ACM Workshop on Encrypted Computing & Applied Homomorphic Cryptography, pp. 45–56 (2019)
8. Boemer, F., Lao, Y., Cammarota, R., Wierzynski, C.: ngraph-he: a graph compiler for deep learning on homomorphically encrypted data. In: Proceedings of the 16th ACM International Conference on Computing Frontiers, pp. 3–13 (2019)
9. Brutzkus, A., Gilad-Bachrach, R., Elisha, O.: Low latency privacy preserving inference. In: International Conference on Machine Learning, pp. 812–821. PMLR (2019)
10. Cai, Y., Zhang, Q., Ning, R., Xin, C., Wu, H.: Hunter: he-friendly structured pruning for efficient privacy-preserving deep learning. In: Proceedings of the 2022 ACM on Asia Conference on Computer and Communications Security, pp. 931–945 (2022)
11. Chabanne, H., de Wargny, A., Milgram, J., Morel, C., Prouff, E.: Privacy-preserving classification on deep neural network. IACR Cryptol. ePrint Arch. **2017**, 35 (2017)
12. Chaudhari, H., Rachuri, R., Suresh, A.: Trident: efficient 4pc framework for privacy preserving machine learning. In: Proceedings 2020 Network and Distributed System Security Symposium. NDSS 2020, Internet Society (2020). https://doi.org/10.14722/ndss.2020.23005, http://dx.doi.org/10.14722/ndss.2020.23005
13. Cheon, J.H., Han, K., Kim, A., Kim, M., Song, Y.: A full RNS variant of approximate homomorphic encryption. In: Cid, C., Jacobson, M.J. (eds.) Selected Areas in Cryptography – SAC 2018: 25th International Conference, Calgary, AB, Canada, August 15–17, 2018, Revised Selected Papers, pp. 347–368. Springer International Publishing, Cham (2019). https://doi.org/10.1007/978-3-030-10970-7_16
14. Choi, W.S., Reagen, B., Wei, G.Y., Brooks, D.: Impala: Low-Latency, Communication-Efficient Private Deep Learning Inference. arXiv preprint arXiv:2205.06437 (2022)

15. Dathathri, R., et al.: CHET: an optimizing compiler for fully-homomorphic neural-network inferencing. In: Proceedings of the 40th ACM SIGPLAN Conference on Programming Language Design and Implementation, pp. 142–156. PLDI 2019, Association for Computing Machinery, New York, NY, USA (Jun 2019). https://doi.org/10.1145/3314221.3314628, https://doi.org/10.1145/3314221.3314628
16. Dilsizian, S.E., Siegel, E.L.: Artificial intelligence in medicine and cardiac imaging: harnessing big data and advanced computing to provide personalized medical diagnosis and treatment. Curr. Cardiol. Rep. **16**, 1–8 (2014)
17. Dowlin, N., Gilad-Bachrach, R., Laine, K., Lauter, K., Naehrig, M., Wernsing, J.: Cryptonets: applying neural networks to encrypted data with high throughput and accuracy. In: International Conference on Machine Learning, pp. 201–210 (2016)
18. Dwork, C., Roth, A.: The algorithmic foundations of differential privacy. Found. Trends Theor. Comput. Sci. **9**(3–4), 211–407 (2014)
19. Goodfellow, I., Bengio, Y., Courville, A.: Deep Learning. MIT Press (2016). http://www.deeplearningbook.org
20. Google, I.: Bard - chat based ai tool from google, powered by palm2. https://bard.google.com/ Accessed 17 Oct 2023
21. Google, I.: Google assitant, your own personal google. https://assistant.google.com/Accessed 17 Oct 2023
22. Grammarly, I.: Grammarly: free writing ai assistance. https://www.grammarly.com/Accessed 17 Oct 2023
23. Hao, M., Li, H., Chen, H., Xing, P., Xu, G., Zhang, T.: Iron: Private Inference on Transformers. In: Advances in Neural Information Processing Systems (2022)
24. Hesamifard, E., Takabi, H., Ghasemi, M.: Cryptodl: Deep neural networks over encrypted data. arXiv preprint arXiv:1711.05189 (2017)
25. Hesamifard, E., Takabi, H., Ghasemi, M.: Deep Neural networks classification over encrypted data. In: Proceedings of the Ninth ACM Conference on Data and Application Security and Privacy, pp. 97–108. ACM, Richardson Texas USA (Mar 2019). https://doi.org/10.1145/3292006.3300044
26. Huang, Z., Lu, W.j., Hong, C., Ding, J.: Cheetah: Lean and Fast Secure $$two-party$$ Deep Neural Network Inference. In: 31st USENIX Security Symposium (USENIX Security 22), pp. 809–826 (2022)
27. Inc., A.: Siri - apple. https://www.apple.com/siri/ Accessed 17 Oct 2023
28. Jiang, X., Kim, M., Lauter, K., Song, Y.: Secure outsourced matrix computation and application to neural networks. In: Proceedings of the 2018 ACM SIGSAC Conference on Computer and Communications Security. pp. 1209–1222. ACM, Toronto Canada (Oct 2018). https://doi.org/10.1145/3243734.3243837
29. Juvekar, C., Vaikuntanathan, V., Chandrakasan, A.: GAZELLE: a low latency framework for secure neural network inference. In: 27th USENIX Security Symposium (USENIX Security 18), pp. 1651–1669 (2018)
30. Kashyap, A., Plis, S., Ritter, P., Keilholz, S.: A deep learning approach to estimating initial conditions of brain network models in reference to measured fmri data. Front. Neurosci. **17** (2023)
31. Kim, D., Park, J., Kim, J., Kim, S., Ahn, J.H.: HyPHEN: A Hybrid Packing Method and Optimizations for Homomorphic Encryption-Based Neural Networks. arXiv preprint arXiv:2302.02407 (2023)
32. Krizhevsky, A., Hinton, G.: Learning multiple layers of features from tiny images,: publisher: Toronto. ON, Canada (2009)
33. Lee, E., et al.: Low-complexity deep convolutional neural networks on fully homomorphic encryption using multiplexed parallel convolutions. In: International Conference on Machine Learning, pp. 12403–12422. PMLR (2022)

34. Lee, J.W., et al.: Privacy-Preserving Machine Learning With Fully Homomorphic Encryption for Deep Neural Network. IEEE Access **10**, 30039–30054 (2022). https://doi.org/10.1109/ACCESS.2022.3159694, conference Name: IEEE Access
35. Li, B., Micciancio, D.: On the security of homomorphic encryption on approximate numbers. In: Canteaut, A., Standaert, F.-X. (eds.) Advances in Cryptology – EUROCRYPT 2021: 40th Annual International Conference on the Theory and Applications of Cryptographic Techniques, Zagreb, Croatia, October 17–21, 2021, Proceedings, Part I, pp. 648–677. Springer International Publishing, Cham (2021). https://doi.org/10.1007/978-3-030-77870-5_23
36. Li, S., et al.: FALCON: a fourier transform based approach for fast and secure convolutional neural network predictions. In: 2020 IEEE/CVF Conference on Computer Vision and Pattern Recognition (CVPR), pp. 8702–8711. IEEE, Seattle, WA, USA (Jun 2020). https://doi.org/10.1109/CVPR42600.2020.00873, https://ieeexplore.ieee.org/document/9156980/
37. Liu, J., Juuti, M., Lu, Y., Asokan, N.: Oblivious neural network predictions via minionn transformations. In: Proceedings of the 2017 ACM SIGSAC Conference on Computer and Communications Security, pp. 619–631 (2017)
38. Mohassel, P., Zhang, Y.: SecureML: a system for scalable privacy-preserving machine learning. In: 2017 IEEE Symposium on Security and Privacy (SP), pp. 19–38 (May 2017). https://doi.org/10.1109/SP.2017.12, iSSN: 2375-1207
39. OpenAI: Chatgpt. https://openai.com/chatgpt Accessed 17 Oct 2023
40. Papernot, N., Song, S., Mironov, I., Raghunathan, A., Talwar, K., Erlingsson, U.: Scalable private learning with pate. arXiv preprint arXiv:1802.08908 (2018)
41. Podschwadt, R., Takabi, D.: Classification of encrypted word embeddings using recurrent neural networks. In: PrivateNLP@ WSDM, pp. 27–31 (2020)
42. Podschwadt, R., Takabi, D.: Non-interactive privacy preserving recurrent neural network prediction with homomorphic encryption. In: 2021 IEEE 14th International Conference on Cloud Computing (CLOUD), pp. 65–70. IEEE (2021)
43. Shivdikar, K., et al.: Accelerating polynomial multiplication for homomorphic encryption on gpus. In: 2022 IEEE International Symposium on Secure and Private Execution Environment Design (SEED), pp. 61–72. IEEE (2022)
44. Smart, N.. P.., Vercauteren, F..: Fully homomorphic SIMD operations. Designs, Codes and Cryptography **71**(1), 57–81 (2014). https://doi.org/10.1007/s10623-012-9720-4
45. Tramèr, F., Zhang, F., Juels, A., Reiter, M.K., Ristenpart, T.: Stealing Machine Learning Models via Prediction $$apis$$. In: 25th USENIX security symposium (USENIX Security 16), pp. 601–618 (2016)
46. Zheng, M., Lou, Q., Jiang, L.: Primer: fast private transformer inference on encrypted data (Mar 2023). arXiv:2303.13679 [cs]

# SNARKProbe: An Automated Security Analysis Framework for zkSNARK Implementations

Yongming Fan[1], Yuquan Xu[1,2], and Christina Garman[1(✉)]

[1] Purdue University, West Lafayette, USA
{fan322,xu1210,clg}@purdue.edu
[2] Georgia Tech, Atlanta, USA

**Abstract.** With the growing interest in privacy-enhancing technologies, we are seeing a complementary growth in the desire to build and deploy complex cryptographic systems that involve techniques like zero-knowledge proofs. Of these, general purpose proof systems like zkSNARKs have seen the most interest, due to their small proof size, fast verification, and expressiveness. Unfortunately, as we have seen with many areas of cryptography, guaranteeing correct implementations can be tricky, as the protocols themselves are complicated and often require substantial low-level manual effort to achieve maximum performance. To help with this problem, and gain better assurances about the correctness and security of already implemented zkSNARK protocols and the privacy-enhancing applications that use them, we design and build `SNARKProbe`, an automated security analysis framework for zkSNARKs that can scan R1CS-based libraries and applications to detect various issues, such as edge case crashing, cryptographic operation errors, and/or inconsistencies with protocol descriptions. `SNARKProbe` leverages a variety of analysis techniques, including fuzzing and SMT solvers. We test the performance of `SNARKProbe` on a variety of different experimental parameters to demonstrate its practicality and reasonable runtime, and we also evaluate its ability to find potential inconsistencies and errors in implementations.

**Keywords:** Cryptography · zkSNARKs · automation · software security

## 1 Introduction

We have seen a growing interest in privacy and privacy-enhancing technologies from the general public [49], which has led to subsequent increased interest from parties that build and deploy the technologies that we use every day, with even the US government expressing interest in ways to best deploy privacy-enhancing technologies for data analytics [45]. One of the key components in many privacy-enhancing protocols are zero-knowledge proofs [37], which are cryptographic algorithms that allow one party (the prover) to prove to another (the verifier) that a statement is true, without revealing any information beyond the


C. Pöpper and L. Batina (Eds.): ACNS 2024, LNCS 14584, pp. 340–372, 2024.
https://doi.org/10.1007/978-3-031-54773-7_14

validity of the statement itself. Of these, one of the most popular instantiations are zkSNARKs (Zero-Knowledge Succinct Non-Interactive Arguments of Knowledge) [26,39,52], because of their small proof size, fast verification, and expressiveness.

Because of this popularity, we have seen an explosion of new zkSNARK protocols and libraries being developed in academia, and substantial interest from industry and other domains in actually deploying these protocols for real world usage [6–8,19,20]. Unfortunately, they can be quite difficult to implement correctly, as the protocols themselves can be complicated and involved, and much of the work to generate a single proof for a single application is often done manually and hand-tuned to ensure maximum performance, with developers often working at the circuit or gate level to design the best protocols. Additionally, as we have seen in the past, deploying complex cryptography has not come without its challenges [35,48,51,56], and applications that use zkSNARKs have not been immune to these either, as Zcash for example has found various cryptographic bugs in different components [1,2,4]. And checking any cryptographic implementation manually can be time consuming and potentially error prone.

While automated techniques like fuzzing have been used to test cryptographic implementations specifically before [21], we cannot use existing cryptographic fuzzers here as they generally test only for known weaknesses in certain schemes and are unable to produce the types of inputs that we need in a cost-effective way. Additionally, most general purpose fuzzing tools cannot detect what we refer to as *cryptographic logic errors*, i.e., errors that might result in an incorrect computation but not a program crash, particularly with regards to zkSNARK libraries.

All of this motivates us to ask the question:

*Can we develop better tooling to automatically check the security of and precisely locate software bugs and cryptographic logic errors in the proof generation processes and libraries of zkSNARK protocols and the applications that use them?*

To help answer this question in the affirmative, we design and build `SNARKProbe` to automatically both check the correctness and consistency of proof programs generated by R1CS-based zkSNARK libraries, as well as inspect the security of the libraries themselves and flag any inconsistencies between a protocol's implementation and its description, no matter how minor[1]. Our primary goal is to make the process as automated as possible, thus reducing the chance of human error in the process, as well as lowering the barrier to entry for usage. We wish to enable even those who might not be cryptographic experts to inspect a library or proof implementation without understanding details of the underlying protocol or specifics of the library. Users need only indicate some configuration settings such as the fuzzer parameters and expected proof statement, and our tool will automatically analyze the library and proof program to detect possible implementation and cryptography related errors.

[1] Note that this is something that professional security audits do flag, as these can lead to potential future problems, see [4].

In order to achieve this, we utilize a combination of techniques. Dynamic analysis allows us to trace real-time data and variable values, as well as handle a variety of different zkSNARK libraries written in different programming languages without needing additional (manual) language specific adaptations. Custom fuzzing techniques allow us to produce a variety of valid or invalid R1CS matrices (i.e., proofs) to exercise the different codepaths in a library. SMT (Satisfiability Modulo Theory) solvers allow us to help verify the consistency of a user-specified set of statement equations (i.e., the desired proof) with the actual R1CS matrix used in the application. And the notion of ideal files and a value checker helps ensure that a library correctly realizes the given underlying protocol.

While one could tackle some of this from a formal analysis approach [15], we view `SNARKProbe` to be complementary, as formal analysis works best for specific, static protocol implementations (like libraries), and we wish to also be able to check application-specific proofs. Formal verification in such a scenario would need to be done for *each individual proof*, which is both time-consuming and requires expertise in such techniques for every project that wishes to use a zkSNARK. `SNARKProbe`, on the other hand, is designed to work with a variety of different protocols and to be easy to run on a given proof implementation in an application, without requiring substantial expertise. We will see later on how a formally verified library for a specific protocol could be adapted as part of `SNARKProbe` to provide stronger guarantees, though we leave this for future work. As such, we believe `SNARKProbe` is a step in the right direction for ensuring the correctness of existing zkSNARK implementations and applications.

We choose to focus on two widely used zkSNARK protocols, Pinocchio [27,52] and Groth16 [39], and four libraries, `libsnark` [3], `Bellman` [10], `arkworks` [14], and `gnark` [13]. `libsnark` implements both Pinocchio and Groth16 in C++, while `Bellman` and `arkworks` implement Groth16 in Rust, and `gnark` implements Groth16 in Go. These represent four of the most popular and widespread open source libraries that have seen real world usage and underpin many projects that use zkSNARKs. This selection also demonstrates the flexibility of `SNARKProbe` to handle different R1CS-based zkSNARK protocols, as well as diverse languages.

In addition to designing and implementing `SNARKProbe`, we tested its performance extensively, using a number of different statement types to test the Constraint Checker, and a wide variety of R1CS matrix sizes and configurations (which are representative of statements of varying complexity) to test Snark-Fuzzer. We demonstrate performance that we believe is both reasonable and scalable for existing zkSNARK use cases[2]. We also evaluated `SNARKProbe`'s ability to detect potential inconsistencies or different types of errors. While we did not find any new exploitable errors, we did find a number of issues across the various libraries that we consider to be potentially unsafe or that might require special care by a developer to navigate correctly.

**Our Contributions.** In this paper we make the following contributions:

[2] And, in fact, in one instance the underlying library was actually unable to scale and run before we ran into any issues with our tool.

- We design `SNARKProbe`, a tool that can automatically check for potential software errors and cryptographic logic errors, as well as for consistency in the implemented proof statement, in R1CS-based zkSNARK libraries.
- We implement and build `SNARKProbe`[3] for two zkSNARK protocols, Pinocchio [27,52] and Groth16 [39], and four libraries, `libsnark` [3], `Bellman` [10], `arkworks` [14], and `gnark` [13], to demonstrate its flexibility and extensibility.
- To the best of our knowledge, we are the first to explore applying fuzzing and other analysis techniques to zkSNARKs specifically.
- We evaluate the performance of `SNARKProbe` in an extensive set of experiments, demonstrating its acceptable performance for real world applications.
- We demonstrate and discuss `SNARKProbe`'s ability to *automatically* catch different types of errors in zkSNARK libraries, finding seven inconsistencies and successfully locating a prior CVE.

**Possible Ethical Considerations.** While our tool did find a few inconsistencies in gadgets and protocol specification versus implementation throughout our testing, all of these issues were either not exploitable, already known, or just require care from a developer when implementing a proof, and as such we do not believe there is anything to disclose.

## 2 Background and Related Work

In this section, we introduce relevant background and prior work.

**zkSNARKs.** In a zero-knowledge protocol [37] a user (the prover) proves a statement to another party (the verifier) without revealing anything about the statement other than that it is true. zkSNARKs (Zero-Knowledge Succinct Non-Interactive Arguments of Knowledge) [26,39,52] are one of the current most popular zero-knowledge proof systems, and have begun to see increasingly complex, real world deployment in a number of privacy-preserving applications [6–8,19,20]. At a very high level, zkSNARKs work as follows. The first step in proof creation is to turn the statement that one wishes to prove into an equivalent form that relies on knowing a solution to some algebraic equations. This representation is then broken down into an arithmetic circuit. To ensure the correct evaluation of the circuit (and thus the proof), a programmer must express a series of constraints on the wires, called a constraint system, which is typically a Rank 1 constraint system or R1CS. zkSNARK libraries often provide an abstraction called a *gadget*, as expressing large programs with constraints can be quite difficult. A gadget allows programmers to specify a series of inputs, hidden internal variables and constraints on the inputs and internal variables. Rather than expressing a large program as many constraints, one can instead express it as some gadgets, and a few constraints binding them together.

**Fuzzing.** Fuzzing is an automated software security testing technique to explore software for bugs that cause incorrect or unexpected results, program crashes,

[3] https://github.com/BARC-Purdue/SNARKProbe.

**Table 1.** Comparison of SNARKProbe and a selection of cryptographic and generic fuzzing tools. A ◐ means achieves in select instances.

| Fuzzer | Adapt to zkSNARK | Error Types | | | Error Location | |
|---|---|---|---|---|---|---|
| | | Program | Logic | | Code | Scheme |
| | | | Crypto | zkSNARK | | |
| AFL [60] | ● | ● | ○ | ○ | ● | ○ |
| CDF [21] | ○ | ● | ◐ | ○ | ○ | ○ |
| SHA-3 Test [46] | ○ | ● | ● | ○ | ○ | ○ |
| TLS-Attacker [57] | ○ | ● | ◐ | ○ | ● | ◐ |
| SNARKProbe | ● | ● | ● | ● | ● | ● |

or in some extreme cases, lead to exploit paths. Fuzzing works by generating inputs and monitoring the program for crashing, assertions, and memory leaks [30] without the need for manual review by developers, security engineers, and auditors. An important part of fuzzing is code coverage, a metric used to evaluate how much of the target program is tested. Early fuzzing systems only generated inputs by mutating a seed input and watching for crashes or errors. Over time, fuzzing test structure has been improved and other techniques have been developed to improve the effectiveness [28,29,36,38,40,59,60].

**SMT Solvers.** Satisfiability modulo theory (SMT) is a complex version of the boolean satisfiability problem (SAT) that can determine if a mathematical equation is satisfiable or unsatisfiable. Z3 (which we choose to use in this paper) is an efficient SMT solver that has been used in various software verification and analysis applications [47]. Typically, SMT solvers such as Z3 can only handle first-order logic, but recent research [23] proposed a pragmatic extension for SMT solvers to support higher-order logic.

### 2.1 Prior Work

There has been work to automate the conversion between proof statement and R1CS [33,41,42,44], but they do not necessarily guarantee the correctness of the translation. Manually writing/editing R1CS is also still popular as it can result in substantial efficiency gains. Such work can help secure new applications but cannot help with the security of existing implementations.

Fuzzing has been used for some cryptographic implementations. Special-purpose fuzzing has been used for TLS [57,58]. CDF [21] targets cryptographic algorithms such as DSA, ECDSA, and RSA. We are inspired in part by these ideas, though we have no known test vectors or reference implementations to compare against and use more targetted input generation techniques.

We provide a comparison of SNARKProbe and the most relevant existing fuzzing tools in Table 1, focusing on the types of errors they are able to catch, if they can precisely locate such errors, and their adaptability to zkSNARKs. Currently, most fuzzing tools are limited to identifying software errors. While some tools such as CDF and SHA-3 Test have the capability to identify cryptographic logic errors, their functionality is restricted and cannot be easily extended. Presently, our SnarkFuzzer stands as the only fuzzing tool capable of detecting both software and cryptographic logic errors for zkSNARKs, accompanied by source code references and protocol location information.

Additionally, an important part of many fuzzers is how they handle code coverage analysis. While off-the-shelf tools like LLVM might seem to fit well for this, as it natively provides a source code line coverage data report [11], this is insufficient for our desired application. Our fuzzer focuses specifically on branch coverage and coverage of critical cryptographic components, not generic line coverage. Additionally, we found that many existing zkSNARK libraries may not work well (or even compile) with LLVM. This motivates our development of the Branch Model and its use of GDB, as existing tools do not suffice.

There has also been prior work on automating the development of cryptographic attacks. Much of this work has focused on side-channels [22,53,54], though it has also seen other applications [25]. Prior work has also sought to automatically deploy existing, known attacks [43]. These are largely orthogonal and do not extend to existing zkSNARK systems.

There is a growing trend towards computer aided cryptography and formal verification of implementations (see [24] for a detailed discussion). Project Everest [15] contains a variety of formally verified software components. While we are seeing increasingly complex protocols being formally verified [55], we have not yet seen these techniques applied to zkSNARKs. We see our work both as a step towards a formally verified zkSNARK implementation, bridging the current gap through the use of heuristic techniques like fuzzing, as well as a complement to it. A formally verified implementation could be used to provide a trustworthy ground truth for our fuzzing techniques, for example. In addition, formal verification is typically targeted at a single implementation, which necessitates re-running the often complicated process for each new application. `SNARKProbe` is designed to streamline the process and make it easy for a user to check a variety of applications or libraries, with little manual effort.

## 3 Overview

Before diving into the details of our design, we give a brief high-level overview of our `SNARKProbe` system, its workflow, and the intended use cases and users.

### 3.1 Users and Use Cases

We view the targeted users of `SNARKProbe` to fall into three main categories: 1. An application user that wishes to evaluate if a given (open-source) application correctly implemented their specified proof statement without having to dig through source code or understand the protocol; 2. Developers who want to build applications using zkSNARKs and wish to gain assurances in the correctness of a library and that a proof they built correctly realizes a given statement;

and 3. Security engineers that want to automatically scan a library/application and detect various issues, such as edge case crashing, cryptographic operation errors, and/or inconsistencies with protocol descriptions, allowing them to focus their time and manual effort on potential issues. `SNARKProbe` helps achieve all these use cases by outputting a full evaluation report that includes a notion of security confidence, any discovered (known) security vulnerabilities or warnings, and potential risks of the target library or proof.

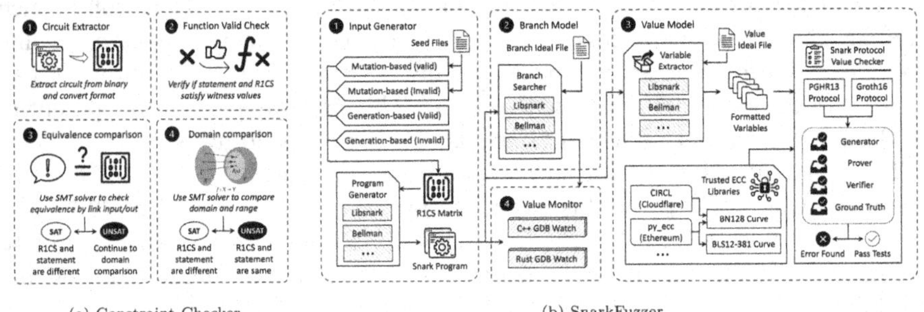


(a) Constraint Checker (b) SnarkFuzzer

**Fig. 1.** Workflow of `SNARKProbe`. White boxes represent subcomponents universal for all zkSNARK libraries, forward diagonal stripes represent those designed for a specific library, and backward diagonal stripes represent those designed for a specific programming language.

### 3.2 Workflow

We now outline the workflow of running `SNARKProbe`, as well as establish terminology, before presenting the details and implementation in subsequent sections. `SNARKProbe` is composed of two broad sub-tools: the Constraint Checker and SnarkFuzzer. These components can operate both independently of each other as well as in sequence, depending on what the user wishes to check.

Recall that at a high level, a zkSNARK proof is generated in two main phases. First (*circuit generation*), the user has a *(proof) statement* that they wish to prove about, which requires converting this statement into a *circuit* that the zkSNARK protocol understands. *R1CS* is a specific form of this that we focus on in this work. Second (*proof generation*), a zkSNARK library takes the circuit (R1CS) as input and produces a proving key, verification key, and a *proof.*

The first step verifies the consistency of a user-specified set of proof statement equations with the actual R1CS matrix used in the application, to ensure that the circuit generation process generates the same proof as the developer states. The Constraint Checker uses an SMT solver to compare the input values, output values, domain, and range of the given statement equations with R1CS matrix to find any errors in the conversion. Figure 1a shows the internal steps of the Constraint Checker, which we discuss in detail in Sect. 4.1.

The second step checks the correctness of the library and proof generation process. Figure 1b shows the steps of SnarkFuzzer, which we discuss in detail in Sect. 4.2. First, the Input Generator produces an R1CS matrix (i.e., proof) using a variety of fuzzing techniques and compiles this into an executable proof program with the selected library, which serves as the input for the Branch Model. Then, the Branch Model investigates the visitation status for each branch during execution and provides feedback to the Input Generator to determine if another input is needed. This coverage feedback fuzzing helps improve the coverage rate of SnarkFuzzer, which improves the chance of catching errors in the target library. Finally, the Value Model re-evaluates the protocol calculations to detect any potential cryptographic logic errors and looks for inconsistencies caused by unexpected value changes or implementation errors.

Together, these two components allow `SNARKProbe` to evaluate the end-to-end correctness and security of a specific implementation of a given proof statement for a given library (or to individually check different parts if desired).

Unlike standard fuzzers, SnarkFuzzer can detect both software and cryptographic logic errors. We consider a *software error* to be a bug or fault in the software that causes unintended behaviors or incorrect performance, such as crashing, overflow, or a system error. A *cryptographic logic error*, on the other hand, is one that causes a program to produce an incorrect result due to errors in the cryptographic protocol implementation, such as incorrect mathematical operations or disregarding the specification. A cryptographic logic error will not cause a software crash or raise an error message, making them much harder to detect. For a basic example, in RSA, software errors might cause a program crash, but cryptographic logic errors are issues where the ciphertext value was not computed correctly ($m^e \mod N$ computed incorrectly) or too large a ciphertext was used (e.g., larger than the modulus).

While we currently focus on R1CS-based zkSNARKS, we believe this high level design can be adapted without major changes to support additional (newer) types of proofs, particularly in the case of SnarkFuzzer, which would largely only involve changing the input generation methodology and format.

**Why Dynamic Analysis?** Dynamic analysis supports our goal of finding cryptographic logic errors by allowing us to trace and extract real-time data and variable values, which we can then use to check for cryptographic protocol conformance and implementation errors. It also allows us to easily support a number of different zkSNARK libraries written in different languages without the need for additional manual intervention, extensions, or program instrumentation by the user, making `SNARKProbe` flexible as well.

## 4 Design and Implementation

In this section, we introduce both the high level goals and concrete implementation decisions, tools, and techniques that allow us to realize `SNARKProbe`. We start with the Constraint Checker and then discuss the various components of SnarkFuzzer. These two sub-tools can be used either in conjunction with each other, or separately, depending on what the developer wishes to check.

### 4.1 Constraint Checker

**Goals:** *The Constraint Checker helps ensure that the realized proof is equivalent to a specified statement. This also allows the Constraint Checker to find errors in flattening and/or gadget use. It achieves this by comparing the equivalence of a user-specified proof statement and the compiled R1CS gates to ensure that the proof generated by the library represents the developer's specified statement*[4].

**Design.** The first step in generating a zkSNARK proof is converting the desired proof statement equations into R1CS. These R1CS gates should have the same domain, range, and output value as input statement equations. To check this, we developed our Constraint Checker, which leverages an SMT solver and associated techniques to verify the equivalence of R1CS gates to the specified proof statement functions[5]. To run the tool, the user only needs to write a short script to define the statement function, primary inputs, and auxiliary inputs in their zkSNARK proof, and everything else then happens automatically. Figure 1a shows the key steps in the Constraint Checker, and we also provide an example in Appendix A.3. We note that our SMT solver could be replaced by any other techniques that allow one to check for function equality and fit the desired goals.

**Implementation.** The Constraint Checker contains two major components—the Circuit Extractor and a three step equivalence check—which we discuss now. We discuss optimizations in Appendix A.1.

*Circuit Extractor.* The Circuit Extractor can extract R1CS gates with private inputs, witness, and gadget relations from an executing zkSNARK binary program. We do this using GDB. We set a GDB breakpoint at the circuit declaration line, convert the circuit to an R1CS matrix when the program reaches the breakpoint, and save the formatted R1CS matrix for equivalence comparison. Automatic extraction both makes the tool more usable and reduces the potential for human errors in the equivalence comparison. Many zkSNARK libraries use Montgomery modular multiplication as an optimization. We also developed a Montgomery representation translator that can convert the Montgomery form to a standard integer format, so that our circuit extractor can produce a z3py (our SMT solver of choice) readable integer format.

After extracting the circuit, the Constraint Checker uses the SMT solver to verify the equivalence of functions through a three step process: a function valid check, equivalence comparison, and domain comparison. If one or more tests fail,

[4] We note that we cannot do anything about the garbage-in-garbage-out problem (for example, the case where a developer implements a proof that misses a necessary case, such as omitting checking if a value is greater than 0). We can just help determine if the specified statement and realized proof are likely equivalent.

[5] We work around the general undecidability of function equality by operating in the more constrained setting (over the finite fields) and adding special rules for primary variables and auxiliary variables.

then we determine that the given statement equation is not equivalent to the produced program. Otherwise, then we can provide assurances that it is highly likely that the proof realizes the specified statement correctly[6].

*Function Valid Check.* As the witness should be a solution in both the statement equations and equations built by the R1CS gates, we first create two SMT solvers $S_1$ and $S_2$ to verify that fact (see Appendix A.2 (b)). The Constraint Checker considers the statement equations and R1CS gates to not be equivalent if the witness is not a valid solution for both.

*Equivalence Comparison.* The equivalence comparison verifies if the statement equations $y_1 = f(x_1)$ and R1CS gates $y_2 = f(x_2)$ have the same output for all the same inputs. First, the Constraint Checker creates a solver $S$, and adds $y_1 = f(x_1)$, $y_2 = f(x_2)$, $x1 = x2$ and $y_1 \neq y_2$ to the solver $S$ (see Appendix A.2 (c)). If $S$ results in `SAT`, then the SMT solver has discovered that the statement equations and R1CS gates have a different output for at least one input and thus considers them not equivalent, and otherwise, it results in `UNSAT`. Like in many other use cases, the Constraint Checker cannot guarantee equivalency if the SMT solver returns `UNSAT` or `UNKNOWN`. Note that the SMT solver may return `UNKNOWN` for a variety of reasons, including running out of memory, or if the quantifier-free fragment is undecidable (such as nonlinear integer arithmetic) or too "expensive" (such as finding primes $p * q = N$ for some $N$).

*Domain Comparison.* The SMT solver cannot directly calculate an equation's domain, but it can find the maximum and minimum values for an equation (Fig. 4a in Appendix A.4 shows an example of different upper and/or lower bounds). We also use the SMT solver to find out if there is a gap between the domains' of the statement equations and R1CS gates, though we cannot guarantee to find all such gaps that may exist (see Appendix A.4 for a detailed discussion).

### 4.2 SnarkFuzzer

**Goals:** *SnarkFuzzer is a smart fuzzing tool with the primary goal of finding potential logic or software errors in zkSNARK libraries. It produces zkSNARK programs with different proofs as input, to detect and catch these errors and provide full (important) code coverage.*

SnarkFuzzer is composed of four major subcomponents: the Input Generator, Branch Model, Value Model, and Value Monitor. The Input Generator is responsible for generating an R1CS matrix and converting it to a zkSNARK program as input for the target library. The Value Model and Value Monitor are designed to detect implementation and cryptography related errors. The Branch Model helps manage branch coverage and provides feedback to help SnarkFuzzer decide

[6] We cannot *guarantee* equivalence due to the fact that the SMT solver might output `UNKNOWN`, as well as possible domain gaps (see Appendix A.4).

if it needs to generate another input program. Figure 1b shows the structure of SnarkFuzzer with both its high level design as well as its implementation details.

**SnarkFuzzer: Input Generator**

**Goals:** *The Input Generator produces valid or invalid R1CS matrices and compiles them into executable proof programs for use by other components as testing inputs. This should be done in a "smart" manner to help better catch errors.*

**Design.** The first step for our fuzzer is the generation of inputs to test a target library. In SnarkFuzzer, these inputs are simply valid or invalid R1CS matrices that represent a variety of (possibly random) proof statements. To improve the chances of catching potential logic or software errors in the library, we desire this input generator to be "smart", in the sense that it should not just randomly generate inputs, but should take into consideration both the concept of valid/invalid proofs, as well as proof or R1CS edge cases. At a high level, the Input Generator generates an R1CS matrix, and then the Program Generator uses this matrix to produce and compile an executable zkSNARK program with a given library. The compiled program will then be used as input for other components, like the Branch Model, Value Model, and Value Monitor. Before generating the R1CS matrix, the Input Generator needs to decide on the size of the generated matrix (number of rows $n_r$ and columns $n_c$) and the number of public inputs $n_p$. This can be done by simply choosing randomly, or in a smarter way by choosing from a specified distribution. The Input Generator can be instantiated with any type of fuzzer that meets the aforementioned goals, giving it the flexibility and adaptability to use new techniques and tools, as they are developed.

**Implementation.** We developed four different methods of input generation to produce these matrices based on mutation-based and generation-based fuzzing. These methods are complementary and all work in tandem to generate the fuzzing inputs (the user can specify the percentage of inputs generated by each method). Each method targets a specific type of R1CS matrix to provide better overall coverage and comes with its own set of unique benefits (and trade-offs).

*Generation-Based Invalid Matrix.* Our generation-based fuzzer is designed to create an R1CS matrix from scratch. Generation-based fuzzing has the advantage of not depending on input seeds, allowing it to function without (user) input. The random number generator will generate $n_r * n_c$ integers as an R1CS matrix and $n_r - 1$ integers as the witness $w$ (since the first value of the witness is always equal to 1), and we use the constraint relation $w \cdot A \times w \cdot B - w \cdot C = 0$ to verify the ground truth of the matrix. This tests a library with possible but unrealistic examples to search for edge case errors that are hard to reach with traditional examples.

*Generation-Based Valid Matrix.* To produce a valid matrix that simulates a real world proof example, the random number generator will generate $n_r - 1$ integers as a witness $w$. Then, a valid matrix will be calculated with z3py based on this witness and the constraints relations in $w \cdot A \times w \cdot B - w \cdot C = 0$. Depending on the actual values in the randomly chosen witness, the complexity of solving the equations to fill out the matrix may vary, but a larger matrix (i.e., larger witness) usually results in a longer generation time. As such, we recommend that for testing large R1CS matrices, the generation-based fuzzer is run once to generate an input seed that can be given to the mutation-based fuzzer.

*Mutation-Based Invalid Matrix.* The mutation-based fuzzer requires an R1CS matrix with a number of public variables as a seed, and then flips values to generate a new matrix. We use Atheris, a mutation-based, coverage-guided fuzzer developed by Google [9]. The seed is converted into a byte array, then Atheris will flip the array, and then it is converted back to a (new) R1CS matrix. Because we have randomly flipped values in the matrix, the R1CS constraint relations will be destroyed, and the matrix will be invalid. This technique can work off of and mutate input examples that might be hard to produce by generation-based fuzzing.

*Mutation-Based Valid Matrix.* Our mutation-based fuzzer can also produce a valid R1CS matrix. Instead of flipping random values, a random number $c$ will be generated, and the new matrix $M$ will be calculated based on the seed matrix $M_0$ as $M = cM_0$. This multiplication will not break the constraint relations, so the new matrix is still valid. This can be used with the generation-based fuzzer to produce valid large R1CS matrices in a short time, thus increasing performance.

**SnarkFuzzer: Ideal Files**

**Goals:** *The ideal files act as a guide for the Branch Model and Value Model to check code coverage and protocol calculations. They contain information related to the source zkSNARK library such as branch locations, variable names, and data types.*

**Design.** Each library and protocol needs two ideal files: an ideal branch file that contains the locations of the branches in a library (automatically generated), and an ideal value file that contains information about the variables in a program (manually generated). Manually creating the ideal value file does not require any specialized knowledge related to zkSNARK protocols, the library, or cryptographic techniques, and the user only needs basic skills such as defining functions, conditions, and assigning variables. These ideal files can be reused for any program using the same protocol and library.

*Ideal Branch File.* An ideal branch file contains protocol-specific information related to the branches in a library. Function calls, if-conditions, and loops are all considered branches. The branch file also contains information about `IMPORTANT` versus `UNIMPORTANT` branches to help the Value Model. Important branches include cryptographic calculations and other core protocol components that we wish to ensure testing and coverage of, while unimportant branches are those that do not involve relevant computation.

*Ideal Value File.* An ideal value file contains location information for all variables that must be used to evaluate the protocol calculation. The Value Model will use line and path information in this file to extract all variables' values. Only variables defined in the official protocol paper should be added to the ideal value file.

**Implementation.** We have already developed the ideal files for Pinocchio and Groth16 in `libsnark` and Groth16 in `Bellman`, `arkworks`, and `gnark`.

*Ideal Branch File.* By default, all branches are marked as `IMPORTANT` and thus covered. We asked four researchers in our group (including people with experience using zkSNARKs and those with only programming experience) to label branches as `IMPORTANT` or `UNIMPORTANT`. To ensure SnarkFuzzer does not miss any critical components, only branches labeled as `UNIMPORTANT` by all four researchers could be marked as `UNIMPORTANT` in our example ideal branch files[7]. We provide an example snippet of an ideal model file for `libsnark` in Appendix B.1.

In order to find uncallable functions, we used a static analysis tool called Doxygen [12] to draw the library functions' call graph. Doxygen can help a user generate the call graph for a library, and by using this call graph, the user can easily find unused and uncallable functions to reduce fuzzing costs.

*Ideal Value File.* The ideal value file contains "official" variable names, variable types, and variable names, path, and line number (the final assignment location for a variable) in the library's source code. We provide an example snippet of an ideal value file for the `libsnark` library in Appendix B.1. While line numbers might change as code is maintained, one should not need to manually create a new file often. If there are only minor or non-cryptographic related changes, our tool will automatically match the new line numbers.

**<u>SnarkFuzzer: Branch Model</u>**

**Goals:** *The Branch Model monitors and records branch visitation status as SnarkFuzzer runs, and informs and stops it after all `IMPORTANT` branches have been covered.*

[7] Incorrectly labeling `UNIMPORTANT` branches as `IMPORTANT` only increases the fuzzing time without affecting the accuracy of the analysis.

**Design.** The Branch Model is used to evaluate if the target library has been fully tested. Traditional fuzzers often work by examining utilized memory bytes in a binary or lines of source code hit to check for program coverage, and then mapping this coverage to an input to determine the next one. However, in a zkSNARK library, it is difficult to correlate the exact relation between a specific branch and values in the input program that could trigger it. Therefore, we instead use the idea of function and condition branches to evaluate coverage.

Since any unvisited branches may cause errors, the Branch Model evaluates each input program to acquire the list of branches that the program visited. The Input Generator will continuously generate new program inputs with different proof statements/matrices until all `IMPORTANT` branches have been visited.

To ensure that we achieve both breadth and depth in code coverage, the Branch Model also works to ensure that each branch is covered multiple times with different inputs, keeping a count of the number of times each `IMPORTANT` branch is hit. We allow the user to define a visitation threshold to balance performance with coverage and confidence. As more inputs are generated, we have a higher chance of finding potential issues in the target library or, conversely, more confidence that the target library is safe, at the cost of runtime.

**Implementation.** Our Branch Model uses GDB breakpoints to investigate the visitation status for each branch defined in the ideal branch file. A GDB breakpoint stops the program whenever the selected location in the program is reached for debugging, and it can be set by line number, function name, or address in the program. When the Input Generator produces a zkSNARK program, the Branch Model sets a GDB breakpoint at the start line for each branch. If a branch is then visited during runtime, GDB will temporarily stop the input program at the corresponding breakpoint. After the program is finished running, the Branch Model records a list of visited branches for the current program. If all important branches have not been visited at least once, or the visitation threshold has not been met, the Branch Model will instruct the Input Generator to generate a new program with a different proof until all important branches have been covered.

**SnarkFuzzer: Value Model**

**Goals:** *The Value Model's goal is to find cryptographic logic errors, such as inconsistencies with the protocol definition or incorrect cryptographic operations.*

**Design.** The Value Model is one of the most important components in SnarkFuzzer, and one of the biggest improvements compared with other fuzzers. Its job is to detect cryptographic logic errors in a library. At a high level, the Value Model must extract all necessary variable values from the input program, which it then feeds to the other components. It achieves this through two major subcomponents: the Value Extractor and Value Checker.

*Value Extractor.* The Value Extractor extracts variables' values from the source zkSNARK program, which are then used in the Value Checker. The ideal value file provides a list of variables that need to be extracted. Then, the Value Extractor recursively extracts these values from the last assignment location in the program and library, and reformats the values to the Value Checker readable format.

*Value Checker.* The Value Checker re-evaluates all protocol calculations and compares these ground-truth values to the values extracted from the input program by the Value Extractor to find any possible logic errors. In the re-evaluation process, the Value Checker will faithfully follow the protocol from the formal specification without any optimization, simplification, or reformatting. To build a trustable re-evaluation process, our Value Checker uses ECC libraries that have been tested and widely used. In the future, this component could be replaced by any trusted evaluation source, such as a formally verified implementation.

**Implementation**

*GDB PrettyPrint.* GDB can display both the structure and value(s) for a variable. However, for more complicated variables GDB displays some unnecessary variable structure and data. Also, different libraries usually have different data structures (even for the "same" variables), and, as such, the Value Checker cannot directly use the raw, unformatted variable value extracted from the library. For example, Figs. 7a, 7b, and 7c in Appendix B.2 show a $G_1$ type variable that represents the same number in both `libsnark`, `Bellman`, and `arkworks` but has different structure and value when printed naively.

To make the Value Checker more universal, we developed a PrettyPrint functionality for each library to convert all data structures into the same format. The goals of PrettyPrint are twofold: 1) to allow the extractor to keep only the necessary values for a variable, and 2) to convert the same types of variables from different libraries into a common universal format that the Value Checker can then accept. Figure 7d in Appendix B.2 shows an example of the PrettyPrint result for the same $G_1$ variable as before.

*Value Extractor.* The Value Extractor extracts all variables defined in the ideal value file using GDB and PrettyPrint. As the ideal value file contains the line number where each variable is assigned, the Value Extractor can automatically set up a breakpoint for each variable immediately after its assignment. Then, when the input program reaches this, the Value Extractor uses PrettyPrint to save the variable's formatted value.

*Value Checker.* We developed the Value Checker for Pinocchio by following [52] and [27] and Groth16 by [39] and [50]. To help ensure accurate re-evaluation of the protocol calculations, the Value Checker uses exactly the same variable names as the original papers, and we follow the protocol description exactly, without any optimizations, to avoid introducing mistakes.

*ECC Libraries.* We use two well-tested elliptic curve libraries to demonstrate diversity and flexibility. py_ecc [31], developed by Ethereum in Python, supports both the BN128 and BLS12-381 curves. CIRCL [32], developed by Cloudflare in Go, supports BLS12-381. Since it is written in Go, we developed the necessary APIs so that our Python-based Value Checker can access the functions. If users would like to test a new zkSNARK library using a curve that py_ecc or CIRCL do not support, they can easily plug it into the Value Checker in this same manner.

**SnarkFuzzer: Value Monitor**

**Goals:** *The Value Monitor detects any unexpected value changes after the extraction of initial variable values from the source program.*

**Design.** While the Value Model extracts all necessary variables' values at the location where the variables are first assigned, and we also need to check if there is a value change after the model extracts these values to ensure consistency between the library and the Value Checker. The Value Monitor can also detect any unexpected side effects caused by the library or dependent functions due to incorrect implementation, out of memory, or other unexpected errors.

**Implementation.** GDB watch allows SnarkFuzzer to monitor value changes in a debugging session with four CPU debug registers called hardware watchpoints. A hardware watchpoint is very efficient, but it does not support larger data structures given the limited debug registers. Software watchpoints will be automatically applied if GDB tries to setup a watchpoint for a variable that cannot be handled by a hardware watchpoint. Unlike hardware watchpoints, software watchpoints are extremely slow, and watching dozens of variables may require unacceptable processing time. For example, using GDB software watch for a single variable `A_query` in `libsnark` takes more than 30 min.

Therefore, we instead used Valgrind, a dynamic analysis tool that analyzes a program to automatically detect memory management and threading bugs. Valgrind has a gdbserver to simulate traditional GDB hardware watchpoints. Simulation still takes longer than pure GDB hardware watchpoints, but the hardware watchpoint simulation is much faster than GDB software watchpoints. Meanwhile, Valgrind hardware watchpoint simulation does not have any limitation on the number and length of variables, so Valgrind can be used for any zkSNARK source program and libraries with complex data structures.

## 5 Performance Evaluation

Our first set of evaluations for `SNARKProbe` explores its performance and scalability. All experiments run on an Intel Core i7-8700 CPU @ 3.20 GHz × 12 with 32 GB of RAM running 64-bit Ubuntu 22.04 LTS.

### 5.1 Performance of the Constraint Checker

We start by testing the Constraint Checker and evaluate its performance on statements with different types of operations and complexities, and present the runtimes in Table 2. There are two runtime results for each experiment. We first recorded the runtime for the SMT solver, which is the most important step in the Constraint Checker, and we also recorded the total runtime, including the processing time of the Circuit Extractor, SMT solver, and other internal evaluations.

**Table 2.** Constraint Checker runtime for different proof statements

| Statement | Equation | Runtime (in seconds) | |
|---|---|---|---|
| | | SMT Solver | Overall |
| Cube | $y = x^3 + x + 5$ | 0.49 | 4.18 |
| Cube with Error | $y = x^3 + x + 5$ | 0.24 | 3.94 |
| Comparison | $x < 60$ | 0.54 | 12.39 |
| SHA-256 Hash | $y = \texttt{sha256}(x)$ | 0.71 | 15.39 |
| Inner Product | $\langle u, v\rangle < c_1 \wedge \langle u, v\rangle > c_2$ | 0.59 | 18.34 |

We tested different types of proofs, including the well-known cube example, a comparison (which requires using a gadget), a hash (a complicated mathematics equation), and a proof with inner product, logical operators, and comparison (which requires multiple gadgets and more complex logic). As expected, as we progress in terms of "complexity", runtime generally increases. Interestingly, the hash proof takes the longest in the SMT solver, demonstrating that there are different notions of "complexity" than just statement size.

We also sought to test if the correctness of the statement checked had any impact on performance. We did this by running two different experiments with the cube proof, one where we model a developer correctly flattening the statement equation into R1CS, and a second where we model a mistake in the flattening that introduces an error. Our Constraint Checker took a shorter time to evaluate the incorrect cube program since the Constraint Checker aborts as soon as it finds an error (such as a different domain or output value).

### 5.2 Performance of SnarkFuzzer

We tested SnarkFuzzer on `libsnark`, `Bellman`, `arkworks`, and `gnark` to evaluate the processing time and performance in different configurations. All experiments run on a single core, except for the Value Monitor which is trivially parallelizable across all cores. We start by evaluating the overall tool to examine the runtime percentage that is dedicated to each sub-component. We then drill down and individually explore the scalability of each sub-component to gain a fuller understanding of SnarkFuzzer's overall scalability.

**Overall Runtime with Different Libraries and Protocols.** We first explore the proportion of total running time that each different facet of SnarkFuzzer takes, and present the results in Fig. 2.

We ran with five different configurations: `libsnark` with Pinocchio, `libsnark` with Groth16, `Bellman` with Groth16, `arkworks` with Groth16, and `gnark` with Groth16. All of these experiments use generation-based fuzzers to produce valid R1CS matrices (the slowest of the four fuzzing methods we provide) with dimensions in [30, 60]. We ran 30 iterations of the Branch Model (since as shown in Fig. 3 that provides reasonable coverage) and calculated the average runtime to complete a full "run"[8] and proof check for each library and protocol.

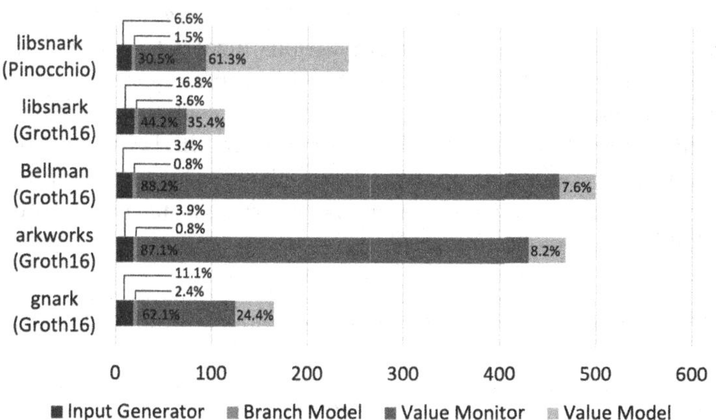


**Fig. 2.** Runtime of each component in SnarkFuzzer with different libraries and protocols, both in terms of actual time as well as percentage of the total.

We observe that for all libraries and protocols, the majority of time is spent in the Value Monitor and Value Model phases. This is somewhat expected, as the cryptographic operations in the Value Model require time to calculate, and Valgrind's simulation hardware watch also introduces substantial overhead. Since Groth16 has fewer elliptic curve and pairing operations than Pinocchio, testing that involves Groth16 costs less time. However, Valgrind spends a longer time executing a program in Rust than a program in C and Go. Since we use Valgrind in the Value Monitor to find and monitor value changes, we see a longer overall runtime with `Bellman` and `arkworks` than `libsnark` and `gnark`.

We do use small R1CS matrices in these experiments, as the primary goal is to demonstrate the runtime proportion for each component. We make a few key observations about this. We noticed that unless one uses only generation-based fuzzing to produce valid inputs, the size of the R1CS matrix (i.e., the proof) will

[8] We define a "full run" to be using the Input Generator to produce one zkSNARK program, analyzing coverage status with the Branch Model, and looking for any software and cryptographic related bugs with the Value Model and Value Monitor.

not substantially affect the performance of the Input Generator. The Branch Model does not work with the R1CS matrix, so different sizes will result in the same runtime. However, a large matrix will significantly increase the runtime of the Value Model and Value Monitor (see Table 4 for more realistic values). For total runtime reference, an R1CS matrix of size 100 × 5000 takes about 940 s to run the complete SnarkFuzzer with our generation-based invalid matrix fuzzer.

**Performance of the Input Generator.** Unlike a mutation-based or generation-based fuzzer for an invalid matrix (which are very quick since they only require straightforward operations), generating a valid R1CS matrix with our generation-based fuzzer requires the SMT solver to produce a matrix based on the random witness array. Thus the processing time depends on the matrix size and random value(s) in the witness list, which generally results in a larger matrix taking longer to process. To validate this, we used our various fuzzers to produce matrices of varying sizes (remember that the rows represent the number of constraints and columns the number of variables). In Table 3, we present the processing time for each method (generally under one second for most methods), which confirms our general intuition. We also note that the Input Generator must compile the input matrix (proof) and source code into a binary program, which can require substantial time that is outside of our control.

**Table 3.** Runtime (in seconds) of the Input Generator to produce R1CS matrices of different sizes.

| Matrix Size | | 5 × 10 | 20 × 40 | 50 × 100 | 50 × 200 |
|---|---|---|---|---|---|
| Generation Based | Invalid Matrix | <0.01 | <0.01 | <0.01 | 0.02 |
| | Valid Matrix | 0.16 | 2.06 | 23.02 | 51.27 |
| Mutation Based | Invalid Matrix | 0.38 | 0.49 | 0.65 | 0.77 |
| | Valid Matrix | <0.01 | <0.01 | <0.01 | 0.02 |

**Performance of the Branch Model.** Next, we explore the coverage ability of the Branch Model in terms of breadth, as well as how quickly we achieve a high percentage of branch coverage. We ran 50 iterations of the Branch Model with `libsnark`, which covers more than 85% of all branches. We stopped our experiments after 50 iterations as SnarkFuzzer did not reach any new branches over the previous 10 prior iterations. Even with this, we note that after roughly 30 iterations we see the breadth of our coverage begin to taper off. A graph can be found in Fig. 3.

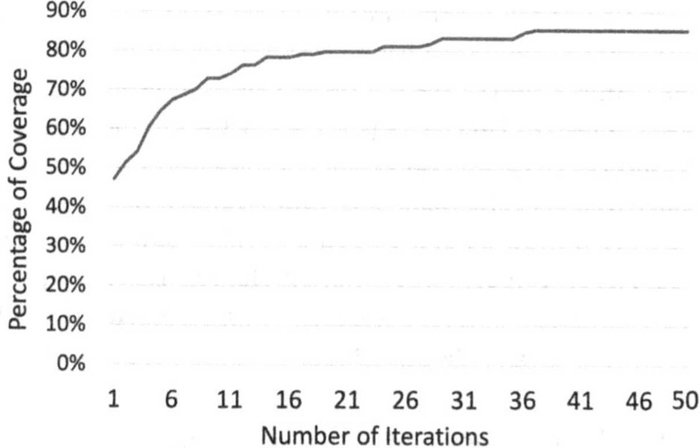


**Fig. 3.** Percentage (breadth) of library coverage after a given number of iterations

**Performance of Value Model and Value Monitor.** The primary effects on overall performance are our Value Model and Value Monitor. Table 4 shows the runtime with different matrix sizes. We expect the size of our matrices to be one of the primary influences on the runtime of these components.

Recall that the computation of the proving key requires calculations with the circuit. Therefore, a larger R1CS matrix will result in longer runtime in our Value Model. At the same time, the shape of the matrix will also affect its runtime. As we can see in Table 4, a matrix of size 20 × 45 takes less time than one of size 30 × 30 or 45 × 20, even though they all contain 900 integers. In fact, the number of variables (columns) plays a greater role than the number of

**Table 4.** Runtime of the Value Model and Value Monitor to process an R1CS matrix of varying size. For example, 10 × 30 is a matrix with 10 variables and 30 constraints.

| Matrix Setting | | Processing Time (in second) | |
|---|---|---|---|
| Matrix Size | Items in Matrix | Value Model | Value Monitor |
| 10 × 10 | 100 | 23.33 | 29.21 |
| 10 × 30 | 300 | 25.96 | 33.09 |
| 30 × 10 | | 32.78 | 34.21 |
| 20 × 45 | 900 | 29.52 | 43.99 |
| 30 × 30 | | 33.01 | 46.30 |
| 45 × 20 | | 40.14 | 47.68 |
| 45 × 60 | 2700 | 41.29 | 81.69 |
| 60 × 45 | | 46.03 | 80.21 |
| 100 × 1500 | 150000 | 200.84 | 223.49 |
| 100 × 5000 | 500000 | 580.97 | 344.83 |

constraints (rows) in Value Model runtime, since this plays a larger role in the size of the proving and verification keys.

Similarly, the Value Monitor requires more time to watch variables in a program with a larger matrix. However, the reason for this is different. Since the runtime of Valgrind depends on the space complexity of a variable, the matrix shape will not have an effect. Instead, the Value Monitor spends more time monitoring a program with a larger matrix, but it takes similar time for programs with the same number of integers but different shapes. For example, each matrix of size $20 \times 45$, $30 \times 30$, and $45 \times 20$ has 900 integers, and the Value Monitor takes around 46 s to run, even though they have a different shape.

**Discussion of Total Runtime.** Our experiments only provide an upper bound on the worst case runtime for SnarkFuzzer. We did not perform any runtime optimizations, and in all of our experiments, we used the slowest options or configurations that we knew of. While SnarkFuzzer does require extra runtime in the Value Monitor and Value Checker for each individual input seed, in comparison to a traditional fuzzer, which might spend hundreds or thousands of core hours to produce inputs, the framework and Branch Model designs allowSnarkFuzzer to find issues with a relatively small number of generated input seeds. In fact, most errors that SnarkFuzzer detected (see Sect. 6) were found with less than ten seeds. Therefore, we view performance to be acceptable for real world usage.

**Table 5.** Summary of the current potential errors and inconsistencies, and previous vulnerabilities, that `SNARKProbe` is able to catch and locate.

| Error/Vulnerability | Type | Affected Component | Program | Found by |
|---|---|---|---|---|
| *Potentially Locatable in Current Libraries* | | | | |
| Incorrect manual flattening by developer | Logic Error | R1CS Circuit | All libraries | ConstraintChecker |
| Multiple gadget misuse | Logic Error | R1CS Circuit | All libraries | ConstraintChecker |
| *Found in Current Libraries* | | | | |
| Incorrect bit/comparison gadget implementation | Logic Error | R1CS Circuit | libsnark | ConstraintChecker |
| Mismatch in circuit generation and usage | Logic Error | R1CS Circuit | All libraries | ConstraintChecker |
| Groth16 pre-pairing computation in Setup | Logic Error | Groth16 Protocol | bellman/arkworks | SnarkFuzzer |
| Inconsistent QAP extension index usage | Logic Error | PGHR13 Protocol | libsnark | SnarkFuzzer |
| Toxic waste not safely destroyed | Logic Error | PGHR13 Protocol | playsnark | SnarkFuzzer |
| Program out of memory with large circuit | Software Error | - | libsnark | SnarkFuzzer |
| *Found in Previous Versions of Libraries* | | | | |
| CVE-2019-7167 | Logic Error | PGHR13 Protocol | libsnark (2018) | SnarkFuzzer |

## 6 Error Catching Evaluation

Our second set of evaluations demonstrates `SNARKProbe`'s ability to *automatically* catch different types of errors in zkSNARK libraries. We test `SNARKProbe` on `libsnark`, `Bellman`, `arkworks`, and `playsnark`, as well as on the circuit generator `Circom`. Additionally, we show how `SNARKProbe` would have caught a previous CVE in the zkSNARK component of Zcash, a popular privacy-preserving cryptocurrency. In total, `SNARKProbe` detected seven inconsistencies in current zkSNARK libraries, successfully *automatically* located the previous vulnerability, and could potentially detect two additional types of errors. We summarize our results in Table 5.

### 6.1 Potentially Locatable in Current Libraries

**Incorrect Flattening.** There is always a possibility that a developer may generate an incorrect R1CS matrix for their circuit, since this process is often done by hand. While we did not find any examples of this in the few applications we tested, consider the following scenario. Take a statement equation like $x^3 + x + 5 = y$ which the developer will typically flatten into `R1CS_gates` with private input $x = 3$ and public input $y = 35$. This set of equations is then equal to $x^3 + x + 5 = 35$. However, the developer *may* incorrectly flatten the statement equation into `R1CS_gates_2`.

$$\texttt{R1CS\_gates} = \begin{cases} x * x = w_1 \\ w_1 * x = w_2 \\ w_2 + x = w_3 \\ w_3 + 5 = y \end{cases} \qquad \texttt{R1CS\_gates\_2} := \begin{cases} x * x = w_1 \\ w_1 * x = w_2 \\ w_2 + 2 * x = w_3 \\ w_3 + 2 = y \end{cases}$$

While `R1CS_gates_2` still satisfies the private input $x = 3$ and public input $y = 35$, causing the underlying library to output an acceptable proof, this flattening does not in fact equal the statement equation $x^3 + x + 5 = y$. Although the statement equation and `R1CS_gates_2` satisfy the witness, and their domains have the same upper and lower bounds, they have a different output range, which our Constraint Checker will catch and flag as an error.

**Combining Multiple Gadgets.** Recall that a gadget is an abstraction that many zkSNARK libraries contain to make developing proofs easier for developers. Multiple gadgets may also be combined to create a single proof. Gadgets are generally created and provided independently, which means that one must combine them with care. For example, say a developer uses the gadgets *greater_than* and *equal_to* to create a proof that a prover has a value which is greater than or equal to a certain number. For this proof, only one input should be used for both gadgets. However, a naive developer may create a proof that has an individual input for each gadget instead of a single input for the entire circuit. In this case, a malicious prover can create a separate program with the same circuit and use two inputs with different values to satisfy each gadget and hence the entire circuit (when in reality these two inputs need to be identical). In this case, our Constraint Checker can detect the inconsistency between the R1CS matrix and statement equations to find potential issues with using multiple gadgets incorrectly.

### 6.2 Found in Current Libraries

**Defective Gadgets.** Gadgets may be implemented incorrectly, causing inconsistencies between the original (desired) statement equation and the R1CS gates generated. Our Constraint Checker is able to find these inconsistencies in its checks for equivalence, regardless of whether a gadget was used or not.

The `comparison_gadget` in `libsnark` uses bit shifting to compare two variables $A$ and $B$ by calculating $2^n + B - A$ and then counting the number of 0 s and 1 s in the resulting bit array (the corresponding R1CS constraints are shown in Appendix C). If the developer incorrectly specifies a bit length smaller than the size of $A$ or $B$, the `comparison_gadget` will not generate the correct R1CS, which may result in a "fake proof"[9]. `libsnark` will not block this behavior or raise any warning messages. Consider a developer that uses the `comparison_gadget` to generate the statement equation $x < 60$ where $x \in \mathbb{F}_p$. The R1CS should then only have a valid solution in $[0, 60)$. However, if an incorrect bit length is provided, we found that all numbers in the range $(21888242871839275222246405745257275088548364400416034343698204186575808494653, p)$ still satisfy this incorrect R1CS, allowing a dishonest prover to generate a valid proof without knowledge of a correct secret value. After our tool flagged this potential issue, on further manual investigation we did see that the `libsnark` source code contains a comment about using the correct bit size, though this could go unnoticed by a novice user or be abused by a malicious one to forge proofs.

**Mismatch Between Circuit Generation and Usage.** In addition to end-to-end libraries, there are a growing number of circuit generators available to assist developers in constructing R1CS/circuits for proof generation, with `Circom` [41] being a widespread example[10]. `Circom` generates R1CS files that can then be utilized by libraries such as `snarkjs` [17], `wasmsnark` [18], and `rapidSnark` [16]. However, during our evaluation process, our Constraint Checker identified a crucial potential issue: the absence of attribute cross-checking between the circuit generator and formal proof generation library.

While the circuit generator may produce valid R1CS that accurately represents the prover's original statement, the proof generation library might, for example, employ a different elliptic curve and finite field to generate the proof by default. Consequently, when operating under distinct elliptic curve and finite field settings, the circuit no longer maintains equivalence with the original statement. This discrepancy can be problematic both for a developer and a verifier who are unaware that a circuit can yield different representations under different elliptic curve configurations. In such cases, the prover can produce a seemingly "valid" proof for the verifier without knowledge of the secret value.

---

[9] One that will verify even though the prover does not actually have a valid witness.

[10] We note that `Circom` is just an example that we tested, and that the same should hold true for other circuit generators as well.

**Groth16 Pre-pairing.** The Groth16 protocol produces $P = g^{\alpha}$ and $Q = h^{\beta}$ as part of Setup, which are subsequently used in Verify to calculate the pairing $e(P, Q)$. However, our Value Checker found that `Bellman` stores the pairing $e(P, Q)$ as part of the verification key instead of $P$ and $Q$. Pre-computing and directly providing $e(P, Q)$ is an optimization that helps make verification more efficient (as pairings are quite slow to calculate). As this is a well-known optimization, we can confidently say that this will not cause any sort of vulnerability, but we err on the side of caution and flag all inconsistencies between the source code and protocol for further review since these can greatly increase the risk of actual vulnerabilities.

**Pinocchio Protocol Inconsistencies.** In the Pinocchio key generator, there exist values $\overrightarrow{A}$, $\overrightarrow{B}$, and $\overrightarrow{C}$ that need to be extended via $A_{m+1} = B_{m+2} = C_{m+3}$ and $A_{m+2} = A_{m+3} = B_{m+1} = B_{m+3} = C_{m+1} = C_{m+2}$ per the specification [27]. However, our Value Checker found that `libsnark` only extended $\overrightarrow{A}$, $\overrightarrow{B}$, and $\overrightarrow{C}$ via $A_{m+1} = B_{m+1} = C_{m+1}$ as an optimization for space complexity. After a review of the `libsnark` source code and protocol, we believe this inconsistency will not lead to a security vulnerability given how the values are used in practice. However, this instance is more subtle and less well-known than the previous one, so while it might not be exploitable, we believe inconsistencies of this nature are still valuable to flag for further review as this might not always be the case.

**Toxic Waste.** As part of the zkSNARK setup process, a set of private parameters informally referred to as "toxic waste" are generated. This toxic waste must be destroyed after the setup process, as possession of it allows one to forge proofs. However, our SnarkFuzzer identified an actual implementation error in a zkSNARK library called `playsnark`, whereby toxic waste is not properly destroyed during the setup phase. `playsnark` [5] serves as a learning playground for proof systems, including Pinocchio and Groth16. While `playsnark` makes no claims that it should be used for security-sensitive applications, we feel that this example still exemplifies valuable use cases for `SNARKProbe`. First, it can indeed catch errors that would be exploitable in real applications. And second, while libraries like `Bellman` and `libsnark` are professionally audited, this will likely not always be the case for all zkSNARK code in production usage in the future (as we have seen in many other domains). Tooling such as `SNARKProbe` can be an invaluable resource for non-experts and small organizations, enabling them to assess the security posture of unaudited zkSNARK libraries, audit their own code throughout the development process, and facilitating informed decisions regarding future security implementations.

**libsnark Out of Memory.** SnarkFuzzer detects a corner-case software error in libsnark. When our Input Generator tried to produce a large R1CS matrix with tens of thousands of variables and constraints, we discovered that libsnark cannot compile and produce a zkSNARK program with such a large R1CS matrix without throwing a segmentation fault or memory error. Intuitively, this occurs because the input matrix we generated was quite dense, i.e., it had a large number of both variables and constraints, as opposed to being quite sparse like most typical R1CS matrices. libsnark's R1CS storage format is clearly not setup to handle such cases. In general, this would not impact the typical usage of the libsnark, as our fuzzer is designed to look for extreme cases like this that might not happen with a typical real world proof statement.

We take this example as a chance to take a step back and revisit our comparison of SnarkFuzzer to a traditional, more generic fuzzer like AFL. As generic memory and software errors such as this have nothing to do with the actual cryptography and zkSNARK logic, traditional fuzzers are also able to detect them. However, it is likely to take a generic fuzzer significantly longer (and many more inputs) to catch such errors, as they lack the context to understand what an "extreme" input means in this instance, and, as we have seen, it is not easy to instrument a fuzzer with this context. Additionally, all previous instances that we discussed would not be detectable by a generic fuzzer, as they are specifically cryptographic logic errors.

### 6.3 Found in Previous Versions of Libraries

**CVE-2019-7167 Problem.** Finally, we discuss how SNARKProbe (specifically SnarkFuzzer) is able to detect real world vulnerabilities by demonstrating its ability to pinpoint a previous CVE. CVE-2019-7167 [34] was found in libsnark through a manual code audit, as part of its usage in the popular privacy-preserving cryptocurrency Zcash [19] (and has since been patched). At a high level, this vulnerability produced a bypass element in the key generation that damaged the soundness of the zkSNARK proof system. To fix this vulnerability, the value of $pk_A^{'}$ must be replaced from $\{A_i(\tau)\alpha_A\rho_A\mathcal{P}\}_{i=0}^{m+3}$ to $\{A_i(\tau)\alpha_A\rho_A\mathcal{P}\}_{i=n+1}^{m+3}$, with all other values the same.

To test this, we downloaded a version of libsnark from 2018 (Commit hash: bf2146b). When running SnarkFuzzer, the Value Checker *automatically* found this inconsistency and vulnerability in key generation. Additionally, while libsnark has since fixed this issue, it did not directly modify the structure of $pk_A^{'}$ in order to keep consistency with the structure of the other proving keys. Therefore, $pk_A^{'}$ still has size $m + 3$ instead of $(m + 3) - (n + 1)$. libsnark just added an extra handler to reformat the $pk_A^{'}$ size in the prover, and while this does not appear to have caused any additional issues, it is unclear if this could result in other corner case issues.

# 7 Conclusion

In this paper we present SNARKProbe, a framework that can automatically and systematically check for potential software errors and cryptographic logic errors, as well as for consistency in the implemented proof statement, in R1CS-based zkSNARK libraries, with little manual input from the user. We demonstrated SNARKProbe's design flexibility by implementing it for multiple different zkSNARK protocols and libraries. In addition, we performed extensive performance evaluations, as well as tested its ability to detect potential errors and inconsistencies. We believe SNARKProbe is a step in the right direction for ensuring the correctness of existing zkSNARK implementations and applications.

**Acknowledgments.** This work was supported by NSF grant CNS-2047991.

# A Additional Information for Constraint Checker

## A.1 An optimization for the SMT solver

The SMT solver may take a while to solve some complicated equations. To reduce the processing time in the equality check, we introduce optimizations and simplify some equations in the R1CS matrix. For example, many libsnark gadgets use bit shifting, which produces the equation $(x*(1+(p-1)*x)) \bmod p = 0$ in R1CS gates. This equation represents $x = 0$ or $x = 1$. For our optimization, if the Constraint Checker detects such a relation, it will be replaced with $0 \leq x \wedge x \leq 1$ where $x \in \mathbb{F}$. These are logically equivalent, but our replacement is much easier for the SMT solver to work with. A real world gadget like the comparison_gadget in libsnark has 16 constraints, and there are 11 constraints representing $x = 0$ or $x = 1$ (see Appendix C).

## A.2 Protocol of the Constraint Checker by the SMT Solver

**(a) Parameters.**

A set of statement equations $E_1$ in size $p$ where equation $e_1^i \in E_1$ and $i \in [1, p]$.

A set of equations $E_2$ converted from R1CS gates in size $q$ where $e_2^i \in E_2$ and $i \in [1, q]$.

$m$ private variables $x_1^i$ in $E_1$ where $i \in [1, m]$ and $n$ private variables $x_2^i$ in $E_2$ where $i \in [1, n]$ and $n \geq m$. A set of auxiliary input $v_x^i$.

$k$ public variables $y_1^i$ in $E_1$ and $k$ public variables $y_2^i$ in $E_2$ where $i \in [1, k]$. A set of primary input $v_y^i$.

A SMT Pro Solver $S$ and Optimizer $O$ with modulus $P$. $0 \leq x_1 < P$, $0 \leq x_2 < P$, $0 \leq y_1 < P$, and $0 \leq y_2 < P$ without optimization.

**(b) Function valid check.**
INPUTS: $E_1$, $E_2$, $S$.
OUTPUTS: Boolean result of function validation.

1. Check and solve the R1CS gates:
   Set a solvers $S_1 \in S$.
   Add $e_1^i \in E_1$ where $i \in [1, p]$ and range of $x_1^i$, $x_2^i$ to $S_1$.
   Solve $S_1$ and get the set of private variables solution as $M_{1_x}^i$ and set of public variables solution as $M_{1_y}^i$.
2. Check and solve the statement equations:
   Set a solvers $S_2 \in S$.
   Add $e_2^i \in E_1$ where $i \in [1, q]$ and range of $y_1^i$, $y_2^i$ to $S_2$.
   Solve $S_2$ and get the set of private variables solution as $M_{2_x}^i$ and set of public variables solution as $M_{2_y}^i$.
3. Output $v_x^i \in M_{1_x}^i$ *AND* $v_x^i \in M_{2_x}^i$ *AND* $v_y^i \in M_{1_y}^i$ *AND* $v_y^i \in M_{2_y}^i$.

**(c) Equivalent comparison.**
INPUTS: $E_1$, $E_2$, $S$.
OUTPUTS: Boolean result of function equality.
Set two solvers $S_1$ and $S_2 \in S$.

1. Comparing with public variables:
   Add $e_1^i \in E_1$ where $i \in [1, p]$ and range of $x_1^i$, $y_1^i$ to $S_1$.
   Add $e_2^i \in E_2$ where $i \in [1, q]$ and range of $x_2^i$, $y_2^i$ to $S_1$.
   Add $x_1^i == x_2^i$ where $i \in [1, m]$ to $S_1$.
   Add $y_1^i \neq y_2^i$ where $i \in [1, k]$ to $S_1$.
   Check if $S_1$ is *SAT*, *UNSAT*, or *UNSURE* as $c_1$.
2. Comparing with Boolean variables:
   Set $b_1$ and $b_2 \in$ BOOLEAN
   Add $b_1 =$ *AND*$(E_1)$ to $S_2$.
   Add $b_2 =$ *AND*$(E_2)$ to $S_2$.
   Add $x_1^i == x_2^i$ where $i \in [1, m]$ to $S_2$.
   Add $y_1^i == y_2^i$ where $i \in [1, k]$ to $S_2$.
   Add $b_1 \neq b_2$ to $S_2$.
   Check if $S_2$ is *SAT*, *UNSAT*, or *UNSURE* as $c_2$.
3. Output ($c_1$ == *UNSAT AND* $c_2$ == *UNSAT*).

**(d) Domain comparison.**
INPUTS: $E_1$, $E_2$, $S$, $O$.
OUTPUTS: Boolean result of domain comparison.

1. Comparing upper and lower bond:
   Add $e_1^i \in E_1$ where $i \in [1, p]$ and range of $x_1^i$, $x_2^i$ to $O$.
   Add $e_2^i \in E_1$ where $i \in [1, q]$ and range of $y_1^i$, $y_2^i$ to $O$.
   Solve the upper bond $u_1$ and lower bond $l_1$ from $O$
   Solve the upper bond $u_2$ and lower bond $l_2$ from $O$
2. Check if R1CS is valid outside statement domain:
   Add *NOT*(*AND*(range of $x_1^i$, $x_2^i$)) to $S$.
   Add $e_2^i \in E_1$ where $i \in [1, q]$ and range of $x_2^i$, $y_2^i$ to $S$.
   Check if $S$ is *SAT*, *UNSAT*, or *UNSURE* as $c$.
3. Output ($c$ == *UNSAT AND* $u_1$ == $u_2$ *AND* $l_1$ == $l_2$).

## A.3 Example Constraint Checker

For the interested reader, we provide an example of our Constraint Checker to show how a developer can run the tool. More examples can be found in our code.

```
x = z3.Int("x")
## Indicate the public variables and private variables
allocate = ["x"]
variables = [x]
## Indicate the statement of a proof
statement = [x < 60]
## Provide the snark program to automatically extract the R1CS matrix
## Developer can also manually provide the R1CS matrix
path = os.path.join(currentdir, "range")
## Call the functions in ConstraintChecker to evaluate the correctness
fcmp = FunctionComparison(path)
```

```
fcmp.allocate(allocate)
fcmp.set_input_sizes(0)
fcmp.addVariables(variables)
fcmp.addStatement(statement)
fcmp.addGadget(gadget1.comparison_gadget("max")) ## Optional
fcmp.addRange(x, z3.And(x < 60))
fcmp.runComparisonTests()
```

## A.4 Domain Gap Issues

The same upper bound and lower bound does not guarantee that statement equations and R1CS gates have the same range. Figure 4c and 4d shows an example of an unmatched domain with the same upper bound and lower bound.

**Domain Gap in Statement Equations**
The ground truth domain of statement equations is known and provided by the user (which means we know the domain gap in the statement equations), the Constraint Checker can use the SMT solver to find if the R1CS gates have solution(s) outside the domain of statement equations (e.g. in the gap). If the SMT solver returns `SAT`, then the domains' of the statement equations and R1CS gates do not match and thus they are not equivalent. This example corresponds to Fig. 4d.

**Domain Gap in R1CS Gates**
Since the domain of the R1CS gates is unknown, the Constraint Checker cannot use the SMT solver to detect an unmatched domain as in the previous example. However, in this instance, the prover likely will not be able to generate a proof for a secret value in the gap because these secret values are not in the domain of R1CS Gates even though they are valid solutions to the original statement equations. That is, the set of allowable input values for the implemented R1CS matrix is a subset of the set of input values for the desired proof statement. Therefore, while this leads to undesirable behavior as the prover cannot generate proofs for the entire valid input range, it does not lead to any exploits or "fake" proofs (i.e., the ability to generate a valid proof without knowledge of the secret value). This example corresponds to Fig. 4c.

We believe this type of gap is very rare, but we still try to find this issue by producing a set of uniform random numbers as input for statement equations and R1CS gates. If the R1CS gates do not have a solution but the statement equations do have a valid solution for an input number, then there is a gap in the statement equations, which is not equivalent to the statement equations' domain. This test does not guarantee finding an existing domain gap, but a larger set of numbers has higher confidence in finding any existing gaps.

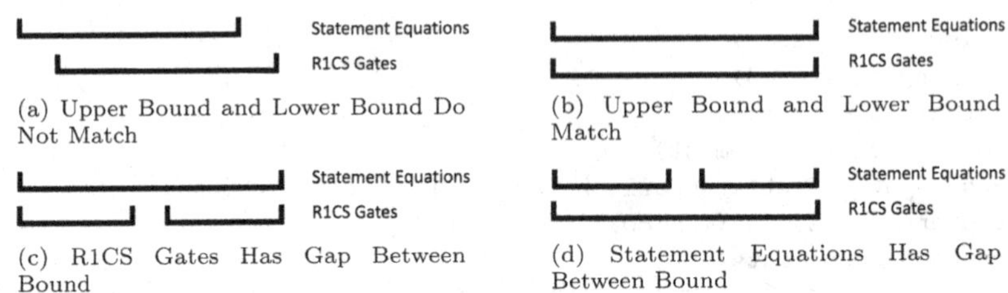


(a) Upper Bound and Lower Bound Do Not Match

(b) Upper Bound and Lower Bound Match

(c) R1CS Gates Has Gap Between Bound

(d) Statement Equations Has Gap Between Bound

**Fig. 4.** Examples of Domain Comparison

# B Additional Information for SnarkFuzzer

## B.1 Example Ideal Model Files

See Figs. 5 and 6.

```
Relative Path: knowledge_commitment/kc_multiexp.tcc
FUNCTION,2,99,127,kc_batch_exp_internal,IMPORTANT
CONDITION,4,117,124,2,IMPORTANT
CONDITION,5,119,123,2,IMPORTANT
RETURN,2,126,126,2,IMPORTANT
```

**Fig. 5.** Example file for the ideal branch file

```
tau,Fr,t,zk_proof_systems/.../r1cs_ppzksnark.tcc,252
rhoA,Fr,rA,zk_proof_systems/.../r1cs_ppzksnark.tcc,300
rhoB,Fr,rB,zk_proof_systems/.../r1cs_ppzksnark.tcc,301
```

**Fig. 6.** Example file for the ideal value file

## B.2 PrettyPrint Example

```
{static wnaf_window_table = {<std::_Vector_base<unsigned long, std::allocator<unsigned long> >> = {_M_impl = {<std::allocator<unsi
gned long>> = {<__gnu_cxx::new_allocator<unsigned long>> = {<No data fields>}, <No data fields>}, <std::_Vector_base<unsigned long
, std::allocator<unsigned long> >::_Vector_impl_data> = {_M_start = 0x5555556f1d90, _M_finish = 0x5555556f1db0, _M_end_of_storage
= 0x5555556f1db0}, <No data fields>}}, <No data fields>}, static fixed_base_exp_window_table = {<std::_Vector_base<unsigned long,
std::allocator<unsigned long> >> = {_M_impl = {<std::allocator<unsigned long>> = {<__gnu_cxx::new_allocator<unsigned long>> = {<No
 data fields>}, <No data fields>}, <std::_Vector_base<unsigned long, std::allocator<unsigned long> >::_Vector_impl_data> = {_M_sta
rt = 0x5555556f0810, _M_finish = 0x5555556f08c0, _M_end_of_storage = 0x5555556f0910}, <No data fields>}}, <No data fields>}, coord
 = {{<mie::local::addsubmul<mie::Fp, mie::local::comparable<mie::Fp, mie::local::hasNegative<mie::Fp, mie::local::inversible<mie::
Fp, mie::local::Empty<mie::Fp> > > > >> = {<mie::local::comparable<mie::Fp, mie::local::hasNegative<mie::Fp, mie::local::inversibl
e<mie::Fp, mie::local::Empty<mie::Fp> > > >> = {<mie::local::hasNegative<mie::Fp, mie::local::inversible<mie::Fp, mie::local::Empt
y<mie::Fp> > >> = {<mie::local::inversible<mie::Fp, mie::local::Empty<mie::Fp> >> = {<mie::local::Empty<mie::Fp>> = {<No data fiel
ds>}, <No data fields>}, <No data fields>}, <No data fields>}, <No data fields>}, v_ = {15230403791020821917, 754611498739239741,
7381016538464732716, 1011752739694698287}}, {<mie::local::addsubmul<mie::Fp, mie::local::comparable<mie::Fp, mie::local::hasNegati
ve<mie::Fp, mie::local::inversible<mie::Fp, mie::local::Empty<mie::Fp> > > > >> = {<mie::local::comparable<mie::Fp, mie::local::ha
sNegative<mie::Fp, mie::local::inversible<mie::Fp, mie::local::Empty<mie::Fp> > > >> = {<mie::local::hasNegative<mie::Fp, mie::loc
al::inversible<mie::Fp, mie::local::Empty<mie::Fp> > >> = {<mie::local::inversible<mie::Fp, mie::local::Empty<mie::Fp> >> = {<mie:
:local::Empty<mie::Fp>> = {<No data fields>}, <No data fields>}, <No data fields>}, <No data fields>}, <No data fields>}, v_ = {12
014063508332092218, 1509222997478479483, 14762033076929465432, 2023505479389396574}}, {<mie::local::addsubmul<mie::Fp, mie::local:
:comparable<mie::Fp, mie::local::hasNegative<mie::Fp, mie::local::inversible<mie::Fp, mie::local::Empty<mie::Fp> > > > >> = {<mie:
:local::comparable<mie::Fp, mie::local::hasNegative<mie::Fp, mie::local::inversible<mie::Fp, mie::local::Empty<mie::Fp> > > >> = {
<mie::local::hasNegative<mie::Fp, mie::local::inversible<mie::Fp, mie::local::Empty<mie::Fp> > >> = {<mie::local::inversible<mie::
Fp, mie::local::Empty<mie::Fp> >> = {<mie::local::Empty<mie::Fp>> = {<No data fields>}, <No data fields>}, <No data fields>}, <No
data fields>}, <No data fields>}, v_ = {15230403791020821917, 754611498739239741, 7381016538464732716, 1011752739694698287}}}}
```

(a) Content without PrettyPrint in `libsnark`

```
pairing::bls12_381::ec::g1::G1Affine {x: pairing::bls12_381::fq::Fq (pairing::bls12_381::fq::FqRepr ([10547801628701281408, 146510
83689357211131, 6481648553651009991, 9048958586612376648, 8036176713143700390, 705443719916985888])), y: pairing::bls12_381::fq::Fq
 (pairing::bls12_381::fq::FqRepr ([8855955297991251329, 16069468485776047325, 12121465487721251295, 18418488638908299805, 16571651
195142601741, 1367670370568535616])), infinity: false}
```

(b) Content without PrettyPrint in `Bellman`

```
ark_ec::models::short_weierstrass::affine::Affine<ark_bls12_381::curves::g1::Config> {x: ark_ff::fields::models::fp::Fp<ark_ff::fi
elds::models::fp::montgomery_backend::MontBackend<ark_bls12_381::fields::fq::FqConfig, 6>, 6> (ark_ff::biginteger::BigInt<6> ([476
2646147170998592, 12788204197850283445, 6937814569682132977, 4601457130438782450, 21258565080345294, 750924354510760241]), core::m
arker::PhantomData<ark_ff::fields::models::fp::montgomery_backend::MontBackend<ark_bls12_381::fields::fq::FqConfig, 6>>), y: ark_f
f::fields::models::fp::Fp<ark_ff::fields::models::fp::montgomery_backend::MontBackend<ark_bls12_381::fields::fq::FqConfig, 6>, 6>
(ark_ff::biginteger::BigInt<6> ([9390487088130527322, 6856353769413480936, 18328620154857584441, 15200026662905747573, 74045709516
95852829, 1485648545527895280]), core::marker::PhantomData<ark_ff::fields::models::fp::montgomery_backend::MontBackend<ark_bls12_3
81::fields::fq::FqConfig, 6>>), infinity: false}
```

(c) Content without PrettyPrint in `arkworks`

```
(780868217653241507189803610308177943005747004655740818420577490519579717155, 9948895334884577511816681179891480858815618120919043
955193642144437020075012)
```

(d) Content with PrettyPrint in any library

**Fig. 7.** Content of variable type G1

# C Equations `comparison_gadget` Represents

$$
\begin{cases}
(w_{14} * (1 + (p-1) * w_{14})) \bmod p = 0 \\
(1024 + w_3 + 2 * w_4 + 4 * w_5 + 8 * w_6 + 16 * w_7 + 32 * \\
\quad w_8 + 64 * w_9 + 128 * w_{10} + 256 * w_{11} + 512 * w_{12}) \\
\quad \bmod p = w_{13} \\
(w_3 * (1 + (p-1) * w_3)) \bmod p = 0 \\
(w_4 * (1 + (p-1) * w_4)) \bmod p = 0 \\
(w_5 * (1 + (p-1) * w_5)) \bmod p = 0 \\
(w_6 * (1 + (p-1) * w_6)) \bmod p = 0 \\
(w_7 * (1 + (p-1) * w_7)) \bmod p = 0 \\
(w_8 * (1 + (p-1) * w_8)) \bmod p = 0 \\
(w_9 * (1 + (p-1) * w_9)) \bmod p = 0 \\
(w_{10} * (1 + (p-1) * w_{10})) \bmod p = 0 \\
(w_{11} * (1 + (p-1) * w_{11})) \bmod p = 0 \\
(w_{12} * (1 + (p-1) * w_{12})) \bmod p = 0 \\
(1024 - 1 * w_1 + w_2) \bmod p = w_{13} \\
(w_{15} * (w_3 + w_4 + w_5 + w_6 + w_7 + w_8 + w_9 + w_{10} + \\
\quad w_{11} + w_{12})) \bmod p = w_{14} \\
((1 + (p-1) * w_{14}) * (w_3 + w_4 + w_5 + w_6 + w_7 + w_8 \\
\quad + w_9 + w_{10} + w_{11} + w_{12})) \bmod p = 0 \\
w_{14} \bmod p = 1
\end{cases}
$$

## References

1. Fixing vulnerabilities in the zcash protocol (2016). https://electriccoin.co/blog/fixing-zcash-vulns/
2. Zcash counterfeiting vulnerability successfully remediated (2019). https://electriccoin.co/blog/zcash-counterfeiting-vulnerability-successfully-remediated/
3. libsnark: a C++ library for zksnark proofs (2020). https://github.com/scipr-lab/libsnark
4. Nu4 cryptographic specification and implementation review (2020). https://research.nccgroup.com/wp-content/uploads/2020/09/NCC_Group_Zcash_ZCHX006_Report_2020-09-03_v2.0.pdf
5. Playsnark: a playground to learn proofs systems (2020). https://github.com/nikkolasg/playsnark
6. Dark forest (2022). https://blog.zkga.me/
7. Zero-knowledge rollups (2022). https://ethereum.org/en/developers/docs/scaling/zk-rollups/
8. Aleo (2023). https://www.aleo.org/
9. atheris, atheris: A coverage-guided, native python fuzzer (2023). https://github.com/google/atheris
10. bellman, a zk-SNARK library (2023). https://github.com/zkcrypto/bellman
11. Clang's source-based code coverage (2023). https://clang.llvm.org/docs/SourceBasedCodeCoverage.html
12. doxygen, doxygen (2023). https://github.com/doxygen/doxygen
13. gnark zk-SNARK library (2023). https://github.com/Consensys/gnark
14. libsnark: A rust implementation of the groth16 zkSNARK (2023). https://github.com/arkworks-rs/groth16
15. Project everest (2023). https://project-everest.github.io/
16. rapidsnark (2023). https://github.com/iden3/rapidsnark
17. snarkjs (2023). https://github.com/iden3/snarkjs
18. wasmsnark (2023). https://github.com/iden3/wasmsnark
19. Zcash (2023). https://z.cash/
20. zksnarks for the world (2023). https://research.protocol.ai/sites/snarks/
21. Aumasson, J.P., Romailler, Y.: Automated testing of crypto software using differential fuzzing. Black Hat USA (2017)
22. Bang, L., Rosner, N., Bultan, T.: Online synthesis of adaptive side-channel attacks based on noisy observations. In: IEEE EuroS&P (2018)
23. Barbosa, H., Reynolds, A., Ouraoui, D.E., Tinelli, C., Barrett, C.: Extending SMT solvers to higher-order logic. In: CADE (2019)
24. Barbosa, M., et al.: SoK: computer-aided cryptography. In: IEEE S&P (2021)
25. Beck, G., Zinkus, M., Green, M.: Automating the development of chosen ciphertext attacks. In: USENIX Security (2020)
26. Ben-Sasson, E., Chiesa, A., Genkin, D., Tromer, E., Virza, M.: SNARKs for C: verifying program executions succinctly and in zero knowledge. Cryptology ePrint Archive, Report 2013/507 (2013)
27. Ben-Sasson, E., Chiesa, A., Tromer, E., Virza, M.: Succinct non-interactive zero knowledge for a von Neumann architecture. In: USENIX Security (2014)
28. Böhme, M., Pham, V.T., Nguyen, M.D., Roychoudhury, A.: Directed greybox fuzzing. In: ACM CCS (2017)
29. Böhme, M., Pham, V.T., Roychoudhury, A.: Coverage-based greybox fuzzing as Markov chain. In: IEEE TSE (2017)

30. Chen, C., Cui, B., Ma, J., Wu, R., Guo, J., Liu, W.: A systematic review of fuzzing techniques. Comput. Secur. **75**, 118–137 (2018)
31. Ethereum: Python implementation of ECC pairing and bn_128 and bls12_381 curve operations. Ethereum, December 2021. https://github.com/ethereum/py_ecc. Accessed Dec 2021
32. Faz-Hernández, A., Kwiatkowski, K.: Introducing CIRCL: An Advanced Cryptographic Library. Cloudflare, June 2019. https://github.com/cloudflare/circl. v1.2.0 Accessed June 2022
33. Fredrikson, M., Livshits, B.: Zø: An optimizing distributing zero-knowledge compiler. In: USENIX Security (2014)
34. Gabizon, A.: AuroraLight: improved prover efficiency and SRS size in a Sonic-like system. Cryptology ePrint Archive, Paper 2019/601 (2019). https://eprint.iacr.org/2019/601
35. Garman, C., Green, M., Kaptchuk, G., Miers, I., Rushanan, M.: Dancing on the lip of the volcano: chosen ciphertext attacks on apple {iMessage}. In: USENIX Security (2016)
36. Godefroid, P., Peleg, H., Singh, R.: Learn&Fuzz: machine learning for input fuzzing. In: ASE (2017)
37. Goldreich, O., Micali, S., Wigderson, A.: Proofs that yield nothing but their validity and a methodology of cryptographic protocol design. In: FOCS (1986)
38. Google: syzkaller - kernel fuzzer (2017). https://github.com/google/syzkaller. Accessed July 2022
39. Groth, J.: On the size of pairing-based non-interactive arguments. In: Fischlin, M., Coron, J.-S. (eds.) EUROCRYPT 2016. LNCS, vol. 9666, pp. 305–326. Springer, Heidelberg (2016). https://doi.org/10.1007/978-3-662-49896-5_11
40. Householder, A.D., Foote, J.M.: Probability-based parameter selection for black-box fuzz testing. Technical report. Carnegie Mellon University, SEI (2012)
41. iden3: circom - Circuit Compiler for ZK Proving Systems (2023). https://github.com/iden3/circom. Accessed Aug 2022
42. Kosba, A.: xJsnark (2022). https://github.com/akosba/xjsnark. Accessed Aug 2022
43. Kupser, D., Mainka, C., Schwenk, J., Somorovsky, J.: How to break XML encryption-automatically. In: USENIX WOOT (2015)
44. o1 labs: snarky (2023). https://github.com/o1-labs/snarky. Accessed Aug 2022
45. Macgillivray, A., deBlanc Knowles, T.: Advancing a vision for privacy enhancing technologies (2022). https://www.whitehouse.gov/ostp/news-updates/2022/06/28/advancing-a-vision-for-privacy-enhancing-technologies/
46. Mouha, N., Raunak, M.S., Kuhn, D.R., Kacker, R.: Finding bugs in cryptographic hash function implementations. IEEE Trans. Reliab. **67**(3), 870–884 (2018)
47. Moura, L.D., Bjørner, N.: Z3: an efficient SMT solver. In: TACAS (2008)
48. Naveed, M., Kamara, S., Wright, C.V.: Inference attacks on property-preserving encrypted databases. In: ACM CCS (2015)
49. Nicas, J., Isaac, M., Frenkel, S.: Millions flock to telegram and signal as fears grow over big tech (2021). https://www.nytimes.com/2021/01/13/technology/telegram-signal-apps-big-tech.html
50. Nitulescu, A.: zk-snarks: a gentle introduction. Technical report (2020)
51. NSA: Patch critical cryptographic vulnerability in Microsoft Windows clients and servers (2020). https://media.defense.gov/2020/Jan/14/2002234275/-1/-1/0/CSA-WINDOWS-10-CRYPT-LIB-20190114.PDF
52. Parno, B., Howell, J., Gentry, C., Raykova, M.: Pinocchio: nearly practical verifiable computation. In: IEEE S&P (2013)

53. Pasareanu, C.S., Phan, Q.S., Malacaria, P.: Multi-run side-channel analysis using Symbolic Execution and Max-SMT. In: IEEE CSF (2016)
54. Phan, Q.S., Bang, L., Pasareanu, C.S., Malacaria, P., Bultan, T.: Synthesis of adaptive side-channel attacks. In: IEEE CSF (2017)
55. Protzenko, J., Beurdouche, B., Merigoux, D., Bhargavan, K.: Formally verified cryptographic web applications in WebAssembly. In: IEEE S&P (2019)
56. Rupprecht, D., Kohls, K., Holz, T., Pöpper, C.: Call me maybe: eavesdropping encrypted LTE calls with ReVoLTE. In: USENIX Security (2020)
57. Somorovsky, J.: Systematic fuzzing and testing of TLS libraries. In: ACM CCS (2016)
58. Walz, A., Sikora, A.: Exploiting dissent: towards fuzzing-based differential black-box testing of TLS implementations. In: IEEE TDSC (2017)
59. Woo, M., Cha, S.K., Gottlieb, S., Brumley, D.: Scheduling black-box mutational fuzzing. In: ACM CCS (2013)
60. Zalewski, M.: American fuzzy lop (2016). https://github.com/mirrorer/afl. v2.52b Accessed July 2022

# Privacy-Preserving Verifiable CNNs

Nuttapong Attrapadung[1(✉)], Goichiro Hanaoaka[1], Ryo Hiromasa[2], Yoshihiro Koseki[2], Takahiro Matsuda[1], Yutaro Nishida[2], Yusuke Sakai[1], Jacob C. N. Schuldt[1], and Satoshi Yasuda[2]

[1] National Institute of Advanced Industrial Science and Technology, Tokyo, Japan
{n.attrapadung,hanaoka-goichiro,t-matsuda,yusuke.sakai, jacob.schuldt}@aist.go.jp

[2] Mitsubishi Electric, Kamakura, Japan
Hiromasa.Ryo@aj.MitsubishiElectric.co.jp,
Koseki.Yoshihiro@ak.MitsubishiElectric.co.jp,
Nishida.Yutaro@da.MitsubishiElectric.co.jp,
Yasuda.Satoshi@ea.MitsubishiElectric.co.jp

**Abstract.** Convolutional neural networks (CNNs) have emerged as one of the most successful deep learning approaches to image recognition and classification. A recent line of research, which includes zkCNN (ACM CCS '21), vCNN (Cryptology ePrint Archive), and ZEN (Cryptology ePrint Archive), aims at protecting the privacy of CNN models by developing publicly verifiable proofs of correct classification which do not leak any information about the underlying CNN models themselves. A shared feature of these schemes is that they require the entity constructing the proof to have access to both the model and the input in the clear. In other words, a client holding a potentially sensitive input is required to reveal this input to the entity holding the CNN model, thereby sacrificing his privacy, to be able to obtain a verifiable proof of correct classification. This is in contrast to the security guarantees provided by secure classification considered in privacy-preserving machine learning, which does not require the client to reveal his input to obtain a (non-verifiable) classification.

In this paper, we propose a privacy-preserving verifiable CNN scheme that overcomes this limitation of the previous schemes by allowing the client to obtain a classification proof without having to reveal his input. The obtained proof allows the client to selectively reveal properties of the obtained classification and his input, which will be verifiable to any third-party verifier. Our scheme is based on the recent notion of collaborative zk-SNARKs by Ozdemir and Boneh (USENIX '22). Specifically, we construct a new collaborative zk-SNARK based on Bulletproofs achieving an efficient maliciously secure proof generation protocol. Based on this, we then present an optimized approach to CNN evaluation. Finally, we demonstrate the feasibility of our approach by measuring the performance of our scheme on a CNN for classifying the MNIST dataset.


C. Pöpper and L. Batina (Eds.): ACNS 2024, LNCS 14584, pp. 373–402, 2024.
https://doi.org/10.1007/978-3-031-54773-7_15

# 1 Introduction

Deep learning has shown itself to be a tremendously useful tool in many application areas, and convolution neural networks (CNNs) in particular have emerged as one of the most successful deep learning techniques for tasks such as image recognition and classification. However, to provide accurate results, CNNs often require a large amount of training data. While this is unproblematic in application areas where training data is readily available, obtaining and correctly labeling sufficient training data in other areas is a challenging task made more difficult by issues related to data ownership. To further complicate matters, the training data, as well as the input data to be classified, might, in some applications, be sensitive, and data holders might be unable to share their data with any other party due to privacy concerns.

Privacy-preserving machine learning aims at addressing these issues by making deep learning techniques applicable to sensitive data which cannot be publicly shared. More specifically, a particular active line of research within this research area focuses on secure *classification* (e.g. see [5,7,9,10,19,24,26,29,36–38] to name just a few works). This allows a server, holding a CNN model $M$ and a client, holding an input $x$, to evaluate the CNN defined by $M$ on $x$, without the server having to disclose $M$ or the client having to reveal $x$ to the server. A different, but closely related line of research focuses on secure *learning* (e.g. see [11,31,32,41]), which enables a set of servers, each holding different datasets, to train a CNN based on the combined dataset, without each server having to reveal his individual dataset. Note that, due to how training is performed in a CNN, secure classification can easily be derived from secure training. While these works allow the entities jointly computing classification or training a CNN model to keep their inputs private, they do not provide *verifiability* i.e. the ability to verify that a given classification result was indeed obtained for input $x$ with respect to a given model $M$.

A recent set of works, specifically ZEN [17], vCNN [28] and zkCNN [30], address this by constructing zero-knowledge succinct non-interactive arguments (zk-SNARGs) for CNN classification. Specifically, these works allow a server holding a CNN model $M$ to commit to this, obtaining the commitment $\mathsf{com}_M$, and subsequently producing a proof $\pi$, that a given input $x$ will lead to a given classification result with respect to the model committed in $\mathsf{com}_M$. Furthermore, neither the input $x$ nor the classification result need to be given in the clear to a potential verifier, but can themselves be contained in commitments, thereby hiding $M$, $x$ and the classification result from the verifier. In other words, letting $y \leftarrow \mathsf{EvalCNN}(M, x)$ denote that the classification result $y$ is obtained by evaluating the CNN model $M$ on input $x$, the proof $\pi$ is informally a zk-SNARG for the language

$$\begin{aligned}\{(\mathsf{com}_M, \mathsf{com}_x, \mathsf{com}_y) \mid \exists M, r_M, x, r_x, y, r_y \text{ s.t.} \\ \mathsf{com}_M = \mathsf{Commit}(M, r_M) \wedge \mathsf{com}_x = \mathsf{Commit}(x, r_x) \wedge \\ \mathsf{com}_y = \mathsf{Commit}(y, r_y) \wedge y = \mathsf{EvalCNN}(M, x)\}\end{aligned}$$

where $\mathsf{Commit}$ denotes the commitment algorithm of a commitment scheme. A potential verifier will of course not gain much information from verifying $\pi$ alone, but a client holding $y$ and $r_y$ can choose to either directly provide $(y, r_y)$ or prove additional properties about $y$ contained in $\mathsf{com}_y$ in a separate proof, thereby choosing what information about $y$ is disclosed while maintaining verifiability of the correctness of the classification result $y$. Overall, this provides a privacy-preserving way for a client to convince a verifier about the correct classification of his input $x$ as well as selective information about $y$ and $x$. To illustrate the usefulness of this type of primitive, [28] highlights the example of using deep learning to diagnose diseases. In this case, a central hospital or medical company will hold the model $M$ and publish $\mathsf{com}_M$, and a patient will obtain input $x$ via some form of examination. Obtaining a diagnosis, i.e. the classification result of $x$ based on $M$, and proof of the above type will allow the patient to show to a third-party e.g. an insurance company, that his diagnosis satisfies the condition of a specific insurance policy, while keeping the exact examination results and corresponding diagnose private.

However, in contrast to secure classification and secure learning, a shared feature of ZEN, vCNN and zkCNN is that the proof generation requires the input $x$ to be available to the entity holding the model. As a consequence, this entity learns both $x$ and the corresponding classification result. In other words, in the example above, the patient will have to sacrifice his privacy with respect to the central hospital or medical company holding $M$, to be able to obtain a privacy-preserving proof verifiable to a third party.

**Our Contribution.** In this paper, we address the above highlighted privacy issue regarding the input $x$ and the obtained classification result.

Specifically, our contribution consists of the following:

- Firstly, we propose a new privacy-preserving notion of a verifiable CNN that allows the model $M$, the input $x$ and the classification result to be kept private.
- Secondly, as a stepping stone towards achieving this notion, we construct a new collaborative zk-SNARK based on Bulletproofs [6].
- Finally, based on our collaborative zk-SNARK, we present a new construction of a verifiable CNN that satisfies our stronger privacy-preserving notion and provide a performance evaluation of this.

In the following, we will provide further details on each of the above items.

**New Privacy-Preserving Notion for Verifiable CNNs.** Our new privacy-preserving notion for verifiable CNNs requires that the model $M$, the input $x$ and the resulting classification are kept private while still ensuring that a publicly verifiable proof of correct classification is obtained. Additionally, our new notion enables the entity holding $x$ to selectively reveal properties of the classification result. The definition of our verifiable CNN notion resembles the notion of a publicly auditable multi-party computation (PA-MPC) introduced by Baum *et al.* [2], and concretely extends the PA-MPC definition by Ozdemir-Boneh [34] to cover randomized functionalities as well as the specialized properties required for our application purpose. More precisely, our definition requires a verifiable CNN to satisfy two main properties. Firstly, a verifiable CNN must implement an interactive proof generation protocol that satisfies the standard notion of maliciously secure MPC, thereby informally guaranteeing that the protocol leaks no information regarding the parties' input besides what can be computed from the protocol output. Here, the output for the party holding the model is defined to be a commitment $\mathsf{com}_y$ to the classification result $y$, whereas the output for the party holding the input is defined to consist of $\mathsf{com}_y$, $y$ and the opening of $\mathsf{com}_y$. Secondly, the proof generation must satisfy the notion of a collaborative zk-SNARK [35]. Note that the witness of the proof, the model and the input, are essentially shared between the parties, and in this setting, a plain zk-SNARK is insufficient since a malicious entity might be able to influence the proof generation in such a way that he can derive information about the other entity's part of the witness from the proof. The above two notions combined ensure that no information leaks regarding the model, the input or the obtained classification result.[1]

**A New zk-SNARK Based on Bulletproofs.** The main tool we use to obtain our concrete construction of a verifiable CNN is a new collaborative zk-SNARK based on Bulletproofs [6] i.e. we construct a new maliciously-secure protocol for the joint generation of Bulletproofs from shared witnesses. As Bulletproofs involve various group operations and in particular commitments, a naive implementation of this would be highly inefficient. However, we observe that a careful setup of the groups over which the computation is performed combined with a corresponding efficient realization of a commitment functionality, will allow efficient joint computation of Bulletproofs. We break up our construction into three relatively simple steps: firstly, we define a new extended arithmetic blackbox (ABB) functionality which provides a setup and commitment functionality tailored to the requirements of Bulletproofs (Sect. 3.1); we then provide an efficient protocol for the joint computation of Bulletproofs based on this (Sect. 3.2); and finally, we show how the extended ABB can be securely realized through an extension of SPDZ [15,40] (Sect. 3.3). We note that as discussed in [35], collaborative zk-SNARK has a number of practical applications, such as healthcare statistics, calculation of credit scores, and audits of financial systems, to name a few, and our Bulletproof-based zk-SNARK provides a new zk-SNARK with a different set of tradeoffs that can be used in these applications

**A New Privacy-Preserving Verifiable CNN.** Based on our new Bulletproof-based collaborative zk-SNARK, we build a new efficient verifiable CNN with succint proofs. The main advantage compared to the existing schemes such as ZEN, vCNN and zkCNN is that our scheme satisfies our new notion of a privacy-preserving verifiable CNN and thereby provides the stronger privacy-preserving properties guaranteed by this. (As highlighted above, the structure of ZEN, vCNN and zkCNN requires the input $x$ to be revealed in the clear to the entity

[1] Here, the model denotes the *parameters* used in the CNN, and like ZEN, vCNN and zkCNN, the *structure* of the CNN (i.e. the number and different types of CNN layers used) is assumed to be public knowledge.

| | Input privacy | Model privacy | Transparent setup | Malicious security | Setting | Optimized for CNNs |
|---|---|---|---|---|---|---|
| CNN-specific schemes | | | | | | |
| zkCNN [30] | ○[1] | ●[1] | ● | N/A[2] | Standalone | ● |
| vCNN [28] | ○[1] | ●[1] | ○ | N/A[2] | Standalone | ● |
| ZEN [17] | ○[1] | ●[1] | ○ | N/A[2] | Standalone | ● |
| pvCNN [42] | ◐[3] | ◐[3] | ○ | N/A[3] | Third-party[3] | ● |
| Ours | ● | ● | ● | ● | Collaborative | ● |
| General-purpose schemes | | | | | | |
| OB22 [35] | ● | ● | ○[4] | ● | Collaborative | ○ |
| DPPSV22 [16] | ● | ● | ● | ○ | Collaborative | ○ |

●: The property is satisfied. ○: The property is not satisfied. ◐: The property is not fully satisfied.

[1] These protocols are standalone algorithms for generating an NIZK proof of CNN classification, and requires plaintext access to model and input. When used as suggested in [30, 28, 17], this leads to model privacy but no input privacy.

[2] These protocols do not use an interactive protocol to generate a proof.

[3] This protocol requires a semi-trusted third-party, see the explanation in Section 1.1.

[4] Ozdemir-Boneh's construction can be instantiated with various zk-SNARKs and the authors highlight that an instantiation based on Fractal [13] enables a transparent setup. However, the authors do not implement an instantiation based on Fractal due to the complexity of this and we thus regard the Ozdemir-Boneh construction not to have transparent setup.

**Fig. 1.** Comparison among verifiable CNN schemes and collaborative zero-knowledge schemes.

holding the model $M$, and hence by design, these schemes cannot provide similar privacy guarantees.) Besides the strong privacy-preserving properties, our construction inherits the transparency property of Bulletproofs i.e. a common reference string (CRS) generated by a trusted party is not required. By maintaining this property of the original Bulletproofs, we ensure that the verifier need not trust any third party to provide an honestly generated CRS. In contrast, we note that both ZEN and vCNN rely on the zk-SNARK by Groth [21], which requires a trusted CRS. Finally, we provide an experimental evaluation of our verifiable CNN construction based on classifying the MNIST dataset.

## 1.1 Related Works

There are several recent works that consider verifiability (in a zero-knowledge manner) of CNN classification, such as vCNN [28], zkCNN [30], and ZEN [17]. Additionally, Kang et al. [22] proposed, among other things, an approach to efficiently generate a zk-SNARK for CNN classification and a protocol for verifying accuracy of a CNN model based on this. However, these works do not achieve the privacy guarantees we are considering in this paper i.e. that model $M$ and the input $x$ are kept private by the entities holding these, and the classification result is only learned by the entity holding $x$. Note that achieving this requires a different structure of the underlying proof generation algorithms which must allow a "joint generation" of a publicly verifiable proof.

The recently proposed pvCNN [42] for privacy-preserving CNN testing is defined in a different setting to the above related works and ours. Specifically, an additionally semi-trusted third party is introduced to perform a (latter) part of the classification computation in *plaintext*. Due to this, some information about the input and CNN model is leaked. In constrast, we aim to not rely on such an external party in this work.

Ozdemir and Boneh [35] introduced the notion of collaborative zk-SNARK which we use in this paper. This is a zk-SNARK system in which the prover's algorithm is distributed among multiple provers who each hold a "witness share" which constitute a valid witness when combined. They also constructed collaborative zk-SNARK protocols from the plain zk-SNARK systems [12,13,18,21], using MPC. We point out that none of these zk-SNARKs, except for Fractal [13], support a transparent setup (i.e. the CRS must be generated by a trusted party). Furthermore, an instantiation using Fractal is not implemented by the authors, as this was deemed too computationally heavy. In contrast, our collaborative zk-SNARK is derived from Bulletproofs [6] and inherits the transparency property from these. Furthermore, [35] also gave an alternative definition of publicly-auditable multi-party computation (PA-MPC) [2] on which our definition of privacy-preserving verifiable CNN is based. See Sect. 4.1 for the details.

Dayama et al. [16] introduced the notion of distributed-prover zero-knowledge protocols, which is a special kind of interactive zero-knowledge protocols in which multiple provers each holding a witness share try to convince the verifier of the validity of an NP statement. Thus, when restricted to the case in which the provers alone can generate a proof verifiable in public non-interactive manner, it is essentially the same notion as collaborative zk-SNARK. They then constructed distributed-prover versions of recent interactive oracle proofs [1,3,6,39] (which can be transformed to zk-SNARKs via the Fiat-Shamir paradigm). In particular, they instantiated a distributed-prover version of Bulletproof [6]. We remark that their constructions assume that there is a special entity among the provers called an aggregator that is assumed to behave semi-honestly, which does not have a counterpart in the collaborative zk-SNARK of [35]. This prevents the constructions from meaningfully achieving malicious security, which we consider in this paper.

Figure 1 shows a comparison between the above mentioned works and ours.

## 2 Preliminaries

**Basic Notation.** For a natural number $n$, we define $[n] := \{1, \ldots, n\}$. For a discrete finite set $S$, $x \leftarrow S$ denotes sampling an element $x$ uniformly at random from $S$.

For a vector $\boldsymbol{a} = (a_1, \ldots, a_n) \in \mathbb{Z}_p^n$ and $1 \leq \ell \leq n$, we use the notations $\boldsymbol{a}_{\leq \ell} = (a_1, \ldots, a_\ell)$ and $\boldsymbol{a}_{\ell+1 \leq} = (a_{\ell+1}, \ldots, a_n)$. For vectors $\boldsymbol{a} = (a_1, \ldots, a_n) \in \mathbb{Z}_p^n$ and $\boldsymbol{b} = (b_1, \ldots, b_n) \in \mathbb{Z}_p^n$, we denote by $\langle \boldsymbol{a}, \boldsymbol{b} \rangle$ the inner product $a_1 b_1 + \cdots + a_n b_n$. We also use the notation of a "vector polynomial" $p(X) = \boldsymbol{p}_0 + \boldsymbol{p}_1 X + \cdots + \boldsymbol{p}_d X^d$ and its inner product $\langle l(X), r(X) \rangle = \sum_{i=0}^{d} \sum_{j=0}^{d'} \langle \boldsymbol{l}_i, \boldsymbol{r}_j \rangle X^{i+j}$ where $l(X) = \boldsymbol{l}_0 + \boldsymbol{l}_1 X + \cdots + \boldsymbol{l}_d X^d$ and $r(X) = \boldsymbol{r}_0 + \boldsymbol{r}_1 X + \cdots + \boldsymbol{r}_{d'} X^{d'}$.

In this paper, $N$ will always denote the number of parties participating in a multi-party computation protocol, and $\lambda$ (given in unary) will always denote the security parameter. PPT stands for *probabilistic polynomial-time*. An efficient algorithm is PPT.

**Convolutional Neural Networks.** In this paper, we consider feedforward convolutional neural networks (CNNs). These networks consist of several *layers*, which each processes the output of the previous layer and forwards the result as input to the next layer. The first layer is the *input* layer, whereas the last layer is the *output* layer, the latter typically assigning a confidence score to each class in a set of classes into which the input is supposed to be classified. While most CNNs can be described using a small set of layer types, the number of layers, the ordering of these, and their exact configuration depend on the specific CNN. In the following, we will outline the abstraction of CNNs we rely on in our definitions related to privacy-preserving verifiable CNNs, and the types of layers we consider the CNNs to consist of.

*CNN Abstraction.* To capture different CNN structures, we will use a generic CNN evaluation algorithm, denoted $\mathsf{EvalCNN}$, with the following syntax:

$$y \leftarrow \mathsf{EvalCNN}(\mathcal{S}, M, x).$$

Here, $\mathcal{S}$ is a representation of the *structure* of the CNN i.e. the used layer types, their ordering and interconnections. $M$ denotes the *model* and consists of the parameters determined by the training of the CNN, and $x$ denotes the input which is to be classified. Finally, $y$ denotes the obtained classification of $x$. The algorithm $\mathsf{EvalCNN}$ is assumed to iteratively evaluate each layer specified in $\mathcal{S}$, applying the corresponding parameters from $M$, and using the obtained result as input for the next layer, until the output layer is reached. The output layer typically defines several classes, and we let the final classification $y$ denote the class with the highest score. In the following description of the layer types we consider, we will highlight what parameters are considered to be part of the model $M$. Note that we will consider the structure $\mathcal{S}$ of the CNN being evaluated to be publicly available.

*Layers.* In this paper, we will consider the following layers.

**Convolution Layer.** A convolution layer divides input variables into mutually overlapped small local regions and computes the inner product of each square and weights (a *filter* or a *kernel*). These inner products consist of the output of the layer. Here, weights are a part of the model $M$.

**Pooling Layer.** Similarly to a convolution layer, a pooling layer divides input variables into mutually overlapped small local regions. For each region, the values are replaced with another value computed from the values in the region. Different subtypes of pooling layers use different replacements. A *max pooling* layer is a typical pooling layer, in which a region is replaced with the maximum of the values in the region. There is no model parameter in pooling layers.

**Activation Function.** An activation function is a non-linear function which is directly applied to each value in the output of a previous layer. A typical activation function is the rectified linear unit (ReLU) function, which maps a negative value to zero and a zero or positive value to the same value.

**Fully Connected Layer.** A fully connected layer, given a set of input values, outputs a set of different values, each of which is the inner product of all the input values and fixed weights. Different outputs use different sets of weights. These sets of weights are a part of $M$.

**SoftMax Function.** The SoftMax function is the typical final layer. This layer is given as input a set of input values which constitutes the confidences of the classifications in that $i$-th value is the confidence for the classification to the $i$-th class. Then this layer normalizes by mapping each confidence to the value between 0 and 1 so that the sum of all values is 1. There is no model parameter in the SoftMax function.

We also note that we can extend our construction to support other types of layers. See further details for Sect. 4.2.

**Secure Multi-party Computation.** We will make use of the standard notion of secure multi-party computation (MPC). Particularly, our main constructions will consider security with abort in the dishonest majority and static corruption setting.

Let $\mathcal{F}$ be a (possibly probabilistic) $N$-input, $N$-output function. An $N$-party computation for $f$ is a protocol among $N$ parties $P_1, \ldots, P_N$ such that each party $P_i$, which takes $x_i$ as input, receives $y_i$ as the result of an execution of the protocol, where $(y_1, \ldots, y_N) \leftarrow \mathcal{F}(x_1, \ldots, x_N)$. (A function computed by a multi-party protocol is often called a *functionality.*)

For security definitions of a multi-party computation protocol, we use the standard definition of security based on the real/ideal paradigm [8,20]. We will consider *security with abort* as a default notion, where a malicious party may obtain the final result while making the protocol abort and preventing honest parties from obtaining the final results. We note that this security notion is sufficient for our purpose. Also, we will consider the *dishonest majority* and *static corruption* setting. The former means that the number $t$ of corrupted parties can be up to $N-1$, and the latter means that the adversary decides the set of corrupted parties before the execution of the protocol. We will also consider semi-honest security, where corrupted parties do not deviate from the protocol specification.

**Definition 1.** *Let $\mathcal{F} : \prod_{i \in [N]} \mathcal{X}_i \rightarrow \prod_{i \in [N]} \mathcal{Y}_i$ be a (possibly probabilistic) efficiently computable function. We say that an $N$-party protocol $\Pi$ for $f$ is* secure with abort *(in the dishonest majority, static corruption setting) if for any PPT adversary $\mathcal{A}$, there exists a PPT ideal-world adversary (also called a simulator) $\mathcal{S}$ such that for any input $\boldsymbol{x} = (x_1, \ldots, x_N) \in \prod_{i \in [N]} \mathcal{X}_i$ and auxiliary-input string $z \in \{0,1\}^*$, the two random variables $\mathsf{real}_{\mathcal{A}}^{\Pi}(\boldsymbol{x}, z)$ and $\mathsf{ideal}_{\mathcal{S}}^{f}(\boldsymbol{x}, z)$ are computationally indistinguishable, where these random variables are defined as follows:*

- *Real execution $\mathsf{real}_{\mathcal{A}}^{\Pi}(\boldsymbol{x}, z)$, generated from an interaction among the set of parties $P_1, \ldots, P_N$ and the adversary $\mathcal{A}$: Given $z$ as input, an adversary $\mathcal{A}$ specifies the set of indices $\mathcal{C} \subset [N]$ of corrupted parties such that $|\mathcal{C}| \leq N-1$, and receives the inputs $\{x_i\}_{i \in \mathcal{C}}$. Then, the protocol $\Pi$ is executed, where during the protocol execution, the behavior of the corrupted parties $P_i$ with $i \in \mathcal{C}$ is determined by $\mathcal{A}$. After the execution, $\mathcal{A}$ outputs an arbitrary string as its final output. $\mathsf{real}_{\mathcal{A}}^{\Pi}(\boldsymbol{x})$ consists of the outputs of all the honest (i.e. uncorrupted) parties concatenated with $\mathcal{A}$'s final output.*
- *Ideal execution $\mathsf{ideal}_{\mathcal{S}}^{\mathcal{F}}(\boldsymbol{x}, z)$, generated from an interaction between the trusted party (for computing $\mathcal{F}$) and the ideal-world adversary $\mathcal{S}$: Given $z$ as*

*input, an ideal-world adversary $\mathcal{S}$ specifies the set of indices $\mathcal{C} \subset [N]$ of corrupted parties such that $|\mathcal{C}| \leq N-1$. At this point, $\mathcal{S}$ may ask the trusted party to abort, in which case, the honest parties' output is forced to be the* abort *symbol. Then, $\mathcal{S}$ give an arbitrary value $x'_i$ (not necessarily $x_i$) for all corrupted indices $i \in \mathcal{C}$. Also, $x'_i = x_i$ is passed to the trusted party for all non-corrupted parties. Then, the trusted party computes $(y_1, \ldots, y_N) \leftarrow \mathcal{F}(x'_1, \ldots, x'_N)$, and gives $(y_i)_{i \in \mathcal{C}}$ to $\mathcal{S}$. For each uncorrupted party index $i \in [N] \setminus \mathcal{C}$, $\mathcal{S}$ decides whether the party $i$ aborts or not. In the former case, $y_i$ is replaced with the* abort *symbol, while $y_i$ is untouched in the latter case. Finally, $\mathcal{S}$ outputs an arbitrary string as its final output.* $\mathsf{ideal}^{\mathcal{F}}_{\mathcal{S}}(\boldsymbol{x}, z)$ *consists of $(y_i)_{i \in [N] \setminus \mathcal{C}}$ concatenated with $\mathcal{S}$'s final output.*

*Furthermore, we say that $\Pi$ is* secure against semi-honest parties *if the above indistinguishability is guaranteed only when the corrupted parties controlled by an adversary $\mathcal{A}$ always follow the protocol specification.*

*Hybrid Model.* We will show the security of our protocols in a hybrid model, where the parties execute a protocol with real messages and also have access to a trusted party computing a subfunctionality for them. The modular sequential composition theorem of [8] states that one can replace the trusted party computing the subfunctionality with a real secure protocol computing the subfunctionality. (This works both security with abort and security against semi-honest parties.) When the subfunctionality is $\mathcal{G}$, we say that the protocol works in the $\mathcal{G}$-hybrid model.

**Privacy-Preserving CNNs.** To be able to define privacy-preserving verifiable CNNs in Sect. 4, we need to first specify what it means for a 2-party protocol to compute a CNN classification in a privacy-preserving manner (without considering verifiability). We define it as a secure 2-party protocol realizing the functionality described in Fig. 2. Note that the functionality is associated with some commitment scheme whose definition is given below.

*Commitments.* A commitment scheme consists of two algorithms $\mathsf{Setup}_{\mathsf{Com}}$ and $\mathsf{Commit}$: $\mathsf{Setup}_{\mathsf{Com}}$ is the setup algorithm that takes a security parameter $1^\lambda$ as input, and outputs a public parameter $\mathsf{pp}$; $\mathsf{Commit}$ is the commitment generation algorithm that takes $\mathsf{pp}$, a message $m$, and a randomness $r$ as input, and outputs a commitmemt $\mathsf{com}$. As usual, we require *hiding* and *binding* for a commitment scheme. The hiding property states that $\mathsf{Commit}(\mathsf{pp}, m_0, r)$ and $\mathsf{Commit}(\mathsf{pp}, m_1, r)$ are indistinguishable for any two messages $m_0$ and $m_1$, where $\mathsf{pp}$ is generated by $\mathsf{Setup}_{\mathsf{Com}}$ and $r$ is chosen uniformly at random; The binding property states that given $\mathsf{pp}$ generated by $\mathsf{Setup}_{\mathsf{Com}}$, it is hard to find a pair $(m_0, r_0)$ and $(m_1, r_1)$ such that $\mathsf{Commit}(\mathsf{pp}, m_0, r_0) = \mathsf{Commit}(\mathsf{pp}, m_1, r_1)$ and $m_0 \neq m_1$.

*Pedersen Commitment.* Our proposed protocol will make use of the Pedersen commitment: Its public parameter consists of two group elements $g, h \in \mathbb{G}$ of prime order $p$. Given a message $m \in \mathbb{Z}_p$ to be committed, choose a randomness $r \in \mathbb{Z}_p$ uniformly at random, and the commitment $\mathsf{com}$ is $\mathsf{com} = g^m \cdot h^r$. It is

$\mathcal{F}^{pCNN}_{\mathsf{Com}}$

This is a 2-party functionality (invoked by $P_1$ and $P_2$) associated with a commitment scheme $\mathsf{Com} = (\mathsf{Setup}_{\mathsf{Com}}, \mathsf{Commit})$. The functionality expects three types of inputs:

- $P_1$'s private inputs, comprising a CNN model $M$ and a randomness $r_M$.
- $P_2$'s private inputs, comprising a CNN input $x$ and a randomness $r_x$.
- public common inputs, consisting of the CNN structure $\mathcal{S}$, a public parameter $\mathsf{pp}$ of the underlying commitment scheme $\mathsf{Com}$, and commitments $\mathsf{com}_M$ and $\mathsf{com}_x$ (which are supposedly generated as $\mathsf{com}_M = \mathsf{Commit}(\mathsf{pp}, M, r_M)$ and $\mathsf{com}_x = \mathsf{Commit}(\mathsf{pp}, x, r_x)$, respectively).

Given the inputs, the functionality performs the following procedure:

1. Compute $y \leftarrow \mathsf{EvalCNN}(\mathcal{S}, M, x)$.
2. Pick $r_y$ randomly, and compute $\mathsf{com}_y \leftarrow \mathsf{Commit}(\mathsf{pp}, y, r_y)$.
3. Output $\mathsf{com}_y$ for $P_1$, and $(y, r_y, \mathsf{com}_y)$ for $P_2$.

**Fig. 2.** Privacy-preserving CNN functionality.

well-known that the Pedersen commitment scheme is perfectly hiding, and computationally binding under the assumption that the discrete logarithm problem is hard in $\mathbb{G}$.

**Collaborative zk-SNARKs.** Here, we recall the definition of a collaborative zk-SNARK formalized by Ozdemir and Boneh [35]. (A large part of this paragraph is taken verbatim from [35].) Let $\mathcal{R} \subseteq \{0,1\} \times \{0,1\}^*$ be a binary relation. A collaborative zk-SNARK for $\mathcal{R}$ consists of $(\mathsf{Setup}, \Pi, \mathsf{Verify})$ each of whose syntax is defined as follows:

- $\mathsf{Setup}$ is the setup algorithm that takes a security parameter $1^\lambda$ as input, and outputs a public parameter $\mathsf{pp}$.
- $\Pi$ is the proof generation protocol, executed among $N$ parties (provers) $P_1, \ldots, P_N$, where the parties have a public parameter $\mathsf{pp}$ and a statement $x$ as public input, and each party $P_i$ has a witness share[2] $w_i$ as private (local) input; As the result of the protocol, the parties output a proof $\pi$. For notational convenience, we denote an execution of the protocol (by honest parties) by $\pi \leftarrow \Pi(\mathsf{pp}, x, \boldsymbol{w})$, where $\boldsymbol{w} = (w_1, \ldots, w_N)$.
- $\mathsf{Verify}$ is the verification algorithm that takes $\mathsf{pp}$, a statement $x$, and a proof $\pi$ as input, and outputs either $\top$ (accept) or $\perp$ (reject).

Note that the verification is non-interactive, and anyone given a statement and a proof can verify the validity of the statement.

A collaborative zk-SNARK in the random oracle model, where each of the algorithms has access to a random oracle $H : X_\lambda \rightarrow Y_\lambda$, is denoted by $(\mathsf{Setup}^H, \Pi^H, \mathsf{Verify}^H)$.

[2] Here, a witness share need not be a share of a secret sharing of a witness.

**Definition 2.** *We require a collaborative zk-SNARK for $\mathcal{R}$ in the random oracle model (where $H$ is modeled as a random oracle),* $(\mathsf{Setup}^H, \Pi^H, \mathsf{Verify}^H)$*, to satisfy the following properties. Below, let $\mathcal{U}(\lambda)$ be the set of all functions from $X_\lambda$ to $Y_\lambda$.*

- Completeness: *For all $(x, \boldsymbol{w}) \in \mathcal{R}$, the following probability is negligible in $\lambda$:*

$$\Pr\left[\begin{array}{l} H \leftarrow \mathcal{U}(\lambda); \\ \mathsf{pp} \leftarrow \mathsf{Setup}^H(1^\lambda); \\ \pi \leftarrow \Pi^H(\mathsf{pp}, x, \boldsymbol{w}) \end{array} : \mathsf{Verify}^H(\mathsf{pp}, x, \pi) = \bot\right].$$

- Knowledge soundness: *For all $x$, for all sets of PPT algorithms $\boldsymbol{P} = (P_1^*, \ldots, P_N^*)$, there exists a PPT extractor* $\mathsf{Ext}$ *and a negligible function $\epsilon$ such that*

$$\Pr\left[\begin{array}{l} H \leftarrow \mathcal{U}(\lambda); \\ \mathsf{pp} \leftarrow \mathsf{Setup}(1^\lambda); \\ \boldsymbol{w} \leftarrow \mathsf{Ext}^{H, \boldsymbol{P}^H}(\mathsf{pp}, x) \end{array} : (x, \boldsymbol{w}) \in \mathcal{R}\right] \geq$$
$$\Pr\left[\begin{array}{l} H \leftarrow \mathcal{U}(\lambda); \\ \mathsf{pp} \leftarrow \mathsf{Setup}(1^\lambda); \\ \pi \leftarrow \boldsymbol{P}^H(\mathsf{pp}, x) \end{array} : \mathsf{Verify}^H(\mathsf{pp}, x, \pi) = \top\right] - \epsilon(\lambda).$$

*Here,* $\mathsf{Ext}^{H, \boldsymbol{P}^H}$ *denotes that* $\mathsf{Ext}$ *has oracle access to $H$ and may re-run the collection of provers $\boldsymbol{P}(\mathsf{pp}, x)$, reprogramming the random oracle $H$ each time, and receiving only the final output produced by $\boldsymbol{P}$.*
- Succinctness: *Proof size and verification time are $o(|\mathcal{R}|)$, where $|\mathcal{R}|$ denotes the size of the description.*
- t-zero-knowledge: *For any PPT adversary $\mathcal{A}$ controlling $k \leq t$ provers: $P_{i_1}, \ldots, P_{i_k}$, there exists a PPT simulator $\mathcal{S}$ such that for all $x$, $\boldsymbol{w}$, and for all PPT distinguishers $\mathcal{D}$,*

$$\left| \Pr\left[\begin{array}{l} H \leftarrow \mathcal{U}(\lambda); \\ \mathsf{pp} \leftarrow \mathsf{Setup}^H(1^\lambda); \\ b \leftarrow \mathcal{R}(x, \boldsymbol{w}); \\ (\mathsf{tr}, \mu) \leftarrow \mathcal{S}^H(\mathsf{pp}, x, w_{i_1}, \ldots, w_{i_k}, b) \end{array} : \mathcal{D}^{H[\mu]}(\mathsf{tr}) = 1\right] \right.$$
$$\left. - \Pr\left[\begin{array}{l} H \leftarrow \mathcal{U}(\lambda); \\ \mathsf{pp} \leftarrow \mathsf{Setup}^H(1^\lambda); \\ \mathsf{tr} \leftarrow \mathsf{View}_{\mathcal{A}}^H(x, \boldsymbol{w}) \end{array} : \mathcal{D}^H(\mathsf{tr}) = 1\right] \right|$$

*is negligible in $\lambda$, where* $\mathsf{tr}$ *denotes a transcript,* $\mathsf{View}_{\mathcal{A}}^H(x, \boldsymbol{w})$ *denotes the view of $\mathcal{A}$ when provers $P_1, \ldots, P_N$ interact with input $x$ and witness $\boldsymbol{w}$ (the honest provers follow $\Pi$, but dishonest ones may not), $\mu$ denotes a partial function from the domain of $H$, and $H[\mu]$ denotes a re-programmed random oracle (by $\mathcal{S}$) that maps $x$ to $\mu(x)$ if $x$ is defined in $\mu$ and $H(x)$ otherwise.*

*If the above indistinguishability is guaranteed to hold only when the corrupted provers follow the protocol specification, we say that a collaborative zk-SNARK is* $t$-zero-knowledge in the presence of semi-honest provers.[3]

## 3 Collaborative Bulletproofs

In this section, we will present our new collaborative zk-SNARK based on Bulletproofs. This will be a crucial tool in our construction of a privacy-preserving verifiable CNN presented in Sect. 4.

Bulletproofs support zero-knowledge arguments for arbitrary arithmetic circuits, which is achieved via a proof for a Hadamard-product relation. More specifically, all 'left' and 'right' inputs to multiplication gates are represented as vectors $\boldsymbol{a}_{\mathrm{L}}$ and $\boldsymbol{a}_{\mathrm{R}}$, respectively, and the output as $\boldsymbol{a}_{\mathrm{O}} = \boldsymbol{a}_{\mathrm{L}} \circ \boldsymbol{a}_{\mathrm{R}}$, where $\circ$ denotes the Hadamard product. By adding additional $Q \leq 2 \cdot n$ constraints (expressed via matrices $\boldsymbol{W}_{\mathrm{L}}, \boldsymbol{W}_{\mathrm{R}}, \boldsymbol{W}_{\mathrm{O}}$), where $n$ is the number of multiplication gates, any arithmetic circuits can be captured (see [4]). Bulletproofs additionally include commitments $V_j$ (and commitment weights $\boldsymbol{W}_{\mathrm{V}}$) as part of the statement. Concretely, for the Bulletproof relation $\mathcal{R}$, a statement $x$ is of the form:

$$\boldsymbol{V} \in \mathbb{G}^m, \boldsymbol{W}_{\mathrm{L}}, \boldsymbol{W}_{\mathrm{R}}, \boldsymbol{W}_{\mathrm{O}} \in \mathbb{Z}_p^{Q \times n}, \boldsymbol{W}_{\mathrm{V}} \in \mathbb{Z}_p^{Q \times m}, \boldsymbol{c} \in \mathbb{Z}_p^{Q}, \tag{1}$$

and a witness $w$ is of the form:

$$\boldsymbol{a}_{\mathrm{L}}, \boldsymbol{a}_{\mathrm{R}}, \boldsymbol{a}_{\mathrm{O}} \in \mathbb{Z}_p^{n}, v_1, \ldots, v_m, \gamma_1, \ldots, \gamma_m \in \mathbb{Z}_p^{m}. \tag{2}$$

Then, $(x, w) \in \mathcal{R}$ if and only if

$$\begin{cases} V_j = g^{v_j} h^{\gamma_j} & (j \in [m]) \\ \boldsymbol{a}_{\mathrm{L}} \circ \boldsymbol{a}_{\mathrm{R}} = \boldsymbol{a}_{\mathrm{O}} & \\ \boldsymbol{W}_{\mathrm{L}} \cdot \boldsymbol{a}_{\mathrm{L}} + \boldsymbol{W}_{\mathrm{R}} \cdot \boldsymbol{a}_{\mathrm{R}} + \boldsymbol{W}_{\mathrm{O}} \cdot \boldsymbol{a}_{\mathrm{O}} = \boldsymbol{W}_{\mathrm{V}} \cdot \boldsymbol{v} + \boldsymbol{c} & \end{cases}, \tag{3}$$

where $\boldsymbol{v} = (v_1, \ldots, v_m)$. Like Bulletproofs, our collaborative zk-SNARK will be for this relation, and we will refer to $x$ (resp. $w$) of the above form as a Bulletproof statement (resp. witness).

We approach our construction gradually, firstly introducing the extended arithmetic black-box abstraction we build our MPC protocol upon in Sect. 3.1, and then the actual protocol construction in Sect. 3.2. Finally, and in Sect. 3.3 we show how the constructed protocol can be realized efficiently for both semi-honest and malicious security, thereby obtaining our collaborative zk-SNARK.

[3] Note that $t$-zero-knowledge in the presence of semi-honest provers still provides the ordinary zero-knowledge property of a (single-prover) zk-SNARK against a malicious verifier (that does not participate in the proof generation protocol).

### 3.1 Extended Arithmetic Black-Box

The arithmetic black-box abstraction (ABB) [14] is a commonly used approach for constructing MPC protocols. It abstracts away the details of tools (e.g. secret-sharing, homomorphic commitments and encryption) and corresponding protocols, and allows us to perform field arithmetic in an ideal "black-box" without explicitly knowing the values of the operands. In this paper, we will only treat an ABB functionality whose underlying field is a prime field, and denote its characteristic by $p$, and for an element $a \in \mathbb{Z}_p$, we use the notation "$[a]$" to mean that $a$ is stored in the black box maintained in the functionality.

As opposed to relying on a standard ABB implementing the most common arithmetic operations, we will define an extended ABB providing additional functionality tailored to the specific computation required in the construction of Bulletproofs. This will in turn simplify and make efficient the ABB-based construction of the protocol for the joint computation of Bulletproofs presented in Sect. 3.2. Specifically, we consider an ABB functionality which is parameterized by a base cyclic group $\mathbb{G}$ of (prime) order $p$.[4] Besides the standard arithmetic operations on stored values, we will allow the computation of multi-exponentiations with respect to a (public) vector of group elements $\boldsymbol{g} = (g_1, \ldots, g_\ell)$ for some $\ell$ i.e. for values $[a_1], \ldots, [a_\ell]$ stored in the ABB, the entities interacting with the ABB will be able to obtain the group element $g_1^{a_1} \cdots g_\ell^{a_\ell} \in \mathbb{G}$. In other words, the extended ABB implements a restricted form of computation over the group elements $\boldsymbol{g}$. This restricted functionality allows the computation of Pedersen-style commitments, which play a crucial role in Bulletproofs. Note that while it would be possible to use generic MPC protocols for exponentiation on top of a standard ABB to achieve a similar functionality, the crucial insight here is that the restricted functionality discussed above can be instantiated very efficiently; see Sect. 3.3 for how we achieve this. Additionally, we require several basic non-linear operations such as equality, max, argmax, and bit-decomposition to be provided by the ABB. These functionalities will be used in our verifiable CNN construction presented in Sect. 4.

The full extended ABB functionality is defined in Fig. 3. To ease the notation, we will for values $[x]$ and $[y]$ stored by the ABB and $a \in \mathbb{Z}_p$ use the notation $[x] + [y]$, $a \cdot [x]$, and $[x] \cdot [y]$ to denote the operations $\mathsf{Add}([x], [y])$, $\mathsf{SMult}(a, [x])$, and $\mathsf{Mult}([x], [y])$, respectively. Furthermore, we will omit the operation "$\cdot$" if it is clear from the context.

### 3.2 Our Construction

We will now present our construction of a collaborative zk-SNARK ($\mathsf{Setup}, \Pi$, $\mathsf{Verify}$) based on Bulletproofs.

Note that in the prover algorithm of Bulletproofs, multi-exponentiation is central and is used for computing the Pedersen-style commitments Bulletproofs

[4] Note that the order $p$ of $\mathbb{G}$ is identical to the characteristic of the field $\mathbb{Z}_p$ which the values in the ABB are elements of. We require $p$ to be of $2\lambda$ bits so that the discrete logarithm problem is hard in $\mathbb{G}$.

$\mathcal{F}_{\mathbb{G}}^{ABB}$

Let $[x]$ denote the identifier for the value $x \in \mathbb{Z}_p$ stored by the functionality. Each of the following operations returns the identifier of the result to all parties unless the output is explicitly defined.

Input($x$): Receive $x \in \mathbb{Z}_p$ from a party and store this.
Rand(): Pick random $z \leftarrow \mathbb{Z}_p$ and store $z$.
Add($[x], [y]$): Compute $z = a + b$ and store $z \in \mathbb{Z}_p$.
SMult($x, [y]$): Compute $z = xy$ and store $z \in \mathbb{Z}_p$.
Mult($[x], [y]$): Compute $z = xy$ and store $z \in \mathbb{Z}_p$.
Com($[x_1], \ldots, [x_\ell], \boldsymbol{g} = (g_1, \ldots, g_\ell) \in \mathbb{G}^\ell$) (for some $\ell$): Compute $Z = g_1^{x_1} \cdots g_\ell^{x_\ell}$ and output $Z \in \mathbb{G}$ to all parties.
EQ($[x], [y]$): Let $z = 1$ if $x = y$ and 0 otherwise. Store $z \in \mathbb{Z}_p$.
Max($[x_1], \ldots, [x_\ell]$) (for some $\ell$): Compute $z = \max_{1 \le i \le \ell} x_i$ and store $z \in \mathbb{Z}_p$.
Argmax($[x_1], \ldots, [x_\ell]$) (for some $\ell$): Compute $z = \arg\max_{1 \le j \le \ell} x_i$ and store $z$.
BitDecomp($[x]$): Compute $(z_0, \ldots, z_{2\lambda-1})$ such that $x = \sum_{i=0}^{2\lambda-1} 2^i z_i$, and store $z_0, \ldots, z_{2\lambda-1} \in \mathbb{Z}_p$.
Output($[x]$): Output $x$ to all parties.
DOutput($[x], i \in [N]$): Output $x$ (only) to the party $P_i$.

**Fig. 3.** Extended arithmetic black-box functionality.

are based on. Computing these is one of the most computationally heavy steps of proof generation, and could be a potential bottleneck when constructing a Bulletproof-based zk-SNARK since the exponents will correspond to witnesses which will be shared among the collaborating parties. However, note that this computation is straightforward to realize when relying on the extended ABB described above, as computing a Pedersen-style commitment can be done via a single call to Com. As a consequence, constructing an efficient prover protocol with respect to the extended ABB becomes a much simpler task (to obtain an efficient realization of the protocol, it will of course be required that the extended ABB itself can be realized efficiently; how this can be done is shown in Sect. 3.3).

In the description of our protocol, we will assume the statement and the corresponding witness are of the form described in Eq. (1) and Eq. (2), respectively, and that the witness is stored (component-wise) in $\mathcal{F}_{\mathbb{G}}^{ABB}$. This will be the case for the application of our protocol in our privacy-preserving verifiable CNN described in Sect. 4. Note, however, that for any arithmetic circuit over $\mathbb{Z}_p$ and a corresponding (witness) input assignment $\boldsymbol{w} = (w_1, \ldots, w_N)$, a representation corresponding to Eq. (1) and Eq. (2) can be computed in a straightforward manner using the functionality of $\mathcal{F}_{\mathbb{G}}^{ABB}$. In the following, we will let $\mathbb{G}$ be a group with $2\lambda$-bit prime order $p$, and $H_1 : \{0,1\}^* \to \mathbb{Z}_p$, $H_2 : \{0,1\}^* \to \mathbb{Z}_p^2$, $H_3 : \{0,1\}^* \to \mathbb{Z}_p \times \mathbb{G}$, and $G : \mathbb{N} \to \mathbb{G}$ be hash functions (modeled as random oracles).

**Setup.** This algorithm generates group elements $g, h \in \mathbb{G}, \boldsymbol{g}, \boldsymbol{h} \in \mathbb{G}^n$ using the hash function $G$, and outputs these as pp.

**Proof Generation Protocol $\Pi$.** Our protocol follows the structure of the original Bulletproofs, and consists of an 'outer' protocol, JointBulletproof shown in Fig. 4, for jointly computing a proof for an arithmetic circuit of the form described in Eq. (1) and Eq. (2), as well as an 'inner' sub-protocol, JointProveIP shown in Fig. 5, for jointly computing a proof for an inner product. The latter is invoked as part of JointBulletproof. Note that compared to the original Bulletproofs, recursion has been eliminated from the inner product computation to avoid complications arising from this in a protocol setting.

Given the Bulletproof statement and the ABB-stored values of a Bulletproof witness, our protocol(s) proceeds by iteratively computing the witness-dependent values required for the next prover message using $\mathcal{F}_{\mathbb{G}}^{ABB}$ (e.g. line (5) and (6) in Fig. 4 or line (3a) in Fig. 5). Then the protocol uses the Com functionality of $\mathcal{F}_{\mathbb{G}}^{ABB}$ to reveal the prover message (e.g. line (8) in Fig. 4 or line (3b) in Fig. 5). Both parties will then hash the revealed prover message (potentially with addition of a public input) to obtain hash values which will be treated as a challenge from the verifier in ordinary Bulletproofs (e.g. line (9) in Fig. 4 or line (3c) in Fig. 5). (Note that this corresponds to the Fiat-Shamir conversion of Bulletproofs to make these non-interactive.) Finally, the challenge will be used in the computation of subsequent prover messages. The protocol continues this until a full Bulletproof is obtained.

A key property here is that all hash values are computed over messages available to both parties in the clear (revealed in Com calls). Hence, the protocol can avoid computing the hash of ABB-stored values, which would have made the protocol prohibitively expensive to evaluate in practice. The only computations that need to be carried out on the ABB-stored values are modular arithmetic over $\mathbb{Z}_p$ and exponentiation over $\mathbb{G}$. The structure of the protocols furthermore highlights the usefulness of the Com functionality of $\mathcal{F}_{\mathbb{G}}^{ABB}$ which plays a crucial role in efficiently instantiating the protocols (see also Sect. 3.3).

Since the operations in the protocols consist of only calls of the functionality in $\mathcal{F}_{\mathbb{G}}^{ABB}$ or local computations by each party, the following theorem can easily be seen to hold.

**Theorem 1.** *The protocol* JointBulletproof *combined with a compiler protocol is a secure-with-abort protocol realizing the proof generation of the Bulletproof zk-SNARK for arithmetic circuits, in the $\mathcal{F}_{\mathbb{G}}^{ABB}$-hybrid model.*

**Verification.** The verification algorithm, VerifyAC, is identical to that of the ordinary Bulletproof zk-SNARK. Due to space limitations, the description is deferred to the full version.

### 3.3 Secure Realization

To realize our Bulletproof-based collaborative zk-SNARK presented in Sect. 3.2, it remains to securely realize the ABB functionality $\mathcal{F}_{\mathbb{G}}^{ABB}$ from Sect. 3.1. Crucially, to maintain the efficiency of the protocol presented in Sect. 3, the $\mathcal{F}_{\mathbb{G}}^{ABB}$

**Public Input:** $\mathsf{pp} = (g, h, \boldsymbol{g}, \boldsymbol{h})$, $\mathsf{stmt} = (\boldsymbol{V}, \boldsymbol{W}_{\mathrm{L}}, \boldsymbol{W}_{\mathrm{R}}, \boldsymbol{W}_{\mathrm{O}}, \boldsymbol{W}_{\mathrm{V}}, \boldsymbol{c})$, where $\boldsymbol{V} \in \mathbb{G}^m$, $\boldsymbol{W}_{\mathrm{L}}, \boldsymbol{W}_{\mathrm{R}}, \boldsymbol{W}_{\mathrm{O}} \in \mathbb{Z}_p^{Q\times n}$, $\boldsymbol{W}_{\mathrm{V}} \in \mathbb{Z}_p^{Q\times m}$, and $\boldsymbol{c} \in \mathbb{Z}_p^Q$.

**Private Input (stored by $\mathcal{F}_{\mathbb{G}}^{ABB}$):** $[\boldsymbol{a}_{\mathrm{L}}]$, $[\boldsymbol{a}_{\mathrm{R}}]$, $[\boldsymbol{a}_{\mathrm{O}}]$, $[v_1], \ldots, [v_m]$, $[\gamma_1], \ldots$, and $[\gamma_m]$, where $\boldsymbol{a}_{\mathrm{L}}, \boldsymbol{a}_{\mathrm{R}}, \boldsymbol{a}_{\mathrm{O}} \in \mathbb{Z}_p^n$ and $v_i, \gamma_i \in \mathbb{Z}_p$.

**The Protocol:**

1. Call Rand to obtain $[\alpha]$, $[\beta]$, $[\rho]$, $[\boldsymbol{s}_{\mathrm{L}}]$, and $[\boldsymbol{s}_{\mathrm{R}}]$, where $\alpha, \beta, \rho \in \mathbb{Z}_p$ and $\boldsymbol{s}_{\mathrm{L}}, \boldsymbol{s}_{\mathrm{R}} \in \mathbb{Z}_p^n$.
2. Call Com to obtain $A_{\mathrm{I}} = h^{\alpha}\boldsymbol{g}^{\boldsymbol{a}_{\mathrm{L}}}\boldsymbol{h}^{\boldsymbol{a}_{\mathrm{R}}}$, $A_{\mathrm{O}} = h^{\beta}\boldsymbol{g}^{\boldsymbol{a}_{\mathrm{O}}}$, and $S = h^{\rho}\boldsymbol{g}^{\boldsymbol{s}_{\mathrm{L}}}\boldsymbol{h}^{\boldsymbol{s}_{\mathrm{R}}}$.
3. Locally compute $(y, z) \leftarrow H_2(\mathsf{pp}, \mathsf{stmt}, A_{\mathrm{I}}, A_{\mathrm{O}}, S)$.
4. Locally compute $\boldsymbol{y}^n \leftarrow (1, y, y^2, \ldots, y^{n-1})$ and $\boldsymbol{z}_{1\leq}^{Q+1} \leftarrow (z, z^2, z^3, \ldots, z^Q)$.
5. Call SMult and Add to obtain $[l](X) \leftarrow [\boldsymbol{a}_{\mathrm{L}}] \cdot X + [\boldsymbol{a}_{\mathrm{O}}] \cdot X^2 + \boldsymbol{y}^{-n} \circ (\boldsymbol{z}_{1\leq}^{Q+1} \cdot \boldsymbol{W}_{\mathrm{R}}) \cdot X + [\boldsymbol{s}_{\mathrm{L}}] \cdot X^3$ and $[r](X) \leftarrow \boldsymbol{y}^n \circ [\boldsymbol{a}_{\mathrm{R}}] \cdot X - \boldsymbol{y}^n + \boldsymbol{z}_{1\leq}^{Q+1} \cdot (\boldsymbol{W}_{\mathrm{L}} \cdot X + \boldsymbol{W}_{\mathrm{O}}) + \boldsymbol{y}^n \circ [\boldsymbol{s}_{\mathrm{R}}] \cdot X^3$.
6. Call Mult and Add to receive $[t](X) = \sum_{i=1}^{6}[t_i] \cdot X^i \leftarrow \langle [l](X), [r](X)\rangle$.
7. Call Rand to obtain $[\tau_i]$ $(i \in \{1, 3, 4, 5, 6\})$, where $\tau_i \in \mathbb{Z}_p$.
8. Call Com to obtain $T_i = g^{t_i}h^{\tau_i}$ $(i \in \{1, 3, 4, 5, 6\})$.
9. Locally compute $x \leftarrow H_1(\mathsf{pp}, \mathsf{stmt}, A_{\mathrm{I}}, A_{\mathrm{O}}, S, T_1, T_3, T_4, T_5, T_6)$.
10. Call SMult and Add to compute $[\boldsymbol{l}] \leftarrow [l](x)$ and $[\boldsymbol{r}] \leftarrow [r](x)$.
11. Call Mult and Add to receive $[\hat{t}] \leftarrow \langle [\boldsymbol{l}], [\boldsymbol{r}]\rangle$.
12. Call SMult and Add to compute $[\tau_{\mathrm{x}}] \leftarrow \sum_{i\in\{1,3,4,5,6\}}[\tau_i] \cdot x^i + x^2 \cdot \langle \boldsymbol{z}_{1\leq}^{Q+1}, \boldsymbol{W}_{\mathrm{V}} \cdot [\boldsymbol{\gamma}]\rangle$ and $[\mu] \leftarrow [\alpha] \cdot x + [\beta] \cdot x^2 + [\rho] \cdot x^3$.
13. Call Output to receive $\tau_{\mathrm{x}}$, $\mu$, $\hat{t}$, $\boldsymbol{l}$, and $\boldsymbol{r}$.
14. Locally compute $h'_i \leftarrow (h_i)^{y^{-i+1}}$ $(i \in \{1, \ldots, n\})$, $W_{\mathrm{L}} \leftarrow (\boldsymbol{h}')^{\boldsymbol{z}_{1\leq}^{Q+1}\cdot \boldsymbol{W}_{\mathrm{L}}}$, $W_{\mathrm{R}} \leftarrow \boldsymbol{g}^{\boldsymbol{y}^{-n}\circ(\boldsymbol{z}_{1\leq}^{Q+1}\cdot \boldsymbol{W}_{\mathrm{R}})}$, $W_{\mathrm{O}} \leftarrow (\boldsymbol{h}')^{\boldsymbol{z}_{1\leq}^{Q+1}\cdot \boldsymbol{W}_{\mathrm{O}}}$, and $P \leftarrow (A_{\mathrm{I}})^x \cdot (A_{\mathrm{O}})^{x^2} \cdot (\boldsymbol{h}')^{-\boldsymbol{y}^n} \cdot (W_{\mathrm{L}})^x \cdot (W_{\mathrm{R}})^x \cdot W_{\mathrm{O}} \cdot S^{x^3}$.
15. Execute the sub-protocol JointProveIP on public input $\boldsymbol{g}$, $\boldsymbol{h}$, $P \cdot h^{-\mu}$, $\hat{t}$, and $\mathsf{aux} = (\mathsf{pp}, \mathsf{stmt}, A_{\mathrm{I}}, A_{\mathrm{O}}, S, T_1, T_3, T_4, T_5, T_6)$, and private input $[\boldsymbol{l}]$ and $[\boldsymbol{r}]$, and then receive $\pi_{\mathsf{IP}}$ as the result.

**Output:** $\pi = (A_{\mathrm{I}}, A_{\mathrm{O}}, S, T_1, T_3, T_4, T_5, T_6, \tau_{\mathrm{x}}, \mu, \hat{t}, \pi_{\mathsf{IP}})$.

**Fig. 4.** Protocol JointBulletproof for jointly generating Bulletproof for arithmetic circuits.

realization must itself be efficient. Note that our goal is to obtain a collaborative zk-SNARK satisfying (malicious) security with abort which is achieved by a secure-with-abort realization of the $\mathcal{F}_{\mathbb{G}}^{ABB}$.

Our starting point is the SPDZ protocol [15] which is a secure-with-abort protocol realizing the standard arithmetic functionalities (as SPDZ is based on additive secret sharing, we will in the following use the notation $[\cdot]$ to denote additive sharing as opposed to a value stored in an abstract ABB). However, SPDZ by itself does not provide an efficient way to instantiate the Com functionality of $\mathcal{F}_{\mathbb{G}}^{ABB}$ which is central to our protocol in Sect. 3. To efficiently realize Com, we make use of an insight by Smart and Alaoui [40] who showed that the SPDZ protocol that can be extended to deal with operations for cyclic groups

**Public Input:** $\boldsymbol{g}$, $\boldsymbol{h} \in \mathbb{G}^n$, $P \in \mathbb{G}$, $c \in \mathbb{Z}_p$, and $\mathsf{aux} \in \{0,1\}^*$.

**Private Input (stored by $\mathcal{F}_{\mathbb{G}}^{ABB}$):** $[\boldsymbol{a}]$, $[\boldsymbol{b}] \in \mathbb{Z}_p^n$.

**The Protocol:**

1. Locally compute $(x, u_0) \leftarrow H_3(\boldsymbol{g}, \boldsymbol{h}, P, c, \mathsf{aux})$.
2. Locally set $\boldsymbol{g}^{(n)} \leftarrow \boldsymbol{g}$, $\boldsymbol{h}^{(n)} \leftarrow \boldsymbol{h}$, $u \leftarrow u_0^x$, and $P^{(n)} \leftarrow P \cdot u_0^{x \cdot c}$, and (implicitly) let $\boldsymbol{a}^{(n)} \leftarrow \boldsymbol{a}$ and $\boldsymbol{b}^{(n)} \leftarrow \boldsymbol{b}$.
3. Repeat the followings for $m = n, n/2, n/2^2, \ldots, 2$.
   (a) Call Mult and Add to receive $[c_{\mathrm{L}}^{(m)}] \leftarrow [\langle \boldsymbol{a}_{\leq m/2}^{(m)}, \boldsymbol{b}_{m/2+1\leq}^{(m)} \rangle]$ and $[c_{\mathrm{R}}^{(m)}] \leftarrow [\langle \boldsymbol{a}_{m/2+1\leq}^{(m)}, \boldsymbol{b}_{\leq m/2}^{(m)} \rangle]$.
   (b) Call Com to receive $L^{(m)} = (\boldsymbol{g}_{m/2+1\leq}^{(m)})^{\boldsymbol{a}_{\leq m/2}^{(m)}} (\boldsymbol{h}_{\leq m/2}^{(m)})^{\boldsymbol{b}_{m/2+1\leq}^{(m)}} u^{c_{\mathrm{L}}^{(m)}}$ and $R^{(m)} = (\boldsymbol{g}_{\leq m/2}^{(m)})^{\boldsymbol{a}_{m/2+1\leq}^{(m)}} (\boldsymbol{h}_{m/2+1\leq}^{(m)})^{\boldsymbol{b}_{\leq m/2}^{(m)}} u^{c_{\mathrm{R}}^{(m)}}$.
   (c) Locally compute $x^{(m)} \leftarrow H_1(L^{(n)}, R^{(n)}, L^{(n/2)}, R^{(n/2)}, \ldots, L^{(m)}, R^{(m)}, \boldsymbol{g}, \boldsymbol{h}, P, c, \mathsf{aux})$.
   (d) Locally compute $\boldsymbol{g}^{(m/2)} \leftarrow (\boldsymbol{g}_{\leq m/2}^{(m)})^{(x^{(m)})^{-1}} (\boldsymbol{g}_{m/2+1\leq}^{(m)})^{x^{(m)}}$, $\boldsymbol{h}^{(m/2)} \leftarrow (\boldsymbol{h}_{\leq m/2}^{(m)})^{x^{(m)}} (\boldsymbol{h}_{m/2+1\leq}^{(m)})^{(x^{(m)})^{-1}}$, and $P^{(m/2)} \leftarrow (L^{(m)})^{(x^{(m)})^2} P^{(m)} (R^{(m)})^{(x^{(m)})^{-2}}$.
   (e) Call SMult and Add to receive $[\boldsymbol{a}^{(m/2)}] \leftarrow [\boldsymbol{a}_{\leq m/2}^{(m)}] \cdot x^{(m)} + [\boldsymbol{a}_{m/2+1\leq}^{(m)}] \cdot (x^{(m)})^{-1}$ and $[\boldsymbol{b}^{(m/2)}] \leftarrow [\boldsymbol{b}_{\leq m/2}^{(m)}] \cdot (x^{(m)})^{-1} + [\boldsymbol{b}_{m/2+1\leq}^{(m)}] \cdot x^{(m)}$.
4. Call Output to receive $\boldsymbol{a}^{(1)}$ and $\boldsymbol{b}^{(1)}$.

**Output:** $\pi_{\mathsf{IP}} = (L^{(n)}, R^{(n)}, L^{(n/2)}, R^{(n/2)}, \ldots, L^{(2)}, R^{(2)}, \boldsymbol{a}^{(1)}, \boldsymbol{b}^{(1)})$.

**Fig. 5.** Protocol JointProveIP for jointly generating Bulletproof for inner products.

over an elliptic curve whose order coincides with that of the underlying field of the SPDZ protocol. While Smart and Alaoui are concerned with implementing full elliptic curve circuit evaluation, the restricted Com functionality required in $\mathcal{F}_{\mathbb{G}}^{ABB}$ is comparably simple and can be implemented very efficiently. Specifically, recall that the main idea of SPDZ is to let each party hold a share of a global MAC key $k \in \mathbb{Z}_p$ i.e. party $i$ holds $[k]_i$ such that $\sum [k]_i = k$. Then each value $x$ (stored in the ABB) is shared among all parties where each share is of the form $([x]_i, [m]_i)$ and $\sum [x]_i = x$ and $\sum [m]_i = k \cdot x$. The parties will then perform any (arithmetic) computation over the shares (consuming multiplication tuples in the process) while maintaining the above format of shares. Finally, when the computation is done, the parities will firstly check correctness of any value opened during the computation and then the computation result by checking $x \cdot k - m = 0$ (for each value $x$). This approach readily extends to our restricted Com functionality. Specifically, given values $a_1, \ldots, a_\ell$ shared among the parties as $([a_i], [m_i])$ where $m_i = ka_i$, each party can *locally* compute

$$X_i = g_1^{[a_1]_i} \cdots g_\ell^{[a_\ell]_i} \quad \text{and} \quad M_i = g_1^{[m_1]_i} \cdots g_\ell^{[m_\ell]_i}.$$

Note that since the characteristic of the field $\mathbb{Z}_p$ the values $a_i$ are (additively) shared over is the same as the order $p$ of the group elements $g_i$, we have that $X = \prod_i X_i = g_1^{a_1} \cdots g_\ell^{a_\ell} = \mathsf{Com}([a]_1, \ldots, [a]_\ell, g_1, \ldots, g_\ell)$. Hence, to open $X$, each party simply broadcasts $X_i$. Finally, to check an opened commitment $X$, the parties check that $X^k - M = 0$ where $M = \prod_i M_i$. It is relatively easy to see that this approach inherits the security properties of SPDZ.

Lastly, the additional non-linear functionalities in $\mathcal{F}_{\mathbb{G}}^{ABB}$ can be realized via standard generic techniques. Specifically, equality and comparison can be efficiently computed by an appropriate combination of addition, multiplication, and output operations supported by a standard ABB functionality, as shown by Nishide and Ohta [33]; Max and argmax can be easily realized using comparison [25]; Bit-decomposition can be also computed using the protocol of [33].

Based on the above, we obtain the following result.

**Theorem 2.** *There exists a secure realization of $\mathcal{F}_{\mathbb{G}}^{ABB}$ based on the above described extension of the SPDZ protocol [15].*

Combining the efficient realization of $\mathcal{F}_{\mathbb{G}}^{ABB}$ with the protocol from Sect. 3.2 provides us with a secure-with-abort protocol for the joint computation of Bulletproofs. As shown by Ozdemir and Boneh [34,35], it is fairly straightforward to show that if a (single-prover) zk-SNARK system is zero-knowledge and has knowledge soundness, and the prover algorithm is computed by a secure-with-abort MPC protocol against $t$ corrupted parties so that each party's private input is a witness share (where the concatenation of all parties' witness shares constitutes a witness), then the resulting protocol is a secure-with-abort collaborative zk-SNARK satisfying $t$-zero-knowledge. Hence, combined with Theorem 1, we obtain the following theorem.

**Theorem 3.** *Our collaborative Bulletproof protocol instantiated with the extended SPDZ protocol [15] is a secure-with-abort collaborative zk-SNARK.*[5]

## 4 Privacy-Preserving Verifiable CNNs

In this section, we will first introduce our formal definition of a privacy-preserving verifiable CNN in Sect. 4.1. Then, we present our proposed privacy-preserving verifiable CNN in Sect. 4.2.

### 4.1 Formal Definition

Our definition of a privacy-preserving verifiable CNN will provide strong privacy guarantees and in particular ensure that no information regarding the CNN model $M$, the input $x$, or the obtained classification will leak to any other party. To achieve this, we require a privacy-preserving verifiable CNN to have similar security properties to publicly-auditable 2-party computation [2]. Informally, a

[5] If a semi-honest MPC protocol for $\mathcal{F}_{\mathbb{G}}^{ABB}$ is used instead of SPDZ, our protocol is still guaranteed to achieve $t$-zero-knowledge in the presence of semi-honest parties.

publicly-auditable multi-party computation is an extension of a secure multi-party computation protocol that, in addition to computing a functionality, can generate a publicly verifiable proof that the output of the protocol is correct with respect to commitments to each party's input. Ozdemir and Boneh [34, 35] gave a definition of publicly auditable multi-party computation based on collaborative ZK, and our definition of privacy-preserving verifiable CNN follows their definitional approach, but with modifications to deal with a probabilistic functionality[6] and to capture the CNN setting we consider here.

Formally, a privacy-preserving verifiable CNN is associated with some commitment scheme $\mathsf{Com} = (\mathsf{Setup}_{\mathsf{Com}}, \mathsf{Commit})$, and consists of $(\mathsf{Setup}, \Pi, \mathsf{Verify})$ each of whose syntax is defined as follows:

- $\mathsf{Setup}$ is the setup algorithm that takes a security parameter $1^\lambda$ as input, and outputs a public parameter $\mathsf{pp}$.
- $\Pi$ is an interactive protocol between two parties $P_1$ (holding a CNN model) and $P_2$ (holding a CNN input). The protocol is executed using three types of inputs:
  - $P_1$'s private inputs: a CNN model $M$ and randomness $r_M$.
  - $P_2$'s private inputs: a CNN input $x$ and randomness $r_x$.
  - public common inputs: the CNN structure $\mathcal{S}$, a public parameter $\mathsf{pp}_{\mathsf{Com}}$ of the underlying commitmemnt scheme $\mathsf{Com}$, and commitments $\mathsf{com}_M$ and $\mathsf{com}_x$ (which are supposedly generated as $\mathsf{com}_M = \mathsf{Commit}(\mathsf{pp}_{\mathsf{Com}}, M, r_M)$ and $\mathsf{com}_x = \mathsf{Commit}(\mathsf{pp}_{\mathsf{Com}}, x, r_x)$, respectively).

  As the results of an execution of the protocol, $P_1$ outputs a commitment $\mathsf{com}_y$ (for the CNN result $y$) and a proof $\pi$, and $P_2$ outputs a CNN output $y$, a randomness $r_y$, a commitment $\mathsf{com}_y$, and a proof $\pi$.
- $\mathsf{Verify}$ is the verification algorithm that takes $\mathsf{pp}$, commitments $(\mathsf{com}_M, \mathsf{com}_x, \mathsf{com}_y)$, and a proof $\pi$ as input, and outputs either $\top$ (accept) or $\bot$ (reject).

**Definition 3.** *A privacy-preserving verfiable CNN* $(\mathsf{Setup}, \Pi, \mathsf{Verify})$ *associated with* $\mathsf{Com} = (\mathsf{Setup}_{\mathsf{Com}}, \mathsf{Commit})$ *is* secure *if it satisfies the following two properties:*

- *Let $\Pi_y$ denote $\Pi$, in which the proof $\pi$ is excluded from each party's output. Then, $\Pi_y$ is a secure-with-abort 2-party protocol for the functionality $\mathcal{F}_{\mathsf{Com}}^{pCNN}$.*
- *Let $\Pi_\pi$ denote $\Pi$, in which only the proof $\pi$ is treated as the output (of both parties). Then,* $(\mathsf{Setup}, \Pi_\pi, \mathsf{Verify})$ *associated with* $\mathsf{Com}$ *satisfies the requirements of a collaborative ZK protocol (Definition 2) for the following relation* $\mathcal{R}$*:*

[6] The definition of publicly-auditable computation in [34, Appendix D] is for a deterministic functionality.

$$\left\{ \underbrace{\left(\mathcal{S}, \mathsf{pp_{Com}}, \mathsf{com}_M, \mathsf{com}_x, \mathsf{com}_y\right)}_{common\ input/output}, \left( \underbrace{(M, r_M)}_{P_1\text{'s input/output}}, \underbrace{(x, r_x, y, r_y)}_{P_2\text{'s input/output}} \right) \right\} \in \mathcal{R}$$

$$\Longleftrightarrow$$

$$\mathsf{com}_M = \mathit{Commit}(\mathsf{pp_{Com}}, M, r_M) \wedge \mathsf{com}_x = \mathit{Commit}(\mathsf{pp_{Com}}, x, r_x) \wedge \mathsf{com}_y = \mathit{Commit}(\mathsf{pp_{Com}}, y, r_y) \wedge y = \mathit{EvalCNN}(\mathcal{S}, M, x). \quad (4)$$

*Furthermore, we say that a privacy-preserving verifiable CNN is* semi-honest secure *if $\Pi_y$ is semi-honest secure and the 1-zero-knowledge property of* (Setup, $\Pi_\pi$, Verify) *is replaced with 1-zero-knowledge property in the presence of semi-honest parties.*

### 4.2 Construction

Our construction of a privacy-preserving verifiable CNN (Setup, $\Pi$, Verify) is based on the collaborative zk-SNARK presented in Sect. 3. In fact, we directly use the Setup and Verify algorithms from Sect. 3 as the corresponding Setup and Verify algorithms for the privacy-preserving verifiable CNN, respectively.

The interactive proof generation protocol itself will be based on an "augmented" CNN computation (which we will describe with respect to the ABB functionality presented in Sect. 3.1). The augmented CNN computation not only computes the classification of an input, but also intermediate variables, which will provide the parties with a witness for proving the correctness of the classification via our collaborative zk-SNARK. We will denote this process as

$$([y], [w]) \leftarrow \mathsf{JointEvalCNN}(\mathcal{S}, [M], [x])$$

using the notation in Sect. 2 where $M$ is the CNN model, $x$ is the CNN input, $y$ is the result of the classification and $w$ is the witness generated in this process (note that the process is deterministic). This process can be divided further into steps corresponding to each layer of the CNN:

$$\begin{aligned}
&([y_1], [w_1]) \leftarrow \mathsf{JointEvalLayer1}([M], [x])\\
&([y_2], [w_2]) \leftarrow \mathsf{JointEvalLayer2}([M], [y_1], [w_1])\\
&\cdots\\
&([y_N], [w_N]) \leftarrow \mathsf{JointEvalLayerN}([M], [y_{N-1}], [w_{N-1}])
\end{aligned}$$

where each algorithm only computes a single layer in the CNN structure $\mathcal{S}$, and $y_i$ and $w_i$ are the output and corresponding witness of layer $i$, respectively. Here we assume that layer $i$ appends its new witness variables to $[w_{i-1}]$ and outputs this concatenation as $[w_i]$ such that the final witness $[w_N]$ contains all witness for the entire classification. In the following, we explain protocols that perform the computations that constitute each layer, e.g., an affine relation between weights, the ReLU relation, or a max pooling relation. Parties execute multiple instances of these protocols to complete the computation of each layer.

This process is finalized by computing a commitment $\mathsf{com}_y$ to the final classification result $y_N$ (the corresponding randomness $r_{\mathsf{com}}$ is given to the party holding $x$). Once this step is completed, the parties will be able to use the final witness $[w_N]$ (which contains the witnesses for all prior layers) to jointly run the JointBulletproof from Sect. 3.2 to obtain a proof for the computed classification.

In the following, we present protocol instantiations for the initialization and each CNN layer described in Sect. 2 which will allow the parties to complete the above outlined steps. Note that we will use fixed-point computation to represent all arithmetic computations done as part of CNN classification. Specifically, a rational number $x_0 + 2^{-d}x_1 \in \mathbb{Q}$ where $x_0 \in \{-2^\ell, \ldots, 2^\ell - 1\}$ and $x_1 \in \{0, \ldots, 2^d - 1\}$ is represented by the integer $2^d x_0 + x_1 \in \mathbb{Z}_p$. Note also that when multiplication is done between two numbers in fixed-point representation, truncation of the last $d$ bits is required to maintain the correct representation of the result.

**Initialization.** The parties will have to generate witness vectors $[\boldsymbol{a}_\mathrm{L}]$, $[\boldsymbol{a}_\mathrm{R}]$,$[\boldsymbol{a}_\mathrm{O}]$, $[v_1]$, ..., $[v_m]$, and $[\gamma_1]$, ..., $[\gamma_m]$, which satisfy Bulletproof's statement Eq. (3). Here, $\boldsymbol{a}_\mathrm{L}$, $\boldsymbol{a}_\mathrm{R}$, and $\boldsymbol{a}_O$ should satisfy the Hadamard product relation $\boldsymbol{a}_\mathrm{L} \circ \boldsymbol{a}_\mathrm{R} = \boldsymbol{a}_\mathrm{O}$ and the $v_j$'s and $\gamma_j$'s are the input values and the randomness used to commit to these in the commitments $V_j = g^{v_j} h^{\gamma_j}$. The parties receive $(M, r_M)$ and $(x, r_x)$ as private input, respectively, as well as public input $(\mathsf{com}_M, \mathsf{com}_x)$, where $\mathsf{com}_M = \mathsf{Commit}(\mathsf{pp}_{\mathsf{Com}}, M, r_M)$ and $\mathsf{com}_x = \mathsf{Commit}(\mathsf{pp}_{\mathsf{Com}}, x, r_x)$. The values $[v_1]$, ..., $[v_m]$, and $[\gamma_1]$, ..., $[\gamma_m]$ are initialized by the parties calling Input of $\mathcal{F}_{\mathbb{G}}^{ABB}$ on the model $M$, $r_M$, the input $x$ and $r_x$. As described above, each of the following layer protocols will append appropriate witnesses to $[\boldsymbol{a}_\mathrm{L}]$, $[\boldsymbol{a}_\mathrm{R}]$, and $[\boldsymbol{a}_\mathrm{O}]$ and add linear relations to be proven among $\boldsymbol{a}_\mathrm{L}$, $\boldsymbol{a}_\mathrm{R}$, $\boldsymbol{a}_\mathrm{O}$, $\boldsymbol{v}$, and $\boldsymbol{c}$. The linear relations will be added by appending extra rows to the matrices $\boldsymbol{W}_\mathrm{L}$, $\boldsymbol{W}_\mathrm{R}$, $\boldsymbol{W}_\mathrm{O}$, $\boldsymbol{W}_\mathrm{V}$, and the vector $\boldsymbol{c}$ (see Eq. (3)). Note that to compute the layers in the model, the parties execute a set of protocols presented below sequentially. In this sequential execution, the output of a protocol is appended to the vector $\boldsymbol{a}_\mathrm{L}$ (as described above, each protocol appends elements to $\boldsymbol{a}_\mathrm{L}$, $\boldsymbol{a}_\mathrm{R}$, and $\boldsymbol{a}_\mathrm{O}$, some of which are intermediate variables and some of which are the output of the protocol). This appended output of the protocol is later used by subsequent protocols. The final classification result $y$ and the randomness used for the commitment $\mathsf{com}_y$ computed in the finalization will be stored in the appropriate $[v_1], \ldots, [v_m]$, and $[\gamma_1], \ldots, [\gamma_m]$ positions. Note that some protocols will additionally require an index to know which part of the witness from the previous layer is used in the computation e.g. the ReLU function takes indices $(i, u) \in \{1, \ldots, n\} \times \{\mathrm{L}, \mathrm{R}, \mathrm{O}\}$ and assumes that the input to the ReLU function is stored at $\boldsymbol{a}_u[i]$.

**Affine and Convolution Layers.** Affine and convolution layers correspond to the computation of an inner product relation (note that average pooling corresponds to an affine layer). The computation is implemented via the JointEvalIP protocol which is given shares of vectors $([\boldsymbol{a}_{u_1}[i_1]], \ldots, [\boldsymbol{a}_{u_m}[i_m]])$, and $([\boldsymbol{a}_{v_1}[j_1]], \ldots, [\boldsymbol{a}_{v_m}[j_m]])$ and a scalar $[\boldsymbol{a}_w[k]]$, and computes the inner product:

$$\boldsymbol{a} = \boldsymbol{a}_w[k] + \sum_{t=1}^{m} \boldsymbol{a}_{u_t}[i_t]\boldsymbol{a}_{v_t}[j_t]$$

where $\boldsymbol{a}_w[k]$ is a constant term that may be utilized by an affine layer and the result $\boldsymbol{a}$ will be appended to the vector $\boldsymbol{a}_{\mathrm{L}}$ during the protocol. The description of JointEvalIP is deferred to the full version, due to the page limitation.

Note that this protocol does not perform the truncation which would normally be required by the fixed-point multiplication. Instead, this truncation will be performed by the following ReLU protocol. Deferring this truncation improves efficiency. Specifically, the computation of an inner product requires multiple multiplications and thus multiple truncations, but if we defer the truncation to the ReLU proof, just a single truncation is sufficient for each inner product.

**ReLU.** The protocol JointEvalReLU computes the ReLU function. Namely, given as input a share $[\boldsymbol{a}_u[i]]$, the protocol computes

$$\boldsymbol{a} = \mathsf{ReLU}(\boldsymbol{a}_u[i])$$

where $\boldsymbol{a}$ will be appended to the vector $\boldsymbol{a}_{\mathrm{L}}$ during the protocol. Recall that ReLU computes the function

$$\mathsf{ReLU}(x) = \begin{cases} 0 \text{ if } x < 0 \\ x \text{ if } x \geq 0 \end{cases}.$$

This is equivalently represented by bit decomposition:

$$\mathsf{ReLU}(x) = x_m \cdot \sum_{i=0}^{m-1} 2^i x_i$$

where $x + 2^m = \sum_{i=0}^{m} 2^i x_i$ with $x_0, \ldots, x_m \in \{0, 1\}$.

To implement this function, the protocol JointEvalReLU utilizes the subprotocol JointEvalRange which computes the bit decomposition of a shared integer in $\mathbb{Z}_p$. The name of the protocol JointEvalRange stems from the witness computed in the protocol is not only a bit decomposition, but can also be viewed as a witness for a range proof i.e. that the input falls into a certain range. The description of the protocols JointEvalReLU and JointEvalRange are deferred to the full version, due to the page limitation.

Note that this protocol truncates the input value by $d$ bits. This truncation is realized by the summation in $\boldsymbol{a}_{\mathrm{R}}[n+1+2\ell+2d+1]$ (Here, the index $n+1+2\ell+2d+1$ comes from the following calculation: The variable $n$ indicates the current number of the multiplication relations, $1+2\ell+2d$ comes from the range proof with $1+2\ell+2d$ bits, and the last 1 comes from an extra multiplication relation for proving the ReLU relation) in the protocol description which runs from $i = d$ to $2\ell + 2d - 1$, by which it truncates the least significant $d$ bits.

**Finalization.** To define the output of a CNN, it is standard to use SoftMax to normalize the output of the last layer. However, since we are only interested in proving the obtained classification, it is sufficient to prove that some given public value is maximum in a given set of values.

The protocol JointEvalFinalize does exactly this. The protocol utilizes the following representation of the maximum relation $y = \max\{x_1, \ldots, x_m\}$: There exists a vector $(z_1, \ldots, z_m)$ satisfying that

$$\begin{aligned} &y = x_1 z_1 + \cdots + x_m z_m, \\ &z_1, \ldots, z_m \in \{0, 1\}, \\ &z_1 + \cdots + z_m = 1, \\ &y - x_1 \geq 0, \ldots, y - x_m \geq 0. \end{aligned}$$

The description of the protocol is deferred to the full version, due to the page limitation.

**Proof Generation.** Upon completion of the finalization described above, the parties simply invoke JointBulletproof (Fig. 4) from Sect. 3.2 using the generated witness $[\boldsymbol{a}_{\mathrm{L}}]$, $[\boldsymbol{a}_{\mathrm{R}}]$, $[\boldsymbol{a}_{\mathrm{O}}]$, $[v_1]$, ..., $[v_m]$, and $[\gamma_1]$, ..., $[\gamma_m]$ as input to collaboratively generate a Bulletproof $\pi$ of correct classification.

**Obtained Proof and Disclosure of Classification Information.** Upon completion of the proof generation protocol, the party holding the input $x$, will obtain a proof $\pi$ with respect to a commitment to the model $\mathsf{com}_M$, a commitment to $x$ and a commitment to the corresponding classification $\mathsf{com}_y$. While this party can present $\pi$ to a third-party verifier, the latter will not gain any information on the classification $y$ by verifying $\pi$, as $\mathsf{com}_y$ hides $y$. This is insufficient in many applications. However, as the party holding $x$ will receive the opening $r_y$ to $\mathsf{com}_y$, he will be able to disclose additional information regarding $y$. One option is simply to reveal both $y$ and $r_y$, which would allow the verifier to check that $y$ is indeed the correct classification result via the commitment scheme. However, a more fine-grained disclosure is possible. Note that $\mathsf{com}_y$ obtained in our verifiable CNN is simply a Pedersen commitment which allows the party holding $x$ to produce an additional Bulletproof $\pi_y$ showing any statement regarding $y$ e.g. that $y$ belong to a set $\mathcal{Y}$ of classification results. This proof can be generated independently and will be logarithmic in the size of the statement. By verifying both $\pi$ and $\pi_y$, a third-party verifier will learn that $y$ has been correctly computed with respect to $M$ and $x$, and that $y$ satisfies the additional statement shown by $\pi_y$, without learning any additional information on $y$.

### 4.3 Security

In the previous subsection, we have presented the procedures for our privacy-preserving verifiable CNN. It is not hard to see that during the protocol, the parties either call commands of $\mathcal{F}_{\mathbb{G}}^{ABB}$, local operations (including hashing on public values), or execute the proof generation protocol of our collaborative

Bulletproof protocol. Note that as the final result of an execution of our protocol, the party $P_1$ (holding a CNN model $M$) finally receives only public values (the commitments to the witnesses and the commitment to the evaluation result $y$ of the CNN, and a proof of the collaborative Bulletproof); and the party $P_2$ (holding a CNN input $x$) will receive the same public values, as well as the CNN evaluation result $y$ and its opening in the clear. Furthermore, the proof generation part of our protocol just invokes the proof generation of our collaborative Bulletproof protocol. Hence, we have the following theorems.

**Theorem 4.** *Let* $(\mathsf{Setup}, \Pi, \mathsf{Verify})$ *be our privacy-preserving verifiable CNN. Let* $\Pi_y$ *denote the interactive protocol* $\Pi$ *of our privacy-preserving verifiable CNN, such that the proof* $\pi$ *is excluded from the output, and let* $\Pi_\pi$ *denote* $\Pi$ *such that the output is restricted to the proof* $\pi$*. Then,* $(\mathsf{Setup}, \Pi_y, \mathsf{Verify})$ *is a secure-with-abort protocol realizing* $\mathcal{F}_{\mathsf{Com}}^{pCNN}$*, in the* $\mathcal{F}_{\mathbb{G}}^{ABB}$*-hybrid model. Furthermore,* $\Pi_\pi$ *is a collaborative zk-SNARK for proving the relation in Eq.* (4).

**Theorem 5.** *Our privacy-preserving verifiable CNN instantiated with the SPDZ protocol [15] with the extension described in Sect. 3 is secure according to Definition 3.*

## 5 Implementation and Comparison

To measure the performance of our approach, we implemented our collaborative zk-SNARK protocol and estimated the performance of our verifiable CNN construction applied to the LeNet CNN [27] and the MNIST dataset [43]. In the following sections we provide the details of this as well as a comparison to related approaches.

### 5.1 Implementation of Collaborative Zk-SNARK

To evaluate the performance of our Bulletproof-based collaborative zk-SNARK, we made an implementation in Rust.[7] Specifically, we implemented the protocol using the elliptic curve library "curve25519-dalek."[8] This library provides group operations on the Edwards and Montgomery forms of Curve25519 and on the prime-order Ristretto group.

We implemented the protocol in the following setting: Firstly, in the protocol, we need to perform two-party multiplications, which require correlated randomness (i.e. Beaver triples). This correlated randomness is assumed to be generated in advance and made available to each party in a preprocessing phase. The cost of this phase can be estimated from [23] and is not included in the timing results presented below. Secondly, each party is implemented as a separate thread on a single server i.e. the implementation of each party is not parallelized. Finally, the communication between the two parties is simulated via the

[7] https://www.rust-lang.org/.

[8] https://doc.dalek.rs/curve25519_dalek/index.html.

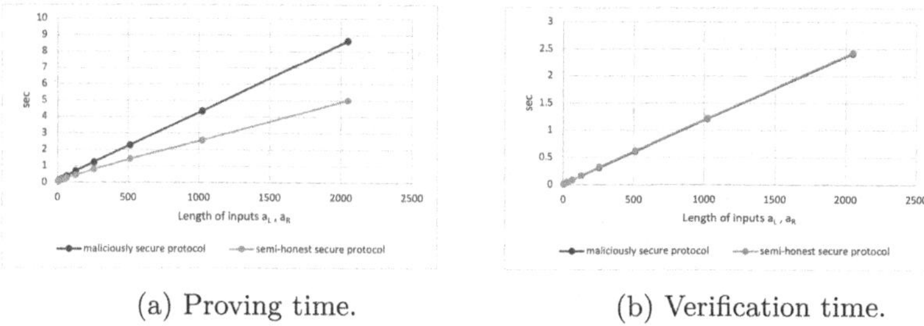


(a) Proving time. (b) Verification time.

**Fig. 6.** Experimental timing results for proofs for inner products.

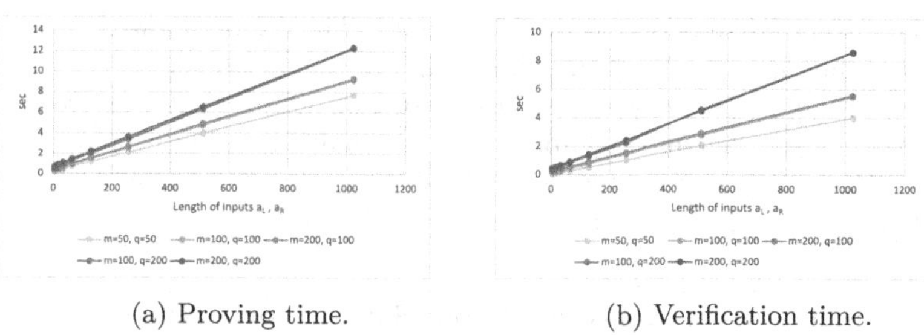


(a) Proving time. (b) Verification time.

**Fig. 7.** Experimental timing results for proofs for arithmetic circuits (malicious security).

"constrained-connection" library[9] set up to simulate a 1 Gbps connection with a round-trip-time of 0.5 ms. All experiments were performed on an Intel i5-7500 CPU @ 3.40 GHz and 16 GB of RAM.

Figure 6 shows the performance of both semi-honest and maliciously secure versions of the sub-protocol JointProveIP (Fig. 5) and its corresponding verification algorithm. (The verification algorithm is exactly that of the ordinary Bulletproofs [6] for inner product relations, and will be given in the full version.) These are for proving and verifying an inner product relation and the horizontal axis "Length of inputs $a_{\mathrm{L}}$, $a_{\mathrm{R}}$" corresponds to the dimension of the vectors in the inner product relation. As the figures show, the processing times increase linearly with the length of the input vectors. Furthermore, note that malicious security is obtained at roughly twice the cost of semi-honest security.

Figure 7 shows the performance of the maliciously-secure proof generation protocol JointBulletproof (Fig. 4) and its verification algorithm of our collaborative zk-SNARK for arithmetic circuits. (As above, the verification algorithm is exactly that of the Bulletproofs [6], and will be given in the full version.) Here, the horizontal axis "Length of inputs $a_{\mathrm{L}}$, $a_{\mathrm{R}}$" corresponds to the number of the multiplications in the proven arithmetic circuit. The parameter $q$ is the number of the additive relations in the proven arithmetic circuit. The parameter $m$ is the size of the committed message, which is, in the CNN application, the sum of

[9] https://docs.rs/constrained-connection/.

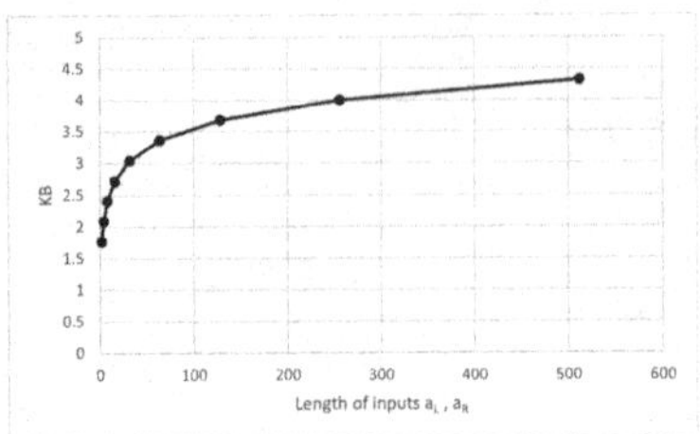


**Fig. 8.** Proof size of arithmetic circuit proofs.

the sizes of the CNN model and the CNN input. The figures show the processing time when the parameters $n$, $m$, and $q$ in the protocol are varied, respectively.

Figure 8 shows the proof size of the protocol. (Note that the proof size is irrespective of whether it is computed by the malicious secure protocol or the semi-honest secure one.) According to the description of the protocol, the proof size depends only on $n$. This measurement confirms this.

### 5.2 Performance Estimate for Proof System for CNN

We will now discuss performance estimates when our protocol is applied to a CNN. For this performance estimation, we use the MNIST dataset [43]. MNIST is a dataset of hand-written digits, and the images are of size $28 \times 28 \times 1$. We use the LeNet network [27] which consists of two convolution layers, two pooling layers, and three fully connected layers. Note that for the purpose of comparison to vCNN and zkCNN, we use average pooling. The parameters of each layer are as follows:

- *Convolution:* Filter Size = 5×5, Stride = 1, Channels = 6
- *Average Pooling:* Filter Size = 2×2, Stride = 2, Channels = 6
- *Convolution:* Filter Size = 5×5, Stride = 1, Channels = 16
- *Average Pooling:* Filter Size = 2×2, Stride = 2, Channels = 16
- *Fully-Connected 1:* Input Size =400, Output Size = 120
- *Fully-Connected 2:* Input Size =120, Output Size = 84
- *Fully-Connected 3:* Input Size =84, Output Size = 10

When applying our protocol for an arithmetic circuit to the classification task of the above model, the parameters in the scheme are $n = m = 2^{19} = 524288$ and $Q = 611878$. We estimate the processing time of the protocol with these parameters based on the measurements in the previous section. As a result, the classification task of the above model takes about 2.9 h, the total communication cost is 236 MB, and the proof size is 7.68 KiB. Finally, based on [23] we estimate that 10 millions multiplications are needed in the on-line protocol and thus 1.7 h are needed for the off-line preprocessing.

| | Algorithm | Model Privacy | Input Privacy | Comm. | Proof Size | Prover Time |
|---|---|---|---|---|---|---|
| Tensorflow | standalone | ○ | ○ | - | - | 0.042ms |
| Groth | standalone | ● | ○ | - | 0.12 KiB | 1.5h |
| vCNN | standalone | ● | ○ | - | 0.34 KiB | 5.5s |
| zkCNN | standalone | ● | ○ | - | 63.6 KiB | 0.5s |
| Ours | interactive | ● | ● | 236 MB | 7.68 KiB | 2.9h |

**Fig. 9.** Comparison of our verifiable CNN to related approaches. ● means the given property is achieved whereas ○ means this is not the case. The prover time for vCNN and zkCNN are from [30], and the time for Groth from [28] (see Sects. 5.1 and 5.3 for more details on all execution environments).

### 5.3 Comparison

Figure 9 shows a comparison between our verifiable CNN and related approaches. We stress that our verifiable CNN is fundamentally different from the related approaches shown in Fig. 9 in that it is an *interactive* protocol, which is required to obtain the strong notion of privacy considered in this paper, whereas the related approachs are all standalone algorithms executed locally by a single party. The results for Tensorflow[10] were obtained by classifying the full MNIST test set of 10000 samples in our local execution environment[11] and computing the average time for a single sample. The results for vCNN and zkCNN are from [30] and obtained on an AMD EPYC 7R32 64-Core CPU, whereas the results for the naive application of the Groth zk-SNARK [21] are from [28] and obtained on an quad-core Intel i5 CPU@3.4GHz (similar to our execution environment). While the measurement of each protocol uses a different computation environment and setup, the hardware differences are not significant for this comparison and the results remain useful for obtaining an overview of the performance of the protocols.

We note that compared to the plain Tensorflow computation, the fastest scheme providing model privacy, zkCNN, is orders of magnitude slower. Compared to zkCNN, our protocol is likewise orders of magnitude slower, but simultaneously provides model and input privacy which zkCNN cannot provide as it is a non-interactive standalone algorithm. This illustrates that protecting the privacy of the CNN input is a challenging task. However, we also note that our scheme is within a factor of two of the prover time for the Groth zk-SNARK when this is straightforwardly applied to ch1LeNet, despite the Groth zk-SNARK being a standalone algorithm. Finally, we note that the proof size of our approach is roughly an order of magnitude smaller than zkCNN, and an order of magnitude larger than vCNN.

These results highlight that it is feasible to provide the stronger notion of privacy we have introduced in this paper, which simultaneously protects the privacy of both CNN model and input. We stress that our implementation is a proof of concept only, and we believe that there is a lot of room for improvement in terms of prover running time by optimizing the implementation.

---

[10] https://www.tensorflow.org/.

[11] MacBook Pro M2 Pro.

**Acknowledgement.** The authors would like to thank the anonymous referees for their valuable comments and helpful suggestions. This work was partially supported by JST CREST Grant Number JPMJCR22M1 and JSPS KAKENHI Grant Number JP18K18055, Japan.

## References

1. Ames, S., Hazay, C., Ishai, Y., Venkitasubramaniam, M.: Ligero: lightweight sublinear arguments without a trusted setup. In: Thuraisingham, B.M., Evans, D., Malkin, T., Xu, D. (eds.) ACM CCS 2017, pp. 2087–2104. ACM Press (2017). https://doi.org/10.1145/3133956.3134104
2. Baum, C., Damgård, I., Orlandi, C.: Publicly auditable secure multi-party computation. In: Abdalla, M., Prisco, R.D. (eds.) SCN 14. LNCS, vol. 8642, pp. 175–196. Springer, Cham (2014). https://doi.org/10.1007/978-3-319-10879-7_11
3. Ben-Sasson, E., Chiesa, A., Riabzev, M., Spooner, N., Virza, M., Ward, N.P.: Aurora: transparent succinct arguments for R1CS. In: Ishai, Y., Rijmen, V. (eds.) EUROCRYPT 2019, Part I. LNCS, vol. 11476, pp. 103–128. Springer, Cham (2019). https://doi.org/10.1007/978-3-030-17653-2_4
4. Bootle, J., Cerulli, A., Chaidos, P., Groth, J., Petit, C.: Efficient zero-knowledge arguments for arithmetic circuits in the discrete log setting. In: Fischlin, M., Coron, J.S. (eds.) EUROCRYPT 2016, Part II. LNCS, vol. 9666, pp. 327–357. Springer, Cham (2016). https://doi.org/10.1007/978-3-662-49896-5_12
5. Bourse, F., Minelli, M., Minihold, M., Paillier, P.: Fast homomorphic evaluation of deep discretized neural networks. In: Shacham, H., Boldyreva, A. (eds.) CRYPTO 2018, Part III. LNCS, vol. 10993, pp. 483–512. Springer, Cham (2018). https://doi.org/10.1007/978-3-319-96878-0_17
6. Bünz, B., Bootle, J., Boneh, D., Poelstra, A., Wuille, P., Maxwell, G.: Bulletproofs: short proofs for confidential transactions and more. In: 2018 IEEE Symposium on Security and Privacy, pp. 315–334. IEEE Computer Society Press (2018). https://doi.org/10.1109/SP.2018.00020
7. Byali, M., Chaudhari, H., Patra, A., Suresh, A.: FLASH: fast and robust framework for privacy-preserving machine learning. Proc. Privacy Enhanc. Technol. **2020**(2), 459–480 (2020). https://doi.org/10.2478/popets-2020-0036
8. Canetti, R.: Security and composition of multiparty cryptographic protocols. J. Cryptol. **13**(1), 143–202 (2000). https://doi.org/10.1007/s001459910006
9. Chandran, N., Gupta, D., Rastogi, A., Sharma, R., Tripathi, S.: EzPC: programmable, efficient, and scalable secure two-party computation for machine learning. Cryptology ePrint Archive, Report 2017/1109 (2017). https://eprint.iacr.org/2017/1109
10. Chaudhari, H., Choudhury, A., Patra, A., Suresh, A.: ASTRA: high throughput 3pc over rings with application to secure prediction. In: Sion, R., Papamanthou, C. (eds.) Proceedings of the 2019 ACM SIGSAC Conference on Cloud Computing Security Workshop, CCSW@CCS 2019, London, 11 November 2019, pp. 81–92. ACM (2019). https://doi.org/10.1145/3338466.3358922
11. Chaudhari, H., Rachuri, R., Suresh, A.: Trident: efficient 4PC framework for privacy preserving machine learning. In: NDSS 2020. The Internet Society (2020)
12. Chiesa, A., Hu, Y., Maller, M., Mishra, P., Vesely, N., Ward, N.P.: Marlin: preprocessing zkSNARKs with universal and updatable SRS. In: Canteaut, A., Ishai, Y. (eds.) EUROCRYPT 2020, Part I. LNCS, vol. 12105, pp. 738–768. Springer (2020). https://doi.org/10.1007/978-3-030-45721-1_26

13. Chiesa, A., Ojha, D., Spooner, N.: Fractal: post-quantum and transparent recursive proofs from holography. In: Canteaut, A., Ishai, Y. (eds.) EUROCRYPT 2020, Part I. LNCS, vol. 12105, pp. 769–793. Springer, Cham (2020). https://doi.org/10.1007/978-3-030-45721-1_27
14. Damgård, I., Nielsen, J.B.: Universally composable efficient multiparty computation from threshold homomorphic encryption. In: Boneh, D. (ed.) CRYPTO 2003. LNCS, vol. 2729, pp. 247–264. Springer, Cham (2003). https://doi.org/10.1007/978-3-540-45146-4_15
15. Damgård, I., Pastro, V., Smart, N.P., Zakarias, S.: Multiparty computation from somewhat homomorphic encryption. In: Safavi-Naini, R., Canetti, R. (eds.) CRYPTO 2012. LNCS, vol. 7417, pp. 643–662. Springer, Cham (2012). https://doi.org/10.1007/978-3-642-32009-5_38
16. Dayama, P., Patra, A., Paul, P., Singh, N., Vinayagamurthy, D.: How to prove any NP statement jointly? Efficient distributed-prover zero-knowledge protocols. PoPETs **2022**(2), 517–556 (2022). https://doi.org/10.2478/popets-2022-0055
17. Feng, B., Qin, L., Zhang, Z., Ding, Y., Chu, S.: ZEN: An optimizing compiler for verifiable, zero-knowledge neural network inferences. Cryptology ePrint Archive, Report 2021/087 (2021). https://eprint.iacr.org/2021/087
18. Gabizon, A., Williamson, Z.J., Ciobotaru, O.: PLONK: permutations over Lagrange-bases for oecumenical noninteractive arguments of knowledge. Cryptology ePrint Archive, Report 2019/953 (2019). https://eprint.iacr.org/2019/953
19. Gilad-Bachrach, R., Dowlin, N., Laine, K., Lauter, K.E., Naehrig, M., Wernsing, J.: Cryptonets: applying neural networks to encrypted data with high throughput and accuracy. In: Balcan, M., Weinberger, K.Q. (eds.) Proceedings of the 33nd International Conference on Machine Learning, ICML 2016. JMLR Workshop and Conference Proceedings, vol. 48, pp. 201–210. JMLR.org (2016)
20. Goldreich, O.: Foundations of Cryptography: Basic Applications, vol. 2. Cambridge University Press, Cambridge (2004)
21. Groth, J.: On the size of pairing-based non-interactive arguments. In: Fischlin, M., Coron, J.S. (eds.) EUROCRYPT 2016, Part II. LNCS, vol. 9666, pp. 305–326. Springer, Heidelberg (2016). https://doi.org/10.1007/978-3-662-49896-5_11
22. Kang, D., Hashimoto, T., Stoica, I., Sun, Y.: Scaling up trustless DNN inference with zero-knowledge proofs. arXiv preprint arXiv:2210.08674 (2022)
23. Keller, M., Orsini, E., Scholl, P.: MASCOT: faster malicious arithmetic secure computation with oblivious transfer. In: Weippl, E.R., Katzenbeisser, S., Kruegel, C., Myers, A.C., Halevi, S. (eds.) ACM CCS 2016, pp. 830–842. ACM Press (2016). https://doi.org/10.1145/2976749.2978357
24. Kitai, H., et al.: MOBIUS: model-oblivious binarized neural networks. IEEE Access **7**, 139021–139034 (2019). https://doi.org/10.1109/ACCESS.2019.2939410
25. Knott, B., Venkataraman, S., Hannun, A.Y., Sengupta, S., Ibrahim, M., van der Maaten, L.: Crypten: secure multi-party computation meets machine learning. In: Ranzato, M., Beygelzimer, A., Dauphin, Y.N., Liang, P., Vaughan, J.W. (eds.) Advances in Neural Information Processing Systems 34: Annual Conference on Neural Information Processing Systems 2021, NeurIPS 2021, pp. 4961–4973 (2021)
26. Koti, N., Pancholi, M., Patra, A., Suresh, A.: SWIFT: super-fast and robust privacy-preserving machine learning. In: Bailey, M., Greenstadt, R. (eds.) USENIX Security 2021, pp. 2651–2668. USENIX Association (2021)
27. Lecun, Y., Bottou, L., Bengio, Y., Haffner, P.: Gradient-based learning applied to document recognition. Proc. IEEE **86**(11), 2278–2324 (1998). https://doi.org/10.1109/5.726791

28. Lee, S., Ko, H., Kim, J., Oh, H.: vCNN: verifiable convolutional neural network. Cryptology ePrint Archive, Report 2020/584 (2020). https://eprint.iacr.org/2020/584
29. Liu, J., Juuti, M., Lu, Y., Asokan, N.: Oblivious neural network predictions via MiniONN transformations. In: Thuraisingham, B.M., Evans, D., Malkin, T., Xu, D. (eds.) ACM CCS 2017, pp. 619–631. ACM Press (2017). https://doi.org/10.1145/3133956.3134056
30. Liu, T., Xie, X., Zhang, Y.: zkCNN: zero knowledge proofs for convolutional neural network predictions and accuracy. In: Vigna, G., Shi, E. (eds.) ACM CCS 2021, pp. 2968–2985. ACM Press (2021). https://doi.org/10.1145/3460120.3485379
31. Mohassel, P., Rindal, P.: $\text{ABY}^3$: a mixed protocol framework for machine learning. In: Lie, D., Mannan, M., Backes, M., Wang, X. (eds.) ACM CCS 2018, pp. 35–52. ACM Press (2018). https://doi.org/10.1145/3243734.3243760
32. Mohassel, P., Zhang, Y.: SecureML: a system for scalable privacy-preserving machine learning. In: 2017 IEEE Symposium on Security and Privacy, pp. 19–38. IEEE Computer Society Press (2017). https://doi.org/10.1109/SP.2017.12
33. Nishide, T., Ohta, K.: Multiparty computation for interval, equality, and comparison without bit-decomposition protocol. In: Okamoto, T., Wang, X. (eds.) PKC 2007. LNCS, vol. 4450, pp. 343–360. Springer, Cham (2007). https://doi.org/10.1007/978-3-540-71677-8_23
34. Ozdemir, A., Boneh, D.: Experimenting with collaborative zk-SNARKs: zero-knowledge proofs for distributed secrets. Cryptology ePrint Archive, Report 2021/1530 (2021). https://eprint.iacr.org/2021/1530
35. Ozdemir, A., Boneh, D.: Experimenting with collaborative zk-SNARKs: zero-knowledge proofs for distributed secrets. In: Butler, K.R.B., Thomas, K. (eds.) USENIX Security 2022, pp. 4291–4308. USENIX Association (2022)
36. Patra, A., Suresh, A.: BLAZE: Blazing fast privacy-preserving machine learning. In: NDSS 2020. The Internet Society (2020)
37. Riazi, M.S., Weinert, C., Tkachenko, O., Songhori, E.M., Schneider, T., Koushanfar, F.: Chameleon: a hybrid secure computation framework for machine learning applications. In: Kim, J., Ahn, G.J., Kim, S., Kim, Y., López, J., Kim, T. (eds.) ASIACCS 18, pp. 707–721. ACM Press (2018)
38. Rouhani, B.D., Riazi, M.S., Koushanfar, F.: Deepsecure: scalable provably-secure deep learning. In: Proceedings of the 55th Annual Design Automation Conference (DAC 2018), pp. 2:1–2:6. ACM (2018). https://doi.org/10.1145/3195970.3196023
39. Setty, S.: Spartan: efficient and general-purpose zkSNARKs without trusted setup. Cryptology ePrint Archive, Report 2019/550 (2019). https://eprint.iacr.org/2019/550
40. Smart, N.P., Talibi Alaoui, Y.: Distributing any elliptic curve based protocol. In: Albrecht, M. (ed.) 17th IMA International Conference on Cryptography and Coding. LNCS, vol. 11929, pp. 342–366. Springer, Cham (2019). https://doi.org/10.1007/978-3-030-35199-1_17
41. Wagh, S., Gupta, D., Chandran, N.: SecureNN: 3-party secure computation for neural network training. PoPETs **2019**(3), 26–49 (2019). https://doi.org/10.2478/popets-2019-0035
42. Weng, J., Weng, J., Tang, G., Yang, A., Li, M., Liu, J.N.: pvcnn: privacy-preserving and verifiable convolutional neural network testing (2022). https://arxiv.org/abs/2201.09186
43. LeCun, Y., Corinna Cortes, C.J.B.: The ch1MNIST database of handwritten digits (2010). http://yann.lecun.com/exdb/mnist/

# A General Framework of Homomorphic Encryption for Multiple Parties with Non-interactive Key-Aggregation

Hyesun Kwak[1(✉)], Dongwon Lee[1], Yongsoo Song[1], and Sameer Wagh[2]

[1] Seoul National University, Seoul, South Korea
{hskwak,dongwonlee95,y.song}@snu.ac.kr
[2] Devron Corporation, Oakland, USA

**Abstract.** Homomorphic Encryption (HE) is a useful primitive for secure computation, but it is not generally applicable when multiple parties are involved, as the authority is solely concentrated in a single party, the secret key owner. To solve this issue, several variants of HE have emerged in the context of multiparty setting, resulting in two major lines of work – Multi-Party HE (MPHE) and Multi-Key HE (MKHE). In short, MPHEs tend to be more efficient, but all parties should be specified at the beginning to collaboratively generate a public key, and the access structure is fixed throughout the entire computation. On the other hand, MKHEs have relatively poor performance but provide better flexibility in that a new party can generate its own key and join the computation anytime.

In this work, we propose a new HE primitive, called Multi-Group HE (MGHE). Stated informally, an MGHE scheme provides seamless integration between MPHE and MKHE, and has the best of both worlds. In an MGHE scheme, a group of parties jointly generates a public key for efficient single-key encryption and homomorphic operations similar to MPHE. However, it also supports computation on encrypted data under different keys, in the MKHE manner. We formalize the security and correctness notions for MGHE and discuss the relation with previous approaches.

We also present a concrete instantiation of MGHE from the BFV scheme and provide a proof-of-concept implementation to demonstrate its performance. In particular, our MGHE construction has a useful property that the key generation is simply done by aggregating individual keys without any interaction between the parties, while all the existing MPHE constructions relied on multi-round key-generation protocols. Finally, we propose a general methodology to build a multi-party computational protocol from our MGHE scheme.

**Keywords:** Multi-Key Homomorphic encryption · Multi-Party Homomorphic Encryption


C. Pöpper and L. Batina (Eds.): ACNS 2024, LNCS 14584, pp. 403–430, 2024.
https://doi.org/10.1007/978-3-031-54773-7_16

# 1 Introduction

Homomorphic Encryption (HE) enables computation over encrypted data without decryption. It prevents the leakage of private information while evaluating data within an untrusted environment. However, HE requires a large resource even when it computes a simple arithmetic operation such as multiplication. As a result, HE is particularly well-suited for implementation in cloud systems that can supply large computing power for evaluation.

A typical HE only supports computations between data encrypted *by the same key*. Consequently, when multiple data owners are involved, it relies on a trusted third party who possesses a key distributed to each party for encryption. Still, this merely transfers the trust problem from the cloud service provider to the new third party and thus does not provide an acceptable solution to this problem. To overcome this challenge, extensive research has explored the use of distributed trust in designing HE schemes involving multiple parties.

In the context of multiple parties, two important lines of HE schemes have emerged: Threshold HE and Multi-Key HE (MKHE). In Threshold HE [5,8,30,31,33], multiple parties collaborate to generate a joint public key, and encryption is performed under this joint key. Threshold HE has a $t$-out-of-$n$ ($t \leq n$) access structure where any $t$ parties can reconstruct the secret key to decrypt the ciphertext. Studies on Threshold HE are again diverged into two different directions: the case where $t < n$ and the case where $t = n$. In our work, we focus on the case when $t = n$, which is referred as Multi-Party HE (MPHE). Like any other Threhold HE schemes, MPHE is comparable to that of the single-key HE schemes since encryption and homomorphic computation are performed in a similar manner with the joint key. However, the set of participants should be determined beforehand and fixed in the preparation phase and no other parties can join the computation in the middle. Moreover, the existing MPHE schemes are based on a multi-round key generation protocol in which the involved parties should interact with each other.

On the other hand, MKHE [12,13,18,29,32,34] features a distributed setup phase where each party independently generates its own key pair, without requiring any information about other participants. The encryption can be done by an individual key, and it allows to perform arithmetic operations on ciphertexts that do not necessarily have to be encrypted under the same key. The main advantage of MKHE lies in its flexibility: it is not necessary to pre-determine the list of participants or the computational task. From the performance perspective, however, the size of ciphertexts increases with the number of involved parties, and so does the complexity of homomorphic operations.

## 1.1 Our Contributions

**Formalization of Multi-group HE.** We propose a novel variant of HE designed for multiple parties, called Multi-Group HE (MGHE), and define its security notion. An MGHE scheme can be viewed as a generalization of both MPHE and MKHE, which enjoys the best of both primitives. In MGHE, a group of parties collaboratively generates a public key that is commonly used among the parties for encryption. Hence, MGHE behaves like an MPHE scheme in a single group. Moreover, an MGHE scheme has the capability to perform arbitrary computations on encrypted data, regardless of whether the input ciphertexts are encrypted under the same group key or not, a crucial property of MKHE.

**Construction of MGHE.** We construct an MGHE scheme and provide a rigorous proof of its semantic security. Our MGHE scheme regards an MPHE ciphertext as a single-key encryption under the joint secret key so that ciphertexts corresponding to different group keys can be operated in a MKHE manner. Consequently, our MGHE scheme has a hierarchical structure where a ciphertext is decryptable by the joint secret keys of the associated groups, each of which is additively shared among the group members. From the perspective of MPHE, it is also the first construction of the MPHE scheme with non-interactive key aggregation where the joint encryption and evaluation keys are obtained from independently generated individual keys by simply summing them.

**Building Multi-party Computation Protocol from MGHE.** We build a round-optimal Multi-Party Computation (MPC) protocol on top of our MGHE scheme, which is naturally derived from the non-interactive key aggregation (setup). We show that the protocol is secure against semi-malicious adversaries in the dishonest majority setting, relying on the semantic security of MGHE.

**Experimental Results.** We implement our MGHE scheme based on both BFV and CKKS and provide a basic benchmark compared to the previous MPHE and MKHE works.

### 1.2 Technical Overview

At the heart of our construction lies a non-interactive key generation algorithm. This allows the joint key of a group to be constructed non-interactively from independently generated keys of the group members. The key generation follows a hybrid construction between MPHE (the encryption key aspects) and MKHE (the relinearization mechanisms).

We assume that each party is identified as a unique index $i$ and let $I$ be a group of parties. The homomorphic property of LWE makes the summation of public and secret key pairs be a valid key pair. To be precise, an MPHE scheme behaves like a single-key HE scheme where the joint secret key $s = \sum_{i \in I} [s]_i$ is additively shared among the members of $I$. We make the Common Random String (CRS) assumption to construct a joint public (encryption) key: given a random polynomial $a \in R_q$, each party $i \in I$ generates $[b]_i = a \cdot [s]_i + [e]_i \pmod q$ for some error $[e]_i$, then the joint public key is obtained as $b = \sum_{i \in I} [b]_i \approx a \cdot s \pmod q$. However, it is more challenging to generate a joint evaluation key, especially a relinearization key, because the relinearization key is usually supposed to be an 'encryption' of $s^2$ which has quadratic structure with respect to the individual secrets $[s]_i$. In the previous constructions [5,31], the key generation procedure involves a multi-round protocol among the parties: (1)

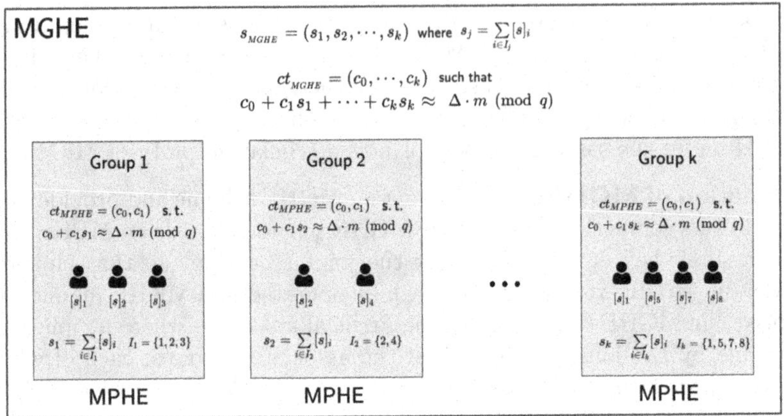


**Fig. 1.** A schematic presenting the overall structure of MGHE schemes. Each boxed group of participants acts as an MPHE scheme. The secret keys and ciphertext equations for each group and the entire set of participants (including between groups) are described above.

parties publish individual encryption keys to build a joint encryption key, then (2) use it to generate 'encryptions' of $[s]_i \cdot s$ and broadcast them to construct a joint evaluation key.

To reduce the multiple rounds of the protocol, we propose a new key generation algorithm which is *nearly linear* with respect to the secret key. This property enables the non-interactive key generation in that each party independently generates and broadcasts its public key $[\mathsf{pk}]_i$ once, which adds up to the joint public (encryption and evaluation) key $\mathsf{pk} = \sum_{i \in I} [\mathsf{pk}]_i$ corresponding to the joint secret $s = \sum_{i \in I} [s]_i$.

To construct our MGHE scheme, we apply this key generation protocol to support homomorphic computation between ciphertexts under different keys. For example, if we perform homomorphic computation on MPHE ciphertexts $\mathsf{ct}_j$ under the joint secret keys $s_j = \sum_{i \in I_j} [s]_i$ of groups $I_j$ for $1 \leq j \leq k$, then it outputs a 'multi-group' ciphertext under the secret $(s_1, \ldots, s_k)$. In particular, the joint public keys of the involved groups themselves are used in the relinearization process of multi-group ciphertexts so that no further interaction is required among the parties. The technical details of our MGHE constructions are described in Sect. 4. Thus, our MGHE scheme behaves as if it is an MKHE scheme in which each key is jointly generated by a group of parties (akin to MPHE). This makes MGHE an ideal generalization of both these HE variants and the hierarchical key structure allows an MGHE scheme to take advantage of strengths of both MPHE and MKHE.

### 1.3 Related Work

We first remark that the terminology for HE-like primitive has not been agreed upon yet in the literature. We use the terms 'MPHE' and 'MKHE' to classify the related works.

Asharov et al. [5] designed the first MPHE scheme from BGV [10]. Mouchet et al. [31] proposed a simplified construction from BFV [9,20] and presented some experimental results. Park [33] recently modified the key generation protocol to reduce the interaction and also suggested a conversion between MPHE and MKHE. To the best of our knowledge, all known MPHE schemes require a multi-round protocol among the parties to generate a shared key pair.

On the other hand, there have been several attempts to construct an MKHE scheme by generalizing single-key HE schemes. López-Alt et al. [29] designed the first MKHE from NTRU [25], and [18,32,34] studied multi-key variants of GSW [22]. Then, Brakerski and Perlman [11] presented an LWE-based MKHE [11], followed by Chen et al. [12] who presented a multi-key variant of TFHE [16]. Other works [13,14] studied MKHE schemes from batched HEs such as BGV [10], BFV [9,20] and CKKS [15]. Ananth et al. [4] proposed a general methodology to design an MKHE scheme in the plain model. The construction is done by combining an oblivious transfer protocol and MKHE schemes with limited functionality or trusted setup.

We remark that some MKHE schemes can be converted into MGHE: if the key generation algorithm of an MKHE scheme has the homomorphic property, then we can simply operate on the public keys of multiple parties to build a shared key for the group. For example, multi-key GSW schemes [18,32,34] hold the condition since GSW does not require an evaluation key for multiplication.

Aloufi et al. [3] combined MPHE and MKHE to perform computation on ciphertexts under two different keys: a joint key of model owners and the other of a client. It can be viewed as a special case of MGHE in which there are two groups consisting of model owners and a client. However, its key generation procedure also involves an interactive protocol to obtain an evaluation key.

Boneh et al. [8] suggested the notion of threshold FHE that has $t$-out-of-$n$ access structure protocol by splitting the secret key into shares. Its key generation is based on a Shamir secret sharing scheme where each party receives a share of the secret key.

## 2 Background

### 2.1 Notation

Let $N$ be a power of two. We denote by $R = \mathbb{Z}[X]/(X^N + 1)$ the ring of integers of the $(2N)$-th cyclotomic field and $R_q = \mathbb{Z}_q[X]/(X^N + 1)$ the residue ring of $R$ modulo an integer $q$. An element of $R$ (or $R_q$) is uniquely represented as a polynomial of degree less than $N$ with coefficients in $\mathbb{Z}$ (or $\mathbb{Z}_q$). We identify $a = \sum_{0 \le i < N} a_i \cdot X^i \in R$ with the vector of its coefficients $(a_0, \ldots, a_{N-1}) \in \mathbb{Z}^N$. For $\sigma > 0$, we denote by $D_\sigma$ a distribution over $R$ which samples $N$ coefficients independently from the discrete Gaussian distribution of variance $\sigma^2$ and $\chi$ as a key distribution.

### 2.2 Ring Learning with Errors

Given the parameters $(N, q, \chi, \sigma)$, consider the samples of the form $b_i = s \cdot a_i + e_i \pmod{q}$ for polynomial number of $i$'s where $a_i \leftarrow U(R_q)$ and $e_i \leftarrow D_\sigma$ for a fixed $s \leftarrow \chi$. The Ring Learning with Errors (RLWE) assumption states that the RLWE samples $(b_i, a_i)$'s are computationally indistinguishable from uniformly random elements of $U(R_q^2)$.

### 2.3 Gadget Decomposition and External Product

A function $h : R_q \to R^d$ is called a *gadget decomposition* if there exists a *gadget vector* $\mathbf{g} = (g_i) \in \mathbb{Z}_q^d$ such that $a = \langle h(a), \mathbf{g} \rangle \pmod{q}$ for all $a \in R_q$. Typical examples are bit decomposition [9,10], digit decomposition [16], and Residue Number System (RNS) based decompositions [6,24]. Our implementation is based on an RNS-friendly decomposition for efficiency.

For $\mu \in R$, we call $\mathbf{U} = (\mathbf{u}_0, \mathbf{u}_1) \in R_q^{d\times 2}$ a *gadget encryption* of $\mu$ under a secret $s$ if $\mathbf{u}_0 + s \cdot \mathbf{u}_1 = \mu \cdot \mathbf{g} + \mathbf{e} \pmod{q}$ for some $\mathbf{e}$ sampled from an error distribution. Chillotti et al. [16] formalized *external product* operation between RLWE and RGSW ciphertexts. We adopt and generalize this concept as follows: for $c \in R_q$ and $\mathbf{v} \in R_q^d$, the external product is defined as $c \boxdot \mathbf{v} := \langle h(c), \mathbf{v} \rangle \pmod{q}$. We also write $c \boxdot \mathbf{U} = (c \boxdot \mathbf{u}_0, c \boxdot \mathbf{u}_1)$ for $\mathbf{U} = (\mathbf{u}_0, \mathbf{u}_1) \in R_q^{d\times 2}$. We note that if $\mathbf{U}$ is a gadget encryption of $\mu$ such that $\mathbf{u}_0 + s \cdot \mathbf{u}_1 = \mu \cdot \mathbf{g} + \mathbf{e} \pmod{q}$ for some $\mathbf{e}$, then the external product $(c_0, c_1) \leftarrow c \boxdot \mathbf{U}$ satisfies that $c_0 + c_1 \cdot s = c \boxdot (\mathbf{u}_0 + s \cdot \mathbf{u}_1) = c \cdot \mu + \langle h(c), \mathbf{e} \rangle \pmod{q}$.

The gadget decomposition technique is widely used in HE schemes to reduce the noise growth of homomorphic operations. In addition, it is often combined with the special modulus technique [21]. Although the special modulus technique is applied to the external product in our implementation, we do not describe it in the main body of this paper for simplicity.

## 3 Formalizing Multi-group Homomorphic Encryption

The ordinary HE schemes support computation on ciphertexts, but the same key should be used for encryption. This major constraint raises the key management problem and makes it difficult to apply the HE technology to a variety of applications. For the last few years, substantial research has been undertaken to solve the issue by distributing the authority of HE system. Currently, there are two main approaches to extend the functionality of HE to the multi-party setting: Threshold HE (ThHE) and Multi-Key HE (MKHE).

First, Threshold HE (e.g. [5,8,30,31,33]) is similar to HE, except the fact that the secret key is shared among several parties. In particular, most studies are dedicated to the case of $t = n$, which we call Multi-party HE (MPHE), while there have been limited results for $t < n$. In practice, ThHE (or MPHE) schemes are derived from single-key HEs by replacing their key-generation algorithms with distributed protocols, while the evaluation procedures remain the same. To the best of our knowledge, all existing schemes require interaction between the parties to build a relinearization key for multiplication. This approach tends to be more efficient, but it is required to fix the parties at the setup phase which cannot change during the entire operation.

Meanwhile, Multi-key HE (e.g. [12,13,18,29,32,34]) is another variant of HE with different pros and cons. In this primitive, each party can generate its own key and use it to encrypt data without any interaction with other users. Moreover, it is possible to evaluate a circuit over ciphertexts under different keys, which results in a multi-key ciphertext decryptable by the associated parties. The MKHE schemes enjoy better flexibility and dynamism since it allows a new party to join the computation anytime. On the other hand, they suffer from relatively poor performance where the space and time complexity grow depending on the number of parties involved in the computation.

In this section, we propose a new variant of HE for multiple parties, called Multi-Group HE (MGHE), which allows the seamless integration of MPHE and MKHE and has the best of both worlds.

### 3.1 Definition

An MGHE scheme consists of several algorithms and protocols below:

- $\texttt{Setup}(1^\lambda, 1^d)$: Given the security parameter $\lambda$ and the maximal level $d$, the setup algorithm generates a public parameter set $\mathsf{pp}$.
- $\texttt{KeyGen}(\{P_i : i \in I\})$: A set of parties $\{P_i : i \in I\}$ execute the key-generation protocol to jointly generate a public key $\mathsf{pk}$. Each party $P_i$ also obtains a secret share $[\mathsf{sk}]_i$.
- $\texttt{Enc}(\mathsf{pk}; m)$: Given a public key $\mathsf{pk}$ and a message $m$, the encryption algorithm returns a ciphertext $\mathsf{ct}$.
- $\texttt{Eval}(\{\mathsf{pk}_1, \ldots, \mathsf{pk}_k; C, \mathsf{ct}_1, \ldots, \mathsf{ct}_k)$: Given a circuit $C$, ciphertexts $\mathsf{ct}_1, \ldots, \mathsf{ct}_k$ and their associated public keys $\mathsf{pk}_1, \ldots, \mathsf{pk}_k$, the evaluation algorithm outputs a ciphertext $\mathsf{ct}$.
- $\texttt{DistDec}(\{P_i : i \in I\}; \mathsf{ct})$. Given a ciphertext $\mathsf{ct}$, the associated parties execute the distributed decryption protocol and recover a message $m$.

First of all, the key-generation protocol can be conducted by a set of parties (which we call a *group*) to build a public key and corresponding secret key shares. A group of parties $\{P_i : i \in I\}$ will be represented as an index set $I$. Unlike MPHE, it is not necessary to specify a group at the setup phase, but any group of parties can execute the protocol at any time. In addition, each party may join several groups and run the key-generation protocol with different parties. A data owner needs to pick a public key in the encrypt algorithm so that the output ciphertext is collaboratively decryptable by the corresponding group of parties. We require that an MGHE scheme is semantically secure in the semi-honest model. In other words, the adversary learns no information about the message if at least one party in the group is honest.

The evaluation algorithm of MGHE allows us to compute a circuit on encrypted messages, which are not necessarily encrypted under the same key.

To be precise, if we evaluate a circuit over ciphertexts associated with groups $I_1, \ldots, I_k$, then the output ciphertext is no longer decryptable by a single group but its decryption requires all parties in $I := I_1 \cup \cdots \cup I_k$ to be involved in the distributed decryption protocol.

In the security game, we assume that the key-generation protocol is executed honestly by the parties. The correctness guarantees that the output of evaluation and decryption protocols in MGHE is same as the result of the evaluation circuit with plain messages. The security of MGHE indicates that when there is at least one honest party among sets of parties, an encryption for that party does not reveal any information about the message.

**Definition 1 (Security).** *Let $I_1, I_2, \ldots, I_k$ be sets of parties and let $I = \cup_{1 \le j \le k} I_j$. Let $A \subseteq I$ denote the set of adversarial parties and $H = I \backslash A$. An MGHE scheme is said to be secure if the advantage of $\mathcal{A}$ in the following game is negligible for any PPT adversary $\mathcal{A}$:*

- The challenger generates a public parameter $\mathsf{pp} \leftarrow \mathtt{Setup}(1^\lambda, 1^d)$.
- The challenger executes the key generation protocol $\mathtt{KeyGen}(\mathsf{pp}, I_j)$ for all $1 \le j \le k$. The challenger sends the public keys $\mathsf{pk}_1, \ldots, \mathsf{pk}_k$ and secret shares $\{[\mathsf{sk}_j]_i : i \in A, 1 \le j \le k\}$ of $A$ to the adversary.
- The adversary chooses messages $m_0, m_1 \in \mathcal{M}$ and picks an index $j$ such that $I_j \not\subseteq A$, and sends them to the challenger. The challenger samples a random bit $b \in \{0,1\}$ and sends $\mathtt{Enc}(\mathsf{pk}_j; m_b)$ back to the adversary.
- The adversary $\mathcal{A}$ outputs a bit $b'$. The advantage is defined as $\left|\Pr[b = b'] - \frac{1}{2}\right|$.

**Definition 2 (Correctness).** *Let $\mathsf{pp} \leftarrow \mathtt{Setup}(1^\lambda, 1^d)$. For $1 \le i \le k$, let $\mathsf{pk}_i \leftarrow \mathtt{KeyGen}(I_i)$ be a public key generated by a set of parties $\{P_j : j \in I_i\}$ and $\mathsf{ct}_i \leftarrow \mathtt{Enc}(\mathsf{pk}_i; m_i)$ be an encryption of a message $m_i$. An MGHE scheme is said to be correct if for any circuit $C : \mathcal{M}^k \to \mathcal{M}$ whose depth is bounded by $d$, the following holds with an overwhelming probability in $\lambda$:*

$$\mathtt{DistDec}\left(\{P_i : i \in \bigcup_{1 \le i \le k} I_i\}; \mathtt{Eval}(\mathsf{pk}_1, \ldots, \mathsf{pk}_k; C, \mathsf{ct}_1, \ldots, \mathsf{ct}_k)\right) = C(m_1, \ldots, m_k).$$

### 3.2 Relations with MPHE and MKHE

Let us explain how MGHE is related with other approaches, MPHE and MKHE. As mentioned before, these primitives differ in various respects such as key structure and functionality. Recall that all parties use the same public key for encryption and evaluation in the MPHE setting, while an MKHE scheme allows each party to generate a key pair independently so that different keys can be involved in the computation.

Our suggestion, the MGHE primitive, can be viewed as a generalization of both primitives. In other words, MPHE and MKHE are special instantiations of MGHE with different group structures. First, suppose that all parties join a single group in the MGHE setting. Then, they share the same key for encryption and the whole evaluation is done within the group, similar to the case of MPHE. Conversely, if each user forms a group alone, then the group key is solely generated and owned by a single party and the evaluation across different parties are performed in the MKHE manner.

Moreover, in these examples, our security definition of MGHE corresponds to the security definitions of MPHE and MKHE. In the single-group case, there is only group to be chosen by the adversary, so the security game is exactly the same as that of MPHE [28]. On the other hand, if every group consists of a single party, then our security game for MGHE defines the ordinary semantic security for (MK)HE.

# 4 MGHE Construction

In this section, we present a concrete instantiation of MGHE from the BFV scheme. Recall that, in the MGHE setting, we can perform computation over ciphertexts which are not necessarily encrypted under the same key. In addition, our idea is easily applicable to design multi-group variants of other HE schemes such as BGV [10] and CKKS [15]. In particular, we implement MGHE schemes from both BFV and CKKS and present experimental results in Sect. 6. We also provide a formal description of multi-group CKKS in Appendix A.1.

In Sects. 4.1 and 4.2, we outline the basic scheme consisting of setup, key generation, encryption, and decryption of the MGHE scheme. In Sects. 4.3 and 4.4, we provide the algorithms of arithmetic operations and automorphism of MGHE, respectively, with its correctness proof and we provide the security analysis of MGHE in Sect. 4.5.

## 4.1 Key Generation

In this section, we describe a key generation procedure of our MGHE scheme. Our scheme is based on the CRS model, *i.e.*, all parties have access to the same random string. A parameter set also includes the RLWE dimensions, ciphertext modulus, the key distribution, as well as the error parameter. We firstly explain the setup phase which is a stage to determine some parameters for further procedures with a certain security level before introducing the key generation.

• $\underline{\texttt{Setup}(1^\lambda)}$: Set the RLWE dimension $N$, the plaintext modulus $t$, the ciphertext modulus $q$, the key distribution $\chi$ over $R$, and the error parameter $\sigma$. Choose a gadget decomposition $h : R_q \to R^d$ with a gadget vector $\mathbf{g} \in R_q^d$. Sample random vectors $\mathbf{a}, \mathbf{u}$ and $\mathbf{k}_1, \ldots, \mathbf{k}_L$ from $U(R_q^d)$ where $L$ is the number of different automorphisms to be used in the evaluation process. Return the public parameter $\mathsf{pp} = (N, t, q, \chi, \sigma, \mathbf{g}, h)$ and common random string $\mathsf{crs} = (\mathbf{a}, \mathbf{u}, \mathbf{k}_1, \ldots, \mathbf{k}_L)$. We write $\Delta = \lfloor q/t \rceil$.

Our scheme generates several CRSs in the setup phase, but this can be implemented efficiently using a keyed pseudo-random function (PRF). This allows us to rely on the CRS assumption for a fixed-size seed, regardless of the number of common random polynomials used for public and automorphism keys.

Recall the definition of MGHE in Sect. 3.1: a group of parties executes the key generation protocol to build a joint public key while each party obtains its own secret. In our construction, the key generation proceeds in two steps of generating individual secret keys and aggregating them into a public key. To be precise, each party $P_i$ first generates its own key pair $([\mathsf{sk}]_i, [\mathsf{pk}]_i)$ and broadcasts the public component $[\mathsf{pk}]_i$. We stress that the generation of an individual key pair can be done locally by each party without any interaction with other parties. In the following step, a public key for a group of parties $\{P_i : i \in I\}$ can be obtained from the individual public keys $[\mathsf{pk}]_i$ of the group members. This aggregation can be done by a public cloud without further interaction between the parties. We note that a public key includes an encryption key, a relinearization key for multiplication and automorphism keys for homomorphic rotation.

Note that the individual key generation can be regarded as a preprocessing phase of the key generation protocol since other parties do not affect and thus each party is able to run this protocol at any time. In addition, even if a party belongs to several groups, the party generates only one key pair of its own and uses it several times to create multiple public keys corresponding to the groups that the party belongs to. It makes our construction more efficient because the party does not need to generate a new key pair for each key aggregation step. We guarantee that the MGHE scheme is secure and the security proof is described in Sect. 4.5.

• $\texttt{IndKeyGen}(P_i; \{\psi_\ell\}_{1\le\ell\le L})$: Each party $P_i$ generates individual secret and public keys as follows:

- Sample $[s]_i \leftarrow \chi$ and set the secret key as $[\mathsf{sk}]_i = s_i$.
- Sample $[r]_i \leftarrow \chi$ and $[\mathbf{e}_0]_i, [\mathbf{e}_1]_i, [\mathbf{e}_2]_i \leftarrow D_\sigma^d$, and compute

$$\begin{aligned}
[\mathbf{b}]_i &= -[s]_i \cdot \mathbf{a} + [\mathbf{e}_0]_i \pmod q,\\
[\mathbf{d}]_i &= -[r]_i \cdot \mathbf{a} + [s]_i \cdot \mathbf{g} + [\mathbf{e}_1]_i \pmod q,\\
[\mathbf{v}]_i &= -[s]_i \cdot \mathbf{u} - [r]_i \cdot \mathbf{g} + [\mathbf{e}_2]_i \pmod q.
\end{aligned}$$

- For given automorphisms $\psi_1, \ldots, \psi_L$, sample $[\mathbf{e}'_\ell]_i \leftarrow D_\sigma^d$ and compute

$$[\mathbf{h}_\ell]_i = -[s]_i \cdot \mathbf{k} + \psi_\ell([s]_i) \cdot \mathbf{g} + [\mathbf{e}'_\ell]_i \pmod q$$

for $1 \le \ell \le L$. Set the public key as $[\mathsf{pk}]_i = ([\mathbf{b}]_i, [\mathbf{d}]_i, [\mathbf{v}]_i, [\mathbf{h}_1]_i, \ldots, [\mathbf{h}_L]_i)$.

• $\texttt{JointKeyGen}(\{[\mathsf{pk}]_i : i \in I\})$: Let $I$ be the index set for a group of parties. Given the collection of public keys $[\mathsf{pk}]_i$ with $i \in I$, compute the public key as $\mathsf{pk} = \sum_{i\in I}[\mathsf{pk}]_i$, *i.e.*, $\mathsf{pk} = (\mathbf{b}, \mathbf{d}, \mathbf{v}, \mathbf{h}_1, \ldots, \mathbf{h}_L) \in R_q^{d\times 4}$ where

$$\mathbf{b} = \sum_{i\in I}[\mathbf{b}]_i, \quad \mathbf{d} = \sum_{i\in I}[\mathbf{d}]_i, \quad \mathbf{v} = \sum_{i\in I}[\mathbf{v}]_i, \text{ and } \mathbf{h}_\ell = \sum_{i\in I}[\mathbf{h}_\ell]_i \pmod q$$

for $1 \leq \ell \leq L$. Specifically, we denote the encryption key as $\mathsf{ek} = (\mathbf{b}[0], \mathbf{a}[0])$, the relinearization key as $\mathsf{rlk} = (\mathbf{b}, \mathbf{d}, \mathbf{v})$, and the automorphism keys as $\mathsf{ak}_\ell = \mathbf{h}_\ell$.

Each component of the public key $[\mathsf{pk}]_i$ forms a gadget encryption with a CRS under the secrets $[s]_i$ or $[r]_i$. We call $s = \sum_{i \in I}[s]_i$ the (implicitly defined) secret key for the group $I$. The individual secrets $[s]_i$ can be viewed as additive shares of $s$. Furthermore, the public key $[\mathsf{pk}]_i$ is *nearly linear* with respect to $[s]_i$ and $[r]_i$ so that the joint public key $\mathsf{pk} = (\mathbf{b}, \mathbf{d}, \mathbf{v}, \mathbf{h}_\ell)_{1 \leq \ell \leq L}$ satisfies the same properties as the individual keys:

$$\mathbf{b} \approx -s \cdot \mathbf{a} \pmod q, \qquad \mathbf{d} \approx -r \cdot \mathbf{a} + s \cdot \mathbf{g} \pmod q$$
$$\mathbf{v} \approx -s \cdot \mathbf{u} - r \cdot \mathbf{g} \pmod q, \qquad \mathbf{h}_\ell \approx -s \cdot \mathbf{k}_\ell + \psi_\ell(s) \cdot \mathbf{g} \pmod q$$

**Non-interactive Key Aggregation.** In the construction of existing MPHE, the main challenge is to generate the relinearization key for a group of parties. To be precise, the relinearization key of BFV is a key-switching key from $s^2$ to $s$, or equivalently, a gadget encryption of $s^2$ under $s$. However, the secret key is additively shared among the parties in the multi-party setting, so it is not easy to generate the relinearization key in a distributed manner due to its quadratic structure. Therefore, the existing MPHE schemes [5,31,33] had a common limitation in that they rely on a multi-round key generation protocol requiring interaction between the parties.

For instance, the public key generation of [33] consists of two steps: all parties broadcast individual encryption keys $[b]_i \approx a \cdot [s]_i \pmod q$ to build a joint encryption key $b = \sum_{i \in I}[b]_i$ first, then use it to generate a gadget encryption of $[s]_i \cdot s$ and aggregate them to build a gadget encryption of $s^2$.

In this work, we solve the issue by introducing a novel key-generation algorithm such that the public key is *nearly linear* with the corresponding secret key. In other words, our relinearization key has a completely different structure where the summation of $[\mathsf{pk}]_i$ for $i \in I$ becomes a valid public key corresponding to the secret $\sum_{i \in I}[\mathsf{sk}]_i$. Our key-generation algorithm is inspired from the idea of Chen et al. [13] introducing the second secret $[r]_i$ to reconstruct the relinearization key structure. Although the prior method is not nearly linear so cannot be directly used in the MPHE construction, we achieve the desired property by making an additional CRS assumption.

Consequently, our MGHE scheme allows each party to independently generate an individual public key once even without any information about other parties, and the public key for a group can be built on the server by simply adding individual public keys. This 'non-interactive' nature of key aggregation offers several advantages, including performance and flexibility. For instance, if a party $P_i$ belongs to several groups, it suffices to generate a single individual public key $[\mathsf{pk}]_i$ and reuse it across all groups, instead of joining the key-general protocol repeatedly once for each group. More discussions on this feature will be given in Sect. 5.1.

### 4.2 Encryption and Decryption

As explained above, the encryption key $\mathsf{ek} = (\mathbf{b}[0], \mathbf{a}[0])$ satisfies $\mathbf{b}[0] + \mathbf{a}[0] \cdot s \approx 0 \pmod{q}$, so it can be viewed as an RLWE instance with secret $s$. Therefore, we use the same BFV encryption and decryption algorithms in our scheme as follows.

• $\underline{\mathtt{Enc}(\mathsf{ek}; m)}$: Given a message $m \in R_p$ and the joint encryption key $\mathsf{ek}$, sample $w \leftarrow \chi$ and $e_0, e_1 \leftarrow D_\sigma$. Return the ciphertext $\mathsf{ct} = w \cdot \mathsf{ek} + (\Delta \cdot m + e_0, e_1) \pmod{q}$.

Suppose that a message $m$ is encrypted using a public key generated by a group of parties $\{P_i : i \in I\}$. Then, the output ciphertext $\mathsf{ct} = (c_0, c_1) \leftarrow \mathtt{Enc}(\mathsf{ek}, m)$ satisfies that $c_0 + c_1 s \approx \Delta m \pmod{q}$ where $s = \sum_{i \in I} [s]_i$ is the secret key for the group $I$. Therefore, it is required to store the information

In our MGHE scheme, it is As we discussed in Sect. 3.1, an MGHE ciphertext holds the references to the associated public keys. In our scheme, each ciphertext stores an ordered set of the involved groups. For example, a fresh ciphertext encrypted by a joint public key $\mathsf{pk} = \sum_{i \in I} [\mathsf{pk}]_i$ is linked to the set containing a single element $I$. More generally, a multi-group encryption of $m$ corresponding an ordered set of $k$ groups $\{I_1, \ldots, I_k\}$ is an $(k+1)$ tuple $\mathsf{ct} = (c_0, c_1, \ldots, c_k) \in R_q^{k+1}$ satisfying $c_0 + c_1 \cdot s_1 + \cdots + c_k \cdot s_k = \Delta \cdot m + e \pmod{q}$ for some error $e$ where $s_j = \sum_{i \in I_j} [s]_i$ is the joint secret key of $I_j$ for $1 \le j \le k$.

Finally, we present a basic (ideal) decryption algorithm and a distributed decryption protocol. For given a ciphertext $\mathsf{ct} = (c_0, \ldots, c_k)$ which is linked to $k$ groups $I_1, \ldots, I_k$, the basic algorithm takes as input the joint secret keys $s_i$ of the associated groups $I_i$ and recovers the plaintext message while the distributed decryption protocol let the parties in $\bigcup_{1 \le j \le k} I_j$ perform the same computation securely in a distributed manner. As we mentioned before, we describe how to set concrete $\sigma'$ for the distributed decryption in Sect. 5.2.

• $\underline{\mathtt{Dec}(\mathsf{sk}_1, \ldots, \mathsf{sk}_k; \mathsf{ct})}$: Given a ciphertext $\mathsf{ct} = (c_0, c_1, \ldots, c_k)$ and joint secret keys $\mathsf{sk}_j = s_j$ for $1 \le j \le k$, return $m = \left\lfloor (t/q) \cdot (c_0 + \sum_{1 \le j \le k} c_j \cdot s_j) \right\rceil \pmod{t}$.

• $\underline{\mathtt{DistDec}(\{[\mathsf{sk}]_i : i \in \cup_{1 \le j \le k} I_j\}, \sigma'; \mathsf{ct})}$: Let $\mathsf{ct} = (c_0, \ldots, c_k)$ be a multi-group ciphertext corresponding to an ordered set of groups $(I_1, \ldots, I_k)$. The distributed decryption protocol consists of the following procedures:

- Partial decryption: Let $I = \cup_{1 \le j \le k} I_j$. Each party $i \in I$ samples $[e']_i \leftarrow D_{\sigma'}$, then broadcasts $[\mu]_i = \left(\sum_{1 \le j \le k,\ i \in I_j} c_j\right) \cdot [s]_i + [e']_i \pmod{q}$.
- Merge: Compute $m = \lfloor (t/q) \cdot (c_0 + \sum_{i \in I} [\mu]_i) \rceil \pmod{t}$.

### 4.3 Arithmetic Operations

Homomorphic operations include a pre-processing step that aligns the components of input ciphertexts as follows. For given two multi-group ciphertexts, we consider the corresponding ordered sets and compute their union,

**Algorithm 1.** Relinearization procedure of MGHE

**Input:** $\mathsf{ct}_{\mathsf{mul}} = (c_{i,j})_{0 \le i,j \le k}$, $\mathsf{rlk}_j = (\mathbf{b}_j, \mathbf{d}_j, \mathbf{v}_j)$ for $1 \le j \le k$.
**Output:** $\mathsf{ct}_{\mathsf{relin}} = (c_j^*)_{0 \le j \le k} \in R_q^{k+1}$.

1: $c_0^* \leftarrow c_{0,0}$
2: **for** $1 \le j \le k$ **do**
3: $\quad c_j^* \leftarrow c_{0,j} + c_{j,0} \pmod q$
4: **end for**
5: **for** $1 \le j \le k$ **do**
6: $\quad c_j^* \leftarrow c_j^* + \sum_{1 \le i \le k} c_{i,j} \boxdot \mathbf{d}_i \pmod q$
7: **end for**
8: **for** $1 \le i \le k$ **do**
9: $\quad c_i'' \leftarrow \sum_{1 \le j \le k} c_{i,j} \boxdot \mathbf{b}_j$
10: $\quad (c_0^*, c_i^*) \leftarrow (c_0^*, c_i^*) + c_i'' \boxdot (\mathbf{v}_i, \mathbf{u}) \pmod q$
11: **end for**

say $\{I_1, \ldots, I_k\}$. Then, we extend the input ciphertexts by padding some zeros and rearranging their components so that both ciphertexts are decryptable with respect to the same secret $\overline{\mathsf{sk}} = (s_1, \ldots, s_k)$ where $s_j$ is the joint secret of group $I_j$, $1 \le j \le k$. We assume that this pre-processing is always performed on the input ciphertext and the output ciphertext is linked to the union $\{I_1, \ldots, I_k\}$ of ordered sets even if it is not explicitly mentioned in the algorithm description.

• $\underline{\texttt{Add}(\mathsf{ct}, \mathsf{ct}')}$: Given two ciphertexts $\mathsf{ct}$ and $\mathsf{ct}'$, return the ciphertext $\mathsf{ct}_{add} = \mathsf{ct} + \mathsf{ct}' \pmod q$.

• $\underline{\texttt{Mult}(\mathsf{rlk}_1, \ldots, \mathsf{rlk}_k; \mathsf{ct}, \mathsf{ct}')}$: Given two multi-group ciphertexts $\mathsf{ct} = (c_0, \ldots, c_k)$, $\mathsf{ct}' = (c_0', \ldots, c_k')$ and $k$ joint relinearization keys $\mathsf{rlk}_1, \ldots, \mathsf{rlk}_k$, compute $\mathsf{ct}_{\mathsf{mul}} = (c_{i,j})_{0 \le i,j \le k}$ where $c_{i,j} = \lfloor (t/q) \cdot c_i c_j' \rceil \pmod q$ for $0 \le i, j \le k$. Return the ciphertext $\mathsf{ct}_{\mathsf{relin}} \leftarrow \texttt{Relin}(\mathsf{rlk}_1, \ldots, \mathsf{rlk}_k; \mathsf{ct}_{\mathsf{mul}})$ where $\texttt{Relin}(\cdot)$ is the relinearization procedure described in Algorithm 1.

We remark that the relinearization algorithm can be shared between our MGHE scheme and the previous MKHE scheme [13] as they have the same ciphertext structure. Our relinearization algorithm is an improvement of the previous method which reduces the number of external products by almost a factor of 2. More formally, the prior algorithm computes lines 8–11 of Algorithm 1 by repeating the following computation iteratively over $1 \le i, j \le k$:

$$(c_0^*, c_i^*) \leftarrow (c_0^*, c_i^*) + (c_{i,j} \boxdot \mathbf{b}_j) \boxdot (\mathbf{v}_i, \mathbf{u}) \pmod q.$$

We observe that $\sum_{1 \le j \le k} c_{i,j} \boxdot \mathbf{b}_j$ is pre-computable and reusable for the relinearization of multiple ciphertext components. This idea consequently reduces the number of external products down to $2k^2 + 2k$ in total, compared to the former method which requires $4k^2$ external products. We refer the reader to Appendix B for details about the noise analysis.

**Correctness of Homomorphic Multiplication.** Suppose that $\mathsf{ct}$ and $\mathsf{ct}'$ are encryptions of $m$ and $m'$ under secret $\overline{\mathsf{sk}} = (s_1, \ldots, s_k)$, respectively, and let

$\mathsf{ct}_{\mathsf{mul}} = (c_{i,j})_{0 \le i,j \le k} = \lfloor (t/q) \cdot \mathsf{ct} \otimes \mathsf{ct}' \rceil \pmod q$. Then, it satisfies following relation: $\langle \mathsf{ct}_{\mathsf{mul}}, (1, \overline{\mathsf{sk}}) \otimes (1, \overline{\mathsf{sk}}) \rangle \approx \Delta \cdot mm' \pmod q$. We claim that if $\mathsf{ct}_{\mathsf{relin}} \leftarrow \mathtt{Relin}(\{\mathsf{rlk}_j\}_{1 \le j \le k}; \mathsf{ct}_{\mathsf{mul}})$, then the output ciphertext $\mathsf{ct}_{\mathsf{relin}} = (c_0^*, \ldots, c_k^*)$ satisfies $c_0^* + \sum_{1 \le j \le k} c_j^* \cdot s_j \approx \sum_{0 \le i,j \le k} c_{i,j} \cdot s_i s_j$ and thereby is a valid encryption of $mm'$.

First, we have

$$c_0^* + \sum_{1 \le j \le k} c_j^* \cdot s_j = c_{0,0} + \sum_{1 \le j \le k} (c_{0,j} + c_{j,0}) \cdot s_j + \sum_{1 \le i,j \le k} (c_{i,j} \boxdot \mathbf{d}_i) \cdot s_j + \sum_{1 \le i \le k} c_i'' \boxdot (\mathbf{v}_i + s_i \cdot \mathbf{u})$$

where $c_i'' = \sum_{1 \le j \le k} c_{i,j} \boxdot \mathbf{b}_j$ from the definition of Algorithm 1.

We also consider the properties $s_j \cdot \mathbf{d}_i \approx -r_i s_i \cdot \mathbf{a} + s_i s_j \cdot \mathbf{g} \approx r_i \cdot \mathbf{b}_j + s_i s_j \cdot \mathbf{g} \pmod q$ and $\mathbf{v}_i + s_i \cdot \mathbf{u} \approx -r_i \cdot \mathbf{g} \pmod q$ of the joint public keys and deduce the following equations:

$$\sum_{1 \le i,j \le k} (c_{i,j} \boxdot \mathbf{d}_i) \cdot s_j \approx \sum_{1 \le i,j \le k} r_i \cdot (c_{i,j} \boxdot \mathbf{b}_j) + \sum_{1 \le i,j \le k} c_{i,j} \cdot s_i s_j \pmod q,$$

$$\sum_{1 \le i \le k} c_i'' \boxdot (\mathbf{v}_i + s_i \cdot \mathbf{u}) \approx - \sum_{1 \le i \le k} r_i \cdot c_i'' = - \sum_{1 \le i,j \le k} r_i \cdot (c_{i,j} \boxdot \mathbf{b}_j) \pmod q.$$

Putting them all together, we obtain

$$c_0^* + \sum_{1 \le j \le k} c_j^* \cdot s_j \approx c_{0,0} + \sum_{1 \le j \le k} (c_{0,i} + c_{i,0}) \cdot s_j + \sum_{1 \le i,j \le k} c_{i,j} \cdot s_i s_j = \sum_{0 \le i,j \le k} c_{i,j} \cdot s_i s_j \pmod q$$

which completes the correctness proof of the relinearization algorithm.

**Asymptotically Faster Multiplication.** Recent research [26] has enhanced the multiplication of BFV and CKKS in MKHE to achieve a linear time complexity. They leverage a newly proposed concept called *homomorphic gadget decomposition*, which satisfies $\langle h(a) \odot h(b), \mathbf{g} \rangle = ab \pmod q$ for $a, b \in R_q$, to replace the term $h(c_{i,j})$ with $h(c_i) \odot h(c_j')$. As our MGHE is a natural extension of MKHE, we can directly adopt their algorithm to both BFV and CKKS. Notably, their multiplication in BFV entails additional (homomorphic) gadget decomposition $\tilde{h} : R_{\tilde{q}} \to R^{\tilde{d}}$ on $\tilde{q} := q^2$ with a gadget vector $h \in R_{\tilde{q}}^{\tilde{d}}$ and the corresponding external product $c \tilde{\boxdot} \mathbf{v} = \left\langle \tilde{h}(c), \mathbf{v} \right\rangle \pmod{\tilde{q}}$. We refer the reader to [26] for further details.

### 4.4 Automorphism

The packing technique of the BFV scheme enables us to encode multiple values in a finite field into a single plaintext polynomial for better efficiency [10]. The (un)packing algorithm has a similar algebraic structure with the canonical embedding map over the cyclotomic field $K = \mathbb{Q}[X]/(X^N + 1)$, and the automorphisms in the Galois group $\mathcal{G}al(K/\mathbb{Q})$ provide special functionality on the plaintext slots such as rotation.

We present a multi-group variant of homomorphic automorphism such that the joint automorphism key is generated non-interactively. Given a multi-group ciphertext $\mathsf{ct} = (c_0, \ldots, c_k)$ linked to $k$ groups $I_1, \ldots, I_k$, the joint automorphism key of $I_j$ is used to perform the key-switching procedure of the $j$-th entry $\psi(c_j)$ during the homomorphic evaluation of $\psi_\ell \in \mathcal{G}\mathsf{al}(K/\mathbb{Q})$. For simplicity, we will describe the case with one automorphism for simplicity in the following sections.

- $\underline{\texttt{Auto}(\mathsf{ak}_1, \ldots, \mathsf{ak}_k; \mathsf{ct})}$: Given a ciphertext $\mathsf{ct} = (c_0, c_1, \ldots, c_k)$ and the joint automorphism keys $\mathsf{ak}_j = \mathbf{h}_j$ for $1 \le j \le k$, compute and return the ciphertext $\mathsf{ct}_{\mathsf{aut}} = (c'_0, c'_1, \ldots, c'_k)$ where $c'_0 = \psi(c_0) + \sum_{1 \le j \le k}(\psi(c_j) \boxdot \mathbf{h}_j) \pmod q$ and $c'_j = \psi(c_j) \boxdot \mathbf{k} \pmod q$ for $1 \le j \le k$.

**Correctness of Homomorphic Automorphism.** We show below the correctness of multi-group homomorphic automorphism algorithm:

$$\begin{aligned} c'_0 + \sum_{1 \le j \le k} c'_j \cdot s_j &= \psi_\ell(c_0) + \sum_{1 \le j \le k} \psi_\ell(c_j) \boxdot (\mathbf{h}_j + s_j \cdot \mathbf{k}) \\ &\approx \psi_\ell(c_0) + \sum_{1 \le j \le k} \psi_\ell(c_j) \cdot \psi_\ell(s_j) = \psi_\ell(c_0 + \sum_{1 \le j \le k} c_j \cdot s_j) \pmod q \end{aligned}$$

where $\mathsf{ct} = (c_0, \ldots, c_k)$ and $\mathsf{ct}_{\mathsf{aut}} = (c'_0, \ldots, c'_k) \leftarrow \texttt{Auto}(\mathbf{h}_1, \ldots, \mathbf{h}_k; \mathsf{ct})$.

### 4.5 Security

In this section, we show that our MGHE scheme achieves a semantic security that we defined in Sect. 3.1 under the RLWE assumption.

**Lemma 1 (Security of MGHE).** *The MGHE scheme described above is semantically secure under the RLWE assumption with parameter* $(n, q, \chi, \sigma)$.

*Proof.* Let $I_i$ be sets such that $I = \cup_{0 \le i \le k} I_i$ and $H = I \backslash A$ for any set $A \subsetneq I$. We define some hybrid games as follows:

- **Game 0:** This is a real world execution of the security game defined in Definition 1.
- **Game 1:** It is similar to **Game 0**, but the challenger samples $[\mathsf{pk}]_i$ uniformly at random from $R_q^{d \times 4}$ for $i \in H$.
- **Game 2:** It is similar to **Game 1**, but the challenger encrypts 0 instead of $m_b$.

Let $[\mathsf{pk}]_i = ([\mathbf{b}]_i, [\mathbf{d}]_i, [\mathbf{v}]_i, [\mathbf{h}]_i)$ be the public key of party $i \in H$. Since $([\mathbf{b}]_i, \mathbf{a})$ and $([\mathbf{v}]_i, \mathbf{u})$ follow the RLWE distribution of secret $[s]_i$, a pair $([\mathbf{b}]_i, [\mathbf{v}]_i)$ is indistinguishable from a uniform distribution over $R_q^{d \times 2}$. In addition, $([\mathbf{d}]_i, \mathbf{a})$ follows the RLWE distribution of secret $[r]_i$, $[\mathbf{d}]_i$ is also indistinguishable from a uniform distribution over $R_q^d$. Meanwhile, $([\mathbf{d}]_i, \mathbf{a})$ and $([\mathbf{v}]_i, \mathbf{u})$ can be viewed as a 'chain' of two gadget encryptions of $[s]_i$ and $-[r]_i$ under secrets $[r]_i$ and $[s]_i$, respectively. Here we make an additional *circular security* assumption which guarantees that our scheme remains secure even if $[\mathbf{d}]_i$, $[\mathbf{v}]_i$, and $[\mathbf{h}]_i$ are public. On the other hand, $[\mathbf{h}]_i$ is an gadget encryption of $\psi([s]_i)$ under $[s]_i$ with a random vector $\mathbf{k}$. Therefore, **Game 0** and **Game 1** are computationally indistinguishable.

In both **Game 1** and **Game 2**, the adversary sends a group index $j$ to the challenger in the security game. The encryption key $\mathbf{b}[0]$ used in these games is given by $\mathbf{b}[0] = \sum_{i \in I_j \cap A} [\mathbf{b}]_i[0] + \sum_{i \in I_j \cap H} [\mathbf{b}]_i[0]$. Since $I_j \cap H$ is non-empty and each $[\mathbf{b}]_i$ is uniformly sampled from $R_q^d$ for all $i \in H$, $\mathbf{b}[0]$ is computationally indistinguishable from a uniform random variable over $R_q$. Thus, under the RLWE assumption, the encryptions of 0 and $m_b$ in both games are also computationally indistinguishable. Therefore, the difference in advantage between these two games is negligible.

According to the aforementioned reasons, we can conclude that the advantage of the adversary in **Game 0** is negligible. Since **Game 0** is a real world-execution game with the MGHE scheme, our MGHE scheme achieves semantic security against semi-malicious corruptions. □

# 5 Constructing MPC from MGHE

The MGHE sheme, being a generalization of both the MKHE and MPHE primitives, can serve as a drop-in replacement for these primitives in any application built with them. As a result, MGHE can be effectively utilized in general 2-round MPC computation [32], outsourced computation applications [31], and distributed machine learning setups [19]. Additionally, it can be employed as a building block in MPC protocols that require varying number of parties [17].

## 5.1 Overview

MPHE and MKHE are both viable options for building an MPC protocol [29,31, 32], but each has limitations that restrict their usefulness in certain applications. For example, MPHE-based MPC protocols require parties to communicate with each other to generate a shared key. On the other hand, MKHE schemes are more time and space intensive than MPHE because ciphertexts expand as they interact with other ciphertexts under different keys. Thus, an MGHE scheme that integrates the strengths of both these schemes can be used to construct round-efficient MPC protocols. In Fig. 2, we describe a high-level structure of an MPC computation in three phases. Here, we assume three entities consisting of key owners, data owners, and a cloud server.

- **[Phase I] Setup:** In the first step of the protocol, key owners generate their key pairs and broadcast the public keys. We can treat this step as an offline phase since these procedures have to be run only once and each party is able to produce a key pair independently. When Phase I is ended, a joint public key is built publicly by summing up the individual public keys without any interaction between the parties.
- **[Phase II] Encryption:** After encrypting inputs with the joint encryption key, the ciphertexts are provided to the server which may be an external entity such as a cloud service provider. In general, semi-honest cloud service providers or parties themselves in MPC may play the role of computing party.

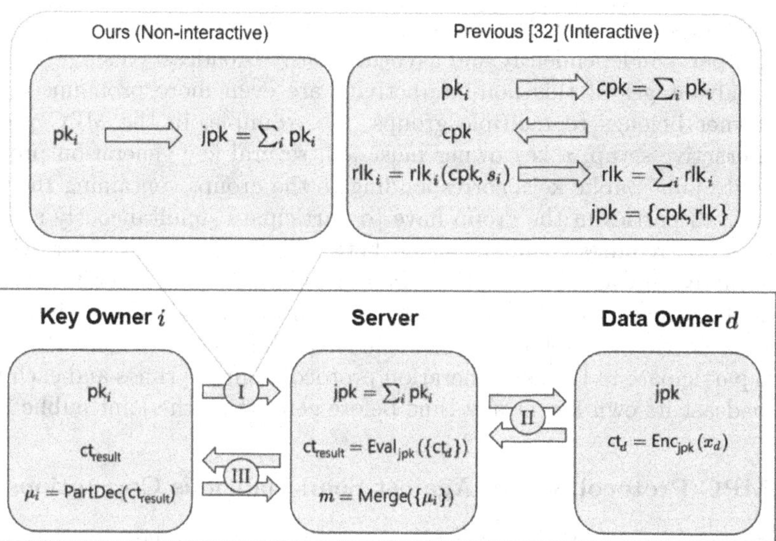


**Fig. 2.** MPC protocol using MGHE and previous work [31]. In [31], cpk and rlk represent the common public key for encryption and evaluation key, respectively. In our MGHE scheme, these keys can be obtained from the joint public key jpk directly.

When Phase II is ended, the circuit is evaluated using the homomorphic properties of the encryption scheme and thus does not require any interaction.

- **[Phase III] Decryption:** When the evaluation is over, we use an interactive protocol known as distributed decryption to securely decrypt the result without revealing the secret key of each party. In the protocol, each party partially decrypts the ciphertext using its own secret key with noise smudging technique [5], and the output message is obtained by adding all of the partially decrypted results.

**Implication of Non-interactive Key Aggregation.** Recall that all prior MPHE yields multi-round key generation in Phase I due to the quadratic structure of the evaluation key with respect to the individual secret keys. In the MPC protocol derived from the previous MPHE, each party broadcasts twice for the key generation: (1) individual encryption key to generate the joint encryption key and (2) individual evaluation key, which is constructed using the joint encryption key, to generate the joint evaluation key. In other words, it requires an interaction between parties for key aggregation during the setup. In our scheme, the novel refactoring of the evaluation key enables the parties to broadcast their keys only once. Each party broadcasts the individual public key, which implicitly contains the shares of the evaluation key. Then, the joint public key is generated publicly to be used for encryption and evaluation. By sharing the individual key pair in the first round itself, each party does not require interaction with other parties in the rest of the process (and can be offline until the decryption process). Thus our setup phase is non-interactive in the sense of Non-Interactive MPC [7,23] that each party independently and asynchronously broadcasts a single message.

The advantages of this non-interactivity are even more pronounced when a key owner belongs to multiple groups. For example, in the MPC protocol with interactive setup, a key owner must join several key generation protocols to generate joint public keys corresponding to the groups containing the party. Moreover, all parties in the group have to participate simultaneously since the key generation requires communications between the parties. However, with the non-interactive key aggregation, the server or the parties can generate joint public keys after each party broadcasts its own public key without any interaction with other parties. Therefore, we can achieve better efficiency since there is no need to participate in the key generation protocol multiple times and each party can broadcast its own key at any time before generating the joint public key.

### 5.2 MPC Protocol Secure Against Semi-malicious Corruptions

We provide a concrete MPC protocol in Fig. 3 for a polynomial-time deterministic circuit $C$. The correctness of the protocol follows from the correctness of the MGHE construction. In this section, we prove the protocol's security against a semi-malicious adversary which the definition is referred from [5]. Note that a semi-malicious adversary follows the honest protocol specification with arbitrary values for their random coins [5,29,32].

To prove the security of the MPC protocol from MGHE, we begin by demonstrating the simulation security [27] of the distributed decryption process in MGHE. For a circuit $C$, let us denote by $B_C$ an error bound of a ciphertext obtained by evaluating the circuit $C$ over fresh ciphertexts. Given $B_C$, we can guarantee the correctness and simulation security of the distributed decryption if $\sigma'$ is exponentially larger than the bound $B_C$.

**Lemma 2 (Correctness of Distributed Decryption).** *Let $n$ be the number of parties in $I = \cup_{1 \le j \le k} I_j$ and $B_{\sigma'}$ be bound of the samples from $D_{\sigma'}$ with non-negligible probability. If $q \ge 2nt(B_C + B_{\sigma'})$, then the distributed decryption procedure* `DistDec` *satisfy correctness.*

*Proof.* Given the partial decryptions $[\mu]_i$ of parties $i \in I$, we have

$$\begin{aligned} c_0 + \sum_{i \in I} \mu_i &= c_0 + \sum_{i \in I} \left( \sum_{1 \le j \le k, i \in I_j} c_j \right) \cdot [s]_i + \sum_{i \in I} [e']_i \\ &= \Delta \cdot m + e + e' \end{aligned}$$

where $e$ is bounded by $nB_C$ and $e' = \sum_{i \in I} [e']_i$ is bounded by $nB_{\sigma'}$. Since $q \ge 2nt(B_C + B_{\sigma'})$, we have $|e + e'| \le q/2t$, which ensures the correctness. □

**Lemma 3 (Security of Distributed Decryption).** *If $\sigma' > 0$ is a real number such that the samples from $D_{\sigma'}$ are larger than $2^\lambda B_C$ without negligible*

**Setup:** A public parameter $\mathsf{pp}$ is generated by $\texttt{Setup}(1^\lambda)$. All parties share the same parameter set.

**Input:** A circuit $C : \mathcal{M}^L \to \mathcal{M}$ where $L$ is the number of inputs. The inputs $x_1, x_2, \ldots, x_L$ are held among the parties.

**The Protocol**

**Phase I:** Let $I$ be the set of parties. Each party $i \in I$ generates a key pair $([\mathsf{sk}]_i, [\mathsf{pk}]_i) \leftarrow \texttt{IndKeyGen}(i)$ and an automorphism key $[\mathsf{ak}]_i \leftarrow \texttt{IndAutKeyGen}([\mathsf{sk}]_i)$, then broadcasts $([\mathsf{pk}]_i, [\mathsf{ak}]_i)$.

**Phase II:**

- Now anybody can compute the joint public and automorphism keys of an arbitrary group. We suppose that the joint keys of $k$ groups $I_1, I_2, \ldots, I_k \subseteq I$ are generated as follows:

$$\mathsf{pk}_j \leftarrow \texttt{JointKeyGen}(\{[\mathsf{pk}]_i : i \in I_j\}),$$
$$\mathsf{ak}_j \leftarrow \texttt{JointAutKeyGen}(\{[\mathsf{ak}]_i : i \in I_j\}).$$

  We denote by $\mathsf{ek}_j$ the encryption key of $I_j$.
- For each $1 \leq \ell \leq L$, the party with input $x_\ell$ encrypts it using a joint public key $\mathsf{pk}_j$ for some $1 \leq j \leq k$ and broadcasts the ciphertexts $\mathsf{ct}_\ell \leftarrow \texttt{Enc}(\mathsf{ek}_j; x_\ell)$.

**Phase III:**

- The circuit $C$ is evaluated as following:

$$\mathsf{ct} \leftarrow \texttt{Eval}(\{\mathsf{pk}_j\}_{1 \leq j \leq k}, \{\mathsf{ak}_j\}_{1 \leq j \leq k}; C, \mathsf{ct}_1, \ldots, \mathsf{ct}_L).$$

- Finally, the parties concurrently take part in the distributed decryption protocol with the error parameter $\sigma'$ to deduce the output $m$:

$$m \leftarrow \texttt{DistDec}(I, \sigma'; \mathsf{ct})$$

**Output:** Return the decrypted message $m$.

**Fig. 3.** $\pi_C$: MPC protocol for a circuit $C$ using MGHE

*probability, then the distributed decryption procedure* DistDec *achieves statistical simulation security against any static semi-malicious adversary corrupting exactly $n-1$ parties.*

*Proof.* Let a party $h$ be the only honest party. We construct a simulator $\mathcal{S}$ against the adversary $\mathcal{A}$ which has an access to the inputs and secret keys of all parties except $h$ and receives the output message $m$ from the ideal functionality. For given evaluated ciphertext $\mathsf{ct} = (c_0, \ldots, c_L)$, the simulator computes and publishes the simulated partial decryption $[\mu]'_h$ of the honest party $h$ using a smudging error $[e']_h^{sm} \leftarrow D_{\sigma'}$:

$$[\mu]'_h = \Delta \cdot m + [e']_h^{sm} - \sum_{i \neq h} \gamma_i - c_0 \tag{1}$$

where $\gamma_i = \left(\sum_{1 \leq j \leq k, i \in I_j} c_j\right) \cdot [s]_i \pmod q$ for $i \neq h$.

Then, the partial decryption of $h$ is generated from the partial decryptions of corrupted parties and the output message as $\Delta \cdot m + [e']_h^{sm} - \sum_{i \neq h} \gamma_i - c_0$. On the other hand, the real partial decryption also can be written as $\Delta \cdot m + e + [e']_h^{sm} - \sum_{i \neq h} \gamma_i - c_0$ where $e$ is the noise in the ciphertext $\mathsf{ct}$. By the smudging lemma [5], the distributions of $[e']_h^{sm}$ and $e + [e']_h^{sm}$ are statistically indistinguishable. It concludes that the simulated partial decryption and the real partial decryption are statistically indistinguishable. □

**Theorem 1 (Security of MPC Protocol).** *Given a poly-time computable deterministic circuit $C$ with $L$ inputs, the protocol $\pi_C$ described in Fig. 3 UC-realizes the circuit $C$ against any static semi-malicious adversary corrupting exactly $n-1$ parties.*

*Proof.* Let a party $h$ be the only honest party. We construct a simulator $\mathcal{S}$ against the adversary $\mathcal{A}$ as follows.

**The Simulator.** In Phase I, the simulator samples the public key of $h$ from uniform distribution over $R_q^{d \times 4}$ instead of $\texttt{IndKeyGen}(h)$. The simulator also plays Phase II honestly on behalf of the honest party, but encrypts 0 instead of the real input from $h$, if any. As the simulator has access to the inputs and secret keys of all parties except $h$ from the witness tape, the simulator can evaluate the circuit $C$ on ciphertexts $\mathsf{ct}_1, \ldots, \mathsf{ct}_L$ and obtain the resulting ciphertext $\mathsf{ct}$. In addition, it also receives the output message $m$ from the ideal functionality. In Phase III, the simulator computes the partial decryption for the party $h$ as same as the simulator introduced in the security proof of Lemma 3.

Now, we define some hybrid games and prove the computational indistinguishability between the real and ideal worlds.

- **The game** $REAL_{(\pi,\mathcal{A},\mathcal{Z})}$: An execution of the protocol $\pi$ in the real world with environment $\mathcal{Z}$ and semi-malicious adversary $\mathcal{A}$.
- **The game** $HYB^1_{(\pi,\mathcal{A},\mathcal{Z})}$: This is the same as $REAL_{(\pi,\mathcal{A},\mathcal{Z})}$ except the output of partial decrpytion of $h$. In Phase III, it publishes the simulated partial decryption which is computed via (1).
- **The game** $HYB^2_{(\pi,\mathcal{A},\mathcal{Z})}$: This is similar to $HYB^1_{(\pi,\mathcal{A},\mathcal{Z})}$, but in Phase II the party $h$ encrypts 0 instead of the real input if any.
- **The game** $IDEAL_{(\mathcal{F},\mathcal{S},\mathcal{Z})}$: It executes the MPC protocol with the simulator $\mathcal{S}$. The difference from $HYB^2_{(\pi,\mathcal{A},\mathcal{Z})}$ is that the public key of $h$ is sampled from a uniform distribution over $R_q^{d \times 4}$ instead of the individual key generation algorithm $\texttt{IndKeyGen}(h)$ in Phase I.

From the above games, we consider the following claims.

**Claim 1.** $REAL_{(\pi,\mathcal{A},\mathcal{Z})}$ and $HYB^1_{(\pi,\mathcal{A},\mathcal{Z})}$ are statistically indistinguishable.

*Proof.* According to the description of the simulator, the partial decryption of $h$ in the game $HYB^1_{(\pi,\mathcal{A},\mathcal{Z})}$ is generated from the partial decryptions of corrupted parties and the output message as $\Delta \cdot m + [e']_h^{sm} - \sum_{i\neq h}\gamma_i - c_0$, while the real partial decryption also can be written as $\Delta \cdot m + e + [e']_h - \sum_{i\neq h}\gamma_i - c_0$ where $e$ is the noise in the ciphertext $\mathsf{ct}$. By Lemma 3, the distributions of $[e']_h^{sm}$ and $e + [e']_h$ are statistically indistinguishable. This indicates that $REAL_{(\pi,\mathcal{A},\mathcal{Z})}$ and $HYB^1_{(\pi,\mathcal{A},\mathcal{Z})}$ are also statistically indistinguishable.

**Claim 2.** $HYB^1_{(\pi,\mathcal{A},\mathcal{Z})}$, $HYB^2_{(\pi,\mathcal{A},\mathcal{Z})}$, and $IDEAL_{(\mathcal{F},\mathcal{S},\mathcal{Z})}$ are computationally indistinguishable.

*Proof.* The differences in three games correspond to the differences in **Game 0**, **Game 1**, and **Game 2** of Lemma 1. In detail, the difference between $HYB^1_{(\pi,\mathcal{A},\mathcal{Z})}$ and $HYB^2_{(\pi,\mathcal{A},\mathcal{Z})}$ is that the party $h$ encrypts the real input in $HYB^1_{(\pi,\mathcal{A},\mathcal{Z})}$ while it encrypts 0 in the game $HYB^2_{(\pi,\mathcal{A},\mathcal{Z})}$, if any. Furthermore, the difference between $HYB^2_{(\pi,\mathcal{A},\mathcal{Z})}$ and $IDEAL_{(\mathcal{F},\mathcal{S},\mathcal{Z})}$ is in the public key $\mathsf{pk}_h$. In $HYB^2_{(\pi,\mathcal{A},\mathcal{Z})}$, $\mathsf{pk}_h$ is a valid public key generated by $h$ while it is sampled from a uniform distribution over $R_q^{d\times 4}$ in the game $IDEAL_{(\mathcal{F},\mathcal{S},\mathcal{Z})}$. Thus, by Lemma 1, the three games $HYB^1_{(\pi,\mathcal{A},\mathcal{Z})}$, $HYB^2_{(\pi,\mathcal{A},\mathcal{Z})}$, and $IDEAL_{(\mathcal{F},\mathcal{S},\mathcal{Z})}$ are computationally indistinguishable.

According to the claims, we conclude that the MPC protocol $\pi_C$ is secure in the semi-malicious model against $n-1$ corrupted parties. □

To handle the arbitrary number of corruptions, we can establish security proof by constructing the extended protocol as outlined in [32]. In addition, we can transform our MPC protocol, which is secure against semi-malicious attackers, into a protocol that offers security against malicious corruptions without introducing any additional rounds. This transformation can be achieved by leveraging non-interactive zero-knowledge proofs, as described in [5].

## 6 Experimental Results

We implement our MGHE scheme based on BFV and CKKS. The source code is written in GO programming language and is built on Lattigo [1] version 2.3.0. We conducted experiments on a system equipped with Intel(R) Core(TM) i9-10900 CPU @ 2.80 GHz and 64 GB RAM. In our implementation, the key distribution $\chi$ samples the coefficients from the ternary set $-1, 0, 1$ with equal probabilities of 0.25 for $-1$ and 1, and a probability of 0.5 for 0. The error parameter is set to $\sigma = 3.2$.

Table 1 shows the execution time of multiplication of our MGHE scheme. The experiment was conducted using two different parameter sets: $(N, \lceil \log pq \rceil) =$

**Table 1.** Performance of our MGHE schemes, the MKHE scheme by Chen et al. [13], and the MPHE scheme by Mouchet et al. [31]: execution times to operate homomorphic multiplication (Mult + Relin), taken in milliseconds (ms). $N$ denotes the dimension of base ring, $n$ and $k$ denote the number of the associated parties and groups (keys), respectively, to the ciphertext. Ours$^+$ refers to our MGHE scheme combined with the technique of [26].

| $N$ | $n$ | $k$ | Mult + Relin | | | | | | | |
|---|---|---|---|---|---|---|---|---|---|---|
| | | | BFV | | | | CKKS | | | |
| | | | Ours | Ours$^+$ | [13] | [31] | Ours | Ours$^+$ | [13] | [31] |
| $2^{14}$ | 1 | 1 | 78.7 | 118.4 | 84.1 | 32.6 | 51.6 | 72.9 | 51.2 | 17.7 |
| | 2 | 1 | 77.9 | 120.4 | – | 33.4 | 50.8 | 75.3 | – | 17.1 |
| | | 2 | 173.4 | 224.4 | 196.2 | – | 122.8 | 133.4 | 139.7 | – |
| | 4 | 1 | 80.1 | 121.6 | – | 32.9 | 51.6 | 76.9 | – | 17.4 |
| | | 2 | 175.3 | 224.1 | – | – | 124.5 | 133.6 | – | – |
| | | 4 | 476.4 | 420.8 | 589.7 | – | 335.8 | 250.5 | 450.7 | – |
| | 8 | 1 | 78.4 | 118.9 | – | 33.3 | 50.8 | 77.2 | – | 17.2 |
| | | 2 | 178.1 | 223.5 | – | – | 123.6 | 135.1 | – | – |
| | | 4 | 461.4 | 422.7 | – | – | 337.1 | 249.4 | – | – |
| | | 8 | 1473.0 | 811.7 | 2014.2 | – | 1081.9 | 495.9 | 1600.7 | – |
| $2^{15}$ | 1 | 1 | 595.9 | 1036.8 | 605.5 | 202.0 | 414.2 | 642.5 | 404.1 | 165.7 |
| | 2 | 1 | 593.1 | 1019.4 | – | 201.5 | 412.9 | 640.7 | – | 170.8 |
| | | 2 | 1308.3 | 1929.8 | 1477.9 | – | 1014.9 | 1094.3 | 1089.7 | – |
| | 4 | 1 | 599.2 | 1024.4 | – | 204.2 | 413.7 | 643.1 | – | 164.6 |
| | | 2 | 1324.9 | 1945.7 | – | – | 1008.4 | 1100.6 | – | – |
| | | 4 | 3556.5 | 4006.8 | 4582.9 | – | 2844.5 | 2177.3 | 3553.1 | – |
| | 8 | 1 | 593.2 | 1033.9 | – | 202.7 | 413.3 | 645.5 | – | 168.7 |
| | | 2 | 1319.8 | 1987.1 | – | – | 1011.4 | 1103.5 | – | – |
| | | 4 | 3515.2 | 3954.5 | – | – | 2825.1 | 2147.2 | – | – |
| | | 8 | 10681.1 | 6871.5 | 15257.5 | – | 9008.9 | 4449.3 | 13052.8 | – |

$(2^{14}, 438)$ and $(2^{15}, 880)$ where $p$ is a special modulus. Both parameter sets ensure a security level of at least 128 bits [2]. Ours shows the performance of Algorithm 1 where a minor optimization is introduced and Ours$^+$ shows that of multiplication algorithm which applies the technique of [26]. As our MGHE supports computation on groups of parties, we measured the performance varying the number of groups.

We also present the performance of the MKHE scheme [13] and MPHE scheme [31] for comparison. Since MKHE and MPHE are instances of MGHE where each group consists of a single party and single group, respectively, the MKHE scheme and MPHE scheme have its results in Table 1 only when $n = k$ and $k = 1$, respectively. Upon comparing the performance of MKHE and our method, the table shows that our multiplication algorithm exhibits slightly faster operation times than previous MKHE. This is due to our approach, as explained in Sect. 4.3, where we reduce the number of external products during the relinearization. Moreover, in the case of a large number of groups, it is even faster than our method when we apply the recent technique introduced in [26]. We also remark that although MPHE shows better performance than other methods, it requires interactions among the parties before the evaluation to generate the joint public key.

## A Construction of MGHE with CKKS

The CKKS supports approximate arithmetic operations for complex numbers. The BFV and CKKS have similar structure, we can easily extend MGHE scheme of the CKKS. The difference is that it adds an error into the plaintext itself and additionally supports the rescaling algorithm to control the size of ciphertext. The ciphertext has a level and it decreases whenever rescaling is performed. To proceed arithmetics between two ciphertexts, they should have same level and it requires bootstrapping when level is low in order to continue evaluation. We are going to provide MGHE scheme without interactive key generation. In this description, we skip setup, key generation, and joint key generation phase since they are same as BFV. Galois automorphism is also not included since it has same procedure with the BFV. We assume the ciphertext modulus $q = \prod_{i=1}^{L} p_i$ for some integers $p_i$ and denote $q_l = \prod_{i=1}^{l} p_i$.

### A.1 MGHE with CKKS

• $\underline{\texttt{MG-CKKS.Enc}(\mathsf{ek}; m)}$: For a joint encryption key $\mathsf{ek}$ and a message $m$, return $\mathsf{ct} \leftarrow \texttt{MP-CKKS.Enc}(\mathsf{ek}; m)$.

• $\underline{\texttt{MG-CKKS.Add}(\mathsf{ct}, \mathsf{ct}')}$: If two given ciphertexts $\mathsf{ct}$ and $\mathsf{ct}'$ has same level, return the ciphertext $\mathsf{ct}_{add} = \mathsf{ct} + \mathsf{ct}' \pmod q$. If not, modify ciphertexts to have same level before the computation.

• $\underline{\texttt{MG-CKKS.Mult}(\{\mathsf{rlk}_j\}_{1\le j\le k}; \mathsf{ct}, \mathsf{ct}')}$: Set $\mathsf{ct}$ and $\mathsf{ct}'$ have same level. Let $\mathsf{ct} = (c_i)_{0\le i\le k}$ and $\mathsf{ct}' = (c_i')_{0\le i\le k}$ be two multi-group ciphertexts and $\{\mathsf{rlk}_j\}_{1\le j\le k}$ the collection of the joint relinearization keys of groups $I_j$ for $1 \le j \le k$. Compute $\mathsf{ct}_{\mathsf{mul}} = (c_{i,j})_{0\le i,j\le k}$ where $c_{i,j} = c_i c_j' \pmod q$ for $0 \le i, j \le k$. Return the ciphertext $\texttt{MG-CKKS.Relin}(\{\mathsf{rlk}_j\}_{1\le j\le k}; \mathsf{ct}_{\mathsf{mul}})$ where $\texttt{MG-CKKS.Relin}(\cdot)$ is the relinearization procedure described in Algorithm 1.

• $\underline{\texttt{MG-CKKS.Rescale}(\mathsf{ct})}$: Given a ciphertext $\mathsf{ct} = (c_0, c_1, \ldots, c_k) \in R_{q_l}^{k+1}$ at level $l$, compute $c_i' = \lfloor p_l^{-1} \cdot c_i \rceil$ for $1 \le i \le k$, and return $\mathsf{ct}' = (c_0', c_1', \ldots, c_k') \in R_{q_l-1}^{k+1}$ which is at level $l-1$.

• $\underline{\texttt{MG-CKKS.Dec}(\{\mathsf{sk}_j\}_{1\le j\le k}; \mathsf{ct})}$: Given a ciphertext $\mathsf{ct} = (c_0, c_1, \ldots, c_k)$ and joint secret keys $\mathsf{sk}_j = s_j$ for $1 \le j \le k$, return $m = \langle \mathsf{ct}, \mathsf{sk}\rangle = (c_0 + \sum_{1\le j\le k} c_i \cdot s_j) \pmod t$.

• $\underline{\texttt{MG-CKKS.DistDec}(\{[\mathsf{sk}_j]_i\}_{1\le j\le k, i\in I_j}, \sigma'; \mathsf{ct})}$: Let $\mathsf{ct} = (c_0, \ldots, c_k)$ be a multi-group ciphertext corresponding to the set of groups $\{I_1, \ldots, I_k\}$ and $[\mathsf{sk}]_i = [s]_i$ be the secret of party $i \in I_j$.

- Partial decryption: For $1 \le j \le k$, each party $i \in I_j$ samples $[e'_j]_i \leftarrow D_{\sigma'}$, then computes and publishes $[\mu_j]_i = c_j \cdot [s]_i + [e'_j]_i \pmod q$.
- Merge: Compute $m = (c_0 + \sum_{1\le j\le k} \sum_{i\in I_j} [\mu_j]_i) \pmod t$.

# B Noise Analysis

Before estimating a noise growth, we specify some distributions for sampling randomness or errors. Let the key distribution $\chi$ be the distribution where each coefficient is sampled from the set $\{0, \pm 1\}$ with probability 0.25 for each of $-1$ and 1 and with probability 0.5 for 0. Set the error distribution $\psi_\ell$ be the discrete Gaussian distribution of variance $\sigma^2$. We also assume that the coefficients of the polynomials are independent zero-mean random variables with the same variances. We denote by $\mathsf{Var}(a) = \mathsf{Var}(a_i)$ the variance of coefficients for random variable $a = \sum_i a_i \cdot X^i$ over the ring $R$. Then the variance of the product $c = a \cdot b$ of two polynomials with degree $n$ can be represented as $\mathsf{Var}(c) = n \cdot \mathsf{Var}(a) \cdot \mathsf{Var}(b)$ if $a$ and $b$ are independent. Similarly, we define variance for a vector $\mathbf{a} \in R^d$ of random variables as $\mathsf{Var}(\mathbf{a}) = \frac{1}{d}\sum_{i=1}^{d} \mathsf{Var}(\mathbf{a}[i])$. We also assume that each ciphertext behaves as if it is a uniform random variable over $R_q^{k+1}$. We analyze the noise growth of $k$-group case, each comprising $N_i$ parties for $1 \le i \le k$.

## B.1 Encryption

Recall that the encryption $\mathsf{ct} = (c_0, c_1) \in R_q^2$ of $m \in R_p$ is $\mathsf{ct} = t \cdot \mathsf{ek} + (\Delta \cdot m + e_0, e_1) \pmod q$ where $t \leftarrow \chi$ and $e_0, e_1 \leftarrow D_\sigma$. For $\mathsf{ek} = (\mathbf{b}[0], \mathbf{a}[0]) \in R_q^2$, we remark that $\mathbf{b}[0] + \mathbf{a}[0] \cdot s = \sum_{i\in I} [\mathbf{e}_0]_i[0]$ and each $[\mathbf{e}_0]_i[0]$ is sampled from $D_\sigma$. Then, it satisfies that $c_0 + c_1 \cdot s = \Delta \cdot m + t(\mathbf{b}[0] + \mathbf{a}[0] \cdot s) + (e_0 + e_1 \cdot s) = \Delta \cdot m + (t \sum_{i\in I} [\mathbf{e}_0]_i[0] + e_0 + e_1 \cdot s) \pmod q$. The encryption noise $e_{\mathsf{enc}} = t\sum_{i\in I}[\mathbf{e}_0]_i[0] + e_0 + e_1 \cdot s$ has the variance of $V_{\mathsf{enc}} = \sigma^2 \cdot (\frac{n|I|}{2} + 1 + \frac{n}{2}) \approx \frac{n\sigma^2(|I|+1)}{2}$.

The CKKS scheme has the same encryption error as the BFV scheme. The only difference is that there is no scaling factor $\Delta$ in the result of decryption.

## B.2 Relinearization

In Algorithm 1 of Sect. 4.3, it satisfies that

$$\begin{aligned}\sum_{1\le i\le k} c''_i \boxdot (\mathbf{v}_i + s_i \cdot \mathbf{u}) &= -\sum_{1\le i\le k} r_i \cdot c''_i + \sum_{1\le i\le k} c''_i \boxdot \mathbf{e}_{i,2} \\ &= -\sum_{1\le i,j\le k} r_i \cdot (c_{i,j} \boxdot \mathbf{b}_j) + \sum_{1\le i\le k} c''_i \boxdot \mathbf{e}_{i,2} \pmod q\end{aligned}$$

and

$$\begin{aligned}
&\sum_{1\le i,j\le k} (c_{i,j} \boxdot \mathbf{d}_i)\cdot s_j \\
&= \sum_{1\le i,j\le k} r_i\cdot (c_{i,j}\boxdot(\mathbf{b}_j - \mathbf{e}_{j,0})) + \sum_{1\le i,j\le k} s_i s_j\cdot c_{i,j} + \sum_{1\le i,j\le k} s_j\cdot(c_{i,j}\boxdot \mathbf{e}_{i,1}) \\
&= \sum_{1\le i,j\le k} r_i\cdot (c_{i,j}\boxdot \mathbf{b}_j) + \sum_{1\le i,j\le k} s_i s_j\cdot c_{i,j} + \sum_{1\le i,j\le k} e'_{i,j} \pmod q
\end{aligned}$$

where $e'_{i,j} = c_{i,j}\boxdot(s_j\cdot \mathbf{e}_{i,1} - r_i\cdot \mathbf{e}_{j,0})$.

We denote by $V_g = \mathsf{Var}(h(a))$ where $a$ is a uniform random variable over $R_q$. Then, the variance of relinearization error $e_{\mathsf{relin}} = \sum_{1\le i\le k} c''_i \boxdot \mathbf{e}_{i,2} + \sum_{1\le i,j\le k} e'_{i,j}$ is obtained as follows:

$$V_{\mathsf{relin}} = ndV_g\sigma^2 \sum_{1\le i\le k} N_i^2 + 2n^2 dV_g\sigma^2 k^2 \sum_{1\le i\le k} N_i^2 \approx 2n^2 dV_g \sigma^2 k \sum_{1\le i\le k} N_i^2$$

In our implementation, we use RNS-friendly decomposition $R_q = \prod_i R_{p_i}$ such that $p_i$'s have the same bit-size. Here, we have $V_g = \frac{1}{12d}\sum_{i=1}^d p_i^2$ for $d = \lceil \log q/\log p_i\rceil$.

## B.3 Multiplication

We again consider $k$-group case, each comprising $N_i$ parties for $1\le i\le k$. Let $\mathsf{ct}_1$ and $\mathsf{ct}_2$ be the input ciphertexts of messages $m_1$ and $m_2$ respectively. Each ciphertext $\mathsf{ct}_i$ satisfies that $\langle \mathsf{ct}_i, \overline{\mathsf{sk}}\rangle = q\cdot I_i + \Delta\cdot m_i + e_i$ for $I_i = \lfloor \frac{1}{q}\langle \mathsf{ct}_i, \overline{\mathsf{sk}}\rangle\rceil$ and some $e_i$. Here, we have the variance $\mathsf{Var}(I_i) \approx \frac{1}{12}(1+\frac{1}{2}kn) \approx \frac{1}{24}kn$ since $\frac{1}{q}\cdot \mathsf{ct}_i$ behaves as an uniform random variable over $\frac{1}{q}\cdot R_q^{k+1}$.

The result of tensor product satisfies that $\langle \mathsf{ct}_1\otimes \mathsf{ct}_2, \overline{\mathsf{sk}}\otimes\overline{\mathsf{sk}}\rangle = \langle \mathsf{ct}_1, \overline{\mathsf{sk}}\rangle\cdot \langle \mathsf{ct}_2, \overline{\mathsf{sk}}\rangle = \Delta^2\cdot m_1 m_2 + q\cdot(I_1 e_2 + I_2 e_1) + \Delta\cdot(m_1 e_2 + m_2 e_1) + e_1 e_2 \pmod{q\cdot\Delta}$ and for $\mathsf{ct}_{\mathsf{mul}} = \left\lfloor \frac{p}{q}\cdot \mathsf{ct}_1\otimes\mathsf{ct}_2\right\rceil$, we have $\langle \mathsf{ct}_{\mathsf{mul}}, \overline{\mathsf{sk}}\otimes\overline{\mathsf{sk}}\rangle = \Delta\cdot m_1 m_2 + p\cdot(I_1 e_2 + I_2 e_1) + (m_1 e_2 + m_2 e_1) + \Delta^{-1}\cdot e_1 e_2 + e_{rd}$ where $e_{rd} = \left\langle \frac{p}{q}\cdot \mathsf{ct}_1\otimes\mathsf{ct}_2 - \mathsf{ct}_{mul}, \overline{\mathsf{sk}}\otimes\overline{\mathsf{sk}}\right\rangle$. That is, the multiplication error is obtained by $e_{\mathsf{mul}} = p\cdot(I_1 e_2 + I_2 e_1) + (m_1 e_2 + m_2 e_1) + \Delta^{-1}\cdot e_1 e_2 + e_{rd}$. From the above equation, the first term $p\cdot(I_1 e_2 + I_2 e_1)$ dominates the whole multiplication error. Therefore, we have the variance of multiplication error by

$$V_{\mathsf{mul}} \approx np^2\cdot(\mathsf{Var}(I_1)\mathsf{Var}(e_2) + \mathsf{Var}(I_2)\mathsf{Var}(e_1)) \approx \frac{1}{24}kn^2p^2(\mathsf{Var}(e_1) + \mathsf{Var}(e_2)).$$

While the relinearization error has a fixed size depending on the parameters, the multiplication error increases by a certain ratio as the computation proceeds. Therefore, the total noise is eventually dominated by the multiplication error unless $(\mathsf{Var}(e_1) + \mathsf{Var}(e_2))$ is very small (e.g. fresh ciphertext).

## References

1. Lattigo v4. ePFL-LDS, Tune Insight SA (2022). https://github.com/tuneinsight/lattigo
2. Albrecht, M., et al.: Homomorphic encryption security standard. Tech. rep., HomomorphicEncryption.org, Toronto, Canada (2018)
3. Aloufi, A., Hu, P., Wong, H.W., Chow, S.S.: Blindfolded evaluation of random forests with multi-key homomorphic encryption. IEEE Trans. Depend. Secure Comput. (2019)
4. Ananth, P., Jain, A., Jin, Z., Malavolta, G.: Multi-key fully-homomorphic encryption in the plain model. In: Pass, R., Pietrzak, K. (eds.) TCC 2020, LNCS, vol. 12550, pp. 28–57. Springer, Cham (2020). https://doi.org/10.1007/978-3-030-64375-1_2
5. Asharov, G., Jain, A., López-Alt, A., Tromer, E., Vaikuntanathan, V., Wichs, D.: Multiparty computation with low communication, computation and interaction via threshold FHE. In: Pointcheval, D., Johansson, T. (eds.) EUROCRYPT 2012. LNCS, vol. 7237, pp. 483–501. Springer, Heidelberg (2012). https://doi.org/10.1007/978-3-642-29011-4_29
6. Bajard, J.-C., Eynard, J., Hasan, M.A., Zucca, V.: A full RNS variant of FV like somewhat homomorphic encryption schemes. In: Avanzi, R., Heys, H. (eds.) SAC 2016. LNCS, vol. 10532, pp. 423–442. Springer, Cham (2017). https://doi.org/10.1007/978-3-319-69453-5_23
7. Beimel, A., Gabizon, A., Ishai, Y., Kushilevitz, E., Meldgaard, S., Paskin-Cherniavsky, A.: Non-interactive secure multiparty computation. In: Garay, J.A., Gennaro, R. (eds.) CRYPTO 2014. LNCS, vol. 8617, pp. 387–404. Springer, Heidelberg (2014). https://doi.org/10.1007/978-3-662-44381-1_22
8. Boneh, D., et al.: Threshold cryptosystems from threshold fully homomorphic encryption. In: Shacham, H., Boldyreva, A. (eds.) CRYPTO 2018. LNCS, vol. 10991, pp. 565–596. Springer, Cham (2018). https://doi.org/10.1007/978-3-319-96884-1_19
9. Brakerski, Z.: Fully homomorphic encryption without modulus switching from classical GapSVP. In: Safavi-Naini, R., Canetti, R. (eds.) CRYPTO 2012. LNCS, vol. 7417, pp. 868–886. Springer, Heidelberg (2012). https://doi.org/10.1007/978-3-642-32009-5_50
10. Brakerski, Z., Gentry, C., Vaikuntanathan, V.: (Leveled) fully homomorphic encryption without bootstrapping. ACM Trans. Comput. Theory **6**(3), 1–36 (2014)
11. Brakerski, Z., Perlman, R.: Lattice-based fully dynamic multi-key FHE with short ciphertexts. In: Robshaw, M., Katz, J. (eds.) CRYPTO 2016. LNCS, vol. 7417, pp. 190–213. Springer, Heidelberg (2016). https://doi.org/10.1007/978-3-662-53018-4_8
12. Chen, H., Chillotti, I., Song, Y.: Multi-key homomorphic encryption from TFHE. In: Galbraith, S.D., Moriai, S. (eds.) ASIACRYPT 2019. LNCS, vol. 11992, pp. 446–472. Springer, Cham (2019). https://doi.org/10.1007/978-3-030-34621-8_16
13. Chen, H., Dai, W., Kim, M., Song, Y.: Efficient multi-key homomorphic encryption with packed ciphertexts with application to oblivious neural network inference. In: Proceedings of the 2019 ACM SIGSAC Conference on Computer and Communications Security, pp. 395–412 (2019)
14. Chen, L., Zhang, Z., Wang, X.: Batched multi-hop multi-key FHE from ring-LWE with compact ciphertext extension. In: Kalai, Y., Reyzin, L. (eds.) Theory of Cryptography. LNCS, vol. 10678, pp. 597–627. Springer, Cham (2017). https://doi.org/10.1007/978-3-319-70503-3_20

15. Cheon, J.H., Kim, A., Kim, M., Song, Y.: Homomorphic encryption for arithmetic of approximate numbers. In: Takagi, T., Peyrin, T. (eds.) ASIACRYPT 2017. LNCS, vol. 10624, pp. 409–437. Springer, Cham (2017). https://doi.org/10.1007/978-3-319-70694-8_15
16. Chillotti, I., Gama, N., Georgieva, M., Izabachène, M.: Faster fully homomorphic encryption: bootstrapping in less than 0.1 seconds. In: Cheon, J.H., Takagi, T. (eds.) ASIACRYPT 2016. LNCS, vol. 10031, pp. 3–33. Springer, Heidelberg (2016). https://doi.org/10.1007/978-3-662-53887-6_1
17. Choudhuri, A.R., Goel, A., Green, M., Jain, A., Kaptchuk, G.: Fluid MPC: secure multiparty computation with dynamic participants. In: Malkin, T., Peikert, C. (eds.) CRYPTO 2021. LNCS, vol. 12826, pp. 94–123. Springer, Cham (2021). https://doi.org/10.1007/978-3-030-84245-1_4
18. Clear, M., McGoldrick, C.: Multi-identity and multi-key leveled FHE from learning with errors. In: Gennaro, R., Robshaw, M. (eds.) CRYPTO 2015. LNCS, vol. 9216, pp. 630–656. Springer, Heidelberg (2015). https://doi.org/10.1007/978-3-662-48000-7_31
19. Damgård, I., Pastro, V., Smart, N., Zakarias, S.: Multiparty computation from somewhat homomorphic encryption. In: Safavi-Naini, R., Canetti, R. (eds.) CRYPTO 2012. LNCS, vol. 7417, pp. 643–662. Springer, Heidelberg (2012). https://doi.org/10.1007/978-3-642-32009-5_38
20. Fan, J., Vercauteren, F.: Somewhat practical fully homomorphic encryption. IACR Cryptol. ePrint Arch. **2012**, 144 (2012)
21. Gentry, C., Halevi, S., Smart, N.P.: Homomorphic evaluation of the AES circuit. In: Safavi-Naini, R., Canetti, R. (eds.) CRYPTO 2012. LNCS, vol. 7417, pp. 850–867. Springer, Heidelberg (2012). https://doi.org/10.1007/978-3-642-32009-5_49
22. Gentry, C., Sahai, A., Waters, B.: Homomorphic encryption from learning with errors: conceptually-simpler, asymptotically-faster, attribute-based. In: Canetti, R., Garay, J.A. (eds.) CRYPTO 2013. LNCS, vol. 8042, pp. 75–92. Springer, Heidelberg (2013). https://doi.org/10.1007/978-3-642-40041-4_5
23. Halevi, S., Ishai, Y., Jain, A., Komargodski, I., Sahai, A., Yogev, E.: Non-interactive multiparty computation without correlated randomness. In: Takagi, T., Peyrin, T. (eds.) ASIACRYPT 2017. LNCS, vol. 10626, pp. 181–211. Springer, Cham (2017). https://doi.org/10.1007/978-3-319-70700-6_7
24. Halevi, S., Polyakov, Y., Shoup, V.: An improved RNS variant of the BFV homomorphic encryption scheme. In: Matsui, M. (ed.) CT-RSA 2019. LNCS, vol. 11405, pp. 83–105. Springer, Cham (2019). https://doi.org/10.1007/978-3-030-12612-4_5
25. Hoffstein, J., Pipher, J., Silverman, J.H.: Ntru: A ring-based public key cryptosystem. In: Buhler, J.P. (ed.) Algorithmic Number Theory. ANTS 1998. LNCS, vol. 1423, pp. 267–288. Springer, Heidelberg (1998). https://doi.org/10.1007/BFb0054868
26. Kim, T., Kwak, H., Lee, D., Seo, J., Song, Y.: Asymptotically faster multi-key homomorphic encryption from homomorphic gadget decomposition. In: Proceedings of the 2023 ACM SIGSAC Conference on Computer and Communications Security, pp. 726–740 (2023)
27. Lindell, Y.: How to simulate it—a tutorial on the simulation proof technique. In: Lindell, Y. (ed.) Tutorials on the Foundations of Cryptography. Information Security and Cryptography. Springer, Cham (2017). https://doi.org/10.1007/978-3-319-57048-8_6
28. López-Alt, A., Tromer, E., Vaikuntanathan, V.: Cloud-assisted multiparty computation from fully homomorphic encryption. Cryptology ePrint Archive (2011)

29. López-Alt, A., Tromer, E., Vaikuntanathan, V.: On-the-fly multiparty computation on the cloud via multikey fully homomorphic encryption. In: Proceedings of the Forty-Fourth Annual ACM Symposium on Theory of Computing, pp. 1219–1234. ACM (2012)
30. Mouchet, C., Bertrand, E., Hubaux, J.P.: An efficient threshold access-structure for rlwe-based multiparty homomorphic encryption. J. Cryptol. **36**(2), 10 (2023)
31. Mouchet, C., Troncoso-Pastoriza, J., Bossuat, J.P., Hubaux, J.P.: Multiparty homomorphic encryption from ring-learning-with-errors. Proc. Privacy Enhanc. Technol. **2021**(4), 291–311 (2021)
32. Mukherjee, P., Wichs, D.: Two round multiparty computation via multi-key FHE. In: Fischlin, M., Coron, J.-S. (eds.) EUROCRYPT 2016. LNCS, vol. 9666, pp. 735–763. Springer, Heidelberg (2016). https://doi.org/10.1007/978-3-662-49896-5_26
33. Park, J.: Homomorphic encryption for multiple users with less communications. IEEE Access **9**, 135915–135926 (2021)
34. Peikert, C., Shiehian, S.: Multi-key FHE from LWE, revisited. In: Hirt, M., Smith, A. (eds.) Theory of Cryptography. LNCS, vol. 9986, pp. 217–238. Springer, Heidelberg (2016). https://doi.org/10.1007/978-3-662-53644-5_9

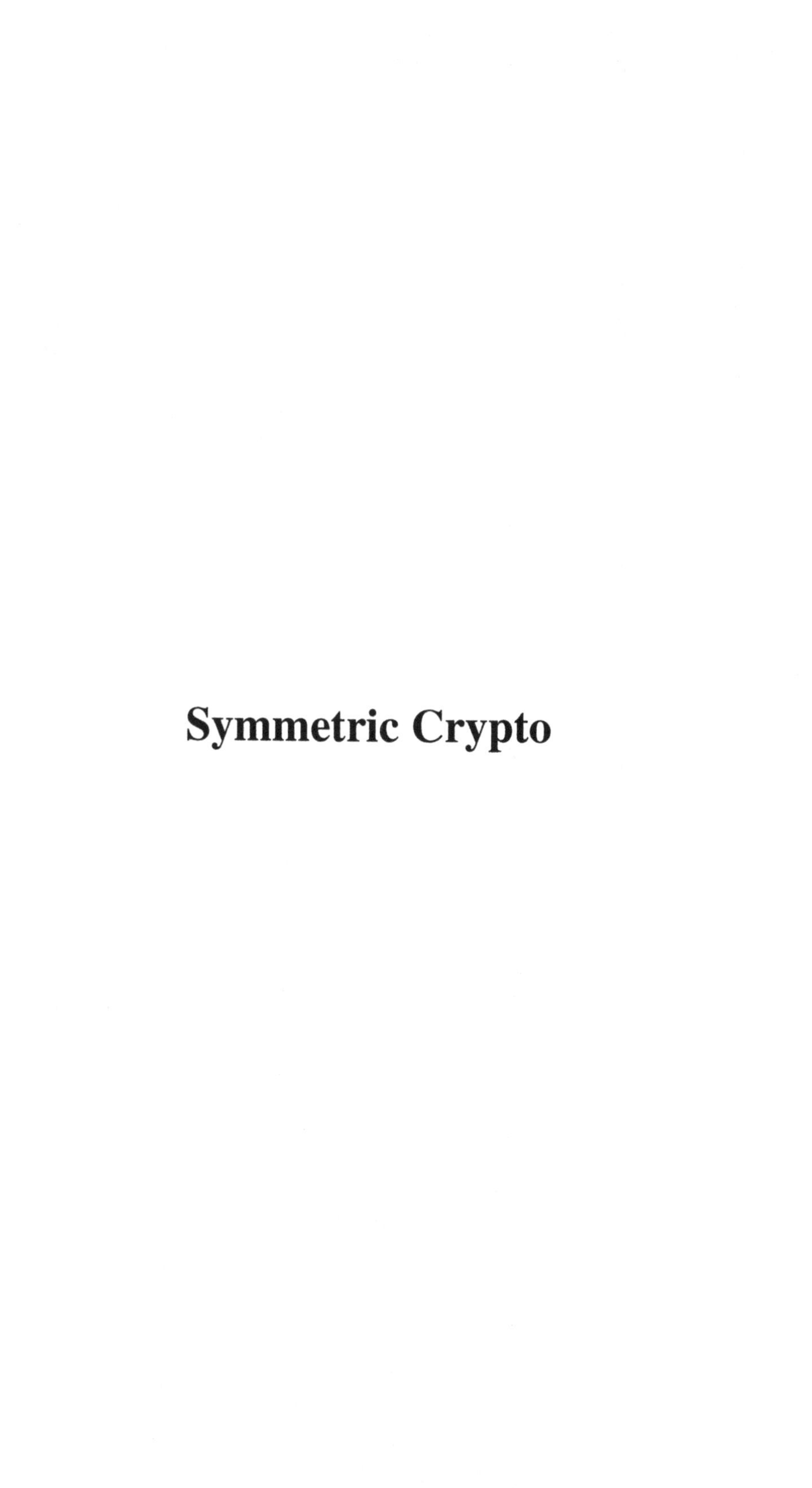

# Symmetric Crypto

# Masked Iterate-Fork-Iterate: A New Design Paradigm for Tweakable Expanding Pseudorandom Function

Elena Andreeva[1(✉)], Benoît Cogliati[2], Virginie Lallemand[3], Marine Minier[3], Antoon Purnal[4], and Arnab Roy[5]

[1] TU Wien, Vienna, Austria
elena.andreeva@tuwien.ac.at
[2] Thales DIS France SAS, Meudon, France
[3] Université de Lorraine, CNRS, Inria, LORIA, Nancy, France
{virginie.lallemand,marine.minier}@loria.fr
[4] KU Leuven, Leuven, Belgium
antoon.purnal@kuleuven.be
[5] University of Innsbruck, Innsbruck, Austria
arnab.roy@uibk.ac.at

**Abstract.** Many modes of operations for block ciphers or tweakable block ciphers do not require invertibility from their underlying primitive. In this work, we study fixed-length Tweakable Pseudorandom Function (TPRF) with large domain expansion, a *novel primitive* that can bring high security and significant performance optimizations in symmetric schemes, such as (authenticated) encryption.

Our first contribution is to introduce a new design paradigm, derived from the Iterate-Fork-Iterate construction, in order to build $n$-to-$\alpha n$-bit ($\alpha \geq 2$), *n-bit secure*, domain expanding TPRF. We dub this new generic composition masked Iterate-Fork-Iterate mIFI. We then propose a concrete TPRF instantiation ButterKnife that expands an $n$-bit input to $8n$-bit output via a public tweak and secret key. ButterKnife is built with high efficiency and security in mind. It is fully parallelizable and based on Deoxys-BC, the AES-based tweakable block cipher used in the authenticated encryption winner algorithm in the defense-in-depth category of the CAESAR competition. We analyze the resistance of ButterKnife to differential, linear, meet-in-the-middle, impossible differentials and rectangle attacks. A special care is taken to the attack scenarios made possible by the multiple branches.

Our next contribution is to design and provably analyze two new TPRF-based deterministic authenticated encryption (DAE) schemes called SAFE and ZAFE that are highly efficient, parallelizable, and offer $(n+\min(n,t))/2$ bits of security, where $n, t$ denote respectively the input block and the tweak sizes of the underlying primitives. We further implement SAFE with ButterKnife to show that it achieves an encryption performance of 1.18 c/B for long messages on Skylake, which is 24% faster than the comparable Crypto'17 TBC-based ZAE DAE. Our second candidate ZAFE, which uses the same authentication pass as ZAE, offers a


C. Pöpper and L. Batina (Eds.): ACNS 2024, LNCS 14584, pp. 433–459, 2024.
https://doi.org/10.1007/978-3-031-54773-7_17

similar level of speedup. Besides, we show that ButterKnife, when used in Counter Mode, is *slightly faster* than AES (0.55 c/B vs 0.63 c/B on Skylake).

**Keywords:** tweakable pseudorandom functions · expanding primitives · deterministic authenticated encryption · beyond-birthday-bound security

## 1 Introduction

**Building Blocks.** Block ciphers (BCs) are fundamental symmetric cryptographic primitives. AES [1] is the most popular block cipher today, a fact that has prompted processor vendors, like Intel and ARM, to equip their products with AES hardware acceleration, enabling excellent software performance. Tweakable block ciphers (TBC) [36] are an extension of BCs by adding a public tweak input. Secure TBCs, similarly to BCs, are modeled as tweak-keyed pseudorandom permutations (TPRPs). TBCs also enable designs with higher security [27,37,43]. Towards building secure TBCs, recent works investigate how to integrate a tweak into the BC. TBC designs like SKINNY [9], the AES-based Deoxys-BC, Joltic-BC and KIASU-BC follow the TWEAKEY [29] design framework.

(Multi)-forkciphers [2,4] (M/FC) are tweakable $n$-to-$\alpha n$ ($\alpha = 2$ for FC) domain-expanding functions with forward, inverse, and a reconstruction functionalities. ForkSkinny [4] is a secure FC instance where each branch realizes a SKINNY TBC. Each branch is an $n$-bit permutation under a fixed key, hence the maximal security is $n/2$ bits, set by the birthday bound. ForkSkinny achieves $2n$-bit domain extension cheaper than 2 SKINNY calls and that allows for performance improvements for authenticated encryption (AE) [4], counter-style (CTR) encryption [2], pseudo-random number generation [6]. Yet, for all these modes, just like in counter mode, the primitive does not need to be invertible. Additionally, they achieve beyond birthday bound (BBB) security which is a sought for security level given the current advancements in computation, resource aggregation in powerful entities, and multi-user security considerations.

A natural candidate for achieving similar security and efficiency optimizations is a $2n$-to-$\alpha n$ domain-expanding function with inherent $n$-bit security. Since a tweakable PRF (TPRF) is equivalent to a PRF with a bigger input space (that subsumes the tweak), the only point of introducing a tweak/block distinction would be to bring down the computational cost of processing changes of these different parts. TPRF can then be built upon existing TBCs that readily support the $2n$-bit input space as compared to $2n$-bit BCs building blocks.

Combining the objectives of building a fixed-length $n$-to-$\alpha n$-bit TPRF and achieving BBB security, in this work we pose the central research question: "*Can we design an efficient, provably and cryptanalytically sound, $n$-bit secure fixed-length $n$-to-$\alpha n$ TPRF for $\alpha \geq 2$ and demonstrate highly efficient, beyond birthday bound secure applications of it in symmetric cryptography?*"

**(Deterministic) Authenticated Encryption.** AE guarantees *both* privacy and authenticity of data. Contemporary AE schemes are *nonce-based*, examples are the OCB [44] and the NIST-recommended [42] GCM [39] and CCM [25] modes. Oftentimes, the nonce may repeat when a user mishandles them, or the device is equipped with a weak or flawed software randomness source, or has a restricted secure storage. The consequences vary from a total loss of confidentiality to forgeability attacks. In some applications, the ciphertext differentiation (of repeated messages) is not wanted, instead the deterministic feature is looked for, e.g. access for encrypted database storage. Similar features might be of use for lightweight AE [7] when devices lack a secure randomness generator or memory. In all these cases one uses deterministic AE or DAE schemes which are nonce misuse-resistant [45] and two-pass, and security-wise leak nothing beyond the repetitions of identical messages.

SIV [45] and its GCM-SIV [24] instantiation are well-known DAEs. A modified version AES-GCM-SIV was defined in RFC 8452 [23]. Although (AES)-GCM-SIV performs close to 1 cpb, it failed to deliver strong security guarantees [26,28]. As a consequence, more recent DAE designs target *beyond birthday bound (BBB)* security. GCM-SIV2 [26] is secure up to about $2^{2n/3}$ queries. The SCT scheme [43] achieves BBB security when nonces do not repeat and its security degrades to the birthday bound with reuse of nonces. The ZAE DAE mode [27] achieves BBB security by processing $n(n+t)/(2n+t)$ input bits per TBC. This was possible due to the use of the ZMAC authentication that "absorbs" $(n+t)$ bits per block. ZAE is instantiated with the Deoxys-BC [31] and SKINNY [9] TBCs. Table 1 summarizes the security and performance of these DAE schemes. Security-wise the ZAE DAE excels and efficiency-wise the AES-GCM-SIV outperforms ZAE (see performance numbers in Table 4). One reason is that using TBCs towards BBB secure DAE comes with a performance penalty compared to BC-based DAE, such as GCM-SIV DAE, admittedly with lower security due to the computational overhead associated with the tweakey processing. Our next research question is: "*How to apply fixed-length TPRFs in DAE schemes to achieve with security comparable to* ZAE *and performance closer to* GCM-SIV?"

**Table 1.** DAE: security against nonce respecting (NR) and nonce-misuse (NM) adversaries and performance for long messages on Intel Skylake. By $n$ we denote the block size, $t$ the tweak size, $Q$ the number of distinct nonces (in enc.), $R$ is the maximal number of nonce repetitions (in enc.), $\sigma$ the total length in blocks of queried messages, $q$ the number of encryption queries, and the maximum message length by $2^{k-1}$ blocks.

| AE Scheme | Security (NR) | Security (NM) | Performance [c/B] |
|---|---|---|---|
| AES-GCM-SIV [22] | $\frac{Q}{2^{n-2k}}$ | $\frac{QR^2}{2^{n-2k}}$ | 0.93 |
| SCT [43] | $\frac{q}{2^n} + \frac{\sigma^2}{2^{n+t}}$ | $\frac{q^2}{2^n} + \frac{R\sigma}{2^t}$ | 1.74 |
| ZAE [27] | $\frac{\sigma^2}{2^{n+\min(n,t)}}$ | $\frac{\sigma^2}{2^{n+\min(n,t)}}$ | 1.46 |
| ZAFE; SAFE [This work] | $\frac{\sigma^2}{2^{n+\min(n,t)}}$ | $\frac{\sigma^2}{2^{n+\min(n,t)}}$ | 1.15; 1.18 |

### 1.1 Contributions

**Novel and Generic $n$-to-$\alpha n$-bit TPRF.** We propose a generic masked Iterate-Fork-Iterate mIFI method for building an $n$-bit secure TPRF. mIFI uses $(\alpha + 1)$ independent permutations, the first one to generate a fork state and the rest for all output branches. The internal fork state masks the outputs of each branch to preclude invertibility. The TPRF has inputs: a key $K$, a tweak $T$, an $n$-bit message $M$; and outputs a ciphertext $C$ of $\alpha n$ bits. The TPRF makes $(\alpha + 1)$ calls to independent random permutations $(\alpha \geq 2)$. The design resembles the iterate-fork-iterate [4] composition. Its proof takes an entirely different approach that is enabled by the application of the $\chi^2$ method [15]. We prove that mIFI is indistinguishable from a uniformly random $\alpha n$-bit string with $n$-bit security. Up to our knowledge, this is the first fixed-length TPRF composition to achieve arbitrary but fixed expansion with $n$-bit security.

**ButterKnife and Cryptanalysis.** The mIFI approach allows us to *efficiently reuse* well-analyzed and optimized TBC components to instantiate our ButterKnife design (in Sect. 3.2). Our design approach is reminiscent of the $n$-to-$n$-bit AES-based (T)PRF [17] method. We use the AES-based Deoxys TBC components due to its robustness in terms of security and its AES internal structure. Deoxys-BC is used in ZAE and the Deoxys [31,32] AE designs. ButterKnife uses a 256-bit tweakey and applies 7 Deoxys-BC-256 rounds until the forking point and another 8 rounds in each of the $\alpha = 8$ fully *parallelizable* branches (see Fig. 1) to expand an $n$-bit input to an $8n$-bit output.

ButterKnife benefits from the cryptanalysis of Deoxys-BC-256. Due to the feed-forward of the 8 output branches in ButterKnife, the security arguments of Deoxys-BC-256 do not directly apply. ButterKnife also benefits from the cryptanalysis of AES-PRF [40]. Our design choices are rooted in the detailed security analysis (in Sect. 4) of our proposal against well-known techniques namely, differential, linear, impossible differential and rectangle attacks.

**Encryption, Authentication and DAE Algorithms.** Towards secure DAE, we propose encryption and authentication schemes of $n$-bit security and tweaks of size $t \geq n$. We introduce FEnc that uses $(n + \min(n, t))$-bit IVs to encrypt on average $m = \alpha n$ bits of plaintext for each call to the underlying expanding TPRF. Our new PRF SFMac takes as inputs $(A, M, K)$ to produce a tag of size $2n$ bits. SFMac uses a GHash-like construction and spends about one multiplication in $\mathsf{GF}(2^{2n})$ to process $2n$ bits of data and two calls to the underlying TPRF for the total data processing. The encryption scheme has optimized message processing due to the use of $\alpha n$ bit outputs from the TPRF (versus $n$-bit outputs for TBCs). Both schemes also support reducing the tag and IV length to any $\lambda \leq 2n$, which is reflected in the security of $\min(\lambda, n + \min(n, t))/2$ bits.

We combine the latter algorithms under the SIV composition [45] to achieve the $n$-bit secure DAE SAFE. Since some platforms do not offer instructions to speed-up finite field multiplication, we also introduce the ZAFE DAE scheme, that combines the TPRF-based encryption from FEnc to the efficient TBC-based ZMAC MAC algorithm. All our designs are parallelizable. The proofs rely on the

H coefficients technique and take advantage of the additional input space that comes from the tweak and of the larger output space to achieve full security using a number of primitive calls that is as small as possible.

**Efficiency.** We implement SAFE and compare it to state-of-the-art DAE schemes. Our results are demonstrated in Table 4. Owing to the large TPRF output at reduced computational cost, our fully parallelizable encryption pass FEnc features significant improvements in throughput ($\approx 58\%$) with respect to ZAE. In the scope of $n$-bit secure DAEs, we observe our proposals SAFE and ZAFE to compare favorably. Our SFMac implementation shows that GHash-style multiplication in $\mathsf{GF}(2^{2n})$ may, depending on the platform, contribute to no less effective SFMac processing than, e.g., ZMAC. Globally, SAFE and ZAFE maintain $n$-bit security, like ZAE, while moving much closer to AES-GCM-SIV in terms of performance (e.g., with 1.15 c/B on Skylake).

**Related Work.** In a parallel work, Dutta *et al.* [19] realize a systematic study of all possible high-level structures to create secure and efficient PRFs with (possibly) variable-length outputs from PRPs. This work complements ours as we focus on a specific design paradigm (mIFI) and use it to propose an actual instantiation with additional cryptanalysis and an optimized implementation.

**Complete Version of the Paper.** We refer to the full version of this paper [3] for missing proofs and any additional resources.

## 2 Preliminaries

### 2.1 General Notation

For every positive integer $n$, we denote by $\{0,1\}^n$ the set of all $n$-bit binary strings, and by $(\{0,1\}^n)^+$ the set of all bit strings whose size is a non-zero multiple of $n$. The set of all bit strings will be denoted by $\{0,1\}^*$, and the empty string by $\epsilon$. For any $M$ in $\{0,1\}^*$, $|M|$ will be the bit length of the string $M$. $M[1]||\dots||M[m] \xleftarrow{n} M$ means that we split $M$ into $m$ blocks of $n$-bit strings, where $m = \lceil |M|/n \rceil$. If $M \notin (\{0,1\}^n)^+$, the one-zero padding is used on $M$ beforehand. For any $T$ in $\{0,1\}^*$, $[T]_n$ denotes the first $n$ bits of $T$ if $|T| \geq n$, or $T||0^{n-|T|}$ otherwise. $M[1]||M[2] \xleftarrow{(n,t)} M$ means that we split the $(n+t)$-bit string $[M]_{n+t}$ into 2 blocks, where $M[1]$ is a $n$-bit string and $M[2]$ a $t$-bit string.

Perm$(n)$ is the set of all permutations of $\{0,1\}^n$. For every positive integer $m, t$ such that $m \geq n$, $\widetilde{\text{Perm}}(t,n)$ is the set of all tweakable permutations of $\{0,1\}^n$ with tweak space $\{0,1\}^t$ and Func$(t,n,m)$ is the set of all tweakable functions from $\{0,1\}^n$ to $\{0,1\}^m$. For any keyed tweakable $P : \mathcal{K} \times \mathcal{T} \times \mathcal{X} \rightarrow \mathcal{Y}$ with key and tweak spaces $\mathcal{K}$ and $\mathcal{T}$, domain $\mathcal{X}$ and range $\mathcal{Y}$, we will indifferently write $P(k,t,x)$, $P_k(t,x)$ or $P_k^t(x)$ for every tuple $(k,t,x)$ in $\mathcal{K} \times \mathcal{T} \times \mathcal{X}$.

As usual, for any positive integers $a, b$ such that $a \geq b$, we denote by $(a)_b$ the falling factorial $a(a-1)\cdots(a-b+1)$, with the convention that $(a)_0 = 1$. Let GF$(2^n)$ be the field of order $2^n$. We identify $n$-bit strings and finite field elements of GF($2^n$) by representing the string $a = a_{n-1}a_{n-2}...a_1a_0$ as the polynomial $a(x) = a_{n-1}x^{n-1} + a_{n-2}x^{n-2} + ... + a_1x + a_0$ and vice versa. For any $a, b$ in $\{0,1\}^n$, their sum $a \oplus b$ is the sum of polynomials $a(x) + b(x)$. $a \otimes b$ or $ab$ is defined with respect to the irreducible polynomial $f(x)$ used to represent GF($2^n$) as $a(x) \cdot b(x) \bmod f(x)$. Thus, we view $\{0,1\}^n$ as the finite field GF($2^n$) with $\oplus$ as field addition and $\otimes$ as field multiplication. Sometimes, we also identify $n$-bit strings with integers in $\{0, \dots, 2^n - 1\}$. In that case, $\boxplus$ and $\boxminus$ denote the addition and subtraction modulo $2^n$. Moreover, we define the $\oplus_t$ operation as follows: for any $x \in \{0,1\}^n$, and any $y \in \{0,1\}^t$, $x \oplus_t y = [x]_t \oplus y$. Note that $|x \oplus_t y| = t$.

### 2.2 The H Coefficients and $\chi^2$ Proof Techniques

We use the H coefficients technique [24] to upper bound the advantage of a computationally unbounded and deterministic distinguisher $D$ with access to a tuple of oracles: $O_{\text{re}}$ (resp. $O_{\text{id}}$) the tuple of real (resp. ideal) world oracles. The advantage of $D$ is defined as

$$\text{Adv}(D) = \left|\Pr\left[D^{O_{\text{re}}} = 1\right] - \Pr\left[D^{O_{\text{id}}} = 1\right]\right|.$$

$D$'s oracles interaction is summarized in the queries transcript $\tau$: $\theta_{\text{id}}$ (resp. $\theta_{\text{re}}$) are obtained by the interaction of $D$ with the ideal (resp. real) world oracles. $\tau$ is *attainable* if and only if $\Pr\left[\theta_{\text{id}} = \tau\right] > 0$. The set of all attainable transcripts is denoted by $\Theta$. Then, one has the following classical lemma.

**Lemma 1** ([13,24]). *Let $\Theta_{\text{bad}}, \Theta_{\text{good}}$ be two sets such that $\Theta = \Theta_{\text{bad}} \sqcup \Theta_{\text{good}}$. If we assume that, for every transcript $\tau$ in $\Theta_{\text{good}}$, one has*

$$\frac{\Pr\left[\theta_{\text{re}} = \tau\right]}{\Pr\left[\theta_{\text{id}} = \tau\right]} \geq 1 - \varepsilon,$$

*then one has* $\text{Adv}(D) \leq \Pr\left[\theta_{\text{id}} \in \Theta_{\text{bad}}\right] + \varepsilon$.

The set $\Theta_{\text{bad}}$ (resp. $\Theta_{\text{good}}$) are the set of *bad* (resp. *good*) transcripts.

In [15], Dai, Hoang, and Tessaro introduced the $\chi^2$ method to upper bound the statistical distance between the probability distributions of two sequences of random variables by computing the expectation of the $\chi^2$ distances of the corresponding conditional distributions of the random variables. Their core result is Lemma 2 that has been used to prove the security of XORP [11,15], encrypted Davies-Meyer [15], and the Swap-Or-Not [15] constructions.

Given a set $\Omega$, let $\mathsf{X} := X^q := (X_1, \dots, X_q)$ and $\mathsf{Y} := Y^q := (Y_1, \dots, Y_q)$ be two random vectors over $\Omega^q$. For $\forall i \in [q]$ and $Z \in \{\mathsf{X}, \mathsf{Y}\}$, we write $\Pr_Z\left[z_i | z^{i-1}\right] := \Pr\left[Z_i = z_i | Z^{i-1} = z^{i-1}\right]$. When $i = 1$, we define $\Pr_Z\left[z_1 | z^0\right] := \Pr\left[Z_1 = z_1\right]$.

**Definition 1.** *Suppose that for every $i$ and every $y^i$ such that* $\Pr\left[Y^i = y^i\right] > 0$, *one also has* $\Pr\left[X^i = y^i\right] > 0$. *For every $z^{i-1}$ in the support of $Y^{i-1}$, the $\chi^2$-distance between these two conditional probability distributions is defined as*

$$\chi^2(z^{i-1}) := \sum_{x_i} \frac{\left(\Pr_{\mathsf{Y}}\left[x_i | z^{i-1}\right] - \Pr_{\mathsf{X}}\left[x_i | z^{i-1}\right]\right)^2}{\Pr_{\mathsf{X}}\left[x_i | z^{i-1}\right]},$$

*where the sum is taken over all* $x_i$ *such that* $\Pr_{\mathsf{X}}\left[x_i|z^{i-1}\right] > 0$.

Before stating the core technical Lemma of the $\chi^2$ method, we recall that the statistical distance between the $\Pr_0$ and $\Pr_1$ distributions whose supports are in a set $\Omega$, is defined as:

$$\|\Pr_0 - \Pr_1\| = \frac{1}{2}\sum_{x\in\Omega} |\Pr_0(x) - \Pr_1(x)|.$$

Besides, the statistical distance also satisfies the following well-known property:

$$\|\Pr_0 - \Pr_1\| = \max_{X\subset\Omega} |\Pr_0(X) - \Pr_1(X)|.$$

**Lemma 2.** *Assuming that the support of* $Y^i$ *is included in the support of* $X^i$ *for every* $i = 1, \ldots, q$, *one has*

$$\|\Pr_{\mathsf{X}} - \Pr_{\mathsf{Y}}\| \leq \left(\frac{1}{2}\sum_{i=1}^{q} \mathbb{E}\left[\chi^2(Y^{i-1})\right]\right)^{\frac{1}{2}}. \quad (1)$$

### 2.3 Security Notions

**Tweakable Pseudorandom Functions/Permutations.** A secure TPRF with tweak $\mathcal{T}$ and input $\mathcal{X}$ spaces, and a secure PRF with input space $\mathcal{T} \times \mathcal{X}$ are identical. We adopt the former due to the different impact of the inputs on performance in our instantiation. When $F$ is a TPRP, we define its tprp security in a similar way to tprf but with respect to the set of all $P$ from $\mathcal{T} \times \mathcal{X}$ to $\mathcal{X}$.

**Definition 2.** *Let* $F : \mathcal{K} \times \mathcal{T} \times \mathcal{X} \to \mathcal{Y}$ *be a TPRF. The advantage of an adversary* $A$ *in breaking the* tprf*-security of* $F$ *is defined as*

$$\mathrm{Adv}_F^{\mathrm{tprf}}(A) = \left|\Pr\left[A^{F_K} = 1\right] - \Pr\left[A^R = 1\right]\right|,$$

*where the probabilities are taken over the random choices of* $A$ *and the uniformly random draw of* $K$ *from* $\mathcal{K}$ *and* $R$ *from the set of all functions from* $\mathcal{T} \times \mathcal{X}$ *to* $\mathcal{Y}$. *When* $\mathcal{T} = \emptyset$, *we recover the standard* prf *security notion.*

**Deterministic AE (DAE).** $\mathsf{DAE} = (\mathcal{K}, \mathcal{AD}, \mathcal{M}, \mathcal{C}, \mathsf{DAE.Enc}, \mathsf{DAE.Dec})$ where $\mathcal{K}, \mathcal{AD}, \mathcal{M}, \mathcal{C}$ are non-empty sets and $\mathsf{DAE.Enc}, \mathsf{DAE.Dec}$ are deterministic algorithms such that:

- $\mathsf{DAE.Enc}$ takes inputs: $K \in \mathcal{K}$, $M \in \mathcal{M}$ and $A \in \mathcal{AD}$; and returns $C \in \mathcal{C}$;
- $\mathsf{DAE.Dec}$ takes inputs $K \in \mathcal{K}$, $C \in \mathcal{C}$ and $A \in \mathcal{AD}$; and returns either a plaintext $M \in \mathcal{M}$, or the special symbol $\perp$ if $C$ is invalid;
- for all $(K, A, M)$ in $(\mathcal{K}, \mathcal{AD}, \mathcal{M})$, $\mathsf{DAE.Dec}_K(A, \mathsf{DAE.Enc}_K(A, M)) = M$.

**Definition 3.** *Let* DAE *be a DAE scheme. The advantage of an adversary A in breaking the* dae*-security of* DAE *is defined as*

$$\mathrm{Adv}^{\mathrm{dae}}_{\mathsf{DAE}}(A) = \left|\Pr\left[A^{\mathsf{DAE.Enc}_K,\mathsf{DAE.Dec}_k} = 1\right] - \Pr\left[A^{\$(\cdot,\cdot),\perp(\cdot,\cdot)} = 1\right]\right|,$$

*where oracle $\perp$ always returns $\perp$, and the probabilities are taken over the random choices of A, the uniformly random draw of K from $\mathcal{K}$, and the randomness of the oracle \$ which returns a uniformly random bit string of the same length as the corresponding output of* DAE.Enc.

**IV-Based Encryption Scheme.** $\mathsf{IVE} = (\mathcal{K}, \mathcal{IV}, \mathcal{M}, \mathcal{C}, \mathsf{IVE.Enc})$ where $\mathcal{K}, \mathcal{IV}, \mathcal{M}, \mathcal{C}$ are non-empty sets and IVE.Enc is a deterministic algorithm such that IVE.Enc takes as inputs: $K \in \mathcal{K}$, an IV $I \in \mathcal{IV}$ and a plaintext $M \in \mathcal{M}$; and returns a ciphertext $C \in \mathcal{C}$. $\mathsf{IVE}^\$$ is the associated randomized algorithm that draws a uniformly random IV from $\mathcal{IV}$.

**Definition 4.** *Let* IVE *be an IV-based encryption scheme. The advantage of an adversary A in breaking the* ive*-security of* IVE *is defined as*

$$\mathrm{Adv}^{\mathsf{ive}}_{\mathsf{IVE}}(A) = \left|\Pr\left[A^{\mathsf{IVE}^\$.\mathsf{Enc}_K} = 1\right] - \Pr\left[A^{\$(\cdot,\cdot)} = 1\right]\right|,$$

*where the first probability is taken over the uniformly random draw of K from $\mathcal{K}$ and oracle \$ returns a uniformly random bit string of the same length as the corresponding output of* IVE.Enc.

## 3 Masked Iterate-Fork-Iterate and ButterKnife

### 3.1 Masked Iterate-Fork-Iterate

mIFI is inspired by the Iterate-Fork-Iterate (IFI) paradigm [4]. The main difference is that we XOR the forking state to all output blocks, see Fig. 1. In existing forkciphers each branch is a TBC which limits their security to the birthday bound. Our simple change makes the construction an $n$-bit secure TPRF ($n$-bit input message), and further boosts the performance benefits of forkciphers. The feed-forward precludes decryption and reconstruction queries.

We then prove the following result.

**Theorem 1.** *Let $\alpha, q$ and $n$ be three strictly positive integers such that $(\alpha+1)q < 2^n$ and let $\mathcal{T}$ be a non-empty set. We denote by $F_0$ the* mIFI *paradigm where $P \xleftarrow{\$} \widetilde{\mathrm{Perm}}([\alpha] \times \mathcal{T}, n)$. Then, for any distinguisher D against the* tprf*-security of $F_0$ that issues at most q queries to its oracle, one has*

$$\mathrm{Adv}^{\mathrm{tprf}}_{F_0}(D) \leq \frac{\sqrt{2(\alpha+1)}q}{2^n}.$$

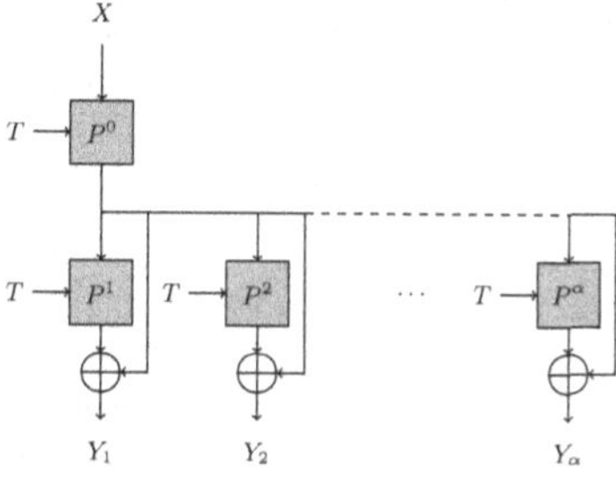


**Fig. 1.** mIFI with a tweakable permutation $P$ and a tweak space $[\alpha] \times \{0,1\}^t$.

*Proof Strategy.* In our proof, we focus on information-theoretical adversaries, that are computationally unbounded, and deterministic without loss of generality. Let $D$ be any distinguisher against the tprf-security of $F_0$ that issues at most $q$ queries to its oracle. We will assume (also w.l.o.g.) that $D$ does not make any redundant queries, and that it always issues exactly $q$ queries.

The first step of the proof is to show that, in the real world, $P$ can be lazily sampled. As long as a random tweakable permutation is queried on a new pair $(T, X)$, the answer can be chosen uniformly at random outside of the set of the previous outputs with the same tweak value $T$. When a new $(T, X)$ is queried to $F_0$, $X$ has never been queried to $P^0(T, \cdot)$. Hence, $Z_0 := P^0(T, X)$ is chosen uniformly at random outside of the set of the $Z_0$ from the previous queries with tweak $T$. Then, the values $Z_i := P^\alpha(T, Y_0)$ can be chosen uniformly at random from the set of values that are different from the previous $Z_i$s with the same tweak. $F_0$ is indistinguishable from $F_1 : \mathcal{T} \times \{0,1\}^n \to \{0,1\}^{\alpha n}$ and $(T, X) \mapsto \|_{i=1}^{\alpha} P^0(T, X) \oplus P^i(T, X)$. Hence, $\mathrm{Adv}_{F_0}^{\mathrm{tprf}}(D) = \mathrm{Adv}_{F_1}^{\mathrm{tprf}}(D)$.

The construction can be seen as a variant of the XORP construction, where independent $P$s are used for each permutation call (with a tweak parameter added). We follow in parts the idea for the proof of [11] and their notation for an $m$-tuple $(x_1, \ldots, x_m)$ as $x^m$. This makes the size of each tuple in the proof easier to follow. First, we reveal additional information to the adversary: 1. in the real world, the intermediate values $Z_0$ will be revealed alongside each query; 2. in the ideal world, a dummy value is chosen uniformly at random in a set of authorized values (the set of all values not colliding with a previous query).

S (resp. R) is the random variable that corresponds to the transcript of the interaction of $D$ with the real (resp. ideal) world oracle. We define both in Algorithms 1 and 2. Recall that $D$ is deterministic, hence, all adversarial queries can be computed from the outputs of the oracle. We make the queries explicit in the transcript in order to make the proof easier to follow.

Note that $D_i[T] = \{0,1\}^n$ and $D = \{0,1\}^n$ cannot occur as we assume $(\alpha+1)q < 2^n$. Thus, for every $y \in \{0,1\}^{\alpha n}$, there exists at least one $z_0$ such that the probability of getting $(y, z_0)$ as an output is non-zero, both in the real and the ideal world. We let $\Omega^q$ (depends on the adversary $D$) denote the set of all transcripts $s^q$ such that $\Pr_{\mathsf{S}}[s^q] > 0$. Such a transcript is parsed as a list of $q$ tuples $(t_i, x_i, y_{1,i} \| \cdots \| y_{\alpha,i}, z_{0,i})$, where: 1. $(t_i, x_i)$ is $D$'s $i$-th query,

**Algorithm 1.** S is the random variable corresponding to the outputs created by the interaction of $D$ with the real-world oracle defined here.

```
variables
    Tables of sets of previous Tweakable Permutation Outputs (D_i[T])_{i∈{0,...,α},T∈𝒯}
end variables

function INITIALIZE
    for i ∈ {0,...,α} do
        for T ∈ 𝒯 do
            D_i[T] ⟵ ∅
        end for
    end for
end function
function QUERY(T,X)
    for i ∈ {0,...,α} do
        if D_i[T] = {0,1}^n then
            return 0^n
        end if
        Z_i ⟵$ {0,1}^n \ D_i[T]
        D_i[T] ⟵ D_i[T] ∪ {Z_i}
    end for
    for i ∈ {0,...,α} do
        Y_i ⟵ Z_0 ⊕ Z_i
    end for
    return (T, X, Y_1‖...‖Y_α, Z_0)
end function
```

**Algorithm 2.** R is the random variable corresponding to the outputs created by the interaction of $D$ with the ideal-world oracle defined here.

```
variables
    Tables of sets of previous Tweakable Permutation Outputs (D_i[T])_{i∈{0,...,α},T∈𝒯}
end variables

function INITIALIZE
    for i ∈ {0,...,α} do
        for T ∈ 𝒯 do
            D_i[T] ← ∅
        end for
    end for
end function
function QUERY(T,X)
    for i ∈ {1,...,α} do
        Y_i ⟵$ {0,1}^n
    end for
    D ⟵ D_0[T]
    for i ∈ {1,...,α} do
        D ⟵ D ∪ (Y_i ⊕ D_i[T])
    end for
    if D = {0,1}^n then
        return 0^n
    end if
    Z_0 ⟵$ {0,1}^n \ D
    D_0[T] ⟵ D_0[T] ∪ {Z_0}
    for i ∈ {1,...,α} do
        D_i[T] ⟵ D_i[T] ∪ {Z_0 ⊕ Y_i}
    end for
    return (T, X, Y_1‖...‖Y_α, Z_0)
end function
```

that deterministically depends on $y_{k,j}$ and $z_{0,j}$ for $j < i$ and $k = 1, \dots, \alpha$; 2. $(y_{1,i}\| \cdots \|y_{\alpha,i}, z_{0,i})$ is the output of $F_1$, which means that, for every $1 \leq i < j \leq q$, if $t_i = t_j$, then $z_{0,i} \neq z_{0,j}$ and $y_{k,i} \oplus z_{0,i} \neq y_{k,j} \oplus z_{0,j}$ for $k = 1, \dots, \alpha$. We have also $\Pr_{\mathsf{R}}[s^q] > 0$ as it would have been possible for the ideal-world oracle to give the same outputs, yet with a different probability. Conversely, any transcript

$r^q$ such that $\Pr_{\mathsf{R}}[r^q] > 0$ also satisfies $\Pr_{\mathsf{S}}[r^q] > 0$. Hence, both distributions have the same support $\Omega^q$, and we can apply the $\chi^2$ technique to S and R to lower bound $\|\Pr_{\mathsf{S}} - \Pr_{\mathsf{R}}\|$. Given that $\mathrm{Adv}^{\mathrm{tprf}}_{F_0}(D) = \mathrm{Adv}^{\mathrm{tprf}}_{F_1}(D) \leq \|\Pr_{\mathsf{S}} - \Pr_{\mathsf{R}}\|$, it allows to conclude the proof of Theorem 1.

The following Lemma is proven in the full version of the paper [3].

**Lemma 1.**

$$\|\Pr_{\mathsf{S}} - \Pr_{\mathsf{R}}\| \leq \frac{\sqrt{2(\alpha+1)}q}{2^n}.$$

### 3.2 Specification of ButterKnife

In order to inherit from both the performance and security arguments of Deoxys-BC, and to serve our design purposes, we modified as few elements of Deoxys-BC as possible in ButterKnife. ButterKnife uses Deoxys-BC that is supported by extensive security analyses [14,38,46], see Table 6. except for the round constants.

ButterKnife uses a 256-bit tweakey and is based on Deoxys-BC-256. $P^0$ contains 7 and $P^j$ $(1 \leq j \leq \alpha = 8)$ contains 8 rounds (15 out of 7 common rounds are iterated to obtain $Y_j$s from $X$), resp. The 128-bit state of ButterKnife is represented as a $4 \times 4$ matrix of bytes. The tweakey is represented as two matrices in the same format. The round operations are:

- AddRoundTweakey (ART) adds the (128-bit) round tweakey to the state,
- SubBytes (SB) transforms each of the 16 bytes by applying the AES Sbox,
- ShiftRows (SR) rotates row $i$ to the left by $i$ positions for $i \in \{0,1,2,3\}$,
- MixColumns (MC) corresponds to the multiplication in $\mathbb{F}_{2^8}$ of each column by the circulant matrix $M = circ(02, 03, 01, 01)$.

A final tweakey addition is done before the final feed forward leading to $Y_j$, $1 \leq j \leq 8$. As in Deoxys, the last MixColumns is not omitted. The tweakey follows the TWEAKEY framework [29]. At round $i$, the tweakey $RTK_i$ is obtained by xoring the state of the two tweakey words with a round constant depending on $i$ and on the branch index $j_b$ ($j_b = 0$ before branching, and $j_b = j \geq 1$ after branching for the branch leading to $Y_j$): $RTK_i = TK_i^1 \oplus TK_i^2 \oplus \mathsf{Rconst}_{j_b,i}$. The number of rounds for ButterKnife and the other parameters are decided by the security analysis (given in Sect. 4). The set of round constants is detailed in Sect. A.

## 4 Security Analysis of ButterKnife

To determine the number of rounds, we examine distinct attack techniques considering the single key and *related-tweakey* adversarial model and aiming for

128-bit security. We recommend a number of rounds before and after branching that is equal or close and that every output $Y_j$ has the same number of rounds. Note the branches of ButterKnife, from $X$ to $Y_j$ ($1 \leq j \leq 8$), follow the Fast-PRF construction [40]. Consequently, parts of the analysis made on the concrete instance AES-PRF in [17] apply to our case. Also, the attacks on ForkAES [5] (exploiting the reconstruction functionality) do not apply to ButterKnife. That is because each branch of ButterKnife is not a permutation of the input, i.e. to obtain a $Y_i$ from a $Y_j$ (for $i \neq j$ and $i, j \geq 1$), is impossible in ButterKnife. Our analysis takes into account that different output branches share the first 7 rounds and that up to our analysis no weakness is induced by this.

### 4.1 Differential Distinguishers

**Scenario I.** One branch of ButterKnife follows Deoxys-BC. The final feed forward and different round constants do no impact the number of active Sboxes of a differential characteristic, and thus the bounds in [14] apply (we recall them in Table 5 in Supplementary Material A).

Let us consider the differential characteristic corresponding to a single branch, w.l.o.g. the first branch producing the outputs $Y_1, Y_1'$ under two distinct tweaks $T, T'$ respectively. Suppose there is a tweakey differential characteristic with probability $p$ observed for 15-round of Deoxys-BC-256 i.e. before adding the feed-forward internal state in ButterKnife, given by ($\boldsymbol{\Delta}_{in} \rightarrow \boldsymbol{\Delta}_1 \rightarrow \ldots \boldsymbol{\Delta} \rightarrow \ldots \widetilde{\boldsymbol{\nabla}}^1$) where $\boldsymbol{\Delta}$ is the difference in the internal state at the round before branching. Then any branch $j$ has a tweakey differential characteristic $\boldsymbol{\Delta}_{in} \rightarrow \boldsymbol{\Delta}_1 \rightarrow \ldots \boldsymbol{\Delta} \rightarrow \ldots \widetilde{\boldsymbol{\nabla}}^j \oplus \boldsymbol{\Delta}$ with probability $p$. Since the S-box used in ButterKnife is differentially 4-uniform, a characteristic with 22 or more active Sboxes does not allow to distinguish the cipher, and thus the previous bounds show that this scenario does not threaten ButterKnife.

**Scenario II.** A second possibility is to obtain information from the difference branch propagation, say the one leading to $Y_i$ and the one to $Y_j$, all computed from $X$. In ButterKnife the difference only comes from the distinct $P^i$ and $P^j$ (see the blue differences on the left in Fig. 2). After branching $\delta = 0$. The question is if the variation between $P^i$ and $P^j$ avoids high probability differential characteristics. The variation comes from the constants added in the tweakey, so in each

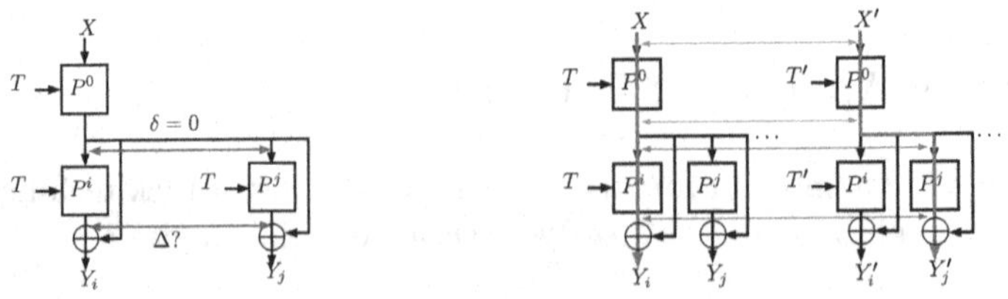


**Fig. 2.** Second and third scenarios for a differential attack.

round the difference is in the third column, and is equal to $(i \oplus j, i \oplus j, i \oplus j, i \oplus j)^T$. Our MILP model of the problem returns the bounds (Table 2) and we obtain that after 3 rounds there are 22 active Sboxes, and that a single characteristic does not allow to distinguish. Moreover, these bounds can easily be shown to not be tight.

**Table 2.** Bounds on the number of active Sboxes in the second scenario.

| rounds after branching | 1 | 2 | 3 | 4 | 5 | 6 | 7 | 8 |
|---|---|---|---|---|---|---|---|---|
| active Sboxes | 4 | 16 | 22 | 22 | 23 | 24 | 25 | 26 |

**Scenario III.** We consider inputs $X$ and $X'$ (under $T$ and $T'$), and look at the difference propagation from the inputs to two different branches. For instance, a difference from $X \oplus X'$ to $Y_i \oplus Y'_j$. (see on the right of Fig. 2). The first part of a characteristic follows the same constraints as in Deoxys-BC, and thus the same bounds as in Table 5 apply. The lower part is more complex, we may have a difference in the internal state, in the tweak, and coming from the round constants. We make a byte-wise MILP model to estimate the number of active Sboxes (Table 3). Note that we did not force a difference in the tweakey nor in the input so that the minimum returned corresponds to characteristics from the previous scenario with no difference in $X$ and $T$.

**Table 3.** Bounds on the number of active Sboxes in the third scenario.

| rounds before + after branching | 2+2 | 3+3 | 4+4 | 5+5 | 6+6 | 7+7 | 7+8 |
|---|---|---|---|---|---|---|---|
| active Sboxes | 2 | 7 | 17 | 22 | 24 | 25 | 26 |

### 4.2 Linear Trails

Any 4 consecutive rounds of ButterKnife have the same property as Deoxys-BC and in AES, that is, activate at least 25 Sboxes. Moreover, the impact of a tweak on the resistance to linear cryptanalysis was studied in detail in [34], with the important conclusion that "tweaking a block cipher with a linear tweak schedule does not introduce any new linear trails".

### 4.3 Meet-in-the-Middle Attacks

AES-PRF [40] has a MitM attack [17] which shows that 7 rounds ($s$ rounds before and $7 - s$ rounds after the feed-forward) can be attacked with time and (chosen plaintext) data complexity $2^{107}$. A single branch in ButterKnife resembles the FastPRF (or AES-PRF) construction. The attack in [17] can also be applied against a single branch of ButterKnife. However, this only compromises 7 out of 15 rounds. The MiTM attack [35] on Deoxys-BC-256 (128-bit key) breaks 8 rounds and is based on the distinguishing technique [16] that is also used in [17]. For ButterKnife (with a 128-bit key), it is possible to break at most 8 rounds.

### 4.4 Impossible Differentials and Zero-Correlation

**Scenario I.** Here, we look at a single branch ($X$ to one of the $Y_i$), which corresponds to the FastPRF construction. The impossible differential technique used against AES-PRF [17] can be applied to any branch of ButterKnife, for a version with $P^j$ ($1 \leq j \leq 8$) of any number of rounds. This is depicted in Fig. 3.

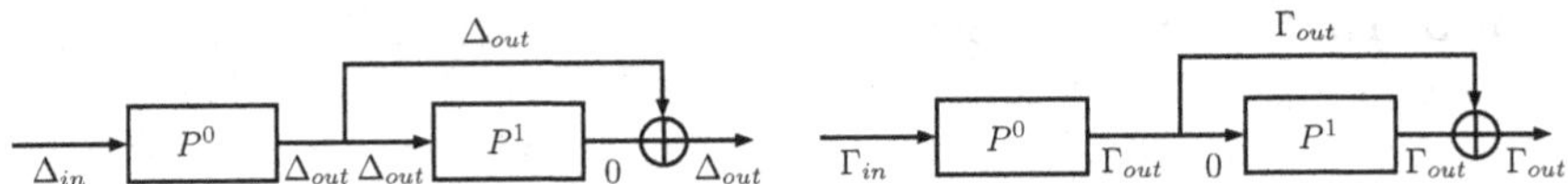


**Fig. 3.** Impossible differential and Zero-correlation attacks (from [17]).

In the single tweakey scenario, $P^j$ cannot cancel a difference: for any non-zero input difference $\Delta_{out}$ the output difference $\neq 0$. If the output difference of $P^0$ is $\Delta_{out}$, we can not have $\Delta_{out}$ after the feed forward. This is a distinguisher, and it can be converted into an attack by positioning the key-recovery rounds in $P^0$. An impossible differential attack [17] against AES-PRF$_{2,8}$ (2 rounds before and 8 rounds after the feed forward) can be mounted. ButterKnife with 7 and 8 rounds before and after feed forward respectively, is secure here as we expect that no more than 3 key recovery rounds can be added. A similar technique can be used to create a zero-correlation linear distinguisher (on the right in Fig. 3) that leads to an attack against AES-PRF$_{2,8}$. We expect that the same number of rounds of ButterKnife can be attacked. We note that like different configurations of AES-PRF in [17], it is possible to attack different round-reduced versions of ButterKnife. For example, corresponding to AES-PRF$_{6,4}$, 6 and 4 rounds before and after feed-forward in ButterKnife, corresponding to AES-PRF$_{7,3}$, 7 and 3 rounds before and after feed forward are possible to attack using zero-correlation attack. However, the full ButterKnife remains secure.

**Scenario II.** The second possible scenario studies two different outputs $Y_i$ and $Y_j$, and thus looks for impossible differences between these two branches. By searching for a trail in a miss in the middle way, our best result reached 3 rounds.

### 4.5 Amplified Boomerang Distinguishers

Given that decryption queries are impossible, we focus on the chosen plaintexts variant of the boomerang attack, or amplified boomerangs [33]. Basic amplified distinguishers are built by splitting the cipher $E$ into[1] $E = E_1 \circ E_0$ and using differentials with probabilities $p$ and $q$ over $E_0$ and $E_1$, respectively. The distinguisher uses messages ($X^i$, $0 \leq i \leq 3$) with two fixed input differences ($X^0 \oplus X^1$ and $X^2 \oplus X^3$), and counts the number of times a specific difference is both in $E(X^0) \oplus E(X^2)$ and $E(X^1) \oplus E(X^3)$. A first estimate gives the probability of a distinguisher based on the previous differentials to be $p^2q^2 2^{-n}$, which is compared to $2^{-2n}$ for the ideal case.

Once again, several scenarios are possible (with the feed forward omitted). The first one (top left in Fig. 4) corresponds to constructing quartets with 4 independent branches built from 4 different inputs ($(X^i, Y^i_j)$ for a fixed $j$ and $0 \leq i \leq 3$). In the best case, the result is the same as for Deoxys-BC. A second possibility is to consider the setting depicted on the top right of Fig. 4 for which a quartet is obtained from 4 different inputs at two different branches (number $i \geq 1$ and $j \geq 1$). By using the bounds by the MILP models for these scenarios, the number of rounds that can be attacked in this setting is 10: the upper trail covers a part $E_0$ made of 3 rounds of $P^0$, while the lower trail covers the next 3 rounds of $P^0$ and 4 rounds of the bottom part. Namely, the first differential characteristic would be in the first differential scenario (3 rounds, 1 active Sbox), and the second differential characteristic would be in the third differential scenario and covers 3 rounds before and 4 rounds after branching, with 9 active Sboxes. Assuming our bounds are tight (as previously, it can be shown that it is not the case) and that each Sbox transition can be done with probability $2^{-6}$, it results in a distinguisher of probability $p^2q^2 2^{-n} = 2^{-12}2^{-108}2^{-128} = 2^{-248}$.

Another setting considers two different inputs and two of their branches (see Fig. 4, bottom left). On the left, we consider the first differential to be starting from the 0 difference, right after branching, while the second differential characteristic is put between the two branches of equal index. A maximum of 12 rounds can be covered: 1 round (4 active Sboxes) after branching, followed by 4 rounds (5 active Sboxes), and since any number of rounds can be added on top (before branching), all 7 can be included. Such a distinguisher has a probability around $2^{-128-108}$. However, a problem here is the difficulty to detect the boomerang once the feed forward is taken into account. To work around this, we consider the setting (on the bottom right in Fig. 4) where the characteristic over $E_0$ is not existing: we consider that a certain difference $\gamma$ appears between the two branching point of two different states and use a (or two different) characteristic(s) from the branching point to the two outputs of equal index, leading to the difference $\Delta$ (or $\Delta_1$ and $\Delta_2$) before the feed forward, and equal to $\Delta \oplus \delta$ (or $\Delta_1 \oplus \delta$ and $\Delta_2 \oplus \delta$) after it. Again, the 7 rounds before branching can be included, and 5 rounds can be considered after branching with 10 active Sboxes, thus reaching a probability close to $2^{-128-120}$.

Given that ButterKnife has 8 rounds after branching, we believe that only reduced round versions could be attacked with this technique.

We provide a discussion on some additional cryptanalysis aspects in Supplementary Material A.1.

[1] Better probability estimates might be obtained with the sandwich technique [18].

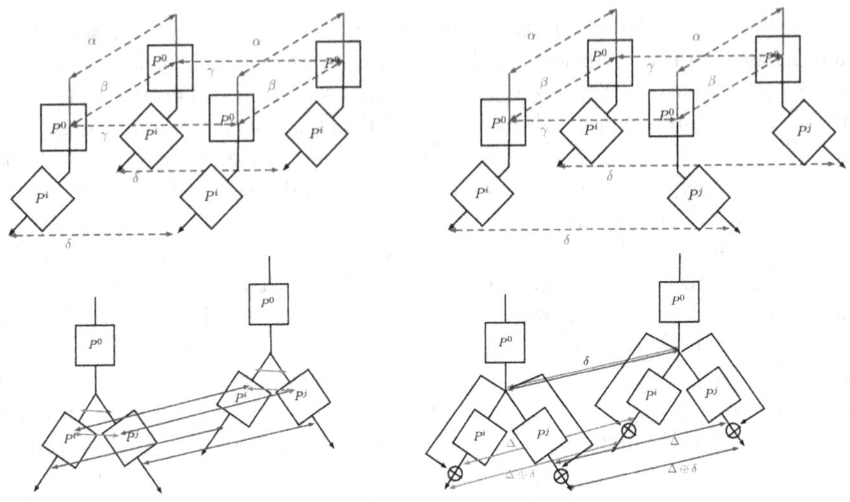

**Fig. 4.** Settings 1, 2, 3 and 4 for the boomerang attack.

## 5 DAE for TPRFs: Security and Performance

TPRFs naturally support CTR-style modes to output a keystream as fast as possible. Conversely, expansion is not a best fit for data absorption. In order to build a fast DAE, one of our proposed authentication mechanisms will be TPRF independent. To this end, we propose 2 DAE constructions: SAFE and ZAFE, that both use a fast TPRF-based CTR-style encryption. SAFE applies a polynomial-based hash function and ZAFE a TBC-based MAC for authentication to enable support for more applications and platforms.

Let $F : \mathcal{K} \times \{0,1\}^{t+1} \times \{0,1\}^n \to \{0,1\}^m$ denote a TPRF with key space $\mathcal{K}$, tweak space $\{0,1\}^{t+1}$, domain $\{0,1\}^n$ and range $\{0,1\}^m$. SAFE and ZAFE offer security level of $(n + \min(n,t))/2$ bits. We implement both schemes with ButterKnife and compare their performance with Deoxys modes of operations.

### 5.1 The SAFE Mode of Operation

Let us fix an integer $\lambda$ such that $\lambda \leq 2n$. SAFE is divided into: 1. FEnc with $\min(\lambda, n+t)$-bit IVs encrypts on average $m$ bits of plaintext for each call to $F$, using a constant tweak; 2. SFMac$[F]$ PRF that takes as input two messages (message and associated data), and processes $2n$ bits of input for every multiplication in $\mathsf{GF}(2^{2n})$. SFMac$[F]$ uses a single call to $F$ during the finalization to output a $\lambda$-bit tag. We combine both primitives via the SIV framework [45] and have both passes computed in parallel. The encryption of $(A, M)$ starts with a $2n$-bit hashing key $L$ derivation from the key via a call to $F$ with the all-zero tweak and message as its inputs. Then, $A$ and $M$ are parsed into $2n$-bit blocks. A $2n$-bit hash $Y$ of $(A, M)$ is computed, the tag $T$ equals $[F_K^{0\|Y[2]}(Y_1)]_\lambda$ where

$Y_1 \| Y_2 \xleftarrow{n,t} Y$. This tag is used as IV in $\mathsf{FEnc}[F]$. $\mathsf{SAFE}$ is specified in Algorithm 3 and the encryption algorithm is illustrated in Fig. 5 in Appendix B. We prove the security of $\mathsf{SAFE}[F]$ via the following theorem.

**Theorem 2.** *Let $n, m, t, \sigma, q, \lambda$ be positive integers such that $m \geq 2n \geq 1$, $q, \sigma < 2^n$ and $\lambda \leq 2n$. Let $F$ be a TPRF with tweak space $\{0,1\}^{t+1}$, domain $\{0,1\}^n$ and range $\{0,1\}^m$. Let also $D$ be an adversary against the* dae*-security of* $\mathsf{SAFE}[F]$ *that runs in time at most* $\mathtt{time}$*, and makes at most $q$ queries for a total of at most $\sigma$ $n$-bit blocks. Then there exists an adversary $B$ against the* prf*-security of $F$ that runs in time at most $\mathtt{time} + O(\sigma)$ and makes at most $\sigma + q + 1$ chosen plaintext queries such that*

$$\mathrm{Adv}^{\mathrm{dae}}_{\mathsf{SAFE}[F]}(A) \leq \mathrm{Adv}^{\mathrm{tprf}}_{F}(B) + \frac{q}{2^\lambda} + \frac{2(q-1)\sigma}{2^{m'}} + \frac{2q\sigma + 2q^2 + \sigma + 4q}{2^{n+\min(n,t)}},$$

*where $m' = \min(\lambda, n+t)$.*

*Proof.* We defer the proof of Theorem 2 to the full version of this work, but we sketch its ingredients here. First, we apply a hybrid argument to replace $F$ by its ideal counterpart. We then use a composition result to split the dae-security in two parts: the prf-security of its authentication pass, and the ive-security of its encryption pass. Both are then studied with the H coefficients technique, and rely on the fact that inputs to $F$ only collide with negligible probabilities.

*Remark 1.* $\lambda$ allows for flexibility of the tag. Also, the bound from Theorem 2 tells us that $\lambda \geq n + \min(n,t)$ is a reasonable choice. When $t + 1 = n$, $\lambda = 2n$ is preferable if $n$ is a multiple of 8 since it will prevent having an unused bit in one byte of the tag.

### 5.2 The ZAFE Mode of Operation

$\mathsf{ZAFE}$ uses a TBC $E : \mathcal{K} \times \{0,1\}^{t'} \times \{0,\ldots,9\} \times \{0,1\}^n \to \{0,1\}^n$ with key space $\mathcal{K}'$, tweak space $\{0,1\}^{t'} \times \{0,\ldots,9\}$, and block space $\{0,1\}^n$. $\mathsf{ZAFE}$ uses a PRF algorithm $\mathsf{ZMAC}$ that processes on average $n+t'$ bits of data per TBC call, and an IV-based encryption scheme $\mathsf{FEnc}$. Note that here both primitives rely on different keys. This is not necessary for $\mathsf{ZAE}$, as both components relied on the same TBC, and could be replaced by two independent tweakable permutations thanks to domain separation. A solution in our case would be to derive both keys from the same master key, by using calls to $F$ in order to generate both subkeys. For the sake of simplicity, we present the 2-key version in Algorithm 4.

We obtain the following result.

**Theorem 3.** *Let $n, m, t, \sigma, q, \lambda$ be positive integers such that $m \geq 2n \geq 1$, $q, \sigma < 2^n$ and $\lambda \leq 2n$. Let $F$ be a TPRF with tweak space $\{0,1\}^{t+1}$, domain $\{0,1\}^n$ and range $\{0,1\}^m$, and let $E : \mathcal{K} \times \{0,1\}^{t'} \times \{0,\ldots,9\} \times \{0,1\}^n \to \{0,1\}^n$ be a TBC with key space $\mathcal{K}'$, tweak space $\{0,1\}^{t+1} \times \{0,\ldots,9\}$, and block space $\{0,1\}^n$. Let also $D$ be an adversary against the* dae*-security of* $\mathsf{ZAFE}[F,E]$ *that runs in time*

**Algorithm 3.** SAFE $[F]$ where $F_K \in \text{Func}(t+1, n, m)$ for every $K$. Here $\otimes$ denotes the multiplication in the field $\mathsf{GF}(2^{2n})$.

```
function SFMac(K,A,M)
    T ⟵ 0^{2n}
    L ⟵ [F_K^{0^{t+1}}(0^n)]_{2n}
    X ⟵ Pad_{10}(A) || Pad_{10}(M)
    X ⟵ X || ⟨|A|⟩_n || ⟨|M|⟩_n
    X[1] || ··· || X[x] ⟵^{2n} X
    for i ⟵ 1, x do
        T ⟵ (T ⊕ X[i]) ⊗ L
    end for
    U || V ⟵^{(n,t)} [T]_{n+t}
    T ⟵ F_K^{0||V}(U)
    return [T]_λ
end function
```

```
function FEnc(K,I,M)
    U || V ⟵^{(n,t)} [I]_{n+t}
    C[1] || ··· || C[c] ⟵^{m} M
    for i ⟵ 1, c do
        C[i] ⟵ C[i] ⊕ [F_K^{1||V}(U ⊞ i−1)]_{|C[i]|}
    end for
    return C[1] || ··· || C[c]
end function
```

```
function SAFE.Enc(K,A,M)
    T ⟵ SFMac(K, A, M)
    IV ⟵ [T]_{min(λ,n+t)}
    C ⟵ FEnc(K, IV, M)
    return (C, T)
end function
```

```
function SAFE.Dec(K,A,C,T)
    IV ⟵ [T]_{min(λ,n+t)}
    M ⟵ FEnc(K, IV, C)
    T' ⟵ SFMac(K, A, M)
    if T = T' then
        return M
    else
        return ⊥
    end if
end function
```

**Algorithm 4.** ZAFE $[F, E]$ where $F_K \in \text{Func}(t+1, n, m)$ for every key $K$, and $E_{K'} \in \text{Perm}(\{0,1\}^{t'} \times \{0,\ldots,9\}, n)$. A formal specification of ZMAC can be found in Appendix C.

```
function ZFMac(K,A,M)
    X ⟵ Pad_{10}(A) || Pad_{10}(M)
    X ⟵ X || ⟨|A|⟩_n || ⟨|M|⟩_n
    T ⟵ ZMAC(K, X)
    return [T]_λ
end function
```

```
function ZAFE.Enc(K,K',A,M)
    T ⟵ ZFMac(K', A, M)
    IV ⟵ [T]_{min(λ,n+t)}
    C ⟵ FEnc(K, IV, M)
    return (C, T)
end function
```

```
function ZAFE.Dec(K,K',A,C,T)
    IV ⟵ [T]_{min(λ,n+t)}
    M ⟵ FEnc(K, IV, C)
    T' ⟵ ZFMac(K', A, M)
    if T = T' then
        return M
    else
        return ⊥
    end if
end function
```

*at most* $\mathtt{time}$*, and makes at most* $q$ *queries for a total of at most* $\sigma$ $n$*-bit blocks. Then there exist an adversary* $B$ *against the* tprf*-security of* $F$ *an adversary* $C$ *against the* tprp*-security of* $E$ *that both run in time at most* $\mathtt{time} + O(\sigma)$ *and make at most* $\sigma + 4q + 2$ *chosen plaintext queries, such that*

$$\text{Adv}^{\text{dae}}_{\mathsf{ZAFE}[F,E]}(A) \leq \text{Adv}^{\text{tprf}}_F(B) + \text{Adv}^{\text{tprp}}_E(C) + \frac{q}{2^\lambda} + \frac{2(q-1)\sigma}{2^{m'}} + \frac{2.5\sigma^2}{2^{n+\min(n,t')}} + 4\left(\frac{q}{2^n}\right)^{3/2},$$

*where* $m' = \min(\lambda, n+t)$.

*Proof.* The proof is very similar to the proof of Theorem 2, and we only highlight the differences here. We first start by applying a hybrid argument to replace both $F$ and $E$ by their ideal counterparts. Then, the variant of [45, Theorem 1] allows us to separate the study of the authentication pass and the encryption pass. Since the latter simply corresponds to FEnc, we can directly reuse the corresponding term from Theorem 2 to upper-bound its ive-advantage. Finally, we upper-bound the prf-security of ZMAC with [27, Theorem 1]. Note that the fact that we truncate the output of ZMAC to $\lambda$ bits does not reduce its security, since a prf-adversary against the truncated version can always be turned into a prf-adversary against the full version, with the same advantage, and a small time complexity overhead.

### 5.3 Implementation Aspects

**Implementation of FEnc and SFMac.** Many contemporary devices support the AES round function in hardware (e.g., AES-NI). Similar to other parallel AES-based modes, SAFE and ZAFE can harness the full power of the AES-NI pipeline for sufficiently long messages [20], or with task-level parallelism [12]. We consider eight simultaneous AES-based primitives (*i.e.*, AES, Deoxys and ButterKnife). Within ButterKnife, all branches are computed independently, and round tweakeys can be precomputed. As the counter is given as an input block to ButterKnife, as opposed to the tweak, the tweakey-schedule only needs to be evaluated once for all calls to the primitive.

For the authentication portion we use the carry-less multiplication instructions (PCLMULQDQ) that are supported on many recent processors, as well as the fast reduction algorithm from [21] to implement the multiplication in the finite field $GF(2^{256})$ (Note that in prior work, it was uncertain whether an implementation in a larger field would maintain competitive performance [27]). In order to keep the reduction algorithm efficient, we used the polynomial $x^{256} + x^{10} + x^5 + x^2 + 1$. Moreover, we aggregate the reduction step by computing the first $\lambda$ powers of the hashing key, and by only reducing once every $\lambda$ multiplications. The optimal value of $\lambda$ depends on the message length and the microarchitecture. Based on experiments, we find $\lambda = 32$ to be an adequate aggregation level.

**Comparisons and Results.** Our SAFE implementations are in C, using compiler intrinsics for AES-NI and PCLMULQDQ instructions. For the encryption pass with ButterKnife, we adapt the Deoxys implementations from [30]. For AES-GCM-SIV, we use assembly-optimized implementations[2] from [22], noting that assembly implementations may further improve the throughput of SAFE/ZAFE as well. To our knowledge, there are no publicly available implementations of ZAE and SCT. Yet, as explored by Iwata et al. [27], the performance of their TBC-based building blocks is well-understood. We adopt their estimation methodology to estimate the performance of ZAFE, and compare our modes with other DAE

[2] Taken from https://github.com/Shay-Gueron/AES-GCM-SIV (September 2021).

**Table 4.** DAEs in cycles per byte (c/B) for 64KiB messages, decoupled in authentication and encryption. ZAE instances use Deoxys-256 and/or Deoxys-384.

| Mode | Security | Skylake (3.2 GHz) | | | Cascade Lake SP (2.7 GHz) | | |
|---|---|---|---|---|---|---|---|
| | | Auth. | Enc. | Total | Auth. | Enc. | Total |
| AES-GCM-SIV [22] | 64 | 0.30 | 0.63 | 0.93 | 0.31 | 0.63 | 0.94 |
| SCT [43] | 64 | 0.87† | 0.87† | 1.74† | 0.87† | 0.87† | 1.74† |
| ZAE (256) [27] | 128 | 0.61† | 0.87† | 1.48† | 0.61† | 0.87† | 1.48† |
| ZAE (384) [27] | 128 | 0.59† | 0.99† | 1.58† | 0.59† | 0.99† | 1.58† |
| ZAE (256-384) [27] | 128 | 0.59† | 0.87† | 1.46† | 0.59† | 0.87† | 1.46† |
| SAFE | **128** | **0.63** | **0.55** | **1.18** | **0.62** | **0.55** | **1.17** |
| ZAFE | **128** | **0.60**† | **0.55** | **1.15**† | **0.60**† | **0.55** | **1.15**† |

(† *are estimates based on measured counter-in-tweak performance*, cf. [27])

schemes (ZAE and SCT). We confirm their long-message estimates for Deoxys counter-in-tweak on Skylake (*i.e.*, 0.87 c/B for Deoxys-256 and 0.99 c/B for Deoxys-384). Like Iwata et al., for random tweak inputs, we apply a penalty of 1.4 for Deoxys-256 and 1.8 for Deoxys-384.

We use the `rdstc(p)` instructions on `x86` to measure performance across 50 batches, each 500 measurements, of which the fastest batch is retained. To reflect practical scenarios and match prior work [22], measurement iterations are preceded by iterations that warm up the instruction and data caches. In addition to Skylake (i5-6500, legacy, 2015), we also evaluate performance of SAFE/ZAFE on the server-grade Cascade Lake SP (Xeon Platinum 8280, server, 2019).

Table 4 gives performance of SAFE/ZAFE w.r.t. comparable schemes (authentication and encryption decoupled). First, ButterKnife itself has excellent performance due to the use of AES rounds (*i.e.*, ≈ 8.875 AES rounds per output block, compared to 14 or 16 for Deoxys). Second, the static tweakey schedule throughout the entire encryption pass compares favorably to a counter in the tweak. As a result, we observe an estimated throughput increase of ≈58% w.r.t. counter-in-tweak with Deoxys-256 (SCT and ZAE) and ≈80% w.r.t. Deoxys-384 (ZAE). ButterKnife is even competitive to AES in counter mode (cf. AES-GCM-SIV). Our SFMac implementation in $GF(2^{256})$ is approximately twice as slow as in $GF(2^{128})$, e.g., as used in AES-GCM-SIV. Our findings suggest that it is at least competitive to ZMAC [27], provided that the platform supports efficient field multiplications (e.g., PCLMULQDQ on x86). On platforms without such hardware support, we expect ZMAC to outperform SFMac (and ZAFE to outperform SAFE). Globally, SAFE/ZAFE outperform current state-of-the-art $n$-bit secure DAE schemes with an estimated 27% on both Skylake and Cascade Lake SP.

# 6 Conclusion

We gave the first $n$-to-$\alpha n$ ($\alpha \geq 2$) domain-expanding mIFI design with $n$-bit security. We proposed the domain-expanding TPRF ButterKnife and supported its security with extensive cryptanalysis. We then designed two provably secure DAE schemes: SAFE and ZAFE, that combine a fast TPRF-based encryption pass with two efficient authentication algorithms. Both schemes come with approximately $n$-bit security and give important efficiency improvements over ZAE when instantiated with ButterKnife.

Natural TPRF candidate applications are nonce-based AE, encryption, data expansion. In a recent work [10] TPRFs are used for constructing an efficient and secure key-derivation function (KDF) which is then implemented in the Signal end-to-end encrypted messaging protocol to demonstrate a significant efficiency gain over the present HMAC-based HKDF solution in Signal. The exploration of the broader security and privacy application scenarios where the use of expanding TPRF can be beneficial is an interesting and novel research direction.

**Acknowledgments.** Elena Andreeva was supported in part by the Austrian Science Fund (FWF) grant SpyCoDe with number 10.55776/F8507-N. Part of this work was written while Benoît Cogliati was affiliated with the CISPA Helmholtz Center for Information Security.

# A Details on ButterKnife

**ButterKnife *Constants.*** In ButterKnife the round constant RC[i] is the AES round constant in the $i$th round as defined below:

$$\mathsf{Rconst}_{j_b,i} = \begin{pmatrix} 1 & \mathtt{RC[i]} & j_b & 0 \\ 2 & \mathtt{RC[i]} & j_b & 0 \\ 4 & \mathtt{RC[i]} & j_b & 0 \\ 8 & \mathtt{RC[i]} & j_b & 0 \end{pmatrix}$$

***Existing Lower Bounds.*** The bounds are summarized in Table 5.

**Table 5.** Lower bounds on the number of active S-boxes in the related-tweakey model for Deoxys-BC-256 [14].

| rounds | 1 | 2 | 3 | 4 | 5 | 6 | 7 | 8 | 9 | 10 | 11 | 12 | 13 | 14 |
|---|---|---|---|---|---|---|---|---|---|---|---|---|---|---|
| Deoxys-BC-256 | 0 | 0 | 1 | 5 | 9 | 12 | 16 | 19 | 23 | 26 | 29 | 32 | 35 | 38 |

***Reminder of the Best Results on Deoxys-BC-256 with 128-bit Key and Tweak.*** The results are summarized in Table 6.

**Table 6.** Some of the best results on Deoxys-BC-256 with 128-bit key and tweak.

| rounds | Technique | Time | Data | Memory | ref. |
|---|---|---|---|---|---|
| 8 | MITM | $2^{113}$ | $2^{113}$ | $2^{97}$ | [35] |
| 9 | RK Imp. dif. | $2^{118}$ | $2^{118}$ | $2^{102}$ | [41] |
| 10 | RK boomerang | $2^{109.1}$ | $2^{98.4}$ | $2^{88}$ | [46] |
| | RK rectangle | $2^{114.2}$ | $2^{114.2}$ | $2^{112.2}$ | [46] |

## A.1 Additional Aspects

In the main body we focused on distinguishers that do not take into account the final feed forward as this final operation makes it hard to mount a key recovery part at the bottom. The key recovery requires to invert rounds in value to access the end of the distinguisher, which is made difficult by the unknown value of the middle internal state. When given the full code book a zero-sum distinguisher can be constructed against one or more branches as described in [40, Appendix A.1] with distinguishing advantage $1 - \frac{1}{2^{128}}$. In an integral attack, adding a round tweakey does not have any impact. This allows an adversary to apply the integral attacks on reduced-round AES to round-reduced ButterKnife also.

Cryptanalysis of ForkCiphers [8] applies as well, but with the difference that the reconstruction setting is not available given that one cannot make decryption queries. A reflection differential distinguishers might exist between two branches, but accessing it and building the required pair is troublesome.

# B Graphical Representation of SAFE

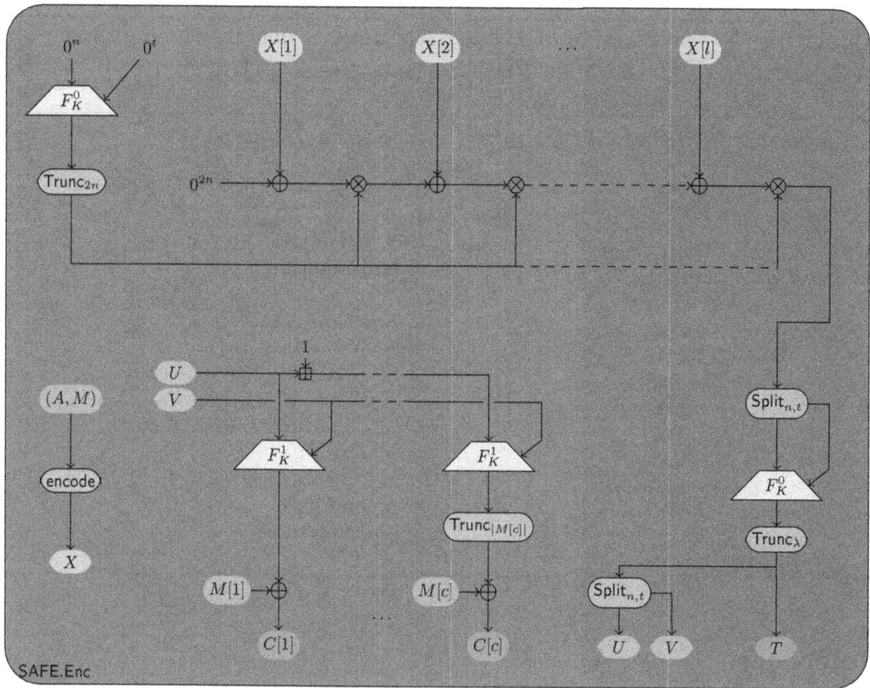


**Fig. 5.** The SAFE authenticated encryption function which, given a plaintext $M$ and associated data $A$, outputs the ciphertext $C$ and the tag $T$. Here $\mathsf{Trunc}_i$ simply truncates its input to $i$ bits if it is longer or fills it with zeroes otherwise, and $\mathsf{Split}_{a,b}$ additionally splits it into its leftmost $a$ bits and rightmost $b$ bits. $\otimes$ denotes the multiplication in $\mathrm{GF}(2^{2n})$. Recall that $\lambda \leq 2n$.

# C ZMAC Pseudocode

**Algorithm 5.** Specification of ZMAC [27]. Here $2a$ denotes the multiplication by the element of the finite field $\mathrm{GF}(2^n)$ that is represented by the polynomial $x$.

**function** ZHASH($K$,$X$)
  $U \leftarrow 0^n$, $V \leftarrow 0^t$
  $L_l \leftarrow E_K^9(0^t, 0^n)$
  $L_r \leftarrow E_K^9(0^{t-1}1, 0^n)$
  $(X[1], \ldots, X[m]) \xleftarrow{n+t} X$
  **for** $i = 1$ to $m$ **do**
    $(X_l, X_r) \xleftarrow{n,t} X[i]$
    $S_l \leftarrow L_l \oplus X_l$
    $S_r \leftarrow L_r \oplus_t X_r$
    $C_l \leftarrow E_K^8(S_r, S_l)$
    $C_r \leftarrow C_l \oplus_t X_r$
    $U \leftarrow 2(U \oplus C_l)$
    $V \leftarrow V \oplus C_r$
    $(L_l, L_l) \leftarrow (2L_l, 2L_l)$
  **end for**
  **return** $(U, V)$
**end function**

**function** ZFIN($K$,$i$,$U$,$V$)
  $Y[1] \longleftarrow E_K^i(V, U) \oplus E_K^{i+1}(V, U)$
  $Y[2] \longleftarrow E_K^{i+2}(V, U) \oplus E_K^{i+3}(V, U)$
  $Y \longleftarrow Y[1] || Y[2]$
  **return** $Y$
**end function**

**function** ZMAC($K$,$M$)
  $X \longleftarrow \mathrm{Pad}_{10}(M)$
  $(U, V) \longleftarrow$ ZHASH$(K, X)$
  **if** $n + t \mid |M|$ **then**
    **return** ZFIN$(K, 0, U, V)$
  **else**
    **return** ZFIN$(K, 4, U, V)$
  **end if**
**end function**

# References


1. Advanced Encryption Standard (AES). National Institute of Standards and Technology, NIST FIPS PUB 197, U.S. Department of Commerce (2001)
2. Andreeva, E., Bhati, A.S., Preneel, B., Vizár, D.: 1, 2, 3, fork: counter mode variants based on a generalized forkcipher. IACR Trans. Symmetric Cryptol. **2021**(3), 1–35 (2021)
3. Andreeva, E., Cogliati, B., Lallemand, V., Minier, M., Purnal, A., Roy, A.: Masked iterate-fork-iterate: a new design paradigm for tweakable expanding pseudorandom function. Cryptology ePrint Archive, Report 2022/1534 (2022). https://eprint.iacr.org/2022/1534
4. Andreeva, E., Lallemand, V., Purnal, A., Reyhanitabar, R., Roy, A., Vizár, D.: Forkcipher: a new primitive for authenticated encryption of very short messages. In: Galbraith, S.D., Moriai, S. (eds.) ASIACRYPT 2019, Part II. LNCS, vol. 11922, pp. 153–182. Springer, Heidelberg (2019). https://doi.org/10.1007/978-3-030-34621-8_6
5. Andreeva, E., Reyhanitabar, R., Varici, K., Vizár, D.: Forking a blockcipher for authenticated encryption of very short messages. Cryptology ePrint Archive, Report 2018/916 (2018). https://eprint.iacr.org/2018/916
6. Andreeva, E., Weninger, A.: A forkcipher-based pseudo-random number generator. In: Tibouchi, M., Wang, X. (eds.) ACNS 2023, Part II. LNCS, vol. 13906, pp. 3–31. Springer, Cham (2023). https://doi.org/10.1007/978-3-031-33491-7_1
7. Banik, S., Bogdanov, A., Luykx, A., Tischhauser, E.: SUNDAE: small universal deterministic authenticated encryption for the internet of things. IACR Trans. Symm. Cryptol. **2018**(3), 1–35 (2018)

8. Banik, S., et al.: Cryptanalysis of ForkAES. In: Deng, R.H., Gauthier-Umaña, V., Ochoa, M., Yung, M. (eds.) ACNS 2019. LNCS, vol. 11464, pp. 43–63. Springer, Heidelberg (2019). https://doi.org/10.1007/978-3-030-21568-2_3
9. Beierle, C., et al.: The SKINNY family of block ciphers and its low-latency variant MANTIS. In: Robshaw, M., Katz, J. (eds.) CRYPTO 2016, Part II. LNCS, vol. 9815, pp. 123–153. Springer, Heidelberg (2016). https://doi.org/10.1007/978-3-662-53008-5_5
10. Bhati, A.S., Dufka, A., Andreeva, E., Roy, A., Preneel, B.: Skye: A Fast KDF based on Expanding PRF and its Application to Signal. Cryptology ePrint Archive, Paper 2023/781 (2023). https://eprint.iacr.org/2023/781. (to appear in ACM ASIACCS)
11. Bhattacharya, S., Nandi, M.: Revisiting variable output length XOR pseudorandom function. IACR Trans. Symmetric Cryptol. **2018**(1), 314–335 (2018)
12. Bogdanov, A., Lauridsen, M.M., Tischhauser, E.: Comb to pipeline: fast software encryption revisited. In: Leander, G. (ed.) FSE 2015. LNCS, vol. 9054, pp. 150–171. Springer, Heidelberg (2015). https://doi.org/10.1007/978-3-662-48116-5_8
13. Chen, S., Steinberger, J.P.: Tight security bounds for key-alternating ciphers. In: Nguyen, P.Q., Oswald, E. (eds.) EUROCRYPT 2014. LNCS, vol. 8441, pp. 327–350. Springer, Heidelberg (2014). https://doi.org/10.1007/978-3-642-55220-5_19
14. Cid, C., Huang, T., Peyrin, T., Sasaki, Y., Song, L.: A security analysis of Deoxys and its internal tweakable block ciphers. IACR Trans. Symm. Cryptol. **2017**(3), 73–107 (2017)
15. Dai, W., Hoang, V.T., Tessaro, S.: Information-theoretic indistinguishability via the chi-squared method. In: Katz, J., Shacham, H. (eds.) CRYPTO 2017. LNCS, vol. 10403, pp. 497–523. Springer, Cham (2017). https://doi.org/10.1007/978-3-319-63697-9_17
16. Demirci, H., Selçuk, A.A.: A meet-in-the-middle attack on 8-round AES. In: Nyberg, K. (ed.) FSE 2008. LNCS, vol. 5086, pp. 116–126. Springer, Heidelberg (2008). https://doi.org/10.1007/978-3-540-71039-4_7
17. Derbez, P., et al.: Cryptanalysis of AES-PRF and its dual. IACR Trans. Symm. Cryptol. **2018**(2), 161–191 (2018)
18. Dunkelman, O., Keller, N., Shamir, A.: A practical-time related-key attack on the KASUMI cryptosystem used in GSM and 3G telephony. In: Rabin, T. (ed.) CRYPTO 2010. LNCS, vol. 6223, pp. 393–410. Springer, Heidelberg (2010). https://doi.org/10.1007/978-3-642-14623-7_21
19. Dutta, A., Guo, J., List, E.: Forking sums of permutations for optimally secure and highly efficient PRFs. Cryptology ePrint Archive, Report 2022/1609 (2022). https://eprint.iacr.org/2022/1609
20. Gueron, S.: Intel's new AES instructions for enhanced performance and security (invited talk). In: Dunkelman, O. (ed.) FSE 2009. LNCS, vol. 5665, pp. 51–66. Springer, Heidelberg (2009). https://doi.org/10.1007/978-3-642-03317-9_4
21. Gueron, S., Kounavis, M.E.: Intel Carry-Less Multiplication Instruction and its Usage for Computing the GCM Mode. Technical report, Intel Corporation (2014). https://software.intel.com/sites/default/files/managed/72/cc/clmul-wp-rev-2.02-2014-04-20.pdf
22. Gueron, S., Langley, A., Lindell, Y.: AES-GCM-SIV: specification and analysis. IACR Cryptol. ePrint Arch. **2017**, 168 (2017)
23. Gueron, S., Langley, A., Lindell, Y.: AES-GCM-SIV: nonce misuse-resistant authenticated encryption. RFC 8452, pp. 1–42 (2019)
24. Gueron, S., Lindell, Y.: GCM-SIV: full nonce misuse-resistant authenticated encryption at under one cycle per byte. In: Ray, I., Li, N., Kruegel, C. (eds.) ACM CCS 2015, pp. 109–119. ACM Press (2015)

25. Housley, R.: Using advanced encryption standard (AES) CCM mode with IPsec encapsulating security payload (ESP). RFC, 4309 (2005)
26. Iwata, T., Minematsu, K.: Stronger security variants of GCM-SIV. IACR Trans. Symm. Cryptol. **2016**(1), 134–157 (2016). https://tosc.iacr.org/index.php/ToSC/article/view/539
27. Iwata, T., Minematsu, K., Peyrin, T., Seurin, Y.: ZMAC: block cipher mode for highly secure message authentication. In: Katz, J., Shacham, H. (eds.) CRYPTO 2017, Part III. LNCS, vol. 10403, pp. 34–65. Springer, Heidelberg (2017). https://doi.org/10.1007/978-3-319-63697-9_2
28. Iwata, T., Seurin, Y.: Reconsidering the security bound of AES-GCM-SIV. IACR Trans. Symm. Cryptol. **2017**(4), 240–267 (2017)
29. Jean, J., Nikolic, I., Peyrin, T.: Tweaks and keys for block ciphers: the TWEAKEY framework. In: Sarkar, P., Iwata, T. (eds.) ASIACRYPT 2014, Part II. LNCS, vol. 8874, pp. 274–288. Springer, Heidelberg (2014). https://doi.org/10.1007/978-3-662-45608-8_15
30. Jean, J., Nikolic, I., Peyrin, T., Seurin, Y.: Deoxys v1. 41. Submitted to CAESAR (2016)
31. Jean, J., Nikolic, I., Peyrin, T., Seurin, Y.: Deoxys v1.43 (2018)
32. Jean, J., Nikolic, I., Peyrin, T., Seurin, Y.: The deoxys AEAD family. J. Cryptol. **34**(3), 31 (2021)
33. Kelsey, J., Kohno, T., Schneier, B.: Amplified boomerang attacks against reduced-round MARS and Serpent. In: Schneier, B. (ed.) FSE 2000. LNCS, vol. 1978, pp. 75–93. Springer, Heidelberg (2001). https://doi.org/10.1007/3-540-44706-7_6
34. Kranz, T., Leander, G., Wiemer, F.: Linear cryptanalysis: key schedules and tweakable block ciphers. IACR Trans. Symm. Cryptol. **2017**(1), 474–505 (2017)
35. Li, R., Jin, C.: Meet-in-the-middle attacks on round-reduced tweakable block cipher Deoxys-BC. IET Inf. Secur. **13**(1), 70–75 (2019)
36. Liskov, M., Rivest, R.L., Wagner, D.: Tweakable block ciphers. In: Yung, M. (ed.) CRYPTO 2002. LNCS, vol. 2442, pp. 31–46. Springer, Heidelberg (2002). https://doi.org/10.1007/3-540-45708-9_3
37. List, E., Nandi, M.: Revisiting full-PRF-secure PMAC and using it for beyond-birthday authenticated encryption. In: Handschuh, H. (ed.) CT-RSA 2017. LNCS, vol. 10159, pp. 258–274. Springer, Heidelberg (2017). https://doi.org/10.1007/978-3-319-52153-4_15
38. Liu, Y., Shi, B., Dawu, G., Zhao, F., Li, W., Liu, Z.: Improved meet-in-the-middle attacks on reduced-round Deoxys-BC-256. Comput. J. **63**(12), 1859–1870 (2020)
39. McGrew, D.A., Viega, J.: The security and performance of the Galois/counter mode (GCM) of operation. In: Canteaut, A., Viswanathan, K. (eds.) INDOCRYPT 2004. LNCS, vol. 3348, pp. 343–355. Springer, Heidelberg (2004). https://doi.org/10.1007/978-3-540-30556-9_27
40. Mennink, B., Neves, S.: Optimal PRFs from blockcipher designs. IACR Trans. Symm. Cryptol. **2017**(3), 228–252 (2017)
41. Moazami, F., Mehrdad, A., Soleimany, H.: Impossible differential cryptanalysis on Deoxys-BC-256. ISC Int. J. Inf. Secur. **10**(2), 93–105 (2018)
42. Dworkin, M.: Recommendation for Block Cipher Modes of Operation: Galois/-Counter Mode (GCM) and GMAC. NIST Special Publication 800-38D (2007)
43. Peyrin, T., Seurin, Y.: Counter-in-tweak: authenticated encryption modes for tweakable block ciphers. In: Robshaw, M., Katz, J. (eds.) CRYPTO 2016, Part I. LNCS, vol. 9814, pp. 33–63. Springer, Heidelberg (2016). https://doi.org/10.1007/978-3-662-53018-4_2

44. Rogaway, P., Bellare, M., Black, J., Krovetz, T.: OCB: a block-cipher mode of operation for efficient authenticated encryption. In: Reiter, M.K., Samarati, P. (eds.) ACM CCS 2001, pp. 196–205. ACM Press (2001)
45. Rogaway, P., Shrimpton, T.: A provable-security treatment of the key-wrap problem. In: Vaudenay, S. (ed.) EUROCRYPT 2006. LNCS, vol. 4004, pp. 373–390. Springer, Heidelberg (2006). https://doi.org/10.1007/11761679_23
46. Zhao, B., Dong, X., Jia, K.: New related-tweakey boomerang and rectangle attacks on Deoxys-BC including BDT effect. IACR Trans. Symm. Cryptol. **2019**(3), 121–151 (2019)

# Generalized Initialization of the Duplex Construction

Christoph Dobraunig[1] and Bart Mennink[2](✉)

[1] Intel Labs, Hillsboro, USA
christoph.dobraunig@intel.com
[2] Radboud University, Nijmegen, The Netherlands
b.mennink@cs.ru.nl

**Abstract.** The duplex construction is already well analyzed with many papers proving its security in the random permutation model. However, so far, the first phase of the duplex, where the state is initialized with a secret key and an initialization vector ($IV$), is typically analyzed in a worst case manner. More detailed, it is always assumed that the adversary is allowed to choose the $IV$ at will. However, in practice, the adversary can be stripped of its power to control the $IV$ in several ways. One prominent way of doing this is the use of a nonce ($IV$) masked with a secret, as done in AES-GCM in TLS 1.3. In this paper, we analyze how the security of the duplex construction changes if restrictions on the choice of the $IV$ are imposed. In particular, we evaluate several strategies that can achieve this, varying from the $IV$ on key case over the global nonce case to the random $IV$ case. We apply our findings to duplex-based encryption and authenticated encryption, compare the different strategies, and discuss the practical applications of our results.

**Keywords:** symmetric cryptography · duplex construction · initialization vector · nonce

## 1 Introduction

The duplex construction of Bertoni et al. [8], the sibling of the sponge construction [7], lends itself to efficiently fulfill many cryptographic tasks including encryption and authenticated encryption. The impact the duplex has on symmetric cryptography has recently been impressively showcased in the NIST lightweight standardization process, where 5 (including the winner) [1,2,11,14, 18] out of 10 algorithms follow the duplex construction or are duplex-inspired. Those schemes are nonce-based authenticated encryption schemes with the property that their security relies just on the uniqueness of the nonce, but not on how it is chosen. The same level of nonce formalism is also followed by the various security proofs of the various different duplex constructions we have seen in literature [8,13,19,23,24]: the proofs in large parts assume an attacker-favorable choice of nonce, or, as called more generally in the duplex, the initialization vector ($IV$).


C. Pöpper and L. Batina (Eds.): ACNS 2024, LNCS 14584, pp. 460–484, 2024.
https://doi.org/10.1007/978-3-031-54773-7_18

However, in practice, it is possible to take the choice over the $IV$ out of the hands of an attacker. One prominent example of how this is done, is the use of an additional secret to mask the nonce ($IV$) with a secret in AES-GCM in TLS 1.3. In this work, we will show that the analogue strategy applies to the duplex construction, with the additional benefit that it can be seen as an increase of the size of the secret key. Since practical applications of the sponge/duplex construction use permutations up to 1600 bits as in SHA-3/Keccak [9], the duplex construction allows for more space in the initialization compared to blockcipher-based modes. Hence, we also analyze other ways of restricting the control on the $IV$ from attackers, e.g., by using globally unique key identifiers, as suggested by Daemen et al. [11].

In our analysis, we will restrict our focus to the very general duplex construction of Daemen et al. [13], but with the rephasing suggested by Mennink [23]. (We also refer to the excellent work of Mennink [23] for a detailed treatment of the duplex in full generality (in his Sect. 3.1) and the role and importance of rephasing (in his Sect. 3.4).) In a nutshell, the duplex consists of an initialization interface, where a $b$-bit state is initialized using a key $K$ and an initialization vector $IV$. Then an arbitrary amount of duplexing calls can be made. Each duplexing call first evaluates a cryptographic $b$-bit permutation $\mathsf{p}$ on the state, then squeezes its $r$ outermost bits of the state (as digest), and it absorbs a $b$-bit message. There is an additional input, namely a flag, that indicates whether the $r$ outermost bits of the message will be added to the outer part of the state, or will overwrite that part. A detailed version of this duplex construction — or, in fact, a construction that generalizes the initialization function as we will discuss shortly — is given in Sect. 3.1.

Daemen et al. [13] derived a general security bound of this duplex construction, which gives an indication of the degree at which the construction is indistinguishable from random depending on a fine-grained set of adversarial resources. Dobraunig and Mennink [19] considered this construction in the leakage resilience setting. A crucial observation in their security analyses is that, intuitively, security of the scheme is guaranteed as long as the intermediate inner parts stay unknown to the adversary and these inner parts never collide. Different keys or different $IV$s will give a different initialization, and thus (likely) different and unpredictable inner parts after evaluation of the permutation. However, current duplex results assume that the attacker has full control over the $IV$, and the influence of initialization calls on the security bound only appears in two terms of the entire security bound:

$$\frac{\mu \cdot N}{2^k} + \frac{\binom{\mu}{2}}{2^k}, \tag{1}$$

where $k$ is the key size, $\mu$ the number of users/keys, and $N$ is the number of permutation queries that the adversary can make. The terms of (1) are the last two terms of (5c) of the bound of Theorem 1, where in general $Q_i \leq \mu$. The first term of (1) comes from the event that the adversary can "guess a key", i.e., it makes a permutation query ($N$ attempts) for one of the $\mu$ $k$-bit keys. The second term comes from "unlucky key collisions", as they would lead to colliding inner parts for different users.[1]

However, as said, these bounds assume that the attacker has fairly full control over the choice of $IV$ and they are merely dominated by the adversarial power in guessing one of the $\mu$ keys. Yet, in practice, restrictions on the $IV$ are quite conceivable. A typical example of this is the idea of masking the $IV$ with a secret, as recently proposed for AES-GCM in TLS 1.3 [25,26]. In detail, for an instantiation of GCM with AES-128, the blockcipher key is of size 128 bits and the nonce of size 96 bits. However, if an attacker would have access to many endpoints that encrypt the same plaintext block with the same nonce under different keys, we end up in a scenario where the same input is encrypted by the underlying blockcipher with different keys. This means that one key used by a pool of users can be recovered considerably faster than a single key in a targeted attack for a single user [10]. This problem gets resolved by masking the nonce with extra key material [5].

**Improved Bounds for Different $IV$ Usages.** The two terms capturing "guessing the key" and "unlucky key collisions" of (1) are tight in the general case, where the attacker is allowed to repeat $IV$s under different keys. However, if this is not the case, these two terms change and can be significantly improved in some use cases. In this paper, we investigate how the security bound of the duplex construction changes if we impose restrictions on the $IV$.

To investigate the exact role of the initialization in the duplex, we first consider a generalization of it in Sect. 3.1. In this generalization, the initialization does not anymore consist of just a concatenation of the key with the $IV$, but instead, we consider initialization as a concatenation of two functions that initialize both parts of the state on input of the key array and an (always unique) index. The generalization seems subtle but is strictly necessary to capture applications that rely on random $IV$s.

Now, using our generalized duplex construction, we consider five different practical cases to initialize the state of the duplex.

- The first case we consider is the globally unique $IV$ in Sect. 4.1. This principle is just the description of the idea of a globally unique key identifier presented by, e.g., Daemen et al. [11]: the $IV$ is unique over all $\mu$ users. Intuitively (but technically the story is a little bit more involved), this ensures that $\mu = 1$ and we get $\frac{N}{2^k} + \frac{0}{2^k}$;
- For the second case, we consider randomly chosen $IV$s in Sect. 4.2. If it can be ensured that the $IV$ is chosen randomly outside the influence of an attacker, the collision of $IV$s for a single user or between different users becomes probabilistic. On the other hand, contrary to the attacker-favorable case where all

[1] We remark that there is a third term influenced by initialization calls, namely the first term of (5c) of Theorem 1. This term is not relevant for the introductory discussion of our work, but is taken into account in the technical analysis; see also Sect. 3.5.

parties may start using as $IV$ an encoding of 0 and count upwards, a randomly chosen $IV$ does improve the bound, although it becomes a bit more technical;
- For the third case, we assume that the involved parties agree on a random offset from which they then count upwards in Sect. 4.3. Compared to the previous case, this eliminates $IV$ collisions of a single user, thus improving the bound further;
- As a fourth scenario, we consider that the $IV$ is masked with additional key material in Sect. 4.4. In contrast to all previous scenarios, the actual choice of the $IV$ does not matter in this case, as long as it is unique per user. This is akin to what is done in TLS 1.3 for AES-GCM [25], which is analyzed in [5]. We show that this is also possible for the duplex, with a potential strong uplift in the security bound, because for the duplex, this has a similar (albeit a bit weaker) effect than just extending the size of the key;
- Finally, we show that the security can further be improved, by combining the ideas of a masked $IV$ (fourth case) with a globally unique $IV$ (first case) in Sect. 4.5.

**Implications.** For all five cases, the precise details/conditions and improved security bounds are given in Sect. 4. We apply the improved bounds to duplex-based stream encryption in Sect. 5 and authenticated encryption in Sect. 6, and we discuss the practical meaning and limitations of the results using a typical parameter set inspired by the NIST Lightweight Cryptography winner Ascon [17, 18] in Sect. 7.

One notable implication of our results mapped to the Ascon parameters is that masking the $IV$ with additional key material indeed gives additional gain in multi-user security. In other words, the improvement observed for AES-GCM [5] *also* works for the keyed duplex. Concretely, if we run a proper duplex-based authenticated encryption scheme with a key and a nonce of 128 bits each, multi-user security improves from roughly $2^{128}/\mu$, where $\mu$ is the number of users, to $2^{256}/Q$, where $Q$ is the total number of online evaluations of the scheme.

That said, our observations demonstrate that masking the $IV$ is *not the only viable* solution for duplex-based modes. Indeed, one can take a larger key and/or a globally unique $IV$ provided the permutation width permits it. Whereas for AES-GCM, the key and nonce size are dominated by the relatively small domain of AES, for duplex-based authenticated encryption schemes the underlying permutation may be large, e.g., 320 bits for Ascon or even 1600 bits for schemes based on the SHA-3 permutation. We can conclude that it highly depends on the size of the underlying permutation which of the proposed solutions fits best.

**Outline.** We describe basic preliminaries in Sect. 2. The duplex construction, including our generalization with respect to the initialization interface, is given in Sect. 3. This section also includes the duplex security model and a copy of the existing security result (adapted to our generalization) of Daemen et al. [13]. We derive improved security bounds for the five types of initialization in Sect. 4.

These improved bounds are then applied to stream encryption in Sect. 5 and authenticated encryption in Sect. 6. Afterwards, we discuss practical implication of our results in Sect. 7 and conclude in Sect. 8.

## 2 Preliminaries

We consider 0 to be a member of $\mathbb{N}$. For a value $n \in \mathbb{N}$, the set of bit strings of length $n$ is defined as $\{0,1\}^n$. We denote $\{0,1\}^* = \cup_{n\in\mathbb{N}}\{0,1\}^n$, and we denote the set of infinitely long strings by $\{0,1\}^\infty$. We define by $\text{perm}(n)$ the set of all permutations $\mathsf{p}$ on $\{0,1\}^n$. For a bit string $X \in \{0,1\}^*$, the length of $X$ is denoted as $|X|$, and for an additional bit string $Y \in \{0,1\}^*$, the concatenation of $X$ and $Y$ is denoted as $X\|Y$ and their bitwise exclusive or (XOR) as $X \oplus Y$ truncated to $\min\{|X|,|Y|\}$ bits. For a finite set $\mathcal{S}$, we denote by $S \xleftarrow{\$} \mathcal{S}$ the uniformly random drawing of an element $S$ from a finite set $\mathcal{S}$.

For $X \in \{0,1\}^n$ and for $m \leq n$, the function $\text{left}_m(X)$ outputs the $m$ leftmost bits of $X$ and $\text{right}_m(X)$ the $m$ rightmost bits of $X$. For $Y \in \{1,\ldots,2^n\}$, we denote by $\text{encode}_n[Y]$ the encoding of $Y$ as an $n$-bit string.

### 2.1 Distinguisher

A distinguisher $\mathsf{D}$ is an algorithm. It is given access to a list of oracles, either $\mathsf{O}$ or $\mathsf{P}$, which we denote as $\mathsf{D}^\mathsf{O}$ or $\mathsf{D}^\mathsf{P}$. It can make queries to its list of oracles, and in the end it outputs a decision bit $b \in \{0,1\}$. We denote by

$$\Delta_\mathsf{D}(\mathsf{O}\,;\,\mathsf{P}) = \left|\mathbf{Pr}\left(\mathsf{D}^\mathsf{O}=1\right) - \mathbf{Pr}\left(\mathsf{D}^\mathsf{P}=1\right)\right|$$

the advantage that distinguisher $\mathsf{D}$ has in distinguishing the lists of oracles $\mathsf{O}$ from $\mathsf{P}$. In our work, distinguishers have unbounded computational power, and we will measure their success probabilities solely by the number of queries made (see also Sect. 3.3).

### 2.2 Multicollision Limit Function

We will use the notion of multicollision limit functions from Daemen et al. [13], which considers a balls-into-bins experiment tailored to sponge constructions.

**Definition 1 (multicollision limit function (mulf)).** *Let $Q, c, r \in \mathbb{N}$. Consider the experiment of throwing $Q$ balls uniformly at random in $2^r$ bins, and let $\nu$ be the maximum number of balls in a single bin. We define the multicollision limit function (mulf) $\nu_{r,c}^Q$ as the smallest natural number $x$ that satisfies*

$$\mathbf{Pr}\left(\nu > x\right) \leq \frac{x}{2^c}\,.$$

The mulf appears a bit artificial, but can be easily bounded. In particular, Daemen et al. [13, Section 6.5] demonstrated that the value $x$ targeted in Definition 1 satisfies

$$\frac{2^b e^{-\lambda}\lambda^x}{(x-\lambda)x!} \leq 1 . \tag{2}$$

where $b = c + r$ and $\lambda = Q/2^r$. We will not dive into detail on how this bound is derived, but will highlight the core idea as we will use it later on. This bound is obtained by observing that for any particular bin, the number of balls in that bin follows the binomial distribution with $n = Q$ trials and probability $p = 1/2^r$, and for large enough values it is upper bounded by a Poisson distribution with mean $\lambda = np = Q/2^r$. We refer to [13, Sect. 6.5] for the detailed reasoning behind (2) and to Mennink [23, Sect. 4.2] for a more detailed discussion of the mulf in general.

## 3 Duplex Construction and Security

We will consider the description of the duplex construction of Daemen et al. [13] and Dobraunig and Mennink [19]. We will, however, adopt the description of Mennink [23], who described the duplex in the more convenient permute-squeeze-absorb phasing (a detailed discussion on the sponge phasing is given in [23, Sect. 3.4]). However, we will not consider this duplex construction as is: we will consider a generalization to be able to properly and rigorously study the initialization of the duplex. Our generalized duplex construction is given in Sect. 3.1. We describe the security model in Sect. 3.2 and an explanation on how to parametrize distinguishers in Sect. 3.3. These two sections are based on [23, Sects. 3.2, 3.3, and 4.1], but generalized to reflect the generalization in the initialization phase. The security result of Daemen et al. [13] for the generalized duplex construction *for the default (baseline) initialization* is given in Sect. 3.4. Finally, in Sect. 3.5 we dive into the security proof of Daemen et al., isolate the parts in the security proof where the initialization plays a role, and re-describe them for our generalized initialization phase.

### 3.1 Construction

Let $b, c, r, k, l, \mu \in \mathbb{N}$ such that $c + r = b$ and $k \leq b$. We describe our generalized version of the keyed duplex construction $\mathsf{KD}$ in Algorithm 1. It operates on a key array $\boldsymbol{K} = (K[1], \ldots, K[\mu]) \in (\{0,1\}^k)^\mu$ consisting of $\mu$ keys, and it is instantiated using a $b$-bit permutation $\mathsf{p} \in \text{perm}(b)$. The construction internally maintains a $b$-bit state $S$, and has two interfaces: $\mathsf{KD.init}$ and $\mathsf{KD.duplex}$. Typical interface calls are depicted in Fig. 1.

**Duplexing Interface.** The duplexing interface $\mathsf{KD.duplex}$ is identical to that of Mennink [23]. The duplexing interface is phased in the permute-squeeze-absorb

**Algorithm 1.** Keyed duplex construction $\mathsf{KD}[\mathsf{p}]_{\boldsymbol{K}}$

**Interface:** KD.init
**Input:** $(\delta, i) \in \{1, \ldots, \mu\} \times \{1, \ldots, 2^l\}$
**Output:** $\varnothing$
$S \leftarrow \mathsf{initL}(\boldsymbol{K}, \delta, i) \parallel \mathsf{initR}(\boldsymbol{K}, \delta, i)$
**return** $\varnothing$

**Interface:** KD.duplex
**Input:** $(\mathit{flag}, P) \in \{\mathit{true}, \mathit{false}\} \times \{0,1\}^b$
**Output:** $Z \in \{0,1\}^r$
$S \leftarrow \mathsf{p}(S)$
$Z \leftarrow \mathrm{left}_r(S)$
$S \leftarrow S \oplus [\mathit{flag}] \cdot (Z \| 0^{b-r}) \oplus P$ ▷ if *flag*, overwrite outer part
**return** $Z$

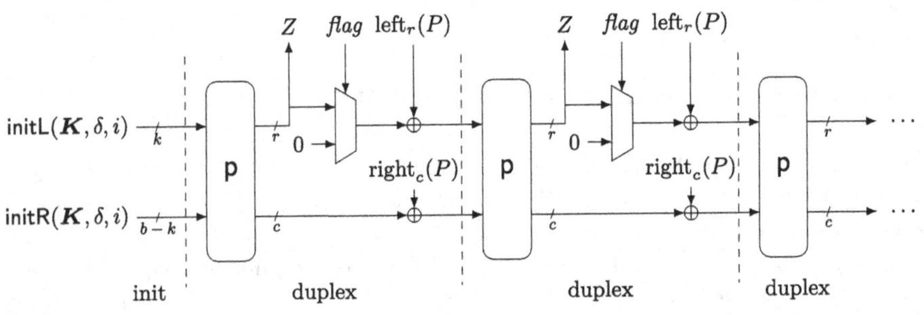


**Fig. 1.** The duplexing interface of KD. The sole difference with the duplexing interface of Mennink [23] is in the initialization.

fashion: first the underlying permutation p is applied on the state $S$. Then, it outputs an $r$-bit block $Z \in \{0,1\}^r$ off the internal state $S$. Finally, it absorbs $P \in \{0,1\}^b$, where the flag $\mathit{flag} \in \{\mathit{true}, \mathit{false}\}$ indicates whether the outer $r$ bits of $P$ are XORed to the outer part of the state (if $\mathit{flag} = \mathit{false}$) or if they overwrite the outer part of the state (if $\mathit{flag} = \mathit{true}$).

**Initialization Interface.** The initialization interface is structurally different from that of Mennink [23], both in the actual inputs that it receives as in the way it processes these inputs. This is done to make it possible to rigorously define and study different initialization approaches. In detail, the initialization interface gets two inputs (apart from the implicit key array $\boldsymbol{K}$), a key index $\delta \in \{1, \ldots, \mu\}$ and an index $i \in \{1, \ldots, 2^l\}$ in such a way that $(\delta, i)$ is always unique. The value $i$ may be a global counter, a counter per $\delta$, or anything else, and this does not yet matter for the specification. Then, KD.init initializes the state as

$$S \leftarrow \mathsf{initL}(\boldsymbol{K}, \delta, i) \parallel \mathsf{initR}(\boldsymbol{K}, \delta, i)$$

for certain initialization functions

$$\begin{aligned}\mathsf{initL} &: (\{0,1\}^k)^\mu \times \{1,\ldots,\mu\} \times \{1,\ldots,2^l\} \mapsto \{0,1\}^k\,,\\ \mathsf{initR} &: (\{0,1\}^k)^\mu \times \{1,\ldots,\mu\} \times \{1,\ldots,2^l\} \mapsto \{0,1\}^{b-k}\,.\end{aligned}$$

It outputs nothing.

**Comparison with Original Duplex.** We remark that this initialization is different from that of Mennink [23] in the fact that his initialization (just like that of [13,19]) got as input the key index $\delta$ and an initialization vector $IV \in \{0,1\}^{b-k}$, and initialized the state as $S \leftarrow \boldsymbol{K}[\delta] \parallel IV$. It can be seen to be covered by restricting the domain of $i$ to $\{1,\ldots,2^{b-k}\}$ and by taking initialization functions

$$\mathsf{initL}(\boldsymbol{K},\delta,i) = \boldsymbol{K}[\delta]\,, \tag{3a}$$

$$\mathsf{initR}(\boldsymbol{K},\delta,i) = \mathrm{encode}_{b-k}[i]\,. \tag{3b}$$

We will refer to this case as the *baseline case.*

## 3.2 Security Model

Daemen et al. [13] described the ideal extendable input function (IXIF) as ideal equivalent for the keyed duplex. We will also consider this function, but adapted to the superficial changes implemented by Mennink [23] and to our generalized initialization of Sect. 3.1. The function is described in Algorithm 2.

The IXIF has the same interface as the keyed duplex. However, it is not based on a key array $\boldsymbol{K}$ and primitive $\mathsf{p}$, but rather on a random oracle $\mathsf{ro} : \{0,1\}^* \times \mathbb{N} \to \{0,1\}^*$ that is defined as follows. Let $\mathsf{ro}_\infty : \{0,1\}^* \to \{0,1\}^\infty$ be a random oracle in the sense of Bellare and Rogaway [4]. For $P \in \{0,1\}^*$, $\mathsf{ro}(P,r)$ outputs the first $r$ bits of $\mathsf{ro}_\infty(P)$. The IXIF additionally maintains a path *path*. In this path, it stores all data input by the user. It is initialized by $\mathrm{encode}_{\log_2 \mu}[\delta] \parallel \mathrm{encode}_l[i]$, and upon each duplexing call the new plaintext block is appended to the path. Duplexing output is generated by evaluating the random oracle on *path*.

The security of the duplex construction is defined as the distance between KD and IXIF. More formally, let $\mathsf{p} \xleftarrow{\$} \mathrm{perm}(b)$ be a random transformation, $\boldsymbol{K} \xleftarrow{\$} (\{0,1\}^k)^\mu$ a random array of keys, and $\mathsf{ro}$ be a random oracle. One considers a distinguisher D that has access to either $(\mathsf{KD}[\mathsf{p}]_{\boldsymbol{K}}, \mathsf{p}^{\pm})$ in the real world or $(\mathsf{IXIF}[\mathsf{ro}], \mathsf{p}^{\pm})$ in the ideal world, where $\pm$ indicates that the distinguisher has two-sided access to the primitive:

$$\mathbf{Adv}_{\mathsf{KD}}(\mathsf{D}) = \Delta_{\mathsf{D}}\left(\mathsf{KD}[\mathsf{p}]_{\boldsymbol{K}}, \mathsf{p}, \mathsf{p}^{-1}\ ;\ \mathsf{IXIF}[\mathsf{ro}], \mathsf{p}, \mathsf{p}^{-1}\right)\,. \tag{4}$$

Without loss of generality, the distinguisher always makes at least one duplexing call after each initialization call.

**Algorithm 2.** Ideal extendable input function $\mathsf{IXIF}[\mathsf{ro}]$

**Interface:** $\mathsf{IXIF.init}$
**Input:** $(\delta, i) \in \{1, \ldots, \mu\} \times \{1, \ldots, 2^l\}$
**Output:** $\varnothing$
  $path \leftarrow \text{encode}_{\log_2 \mu}[\delta] \parallel \text{encode}_l[i]$
  **return** $\varnothing$

**Interface:** $\mathsf{IXIF.duplex}$
**Input:** $(flag, P) \in \{true, false\} \times \{0,1\}^b$
**Output:** $Z \in \{0,1\}^r$
  $Z \leftarrow \mathsf{ro}(path, r)$
  $path \leftarrow path \parallel ([flag] \cdot (Z \| 0^{b-r}) \oplus P)$
  ▷ if *flag*, overwrite outer part
  **return** $Z$

### 3.3 Parameterization of Distinguishers

The three main measures to quantify the resources of $\mathsf{D}$ are the number of queries it can make to its oracles:

- $Q$: the number of distinct initialization queries;
- $M$: the number of distinct duplexing queries;
- $N$: the number of distinct primitive queries.

The number of initialization calls are further refined in the maximum number of calls per $\delta$ and per $i$, and per $(\delta, i)$:

- $Q_\delta$: the maximum number of initialization queries for a single $\delta$;
- $Q_i$: the maximum number of initialization calls for a single $i$;
- $Q_{\delta,i}$: the maximum number of initialization calls for a single $\delta, i$.

We remark that earlier works [13,19] used $Q_{IV}$ as the maximum number of initialization calls for a single $IV$ (or more broadly seen, for a single inner part). This notation is deprecated, as we will consider different inner parts that depend only on $\delta$, on $i$, on $(\delta, i)$, or on neither of them.

Finally, different evaluations of the duplex can be the same up to a common prefix, and common subpaths can actually benefit the distinguisher. To measure the degree in which it could help the distinguisher, we will define a path *path* that keeps track of the data that got absorbed in the duplex up to the point that the cryptographic primitive ($\mathsf{p}$ in the real world and $\mathsf{ro}$ in the ideal world) is evaluated. For an initialization call $(\delta, i) \mapsto \varnothing$, the associated path is defined as $path = \text{encode}_{\log_2 \mu}[\delta] \parallel \text{encode}_l[i]$. For each duplexing call $(flag, P) \mapsto Z$, the value $[flag] \cdot (Z \| 0^{b-r}) \oplus P$ is appended to the path of the previous construction query. In order to reason about duplexing calls, we will also define a *subpath* of a *path*, which is the path leading to the particular duplexing call. In other words, for a path *path*, its *subpath* is simply *path* with the last $b$ bits removed. Using this terminology, we define additional measures:

- $L$: the number of duplexing calls with repeated subpath, i.e., $M$ minus the number of distinct subpaths;
- $\Omega$: the number of duplexing queries with *flag* = *true*.

### 3.4 Security of Baseline Case

As the current duplex construction of Sect. 3.1 has a more general initialization than that of Daemen et al. [13], we cannot translate their security result to the current duplex construction. Nevertheless, the duplex construction of Daemen et al. is in fact the baseline case, i.e., our duplex construction but with the initialization functions of (3). For this baseline case, we can thus carry over the result of Daemen et al. [13]:

**Theorem 1 (security of duplex construction** [13]**).** *Let* $b, c, r, k, l, \mu \in \mathbb{N}$, *with* $c + r = b$, *and* $k \leq b$. *Let* $\mathsf{p} \xleftarrow{\$} \mathrm{perm}(b)$ *be a random permutation, and* $\boldsymbol{K} \xleftarrow{\$} (\{0,1\}^k)^\mu$ *a random array of keys. For any distinguisher* $\mathsf{D}$ *quantified as in Sect. 3.3 and with* $M + N \leq 0.1 \cdot 2^c$,

$$\mathbf{Adv}_{\mathsf{KD}}(\mathsf{D}) \leq \frac{(L+\Omega)N}{2^c} + \frac{2\nu_{r,c}^{2(M-L)}(N+1)}{2^c} + \frac{\binom{L+\Omega+1}{2}}{2^c} \tag{5a}$$

$$+ \frac{(M-L-Q)Q}{2^b - Q} + \frac{M(M-L-1)}{2^b} \tag{5b}$$

$$+ \frac{Q(M-L-Q)}{2^{\min\{c+k,b\}}} + \frac{Q_i N}{2^k} + \frac{\binom{\mu}{2}}{2^k}\,. \tag{5c}$$

### 3.5 Role of Initialization Vector

The bound of Theorem 1 is rather involved, but the part that matters for our analysis is only (5c). In detail, these three terms are related to key guessing or key hitting problems that may occur in a security game and that involve the initialization of the duplex. These three terms correspond to three bad events in the analysis of Daemen et al., namely (in this order) [13, (22)], [13, (20)], and [13, (23)]. We will restate those (and exactly those) bad events, but updated[2] for the initialization interface of our duplex of Sect. 3.1 and with conveniently identifiable names:

$\mathsf{col}_{\mathsf{init}}^{\mathsf{duplex}}$ **(corresponding to** [13, **(22)**]**):** There exists an initialization call $(\delta, i)$ to $\mathsf{KD.init}$ and a duplex evaluation $(s, t)$ of $\mathsf{p}$ within $\mathsf{KD.duplex}$ such that $\mathsf{initL}(\boldsymbol{K}, \delta, i) \parallel \mathsf{initR}(\boldsymbol{K}, \delta, i) = s \oplus 0^r \| \kappa$, where $\kappa$ is a random $c$-bit dummy key;

$\mathsf{col}_{\mathsf{init}}^{\mathsf{prim}}$ **(corresponding to** [13, **(20)**]**):** There exists an initialization call $(\delta, i)$ to $\mathsf{KD.init}$ and a primitive evaluation $(x, y)$ of $\mathsf{p}$ such that $\mathsf{initL}(\boldsymbol{K}, \delta, i) \parallel \mathsf{initR}(\boldsymbol{K}, \delta, i) = x$;

[2] The update is fairly straightforward, merely replacing $\boldsymbol{K}[\delta] \parallel IV$ with $\mathsf{initL}(\boldsymbol{K}, \delta, i) \parallel \mathsf{initR}(\boldsymbol{K}, \delta, i)$.

**Table 1.** Different types of $IV$ generation cases considered in this work, and a reference to their security analyses. Here, $RIV$ stands for "random $IV$" for each evaluation, and $RIV_\delta$ is a unique random $IV$ per user (independently distributed for each user). They are of length $n$ bits, and 0-padded.

| case | $\mathsf{initL}(\boldsymbol{K},\delta,i)$ | $\mathsf{initR}(\boldsymbol{K},\delta,i)$ | restriction | reference |
|---|---|---|---|---|
| baseline | $\boldsymbol{K}[\delta]$ | $\mathrm{encode}_{b-k}[i]$ | $l \leq b-k$ | Sect. 3.4 |
| globally unique $IV$ | $\boldsymbol{K}[\delta]$ | $\mathrm{encode}_{b-k}[(\delta,i)]$ | $\log_2 \mu + l \leq b-k$ | Sect. 4.1 |
| random $IV$ | $\boldsymbol{K}[\delta]$ | $RIV \| 0^{b-k-n}$ | — | Sect. 4.2 |
| quasi-random $IV$ | $\boldsymbol{K}[\delta]$ | $(RIV_\delta \oplus \mathrm{encode}_n[i]) \| 0^{b-k-n}$ | $i$ counter, $l \leq n$ | Sect. 4.3 |
| $IV$ on key | $\boldsymbol{K}[\delta] \oplus \mathrm{encode}_k[i]$ | $0^{b-k}$ | $l \leq k$ | Sect. 4.4 |
| globally unique $IV$ on key | $\boldsymbol{K}[\delta] \oplus \mathrm{encode}_k[i]$ | $\mathrm{encode}_{b-k}[\delta]$ | $l \leq k$, $\log_2 \mu \leq b-k$ | Sect. 4.5 |

$\mathbf{col}_{\mathsf{init}}^{\mathsf{init}}$ **(corresponding to** [13, **(23)**]**):** There exist two distinct initialization calls $(\delta,i),(\delta',i')$ to $\mathsf{KD.init}$ such that
$\mathsf{initL}(\boldsymbol{K},\delta,i) \parallel \mathsf{initR}(\boldsymbol{K},\delta,i) = \mathsf{initL}(\boldsymbol{K},\delta',i') \parallel \mathsf{initR}(\boldsymbol{K},\delta',i')$.

We recall from Sect. 3.3 that the distinguisher makes at most $Q$ initialization calls, where at most $Q_i$ are made for a single $i$, at most $M-Q$ duplex calls, and at most $N$ primitive calls. Using this, we can easily obtain that $\mathbf{col}_{\mathsf{init}}^{\mathsf{prim}}$ happens with probability at most $\frac{Q_i N}{2^k}$ and $\mathbf{col}_{\mathsf{init}}^{\mathsf{init}}$ with probability at most $\frac{\binom{\mu}{2}}{2^k}$. Event $\mathbf{col}_{\mathsf{init}}^{\mathsf{duplex}}$, finally, occurs with probability at most $\frac{Q(M-L-Q)}{2^{\min\{c+k,b\}}}$, where the presence of $-L$ in the numerator is for technical reasons that are irrelevant for the remainder of the work.

# 4 Improvements Under Specific $IV$ Generation

We will discuss improvements of the security bound of Theorem 1, and in particular the terms in equation (5c), in case of various types of $IV$ conventions, as outlined in Table 1. Here, $RIV$ is an independently drawn random $IV$ each evaluation and $RIV_\delta$ is a random $IV$ independently drawn per user.

## 4.1 Globally Unique $IV$

A globally unique $IV$, in this context, means that different users never employ the same $IV$. In Table 1, this is formally defined by using an encoding function for $\mathsf{initR}$ that encodes *both* the $\delta \in \{1,\ldots,\mu\}$ and the $i \in \{1,\ldots,2^l\}$, where we require that $\log_2 \mu + l \leq b-k$. As $\mathsf{KD}$ is never initialized twice for the same $(\delta,i)$, the rightmost $b-k$ bits of the initialization will always be distinct.

This use case is in fact the easiest one to consider, as it allows to derive quite strong improved bounds on the relevant bad events of [13] as outlined in Sect. 3.5:

$\mathbf{col}_{\mathsf{init}}^{\mathsf{duplex}}$: The analysis of this event remains mostly unchanged. The reason is that the dummy key $\kappa$ "blinds" the rightmost $c$ bits of $\mathsf{initR}(\boldsymbol{K},\delta,i) =$

$\text{encode}_{b-k}[(\delta, i)]$ anyway. A small improvement may be possible in case the blinding is incomplete, i.e., if $|\mathsf{initR}(\boldsymbol{K}, \delta, i)| = b-k > c$, but the improvement is negligible as, even though $\mathsf{initR}(\boldsymbol{K}, \delta, i)$ is distinct for each input $(\delta, i)$, they may collide on their left $b-k-c$ bits and we cannot rely on their uniqueness;

$\mathsf{col}_{\mathsf{init}}^{\mathsf{prim}}$: Consider any primitive evaluation $(x, y)$. In case of a globally unique $IV$, $\mathsf{initR}(\boldsymbol{K}, \delta, i) = \text{encode}_{b-k}[(\delta, i)]$ is distinct for each input $(\delta, i)$. This means that there is only 1 initialization call $(\delta, i)$ that satisfies $\text{right}_{b-k}(x) = \mathsf{initR}(\boldsymbol{K}, \delta, i)$. For this initialization call, we have $\text{left}_k(x) = \mathsf{initL}(\boldsymbol{K}, \delta, i)$ with probability $1/2^k$. (For inverse queries, the probability is strictly smaller as also $\text{right}_{b-k}(x) = \mathsf{initR}(\boldsymbol{K}, \delta, i)$ needs to hold, and it holds only with probability less than 1.) Summing over all initialization calls, we obtain that this bad event occurs with probability at most $N/2^k$;

$\mathsf{col}_{\mathsf{init}}^{\mathsf{init}}$: In the case of a globally unique $IV$, we have $\mathsf{initR}(\boldsymbol{K}, \delta, i) \neq \mathsf{initR}(\boldsymbol{K}, \delta', i')$ for any two distinct initialization calls, and hence this bad event occurs with probability 0.

In the case of a globally unique $IV$, we can thus replace (5c) of Theorem 1 by:

$$\frac{Q(M-L-Q)}{2^{\min\{c+k,b\}}} + \frac{N}{2^k}. \tag{6}$$

### 4.2 Random *IV*

In the case of random $IV$ generation, we will consider a setting where each user will always select the right part of the state, $\mathsf{initR}(\boldsymbol{K}, \delta, i)$ uniformly randomly from $\{0,1\}^n$ with $n \leq b-k$, denoted as $RIV$ in Table 1.

The analysis is a bit different to that of Sect. 4.1. To wit, for the case of a globally unique $IV$, event $\mathsf{col}_{\mathsf{init}}^{\mathsf{prim}}$ was very similar to the original analysis of [13], and for event $\mathsf{col}_{\mathsf{init}}^{\mathsf{init}}$ it sufficed to observe that [13] made the assumption that the $IV$ is always chosen in favor of the attacker. Now, in the case of random $IV$s, the situation changes in that (i) $IV$s may repeat, and (ii) there is no clear bound on the maximum occurrence of a single $IV$. The latter issue is particularly problematic as we cannot claim a clear upper bound on the maximum number of initialization calls for a single inner part (formally known as $Q_{IV}$ (see Sect. 3.3)). Instead, we will have to employ a probabilistic argument using the mulf (Definition 1). In detail, we will obtain the following improved bounds on the three relevant bad events of [13] as outlined in Sect. 3.5:

$\mathsf{col}_{\mathsf{init}}^{\mathsf{duplex}}$: This event remains mostly unchanged, for the same reason as in Sect. 4.1;

$\mathsf{col}_{\mathsf{init}}^{\mathsf{prim}}$: Consider any primitive evaluation $(x, y)$. As the $RIV$s are chosen uniformly at random, we can use the mulf $\nu_{n,k}^{Q}$ on the maximum multicollision on $RIV$ (note that the $RIV$ is of size $n \leq b-k$ bits). More detailed, assume the highest occurrence of an inner part of $RIV$ is $\nu$, then there are at most $\nu$ initialization calls $(\delta, i)$ that satisfy $\text{right}_{b-k}(x) = \mathsf{initR}(\boldsymbol{K}, \delta, i)$. For those specific initialization calls, we have $\text{left}_k(x) = \text{initL}(\boldsymbol{K}, \delta, i)$ with probability $\nu/2^k$. (As before, for inverse queries, the probability is strictly smaller.) Summing over all initialization calls, we obtain that this bad event occurs with probability at most $\nu N/2^k$. We then select the term $\nu$ so that the sum of this term and the probability of a $\nu$-collision is small, and this minimum is achieved for the mulf $\nu_{n,k}^Q$:

$$\min_{\nu} \frac{\nu N}{2^k} + \mathbf{Pr}\left(\nu > \nu_{n,k}^Q\right) \leq \frac{\nu_{n,k}^Q \cdot (N+1)}{2^k};$$

$\mathbf{col}_{\mathbf{init}}^{\mathbf{init}}$: In the original proof, the authors simply assumed that the $IV$ was always chosen in favor of the attacker, and the bad event simplified to a simple key collision in $\text{initL}(\boldsymbol{K}, \delta, i)$. Now, not only the $k$-bit keys $\text{initL}(\boldsymbol{K}, \delta, i) = K[\delta]$ and $\text{initL}(\boldsymbol{K}, \delta', i') = K[\delta']$ are randomly distributed but also the $n$-bit $IV$s $\text{initR}(\boldsymbol{K}, \delta, i) = RIV \| 0^{b-k-n}$ and $\text{initR}(\boldsymbol{K}, \delta', i') = RIV' \| 0^{b-k-n}$ (here, the accent is put in $RIV'$ to make the distinction clear). This leads to a more complex analysis of $\mathbf{col}_{\mathbf{init}}^{\mathbf{init}}$, and we have to distinguish depending on whether $\delta = \delta'$ or not:

- $\delta = \delta'$: in this case, $K[\delta] = K[\delta']$ by default, but $RIV = RIV'$ with probability $1/2^n$;
- $\delta \neq \delta'$: in this case $K[\delta] \| RIV = K[\delta'] \| RIV'$ with probability at most $1/2^{k+n}$.[3]

There are at most $\mu\binom{Q_\delta}{2}$ tuples $\{(\delta, i), (\delta', i')\}$ of the former category and at most $\binom{Q}{2}$ tuples of the second category. The bad event is thus set with probability at most $\mu\binom{Q_\delta}{2}/2^n + \binom{Q}{2}/2^{k+n}$.

In the case of a random $IV$, we can thus replace (5c) of Theorem 1 by:

$$\frac{Q(M-L-Q)}{2^{\min\{c+k,b\}}} + \frac{\nu_{b-k,k}^Q \cdot (N+1)}{2^k} + \frac{\mu\binom{Q_\delta}{2}}{2^n} + \frac{\binom{Q}{2}}{2^{k+n}}. \tag{7}$$

### 4.3 Quasi-Random $IV$

The case of a quasi-random $IV$ is a subtle combination of the globally unique $IV$ and a random $IV$. In detail, we consider a setting where each user $\delta$ uses a counter starting from a random offset $RIV_\delta$. For example, in a simplified case of two users Alice and Bob, Alice will be assigned a random initialization vector $RIV_A \xleftarrow{\$} \{0,1\}^n$ and will use $\{RIV_A \oplus \text{encode}_n[1], RIV_A \oplus \text{encode}_n[2]), \ldots\}$ padded with $0^{b-k-n}$, whereas Bob will be assigned a random initialization vector $RIV_B \xleftarrow{\$} \{0,1\}^n$ and will use $\{RIV_B \oplus \text{encode}_n[1], RIV_B \oplus \text{encode}_n[2], \ldots\}$ padded with $0^{b-k-n}$.

The security analysis, for this case, becomes much more subtle. Indeed, the initialization vectors ($RIV_A$ and $RIV_B$ in above use case) are random, but the

[3] This could be improved by conditioning on which keys in $\boldsymbol{K}$ actually collide, but the gain in following this avenue is negligible as this is not the main term anyway.

following $IV$s have no randomness *given* the initial ones. To resolve the issue, we need to define a variant of the mulf of Definition 1, namely one that considers collisions in *sets*.

**Definition 2 (sequence multicollision limit function (smulf)).** *Let $Q_i, Q_\delta$, $c$, $r \in \mathbb{N}$. Consider the experiment of throwing $Q_i$ balls uniformly at random in $2^r$ bins and for each of the randomly thrown balls, throwing a ball in the $Q_\delta$ subsequent bins, and let $\nu$ be the maximum number of balls in a single bin. We define the sequence multicollision limit function (smulf) $\bar{\nu}_{r,c}^{Q_i,Q_\delta}$ as the smallest natural number $x$ that satisfies*

$$\mathbf{Pr}\left(\nu > x\right) \leq \frac{x}{2^c} .$$

Intuitively, the smulf on parameters $Q_i, Q_\delta$ is at most the mulf on parameter $Q_i Q_\delta$. As a matter of fact, it can be argued that the value $x$ targeted in Definition 2 also satisfies (2), but with adjusted $\lambda$. The reason is almost identical to that of [13, Section 6.5]. In detail, they observe that $\mathbf{Pr}\left(\nu > x\right) \leq 2^r \mathbf{Pr}\left(X > x\right)$, where $\mathbf{Pr}\left(X > x\right)$ is the probability that any particular bin has more than $x$ balls, then they observe that the number of balls in a particular bin is binomially distributed with $n = Q$ trials and success probability $p = 1/2^r$, and finally they observe that for sufficiently large parameters this is upper bounded by a Poisson distribution with mean $\lambda = np = Q/2^r$. In the case of the smulf of Definition 2, the same story applies with the difference that the number of balls in a particular bin is now binomially distributed with $n = Q_i$ trials and success probability $p = Q_\delta/2^r$, which can be upper bounded by a Poisson distribution with mean $\lambda = np = Q_i Q_\delta/2^r$.

Using the definition of the smulf, can derive the following improved bounds on the three relevant bad events of [13] as outlined in Sect. 3.5:

$\mathsf{col}_{\mathsf{init}}^{\mathsf{duplex}}$: This event remains mostly unchanged, for the same reason as in Sect. 4.1;

$\mathsf{col}_{\mathsf{init}}^{\mathsf{prim}}$: The first part of the analysis is identical to that of Sect. 4.2. Consider any primitive evaluation $(x, y)$. Denoting the highest occurrence of an inner part of $RIV_\delta \oplus \mathsf{encode}_n[i]$ by $\nu$, then there are at most $\nu$ initialization calls $(\delta, i)$ that satisfy $\mathsf{right}_{b-k}(x) = \mathsf{initR}(\boldsymbol{K}, \delta, i)$, and the bad event occurs with probability at most $\nu N/2^k$. We then select the term $\nu$ so that the sum of this term and the probability of a $\nu$-collision is small, and this minimum is achieved for the smulf $\bar{\nu}_{n,k}^{Q_i,Q_\delta}$ on sets defined by $RIV_\delta$ for $\delta \in \{1, \ldots, \mu\}$:

$$\min_{\nu} \frac{\nu N}{2^k} + \mathbf{Pr}\left(\nu > \bar{\nu}_{n,k}^{Q_i,Q_\delta}\right) \leq \frac{\bar{\nu}_{n,k}^{Q_i,Q_\delta} \cdot (N+1)}{2^k} ;$$

$\mathsf{col}_{\mathsf{init}}^{\mathsf{init}}$: The analysis of Sect. 4.2 mostly carries over, a difficulty occurs in that we have to investigate the probability that two sets (with specific distributions) collide or not. Note that the $k$-bit keys $\mathsf{initL}(\boldsymbol{K}, \delta, i) = K[\delta]$ and $\mathsf{initL}(\boldsymbol{K}, \delta', i') = K[\delta']$ are randomly distributed but the $n$-bit $IV$s satisfy

$\mathsf{initR}(\boldsymbol{K}, \delta, i) = (RIV_\delta \oplus \mathrm{encode}_n[i])\|0^{b-k-n}$ and $\mathsf{initR}(\boldsymbol{K}, \delta', i') = (RIV_{\delta'} \oplus \mathrm{encode}_n[i'])\|0^{b-k-n}$ for counters $i, i' \leq Q_\delta$. We again distinguish depending on whether $\delta = \delta'$ or not:

- $\delta = \delta'$: in this case, $K[\delta] = K[\delta']$ by default, but $RIV_\delta = RIV_{\delta'}$ and $\mathrm{encode}_n[i] \neq \mathrm{encode}_n[i']$, so the initializations collide with probability 0;
- $\delta \neq \delta'$: in this case $K[\delta] = K[\delta']$ with probability $1/2^k$. For $RIV_\delta \oplus \mathrm{encode}_n[i] = RIV_{\delta'} \oplus \mathrm{encode}_n[i']$, we can observe that any pair $(\delta, i), (\delta', i')$ fixes $\mathrm{encode}_n[i]$ and $\mathrm{encode}_n[i']$ and thus collides with probability $1/2^n$. We can tighten this by only focusing on $\delta$ and $\delta'$. Per $\delta$, there are at most $Q_\delta$ consecutive values $i$. Thus, the sets

$$\{RIV_\delta \oplus \mathrm{encode}_n[1], RIV_\delta \oplus \mathrm{encode}_n[2], \ldots\},$$
$$\{RIV_{\delta'} \oplus \mathrm{encode}_n[1], RIV_{\delta'} \oplus \mathrm{encode}_n[2], \ldots\}$$

overlap with probability at most $(2Q_\delta - 1)/2^n$.

There are at most $\binom{\mu}{2}$ different choices $\{\delta, \delta'\}$ for bounding the second category. The bad event thus occurs with probability at most $\binom{\mu}{2}(2Q_\delta - 1)/2^{k+n}$.

In the case of a quasi-random $IV$, we can thus replace (5c) of Theorem 1 by:

$$\frac{Q(M-L-Q)}{2^{\min\{c+k,b\}}} + \frac{\bar{\nu}_{n,k}^{Q_i,Q_\delta} \cdot (N+1)}{2^k} + \frac{\binom{\mu}{2}(2Q_\delta - 1)}{2^{k+n}}. \tag{8}$$

### 4.4 *IV* on Key

The case of an $IV$ added to the key is structurally different from previous ones. In detail, we will consider a setting where an $IV$ is added to a user's key $\boldsymbol{K}[\delta]$: $\mathsf{initL}(\boldsymbol{K}, \delta, i) = \boldsymbol{K}[\delta] \oplus \mathrm{encode}_k[i]$. The right part of the initialization stays blank.

The analysis is a bit different to the previous ones, but not necessarily harder, simply as it leads to a similar query trade-off that can already be observed in the Even-Mansour construction [21]. We will see that event $\mathsf{col}_{\mathsf{init}}^{\mathsf{prim}}$ introduces a multiplicative term between initialization and primitive queries. Event $\mathsf{col}_{\mathsf{init}}^{\mathsf{init}}$ corresponds to two different initializations for which $\boldsymbol{K}[\delta] \oplus \mathrm{encode}_k[i]$ and $\boldsymbol{K}[\delta'] \oplus \mathrm{encode}_k[i']$ collide (looking ahead, in the case of Sect. 4.5 the latter case is avoided by encoding the user index in the right part of the initial state). In detail, we will obtain the following bounds on the three relevant bad events of [13] as outlined in Sect. 3.5:

$\mathsf{col}_{\mathsf{init}}^{\mathsf{duplex}}$: This event remains mostly unchanged, for the same reason as in Sect. 4.1;

$\mathsf{col}_{\mathsf{init}}^{\mathsf{prim}}$: Consider any primitive evaluation $(x, y)$, without loss of generality satisfying $\mathrm{right}_{b-k}(x) = 0^{b-k}$. For any initialization query, the probability that $\mathrm{left}_k(x) = \boldsymbol{K}[\delta] \oplus \mathrm{encode}_k[i]$ is the same as the probability that $\mathrm{left}_k(x) \oplus \mathrm{encode}_k[i] = \boldsymbol{K}[\delta]$, which entirely depends on the randomness of the key and is $1/2^k$. (As before, for inverse queries, the probability is strictly smaller.) Summing over all primitive queries and all initialization queries, the bad event is set with probability at most $QN/2^k$;

$\mathbf{col}_{\mathsf{init}}^{\mathsf{init}}$: For any two initialization calls, the $(b-k)$-bit outer parts $\mathsf{initR}(\boldsymbol{K}, \delta, i)$ always equal $0^{b-k}$. For any two initialization queries, we have to consider collisions between $\mathsf{initL}(\boldsymbol{K}, \delta, i) = \boldsymbol{K}[\delta] \oplus \text{encode}_k[i]$ and $\mathsf{initL}(\boldsymbol{K}, \delta', i') = \boldsymbol{K}[\delta'] \oplus \text{encode}_k[i']$. Again, the probability that $\boldsymbol{K}[\delta] \oplus \text{encode}_k[i] = \boldsymbol{K}[\delta'] \oplus \text{encode}_k[i']$ is the same to the probability that $\boldsymbol{K}[\delta] \oplus \boldsymbol{K}[\delta'] = \text{encode}_k[i] \oplus \text{encode}_k[i']$. This probability $1/2^k$ due to $\boldsymbol{K}[\delta]$ and $\boldsymbol{K}[\delta']$ being randomly chosen. The bad event is thus set with probability at most $\binom{Q}{2}/2^k$.

In the case of an $IV$ on the key, we can thus replace (5c) of Theorem 1 by:

$$\frac{Q(M-L-Q)}{2^{\min\{c+k,b\}}} + \frac{QN}{2^k} + \frac{\binom{Q}{2}}{2^k}. \tag{9}$$

### 4.5 Globally Unique $IV$ on Key

In this section, we extend the case of Sect. 4.4 to a globally unique $IV$ on the key, where "global" refers to the fact that the inner part of the initialization is an encoding of the user: $\mathsf{initL}(\boldsymbol{K}, \delta, i) = \boldsymbol{K}[\delta] \oplus \text{encode}_k[i]$ as before but $\mathsf{initR}(\boldsymbol{K}, \delta, i) = \text{encode}_{b-k}[\delta]$.

By encoding the user index into the outer part, key collisions among different users do not matter anymore for the security, only colliding $IV$'s for a fixed user. This affects the analysis of both $\mathbf{col}_{\mathsf{init}}^{\mathsf{prim}}$ and $\mathbf{col}_{\mathsf{init}}^{\mathsf{init}}$. In detail, we will obtain the following improved bounds on the three relevant bad events of [13] as outlined in Sect. 3.5:

$\mathbf{col}_{\mathsf{init}}^{\mathsf{duplex}}$: This event remains mostly unchanged, for the same reason as in Sect. 4.1;

$\mathbf{col}_{\mathsf{init}}^{\mathsf{prim}}$: Consider any primitive evaluation $(x, y)$. Let $\delta$ be such that $\text{right}_{b-k}(x) = \text{encode}_{b-k}[\delta]$. By assumption, there are at most $Q_\delta$ initialization queries for this particular $\delta$. For any of those queries, the probability that $\text{left}_k(x) = \mathsf{initL}(\boldsymbol{K}, \delta, i) = \boldsymbol{K}[\delta] \oplus \text{encode}_k[i]$ is $1/2^k$. (As before, for inverse queries, the probability is strictly smaller.) Summing over all primitive queries and all $Q_\delta$ initialization queries, the bad event is set with probability at most $Q_\delta N/2^k$;

$\mathbf{col}_{\mathsf{init}}^{\mathsf{init}}$: Clearly, if $\delta \neq \delta'$, then $\mathsf{initR}(\boldsymbol{K}, \delta, i) \neq \mathsf{initR}(\boldsymbol{K}, \delta', i')$ and the bad event cannot be set. On the other hand, if $\delta = \delta'$, the right part of the initial states are equal, and the left parts $\mathsf{initL}(\boldsymbol{K}, \delta, i) = \boldsymbol{K}[\delta] \oplus \text{encode}_k[i]$ and $\mathsf{initL}(\boldsymbol{K}, \delta', i') = \boldsymbol{K}[\delta'] \oplus \text{encode}_k[i']$ collide with probability $1/2^k$. There are at most $\mu\binom{Q_\delta}{2}$ tuples $\{(\delta, i), (\delta', i')\}$ such that $\delta = \delta'$. Summing over all these queries, the bad event is set with probability at most $\mu\binom{Q_\delta}{2}/2^k$.

In the case of a globally unique $IV$ on the key, we can thus replace (5c) of Theorem 1 by:

$$\frac{Q(M-L-Q)}{2^{\min\{c+k,b\}}} + \frac{Q_\delta N}{2^k} + \frac{\mu\binom{Q_\delta}{2}}{2^k}. \tag{10}$$

# 5 Stream Encryption

We will consider one of the most elementary use case of the duplex, namely (sequential) stream encryption, following Mennink [23, Section 7]. The construction and its security model are outlined in Sect. 5.1, and we discuss its security under different types of initialization in Sect. 5.2.

## 5.1 Construction and Security Model

Consider the stream cipher $\mathsf{SC} : \{0,1\}^k \times \{1,\ldots,2^l\} \times \mathbb{N} \to \{0,1\}^*$, that gets as input a $k$-bit key $K$, an index value $i \in \{1,\ldots,2^l\}$, and a requested output length $\ell$, and that outputs a key stream $S$ of length $\ell$ bits. It is defined using the duplex as follows:

- Initialize the keyed duplex of Algorithm 1 with permutation $\mathsf{p}$ and key array $\boldsymbol{K} = (K)$;
- Evaluate $\mathsf{KD.init}(1, i)$;
- Evaluate $\mathsf{KD.duplex}(\mathit{false}, 0^b)$ for exactly $\lceil \ell/r \rceil$ times, concatenate their outputs, and truncate this string to $\ell$ bits to obtain $S$.

The scheme is depicted in the multi-user setting in Fig. 2. We note that this is a very natural way of duplex-based stream generation; a variant of it (with a significantly more involved initialization to suit side-channel resilience) can be observed in ISAP v2 [14–16] and in Asakey [20].

We will consider its security as indistinguishability from a random function in the multi-user setting. Let $\mathsf{p} \xleftarrow{\$} \mathrm{perm}(b)$ be a random permutation. Let $\boldsymbol{K} \xleftarrow{\$} (\{0,1\}^k)^\mu$ be a random array of keys and $(\$_j)_{j=1}^{\mu}$ be functions that for each input $i \in \{1,\ldots,2^l\}$ define a random string of infinite length and on input of a tuple $(i, \ell)$ return the first $\ell$ bits of the string related to input $i$. Let case $\in$ {baseline, global, random, quasirandom, onkey, globalonkey} describe the type of initialization, corresponding to the six cases outlined in Table 1.

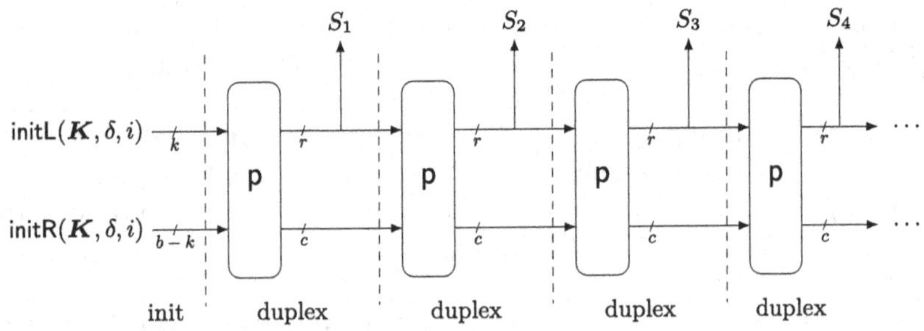


**Fig. 2.** Stream cipher SC in the multi-user setting. The function gets as input a key array $\boldsymbol{K}$, key index $\delta$, and index $i$. It outputs keystream blocks $(S_1, S_2, \ldots)$. The actual number of output blocks is determined by an additional input parameter $\ell$. The sole difference with the sequential keystream generation construction of Mennink [23] is in the initialization.

We define the multi-user security of SC under initialization type case as

$$\mathbf{Adv}_{\mathsf{SC}}^{\mu\text{-prf-case}} = \Delta_{\mathsf{D}}\left( (\mathsf{SC}[\mathsf{p}]_{\boldsymbol{K}_j})_{j=1}^{\mu}, \mathsf{p}^{\pm} \; ; \; (\$_j)_{j=1}^{\mu}, \mathsf{p}^{\pm} \right) . \tag{11}$$

### 5.2 Security Under Different Initializations

We will consider a distinguisher that can make $Q$ initialization queries (i.e., $Q$ queries to its construction oracle), $M$ duplexing queries (i.e., the $Q$ queries are of total length $M$ duplexing calls), and $N$ primitive queries, in accordance with Sect. 3.3. For the refined values of $Q$, we have that $Q_\delta \leq \min\{2^l, Q\}$, $Q_i \leq \mu$, and $Q_{\delta,i} = 1$. Finally, just like in [23, Section 7], all queries start with a new $i$ (so $L = 0$) and all duplexing calls are for *flag* = *false* (so $\Omega = 0$).

We obtain the following general bound over all cases:

$$\mathbf{Adv}_{\mathsf{SC}}^{\mu\text{-prf-case}}(\mathsf{D}) \leq \frac{2\nu_{r,c}^{2M}(N+1)}{2^c} + \frac{(M-Q)Q}{2^b - Q} + \frac{M(M-1)}{2^b} \tag{12a}$$

$$+ \frac{Q(M-Q)}{2^{\min\{c+k,b\}}} + \Xi^{\text{case}} . \tag{12b}$$

The first part (12a) is the same for all different initializations and corresponds to (5a) and (5b). Part (12b) corresponds to (5c), which is actually improved for the specific cases:

$$\Xi^{\text{case}} = \begin{cases} \frac{\mu N}{2^k} + \frac{\binom{\mu}{2}}{2^k} & (\text{case} = \text{baseline}), \\ \frac{N}{2^k} & (\text{case} = \text{global}), \\ \frac{\nu_{n,k}^{Q} \cdot (N+1)}{2^k} + \frac{\mu \binom{\min\{2^l, Q\}}{2}}{2^n} + \frac{\binom{Q}{2}}{2^{k+n}} & (\text{case} = \text{random}), \\ \frac{\bar{\nu}_{n,k}^{\mu, \min\{2^l, Q\}} \cdot (N+1)}{2^k} + \frac{\binom{\mu}{2}(2\min\{2^l, Q\} - 1)}{2^{k+n}} & (\text{case} = \text{quasirandom}), \\ \frac{QN}{2^k} + \frac{\binom{Q}{2}}{2^k} & (\text{case} = \text{onkey}), \\ \frac{\min\{2^l, Q\} N}{2^k} + \frac{\mu \binom{\min\{2^l, Q\}}{2}}{2^k} & (\text{case} = \text{globalonkey}), \end{cases} \tag{13}$$

which are based on (5c), (6), (7), (8), (9), and (10), respectively.

## 6 Authenticated Encryption

The main raison d'être of the duplex construction is authenticated encryption. We will consider the MonkeySpongeWrap construction as described by Mennink [23, Section 9], which generalizes the original SpongeWrap construction [8]. However, we do so including our generalized initialization. The construction and its security model are outlined in Sect. 6.1, and we discuss its security under different types of initialization in Sect. 6.2.

### 6.1 Construction and Security Model

Consider the authenticated encryption scheme $\mathsf{AE} : \{0,1\}^k \times \{1,\ldots,2^l\} \times \{0,1\}^* \times \{0,1\}^* \to \{0,1\}^* \times \{0,1\}^t$, that gets as input a $k$-bit key $K$, an index value $i \in \{1,\ldots,2^l\}$, arbitrary length associated data $A$, and arbitrary length message $P$, and that outputs a ciphertext $C$ of size $|P|$ bits and a tag $T$ of size $t$ bits. It is defined using the duplex as follows:

- Initialize the keyed duplex of Algorithm 1 with permutation $\mathsf{p}$ and key array $\boldsymbol{K} = (K)$;
- Evaluate $\mathsf{KD.init}(1, i)$;
- Append a single 1 and a sufficient number of 0s to $A$ to obtain $r$-bit associated data blocks $(A_1,\ldots,A_v)$, and for each block, evaluate $\mathsf{KD.duplex}(\mathit{false}, A_i\|0\|0^{c-1})$ and discard the output;
- Append a single 1 and a sufficient number of 0s to $M$ to obtain $r$-bit plaintext blocks $(P_1,\ldots,P_w)$, and, for each block, evaluate $\mathsf{KD.duplex}(\mathit{false}, P_i\|1\|0^{c-1})$ and XOR the output with $P_i$ to obtain $C_i$;
- Evaluate $\mathsf{KD.duplex}(\mathit{false}, 0^b)$ for exactly $\lceil t/r \rceil$ times, concatenate their outputs, and truncate this string to $t$ bits to obtain $T$.

The scheme is depicted in the multi-user setting in Fig. 3. This variant of authenticated encryption can be observed in various NIST candidates, most notably Xoodyak [11,12] and Gimli [6]. We refer to [23, Section 9] for a more detailed algorithmic description as well as a discussion of the inverse $\mathsf{AE}^{-1}$.

We will consider its security as indistinguishability from ideal in the multi-user setting. Here, we consider the ideal setting as the scheme that upon encryption, always outputs random strings, and upon decryption always outputs the failure symbol $\bot$, assuming that the distinguisher never relays an encryption output to the decryption oracle. Let $\mathsf{p} \xleftarrow{\$} \mathrm{perm}(b)$ be a random permutation. Let $\boldsymbol{K} \xleftarrow{\$} (\{0,1\}^k)^\mu$ be a random array of keys and $(\$_j)_{j=1}^\mu$ be functions that for each input $i \in \{1,\ldots,2^l\}$ define a random string of infinite length and on input of a tuple $(i, A, P)$ return the first $|P| + t$ bits of the string related to input $i$. Let $\bot$ be the function that always returns the failure symbol $\bot$. Let $\text{case} \in \{\text{baseline}, \text{global}, \text{random}, \text{quasirandom}, \text{onkey}, \text{globalonkey}\}$ describe the type of initialization, corresponding to the six cases outlined in Table 1.

We define the multi-user security of $\mathsf{AE}$ under initialization type case as

$$\mathbf{Adv}_{\mathsf{AE}}^{\mu\text{-ae-case}} = \Delta_{\mathsf{D}}\left((\mathsf{AE}[\mathsf{p}]_{\boldsymbol{K}_j}, \mathsf{AE}[\mathsf{p}]_{\boldsymbol{K}_j}^{-1})_{j=1}^\mu, \mathsf{p}^\pm \; ; \; (\$_j, \bot)_{j=1}^\mu, \mathsf{p}^\pm\right). \qquad (14)$$

Distinguisher $\mathsf{D}$ is not allowed to repeat an index for encryption queries but it may do so for decryption queries. In the (quasi-)random $IV$ case we assume that the oracle maintains a table to re-use earlier $RIV$ or $RIV_\delta$ in case of repeated indices. It is not allowed to relay an encryption output to the decryption oracle.

### 6.2 Security Under Different Initializations

We will consider a distinguisher that can make $Q$ initialization queries (i.e., $Q$ queries to its construction oracle), split into $Q_e$ encryption and $Q_d$ decryption

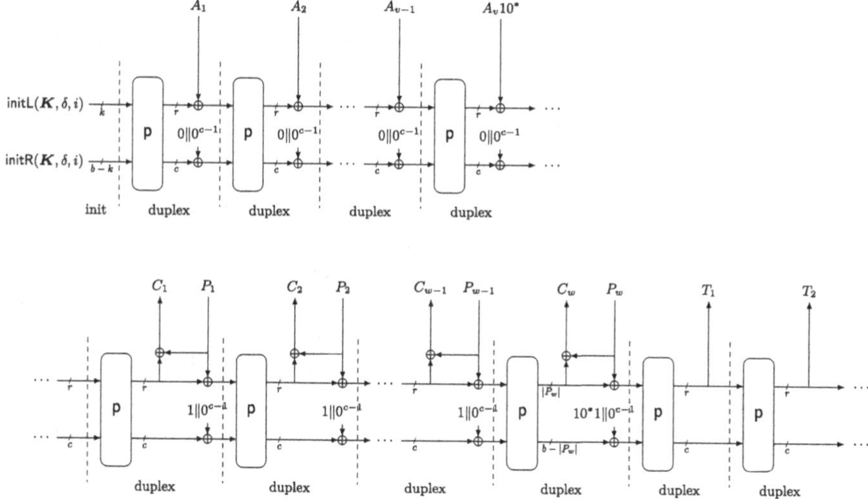


**Fig. 3.** Authenticated encryption scheme AE in the multi-user setting. The function gets as input a key array $\boldsymbol{K}$, key index $\delta$, index $i$, associated data blocks $(A_1, A_2, \ldots, A_v)$, and plaintext blocks $(P_1, P_2, \ldots, P_w)$ (the last blocks of associated data and plaintext may be partial). It outputs a ciphertext $C = (C_1, C_2, \ldots, C_w)$ of size $|P|$ bits and tag blocks $(T_1, T_2, \ldots)$ truncated to $t$ bits (the last blocks of ciphertext and tag may be partial). The sole difference with the MonkeySpongeWrap construction of Mennink [23] is in the initialization.

queries, $M$ duplexing queries (i.e., the $Q$ queries are of total length $M$ duplexing calls), again split into $M_e$ encryption and $M_d$ decryption queries, and $N$ primitive queries, in accordance with Sect. 3.3. For the refined values of $Q$, we have that $Q_\delta \leq \min\{2^l, Q\}$, $Q_i \leq \mu$, and $Q_{\delta,i} = 1$. Finally, just like in [23, Section 9], all encryption queries start with a new $i$, but decryption queries may repeat $i$ (so $L \leq Q_d$) and all duplexing encryption calls are for *flag* = *false* but duplexing decryption calls may be for *flag* = *true* (so $\Omega \leq M_d - 2Q_d$).

We obtain the following general bound over all cases:

$$\mathbf{Adv}_{\mathsf{AE}}^{\mu\text{-ae-case}}(\mathsf{D}) \leq \frac{2\nu_{r,c}^{2M}(N+1)}{2^c} + \frac{(M-Q)Q}{2^b - Q} + \frac{M(M-1)}{2^b} \tag{15a}$$

$$+ \frac{M_d N + \binom{M_d}{2}}{2^c} + \frac{Q_d}{2^t} \tag{15b}$$

$$+ \frac{Q(M-Q)}{2^{\min\{c+k,b\}}} + \Xi^{\text{case}}. \tag{15c}$$

The first part (15a) is identical to what we saw for stream encryption in (12a) as derived from (5a) and (5b). The second part (15b) has an additional fraction coming from (5a) due to the fact that now $L + \Omega$ may be as high as $M_d - Q_d$, and an additional term $Q_d/2^t$ corresponding to random tag guesses (refer to [23,

Theorem 7]). The third part (15c) corresponds to (5c) and is identical to (12b). As such, the term $\Xi^{\text{case}}$ is actually the same as for encryption, i.e., as in (13).

## 7 Practical Implications

Given the improved bounds of Sect. 4 and its generic application to duplex-based stream encryption in Sect. 5 and authenticated encryption in Sect. 6, we next discuss the practical implications (and limitations) of the different strategies to choose the *IV*/nonce. We will perform this discussion using a typical parameters set, namely $b = 320$, $r = 64$, $c = 256$, $k = 128$, and a 128-bit *IV*. This parameter set is analogue to the NIST Lightweight Cryptography winner Ascon-128 [17,18].

Note that, in practice, we can assume that the entity that performs the encryption chooses the *IV* outside the influence of a potential adversary. However, for decryption, an adversary can potentially manipulate the transmitted *IV*.

### 7.1 Baseline

For the baseline version, we assume that an attacker can manipulate the *IV* anyway. In this case, we get as a bound following Sect. 5.2 (similar for authenticated encryption following Sect. 6.2):

$$\frac{2\nu_{r,c}^{2M}(N+1)}{2^{256}} + \frac{(M-Q)Q}{2^{320}-Q} + \frac{M(M-1)}{2^{320}} + \frac{Q(M-Q)}{2^{320}} + \Xi^{\text{baseline}}, \tag{16}$$

with

$$\Xi^{\text{baseline}} = \frac{\mu N}{2^{128}} + \frac{\binom{\mu}{2}}{2^{128}}.$$

For practical settings, $\Xi^{\text{baseline}}$ likely dominates the bound.

### 7.2 Globally Unique *IV*

If a globally unique *IV* is used, the bound is independent of the number of users and we get (16) but instead with

$$\Xi^{\text{global}} = \frac{N}{2^{128}}.$$

However, in practice, the question is how to ensure the use of a globally unique *IV*. Ensuring a globally unique *IV* with just 128 bits seems to be unrealistic. One way would be to allocate a bit more space and separate the *IV* into a unique identifier per key and an actual nonce per transmission akin to [11]. Assuming the unique identifier is randomly chosen like the key during the key setup, it also does not have to be transmitted. To be sure that the identifier is unique, it is probably wise to use a 256-bit value. Combined with a 128-bit key and a 128-bit actual nonce, relying on a globally unique *IV* seems to be a viable choice for permutations with $b \geq 512$ bits.

### 7.3 Random $IV$

Considering a random $IV$, we get (16) but instead with

$$\Xi^{\text{random}} = \frac{\nu^{Q}_{128,128} \cdot (N+1)}{2^{128}} + \frac{\mu\binom{\min\{2^l,Q\}}{2}}{2^{128}} + \frac{\binom{Q}{2}}{2^{256}}.$$

Here, we must ensure the decryption party has authentic access to the random $IV$ chosen by the encrypting party. This is in practice often not the case for single-pass (authenticated) encryption schemes. In some two-pass schemes like encrypt-then-MAC [3,22], the authenticity of the random $IV$ can be verified before decryption starts as it is done for, e.g., ISAP v2 [14–16]. However, in this case the MAC verification cannot rely on the randomness of the $IV$ for security reasons.

### 7.4 Quasi-Random $IV$

With the quasi-random $IV$ we get (16) but instead with

$$\Xi^{\text{quasirandom}} = \frac{\bar{\nu}^{\mu,\min\{2^l,Q\}}_{128,128} \cdot (N+1)}{2^{128}} + \frac{\binom{\mu}{2}(2\min\{2^l,Q\}-1)}{2^{256}}.$$

In practice, such a scheme could be realized by setting up the random starting point of the $IV$ during the setup of the keys and then both communicating parties count upwards per message. In essence, this then works similarly to the method described in Sect. 7.2. However, it can be easily realized with smaller permutations.

### 7.5 $IV$ on Key

With the $IV$ on key scheme, we want to essentially picture what happens in TLS 1.3 for AES-GCM [25] which is analyzed in [5]. In principle, we have additional key material that masks the $IV$. When doing this in a duplex-based scheme, one can potentially profit more from having this additional key material compared to AES-GCM since it effectively extends the key. In our example, we would move from a 128-bit key and a 128-bit $IV$ to a 128-bit $IV$ on 256-bit key scheme, and we get (16) but instead with

$$\Xi^{\text{onkey}} = \frac{QN}{2^{256}} + \frac{\binom{Q}{2}}{2^{256}}.$$

One may wonder why to define the $IV$ usage this way and not just concatenate a larger key with the $IV$. First, having an additional key to mask the $IV$ can be agreed on protocol level without changing the underlying scheme. Second, for small permutations, like in our 320-bit example, there must be some overlap between a 256-bit key and a 128-bit $IV$.

### 7.6 Globally Unique *IV* on Key

This is the extension of Sect. 7.5, which in practice would require additional space to fit a unique partial $IV$. This would then lead to (16) but instead with

$$\Xi^{\text{globalonkey}} = \frac{\min\{2^l, Q\}N}{2^{256}} + \frac{\mu\binom{\min\{2^l,Q\}}{2}}{2^{256}}.$$

## 8 Conclusion

In this paper, we have shown that different ways to initialize the state of a duplex can lead to a significant improvement in the security bound considering multi-user setting. What is even more interesting is that many approaches we discuss, like masking the $IV$ with an additional key, can be retrofitted on protocol level without changing the specification of the underlying algorithm. However, one still has to consider that the proofs are done in the random permutation model. Concretely, this means that for an actual instantiation of the duplex, assuming that it uses a permutation designed for 128-bit security, using the $IV$ on key method (of Sect. 4.4) with a 256-bit key might not necessarily result in 256-bit security. Overall, care must be taken when instantiating a permutation-based cryptographic construction with any actual permutation.

**Acknowledgements.** We want to thank the authors of [13] for the many insightful discussions. Bart Mennink is supported by the Netherlands Organisation for Scientific Research (NWO) under grant VI.Vidi.203.099.

## References

1. Bao, Z., et al.: PHOTON-beetle authenticated encryption and hash family. Finalist of NIST lightweight cryptography standardization process (2021)
2. Beierle, C., et al.: Lightweight AEAD and hashing using the sparkle permutation family. IACR Trans. Symmetric Cryptol. **2020**(S1), 208–261 (2020). https://doi.org/10.13154/tosc.v2020.iS1.208-261
3. Bellare, M., Namprempre, C.: Authenticated Encryption: relations among notions and analysis of the generic composition paradigm. In: Okamoto, T. (ed.) ASIACRYPT 2000. LNCS, vol. 1976, pp. 531–545. Springer, Heidelberg (2000). https://doi.org/10.1007/3-540-44448-3_41
4. Bellare, M., Rogaway, P.: Random oracles are practical: a paradigm for designing efficient protocols. In: Denning, D.E., Pyle, R., Ganesan, R., Sandhu, R.S., Ashby, V. (eds.) CCS 1993, Proceedings of the 1st ACM Conference on Computer and Communications Security, Fairfax, Virginia, USA, 3–5 November 1993, pp. 62–73. ACM (1993). https://doi.org/10.1145/168588.168596
5. Bellare, M., Tackmann, B.: The Multi-user security of authenticated encryption: AES-GCM in TLS 1.3. In: Robshaw, M., Katz, J. (eds.) CRYPTO 2016. LNCS, vol. 9814, pp. 247–276. Springer, Heidelberg (2016). https://doi.org/10.1007/978-3-662-53018-4_10

6. Bernstein, D.J., et al.: Gimli: second round submission to NIST lightweight cryptography (2019)
7. Bertoni, G., Daemen, J., Peeters, M., Van Assche, G.: Sponge functions. In: Ecrypt Hash Workshop 2007 (2007)
8. Bertoni, G., Daemen, J., Peeters, M., Van Assche, G.: Duplexing the Sponge: single-pass authenticated encryption and other applications. In: Miri, A., Vaudenay, S. (eds.) SAC 2011. LNCS, vol. 7118, pp. 320–337. Springer, Heidelberg (2012). https://doi.org/10.1007/978-3-642-28496-0_19
9. Bertoni, G., Daemen, J., Peeters, M., Van Assche, G.: The KECCAK SHA-3 submission. SHA-3 competition (round 3) (2011)
10. Biham, E.: How to decrypt or even substitute DES-encrypted messages in $2^{28}$ steps. Inf. Process. Lett. **84**(3), 117–124 (2002). https://doi.org/10.1016/S0020-0190(02)00269-7
11. Daemen, J., Hoffert, S., Peeters, M., Van Assche, G., Van Keer, R.: Xoodyak, a lightweight cryptographic scheme. IACR Trans. Symmetric Cryptol. **2020**(S1), 60–87 (2020). https://doi.org/10.13154/tosc.v2020.iS1.60-87
12. Daemen, J., Hoffert, S., Peeters, M., Van Assche, G., Van Keer, R.: Xoodyak, a lightweight cryptographic scheme. Final Round Submission to NIST Lightweight Cryptography (2021)
13. Daemen, J., Mennink, B., Van Assche, G.: Full-State keyed duplex with built-in multi-user support. In: Takagi, T., Peyrin, T. (eds.) ASIACRYPT 2017. LNCS, vol. 10625, pp. 606–637. Springer, Cham (2017). https://doi.org/10.1007/978-3-319-70697-9_21
14. Dobraunig, C., et al.: ISAP v2.0. IACR Trans. Symmetric Cryptol. **2020**(S1), 390–416 (2020). https://doi.org/10.13154/tosc.v2020.iS1.390-416
15. Dobraunig, C., et al.: ISAP v2. Final round submission to NIST lightweight cryptography (2021)
16. Dobraunig, C., Eichlseder, M., Mangard, S., Mendel, F., Unterluggauer, T.: ISAP - towards side-channel secure authenticated encryption. IACR Trans. Symmetric Cryptol. **2017**(1), 80–105 (2017). https://doi.org/10.13154/tosc.v2017.i1.80-105
17. Dobraunig, C., Eichlseder, M., Mendel, F., Schläffer, M.: ASCON v1.2. Winning submission to NIST lightweight cryptography (2021)
18. Dobraunig, C., Eichlseder, M., Mendel, F., Schläffer, M.: ASCON v1.2: lightweight authenticated encryption and hashing. J. Cryptol. **34**(3), 33 (2021). https://doi.org/10.1007/s00145-021-09398-9
19. Dobraunig, C., Mennink, B.: Leakage resilience of the duplex construction. In: Galbraith, S.D., Moriai, S. (eds.) ASIACRYPT 2019. LNCS, vol. 11923, pp. 225–255. Springer, Cham (2019). https://doi.org/10.1007/978-3-030-34618-8_8
20. Dobraunig, C., Mennink, B., Primas, R.: Leakage and tamper resilient permutation-based cryptography. In: Yin, H., Stavrou, A., Cremers, C., Shi, E. (eds.) Proceedings of the 2022 ACM SIGSAC Conference on Computer and Communications Security, CCS 2022, Los Angeles, CA, USA, 7–11 November 2022, pp. 859–873. ACM (2022). https://doi.org/10.1145/3548606.3560635
21. Even, S., Mansour, Y.: A construction of a cipher from a single pseudorandom permutation. J. Cryptol. **10**(3), 151–162 (1997). https://doi.org/10.1007/s001459900025
22. Krawczyk, H.: The Order of encryption and authentication for protecting communications (or: How Secure Is SSL?). In: Kilian, J. (ed.) CRYPTO 2001. LNCS, vol. 2139, pp. 310–331. Springer, Heidelberg (2001). https://doi.org/10.1007/3-540-44647-8_19

23. Mennink, B.: Understanding the duplex and its security. IACR Trans. Symmetric Cryptol. **2023**(2), 1–46 (2023). https://doi.org/10.46586/tosc.v2023.i2.1-46
24. Mennink, B., Reyhanitabar, R., Vizár, D.: Security of full-state keyed sponge and duplex: applications to authenticated encryption. In: Iwata, T., Cheon, J.H. (eds.) ASIACRYPT 2015. LNCS, vol. 9453, pp. 465–489. Springer, Heidelberg (2015). https://doi.org/10.1007/978-3-662-48800-3_19
25. Rescorla, E.: The Transport layer security (TLS) protocol version 1.3. RFC 8446 (2018). https://www.rfc-editor.org/info/rfc8446
26. Smith, B.: Re: [TLS] Pull Request: removing the AEAD explicit IV. Mail to IETF TLS Working Group (2015). https://mailarchive.ietf.org/arch/msg/tls/2BLiJrJxKveoVjRCZhvkgGq-ksg

# Alternative Key Schedules for the AES

Christina Boura[1(✉)], Patrick Derbez[2], and Margot Funk[1]

[1] Université Paris-Saclay, UVSQ, CNRS, Laboratoire de mathématiques de Versailles, 78000 Versailles, France
{christina.boura,margot.funk}@uvsq.fr

[2] Univ Rennes, Inria, CNRS, IRISA, Rennes, France
patrick.derbez@irisa.fr

**Abstract.** The AES block cipher is today the most important and analyzed symmetric algorithm. While all versions of the AES are known to be secure in the single-key setting, this is not the case in the related-key scenario. In this article we try to answer the question whether the AES would resist better differential-like related-key attacks if the key schedule was different. For this, we search for alternative permutation-based key schedules by extending the work of Khoo et al. at ToSC 2017 and Derbez et al. at SAC 2018. We first show that the model of Derbez et al. was flawed. Then, we develop different approaches together with MILP-based tools to find good permutations that could be used as the key schedule for AES-128, AES-192 and AES-256. Our methods permitted to find permutations that outperform the permutation exhibited by Khoo et al. for AES-128. Moreover, our new approach based on two MILP models that call one another allowed us to handle a larger search space and thus to search for alternative key schedules for the two bigger versions of AES. This method permitted us to find permutations for AES-192 and AES-256 that provide better resistance to related-key differential attacks. Most importantly, we showed that these variants can resist full-round boomerang attacks.

**Keywords:** AES · key schedule MILP · related-key attacks · differential cryptanalysis

## 1 Introduction

The Rijndael family of block ciphers was designed by Joan Daemen and Vincent Rijmen in the late 90's. In 2000, the National Institute of Standards and Technology (NIST) selected three members of this family of ciphers to replace the DES and to form what is known today as the Advanced Encryption Standard (AES) [10]. In the standardized version, the block size is equal to 128 bits and the key size can be 128, 192 or 256 bits. The AES is considered today as the

All authors were partially supported by the French Agence Nationale de la Recherche through the OREO project under Contract ANR-22-CE39-0015.


C. Pöpper and L. Batina (Eds.): ACNS 2024, LNCS 14584, pp. 485–506, 2024.
https://doi.org/10.1007/978-3-031-54773-7_19

most important and widely deployed symmetric primitive and its elegant design inspired several others through the years.

After almost 25 years of intense analysis and scrutiny, all three versions, i.e. AES-128, AES-192 and AES-256, are still considered secure in the single-key scenario. However, in the related-key setting, the two bigger variants of the AES were shown to be much weaker. In 2009, Biryuvov et al. discovered full-round related-key boomerang attacks, with respectively $2^{99.5}$ time and data complexity for AES-256 and $2^{123}$ data and $2^{176}$ time complexity for AES-192 [2,3]. More attacks on AES-192 or AES-256, breaking all rounds or a high number of them, were described later, notably boomerang attacks [8,12], differential meet-in-the-middle attacks [5] or attacks exploiting other properties [11].

The design of the AES round function, including its S-box as well as the MixColumns operation, was done with concrete criteria in mind and was based on solid mathematical arguments borrowed from the theory of Boolean functions and error-correcting codes. On the other hand, the design of the key schedule was much more ad-hoc with much less precise and formal security arguments employed. Mainly, the authors wanted the key schedule to be "different enough" from the round function. It is today considered that this component is responsible for the weaknesses discovered on the biggest versions in the related-key setting.

Even if the AES was not designed with related-key security in mind, the importance of this design necessitates that its security is analyzed even in weaker scenarios in which the adversary has access to data encrypted through related keys. In parallel, a natural question that is often asked for such important targets, is whether replacing a particular component of the cipher would make it more resistant to attacks the original version is not so strong against. As the AES is weaker than expected against related-key attacks of differential nature, i.e. attacks exploiting the existence of high-probability differential characteristics, it is therefore interesting to see whether the level of security would increase against such attacks if the original key schedule of AES was replaced by an alternative one.

This question was first investigated by Nikolic in [18] just after the attacks on the full AES-192 and the full AES-256 in the related-key setting got published. In this paper, Nikolic proposed to tweak the original key schedule of all three versions of the AES by adding more rotations and some additional S-box applications but keeping a global structure quite close to the original key schedule. Much later, Khoo et al. focused only on the smallest AES version and presented an alternative key schedule for AES-128 that could ensure pure differential truncated characteristics with more active S-boxes in the related-key setting than the original key schedule [15]. A very interesting approach in this paper is that the proposed key schedule consisted of a simple byte permutation of the 16 bytes of the key state and offered for this reason excellent performances in both software and hardware. This work was further extended by Derbez et al. who automated the search for good permutations to replace the key schedule of AES-128 and used a constraint programming (CP) model to evaluate the minimum number of active S-boxes of an AES-128 cipher with a modified key schedule [9]. This permitted them to find the first permutation reaching at least 16 active S-boxes for 5 rounds of AES-128 and a different permutation that could reach at least 20 active S-boxes for 6 rounds, thus improving the results of [15].

**Our Contributions.** In this paper we focus on the design of alternative key schedules for all three versions of the AES. Similarly to what was done in [15] and [9], we only analyzed key schedules that are built as a byte permutation of the key state, as these key schedules have excellent implementation properties. We first prove that the CP-model used in [9] is flawed and thus all the results obtained in this paper are wrong. Then, we build our own MILP model to compute the minimum number of active S-boxes for a modified AES and investigate several strategies to search for good permutation-based key schedules. Our first strategy improves the method used in [9] which consisted in searching for good permutations by decomposing them into disjoint cycles. The idea is to build a permutation cycle by cycle and early abort when we are sure a partially formed permutation cannot be extended to a strong one. This method works well for AES-128 and permitted us to obtain many different permutations that could reach 15 active S-boxes for 5 rounds and 20 active S-boxes for 6 rounds, leading thus to better permutations than the one designed by Khoo et al. in [15]. However, this method scales badly for the other two variants. For this reason, we propose a different strategy based on two MILP models that call each other. The first model starts to search for a key schedule by having as its only constraint that this key schedule should be a permutation. This model then calls a second model that computes the minimum number of active S-boxes of any characteristic of the AES with key schedule the one found by the first model. If a characteristic activating less S-boxes than the desired bound is found, then this second model calls again the first one by adding to it extra constraints for the key schedule to prevent that such a weak characteristic reappears. This is done until a good permutation is found or until the problem has no solution. This method is efficient, as each time the first model is called, extra constraints are added on the top of the previous ones, restricting the search space more and more. This strategy permitted us to find strong permutations that can be used as the key schedule for all three AES variants. In particular, we show in the last part of this article, that the key schedules we propose would permit AES-192 and AES-256 to resist full-round boomerang attacks in the related-key setting.

The rest of the paper is organized as follows. Section 2 provides a brief description of the AES, introduces some preliminary notions on differential characteristics and introduces the Mixed Integer Linear Programming (MILP) principle. In Sect. 3 we recall previous results on alternative key schedules for the AES and prove that the results of [9] are wrong. Then, in Sect. 4 we describe our first method based on the decomposition of a permutation into cycles for AES-128. Section 5 presents our new method based on the two MILP models that call each other. Finally, our results for all versions of the AES are summarized and discussed in Sect. 6.

Our code is available at:

https://github.com/pderbez/acns2024/

## 2 Background

### 2.1 Description of the AES

The **AES** is a Substitution Permutation Network that processes data blocks of 128 bits, using keys of 128, 192 or 256 bits. The number of rounds $N_r$ depends on the key size. It is $N_r = 10$ for AES-128, $N_r = 12$ for AES-192 and $N_r = 14$ for AES-256. From the initial master key, $N_r + 1$ round subkeys of 128 bits are generated with a key schedule algorithm that is composed of XORs and the application of an 8-bit S-box (the same as in the round function). We refer the reader to [10] for the detailed specification of the key schedule.

Both the internal block state and each 128-bit subkey can be represented by an array of $4 \times 4$ bytes. We will use the numbering below to refer to the bytes of such a state.

| | 0 | 1 | 2 | 3 |
|---|---|---|---|---|
| 0 | 0 | 1 | 2 | 3 |
| 1 | 4 | 5 | 6 | 7 |
| 2 | 8 | 9 | 10 | 11 |
| 3 | 12 | 13 | 14 | 15 |

After an initial subkey addition, the state is transformed by iterating a round function composed of four byte-oriented transformations as depicted in Fig. 1. SubBytes (SB) applies to each byte of the state the same non-linear bijection called S-box. ShiftRows (SR) shifts the $i$-th row by $i$ bytes to the left. MixColumns (MC) transforms each column of the state by multiplying it by an MDS (Maximum Distance Separable) matrix. Finally, AddRoundKey (ARK) XORs the state with the round subkey. For the last round, the MixColumns operation is omitted.

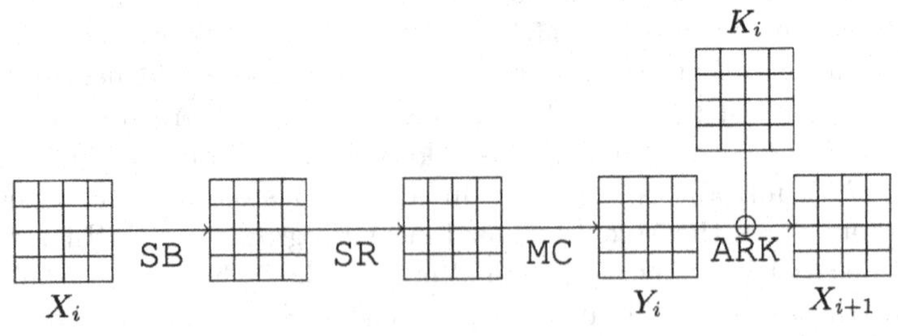


**Fig. 1.** The AES round function. $X_1$ is obtained by xoring the input block and the subkey $K_0$. The output block is $X_{N_r+1}$. MC is omitted for the last round.

## 2.2 AES Differential Characteristics

Differential cryptanalysis is a classical technique for symmetric primitives introduced in 1990 by Biham and Shamir [1]. The idea of this technique is to study the propagation of an input difference through several rounds of the cipher. In order for a cipher to be immune against this family of attacks, there should not exist an input difference $a$ that propagates to an output difference $b$ with a probability higher than expected for a random permutation. Such couples of input/output differences $(a, b)$ are called *differentials*. Computing the exact probability of a differential is a very hard computational problem. In practice, we search to approximate this probability by studying sequences of differences $(a = \delta_0, \delta_1, \ldots, \delta_R = b)$ that start from the difference $a$ and end with the difference $b$, and that we call *differential characteristics*. As the number of differential characteristics is too high to be exhausted, a common search method is to use a *truncated* representation of the characteristics [16]. This approach that works particularly well for word-oriented ciphers consists in abstracting each word by a Boolean value that indicates whether this word is *active*, i.e. has a non-zero difference on it, or *inactive*. Furthermore, we say that an S-box is active if there exists a non-zero difference at its input. The number of active S-boxes of a differential characteristic is an important quantity as, combined with the maximum differential probability of a non-trivial transition through the S-box, permits to provide an upper bound on the probability of any differential characteristic following the truncated pattern. The higher the number of active S-boxes, the lower the probability of a characteristic can be.

The authors of the AES employed an approach known as the *wide-trail strategy* [7] to ensure that all characteristics have, after a certain number of rounds, a relatively high number of active S-boxes. Thanks to this, the AES can be proven immune to classical differential attacks in the single-key setting. On the other hand, the attacks of Biryukov et al. [3,4] and the works that followed showed that if differences are permitted in the key, then there exist related-key characteristics with much less active S-boxes than classical characteristics of the same length.

**Modeling the Propagation of Truncated Differences Through the AES.** Modeling the propagation of truncated differences on the AES can be done quite easily by exploiting the byte-oriented structure of the cipher. A state in a truncated differential of the AES is seen as the concatenation of 16 Boolean variables, each indicating whether the corresponding byte is active or inactive. Then the activity pattern of a byte does not change after the application of the S-box, as this operation is bijective. ShiftRows is a simple reorganization of the bytes inside the state and for MixColumns we use the fact that the matrix is MDS and that its branch number is 5. This means that the sum of the active bytes in a column before and after the application of the matrix is 0 if the column is inactive and at least 5 if the column is active. Finally, we model the AddRoundKey operation, by supposing that the XOR of two active bytes can give an active byte or an inactive byte. We call a *pure* truncated differential characteristic a sequence of truncated differences that respect these propagation rules. A truncated related-key characteristic for 3 rounds of AES-128 is depicted in Fig. 2.

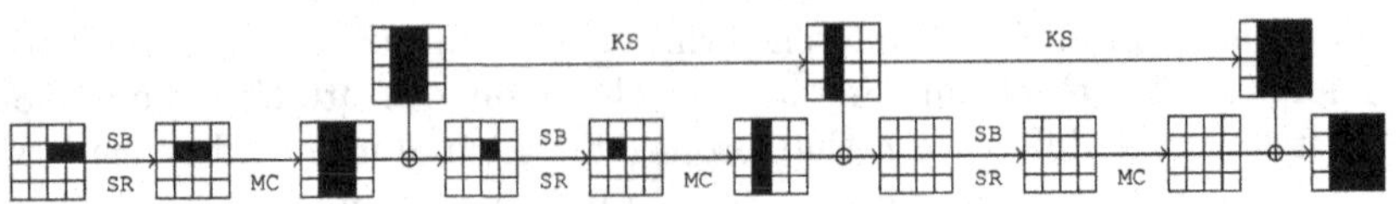


**Fig. 2.** A 3-round related key characteristic for AES-128 (drawn with the library [14]).

**Invalid Truncated Differential Characteristics.** It can happen that a truncated differential characteristic that follows the propagation rules described above cannot be instantiated with real differences. Such characteristics are called *invalid*. Some invalid characteristics can however directly be avoided by exploiting linear relations between the round function and the key schedule. An example of an invalid truncated differential characteristic is shown in Fig. 3.

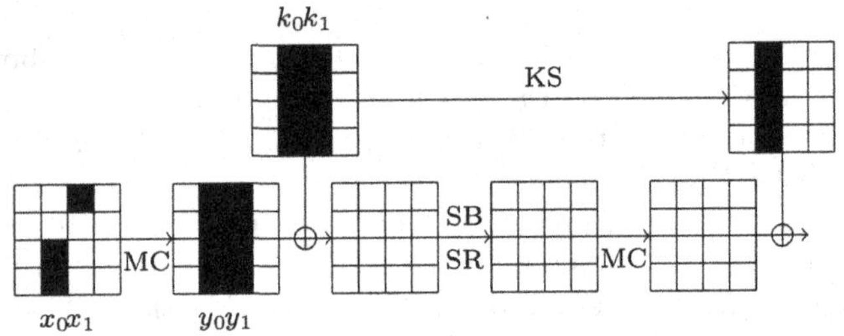


**Fig. 3.** Example of a linear incompatibility. The key schedule's transition is only possible if the subkeys' active columns $k_0$ and $k_1$ are equal. This equality also implies an equality between the columns $y_0$ and $y_1$. This contradicts the fact that the columns $x_0$ and $x_1$ are different.

A common method to remove such invalid characteristics consists in writing down a system of equations including all or a subset of linear relations resulting from the round function and the key schedule and apply linear algebra to it.

### 2.3 Mixed Integer Linear Programming

A well-known method to get a lower bound on the number of active S-boxes of a differential characteristic consists in reducing the problem to a Constraint Optimization Problem (COP) than can be solved by a dedicated solver. Among all existing methods, the MILP (Mixed Integer Linear Program) approach became during the last decade particularly popular among cryptographers. This approach was used for the first time by Mouha et al. in [17] and by Wu and Wang in [19] to prove, among others, lower bounds on the minimal number of active S-boxes for the AES in the single key setting. In a MILP model the variables are either integers or real numbers, the constraints are linear inequalities and the objective function, if any, is a linear function of the variables. The goal is to find values for the variables such that all the constraints are satisfied and such that the objective function is optimized (i.e. maximized or minimized). This modeling technique is particularly well suited for byte-oriented ciphers like the AES: each byte is abstracted by a Boolean that indicates whether this byte is active or not; the objective function simply corresponds to the sum of all the variables that go through an S-box and each of the byte-oriented operations can easily be encoded. For instance, the XOR of 3 bytes $a$, $b$ and $c$ can be modeled with 3 linear inequalities (see Algorithm 1).

**Algorithm 1:** `XOR(model, a, b, c)`

```
model.addConstr(1 - a + b + c ≥ 1)
model.addConstr(a + 1 - b + c ≥ 1)
model.addConstr(a + b + 1 - c ≥ 1)
```

The constraints for the basic model for the AES are described in Algorithms 2 and 3 with the same notations as in Fig. 1 (i.e. for $1 \leq r \leq R$, $X_r$ refers to the state after the AddRoundKey operation of round r-1, $Y_r$ corresponds to the state after the MixColumns operation and $K_r$ is the subkey used in round r). The objective function to be minimized is returned by the function getSboxes. This basic model allows one to easily get a bound on the number of active S-boxes. However, all the truncated characteristics that are solutions of the model cannot be instantiated into actual characteristics. In particular, inconsistencies may come from the fact that encoding a set of linear equations between variables does not encode the vector space spanned by these equations. A first approach to reduce the number of invalid trails is to add extra variables and constraints to the model. Another approach, used by Derbez et al. in [8] is to perform linear algebra to check if the solution found by the solver respects the whole system of linear equations induced by the cipher. When a linear inconsistency is detected, the authors of [8] used the callback functionality of the solver Gurobi [13] to add new constraints during the solving process in order to prevent this inconsistency for the upcoming solutions.

**Algorithm 2:** `addConstrForAddRoundKey(model, R)`

```
for r = 1...R-1 do
    for i = 0...15 do
        XOR(model, X_{r+1}[i], K_r[i], Y_r[i])
```

**Algorithm 3:** `addConstrForShiftRowsMixColumns(model, R)`

```
for r = 1...R−1 do
    for c = 0...3 do
        e ← 0
        for i = 0...3 do
            e ← e + Y_r[c + 4i]
            e ← e + X_r[(c + i) mod 4 + 4i]
        Let f be a dummy binary variable
        model.addConstr(e ≤ 8f)
        model.addConstr(e ≥ 5f)
```

**Algorithm 4:** `getSboxes(model, R)`

```
output: The number of active S-boxes
Sboxes ← 0
for r = 1... R do
    for i = 0...15 do
        Sboxes ← Sboxes + X_r[i]
return Sboxes
```

## 3 Permutation-Based Key Schedules for the AES

While the AES is secure in the single key model, its two bigger variants were shown to be vulnerable to full-round related-key attacks that exploit the existence of high probability differential characteristics for some number of rounds [2,3]. It is widely admitted today that the success of these attacks is mainly due to weaknesses in the key schedules of AES-192 and AES-256. Furthermore, while the design of the AES round function was based on solid mathematical properties, the design of the key schedule was done with much less formal criteria in mind. It is therefore natural to ask the question whether an alternative key schedule design could strengthen the resistance of the AES against related-key differential-like attacks.

A natural idea for designing an alternative key schedule is to use a simple byte-permutation of the master key. This design choice is clearly relevant, as key schedules of this type offer excellent implementation properties both in software and hardware. This idea was investigated notably by Khoo et al. in [15], where the authors searched (among others) to replace the key schedule of AES-128 by a key schedule of this type with the goal of increasing the minimal number of active S-boxes of any differential characteristic after some rounds. The main result of this part of their paper is the discovery of a byte-permutation that could play the role of the AES-128 key schedule and that permits to reach more active S-boxes in the pure related-key setting starting from the third round. This permutation is:

$$\begin{pmatrix} 0 & 1 & 2 & 3 \\ 4 & 5 & 6 & 7 \\ 8 & 9 & 10 & 11 \\ 12 & 13 & 14 & 15 \end{pmatrix} \longrightarrow \begin{pmatrix} 14 & 15 & 12 & 13 \\ 3 & 0 & 1 & 2 \\ 4 & 5 & 6 & 7 \\ 8 & 9 & 10 & 11 \end{pmatrix},$$

and its table representation is

$$P_1 = (\texttt{5, 6, 7, 4, 8, 9, 10, 11, 12, 13, 14, 15, 2, 3, 0, 1}).$$

This key schedule permits to achieve at least 5, 10, 14, 18 and 21 active S-boxes after respectively 3, 4, 5, 6 and 7 rounds of computation in the pure truncated differential setting, i.e. when linear inconsistencies are not taken into account. To compare, the original `AES-128` key schedule leads to only 3, 9, 11 and 13 active S-boxes for the same number of rounds in the same setting. To design this permutation, the authors of [15] started from their human-readable proof of the bound on 3 rounds of `AES-128` and searched for modifications in the design that could increase the minimum number of active S-boxes.

The problem of finding a byte-permutation to replace the key schedule of `AES`, was then further analyzed by Derbez et al. in [9]. First, they showed that, without considering linear inconsistencies, the permutation from [15] is optimal by exhibiting differential characteristics that hold for any permutation and reaching the corresponding number of active S-boxes. Then, they introduced the idea to use a more automated approach to search for good permutations and to consider the underlying equations as well, hence removing all linearly inconsistent truncated characteristics. For this search, to test the minimum number of active S-boxes of `AES-128` with a permutation playing the role of the key schedule could achieve, the authors wrote up a Constraint Programming (CP) model. As a result, they provided permutations achieving a better security than the one from [15] and gave upper bounds on the minimum number of active S-boxes a permutation could reach. More precisely, the authors proposed the permutation

$$P_2 = (\texttt{4, 1, 10, 6, 7, 9, 3, 11, 8, 2, 14, 15, 12, 13, 5, 0}),$$

that could reach at least 16 active S-boxes for 5 rounds and the permutation

$$P_3 = (\texttt{14, 5, 0, 7, 4, 3, 6, 15, 9, 2, 1, 11, 13, 8, 10, 12})$$

that could reach at least 20 active S-boxes for 6 rounds.

### 3.1 Analyzing the Results of [9]

We wrote a simple MILP model to compute the minimum number of active S-boxes that could be achieved by any truncated differential characteristic for `AES-128` with a given permutation-based key schedule. The constraints to add to the model are described in Algorithms 2, 3 and 5 and the objective function to minimize (i.e. the number of active Sboxes) is returned by the function `getSboxes`. We also handled linear dependencies of the truncated differential characteristics with the same method as Derbez et al. in [8].

**Algorithm 5:** `addConstrForKeySchedule128(model, R, P)`

```
for r = 2...R-1 do
    for i = 0...15 do
        model.addConstr(K_r[P(i)] = K_{r-1}[i])
```

With this MILP model, we confirmed the bounds for the permutation $P_1$ built in [15] in the pure truncated differential model announced by the authors and showed, that by taking linear dependencies into account, this permutation actually leads to at least 19 active S-boxes for 6 rounds (see Table 5 of [15]).

However, we were not able to confirm any of the results of [9] obtained with their CP model. We checked the two proposed permutations $P_2$ and $P_3$ with our MILP model and we got that the minimum number of active S-boxes reached was much smaller than what the authors announced. More precisely, we discovered that the permutation $P_2$ led to a minimum number of 10 active S-boxes after 5 rounds instead of the 16 S-boxes announced, and that $P_3$ resulted in at least 17 active S-boxes after 6 rounds instead of the claimed 20 active S-boxes. As a proof, we provide an example of a truncated differential characteristic with 10 active S-boxes for 5 rounds with the permutation $P_2$ in Fig. 4 and a characteristic with 17 active S-boxes for 6 rounds with the permutation $P_3$ is given in Fig. 5. The above prove that the CP model used in [9] was flawed and thus none of the results of that paper can be considered as correct[1]. For example, the "proof" that there exists no permutation for the key schedule permitting to reach a minimum of 18 active S-boxes after 5 rounds of AES-128, cannot be trusted anymore as this proof was computational and the computations were based on the badly flawed CP model.

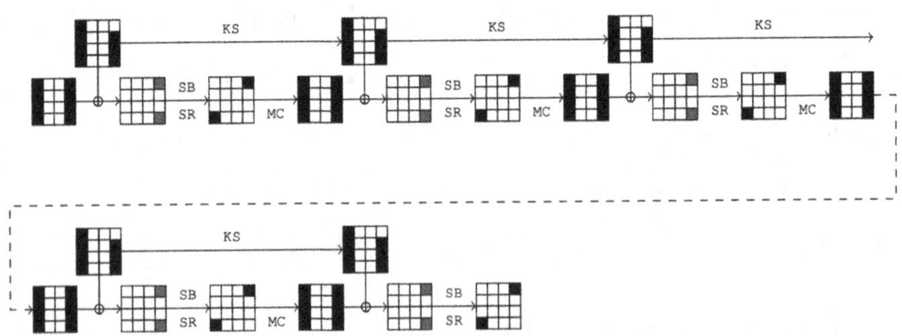


**Fig. 4.** Example of a truncated differential characteristic with 10 active S-boxes (in red) for 5 rounds with the permutation $P_2$. (Color figure online)

[1] We contacted the authors of [9] to let them know about our findings and after verification they confirmed there is indeed a problem with their CP model and that the results of this paper should be considered as flawed.

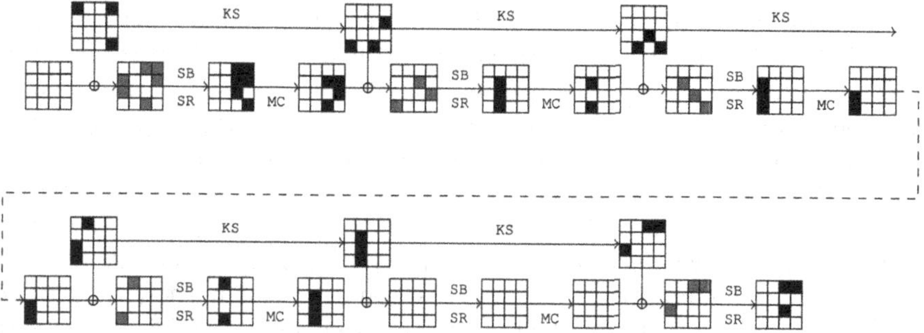


**Fig. 5.** Example of a truncated characteristic with 17 active S-boxes (in red) for 6 rounds with the permutation $P_3$. (Color figure online)

# 4 A Cycle-Decomposition Approach to Search for Good Key Schedules

Once we saw that the results of [9] were wrong, we decided to search ourselves for alternative permutation-based key schedules for AES-128. We describe in this section the method we used to do so. This method is based on the decomposition of a permutation in its disjoint cycles and is inspired from what was done in [9]. As we will see, this method is efficient for AES-128 but is too expensive for AES-192 and AES-256. Thus, we develop a different approach in Sect. 5 that we successfully adapt to all three AES variants.

## 4.1 Description of the Method

The idea on which the method is based is the following. It is a well known fact that any permutation can be decomposed in cycles in a unique way. For example, the permutation $P_1$ above can be written as (0, 5, 9, 13, 3, 4, 8, 12, 2, 7, 11, 15, 1, 6, 10, 14) and consists of a single cycle of length 16, while the permutation $P_2$ can be written as (0, 4, 7, 11, 15)(2, 10, 14, 5, 9)(3, 6)(1)(8)(12)(13) and is thus decomposed in 2 cycles of length 5, a cycle of length 2 and four cycles of length 1. Viewing a permutation as a composition of cycles has an important advantage: it is possible to evaluate the quality of a permutation to play the role of the key schedule by only partially defining its decomposition in cycles. Suppose for example, that we want to verify if a permutation that has in its decomposition the cycle (0, 2, 7, 13, 15) can lead to a minimum of 15 active S-boxes after 5 rounds. Then we can write a MILP model for which the key schedule is only partially defined and the only permitted active bytes in the first subkey are among the bytes 0, 2, 7, 13 and 15. The cycle structure permits us to know where these active bytes will be moved to by the key schedule in any of the following subkeys. If the MILP program manages to find a valid differential characteristic with less than 15 active S-boxes then we know that we can throw away all permutations that have this cycle as part of their decomposition.

Moreover, we do not need to restrict ourselves to complete cycles and can check with this method permutations for which we have only partially specified a cycle they contain. To give an example, suppose we want to evaluate a permutation that has in its decomposition the partially defined cycle (0, 2, 7, 13, 15, ...). If the partially defined cycle is at least as long as the number of rounds we want to find a bound for, we can still partially evaluate its strength, by activating only bytes in the key for which the partial knowledge of the incomplete cycle permits us to propagate through all subkeys that are needed for the computation. If our target is again at least 15 active S-boxes for 5 rounds and if this partial evaluation permits to exhibit a characteristic with less than 15 active S-boxes, we know that we can remove all permutations that have inside cycles containing the trail $0 \rightarrow 2 \rightarrow 7 \rightarrow 13 \rightarrow 15$.

We describe now our global approach for this method. This approach is based on the recursive Algorithm 6. This algorithm takes as input the number of rounds `r` to analyze, a target bound `b` for the minimum number of active S-boxes, a table $P_{KS}$ corresponding to the partially specified permutation the algorithm is working on, an element `x` for which we want to fix the image by the permutation and a variable `length` corresponding to the actual length of the cycle the algorithm is working on.

The first call to the algorithm is done for `x` $= 0$ and `length = 1`. The algorithm first checks (line 1) if the image of `x` has been fixed. If this is the case, meaning that the cycle is complete, the MILP-based routine `EvaluatePerm`($P_{KS}$) checks whether the partial knowledge of $P_{KS}$ permits to exhibit a characteristic activating less than `b` S-boxes. At this step, with the method of Derbez et al. in [8], we also detect linear inconsistencies using linear algebra and handle them using the callback functionality of the solver Gurobi. If a valid characteristic is found, then the algorithm returns to the instance that called it as this means that this partially defined cycle decomposition can never lead to permutations reaching more than `b` active S-boxes. On the other hand, if the routine `EvaluatePerm`($P_{KS}$) returns a value higher or equal to the bound `b`, then if $P_{KS}$ is entirely specified (line 4) this means that a permutation with the desired property has been found. If there are still values that remain to be fixed, the algorithm will start working on a new cycle, by choosing as the beginning of this new cycle the first available element `y` (line 7).

Finally, if the image of `x` has not yet been fixed meaning that the cycle is not yet complete (line 9), then if the current length of the cycle is long enough to permit an evaluation of the permutation, the routine `EvaluatePerm`($PK_S$) is called (line 10). If the return value is smaller than `b` then this partially defined cycle is abandoned. Otherwise, the next available value `y` is chosen to continue the cycle (line 12), the image of `x` is set to `y` and the search continues (line 13).

**An Improvement.** The basic algorithm described above can be improved by taking into account the column symmetry. Indeed let $P_{KS}$ be a permutation for the key schedule and let $P_{\ggg}$ a permutation that shifts the columns of $P_{KS}$. Then, both the permutations $P_{KS}$ and $P_{\ggg} \circ P_{KS} \circ P_{\ggg}^{-1}$ are equivalent and

**Algorithm 6:** `CycleSearch(r, b, P_KS, x, length)`

```
output: All permutations reaching at least b active S-boxes for r rounds of
        AES-128
if P_KS[x] has been fixed then
    if EvaluatePerm(P_KS) < b then
        return
    if all the images of P_KS have been fixed then
        return P_KS
    else
        Choose the next available value y to start a new cycle.
        CycleSearch(r,b,P_KS,y,1)
else
    if length >= r-1 and EvaluatePerm(P_KS) < b then
        return
    Find the next available value y to continue the cycle.
    P_KS[x] = y
    CycleSearch(r,b,P_KS,y,length + 1)
```

lead to exactly the same bounds. We have incorporated this observation to our algorithm to decrease the search space.

## 5 Double-MILP Model for Permutations

The strategy we presented in Sect. 4 can be hardly adapted to the bigger variants of the AES. The reason is that the search space becomes too big, as it necessitates going through permutations of 24 bytes for AES-192 and 32 bytes for AES-256. For this reason, we present here an entirely different strategy to find good alternative permutation-based key schedules that we applied to all AES versions. This method combines a first MILP model to generate permutations with a second MILP model to evaluate the generated permutations. The aim of the second model is twofold. First, it detects when a permutation leads to the desired minimum number of active S-boxes. Second, it identifies bad subkeys patterns that a good permutation should prevent. This information is used to refine the constraints of the first model.

In the following, to simplify the notations, we only describe our algorithms for the case of AES-128. Note that they can be extended to AES-192 and AES-256 in a rather straightforward way.

Algorithm 7 summarizes the overall search process. For the initialization of the model m1 that generates permutations, we add constraints to restrict the solutions of m1 to permutation matrices of size $16 \times 16$. Some extra empirical constraints can possibly be added at this step (see discussion below). Then, we generate a permutation with the model m1 and evaluate it with the function evaluateP128. If the key schedule defined by this permutation allows a differential characteristic with too few active S-boxes, the function evaluateP128 outputs a bad subkey pattern to be removed by calling the function addConstrToRemoveKeyPattern128. The form of this bad subkey pattern and the constraints to remove it will be detailed below. We repeat this until there is no more permutation matrix satisfying the constraints in m1 or until a permutation guarantying nbWantedSboxes after R rounds of AES-128 is found.

**Algorithm 7:** searchP128(R, nbWantedSboxes)

```
Initialize a model m1
▷ Ensure that P is a permutation matrix.
e1 ← 0
e2 ← 0
for i = 0...15 do
    for j = 0...15 do
        e1 ← e1 + P[i][j]
        e2 ← e2 + P[j][i]
m1.addConstr(e1 = 1)
m1.addConstr(e2 = 1)
▷ Generate a permutation P with the model m1 and test it
while True do
    m1.optimize()
    if No solution found then
        return
    P ← m1.getASolution()
    badKeyPattern ← evaluateP128(P, nbWantedSboxes, R)
    if badKeyPattern = ∅ then
        // P guarantees nbWantedSboxes after R rounds
        return P
    addConstrToRemoveKeyPattern128(m1, badKeyPattern)
```

The function evaluateP128 describes a basic MILP model similar to the one we used for Algorithm 6. However, note that we do not optimize the number of active S-boxes. Instead, we only add a constraint to know whether there exists a truncated differential characteristic activating less than nbWantedSboxes S-boxes. Then, if such a truncated differential characteristic exists, the model will minimize the number of active bytes in the master key. This is directly related to the number of permutations for which the characteristic does hold. Indeed, we observed that in practice, valid truncated characteristics have few active key bytes (hardly more than 6) and thus, lower this number is, higher the number

**Algorithm 8:** `evaluateP128(P, nbWantedSboxes, R)`

**output:**
- ∅ if there is no `R`-round characteristic with less than `NbWantedSboxes` when the alternative `AES-128` key schedule is based on the permutation `P`,
- A tuple of subkeys which leads to a characteristic with less than `NbWantedSboxes` and which minimizes the number of active bytes in the master key otherwise.

```
Initialize a model m2.
▷ Key schedule and round constraints
addConstrForKeySchedule128(m2, R, P)
addConstrForShiftRowsMixColumns(m2, R)
addConstrForAddRoundKey(m2, R)
▷ Number of active Sboxes
Sboxes ← getSboxes(m2, R)
m2.addConstr(sboxes ≥ 1)
m2.addConstr(sboxes ≤ nbWantedSboxes)
▷ Number of active bytes in the master key for AES-128
obj ← 0
for i = 0...15 do
    obj ← obj + K1[i]
m2.addConstr(obj ≥ 1)
▷ Minimize the objective function
▷ Handle linear inconsistencies with the callback functionality of Gurobi
m2.minimize(obj)
if No solution found then
    return ∅
else
    badKeyPattern ← (K1, K2, K3, ..., KR−1)
    return badKeyPattern
```

of permutations satisfying the pattern and as a consequence, higher the number of permutations removed by the constraint will be. Of course, this is not always true but remains a quite reasonable assumption.

**Algorithm 9:** `addConstrToRemoveKeyPattern128(m1,(K1,K2,...,KR−1))`

```
e ← 0
for r = 1,..., R-2 do
    for a such that Kr[a] is an active byte do
        bound ← bound + 1
        for b such that Kr+1[b] is an active byte do
            e ← e + P[a][b]
m1.addConstr(e ≤ bound -1)
```

**Removing Patterns.** In order to better explain how we exploit a particular "bad" truncated differential characteristic to reduce the search space of possible permutations, let us focus on a simple example. For this, we denote by $P$ the permutation that plays the role of the key schedule, and we write $P^2 = P \circ P$, $P^3 = P \circ P \circ P$, etc. Further, we suppose that $M_P$ represents the permutation matrix associated to $P$, that is $M_P[i][j] = 1$ if $P(i) = j$ and is 0 otherwise. Assume now for instance that the active bytes of the characteristic are $\{0, 1\}$ on the first subkey and $\{2, 6\}$ on the second one and that $P(0) = 2$ and $P(1) = 6$. A naive way to discard the permutations leading to the exact same truncated characteristic is to forbid either $P(0) = 2$ or $P(1) = 6$. This can be easily done by adding the constraint $M_P[0][2] + M_P[1][6] \leq 1$. However, in many cases we can safely remove the transition $P(\{0, 1\}) = \{2, 6\}$, which includes, among others, the configuration $P(0) = 6$ and $P(1) = 2$. Being allowed to remove the transition from the first set to the second one, depends on the characteristic and more precisely on the relation between the active key bytes. If the characteristic is valid if and only if $\Delta k_0[0] = \alpha \Delta k_0[1]$ with $\alpha \neq \alpha^{-1}$, then we cannot ensure that swapping the images of $P(0)$ and $P(1)$ will not affect the validity of the truncated characteristic and thus we cannot discard the transition $P(\{0, 1\}) = \{2, 6\}$. On another hand, whenever $\alpha = \alpha^{-1}$ or if both $\Delta k_0[0]$ and $\Delta k_0[1]$ can be chosen independently, we can immediately forbid the transition between both sets by adding the constraint $M_P[0][2] + M_P[0][6] + M_P[1][2] + M_P[1][6] \leq 1$. In practice, two key bytes have to be related only to satisfy linear constraints on specific rounds but rarely on all the rounds. As a consequence, given a truncated differential characteristic, the corresponding constraint added to discard it consists in forbidding at least one transition between the sets of active bytes on two consecutive subkeys or at least one transition between actual values for powers of $P$.

Note that the accurate constraint makes the model more complicated since we might need to add constraints on $P^2$, $P^3$, etc. Removing the constraints on them, and by then potentially discarding good permutations, leads to a simpler and faster model which can be useful as a heuristic search algorithm. This is actually the version we used for the two bigger versions of AES since exhausting the whole search space would have been out of reach anyway.

**An Additional Constraint for AES-128.** We tried to add several constraints to the MILP model that generates permutations for AES-128 in order to restrict the search space while ensuring good properties. One of them permitted us to find permutations that outperform the permutation in [15]. This constraint is as follows: a byte of the state cannot be sent by the permutation to a column where the ShiftRows (SR) permutation would send it. For example byte 0 cannot be sent by the permutation to the first column while byte 4 cannot be sent to the last column. This constraint, while being simple, is quite natural as it tries to minimize the overlapping between ShiftRows and the key schedule in order to avoid cancellations between the state and the key addition. As a result we noticed that the permutation $P_1$ found in [15] was actually quite common as we were able to generate a very high number of permutations achieving a minimum of 14 active S-boxes after 5 rounds and a minimum of 19 active S-boxes after 6 rounds. More importantly, we were also able to generate permutations achieving a minimum of 15 active S-boxes after 5 rounds and at least 20 active S-boxes after 6 rounds.

## 6 Results

In this section we present the results we obtained with the algorithms and models described in the previous sections.

### 6.1 Results for AES-128

We obtained several permutations reaching at least 20 active S-boxes for 6 rounds. We present two such permutations, respectively denoted by $P_4$ and $P_5$. The permutation $P_4$ was discovered with the method of Sect. 4, while $P_5$ was found with the method of Sect. 5.

$$P_4 = (6, 0, 4, 9, 13, 10, 8, 3, 7, 12, 15, 14, 11, 5, 1, 2)$$
$$P_5 = (3, 15, 11, 8, 2, 1, 10, 5, 4, 0, 9, 7, 6, 12, 13, 14)$$

The bounds for 2 to 7 rounds for these two permutations are given in Table 1. These permutations can be compared to $P_1$ given in [15] and to $P_2$ and $P_3$ given in [9]. These permutations $P_4$ and $P_5$ achieve better differential bounds than the one proposed by Khoo et al. but none of them is strictly better. Still, permutation $P_4$ reaches similar or higher bounds up to 6 rounds and ensures that no differential characteristic with a probability higher than $2^{-128}$ does exist on 7 rounds (assuming the best probability of a non-trivial transition through the S-box is $2^{-6}$ as for AES).

**Table 1.** Bounds on the minimal number of active S-boxes for 2 to 7 rounds for our permutations $P_4$ and $P_5$ and for the three permutations given previously by Khoo et al. [15] and Derbez et al. [9].

| Rounds | 2 | 3 | 4 | 5 | 6 | 7 | Ref. |
|---|---|---|---|---|---|---|---|
| $P_1$ | 1 | 5 | 10 | 14 | 19 | 23 | [15] |
| $P_2$ | 1 | 3 | 7 | 10 | 12 | 14 | [9] |
| $P_3$ | 1 | 3 | 7 | 11 | 17 | 22 | [9] |
| $P_4$ | 1 | 5 | 9 | 15 | 20 | 23 | Sect. 4 |
| $P_5$ | 1 | 5 | 10 | 14 | 20 | 22 | Sect. 5 |

**Other Results and Open Problems.** We used Algorithm 6 on a cluster equipped with 128 cores to scan the space of all permutations and show that there does not exist a permutation that could lead to 18 active S-boxes for 5 rounds. We also searched with both methods of Sect. 4 and Sect. 5 to find permutations that could give at least 16 S-boxes for 5 rounds or at least 21 S-boxes for 6 rounds, but we were not able to find any such permutation. It is thus an open problem if such permutations exist.

### 6.2 Results for AES-192 and AES-256

For the first time, we investigate how a permutation as a key schedule could affect the resistance against differential cryptanalysis for the two bigger versions of AES. Because the search space is very big for those two variants, we only used the approach described in Sect. 5. Actually, it was surprisingly easy to obtain permutations leading to much stronger variants than with the original key schedules. In particular, while 9 and 13 rounds respectively are required to ensure the non-existence of differential distinguishers on both the 192 and 256-bit versions of AES, we found permutations for which only 8 and 9 rounds are enough[2]. For AES-256 this is 4 rounds less, something we believe is quite impressive and supports the belief that the key schedule for this version was far from being optimal with respect to differential cryptanalysis.

The two permutations we propose for these two versions are:

$$\begin{aligned} P_{192} &= \{2, 17, 19, 9, 13, 12, 23, 0, 4, 21, 18, 16, 10, 20, 22, 1, 11, 3, 7, 5, \\ &\quad 15, 6, 14, 8\} \\ P_{256} &= \{27, 16, 9, 25, 11, 13, 14, 18, 22, 21, 19, 23, 28, 31, 29, 3, 2, 15, 8, \\ &\quad 24, 17, 1, 26, 0, 7, 20, 10, 4, 6, 30, 12, 5\} \end{aligned}$$

These two permutations are visualized below by showing how the bytes are re-arranged inside the key state:

$$\begin{pmatrix} 0 & 1 & 2 & 3 & 4 & 5 \\ 6 & 7 & 8 & 9 & 10 & 11 \\ 12 & 13 & 14 & 15 & 16 & 17 \\ 18 & 19 & 20 & 21 & 22 & 23 \end{pmatrix} \longrightarrow \begin{pmatrix} 7 & 15 & 0 & 17 & 8 & 19 \\ 21 & 18 & 23 & 3 & 12 & 16 \\ 5 & 4 & 22 & 20 & 11 & 1 \\ 10 & 2 & 13 & 9 & 14 & 6 \end{pmatrix}$$

$$\begin{pmatrix} 0 & 1 & 2 & 3 & 4 & 5 & 6 & 7 \\ 8 & 9 & 10 & 11 & 12 & 13 & 14 & 15 \\ 16 & 17 & 18 & 19 & 20 & 21 & 22 & 23 \\ 24 & 25 & 26 & 27 & 28 & 29 & 30 & 31 \end{pmatrix} \longrightarrow \begin{pmatrix} 23 & 21 & 16 & 15 & 27 & 31 & 28 & 24 \\ 18 & 2 & 26 & 4 & 30 & 5 & 6 & 17 \\ 1 & 20 & 7 & 10 & 25 & 9 & 8 & 11 \\ 19 & 3 & 22 & 0 & 12 & 14 & 29 & 13 \end{pmatrix}$$

As already stated in the introduction, it is well-known that there exist related-key boomerang attacks on the full AES-192 and on the full AES-256. A boomerang distinguisher is composed of two differentials and its probability

[2] Note that the bounds are computed assuming the master key is filled into the first round keys. Shifting the round keys does slightly modify some of the bounds.

mostly depends on the probability of the underlying differentials. Let denote by $n_r$ the minimum number of active S-boxes after $r$ rounds. A first approximation of the probability of a boomerang characteristic on $R$-round AES would be $\min_r 2^{-6\times 2(n_r+n_{R-r})}$. While we know this formula is not accurate, especially since the work of Cid et al. regarding Boomerang Connectivity Table (BCT) [6], it still gives the intuition that $n_r+n_{R-r}$ should be as high as possible to ensure good resistance against boomerang attacks. Hence, when searching for replacement permutations for both AES-192 and AES-256 we tried to reach 22 active S-boxes with as few rounds as possible and to optimize $\min_r n_r+n_{R-r}$ for several values of $R$. Since most boomerang attacks only add few rounds around their inner distinguisher, we primarily focused on $R = 10$ for AES-192 and $R = 12$ for AES-256. We also decided empirically to favor 5 and 6 rounds respectively to decide between two permutations (Table 2).

**Table 2.** Bounds on the minimal number of active S-boxes for 2 to 10 rounds for the permutations $P_{192}$ and $P_{256}$.

| Rounds | 2 | 3 | 4 | 5 | 6 | 7 | 8 | 9 | 10 |
|---|---|---|---|---|---|---|---|---|---|
| $P_{192}$ | 0 | 1 | 5 | 10 | 13 | 17 | 22 | 25 | 28 |
| $P_{256}$ | 0 | 1 | 2 | 5 | 10 | 14 | 16 | 22 | 26 |

To test our permutations against boomerang cryptanalysis we modified the MILP model proposed in [8] to handle a linear key schedule. We also removed the part of the model related to the key recovery process since the complete model was too slow to finish in a reasonable time. Hence we only searched for the number of rounds after which there is no boomerang characteristic with a probability higher than $2^{-128}$. As a result we obtain that 10 rounds are enough for AES-192 and 11 rounds for AES-256. This is much better than with the original versions of the key schedule and it is highly unlikely that our variants could be fully broken by this cryptanalysis technique. We believe this result is important since it supports that the number of rounds set by the designers for all the different versions would have been enough to ensure full security of the AES family.

**Generic Bounds for Reduced-Round AES-192 and AES-256.** By looking at the bounds obtained for AES-192 and AES-256, one may wonder if it is possible to establish in a generic way bounds on the minimum number of active S-boxes for a modified AES with a permutation-based key schedule. As we show in Proposition 1 such bounds can be easily obtained for a small number of rounds and are valid for any key schedule of this form.

**Proposition 1.** *For* AES-256 *or* AES-192 *used with a permutation-based key schedule there always exist a 4-round differential characteristic with 5 or less active S-boxes and a 2-round differential characteristic with 0 active S-box. Moreover for* AES-256 *(resp.* AES-192*) there exists a 3-round differential characteristic with 1 (resp. less than 2) active S-boxes.*

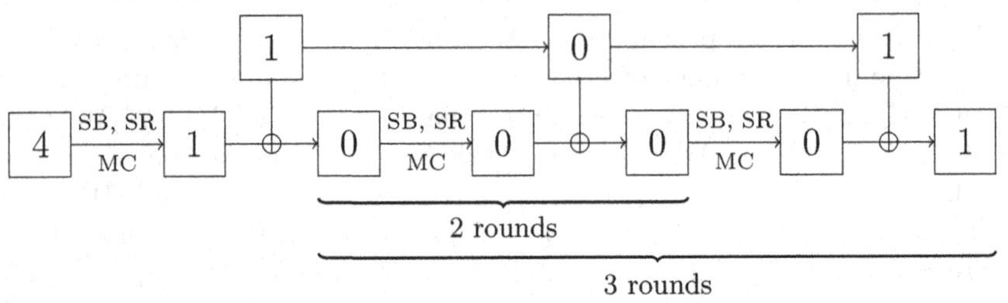


**Fig. 6.** A 4-round differential characteristic. The numerals represent the number of active bytes. They are depicted in red if these bytes go through an S-box. (Color figure online)

*Proof.* Let us denote by $w(K_i)$ the number of active bytes of a subkey $K_i$. For any permutation-based key schedule for AES-256 there exist

- a configuration such that $(w(K_1), w(K_2), w(K_3)) \in \{(1,0,0),(1,0,1)\}$;
- a configuration such that $((w(K_1), w(K_2)) = (0,1)$.

For any permutation-based key schedule for AES-192 there exist

- a configuration such that $((w(K_1), w(K_2), w(K_3)) = (1,0,1)$;
- a configuration such that $((w(K_1), w(K_2)) \in \{(0,1),(0,2)\}$.

Together with Fig. 6, the following table finishes the proof.

| # rounds | $w(K_1)$ | $w(K_2)$ | $w(K_3)$ | # active S-boxes that can be reached |
|---|---|---|---|---|
| 4 | 1 | 0 | 1 | 5 (see the 4 rounds of Fig. 6) |
| 4 | 1 | 0 | 0 | 4 (change the last subkey of the 4 rounds) |
| 3 | 0 | 1 | | 1 (see the 3 rounds of Fig. 6) |
| 3 | 0 | 2 | | 2 (change the last subkey of the 3 rounds) |
| 2 | 0 | | | 0 (see the 2 rounds of Fig. 6) |

## 7 Conclusion and Open Problems

We investigate in this work two strategies to find, in an automated way, alternative permutation-based key schedules for AES that resist differential related-key attacks. The first one is based as in [9] on a cycle decomposition of permutations. The other one is based on two nested MILP models that generate and test permutations. We were able to confirm the results of [15] with our tool, which is an indication that our program is correct. Further, we analyzed the differential characteristics matching the lower bound and verified that for none of them removing one of their active S-boxes was possible, which is another indication that the bounds obtained are exact. These arguments do not form of course a formal proof, but providing such a proof is extremely difficult.

Our work is a step forward to the understanding of how to design good key schedules and raises new questions. First, regarding our double-MILP model, it is natural to ask whether adding some extra constraints to the model that generates permutations can improve the search. For AES-128 we tried to add several constraints related to the composition of permutations and their relations to the ShiftRows operation. It was in fact the simplest one that gave the best results. For the other versions of AES, as there is a discrepancy between the size of the permutation and the size of the subkeys, it is not clear what would good constraints for these cases be. More generally, more research efforts are needed to better understand how good key schedules for block ciphers and tweakable block ciphers should be designed and what the design criteria should be.

## References


1. Biham, E., Shamir, A.: Differential cryptanalysis of DES-like cryptosystems. In: Menezes, A.J., Vanstone, S.A. (eds.) CRYPTO 1990. LNCS, vol. 537, pp. 2–21. Springer, Heidelberg (1991). https://doi.org/10.1007/3-540-38424-3_1
2. Biryukov, A., Khovratovich, D.: Related-key cryptanalysis of the full AES-192 and AES-256. In: Matsui, M. (ed.) ASIACRYPT 2009. LNCS, vol. 5912, pp. 1–18. Springer, Heidelberg (2009). https://doi.org/10.1007/978-3-642-10366-7_1
3. Biryukov, A., Khovratovich, D., Nikolić, I.: Distinguisher and related-key attack on the full AES-256. In: Halevi, S. (ed.) CRYPTO 2009. LNCS, vol. 5677, pp. 231–249. Springer, Heidelberg (2009). https://doi.org/10.1007/978-3-642-03356-8_14
4. Biryukov, A., Nikolić, I.: Automatic search for related-key differential characteristics in byte-oriented block ciphers: application to AES, Camellia, Khazad and others. In: Gilbert, H. (ed.) EUROCRYPT 2010. LNCS, vol. 6110, pp. 322–344. Springer, Heidelberg (2010). https://doi.org/10.1007/978-3-642-13190-5_17
5. Boura, C., David, N., Derbez, P., Leander, G., Naya-Plasencia, M.: Differential meet-in-the-middle cryptanalysis. In: Handschuh, H., Lysyanskaya, A. (eds.) CRYPTO 2023, Part III. LNCS, vol. 14083, pp. 240–272. Springer, Cham (2023). https://doi.org/10.1007/978-3-031-38548-3_9
6. Cid, C., Huang, T., Peyrin, T., Sasaki, Y., Song, L.: Boomerang connectivity table: a new cryptanalysis tool. In: Nielsen, J.B., Rijmen, V. (eds.) EUROCRYPT 2018, Part II. LNCS, vol. 10821, pp. 683–714. Springer, Cham (2018). https://doi.org/10.1007/978-3-319-78375-8_22
7. Daemen, J., Rijmen, V.: The wide trail design strategy. In: Honary, B. (ed.) Cryptography and Coding 2001. LNCS, vol. 2260, pp. 222–238. Springer, Heidelberg (2001). https://doi.org/10.1007/3-540-45325-3_20
8. Derbez, P., Euler, M., Fouque, P., Nguyen, P.H.: Revisiting related-key boomerang attacks on AES using computer-aided tool. In: Agrawal, S., Lin, D. (eds.) ASIACRYPT 2022, Part III. LNCS, vol. 13793, pp. 68–88. Springer, Cham (2022). https://doi.org/10.1007/978-3-031-22969-5_3
9. Derbez, P., Fouque, P., Jean, J., Lambin, B.: Variants of the AES key schedule for better truncated differential bounds. In: Cid, C., Jacobson Jr., M. (eds.) SAC 2018. LNCS, vol. 11349, pp. 27–49. Springer, Cham (2018). https://doi.org/10.1007/978-3-030-10970-7_2

10. FIPS 197: Announcing the Advanced Encryption Standard (AES). National Institute for Standards and Technology, Gaithersburg, MD, USA, November 2001
11. Gérault, D., Lafourcade, P., Minier, M., Solnon, C.: Computing AES related-key differential characteristics with constraint programming. Artif. Intell. **278**, 103183 (2020)
12. Guo, J., Song, L., Wang, H.: Key structures: improved related-key boomerang attack against the full AES-256. In: Nguyen, K., Yang, G., Guo, F., Susilo, W. (eds.) ACISP 2022. LNCS, vol. 13494, pp. 3–23. Springer, Cham (2022). https://doi.org/10.1007/978-3-031-22301-3_1
13. Gurobi Optimization, LLC: Gurobi Optimizer Reference Manual (2023). https://www.gurobi.com
14. Jean, J.: TikZ for Cryptographers (2016). https://www.iacr.org/authors/tikz/
15. Khoo, K., Lee, E., Peyrin, T., Sim, S.M.: Human-readable proof of the related-key security of AES-128. IACR Trans. Symmetric Cryptol. **2017**(2), 59–83 (2017)
16. Knudsen, L.R.: Truncated and higher order differentials. In: Preneel, B. (ed.) FSE 1994. LNCS, vol. 1008, pp. 196–211. Springer, Heidelberg (1995). https://doi.org/10.1007/3-540-60590-8_16
17. Mouha, N., Wang, Q., Gu, D., Preneel, B.: Differential and linear cryptanalysis using mixed-integer linear programming. In: Wu, C., Yung, M., Lin, D. (eds.) Inscrypt 2011. LNCS, vol. 7537, pp. 57–76. Springer, Cham (2011). https://doi.org/10.1007/978-3-642-34704-7_5
18. Nikolic, I.: Tweaking AES. In: Biryukov, A., Gong, G., Stinson, D.R. (eds.) SAC 2010. LNCS, vol. 6544, pp. 198–210. Springer, Cham (2010). https://doi.org/10.1007/978-3-642-19574-7_14
19. Wang, N., Jin, C.: Security evaluation against differential and linear cryptanalyses for Feistel ciphers. Front. Comput. Sci. China **3**(4), 494–502 (2009)

# Author Index





C. Pöpper and L. Batina (Eds.): ACNS 2024, LNCS 14584, pp. 507–509, 2024.
https://doi.org/10.1007/978-3-031-54773-7

Printed in the United States
by Baker & Taylor Publisher Services